Sex, Love, Race

Crossing Boundaries in North American History

EDITED BY

Martha Hodes

New York University Press

NEW YORK AND LONDON

NEW YORK UNIVERSITY PRESS
New York and London

Library of Congress Cataloging-in-Publication Data
Sex, love, race : crossing boundaries in North American history /
edited by Martha Hodes.
p. cm.
Includes bibliographical references and index.
ISBN 0-8147-3556-8 (clothbound : alk. paper). — ISBN
0-8147-3557-6 (paperback : alk. paper)
1. Sex customs—North America—History. 2. North America—Race
relations—History. 3. Interracial marriage—North America—
History. 4. Family—North America—History. I. Hodes, Martha
Elizabeth.
HQ18.N6S49 1999
306.7'097—dc21   98-27705
CIP

New York University Press books are printed on acid-free paper,
and their binding materials are chosen for strength and durability.

Manufactured in the United States of America

10 9 8 7 6 5 4 3 2 1

This book is for
Matthew Jacob Ji Huhng Choi

Contents

Acknowledgments

I thank each of the authors for such admirable combinations of creativity and diligence; Niko Pfund for his vision and energy; Despina Gimbel for her keen editorial eyes; and New York University for a Goddard Fellowship that permitted time for this project. I offer special gratitude to Bruce Dorsey for his steadily everboundless love and to Timothy Dorsey for letting me into his life and his heart. This book is dedicated to my nephew, at this writing a young boy already navigating the shoals of racial categories.

Material from Peter W. Bardaglio, " 'Shamefull Matches': The Regulation of Interracial Sex and Marriage in the South before 1900" originally appeared in *Reconstructing the Household: Families, Sex, and the Law in the Nineteenth-Century South*, © 1995 by the University of North Carolina Press, and is reprinted with permission.

Material in Josephine Boyd Bradley and Kent Anderson Leslie, "White Pain Pollen: An Elite Biracial Daughter's Quandary" originally appeared in Kent Anderson Leslie, *Woman of Color, Daughter of Privilege: Amanda America Dickson, 1849–1893*, © 1995 by the University of Georgia Press, and is reprinted with permission.

Thomas E. Buckley, S.J., "Unfixing Race: Class, Power, and Identity in an Interracial Family" originally appeared in *Virginia Magazine of History and Biography* 102, no. 3 (July 1994): 349–80, and is reprinted with permission of the Virginia Historical Society.

A version of Victoria E. Bynum, "Misshapen Identity: Memory, Folklore, and the Legend of Rachel Knight" originally appeared in *Discovering the Women in Slavery: Emancipating Perspectives on the American Past*, ed. Patricia Morton, © 1996 by the University of Georgia Press, and is reprinted with permission.

Laura F. Edwards, "The Disappearance of Susan Daniel and Henderson Cooper: Gender and Narratives of Political Conflict in the Reconstruction-Era U.S. South" is reprinted from *Feminist Studies* 22, no. 2 (summer 1996): 363–86, by permission of the publisher, *Feminist Studies*, Inc., c/o Department of Women's Studies, University of Maryland, College Park, MD 20742.

Estelle B. Freedman, "The Prison Lesbian: Race, Class, and the Construction of the Aggressive Female Homosexual, 1915–1965" is reprinted from *Feminist Studies* 22, no. 2 (summer 1996): 397–423, by permission of the publisher, *Feminist Studies*,

Inc., c/o Department of Women's Studies, University of Maryland, College Park, MD 20742.

A version of Gary B. Nash, "The Hidden History of Mestizo America" originally appeared in *Journal of American History* 82, no. 3 (December 1995): 941–62, and is reprinted with permission.

Peggy Pascoe, "Miscegenation Law, Court Cases, and Ideologies of 'Race' in Twentieth-Century America" originally appeared in *Journal of American History* 83, no. 1 (June 1996): 44–69, and is reprinted with permission.

Bryant Simon, "The Appeal of Cole Blease of South Carolina: Race, Class, and Sex in the New South" originally appeared in *Journal of Southern History* 62, no. 1 (February 1996): 57–86, © 1996 by the Southern Historical Association, and is reprinted by permission of the managing editor.

Chap. 23. Excerpts from *The Desegregated Heart: A Virginian's Stand in Time of Transition,* by Sarah Patton Boyle, © 1962, 1990 by Sarah Patton Boyle. By permission of William Morrow and Company, Inc.

Contributors

Barbara Bair is the associate editor of the Jane Addams Papers Project, Department of History, Duke University, and one of the editors of the Marcus Garvey and Universal Negro Improvement Association Papers for the University of California Press. Her most recent book is *Though Justice Sleeps: African Americans, 1880–1900* (New York: Oxford University Press, 1990).

Peter W. Bardaglio is the Elizabeth Conolly Todd Associate Professor of History at Goucher College. His book, *Reconstructing the Household: Families, Sex, and the Law in the Nineteenth-Century South* (Chapel Hill: University of North Carolina Press, 1995), was awarded the James Rawley Prize from the Organization of American Historians.

Sharon Block is an assistant professor of history at the University of Iowa. Her essay in this volume was written while she was a post-doctoral and National Endowment for the Humanities Fellow at the Omohundro Institute of Early American History and Culture. She is completing a book entitled *He Said I Must: Coerced Sex in Early America,* to be published by the University of North Carolina Press.

Josephine Boyd Bradley is an adjunct professor with the graduate program in Africana women's studies at Clark Atlanta University. Her current research focuses on African American men as single parents and identification ideology of African American women on white college campuses.

Thomas E. Buckley, S. J., is a professor of American religious history at the Jesuit School of Theology at Berkeley/Graduate Theological Union. He has recently completed a book-length manuscript entitled *"The Great Catastrophe of My Life": Divorce in the Old South.*

Victoria E. Bynum is an associate professor of history at Southwest Texas State University. She is the author of *Unruly Women: The Politics of Social and Sexual Control* (Chapel Hill: University of North Carolina Press, 1992) and is working on a book entitled *Mississippi's Longest Civil War: Memory, Community, and the "Free State of Jones,"* to be published by the University of North Carolina Press.

Leslie K. Dunlap is a doctoral candidate in the department of history at Northwestern University. She is completing a dissertation entitled "Race and Women's Political Activism in the Age of Reform, 1877–1932."

Laura F. Edwards is an assistant professor of history at the University of California-Los Angeles. She is the author of *Gendered Strife and Confusion: The Political Culture of Reconstruction* (Urbana: University of Illinois Press, 1997).

Estelle B. Freedman is a professor of history and chair of the program in feminist studies at Stanford University. She is the author of *Their Sisters' Keepers: Women's Prison Reform in America, 1830–1930* (Ann Arbor: University of Michigan Press, 1981) and *Maternal Justice: Miriam Van Waters and the Female Reform Tradition* (Chicago: University of Chicago Press, 1996), and the coauthor, with John D'Emilio, of *Intimate Matters: A History of Sexuality in America* (rev. ed., Chicago: University of Chicago Press, 1998).

Richard Godbeer is an associate professor of history at the University of California-Riverside, and the author of *The Devil's Dominion: Magic and Religion in Early New England* (New York: Cambridge University Press, 1992). He is working on a book exploring attitudes toward sex in early America.

Leslie M. Harris is an assistant professor of history at Emory University. She is at work on a book entitled *Creating the African-American Working Class in New York City, 1626–1863*.

Martha Hodes is an assistant professor of history at New York University. Her book, *White Women, Black Men: Illicit Sex in the Nineteenth-Century South* (New Haven: Yale University Press, 1997), was awarded the Allan Nevins Prize of the Society of American Historians.

Graham Russell Hodges is a professor of history at Colgate University. He is most recently the author of *Slavery and Freedom in the Rural North: African Americans in Monmouth County, New Jersey, 1660–1860* (Madison, Wisc.: Madison House Books, 1997) and the editor of *Robert Roberts's House Servant's Directory* (Armonk, N.Y.: M. E. Sharpe, 1997).

Kent Anderson Leslie is the administrative director of women's studies and an adjunct professor of women's history and literature in the University College of Oglethorpe University. She is the author of *Woman of Color, Daughter of Privilege: Amanda America Dickson, 1849–1893* (Athens: University of Georgia Press, 1995) and is working on an oral history project with the Afro-Caribbean Women's Association in Bluefields, Nicaragua.

Daniel R. Mandell was a National Endowment for the Humanities Fellow in 1996–97 and is the author of *Behind the Frontier: Indians in Eighteenth-Century Eastern Massachusetts* (Lincoln: University of Nebraska Press, 1996). He is working on a book tentatively entitled *Ethnic Boundaries and Racial Walls: Indians, Blacks, and Whites in Southern New England,* to be published by Johns Hopkins University Press.

Pablo Mitchell is a doctoral candidate in the department of history at the University of Michigan. He is writing a dissertation on marriage, intermarriage, and economic transformation in territorial New Mexico, 1880–1920.

Gary B. Nash is a professor of history at the University of California-Los Angeles and the director of the National Center for History in the Schools. He is the author of many books and essays on early American history, and most recently of *History on Trial: Culture Wars and the Teaching of the Past*, with Charlotte Crabtree and Ross Dunn (New York: Alfred A. Knopf, 1997) and *Forbidden Love: The Secret History of Mixed-Race America* (New York: Henry Holt, 1998).

Scott Nelson is an assistant professor of history at the College of William and Mary. His book, *An Iron Confederacy: Southern Railways, Klan Violence, and the Reconstruction of the South,* will be published by the University of North Carolina Press. He is at work on a book about manhood in Civil War prisons.

Peggy Pascoe is an associate professor of history and the Beekman Chair of Northwest and Pacific History at the University of Oregon. She is the author of *Relations of Rescue: The Search for Female Moral Authority in the American West, 1874–1939* (New York: Oxford University Press, 1990) and is writing a history of miscegenation law in the United States from the Civil War to the present. Her essay in this volume won the 1997 ABC-CLIO America: History and Life Prize.

Jennifer Ritterhouse is a doctoral candidate in the department of history at the University of North Carolina-Chapel Hill. She is completing a dissertation on the racial socialization of children in the Jim Crow South.

Hannah Rosen is a doctoral candidate in the department of history at the University of Chicago. She is completing a dissertation on the political dimensions of sexual violence during Reconstruction in the southern United States.

Bryant Simon is an assistant professor of history at the University of Georgia. He is the author of *A Fabric of Defeat: The Politics of South Carolina Textile Workers, 1910–1948* (Chapel Hill: University of North Carolina Press, 1998).

Lyde Cullen Sizer is an assistant professor at Sarah Lawrence College, where she teaches cultural and intellectual history. She is working on a book entitled *"A Revolution in Woman Herself": Northern Women Writers and the American Civil War* and a collection of documents entitled *Between the Lines: Confederate Women's Spy Narratives.*

Jennifer M. Spear is a doctoral candidate in the department of history at the University of Minnesota. She is writing a dissertation entitled " 'Whiteness and the Purity of Blood': Race, Sexuality, and Cultural Identity in Colonial Louisiana, 1699–1795."

Henry Yu is an assistant professor of history at the University of California-Los Angeles and a member of the Asian American Studies Center at UCLA. His book, *Thinking about "Orientals": Race, Migration, and the Production of Ex-*

otic Knowledge in Modern America, will be published by Oxford University Press.

Jonathan Zimmerman is an assistant professor of educational history, School of Education, New York University. His book, *Distilling Democracy: Alcohol Education in America's Public Schools, 1880–1925*, will be published by the University Press of Kansas.

Introduction
Interconnecting and Diverging Narratives

Martha Hodes

Any investigation of sex and love across racial boundaries in North America yields a record of violent encounters, devoted relationships, legal battles, political struggles, commercial exchanges, class antipathy, radical and conservative activism, and intellectual ferment. The actors are innocent people castigated or criminals never accused. They are poor, middling, and elite; their worlds extend from the South and Southwest to the North and West, and span from the earliest invasions and settlements to the modern day. Accordingly, the chapters in this volume form interconnecting narratives of coercion and persecution, affection and ambivalence. At the same time, the multiple voices of transgressors, victims, and authorities—voices that are defiant, lonely, hateful, evasive—preclude the crafting of one master narrative.

Searching and researching, the authors worked with evidence both direct and elusive. Some sifted through an abundance of published materials, while others pieced together fragments of manuscripts. Different authors consequently employ varying strategies. Some reconstruct an individual life, an unusual episode, a particular neighborhood at a certain time, or a representative crime. Others interrogate broader sweeps of legal records or the writings of travelers or reformers. Some examine the voices of the powerful—say, judges or missionaries—not only to discern dominant attitudes, but also to recover the experiences of subordinated classes. Others are able to listen more directly to marginal voices through, for example, trial testimony or political protests. A number of authors have conducted oral histories to call forth the memories of protagonists or their descendants.

Two streams converge in this volume—streams that reflect as much about the practice of American history as they do about that history itself. First, the investigations here chart the shifting production and construction of racial categories in American history, and indeed of the concept of "race" itself.[1] Second, the history of racial categories is often a history of sexuality as well, for it is partly as a result of the taboos against boundary crossing that such categories are invented. Moreover, the history of sexuality is a field in which concepts and definitions likewise change across time.[2] While the chapters in this volume are united in their focus on race and sex, each one encompasses any number of other historical problems as well: gender, family, class, religion, national identity, sexual orientation, politics, economy, law, crime, friendship, love. It is for this reason that the essays appear in roughly chronological order rather than under thematic headings.[3]

The language of race and sex is a good indicator of the ever-changing nature of these historical constructions. Different historical actors have formulated descriptors of race in diverse ways, evident in documents from the census to scientific treatises to novels. Different scholars likewise select and create particular words and phrases to connote racial categories. Some invoke familiar terminology; others aim to challenge that terminology in a variety of ways. This pertains not only to the myriad of expressions that signify the mixture of ancestry ("biracial," "mulatto," "mestizo," "coyote"), but also to terms that may seem more straightforward ("black," "white," "race").

Instability and choice also characterize the language of sex and sexuality. Documents from institutional records to personal writings reveal the multifarious—and often oblique—ways in which those in the past have described, for example, sexual violence or heterosexual intercourse. Again, historians echo, select, and formulate descriptors for the experiences they uncover, navigating between the familiar and the innovative: rape or prostitution or homosexuality might alternatively be described as coerced sex or commercial sex or same-sex intimacy. Descriptions for the sexual crossing of racial categories are, of course, many and varied. "Métissage," "amalgamation," "miscegenation," "interracial sex": each word or phrase carries its own layers of history and contextual meanings.

The essays in this volume, spanning from the 1690s to the 1970s, resonate with various contemporary dilemma. These range from the reception of marriages across racial boundaries by majority and minority communities to the unequal legal treatment of people of color who are victims of sexual violence, or who are accused of sexual violence. As many of the essays demonstrate, the fates and struggles of children of mixed ancestry produce some of the most complex questions—how best to describe those children in the U.S. census, for example, or the ethics of adoption across racial lines. As such, these essays inspire new questions and spark new ways of thinking about race and sex, both historically and in the present day.

Scanning the table of contents, readers will see that the majority of essays focus on encounters across the black-white color line. This reflects the persistence of a vision of "race" in North America that refers largely (or only) to those of European and African ancestries, and in turn, the reflection of that vision within the academy. It is precisely because of this dominant vision, intertwined with the particular history of black-white relations in North America, that the undertaking of this scholarship is so crucial. Indeed, while a great deal of work yet remains to be done in this field, it is imperative as well that scholars investigate historical categories of race beyond the black-white duality in North American culture. A number of the essays in this volume form a part of that endeavor.

Abiding questions about center and periphery in the writing of history also come into play in explorations of race and sexuality in North American history. Many of the scholars here have listened to obscure historical voices and thus tell and interpret stories heretofore untold. Such shifting of perspective may point to new and more complicated syntheses or, on the contrary, may force the ultimate rejection of synthesis. In either scenario, the writing and rewriting of histories of race and sexuality can serve to exchange margins for center. Such exchanges in turn call into question rigid categories of public and private. In many of the essays that follow, the authors illuminate permeable boundaries between the household, marriage, or sex on the one hand, and politics, diplomacy, or the market on the other.[4] By exploring all of these permeable boundaries—among racial categories, experiences of sex, margin, and center—the work in this volume begins to illuminate the manifold histories of race and sex in North America.

In the first chapter of *Sex, Love, Race,* Gary B. Nash surveys mixture across the North American continent from the colonial era through the twentieth century. Nash posits a "hidden history" of those who have defied dominant ideology, asserting the increasing difficulty of sustaining racial markers in the modern nation. Heeding tensions between multiculturalism and cultural identity, Nash ultimately calls for creative reconceptualizations of rigid ideas about race in the United States. The chapters that follow speak to the histories, possibilities, and dilemmas therein.

Four essays focus on colonial America. The authors here treat encounters among American Indians, Europeans, Africans, and African Americans, discussing broad concerns of property, religion, gender, and sexuality. Jennifer M. Spear finds discourses about civilization to be closely intertwined with concerns about property and identity as she sifts through constructions of racial boundaries by French colonizers in Louisiana. Paying close attention to both cultural and demographic factors, Spear examines the ways in which secular and religious authorities attempted to manage sex and marriage between French men and Indian women in the name of creating a stable colony. While Indian and French women left no records, Spear inverts other voices to speculate about their experiences.

Taking up the mid-Atlantic, Graham Russell Hodges illuminates shifting attitudes about Christianity and race by delving into a scandalous case of slander in colonial New York. When a Dutch-speaking African American servant accused her master, a German Lutheran pastor, of fathering her child, she was brought to trial in a church that embraced both racial slavery and members of African descent. Hodges charts increasingly hostile relations between blacks and whites in a community that had once sanctioned unions across racial bounds.

Moving farther north, Daniel R. Mandell explores emerging identities in colonial New England by investigating the life of one Indian woman and her successive common-law marriages to two men of African ancestry. By scrutinizing conflicts over labor, land, and gender, Mandell discerns possible motivations for such unions—which were becoming increasingly frequent—and reflects upon the consequences for both Indian and African American communities. The author pays special attention to the choices made by the children in regard to identity and community.

Richard Godbeer demonstrates that sex on the colonial southern frontier played a role equal in importance to economic, diplomatic, and military encounters. Allowing often promiscuous Englishmen to speak for themselves, Godbeer discovers liaisons with Native women that are violent and consensual, short-term and stable, commercial and romantic. Disjunctures between preconception and experience allow Godbeer to trace the sentiments and strategies of Native women, and to draw suggestive conclusions about the contradictory sexual ideas and behaviors of white men in colonial America.

In the realm of formal law, Peter W. Bardaglio detects patterns and variations alike as he closely reads southern statutes and appellate court decisions concerning sex and marriage across the black-white color line. By examining the anxieties of white lawmakers from the colonial period through the end of the nineteenth century, Bardaglio maps expanding state intervention and illuminates the role of statutory law in both reflecting and shaping dominant ideas and fears about race and sexuality, most especially in the transition from slavery to freedom.

Four authors inquire into episodes about violence, marriage, and love between African Americans and whites in the early national and antebellum periods. Sharon Block rereads force and consent in the lives of black and white female laborers in the early Republic. Invoking the respective cases of an indentured servant and a slave, Block argues that masters could erode the sexual agency of bound women and subsequently control public interpretations of sexual coercion. Yet the documents also indicate the parallel ways in which these women could resist and negotiate—alongside the disparate treatment accorded black and white women under the law.

Thomas E. Buckley considers the central role of class as he reconstructs the world of a slaveholding free man of color in antebellum Virginia. The protagonist, Robert Wright, married and divorced one white woman, then formed a partnership with another; both unions were accepted by neighboring white slaveholders. Moreover, after Wright's death, family members of African descent asserted their property rights, and often won their cases, in various legal battles. Racial identity in the slave South, Buckley proves, could thus be mediated in unusual ways by class status.

Studying the urban North, Leslie M. Harris charts the triumph of racist discourses surrounding consensual sex between blacks and whites. Harris finds that as black and white abolitionists worked together in New York City, their opponents portrayed such cooperation as tantamount to "amalgamation." Following the anti-abolitionist violence of 1834 and the retreat of radicals on the marriage issue, conservatives targeted working-class blacks and Irish immigrants in their discussions of morality and criminality. The city's bloody 1863 draft riot marked the triumph of an anti-amalgamation discourse.

The protagonist of Josephine Boyd Bradley and Kent Anderson Leslie's essay is a woman who forged an identity outside of standard racial classifications. The daughter of a slave who was raped by her master, Amanda America Dickson grew up in her white father's household in Georgia's Black Belt, inherited his estate, married a white man, and died wealthy. Through their meticulous investigations of the white family, the enslaved mother, and the privileged daughter, the authors pose questions about love and explore the elusive terrain of motivation and agency in the South during and after slavery.

The next five essays treat relations and confrontations between blacks and whites in the volatile era of the Civil War and Reconstruction. Working back from a mid-twentieth-century court case about the crime of miscegenation, Victoria E. Bynum reclaims the life of Rachel Knight, a slave of mixed ancestry who participated in an anti-Confederate uprising of white deserters in Mississippi. Interrogating history's relationship to racist local legends and folklore, Bynum uncovers a story that involves both master-slave sexual exploitation and post-war marriages that created a still-contested community of so-called white Negroes.

Lyde Cullen Sizer finds visions of racial harmony in tandem with persistent white supremacy in the war novels of three abolitionist women. Published during the early years of Reconstruction, the works of Lydia Maria Child, Anna Dickinson, and Rebecca Harding Davis all involve consensual relationships between white and black characters. Treating the works as political texts, Sizer scrutinizes the authors' visions of sectional reconciliation as well as the mixed responses of white readers to these manifestos.

Turning south, Hannah Rosen considers the meaning of sexual violence to trace changing dynamics of power immediately after the Civil War. By closely reading the testimony of freedwomen who were assaulted during the Memphis Riot of 1866, Rosen locates black women's agency both in their resistance to white ideology and in their claims to citizenship and public space. At the same time probing the actions and justifications of the white rapists, Rosen examines shifting white ideas about black and white womanhood and manhood.

Laura F. Edwards analyzes intertwinings of rape and politics in the Reconstruction South through a North Carolina case involving a black man and a poor white woman. Moving between public and private contexts, Edwards explores the relation of power to both gender and class in the narratives that ensued, as well as efforts to challenge those elite scripts: while black and poor white women began to prosecute men for sexual violence, their menfolk worked to protect their families from both economic and sexual exploitation.

Scott Nelson also considers reconfigurations of power in public and private, this time from the vantage point of livestock markets in the Reconstruction South. Sale days in one South Carolina county reflected social boundaries, with concentric rings of trade ranging from an inner circle around the courthouse to a "black" market on the margins. Nelson assesses local geographical shifts after the Civil War, connecting these changes specifically to the lives of two African American coachmen targeted by the Klan precisely as they gained community power.

Four authors consider episodes in the last decades of the nineteenth century and the first decades of the twentieth. The scholarship here reaches into arenas beyond both the categories of black and white and the category of heterosexuality. Pablo Mitchell argues for the critical role of gender and sexuality in the consolidation of power as he investigates strategies of marriage in turn-of-the-century New Mexico. A series of cross-cultural unions led to a half century of inheritance disputes, and Mitchell links these economic entanglements to transformations that accompanied the emergence of a Hispano-Anglo elite. Mitchell's protagonist is the likely-gay son of an Anglo doctor and an Indian servant woman, a man who himself defied precise racial, religious, and sexual categorization.

Leslie K. Dunlap uncovers a moment in history in which the sexual conduct of presumably respectable white men was targeted for surveillance. As part of national sex reform efforts by the Women's Christian Temperance Union, white southern women led campaigns to raise the age of consent in rape laws, defending black girls and women against white men. Yet as Dunlap listens to the voices of black activists as well as to those of the reformers' opponents, she discerns shifting, and increasingly racist, motives on the part of the campaigners.

Bryant Simon connects sex and race to popular politics in an essay that opens with an elusive sexual encounter between two black men and one white man in the early twentieth-century South. Simon considers the accusation of sexual assault, and the subsequent lynching of the black men, in light of the antireform platform in South Carolina that appealed to the region's new class of white mill hands. In so doing, Simon explores links among industrialization, threats to white working-class masculinity, and relations of race and gender in the New South.

Barbara Bair inquires into an unusual alliance between Garveyite black nationalists and white supremacists in her examination of campaigns supporting a 1924 Virginia law intended to prohibit racial mixing. Whereas Garveyites metaphorically invoked the bodies of black women, white supremacists invoked those of white women in their respective goals of a black empire and a glorified Anglo-Saxonism. The control of women's racialized bodies, Bair argues, was deeply implicated in both conservative and radical visions of race and political power.

The last five chapters move into the mid- and late twentieth century, continuing the expansion into broader categories of race and sexual orientation. Estelle B. Freedman examines constructions of black and white lesbians in her study of relationships across the color line in women's prisons. Reading criminology literature and interpreting the records of the Massachusetts Reformatory for Women, Freedman finds denial, toleration, and increasing anxiety on the part of authorities, and traces complex relationships among sexual identity, sexual agency, race, and class in the emergence of the idea of the dangerous prison lesbian in modern America.

Henry Yu casts a critical eye on the fascination of social scientists with sex and marriage between Americans of Asian ancestry and Americans of European ancestry in the twentieth century. Dissecting attendant sociological theories of race and culture from the 1920s through the 1970s, Yu simultaneously untangles ideas about exoticism and assimilation, cultural difference and physical markers, and places these ever shifting ideologies in the context of various visions of America.

From a legal angle, Peggy Pascoe maps out discourses about race that coexisted with modern social science. Analyzing four twentieth-century miscegenation cases, Pascoe argues that the emerging nonrecognition of race amounted to a racial ideology in its own right. Pascoe explores the legal uses of this ideology, the ways in which such ideas were reshaped in courtrooms, and the culmination of this modernist ideology in the famous 1967 Supreme Court case of *Loving v. Virginia*. She ends by reflecting on the present-day legacies of the idea of nonrecognition.

The South in the 1950s and 1960s is the setting for Jennifer Ritterhouse's study of a deep, though by no means untroubled, friendship between a white woman and an African American man. The newspaper editor T. J. Sellers unflinchingly criticized

Sarah Patton Boyle's paternalistic liberalism, reaching Boyle precisely because he understood the cold lessons she had to learn as she moved from gradualism to civil rights activism. This uncommon relationship across lines of race and gender, as re-created by Ritterhouse, indicates perhaps greater conflict and disillusionment than it does progress.

Moving into the late twentieth century, Jonathan Zimmerman looks closely at romantic relationships between black and white American Peace Corps volunteers working in Africa. Although such liaisons were accepted with some equanimity overseas, black volunteers not surprisingly encountered difficulties upon their return home. Zimmerman places these conflicts in the political context of the 1960s, discovering not only that the Peace Corps discouraged black-white romances, but also that black activists at home responded with hostility, at least at first.

Some of the questions raised in the connecting and diverging narratives of *Sex, Love, Race* may be answered definitively. Others will be answered partially, suggestively, or tentatively. Still others will be explored but remain unanswered until investigated in future scholarship. Indeed, it is the intention of this collection to inspire others to think about and take up the stories that remain to be written about traversing and transgressing invented racial boundaries throughout history.[5]

NOTES

1. On the historical construction of race, see, for example, W. E. B. Du Bois, *Dusk of Dawn: An Essay toward an Autobiography of a Race Concept* (1940; reprint, New York: Schocken, 1968); Barbara J. Fields, "Ideology and Race in American History," in *Region, Race, and Reconstruction: Essays in Honor of C. Vann Woodward*, ed. J. Morgan Kousser and James M. McPherson (New York: Oxford University Press, 1982); idem, "Slavery, Race and Ideology in the United States of America," *New Left Review* 181 (1990): 95–118; Lucius Outlaw, "Toward a Critical Theory of 'Race,' " in *Anatomy of Racism*, ed. David Theo Goldberg (Minneapolis: University of Minnesota Press, 1990); essays in Henry Louis Gates, Jr., ed., *"Race," Writing, and Difference* (Chicago: University of Chicago Press, 1986); Paul R. Spickard, "The Illogic of American Racial Categories," in *Racially Mixed People in America*, ed. Maria P. P. Root (Newbury Park, Calif.: Sage, 1992); Audrey Smedley, *Race in North America: Origin and Evolution of a Worldview* (Boulder: Westview, 1993); Michael Omi and Howard Winant, *Racial Formation in the United States from the 1960s to the 1990s* (New York: Routledge, 1994), chaps. 1–4; Howard Winant, *Racial Conditions: Politics, Theory, Comparisons* (Minneapolis: University of Minnesota Press, 1994), chap. 2; Naomi Zack, *Race and Mixed Race* (Philadelphia: Temple University Press, 1993), chaps. 1–4; Thomas C. Holt, "Marking: Race, Race-Making, and the Writing of History," *American Historical Review* 100 (1995): 1–20.

2. On the historical construction of sexuality, see, for example, Michel Foucault, *The History of Sexuality*, vol. 1, *An Introduction*, trans. Robert Hurley (New York: Vintage, 1980); Ann Snitow, Christine Stansell, and Sharon Thompson, introduction to *Powers of Desire: The Politics of Sexuality*, ed. Ann Snitow, Christine Stansell, and Sharon Thompson (New York: Monthly Review Press, 1983); Robert Padgug, "Sexual Matters: On Conceptualizing Sexuality," in *Hidden from History: Reclaiming the Gay and Lesbian Past*, ed. Martin Duberman, Martha Vicinus, and George Chauncey, Jr. (New York: Meridian, 1990); David

Halperin, "Is There a History of Sexuality?" in *The Lesbian and Gay Studies Reader*, ed. Henry Abelove, Michèle Aina Barale, and David M. Halperin (New York: Routledge, 1993); Carolyn J. Dean, "The Productive Hypothesis: Foucault, Gender, and the History of Sexuality," *History and Theory* 33 (1994): 271–96.

3. Readers may consult individual essays for fuller bibliographies, but a sampling of pioneering works at the crossroads of the study of race and sex includes Carter G. Woodson, "The Beginnings of the Miscegenation of the Whites and Blacks," *Journal of Negro History* 3 (1918): 335–53; Joel A. Rogers, *Sex and Race: A History of White, Negro, and Indian Miscegenation in the Two Americas*, 3 vols. (New York: H. M. Rogers, 1940–44); James Hugo Johnston, *Race Relations in Virginia and Miscegenation in the South, 1776–1860* (Amherst: University of Massachusetts Press, 1970); Jacquelyn Dowd Hall, *Revolt against Chivalry: Jessie Daniel Ames and the Women's Campaign against Lynching* (1979; rev. ed., New York: Columbia University Press, 1993); idem, " 'The Mind That Burns in Each Body': Women, Rape, and Racial Violence," in *Powers of Desire*, ed. Snitow, Stansell, and Thompson; Richard H. Steckel, "Miscegenation and the American Slave Schedules," *Journal of Interdisciplinary History* 11 (1980): 251–63; Joel Williamson, *New People: Miscegenation and Mulattoes in the United States* (New York: Free Press, 1980); Alice Walker, "Advancing Luna—and Ida B. Wells," in *You Can't Keep a Good Woman Down* (New York: Harcourt Brace Jovanovich, 1981); Dick Megumi Ogumi, "Asians and California's Anti-Miscegenation Laws," in *Asian and Pacific American Experiences: Women's Perspectives*, ed. Nobuya Tsuchida (Minneapolis: Asian/Pacific American Learning Resource Center and General College, University of Minnesota, 1982); Karen A. Getman, "Sexual Control in the Slaveholding South: The Implementation and Maintenance of a Racial Caste System," *Harvard Women's Law Journal* 7 (1984) : 115–52; Patricia Morton, "From Invisible Man to 'New People': The Recent Discovery of American Mulattoes," *Phylon* 46 (1985): 106–22.

A sampling of more recent works includes Jack D. Forbes, *Black Africans and Native Americans: Color, Race and Caste in the Evolution of Red-Black Peoples* (New York: Basil Blackwell, 1988); Nell Irvin Painter, " 'Social Equality,' Miscegenation, Labor, and Power," in *The Evolution of Southern Culture*, ed. Numan V. Bartley (Athens: University of Georgia Press, 1988); Paul R. Spickard, *Mixed Blood: Intermarriage and Ethnic Identity in Twentieth-Century America* (Madison: University of Wisconsin Press, 1989); Ramón A. Gutiérrez, *When Jesus Came, the Corn Mothers Went Away: Marriage, Sexuality, and Power in New Mexico, 1600–1846* (Stanford: Stanford University Press, 1991); W. Fitzhugh Brundage, *Lynching in the New South: Georgia and Virginia, 1880–1930* (Urbana: University of Illinois Press, 1993); Gail Bederman, " 'Civilization,' the Decline of Middle-Class Manliness, and Ida B. Wells's Antilynching Campaign (1892–94)," *Radical History Review* 52 (1992): 5–30; Robyn Wiegman, "The Anatomy of Lynching," in *American Sexual Politics: Sex, Gender, and Race since the Civil War*, ed. John C. Fout and Maura Shaw Tantillo (Chicago: University of Chicago Press, 1993); Tomás Almaguer, *Racial Fault Lines: The Historical Origins of White Supremacy in California* (Berkeley: University of California Press, 1994); James Goodman, *Stories of Scottsboro* (New York: Pantheon, 1994); Colleen Fong and Judy Yung, "In Search of the Right Spouse: Interracial Marriage among Chinese and Japanese Americans," *Amerasia Journal* 21 (1995–96): 77–98; Larry Hijame Shinagawa and Gin Yong Pang, "Asian American Panethnicity and Intermarriage," *Amerasia Journal* 22 (1996): 127–52; Carolyn J. Powell, "In Remembrance of Mira: Reflections on the Death of a Slave Woman," and Hélène Lecaudey, "Behind the Mask: Ex-Slave Women and Interracial Sexual Relations," in *Discovering the Women in Slavery: Emancipating Perspectives on the American Past*, ed. Patricia Morton (Athens: University of Georgia Press, 1996); Kevin J. Mumford, *Interzones: Black/White Sex Districts in Chicago and New York in the Early Twentieth*

Century (New York: Columbia University Press, 1997); Annette Gordon-Reed, *Thomas Jefferson and Sally Hemings: An American Controversy* (Charlottesville: University Press of Virginia, 1997); Martha Hodes, *White Women, Black Men: Illicit Sex in the Nineteenth-Century South* (New Haven: Yale University Press, 1997); William S. Penn, ed., *As We Are Now: Mixblood Essays on Race and Identity* (Berkeley: University of California Press, 1997); Naomi Zack, ed., *Race/Sex: Their Sameness, Difference, and Interplay* (New York: Routledge, 1997).

4. See, for example, Thomas Bender, "Wholes and Parts: The Need for Synthesis in American History," *Journal of American History* 73 (1986): 120–36; David Thelen, Nell Irvin Painter, Richard Wightman Fox, Roy Rosensweig, and Thomas Bender, "A Roundtable: Synthesis in American History," *Journal of American History* 74 (1987): 107–30; Eric H. Monkkonen, "The Dangers of Synthesis," *American Historical Review* 91 (1986): 1146–57; Thomas Bender, " 'Venturesome and Cautious': American History in the 1990s," *Journal of American History* 81 (1994): 992–1003; Dorothy Ross, "Grand Narrative in American Historical Writing: From Romance to Uncertainty," *American Historical Review* 100 (1995): 651–77.

On public and private, see, for example, Joan W. Scott, "Gender: A Useful Category of Historical Analysis," in *Gender and the Politics of History* (New York: Columbia University Press, 1988), 28–50; Carole Pateman, "Feminist Critiques of the Public/Private Dichotomy," in *The Disorder of Women: Democracy, Feminism and Political Theory* (Stanford: Stanford University Press, 1989); Susan M. Reverby and Dorothy O. Helly, "Introduction: Converging on History," in *Gendered Domains: Rethinking Public and Private in Women's History*, ed. Dorothy O. Helly and Susan M. Reverby (Ithaca: Cornell University Press, 1992); Lawrence E. Klein, "Gender and the Public/Private Distinction in the Eighteenth Century: Some Questions about Evidence and Analytic Procedure," *Eighteenth-Century Studies* 29 (1995): 97–109. For a fine example, see Elsa Barkley Brown, "Negotiating and Transforming the Public Sphere: African American Political Life in the Transition from Slavery to Freedom," *Public Culture* 7 (1994): 107–46.

5. Historians of race and sexuality in North America might increasingly cast their nets across national borders, from both comparative and transnational perspectives. See Frederick Cooper, "Race, Ideology, and the Perils of Comparative History," *American Historical Review* 101 (1996): 1122–38; George M. Fredrickson, *The Comparative Imagination: On the History of Racism, Nationalism, and Social Movements* (Berkeley: University of California Press, 1997); Akira Iriye, "The Internationalization of History," *American Historical Review* 94 (1989): 1–10; Ian Tyrrell, "American Exceptionalism in an Age of International History," *American Historical Review* 96 (1991): 1031–55; Michael McGerr, "The Price of Transnational History," *American Historical Review* 96 (1991): 1056–72; Michael Kammen, "The Problem of American Exceptionalism: A Reconsideration," *American Quarterly* 45 (1993): 1–43; John Higham, "The Future of American History," *Journal of American History* 80 (1994): 1289–1309.

Chapter One

The Hidden History of Mestizo America

Gary B. Nash

La Nature aime les croisements (Nature loves cross-breedings).

—Ralph Waldo Emerson

On a dank January evening in London in 1617, the audience was distracted from a performance of Ben Johnson's *Vision of Delight* by the persons sitting next to King James I and Queen Anne: a dashing adventurer who had just returned from the outer edge of the fledgling English empire and his new wife, ten years his junior. The king's guests were John Rolfe and his wife, Rebecca—a name newly invented to anglicize the daughter of another king who ruled over a domain as big and populous as a north English county. She was Pocahontas, the daughter of Powhatan.[1] The first recorded interracial marriage in American history had taken place because Rebecca's father and the English leaders in the colony of Virginia were eager to bring about a détente after a decade of abrasive and sometimes bloody European-Algonkian contact on the shores of the Chesapeake Bay.

The Rolfe-Pocahontas marriage might have become the embryo of a mestizo United States.[2] I use the term "mestizo" in the original sense—referring to racial intermixture of all kinds. In the early seventeenth century, negative ideas about miscegenation had hardly formed; indeed, the word itself did not appear for another two and a half centuries. King James was not worried about interracial marriage. He fretted only about whether a commoner such as Rolfe was entitled to wed the daughter of a king. Nearly a century later, Robert Beverley's *History and Present State of Virginia* (1705) described Indian women as "generally beautiful, possessing uncommon delicacy of shape and features," and he regretted that Rolfe's intermarriage was not followed by many more.[3]

William Byrd, writing at the same time, was still commending what he called the "modern policy" of racial intermarriage employed in French Canada and Louisiana by which alliances rather than warfare were effected. Byrd confessed his preference for light-skinned women (a woman's skin color, however, rarely curbed his sexual appetite), but he was sure that English "false delicacy" blocked a "prudent alliance" that might have saved Virginians much tragedy. Most colonies saw no reason to ban intermarriage with Native Americans (North Carolina was the exception).[4]

In 1784 Patrick Henry nearly pushed through the Virginia legislature a law offering bounties for white-Indian marriages and free public education for interracial children. In the third year of his presidency, Thomas Jefferson pleaded "to let our settlements and theirs [Indians'] meet and blend together, to intermix, and become one people." Six years later, just before returning to Monticello, Jefferson promised a group of western Indian chiefs, "you will unite yourselves with us . . . and we shall all be Americans; you will mix with us by marriage, your blood will run in our veins, and will spread with us over this great island."[5]

In 1809, almost two hundred years after Pocahontas sat in the theater with James I, the sixteen-year-old Sam Houston, taking a page from the book of Benjamin Franklin, ran away from his autocratic older brothers. The teenage Franklin fled south from Boston to Philadelphia, but Houston made his way west to Hiwassee Island in western Tennessee. There he took up life among the Cherokees and was soon adopted by Ooleteka, who would become the Cherokee chief in 1820. Reappearing in white society in 1812, Houston launched a tumultuous, alcohol-laced, violent, and roller-coaster political career, but he retained his yen for the Cherokee life. After his disastrous first marriage at age thirty-six, he rejoined the Cherokee, became the ambassador of the Cherokee nation to Washington (in which office he wore Indian regalia) in 1829, and married Ooleteka's niece, the widowed, mixed-blood Cherokee woman Tiana Rogers Gentry.[6]

Until recently, official biographies of Houston omitted this Cherokee marriage. His drunken arrogance soon led to exile from the Cherokee nation, where he had been known as "the big drunk"; he left his Cherokee wife and headed for Texas to fight and speculate his way to fame. In 1836, as president of Texas, Houston convinced Chief Bowles, leader of the numerous Cherokees who had migrated there, to cast their lot with the provisional American government against the armed and dissatisfied Mexican residents. Houston hoped to cement an alliance between Cherokees and whites that would combine Texas and northern Mexico into a vast territory with plenty of land both for a new Cherokee homeland and for Anglo-Texan settlers. After all, the Cherokees had fought alongside Andrew Jackson, Houston's friend, against the Creeks in the battle of Horseshoe Bend near New Orleans—the climactic battle in the War of 1812.[7]

In both Virginia and Texas, prejudice and violence blocked the way toward what might have become a mixed-race American republic. Pocahontas died after boarding ship in England in 1617—bound for Virginia—with Rolfe and their infant son. With his mixed-race son, Rolfe reached Virginia, married again in 1620, and two years later died in an all-out assault mounted by Opechancanough, the half-brother of Pocahontas's father. This attack killed off one-third of the tobacco planters, and intermarriage in Virginia thereafter was a rarity.[8]

Two centuries later, after Houston worked to protect the Cherokees from white settler racism and violence in Texas, his successor as president of the Lone Star Republic, Mirabeau Buonaparte Lamar, called for a policy of Cherokee expulsion or extinction. In 1839, when the Texas army attacked the defiant Cherokees, Hous-

Fig. 1.1 Sam Houston made a point of dressing in full Indian regalia on his two trips to Washington as an ambassador for the Cherokee nation. Through clothing, Houston presented himself as "Indian"—in effect, announcing his new identity and obliging American political leaders to accept him on Cherokee terms. Courtesy San Jacinto Museum of History, Houston, Texas.

ton's old friend Chief Bowles died holding a sword inscribed by Houston. On the battlefield a Cherokee warrior removed a metal canister held by a cord around Chief Bowles's neck that contained the treaty, drafted and signed by Houston, that guaranteed the Cherokee lands in Texas forever.[9]

Other forerunners of a mestizo nation were more successful. English, French, and Spanish fur traders in North America, from the early 1600s to the late 1800s, were typically married to Indian women. They became the very symbol of mestizo America—*métissage* is the French term (comparable to the Spanish *mestizaje*) for the joining of English or French traders and their Indian wives, and their offspring were *métis*.[10] Irish trader John Johnson could hardly have done business in Indian villages without his Ojibway wife O-shaw-gus-co-day-wayquak, daughter of an Ojibway leader. Nor could Michael Laframboise, a French immigrant, whose Okanogay wife paved the way for his trading with the Indians in Oregon Territory. Laframboise boasted about having a high-ranking wife in every Indian tribe inhabiting the region he worked as a trapper. He was apparently the only man "who moved with solitary security from one Umpqua village to another." The fabled Jim Bridger married three times, each time to an Indian woman, once to the daughter of Chief Washakie of the Shoshone. Equally fabled Kit Carson had four wives: an Arapaho, a Cheyenne, a Mexican, and a Taos-born Indian-Mexican woman.[11]

The fur traders, trappers, and trail blazers are poignant examples of a frontier that should be conceptualized as a zone of deep intercultural contacts rather than as a line that divided two societies, one advanced and the other primitive. The frontier, as it involved white settlers and native peoples, is indelibly etched in our national consciousness as a battleground, but it was also a cultural merging ground and a marrying ground. Nobody left the frontier cultural encounters unchanged.[12]

Two further examples of *mestizaje*, one from the nineteenth century and one from the twentieth, illustrate the "in-betweenness" of many who confounded the official racial taxonomy of the United States. The first example is in the mixing of American Indians and African Americans. In every part of eastern North America from the 1600s to the 1800s, escaping African slaves sought refuge among Native Americans, relying on a natural affinity between oppressed peoples. White colonists, fearing an alliance of red and black peoples, strenuously promoted hatred between Indians and Africans, offering bounties to Indians who captured escaping Africans and trying to convince Indians that Africans were a detestable people. Nonetheless, the bloodlines of Cherokees and Mandingo, Creeks and Fula, Choctaws and Ashanti became mixed as fugitive slaves disappeared into Indian society. The Africans took Indian spouses, produced children of mixed blood, and contributed to Afro-Indian transculturation.[13]

The revolutionary era was neatly bracketed by two Afro-Indians. The first blood shed, in the Boston Massacre of 1774, was that of Crispus Attucks, whose father was black and his mother Indian. In the aftermath of the Revolution, it was Paul Cuffe, son of an African father and Wampanoag mother, who planned the repatriation of black Yankees to Sierra Leone after concluding that it was nearly impossible for New England's blacks to find a life of liberty and happiness in the new Republic.[14]

Fig. 1.2 Joseph Rolette, who represented the Pembina Métis in the Minnesota territorial legislature during the 1850s, is dressed here in classic Métis fashion. His European hat, tie, hunting knife, and coat and Indian pants, moccasins, and tobacco pouch symbolize his mixed-race identity. Anonymous artist. Courtesy Minnesota Historical Society.

Up and down the seaboard, Indian-African intermixing continued. The whaling boat crews of Nantucket Island had many African-Indians, including the harpooners celebrated by Herman Melville. On the peninsula comprising Delaware, eastern Maryland, and eastern Virginia, deep-rooted mixtures of red, white, and black peoples created triracial communities. Still today, from Alabama to New York, the Lumbees, Red Bones, Wesorts, Brass Ankles, and many other triracial societies maintain their distinctive identities.[15]

African-Indian intermixture was furthered by the Cherokee adoption of black slavery, which grew slowly in the eighteenth century but increased rapidly in the early nineteenth century when the Cherokee strategy for survival staked its future on adopting key white institutions: a constitution, literacy, family farming, Christianity—and black slavery. By the 1830s, about one-fourth of all Cherokees were intermixed, mostly with whites but many with blacks. Chulio, the famous Cherokee chief and warrior, married three times, first a Cherokee, then a white woman, finally one of his black slave women. The Cherokee attempts to protect their homelands extended even to passing a law in 1824 forbidding intermarriage with African Americans, but this did not stop black-Cherokee liaisons. Today, many thousands of Americans claim both African and Cherokee descent.[16]

A second example of *mestizaje* can be found in the history of agriculture in California's San Joaquin and Imperial valleys. In the early twentieth century, the landowners of the flourishing agricultural industry were no longer able to bring in new Chinese and Japanese contract laborers because of immigration restrictions. The cotton, fruit, and vegetable growers turned to Korea, the Philippines, and South Asia for labor. Among the immigrants were nearly seven thousand Sikhs from the Punjab. Arriving as single men or as married men who could not bring their wives and children, the Punjabis faced the creeping glacier of antimiscegenation that left them in a racial catch-22: they could not bring Sikh women with them, and California law prohibited marriage between people of different races, as races were defined in this period. By the end of World War I, however, the Sikhs were finding that county clerks would issue marriage licenses to people of different "races" so long as they had a similar skin color. This softness in the application of the law soon led to marriages between Punjabis and Mexicans, who had been crossing the border in large numbers since the Mexican Revolution of 1911.[17]

Between 1913 and 1948—the latter date the abrogation of California's law prohibiting racial intermarriage—80 percent of the Asian Indian men in California married Hispanic women. To this day, several thousand of the children and grandchildren of these Punjabi-Hispanic marriages, which involved vows between Muslims and Catholics or Hindus and Catholics, can be found in Imperial Valley and San Joaquin Valley towns. Many of the families can still be found under the name Singh—the most common Sikh surname—but most have Hispanic first names, representing the mixed cultural heritage that emerged. Hindu temples and Muslim mosques can be found all over the San Joaquin and Imperial valleys. What an exclamation point this hybridizing of people adds to Frederick Jackson Turner's dictum that "In the crucible of the frontier the immigrants were Americanized, liberated, and fused into a mixed race, English in neither nationality nor characteristics." (Since the new immigration law of 1965, California's population of Asian Indians has grown from a few thousand to over a hundred thousand, which has reconstituted and revitalized Punjabi culture and identity. Tension between the new Punjabis and Hispanic-Punjabi people has arisen in San Joaquin Valley cities; thus begins again the process of "contesting and negotiating ethnic identity within marriages, within families, and in arenas beyond the family," as Karen Leonard has written.)[18]

The numbers of Mexican–Asian Indian Californians involved are not very significant, but they represent a powerful theme in American history that has been largely hidden—that people of many kinds, in every era and in every region of this country, have found loopholes in the ruling system of racial division and classification.[19] The silence in our history books on the topic of multiraciality reflects the antimiscegenist attitudes supported by the law. In fact, about three-quarters of African Americans today are multiracial, and perhaps one-third have some Indian ancestry. Virtually all Latino Americans are multiracial, so are almost all Filipino Americans, so are a large majority of American Indians, and millions of whites have multiracial roots.[20]

Far more common than is generally recognized are interracial marriages that resulted in pivotal chapters of American history. Such is the case of Lucy and Albert Parsons. Born in Buffalo Creek, Texas, in 1853, Lucía Gonzalez, whose heritage was black and Creek as well as Mexican, married Albert Parsons, who had been a Confederate scout in the Civil War. In marrying Lucía Gonzalez in 1871, Parsons turned his back on his brother, editor of a white supremacist newspaper in Texas. William Parsons, at about the same time, expressed his disgust for "the *mongrel results* which have so universally attended emancipation, and the fraternization of the races throughout the Spanish Republics of the two American Continents." From this interracial marriage came two racially mixed children but also one of the most dramatic stories in labor history. Lucy, as she was known, and Albert joined the Socialist Labor Party and became leading activists in Chicago in the 1877 railroad strike. Ten years later, Albert was executed as one of the anarchists charged with inciting the Haymarket Square riot in Chicago in 1886. But Lucy, a spellbinding speaker with flashing eyes and a trenchant pen, carried forth the radical labor message for another fifty-five years until she died in the 1940s. She is listed in Hispanic and black American biographical indexes—under different names. In *Black Women in America* she is listed as Lucy Parsons: the "first Black woman to play a prominent role in the American Left," although her triracial heritage is acknowledged. In *Mexican American Biographies*, she is listed as Lucía Gonzalez Parsons, under *G*.[21]

This brings us to a consideration of the virulent racial ideology that arose among the dominant Euro-Americans and that profoundly affected people of color. How most Americans came to believe that character and culture are literally carried in the blood, and how the idea of racial mixture was almost banished officially, has its own history. How would it come to happen, as Barbara Fields has expressed it, that a white woman can give birth to a black child but a black woman can never give birth to a white child?[22] How would it come to be that the children of Indian-white marriages would contemptuously be referred to by whites as half-breeds, while the parallel terms in French and Spanish—*méti* and *mestizo*—carried no such negative connotations?

The sequence of legal definitions of blacks in Virginia demonstrates this progression. In 1785, the revolutionary generation defined a black person as anyone with a black parent or grandparent, thus conferring whiteness on whomever was less than one-quarter black. Virginia changed the law 125 years later to define as "Negro," as the term then was used, anyone who was at least one-sixteenth black. In 1930, Virginia adopted the notorious "one-drop" law—defining as black anyone with one drop of African blood, however that might have been determined.

A comparison of the early histories of Spanish and English colonizers in this hemisphere is instructive. In Spanish America from the time of the Columbian voyages, Spanish males, living overwhelmingly without Spanish women, began to mix with indigenous women. This was especially facilitated by *repartimento*, by which Indian peoples were made subject to Spanish conquerors and brought into close contact as tribute laborers. Through concubinage and intermarriage, Indian women became enmeshed in Spanish life, and their mestizo offspring were usually recognized for exactly what they were—mixed-race children. Mestizos, outnumbering Spaniards in New Spain as early as 1650, were to play a large role in the later stages of colonization and conquest. Today most of the Mexican population is mestizo—testimony to the early assimilation of much of the Indian population.[23]

The history of Spanish-African mixing is similar. The Spanish brought enslaved Africans to their colonies much earlier than did the English in North America, and they brought Africans in larger numbers proportionate to the European population. The Africans served as artisans and supervisors of Native American slaves, which gave many of them a status much above that of the field laborer. And in the relative absence of Spanish women, Spanish-African intermixing flourished.[24]

Thus, the demographic and economic factors arising out of the Spanish colonizing experience, prompted by incessant contact with dark-skinned Muslims over centuries of Islamic expansion into Spain, created continuous racial blending and a mingled civilization. With no prohibitions against interracial contact and interracial marriage, Spanish, African, and Indian people became extensively intermixed.

A series of family portraits produced in Mexico in the eighteenth century provides a fascinating record of the grafting of racial backgrounds onto the Enlightenment passion for classification as well as its keen interest in the human condition. This genre of paintings, known as *las castas*, marked the first time that Mexican artists chose to represent their own surroundings rather than using European models; some consider this body of paintings a self-portrait of Mexican society. On the other hand, the most important clientele for *las castas* were Spanish visitors who wanted to take a Mexican souvenir back to Europe. Exoticism, therefore, also played a role. Nonetheless, these paintings provide an important glimpse into the everyday life of eighteenth-century Mexico and show that the Mexicans were eager to advertise the remarkable blending of races as virtually the signature of Spain's conquest of the southern half of the Americas. María Concepción García Sáiz has recovered a total of fifty-nine series of the "caste paintings," which she has determined to be the work of seven artists. Further research has brought many other caste paintings to light.[25]

Las castas provide a carefully delineated classification scheme for the various kinds and degrees of racial mingling. A Spanish and Indian couple, for example, had a mestizo child. Mestizo and Spanish mates produced castizo children. African and Spanish parents created mulatto children. The offspring of Spanish and mulatto was a morisco. The child of morisco and Spanish was a chino, or albino. A chino and Indian pair had a child that was termed *salta atras*, literally, to jump back (away from Spanish blood). And so forth, even to the point of racial entanglements so perplexing that the resulting persons were *tente en el aire*, "you grope in the air," or *no te entiendo*, "I don't get you"—a mixing of blood impossible to unscramble.[26]

It is foolish to overromanticize this mixing of blood. On the positive side, the caste paintings of interracial families—mostly portrayed in serene domestic and workaday settings—invited tolerance, common compassion, and some understanding of "the fundamental cohesion of the human race."[27] Surely the widespread distribution of these caste paintings spread the notion in Spain, where many of the paintings are found today, that interracial mixing was not repugnant; it was rather the natural human mingling that occurred when three worlds met.

Yet the caste paintings also tell us of the careful attention to racial distinctions that discloses the Spaniards' sense of racial superiority. They portray what has been called a "pigmentocratic system," in which social and economic status depended largely on skin color.[28] A Spaniard in Mexico explained, "If the mixed-blood is the offspring of a Spaniard and an Indian, the stigma disappears at the third step in descent . . . [whereas] a mulatto can never leave his condition of mixed blood but rather it is the Spanish element that is lost and absorbed into the condition of a Negro."

Some caste paintings registered domestic discord, and they are especially revealing in associating marital turbulence with the mixing of African and Indian bloodstreams, whereas the dark-skinned African or Indian who married a Spaniard could count on a child with a favorable temperament. In one *castas* series, for example, one painting is inscribed, "In the Americas people of different colours, customs, temperaments, and languages are born: Born of the Spaniard and the Indian woman is a Mestizo, who is generally humble, tranquil and straightforward." Another painting proclaims, "The pride and sharp wits of the Mulatto are instilled by his white father and black mother." But in another family portrait, "the Jibaro born of Indian mother and Calpamulato father is restless and almost always arrogant"; in yet another, "from Lobo and Indian woman, the Cambujo is usually slow, lazy, and cumbersome."[29]

In British American colonies, we can find no such pictures acknowledging racially mixed families or classifying them by degrees of mixture. Indeed, artists and publishers of such caste paintings would probably have been expelled from colonial towns (while going broke). The reason is not that racial intermingling was emotionally or sensuously unacceptable; rather, it was ideologically repugnant. Male settlers had strong objections not to sexual relations (most often coercive) with African women, but to giving the offspring of such interracial liaisons a half- or partway

Fig. 1.3 One can imagine how this sixteen-part painting of racial mixing in Nueva España would have occasioned interest if hung on the wall of a merchant of Seville in about 1750. Today, many such paintings are in private collections in Spain, Mexico, France, and the United States. Courtesy National Institute of Anthropology and History, Mexico City, Mexico.

Fig. 1.4 Marriage between a Spanish woman and an African man produced both a mulatto child and a serene domestic environment in this caste painting. Reprinted from María Concepción García Sáiz, *Las castas Mexicanas: Un genero pictorico americano*, 226.

status in society.[30] Also, English males, coming largely with families or with access to European females, had little compulsion to consort with Native American women. Nor, in the main, were English colonizers powerful enough to subject the Native American peoples or to extract tribute labor from them. In English North America, a very different demographic, economic, and ideological context planted the seeds of the racial binary thinking that became the basis of what has been called a white *Herrenvolk* democracy.[31]

The master ideology of the North American master class was not uncontested, however. Largely unnoticed by historians were many people who conducted their lives, formed families, raised children, and created their own identities in ways that defied the official racial ideology. Originating with the first interracial encounters, the mestizo counter-ideology stood in constant, shifting tension with the doctrine of racial purity. Most of its adherents were people who issued no tracts, passed no laws, and preached no sermons, but they announced their ideas, values, and racial preferences with their feet. Some of these racial boundary jumpers were the so-called white Indians, such as John Hunter, who grew up among the Kickapoos, Kansas, and Osages. Several thousand Americans who were captured by Indians in white-Indian warfare chose to remain in Indian society. To the horror of white cultural leaders, many married there. Precious few Indians took the reverse route of choosing to remain in white society after exposure to it. Crèvecoeur, in his celebrated *Letters from an American Farmer* (1782), wrote of the Indians, "There must be in their social bond something singularly captivating, and far superior to anything to be boasted of among us; for thousands of Europeans are Indians, and we have no examples of even one of those aborigines having from choice become Europeans."[32]

Also confounding the ideology of racial separation was an American universalism that posited "a social vision and a definition of nationhood" that grounded "public life and institutions not on an exclusive heritage but on natural rights."[33] The American revolutionists abandoned this Enlightenment universalism when they backed away from what they knew was the impossibility of creating a free republic based on inalienable rights while they perpetuated slave labor. Despite this massive contradiction, which has disfigured all subsequent American history, the belief persisted, at least in some quarters, that the fusion of peoples across ethnic and racial lines could produce a more vigorous society. Two generations after the Revolution, William Lloyd Garrison predicted in 1831 that "the time is assuredly hastening . . .

Fig. 1.5 This caste painting of a violent mulatto woman attacking her *coyote* mestizo husband seems to warn against racial intermixture. The child of this union, labeled "Ahí te estás," or "Stay where you are," is evidently expected to carry out her parents' discord in similarly threatening behavior. Reprinted from García Sáiz, *Las castas Mexicanas*, 229.

when the distinctions of color will be as little consulted as the height and bulk of the body, when colored men shall be found in our legislative halls and stand on perfect equality with whites." Herman Melville proclaimed in *Redburn* (1849), "You can not spill a drop of American blood without spilling the blood of the whole world. . . . On this Western Hemisphere all tribes and people are forming into one federated whole." In *The Confidence Man*, Melville's shadowy figure asks, "What are you? What am I? Nobody knows who anybody is."[34]

Most white Americans had no intention of federating across racial lines and were doing their best to discourage such commingling as Garrison predicted. Yet Melville's vision commanded considerable respect. Boston's Ralph Waldo Emerson echoed it: "a new compound more precious than any" is being melded into an "asylum of all nations" where "the energy of Irish, Germans, Swedes, Poles, & Cossacks, & all the European tribes—of the Africans, & of the Polynesians, will construct a new race as vigorous as the new Europe which came out of the smelting pot of the Dark Ages." Wendell Phillips, the thundering abolitionist from Boston, approvingly spoke of "The United States of the United Races" in 1853; he dwelt on the same point in 1863 when the nation was immersed in a cataclysmic bloodletting. The intensely Christian Phillips envisioned an alchemical laboratory for a new and extraordinarily vital race. He imagined "the melting of the Negro into the various races that congregate on the continent" in "gradual and harmonizing union, in honorable marriage. In my nationality," he proclaimed, "there is but one idea—the harmonious and equal mingling of all races. No nation ever became great which was born of one blood."[35]

The power of these cosmopolitan proclamations might have found their rendezvous with destiny on January 1, 1863, when Abraham Lincoln's Emancipation Proclamation unshackled four million black Americans. But the promise of cashing in the revolutionary generation's promissory note crumbled before a stiff-backed white national consciousness that gathered momentum in the nineteenth century. Antiamalgamationists were carrying the day, blackface minstrelsy was ridiculing free black life, and phrenologists were promulgating the doctrine of the genetically deficient dark-skinned races.

By the early twentieth century, the white middle and upper classes in the United States began to retreat to exclusive suburbs, indulge in a fetish of genealogy, and invent a comforting history of Anglo-Saxonism. At the same time, anthropometric studies stood Wendell Phillips's idea of a cosmopolitan intermixed race on its head. From an outpouring of purportedly scientific research, Americans learned that racial mixing produced sterile and anemic offspring that would lead American society toward a Darwinian fate of racial unfitness. In this way, studies of race bulwarked the racial ideology of the period, "greatly strengthening popular prejudice by clothing it," as one historian has written, "in the mantle of academic and scientific authority."[36]

In the early twentieth century, racial intermingling dropped precipitously as a new white orthodoxy depicted mixed-race people as degenerate and racial amalgamation as a prescription for national suicide. Frenzied opposition to racial intermarriage reached its height as the eugenics movement, which referred to racial mixing in such terms as "hybrid degeneracy" and "mongrelization," swept the country. Paradoxically, this occurred in the so-called Progressive Era. The herald of the eugenics movement was an eastern establishment lawyer who bore the name of two presidents. Madison Grant was reared at Yale and Columbia and became, avocationally, a traveler, writer, and zoologist. His special passion was preserving the treasures of America: the buffalo, the redwoods, and the white race. Gunnar Myrdal would later call him "the high priest of racialism in America." In *The Passing of the Great Race* (1916), Grant brought to fever pitch the white fear that the intellectual and moral attainments of the white race would be destroyed by racial intermixing. The progeny of mixed unions would inevitably degenerate to the lower type. "The cross between white and Indian is an Indian," he wrote; "the cross between a white man and a Negro is a Negro; the cross between a white man and a Hindu is a Hindu; the cross between any of the three European races and a Jew is a Jew."[37]

The Progressives were notably unprogressive on the topic of racial fusion; their "melting pot" ideal was limited to Americanizing the European immigrants and had nothing to do with racial mixing. But at least some on their radical wing kept alive the idea of a federated, transnational, transracial democratic culture. Some colleges launched courses on race relations, and social scientists, led by Robert E. Park at the University of Chicago, began studying the cultures of ethnic minorities. From this research came a model of stages of cultural interaction that in theory led relentlessly to racial amalgamation.[38]

The clarion voice of mestizo America belonged to a brilliant young Anglo-Saxon man of letters whose twisted body contained a gigantic mind. Writing in 1916, Randolph Bourne—a contemporary of Madison Grant—told of "hard-hearted old Brahmins virtuously indignant at the spectacle of the immigrant refusing to be melted," as World War I brought to the surface "vigorous nationalistic and cultural movements in this country." Thoroughly Brahmin himself in background, Bourne preached that the nation would never achieve greatness and never build on its own founding principles by washing out of its immigrant masses all that they came from and all they wished to preserve. The melting pot, Bourne charged, was a failure as a program for Anglo-Saxon cultural conversion; American nationalism could find its destiny as internationalism. In fact, he argued, "we have all unawares been building up the first international nation."[39]

As World War I was raging, Bourne was already celebrating a polycentric American culture in which cultural identity would become "based partly on descent and partly on consent." This "transnationality," wrote Bourne, would be "a weaving back and forth, with the other lands, of many threads of all sizes and colors. Any movement which attempts to thwart this weaving, or to dye the fabric any one color, or disentangle the threads of the strands, is false to this cosmopolitan vision." Bourne addressed the question of race gingerly, although he welcomed the "migratory [Mexican] alien who has lived with us and caught the pioneer spirit and a sense of new social vistas." But he was extraordinary in an era when race relations reached their nadir in American history. Though his bloodlines were intensely Anglo-Saxon, Bourne burned with conviction that the nation would impoverish itself if Anglo-Saxon obsessionism sucked the essence out of the varied American peoples. "He, if anyone, in the days to come," wrote Van Wyck Brooks, "would have conjured out of our dry soil the green shoots of a beautiful and a characteristic literature; he knew that soil so well, and why it was dry, and how it ought to be irrigated."[40] The modern American identity could never be reduced to a single monochromatic lineage. Instead, the cultural identity of Americans had to be repeatedly reforged and refashioned as people of different backgrounds, ancestral roots, and cultural leanings came into contact with each other, both inside and outside of marriage.

Bourne died in the 1918 influenza epidemic at age thirty-two. What nearly died with him were hopes for transcending Anglo-Saxonism and also transcending a cultural pluralism that envisioned a United States full of durable ethnic blocs. A militant nationalism, fed by fears of revolutionary bolshevism in Russia, now coursed through the nation. After World War I, criminalization of dissent, deportation of aliens, the rise of the Ku Klux Klan, and a sudden slamming shut of the doors of immigration gave resonance to the trumpet of Madison Grant rather than to that of Randolph Bourne.

Bourne's transnational America would have to await another world war and a cold war that followed it. In the interwar era, an even more utopian vision of a thoroughly intermixed cosmic race was promoted by the Mexican José Vasconcelos and by the French anthropologist Pierre Teilhard de Chardin. But these visionaries, eerily echoing Wendell Phillips, were read only by fellow mystics and yearners for universal unity. In the United States, they had scant popular appeal. Only in cosmopolitan centers, especially New York, did the words of Vasconcelos, expressed in *La Raza Cósmica* (1925), have currency: "the future race," he wrote, "the definitive race, the synthetical race, the integral race, [will] be made up of the genius and the blood of all peoples and, for that reason, more capable of free brotherhood and of a truly universal vision."[41]

The vision of Bourne, Vasconcelos, and Teilhard de Chardin would be taken up most eloquently a couple of generations later by a man who was born halfway around the world in a vastly different culture. Bourne would have appreciated Salman Rushdie. Writing in defense of *The Satanic Verses* (1988), which inspired cultural and religious essentialists to offer one million dollars to snuff out his voice, Rushdie explains that it was

> written from the very experience of uprooting, disjuncture and metamorphosis . . . that is the migrant condition, and from which, I believe, can be derived a metaphor for all humanity.
>
> Standing at the centre of the novel is a group of characters most of whom are British Muslims, or not particularly religious persons of Muslim background, struggling with just the sort of great problems that have arisen to surround the book, problems of hybridization and ghettoization, of reconciling the old and the new. Those who oppose the novel most vociferously today are of the opinion that intermingling with a different culture will inevitably weaken and ruin their own. I am of the opposite opinion. *The Satanic Verses* celebrates hybridity, impurity, intermingling, the transformation that comes of new and unexpected combinations of human beings, cultures, ideas, politics,

movies, songs. It rejoices in mongrelization and fears the absolutism of the Pure. *Mélange*, hotchpotch, a bit of this and a bit of that is *how newness enters the world. It is* the great possibility that mass migration gives the world, and I have tried to embrace it. *The Satanic Verses* is for change-by-fusion, change-by-conjoining. It is a love-song to our mongrel selves.[42]

The Satanic Verses has a special vibrancy today in view of how wide the doors of immigration to the United States have swung since 1965. The flow of immigrants now exceeds one million each year, with another quarter million illegal immigrants joining them. These newcomers are overwhelmingly Asian and Latino, but many thousands more each year are coming from Africa—on an airborne "middle passage" of a very different kind. Quite remarkably, it was the cold war that was responsible for prying open the doors of immigration. As secretary of state Dean Rusk argued in 1965, the United States must end its racist immigration restriction laws of the 1920s because they undermined the nation's need to offer nonwhite Third World nations an alternative to communism. The immigration laws of 1965 and 1991 have changed the face of this country. Today only one in five Americans is of British descent.

Accompanying this demographic tectonic plate shift has been another great phenomenon of our own time—the breaking down of the social, religious, emotional, and marital barriers that have separated people of different homelands, hues, and histories in the United States. The invisible Berlin Wall, the racial wall, is being dismantled stone by stone.[43] The laws prohibiting miscegenation began to fall in western states in the late 1940s, and in the South after the landmark *Loving v. Virginia* Supreme Court decision in 1967. Today, in Hawaii, 60 percent of babies born each year are of mixed race. In Los Angeles County, the rise in the percentage of Japanese American women who marry out of their ethnic group has risen from one of every ten in the 1950s to two of three today. Similar trends pertain to other Asian American groups. Seventy percent of American Indians tie bonds with mates who are not Indian.[44] Even the most enduring nightmare of Euroamerica—racial intermarriage between black and white partners—is no longer extraordinary. Outside the South, more than ten percent of all African American males today marry nonblack women, and black-white marriages nationwide have tripled since 1970. Mestizo America is a happening thing. A multiracial baby boom is occurring in America today.[45]

Human emotions—the attraction of people to each other regardless of race and religion and much else—have run ahead of ideology and have often caused identity confusion and anguish. As so often in history, young people have taken the lead. They have founded organizations that have such names as Interracial, Intercultural Pride in Berkeley, Multiracial Americans of Southern California in Los Angeles, and the Biracial Family Network in Chicago. These people resist racial reductionism, a one-dimensional construction of their identity, and insist that identity has many layers, racial and otherwise.[46]

There is nothing new about crossing racial boundaries; what is new is the frequency of border crossings and boundary hoppings and the refusal to bow to the thorn-filled American concept, perhaps unknown outside the United States, that each person has a race but only one.[47] Racial blending is undermining the master idea that race is an irreducible marker among diverse peoples—an idea in any case that always has been socially constructed and has no scientific validity. (In this century, revivals of purportedly scientifically provable racial categories have surfaced every generation or so. Ideas die hard, especially when they are socially and politically useful.) Twenty-five years ago, it would have been unthinkable for Time-Life to publish a computer-created chart of racial synthesizing; seventy-five years ago, an issue on *The New Face of America* might have put *Time* out of business for promoting racial impurity.[48]

Pride in racial mixing and pride in descent from different races have historical roots, though they are not very deep in this country. In the early twentieth century, biracial couples founded Manasseh clubs in Milwaukee and Chicago, named after the half-Egyptian son of the Old Testament's Joseph. In the 1940s, Los Angeles had its Miscegenation Club to help multiracial couples and their children to "affirm both their heritages."[49] These are the pioneers of the suppressed and scorned Americans who dared to oppose the relentless bichromatism that entrapped white and black Americans alike.

Uncovering the shrouded past of mestizo America bears on the ongoing pursuit of *e pluribus unum* in this nation—the search for creating commonality out of diversity. Few would argue in favor of universal intermarriage to achieve *e pluribus unum;* all our grandchildren would be gray, tan, or tawny, and ethnic or racial identity formation would be irrelevant. What we do need in our passionate and sometimes violent arguments about American culture and identity, about courses, canons, and holidays, about entitlements and compensatory programs, is a social and intellectual construction of a mestizo America. This construction can find enlightenment and derive sustenance from a hidden chapter of the nation's submerged and tangled mestizo past.

In today's multicultural wars, the tendency has been to define one's identity and therefore one's politics by race or ethnicity. "Multiculturalism" is a slippery term that is used in various and often contradictory ways. When multiculturalism is used simply as multiracialism and as such pretends that culture can be transmitted through genes, it fosters identity politics that absolutize racial differences. Multiculturalism as multiracialism clouds the complicated business of acquiring and transmitting culture. Still worse, when multiculturalism is construed simply as multiracialism, it has led toward a definitional absolutism that has unwittingly defeated egalitarian and humanitarian goals by smothering inequalities of class and fueling interethnic and interracial tensions that give more powerful groups opportunities to manipulate these divisions. Racial absolutism—the enemy of *mestizaje*—insists that racial difference is the alpha and omega of intellectual discourse and politics and, therefore, of social action. This has diverted attention from the intensifying social and economic inequality that surely threatens a democratic polity.[50]

Of course, arguments about culture are about power, and hence the kind of multiculturalism that insists on studying self-contained and absolutized racial groups is meant to effect a redistribution of power. All of this began as a legitimate claim to dignity, as a way of shattering the walls of exclusion, domination, and derogation, as an insistence on recognition and representation, and as a strategy for overcoming psychological damage. Ethnic and racial group identity long ago emerged in response to the power of white supremacist America, and at many points in our history ethnic and racial politics have been indispensable in the social reform movements that have brought American society closer to realizing its founding principles. In the past, most historians have supported ethnoracial communities as what David Hollinger calls "vital sites for the formation, articulation, and sustenance of cultural values, social identities, and political power."[51] But many of us have always assumed that cultural particularisms would be vital repositories of political strength and cultural wisdom so long as they did not become brittle and self-contained and so long as they held to a long-term agenda of forging a unified, comprehensive, cosmopolitan, cross-ethnic, and cross-racial community.

Today we need to ask about the costs of the rigidifying of ethnoracial particularisms. The specters of Sarajevo, Sri Lanka, and Somalia fill us with haunting images and dark forebodings. But the unleashing of ancient ethnic and religious hatreds that has quickly followed the toppling of centralized authority around the world is not the main reason for rethinking our own situation. More relevant to our unique historical development is the possibility that we are best served by imagining new ways of transcending America's Achilles' heel of race, now that a certain amount of progress has been achieved in living up to our own credo, especially since the freedom struggles of the 1960s. What we need is a pan-ethnic, pan-racial, antiracist sensibility. Only through hybridity—not only in physical race crossing but in our minds as a shared pride in and identity with hybridity—can our nation break "the stranglehold that racialist hermeneutics has over cultural identity."[52]

Historians know how Anglo-chauvinists invented a racial typology and racial categorization to exclude and exploit many of America's peoples; but now we see that historians will need to write about how an ideology has arisen in this era among excluded groups to celebrate racial difference and even to insist on the viciously racist one-drop rule to preserve entitlements. The ethnoracial element in self-identity is not likely to disappear quickly because jobs and dollars, as well as demonstrating discrimination in many forms, depend upon legislative mandates based on racial categories that classify people by skin color and genetic ancestry.[53] Yet affiliation by voluntary consent rather than prescribed descent is an unstoppable process that is being carried forward on a mighty wave of personal lives, mate choices, and mixed-race progeny.[54] When it receives its proper due, the hidden history of mestizo America may help to produce a more cosmopolitan and just America as we approach the end of the century; but this can happen only if this nation will live up to its foundational principles of freedom, equality, and social justice.

NOTES

This essay was delivered as the presidential address at the national meeting of the Organization of American Historians in Washington, March 31, 1995. For shrewd critiques of this essay, I am indebted to Carlos Cortez, David Hollinger, J. Jorge Klor de Alva, and Jeffrey Prager. For research assistance, I am indebted to Edith Sparks.

1. For historical accounts of the Pocahontas-Rolfe union, see, for example, Philip L. Barbour, *Pocahontas and Her World: A Chronicle of America's First Settlement in Which Is Related the Story of the Indians and the Englishmen, Particularly Captain John Smith, Captain Samuel Argall, and Master John Rolfe* (Boston, 1970); Grace Steele Woodward, *Pocahontas* (Norman, 1969); and Karen Ordahl Kupperman, *Settling with the Indians: The Meeting of English and Indian Cultures in America, 1580–1640* (Totowa, 1980).

2. For the term "mestizo America" (which I have changed to mestizo United States to avoid equating the United States with the Americas), I am indebted to Brewton Berry, "America's Mestizos," in *The Blending of Races: Marginality and Identity in World Perspective*, ed. Noel P. Gist and Anthony G. Dworkin (New York, 1972).

3. The earliest known appearance of the word "miscegenation," defined as the "mixture of races [and] especially the sexual union of whites with Negroes," was in the title of a book by David Goodman Croly and George Wakeman, *Miscegenation: The Theory of the Blending of the Races, Applied to the American White Man and Negro* (1863; reprint, New York, 1984); *Oxford English Dictionary*, 2d ed., s.v. "miscegenation." Robert Beverley, *History and Present State of Virginia*, ed. Louis B. Wright (Williamsburg, 1947), 159, 38–39.

4. William K. Boyd, ed., *William Byrd's Histories of the Dividing Line betwixt Virginia and North Carolina* (Raleigh, 1929), 3–4. For colonial American attitudes toward white-African unions, see Winthrop D. Jordan, *White over Black: American Attitudes toward the Negro, 1550–1812* (Chapel Hill, 1968), 136–78, 461–75; and Leon A. Higginbotham, *In the Matter of Color: Race and the American Legal Process* (New York, 1978).

5. Thomas Jefferson quoted in Richard Drinnon, *Facing West: The Metaphysics of Indian-Hating and Empire-Building* (Minneapolis, 1980), 83. Thomas Jefferson, "Advice to Indian Chiefs: To Captain Hendrick, the Delawares, Mohicans and Munries," Washington, Dec. 21, 1808, in *Thomas Jefferson: Letters and Addresses*, ed. William B. Parker (New York, 1908), 190.

6. Sam Houston's connection with the Cherokees is most thoroughly recounted in Jack Gregory and Rennard Strickland, *Sam Houston with the Cherokees, 1829–1833* (Austin, 1967). For Houston's relationships with Indian women, see 82–87, 106–07.

7. A more recent biographical account of Houston, which also documents his Cherokee relationships, is Marshall De Bruhl, *Sword of San Jacinto: A Life of Sam Houston* (New York, 1993), esp. 105–41.

8. J. Frederick Fausz, "An 'Abundance of Blood Shed on Both Sides': England's First Indian War, 1609–1614," *Virginia Magazine of History and Biography* 98 (January 1990): 3–56.

9. De Bruhl, *Sword of San Jacinto*, 264.

10. For general treatments of racial blending, see Joel Williamson, *New People: Miscegenation and Mulattoes in the United States* (New York, 1980); Albert Murray, *The Omni-Americans: New Perspectives on Black Experience and American Culture* (New York, 1970); Paul Spickard, *Mixed Blood: Intermarriage and Ethnic Identity in Twentieth-Century America* (Madison, 1989); and Maria. P. P. Root, ed., *Racially Mixed People in America* (Newbury Park, 1992). On European-Indian intermarriage, see, for example, Jacqueline Peterson, "Women Dreaming: The Religiopsychology of Indian-White Marriages and the Rise of a Métis Culture," in *Western Women: Their Land, Their Lives*, ed. Lillian Schlissel, Vicki L. Ruiz, and Janice Monk (Albuquerque, 1988), 49–68; and John Mack Faragher, "The Custom of the Country: Cross-Cultural Marriage in the Far Western Fur Trade," in *Western*

Women, ed. Schlissel, Ruiz, and Monk, 199–215. For an introduction to the growing literature on the Métis, particularly on people of mixed Indian and European descent identifying themselves collectively as distinct from both Indian and white communities, see Jacqueline Peterson and Jennifer S. H. Brown, eds., *The New Peoples: Being and Becoming Métis in North America* (Winnipeg, 1985).

11. For John Johnson, see Faragher, "Custom of the Country." Doyce B. Nunis, Jr., "Michael Laframboise," in *The Mountain Men and the Fur Trade of the Far West: Biographical Sketches of the Participants by Scholars of the Subject and with Introductions by the Editor*, ed. LeRoy R. Hafen (Glendale, 1968), 147. Gene Caeser, *King of the Mountain Men: The Life of Jim Bridger* (New York, 1961); Faragher, "Custom of the Country." For an account of Kit Carson's marriages, see, for example, Thelma S. Guild and Harvey L. Carter, *Kit Carson: A Pattern for Heroes* (Lincoln, 1984), 69, 95, 106–07, 168.

12. See, for example, William R. Swagerty, "Marriage and Settlement Patterns of Rocky Mountain Trappers and Traders," *Western Historical Quarterly* 11 (April 1980): 159–80; Richard White, *The Middle Ground: Indians, Empires, and Republics in the Great Lakes Region, 1650–1815* (Cambridge, 1991); and Patricia Limerick, *The Legacy of Conquest: The Unbroken Past of the American West* (New York, 1987).

13. For historical accounts of Afro-Indian intercultural contact, see Kenneth W. Porter, *The Negro on the American Frontier* (New York, 1971); Richard Halliburton, Jr., *Red over Black: Black Slavery among the Cherokee Indians* (Westport, 1977); Theda Perdue, *Slavery and the Evolution of Cherokee Society, 1540–1866* (Knoxville, 1979); Daniel F. Littlefield, *Africans and Creeks from the Colonial Period to the Civil War* (Westport, 1976); and Jack D. Forbes, *Black Africans and Native Americans: Color, Race, and Caste in the Evolution of Red-Black Peoples* (Oxford, 1988).

14. See Lamont D. Thomas, *Rise to Be a People: A Biography of Paul Cuffe* (Urbana, 1986).

15. William S. Pollitzer, "The Physical Anthropology and Genetics of Marginal People of the Southeastern United States," *American Anthropologist* 74 (June 1972): 719–34; Joseph Douglas Deal, *Race and Class in Colonial Virginia: Indians, Englishmen, and Africans during the Seventeenth Century* (Ann Arbor, 1981); Brewton Berry, *Almost White: A Study of Certain Racial Hybrids in the Eastern United States* (New York, 1963); and K. I. Blu, *The Lumbee Problem: The Making of an American Indian People* (New York, 1980).

16. One of the latest of many studies on social and cultural Cherokee transformation after the American Revolution is William G. McLoughlin, *Cherokee Renascence in the New Republic* (Princeton, 1986), esp. 67–70, 331–39, 343–45. Cherokee Advocate Office, *Laws of the Cherokee Nation: Adopted by the Council at Various Periods, Printed for the Benefit of the Nation* (1852; Wilmington, 1973), 38. For an example of African Americans who became Indian without actually mixing their blood, see Kevin Mulroy, *Freedom on the Border: The Seminole Maroons in Florida, the Indian Territory, Coahuila, and Texas* (Lubbock, 1993).

17. Karen Isaksen Leonard, *Making Ethnic Choices: California's Punjabi Mexican Americans* (Philadelphia, 1992).

18. Frederick Jackson Turner, "The Significance of the Frontier in American History," reprinted in *Rereading Frederick Jackson Turner*, ed. John Mack Faragher (New York, 1994), 47. Leonard, *Making Ethnic Choices*, 203. For widespread racial intermarriage of Mexican Americans, see Peter Skerry, *Mexican-Americans: The Ambivalent Minority* (New York, 1993).

19. See, for another example, Marilyn Halter, *Between Race and Ethnicity: Cape Verdean American Immigrants, 1860–1965* (Urbana, 1993).

20. Root, *Racially Mixed People in America*, 9. In 1918 the U.S. Census Bureau accepted the estimate that three of every four black Americans were of mixed ancestry: see Williamson, *New People*, 111.

21. William Parsons quoted in Carolyn Ashbaugh, *Lucy Parsons: American Revolutionary* (Chicago, 1976), 13. Darlene Clark Hine, ed., *Black Women in America*, 2 vols. (Brooklyn, 1993), 2:909–10. Matt S. Meier, *Mexican American Biographies: A Historical Dictionary, 1836–1987* (New York, 1988), 96–97.

22. Barbara J. Fields, "Ideology and Race in American History," in *Region, Race, and Reconstruction*, ed. J. Morgan Kousser and James M. McPherson (New York, 1982), 149.

23. Literature on Spanish-Indian relations in the New World includes Magnus Mörner, *Race Mixture in the History of Latin America* (Boston, 1967); Marvin Harris, *Patterns of Race in the Americas* (New York, 1964); and Colin MacKay MacLachlan, *The Forging of the Cosmic Race: A Reinterpretation of Colonial Mexico* (Berkeley, 1980).

24. See, for example, Colin A. Palmer, *Slaves of the White God: Blacks in Mexico, 1570–1650* (Cambridge, Mass., 1976).

25. See María Concepción García Sáiz, *Las castas Mexicanas: Un genero pictorico americano* (The Mexican castes: A painting genre) ([Milan], 1989); Nicolas Leon, *Las castas del Mexico colonial o Nueva España* (The castes of colonial Mexico or New Spain) (n.p., 1924); Ilona Katzew, *New World Orders: Casta Painting and Colonial Latin America* (New York, 1996).

26. García Sáiz, *Castas Mexicanas*, 24–29.

27. Ibid., 10.

28. The term "pigmentocratic system" is used in Mörner, *Race Mixture*, 54; Mörner adapted it from the word "pigmentocracy," first used in Alejandro Lipshütz, *El indoamericanismo y el problema racial en las Américas* (Indian-Americanism and the racial problem in the Americas) (Santiago de Chile, 1944), 75. Alexander von Humboldt quoted in Katzew, *New World Orders*, 9.

29. García Sáiz, *Castas Mexicanas*, 103–11.

30. Jordan, *White over Black*, 167–78.

31. The term "white Herrenvolk democracy" was adapted by George Fredrickson, *The Black Image in the White Mind: The Debate on Afro-American Character and Destiny, 1817–1914* (New York, 1971), 61, from its originator, the sociologist Pierre L. van den Berghe, *Race and Racism: A Comparative Perspective* (New York, 1967), 17–18.

32. Richard Drinnon, *White Savage: The Case of John Dunn Hunter* (New York, 1972), 7–8. On "Indianization" of European colonists, see Alden T. Vaughan and Daniel K. Richter, "Crossing the Cultural Divide: Indians and New Englanders, 1605–1763," *Proceedings of the American Antiquarian Society* 90, part 1 (1980): 23–99; Marius Barbeau, "Indian Captivities," *Proceedings of the American Philosophical Society* 94 (Dec. 1950): 522–48; A. Irving Hallowell, "American Indians, White and Black: The Phenomenon of Transculturalization," *Current Anthropology* 4 (December 1963): 519–31; J. Norman Heard, *White into Red: A Study of the Assimilation of White Persons Captured by Indians* (Metuchen, 1973); and James Axtell, "The White Indians of Colonial America," *William and Mary Quarterly*, 32 (January 1975): 55–88. J. Hector St. John Crèvecoeur, *Letters from an American Farmer* (New York, 1957), 208–09.

33. John Higham, "Multiculturalism and Universalism: A History and Critique," *American Quarterly* 45, no. 2 (1993): 197.

34. Garrison, in *The Liberator*, April 2, 1831. Herman Melville, *Redburn: His First Voyage, Being the Sailor-Boy Confessions and Reminiscences of the Son-of-a-Gentleman, in*

the Merchant Service (1849; Evanston, 1969), 169. idem, *The Confidence Man: His Masquerade* (1857; New York, 1954), 216.

35. Ralph Waldo Emerson, *Emerson in His Journals*, ed. Joel Porte (Cambridge, Mass., 1982), 347. Wendell Phillips, "The United States of the United Races," *National Era* 7 (September 1853): 146; the 1863 passage is quoted in Gilbert Osofsky, "Wendell Phillips and the Quest for a New American Identity," *Canadian Review of Studies in Nationalism* (Charlottetown) 1 (fall 1973): 37–39.

36. John G. Mencke, *Mulattoes and Race Mixture: American Attitudes and Images, 1865–1918* (Ann Arbor, 1979), 99.

37. Historical accounts of the eugenics movement include George Fredrickson, *The Arrogance of Race: Historical Perspectives on Slavery, Racism, and Social Inequality* (Middletown, 1988); William Stanton, *The Leopard's Spots: Scientific Attitudes toward Race in America, 1815–1859* (Chicago, 1960); and George W. Stocking, *Race, Culture and Evolution: Essays in the History of Anthropology* (New York, 1968). For a historical account of nativism in the Progressive Era, see, for example, John Higham, *Strangers in the Land: Patterns of American Nativism, 1860–1925* (New Brunswick, 1955). For racism in the Progressive Era, see, for example, Ray Stannard Baker, *Following the Color Line: American Negro Citizenship in the Progressive Era* (New York, 1964); John Dittmer, *Black Georgia in the Progressive Era, 1900–1920* (Urbana, 1977); and Noralee Frankel and Nancy S. Dye, eds., *Gender, Class, Race, and Reform in the Progressive Era* (Lexington, 1991). Gunnar Myrdal, *An American Dilemma: The Negro Problem and Modern Democracy*, 2 vols. (New York, 1944), 114. Madison Grant, *The Passing of the Great Race* (1916; New York, 1921), 17–18; quoted in Myrdal, *American Dilemma*, 114.

38. See R. Fred Wacker, *Ethnicity, Pluralism, and Race: Race Relations Theory in America before Myrdal* (Westport, 1983); and Henry Yu, "Thinking about Orientals: Modernity, Social Science, and Asians in Twentieth-Century America" (Ph.D. diss., Princeton University, 1995), 78–91.

39. Randolph S. Bourne, "Trans-National America," *Atlantic Monthly* 118 (July 1916), reprinted in Randolph S. Bourne, *War and the Intellectuals: Essays, 1915–1919*, ed. Carl Resek (New York, 1964), 107, 117. For secondary literature on Randolph Bourne, see Leslie J. Vaughn, "Cosmopolitanism, Ethnicity and American Identity: Randolph Bourne's 'Trans-National America,' " *Journal of American Studies* 25 (December 1991): 443–59; Bruce Clayton, *Forgotten Prophet: The Life of Randolph Bourne* (Baton Rouge, 1984); and Werner Sollors, *Beyond Ethnicity: Consent and Descent in American Culture* (New York, 1986). For collections of Bourne's own writings, see Olaf Hansen, ed., *The Radical Will: Selected Writings of Randolph Bourne, 1911–1918* (New York, 1977); and Bourne, *War and the Intellectuals*, ed. Resek.

40. Vaughn, "Cosmopolitanism, Ethnicity, and American Identity," 452. Bourne, "Trans-National America," 121. Van Wyck Brooks quoted in John Adam Moreau, *Randolph Bourne: Legend and Reality* (Washington, D.C., 1966), 205.

41. José Vasconcelos, *La Raza Cósmica* (The cosmic race), bilingual edition, trans. Didier Tisdel Jaén (Los Angeles, 1979), 18.

42. Salman Rushdie, *Imaginary Homelands: Essays and Criticism, 1981–1991* (London, 1991), 394.

43. For an early campaign against laws prohibiting racial intermarriage, see Louis Ruchames, "Race, Marriage, and Abolition in Massachusetts," *Journal of Negro History* 40 (July 1955): 250–73.

44. H. H. L. Kitano et al., "Asian-American Interracial Marriage," *Journal of Marriage*

and the Family 46 (February 1984): 179–90; Mark Nagler, "North American Indians and Intermarriage," in *Interracial Marriage: Expectations and Realities*, ed. Irving S. Stuart and Lawrence Edwin (New York, 1973), 280–95.

45. M. Belinda Tucker and Claudia Mitchell-Kernan, "New Trends in Black American Interracial Marriage: The Social Structural Context," *Journal of Marriage and the Family* 52 (February 1990): 209–18; *New York Times*, Dec. 2, 1991, A1, B6; and Paul Ruffins, "Interracial Coalitions," *Atlantic* 265 (June 1990): 28–34. Scholarly investigations of racial intermarriage are increasing rapidly. See, for example, Edward Murguía, *Chicano Intermarriage: A Theoretical and Empirical Study* (San Antonio, 1982); Stanley Leberson and Mary C. Waters, *From Many Strands: Ethnic and Racial Groups in Contemporary America* (New York, 1988); Kathy Y. Russel, Midge Wilson, and Robert E. Hall, *The Color Complex: The Politics of Skin Color among African Americans* (New York, 1992); and various essays in Root, *Racially Mixed People in America*.

46. G. Reginald Daniel, "Beyond Black and White: The New Multiracial Consciousness," in *Racially Mixed People in America*, ed. Root, 333–41.

47. See Spickard, *Mixed Blood*; Root, *Racially Mixed People in America*; and F. James Davis, *Who Is Black? One Nation's Definition* (University Park, 1991).

48. Paul R. Spickard, "The Illogic of American Racial Categories," in *Racially Mixed People in America*, ed. Root, 12–23. For the latest revival of race as a biological category, see Richard J. Herrnstein and Charles Murray, *The Bell Curve: Intelligence and Class Structure in American Life* (New York, 1994); for the onslaught of criticism that their argument has received, see Russell Jacoby and Naomi Glauberman, eds., *The* Bell Curve *Debate: History, Documents, Opinions* (New York, 1995). "Rebirth of a Nation, Computer-Style," chart, in *The New Face of America*, special issue *Time* 142 (fall 1993): 66–67.

49. Daniel, "Beyond Black and White," 335.

50. In these comments and those below, I have been influenced by Philip Gleason, *Speaking of Diversity: Language and Ethnicity in Twentieth-Century America* (Baltimore, 1992); Higham, "Multiculturalism and Universalism"; and David Hollinger, "How Wide the Circle of the 'We'? American Intellectuals and the Problem of the Ethos since World War II," *American Historical Review* 98 (April 1993): 317–37.

51. Hollinger, "How Wide the Circle of the 'We'?" 322.

52. J. Jorge Klor de Alva, "Beyond Black, Brown, or White: Cultural Diversity, Strategic Hybridity, and the Future of Democracy" (paper presented at the Bohen Foundation, New York, N.Y., Feb. 11, 1994) 23. See also Todd Gitlin, "From Universality to Difference: Notes on the Idea of the Fragmentation of the Left," *Contention* 5 (winter 1993): 15–40; and David Hollinger, "Post-Ethnic America," *Contention* 4 (fall 1992): 79–96.

53. Lawrence Wright, "One Drop of Blood," *New Yorker*, July 25, 1994, 46–55.

54. Sollors, *Beyond Ethnicity*.

Part I

Colonial Era

Chapter Two

"They Need Wives"
Métissage and the Regulation of Sexuality in French Louisiana, 1699–1730

Jennifer M. Spear

> There are here . . . young men and soldiers who are in
> a position to undertake farms. They need wives. I know
> only this one way to hold them.
> —Jean-Baptiste Martin d'Artaguiette, 1710

When the French colonization of Louisiana began in the early eighteenth century, *commissaire ordonnateur* d'Artaguiette and other Louisiana administrators were faced with a problem they believed could be solved only by increasing the immigration of single Frenchwomen into the colony.[1] From 1699 through the 1720s, administrators and missionaries were constantly concerned with the "concubinage among the backwoodsmen and soldiers" with Indian women.[2] These secular and religious officials believed that relationships between Frenchmen and Indian women were "retard[ing] the growth of this colony" by discouraging male Louisiana colonists from settling down and establishing themselves as farmers.[3] Similarly, they feared "losing" French Louisianians to the Indians' "alternative form of society for sex and recreation."[4] Officials believed that the presence of more Frenchwomen would allow the backwoodsmen, *engagés*, or indentured servants,[5] and discharged soldiers to find wives among the European population and, in turn, that the resulting marriages to European women would encourage the establishment of a stable and self-sufficient colony. In this essay, I examine the ways in which Louisiana administrators and missionaries constructed the presence of sexual relations between Frenchmen and Indian women as a hindrance in their attempts to create a European colony, and how they came to believe that Frenchwomen could become the colony's saviors. Their reactions to métissage, or interracial unions, and their reasons for turning to Frenchwomen were greatly influenced by how they constructed cultural difference and by their desire to manage sexuality: of Europeans, both male and female, and of Indians.[6]

Historians who have addressed the issue of métissage in the American colonies have generally stressed either culture or demography in accounting for the presence or absence of these relationships. For the proponents of the cultural attitudes explanation, historical experiences of interacting with peoples of different cultures led to an openness to métissage,[7] while the demographically inclined historians argue that demographic factors, particularly gender ratios among the European population and the ratios of Africans, Indians, and Europeans in any specific place determined whether European men engaged in relationships with Indian or African women.[8] Both of these explanations, however, focus on the critical factors among the European populations, leaving the non-European women involved in these relationships passive and voiceless.[9] In addition, traditional explanations of métissage have not addressed the role of sexuality in the establishment of European colonies in the Americas.[10] Rather than looking for a purely cultural or demographic explanation, I believe that a dialectical relationship existed between demographic conditions and cultural attitudes; each influenced and reacted to the other. It is precisely this dialectic that we need to examine in order to understand not just the presence of these relationships but also the discourse surrounding them and the offspring created by them.

In the context of colonial Louisiana, historians have disagreed over the frequency and importance of métissage.[11] While it is unlikely, given the nature of the evidence, that the frequency of these relationships will ever be accurately pinned down, métissage is worthy of study because it has a significance beyond its numbers. As I will argue, religious and secular officials perceived métissage as a threat to the establishment of a French colony in Louisiana. An examination of the discourse and practice of métissage illuminates, in the words of Ann Stoler, the "precarious vulnerabilities of imperial systems of control."[12]

France's interest in Louisiana originated in New France and flowed down the Mississippi River to the Gulf of Mexico; in many ways, its early development echoed that of New France. In 1682 Robert Cavelier, sieur de La Salle, traveled from New France down the Mississippi to its mouth, claiming all the lands drained by the river for France and naming this territory in honor of Louis XIV. The first French colony, on the Gulf Coast of present-day Texas, failed, but France's desire to colonize Louisiana continued. International rivalry with Spain and England impelled the Ministry of the Navy, which oversaw the French colonies, to argue that France needed to establish its claim to the territory through settlement in order to contain English and Spanish expansion across the North American continent. By controlling the St. Lawrence and Mississippi Rivers, France could control the interior of the continent.[13] The ministry also believed that a military base along the Gulf of Mexico could help protect France's sugar-rich West Indian islands. Finally, mercantilists saw the vast territory as a potential supplier of raw materials and a future market for French-manufactured goods. Thus in 1699 the Canadian Pierre Le Moyne, sieur d'Iberville, accompanied by his brother, Jean Baptiste Le Moyne, sieur de Bienville, established the first permanent French encampment near present-day Biloxi.[14]

Along with Iberville and Bienville, many of the earliest Euro-Louisianians came by way of New France, and they were overwhelmingly male. Because imperialist and militarist intentions predominated in the early years, the French population of Louisiana was scattered, and most of the first colonists were military personnel. Indeed, the first extant census of 1700 lists 125 men, including 42 military personnel and 61 Canadians, and no women, living at Biloxi.[15] The censuses of 1704 and 1708 also show a predominantly military presence.[16] After the military personnel, the largest group of Euro-Louisianians consisted of trappers, hunters, and *coureurs de bois*.[17] This predominance of men, and the fact that many were from New France, had a profound impact on the formation of relationships with local Indian women.

However, it was not just demographic imbalances among Euro-Louisianians that encouraged métissage. The Canadian immigrants brought with them cultural attitudes and a history of interactions with Indians that differed from those of their French *confrères*, or counterparts. Coming from the frontier society of New France, these Canadians were used to a certain degree of personal freedom. Governor Bienville complained about these "young men who have left Canada on account of [their] wildness," while d'Artaguiette accused them of being "naturally lazy; they fled from Canada only for lawlessness and idleness."[18] But the harshest words came from Bienville's successor, Antoine de Lamothe Cadillac, who described them as "a heap of the dregs from Canada, jailbirds without subordination for religion and for government," despite the fact that he himself had spent his adult life in New France.[19]

This perception of the Canadians' lawlessness and insubordination stemmed partially from their intimate associations with Indians and their apparent acceptance of an "Indian way of life."[20] This was particularly true of the hunters, trappers, and *coureurs de bois* who had quickly learned to adapt to Indian customs and norms in order to facilitate trade. These customs often included integrating themselves into Indian trade and kinship networks through marriage to Indian women.[21] When Bienville complained in 1706, "several marriages of Frenchmen with Indian women [had been] performed by the missionaries who are among the Indians," it is likely that they were these types of marriages.[22]

In addition to these individual alliances designed to facilitate trade, there were official practices that broke down the cultural barriers between European men and Louisiana Indians and encouraged personal, and perhaps intimate, contact between the Frenchmen and Indian women. The first was the custom of sending young French boys, usually orphans, to live in Indian villages to learn their languages in order to later serve as diplomatic go-betweens or interpreters.[23] Iberville and Bienville also intended these boys to become "cultural spies," as Bienville noted that a boy he left with the Chickasaw "can write and informs me often about what is happening in this village."[24] Yet, as historians have noted of New France, it is very likely that this practice led, "in many cases, [to the formation of] a taste for the life they never would lose."[25]

The custom of sending soldiers and other colonists to live in Indian villages during times of famine also broke down cultural barriers. Although France was supposed to be sending regular provisions to its colony, shipments often never arrived or were delayed, and the foods spoiled.[26] Several Euro-Louisianians spent a winter with the Colapissas and Nassitoches in 1706, when Bienville, "seeing that the food supplies were fast diminishing and that no vessel was on the way to bring some, gave permission to several persons of the garrison to go hunting or to go live as best they could among the savage nations friendly to the French."[27] Until Louisiana achieved self-sufficiency, its European residents were dependent on local Indians, especially for food supplies, and administrators occasionally had to disperse the colonists among Indian villages. Bienville was "obliged to send the entire garrison into the woods . . . to seek a living among the Indians" again in 1713.[28] Six years later, because of great want at the fort, the commandant of Biloxi was forced to send his men "to the nearest Indians of the country . . . who received them with great pleasure, and supported them quite well."[29] Upon his arrival as governor in 1713, Cadillac was not pleased to find "all the garrison in the woods among the Indians who have kept them alive as well as they could." Even the officers, he wrote, were reduced to a "deplorable condition" living among the Indians.[30]

André Pénicaut was one of those who stayed with the Colapissas and Nassitoches in the winter of 1706, a stay that he recalled in a narrative published in 1723. When he and fellow colonists arrived at the village, "they embraced us, the men as well as the women and girls, all [were] delighted to see us come to stay with them." Pénicaut lodged with the chief of the Nassitoches and wrote that he

> was not sorry . . . for in his house I received every possible favor. He had two daughters that were the most beautiful of all the savage girls in the district. The older one was twenty; she was called Oulchogonime, which in their language means the good daughter. The second was only eighteen, but was much taller than her older sister. She was named Ouilchil, which means the pretty spinner.

By February 1707, Bienville sent out word for all the Frenchmen to return to Mobile, causing Pénicaut and his colleagues to "bec[o]me quite melancholy." Upon returning to Mobile, however, they were pleased "to behold the provisions that had come for us and to find wine in the lot, which we had not had among the Colapissas. The wine consoled us for the loss of the favors of their girls."[31] While never explicitly stating that he or his fellow Frenchmen engaged in sexual relationships with Colapissas or Nassitoches women, Pénicaut did refer to a kiss between his host's older daughter and Picard, a fellow Frenchmen, claiming, "I was not so sorry about this as I would have been if it had been the younger daughter kissing him."[32] Whether or not sexual relations took place, these occasional stays in Indian villages fostered a familiarity between Indians and Frenchmen that officials would rather have done without.

In *The History of Louisiana*, Antoine Simon Le Page du Pratz, who lived in Louisiana from 1718 to 1734, indicated that at least some Frenchmen were spending more time interacting with Indian women than they were with Indian men. In describing the Natchez Indians, he wrote,

> Tho' the women speak the same language with the men, yet, in their manner of pronunciation, they often soften and smooth the words, whereas the speech of men is more grave and serious. The French, by chiefly frequenting the women, contracted

their manner of speaking, which was ridiculed as an effeminacy by the women, as well as the men, among the natives.[33]

Le Page du Pratz's comment also suggests the presence of a gendered frontier along which Indians and Europeans interacted. In this instance, the Natchez language was spoken differently by men and women—a difference not understood by the French and one that likely led to misunderstandings and conflicts.[34]

While European men like Pénicaut and Le Page du Pratz have left evidence of their interactions with Indian women, no Indian women left records of their reasons for engaging in relationships with European men. Some Indian women may have initiated relationships with French traders because it gave them access to European goods that they had grown to rely on; as conduits of these goods, they may have gained status in their own communities.[35] In addition, Indian fathers may have desired military and trade alliances, as seen in Jesuit Father le Petit's comment that the Illinois were "inviolably attached to the French, by alliances which many of that Nation had contracted with them, in espousing their daughters."[36] Pointing to another possible motivation, Le Page du Pratz claimed that a Natchez chief's wife begged him to marry her daughter "that I might have it in my power to civilize their nation by abolishing their inhuman customs, and introducing those of the French."[37] While it is possible that this exchange took place, it is most likely that Le Page du Pratz interpreted the Natchez woman's reasons, which may have concerned economic or political alliance building, through his own ethnocentric lenses, placing himself in the role of the "civilizing" European. Another possible reading is that the Natchez, like Iberville and Bienville, wanted to plant "cultural spies" among the French.

These practices of sending French boys and colonists to Indian villages for education and survival, respectively, as well as the marriages between Indian women and European traders took place in Indian villages. Other interactions between Indian women and European men took place within the French establishments and demonstrate how sites of contact played a role in determining the nature of these relationships. Interactions that took place within Indian villages were more likely to be consensual, while those occurring in French villages were more likely to be exploitative. As early as 1710, there was a thriving black market in Indian slave women, supplied by Indians in the interior and by raids on nearby villages undertaken by Canadian and Frenchmen themselves. Le Page du Pratz purchased a Chitimacha woman "in order to have a person who could dress our victuals." This unnamed woman remained with him for many years, even refusing her father's offer to buy her back.[38] Le Page du Pratz was not the only one; according to the censuses of 1721, there were 51 Indian slaves in the New Orleans area and 139 in the Mobile-Biloxi area.[39] Although these censuses do not list the gender of the Indian slaves, later censuses document that female Indian slaves outnumbered male ones by almost two to one.[40]

While Le Page du Pratz and others claimed to be seeking domestic help when they bought Indian slaves, Cadillac, among others, was not convinced that this was the real reason European men kept female slaves. In 1713 he noted that "The

Canadians and the soldiers who are not married have female Indian slaves and insist that they cannot dispense with having them to do their washing and to do their cooking or to make their sagamity and to keep their cabins." However, Cadillac argued, if these slaves were only serving as domestic help, "it ought not to prevent the soldiers from going to confessional, or the Canadians either."[41] Cadillac believed that European men were buying Indian slave women to serve as concubines rather than for domestic help.

Father Henry de la Vente, the curate of Mobile, agreed with Cadillac that female Indian slavery was thinly disguised concubinage. Complaining about the religious and moral turpitude he observed among Euro-Louisianians, he wrote, "They prefer to maintain scandalous concubinages with young Indian women, driven by their proclivity for the extremes of licentiousness. They have bought them under the pretext of keeping them as servants, but actually to seduce them, as they in fact have done."[42] Sister Marie-Madeleine Hachard, an Ursuline nun, echoed la Vente's concern when she wrote that "not only debauchery, but dishonesty and all the other vices reign here more than elsewhere."[43]

Although in this instance Cadillac, the secular governor, and la Vente, a religious curate, agreed, generally secular and religious opinions on the two forms of métissage differed. Religious officials were concerned with converting Indian souls and maintaining religiosity among the Euro-Louisianians. They believed that marriage, a relationship sanctified by European church and state, could serve as a "civilizing" vehicle, leading to the cultural colonization of Indian women and their children. Concubinage, by contrast, would encourage licentiousness among both Indians and Euro-Louisianians, resulting in the Indianization of the latter. Secular officials, on the other hand, feared that promoting or even allowing Indian-European marriages legitimated an alternative and potentially destabilizing way of life. These differences are most apparent in the decade-long conflict between la Vente and secular officials, particularly Bienville and d'Artaguiette's successor as *commissaire ordonnateur*, Jean-Baptiste du Bois Duclos, over which form of métissage was worse—marriage or concubinage—and what actions needed to be taken to limit its effects.[44] The debate began when la Vente sought official sanction from Louisiana administrators and from the superiors of the foreign missions for the marriages he and his priests had performed between European men and Indian women.[45]

La Vente believed that allowing Indian-European marriages would discourage French and Canadian men from "maintain[ing] scandalous concubinages." In his 1713 or 1714 "Memoir on the Conduct of the French in Louisiana," he argued that because these men could not, or would not, "bind [themselves] to any woman through a legitimate marriage," they resorted to concubinage and that this state of affairs led to "the public and habitual lack of religion in which they have languished for so long."[46] In his proposal to legitimate Indian-European relationships, la Vente was building on past policies of both missionaries and secular officials in New France. Since 1648, missionaries had been struggling to control the relationships between French fur traders and Indian women and thought that legitimating them through marriage would do so. Jean-Baptiste Colbert, French Minister of the Navy in the 1660s, "urged very strongly that the native Indian population be Christianized, civilized, and constrained to settle and intermarry with the French," instituting a policy of Frenchification. In 1699 Iberville, then a naval captain in New France, received permission from King Louis XIV "to allow the French who will settle in this country to marry Indian girls" as long as the latter were Christianized. When Cadillac planned the founding of Detroit in 1700, he proposed that it be a colony of both Europeans and Indians and encouraged intermarriage in order to "form one people." Yet all these attempts at Frenchification failed as Canadian men tended to adopt Indian ways and the Indians were not attracted by European "civilization."[47]

Bienville probably had these past failures in mind when he opposed la Vente's proposal, claiming that la Vente was responsible for "authorizing [the Frenchmen who are scattered among the Indians] to live there as libertines under the pretext that they have wives among them."[48] Although he had occasionally sent soldiers and colonists to live temporarily among the Indians, Bienville believed that for the successful colonization of Louisiana, Frenchmen needed to reside in French settlements, under French authority, and not with the Indians on a permanent or even semipermanent basis. Louis XIV apparently concurred with Bienville's plans, as he instructed his newly appointed governor, sieur de Muy, to "inquire whether all these backwoodsmen have really withdrawn, and in case some of them have remained that [de Muy] makes them return."[49] Although the king did not authorize la Vente's proposal, neither did he state unequivocally that these relationships should be stopped. While no French or Louisiana officials prohibited these relationships outright, in 1735 the Superior Council did order that all métissage marriages be approved by the state, indicating that secular officials were concerned with regulating, rather than prohibiting, such relationships.[50]

Perhaps anticipating Bienville's opposition to legitimating French-Indian marriages, la Vente also requested that officials "issue an ordinance to forbid the French of Mobile from taking Indian women as slaves and especially from living with them under the same roof in concubinage."[51] Cadillac concurred, arguing that all unmarried military men, "from the governor to the lowest officers," should be permitted only male slaves. He recommended that "In regard to their washing we shall be able to find Frenchwomen who will take charge of it for the whole garrison and instead of Indian women, by deducting a fair salary from the pay of the officers and soldiers."[52]

Bienville, however, was not inclined to agree with la Vente in his attack on concubinage. He claimed that it would be difficult to implement, as "Everybody represents to me the indispensable need that they have of taking care of their households and backyards." Even though he thought la Vente was deliberately trying to "annoy the officers and colonists," Bienville did succumb in that he "oblig[ed] all those who are concerned to send [the female slaves] to sleep in the houses in which there are Frenchwomen," a move that, he claimed, "does not fail to be a very great inconvenience for [the masters]."[53]

While secular administrators may not have encouraged or desired these relationships, they preferred to turn a blind eye to illicit and presumably transitory ones rather than legitimate them through marriage. Their fear was that marriage to Indians would Indianize the French colonists and prevent the establishment of a stable colony. Unlike the missionaries, who stressed the power of European social institutions such as marriage to convert and "civilize" Indians, secular administrators believed that cultural differences overrode the supposedly civilizing influences of marriage. Duclos pointed to a few examples of Indian-French marriages that had survived, though

> not because [the wives] have become Frenchified, if one may use that term, but it is because those who have married them have themselves become almost Indian, residing among them and living in their manner, so that these Indian women have changed nothing or at least very little in their manner of living.[54]

Louisiana officials feared "losing" male Euro-Louisianians to an Indian way of life partly because their constructions of Indian sexuality and marriage practices conflicted with their notions of how to create a stable European society.

Many male European commentators in early Louisiana perceived Indian women as more sexual or more promiscuous than European women (or at least the ideal European woman). One of the first things many commented on was the relative nudity among Indians. In describing the first time he met the Bayogoulas, Iberville wrote,

> The women wear only a sash of bark, most of which are red and white. . . . They are sufficiently concealed by this garment, the strands in continuous motion. Many girls six to seven years of age do not wear sashes; they conceal their nakedness with a small bundle of moss, held by a string which runs between the thighs and is fastened to a waistband.[55]

Pénicaut commented that Pascagoulas women wore only "a single hank of moss which passed between their legs and covered their nakedness, the rest of their bodies being quite nude."[56] For Europeans, nakedness was an indication of an unrestrained sexuality.[57]

Polygamy was also seen by the French as representative of immorality. Bernard Diron d'Artaguiette, commandant at Mobile and the *commissaire ordonnateur*'s younger brother, claimed that "polygamy is in practice here [by the Natchez] and among all the Indian nations which I have seen." Chiefs and other elite men contracted marriages with several women in order to build economic and political alliances, and as an indication of status and power. For Diron d'Artaguiette, however, polygamy and an unrestrained Indian sexuality were linked because he believed that the former led to women's ability to leave their husbands "without the least complaint being made by those whom they leave."[58] Duclos also pointed to women's apparent sexual freedom in his opposition to la Vente's proposal, claiming,

> we shall find very few Indian women who will be willing to marry Frenchmen. Accustomed to a certain sort of dissolute life that they lead in their villages and to leave the husbands with whom they are not pleased in order to take others they will never be able to accustom themselves and even less to remain with them the rest of their lives. . . . Furthermore it happens very often that they leave their French husbands and go and remarry Indians in other villages.[59]

Commissaire ordonnateur d'Artaguiette agreed, arguing that Indian wives "would also leave [their French husbands] at the least trouble as has already been seen in the cases of two or three."[60] This ability to change spouses "when it seems good to them" resulted, according to Father le Petit, in an "indifference to the conjugal union."[61] In the minds of Louisiana administrators, the instability of Indian marriages would carry over to Indian-French marriages and undermine their struggle to establish a secure colony.

The perceived ease of divorce or separation was one of the most disturbing aspects of Indian society for the French commentators, as it indicated a female sexuality far more independent than they were used to. Diron d'Artaguiette noted that young girls were taught that they were "the mistresses of their own bodies (to use their own expression)."[62] Taken as a whole, European commentators saw Indian women as "lustful and devoid of restraint," "naturally inclined towards love," and willing to prostitute themselves to "the Frenchmen, to whom they refuse none of their favors, in return for a few glass beads or other trifles."[63] But it was not just Indian women's sexuality that was blamed for encouraging métissage. D'Artaguiette also pointed to the "stimulating" climate and to the backwoodsmen and soldiers who were "young men for the most part Canadians, that is to say very vigorous."[64]

Some administrators complained that French and Canadian men would select local Indian women over Frenchwomen if they had the choice. Cadillac wrote that many colonists were "addicted to vice principally with Indian women whom they prefer to Frenchwomen." He derided one particular colonist as "a prime fool, a backwoodsman and a real debauchée, unprincipled and insubordinate, married in Canada, very much devoted to the Indian women."[65] The naval officer Tivas de Gourville described the Canadians as "hunters and backwoodsmen who are of a strong and vigorous age and temperament . . . who like the sex, and not finding any who can hold them, as wanderers among the Indian nations and satisfy their passions with the daughters of these Indians." This behavior, de Gourville continued, "retards the growth of this colony."[66] The recipient of this memoir, Jérôme Phélypeaux de Pontchartrain, the French Minister of the Navy, suggested that the way to prevent this retardation was "to send women" from France.[67]

Given these constructions of Indian women's and Canadian men's sexuality, administrators and missionaries feared the results of métissage on a number of levels, stemming not only from the desire to regulate Indians but also from the need to regulate the Euro-Louisianians. As Ann Stoler has argued in regard to French Indochina and the Dutch East Indies, "it was through the policing of sex that subordinate European military and civil servants were kept in line and that racial boundaries were thus maintained."[68] The administrators' greatest concern was how these relationships would affect the establishment of Louisiana as an economically viable colony. La Chaise complained that "None of those voyageurs clear any group or make any settlements."[69] Relationships, let alone sanctioned marriages, with Indian women were not seen by administrators as conducive to creating stable families. D'Artaguiette argued that marriages to Indian women would "not cause . . . any great change at all in the Indians," but would encourage Frenchmen to lead "with these wives a life as nomadic as before," although he did admit that he knew of two or three examples in which the Indian wife was apparently adapting to European culture.[70] Duclos also argued that it would not "be conducive to the welfare of the colony to permit these marriages."[71]

Administrators were less concerned with the morality of the colonists, although they did complain about the Canadian men's licentiousness, and preferred that Euro-Louisianians engage in immoral but fleeting relationships with Indian women rather than have those relationships sanctified and made permanent. The missionaries, on the other hand, were greatly concerned with the moral state of the colony, its colonists, and its indigenous inhabitants. La Vente complained about the lack of Frenchmen attending religious services, but he did not want Frenchmen living in concubinage to receive the Sacrament at Easter.[72] While both religious and secular officials wanted to see the successful colonization of Louisiana, they disagreed over the method to achieve this goal. For the administrators, the presence of Indians offered the French settlers an alternative way of life that needed to be discouraged.[73] The missionaries, on the other hand, were more concerned with breaking down Indian culture and assimilating individual Indians into French "civilization." Regardless of experiences in New France, they still believed the Frenchification of Indian women would follow from marriages with Frenchmen. At the same time, they were opposed to illicit relationships of any kind.

For Louisiana *habitants*, the key issue regarding these marriages was the question of succession, illustrating the centrality of property in European conceptions of marriage. Under French law, an Indian widow was entitled to receive half of her French husband's estates, and if there were no children the property acquired during the marriage went to her Indian heirs, rather than to her husband's French heirs. *Habitants* complained that many of these "Indian heirs frequently ran away with what was left by the deceased," and that it was impossible to force them to make good on debts held against the estates. They petitioned the Superior Council "that what had been acquired by the French should remain to the French, and not go to the huts of barbarians." In 1728 the Superior Council decreed that a Frenchman should be appointed as tutor, if there were children, or, if there were none, as curate, who would control the property left by Frenchmen to their Indian wives and children. With or without children, the widow would receive a pension of one-third of the estate. This decree included a provision "that this pension should cease in case she returned to dwell among her tribe."[74]

Although these concerns were articulated in terms of property rights, questions of French identity, citizenship, and nationality permeated the legal discourse. Would the children of French-Indian marriages be Indian? Would they be French? Or would they be something new, a people in between? Duclos opposed la Vente's proposal, arguing, "experience shows every day that the children that come from such marriages are of an extremely dark complexion," causing the adulteration of "the whiteness and purity of the blood in the children." If these were the only children born in Louisiana, "it would become a colony of halfbreeds who are naturally idlers, libertines and even more rascals as those of Peru, Mexico and the other Spanish colonies give evidence."[75] While the Superior of Foreign Missions to whom la Vente wrote had no objections to Indian-French marriages, "there was still a fear of mingling by these marriages good blood with bad and of producing in the colony only children of a hard and idle character."[76] It was not only Euro-Louisianians who worried about the results of Indian-French marriages or cultural intermingling more generally. One Natchez elder also expressed anxiety regarding purity of blood, blaming Frenchmen for "debauch[ing] the young women, and taint[ing] the blood of the nation." This elder also accused the French of making Natchez women "vain and idle." Stung Serpent, another Natchez, concurred: "our women were more laborious and less vain than they are now."[77]

These concerns over "purity of blood" and "half-breeds" illuminate the racial boundaries that the French in Louisiana were constructing. When the Bayougoulas offered women to Iberville and his party in 1700, Iberville "made them understand that their skin—red and tanned—should not come close to that of the French, which was white."[78] Color here was an indicator of social and sexual distance. In his original proposal, la Vente himself distinguished between the southern Indians and the northern ones, who were "whiter, more laborious, cleverer, neater in the household work and more docile than those of the south": in other words, more akin to the construction of European women.[79] Pénicaut also drew implicit comparisons between white and Indian womanhood. Describing Tourimas and Capas women, he wrote that "they are quite pretty and white-complexioned."[80]

In a long comparison of the Nassitoches and Colapissas, Pénicaut wrote,

> The Nassitoches are handsomer and have better figures than the Colapissas, because the Colapissas' bodies, men's and women's, are all tattooed. They prick almost their entire bodies with needles and rub the pricks with willow ash crushed quite fine, which causes no inflammation of the punctures. The arms and faces of Colapissas women and girls are tattooed in this way, which disfigures them hideously; but the Nassitoches, men as well as women and girls, make no use of such punctures, which they loathe. That is why they are so much better looking; *besides, they are naturally whiter.*[81]

Here Pénicaut conflated race, savagery, civilization, and beauty, inscribing them onto the body. While the last line seems almost an afterthought, "whiteness" lies at the center of Pénicaut's aesthetic.[82] For the French colonizing Louisiana, a discourse of color, embodying racial and cultural differences, was present from the start: a discourse shaped by previous French experiences in New France and by knowledge of Spanish and English colonization elsewhere in the New World.

Constructions of unrestrained sexuality of both Indian women and some European men, together with the racialized fears of "mixing blood," led secular officials to oppose any proposals that would legitimate marriages between Indian women and European men, thereby in some ways legitimating a non-European way of life. The Navy Council at Louvre agreed, declaring that "Marriages of this sort must be prevented as much as possible and girls will be sent from here when it will be possible to do so."[83] Some of the blame for these relationships was laid at the feet of the "vigorous" backwoodsmen, Canadians, and soldiers, but administrators, clerics, and other commentators also believed that these men could be reformed and redeemed through marriage to Frenchwomen. As d'Artaguiette wrote to Pontchartrain, the young men and soldiers "need wives. I know only this one way to hold them."[84]

When the complaints about métissage were reported to Pontchartrain in 1712, he noted that "We ought to send women."[85] Over and over, Louisiana administrators wrote to France begging for more Frenchwomen, stressing that only marriage to Frenchwomen would encourage the young settlers, many of them discharged soldiers or backwoodsmen, to establish farms. In addition, several administrators, including d'Artaguiette, argued that "of all the remedies [to check the course of concubinage] the most sure is to send women there."[86] According to François de Mandeville, the discharged Canadians themselves responded to the suggestion that they "work at the cultivation of the land. . . . with a common voice that . . . being unmarried, they would not settle down." He suggested that "if about forty girls who would provide for themselves were sent there, they would first get married and being married they would work to support their families in mutual rivalry."[87] While Bienville and la Vente disagreed over the appropriateness of marriages between Indian women and Frenchmen, both believed that the immigration of European women was the best solution. In 1710 la Vente returned to France and, participating in the recruitment effort, relayed the concerns of d'Artaguiette and others about "the necessity that exists for having girls to draw in [to the settlements] the backwoodsmen."[88]

France had previous experiences in recruiting women for the colonies. Between 1662 and 1673, authorities sent more than seven hundred women to New France in order to "satisfy the colony's need for marriageable women." These women, known as the *filles du roi*, or the king's girls, since their dowries were provided by the Crown, were usually orphans and often illiterate. They were mostly recruited from the Hôpital Général du Paris, which served as a house of detention and correction for prostitutes, vagrants, kept women, and other criminals but was also an orphanage. More than 80 percent married within six months of arrival.[89] Marie de l'Incarnation, an Ursuline nun based in Montreal, wrote in 1668, "Ninety-two girls have come from France this year, who are already married (for the most part) to soldiers or labourers, who are given a habitation and food for eight months so they can clear fields to maintain themselves."[90]

At first, Louisiana officials requested any woman and every woman. De Gourville suggested recruiting women from the Paris asylums, who would not be missed. To persuade these women to emigrate, he recommended giving them free passage and eighteen to twenty months of subsistence.[91] Other Louisiana administrators wanted "hard-working people and girls" who would be able to perform the labor necessary in a young colony: cultivating the land, reproducing, and teaching the Indian men and women.[92] D'Artaguiette wrote that the best immigrants would be "families of farmers, selecting those in which there are many girls who would be married to Canadians." Not only would this "make that many more settlers" (presumably the immigrants and their future offspring), but, d'Artaguiette claimed, "That is the only way to put at one stroke the establishments of this colony in a position to do without the assistance from France for material existence."[93] They were at least partially successful in recruiting some "hard-working girls," as indicated by the passenger list for the *Loire*, which left France in 1720, carrying dressmakers, bakers, cooks, and laundresses.[94]

After some experience, Louisiana administrators became more selective about what sorts of European women they wanted sent, although they also spread their geographical net wider. As d'Artaguiette noted,

> It has cost the King a great deal to send those that are here. It does not seem to me necessary to send any more of that sort but rather daughters of farmers and the like who [are] rid of vain show and vanity or else those who are not acquainted with it at all. While going to the expense of equipping a ship for this mission one could also put on it thirty or forty good farmers, selecting those who have the largest numbers of daughters, sisters or nieces, or to give permission to those of Canada who would like to come and settle here, likewise to those of Detroit if that post is abandoned.[95]

The ideal female immigrants, in the minds of Louisiana officials, then, were farmers' daughters who were used to hard work and would not be distracted by vanity.

French officials did not ignore these requests. In 1704 Pontchartrain wrote to Bienville notifying him that the *Pélican* was on its way to Louisiana, carrying "twenty girls to be married to the Canadians and others who have begun to make themselves homes on the Mobile in order that this colony may be firmly established."[96] This was the first shipment of *épouseuses*, or women specifically sent "to marry and civilize the rough woodsmen and populate the wilderness."[97] The *Pélican* and its twenty *épouseuses* were followed by the *Baron de la Fosse* in 1713, bringing Cadillac, his wife and children, and several "Breton girls, who had come of their own accord."[98] Immigration picked up between 1718 and 1721 with the arrival of 7,020 Europeans, including 1,215 women.[99] Shipments of *épouseuses* ended in 1728 with the arrival of the *filles à cassette*, or "casket girls," named after the casket of dress articles they were given for their new lives in Louisiana.[100]

While Louisiana officials had high expectations for these women, not all who arrived as *épouseuses* in Louisiana were, in the words of one Louisiana historian, "the best women for founding a colony."[101] Scholars have estimated that between one-fifth and one-half were prostitutes.[102] Anecdotal evidence indicates that many, especially those who arrived in the 1720s, had been recruited from the Hôpital Général du Paris, which had also supplied many of the *filles du roi* for New France. Because it was still a house of detention and correction, Louisiana settlers were concerned that the recruits were all "fallen women." Father du Poisson wrote ironically that the incoming women were "taken from the hospitals of Paris, or from the salpêtrière, or other places of equally good repute, who find that the laws of marriage are too severe, and the management of a house too irksome."[103] Chassin, an officer in the Illinois country, complained that the women being sent were unsuitable for officers to marry.

> Several are becoming impatient but we let them grumble. The Company has already sent four or five hundred girls but officers and those who hold any rank cannot make

up their minds to marry such girls who in addition to the bad reputations that they bring from France give reason to fear that some also bring remnants of infirmities of which they have been imperfectly healed.

He suggested that girls be recruited from Canada, but he feared that was not a perfect solution since "a libertine who came here from that country makes us fear that among those who might come from there might be some of the same sort."[104]

Officials were not unaware of these concerns. When Minister of the Navy Colbert instituted subsidized immigration for women into New France, he looked for "marriageable girls whose backgrounds had been investigated to ensure that they were morally healthy as well as physically fit." Pontchartrain, echoing his predecessor, claimed that the *Pélican* "girls have been brought up in virtue and piety" and had been recruited from "places that cannot be suspected of any dissoluteness," so that "none at all may be sent except those of recognized and irreproachable virtue." He ordered Bienville to "be careful to establish them as best you can and to marry them off to men capable of supporting them with some sort of comfort."[105] Pénicaut noted that the *Pélican* women "were quite well behaved, and so they had no trouble finding husbands."[106]

A later group of women who arrived aboard the *Baron* in 1713 were not so well received, as they landed under a cloud of rumor and scandal.[107] The *épouseuses* aboard the *Baron* were under the chaperonage of Cadillac and his wife. Cadillac accused the ship's crew of misbehaving toward these women, particularly condemning Sieur de Richebourg as "a man who indulges in all sorts of debaucheries. . . . seduc[ing] my wife's chambermaid." Some of the Canadians on board the same vessel, "being witnesses of what happened in regard to them, spoke ill of them as soon as they landed." As a result, only two of the twelve women had married by October. It was not only rumors that hindered these women's marriages, however. Duclos commented that they were "extremely ugly," while Cadillac noted, "these girls are very poor having neither linen nor clothes nor beauty."[108] One historian has asserted that, faced with these "unprepossessing" women, bachelors returned to the woods, preferring Indian women to the new arrivals.[109]

It is not clear who were the intended husbands for the *Baron* women. The initial calls had been for wives for the discharged soldiers, yet Cadillac recommended that "it would be well to marry off several of these girls to soldiers who are courting them and who could support them, for fear that they may be debauched since they are quite destitute."[110] Again, a year later, Cadillac issued a request for women "suitable for marriage to officers and refined and educated colonists."[111]

Not all the Hôpital recruits would have been prostitutes or other criminals. When the *Maréchal de Villars* arrived in 1719, it brought twenty "girls from the poorhouse of La Rochelle." These women were fourteen to twenty-seven years old; the ages at which they had been left at the poorhouse ranged from birth to fourteen.[112] Pénicaut similarly described the girls he saw arrive in 1721 as fourteen to fifteen years old and having been "brought up in this house from infancy," indicating that these girls were probably the orphaned or abandoned children of the women detained at the Hôpital. They arrived chaperoned by Sister Gertrude and, like the *filles à cassette*, arrived with a chest of clothing and accessories.[113] The *filles à cassette* themselves were given into the care of the Ursuline nuns and received an allowance from the Crown until they married.[114]

Many of these women did not come voluntarily to Louisiana. In 1719 ninety-five women arrived aboard the *Mutine*, "sent by the king," while thirty-eight "exiled women" arrived aboard the *Deux Frères* and *Duc de Noailles*.[115] Working against voluntary emigration to Louisiana was the fact that the colony suffered from an unsavory reputation among the common people of France.[116] Conditions in Louisiana were those of a frontier society that had not yet become self-sufficient. Death rates were high for incoming immigrants, and settlers still relied on shipments of provisions from France for wine, clothing, and food staples.[117] When they first arrived in Louisiana, the women, according to Dumont de Montigny, "were lodged in the same house, with a sentinel at the door. Leave was given to see them by day and make a selection, but as soon as it was dark, entrance to the house was forbidden to all persons."[118] The unpleasantness of being on display as bachelors paraded past was compounded by those such as Pénicaut who referred to the *épouseuses* as "merchandise that was soon distributed, so great was the dearth of it in the country."[119]

It is not clear how many women found husbands and how many settlers were deterred by rumors of impurity or the "unattractiveness" of the women. Dumont de Montigny reported that "These girls were not long in being provided for and married. . . . In fact, had there arrived at the time as many girls as there were soldiers and workmen on the island, not one would have remained without a husband."[120] There was at least one woman, however, who apparently refused to marry. In 1706, two years after the arrival of the *Pélican*, Bienville complained that "There is one of the twenty girls who were sent to Mobile who is quite unwilling to marry." He wrote to Pontchartrain requesting permission to "oblige . . . her to do so like the others since there are several good suitors who are sighing for her."[121] Louis XIV granted governor-elect de Muy permission to "oblige her to do so" under the threat of being returned to France. The king did allow de Muy to determine for himself whether she could be "useful to the colony while living as she does either for the instruction of the daughters of the inhabitants in the principles of religion or to teach them to work." If de Muy determined that this unnamed woman would be useful, he could postpone her forced return to France.[122] Just as French male immigrants to New France had found freedom from Old World customs and mores, so too did Frenchwomen who emigrated to Louisiana.

Some of these imported women did establish themselves in the colony and occasionally became matriarchs among the "first families."[123] While some of these women were promised support by the Company of the Indies until they got married, others supported themselves in a variety of ways, including prostitution.[124] Cadillac complained of one woman who was "selling herself to all comers, the Indians just like the whites."[125] Unfortunately for the Louisiana administrators who espoused the civilizing effects that Frenchwomen would have on Louisiana, the colony seems to have had the opposite effect on some Frenchwomen. Périer and Salmon acknowledged that conditions in the colony did not help in preventing single women, especially orphan girls, from resorting to vice.[126]

La Chaise complained in 1725 that "there are many other women . . . who have no husbands and who are ruining the colony"; he recommended that all the immigrants who had been forced to Louisiana, men and women, be returned to France.[127] A few months later, the Council of Louisiana argued for "the necessity of purging the colony of . . . a number of women of bad life who are entirely lost."[128] Other women were destined to end up where they began. In 1727 Governor Périer and *commissaire ordonnateur* la Chaise noted, "There are many women and girls of bad life here," and recommended the building of "a house of correction here in order to put in it the women and girls of bad lives who cause a public scandal."[129] Périer asked the Ursuline nuns to "take care of the girls and women of evil life," illustrating that "issues of sexual management" included control of Frenchwomen as well as of Euro-Louisianian men and Indian women.[130] While administrators had previously believed that Frenchwomen would secure the establishment of families and farms in Louisiana, by the late 1720s, they found themselves faced with women who, in the words of la Chaise, "are useless and who do nothing but cause disorder."[131]

Even with the increased population of Frenchwomen, administrators and clerics were unable to eradicate métissage between Indian women and Euro-Louisianian men as both concubinage and marriages continued to occur. Father Raphäel complained in 1726 that while "the number of those who maintain young Indian women . . . to satisfy their intemperance is considerably diminished, there still remain enough to scandalize the church and to require an effective remedy."[132] One of these relationships that was apparently legalized through marriage came to light in 1725, when Peltier de Franchomme petitioned for a new marriage certificate, claiming that the original had been devoured by rats. During testimony heard confirming the marriage, the Superior Council noted that Madame Franchomme's unmarried name was Marguerite Ouaquamo Ouoana, a name, according to the council, with "an Indian semblance."[133] In 1745 another marriage appeared in the Superior Council records in the will of Charles Hegron. Hegron bequeathed half his estate to "François, an Indian woman, his legitimate wife." The remainder of the estate was to be "divided between his two children, the issue of his legitimate marriage." Hegron's concern with stressing the legitimacy of his marriage, and therefore of his children, probably stemmed from a fear that his fellow Euro-Louisianians would not accept the legitimacy of his bequests to his Indian wife and children. Indeed, the Superior Council did appoint a tutor for his widow, determining that she was incompetent to manage the estate herself.[134] Relationships between Indian women and Euro-Louisianian men continued throughout the eighteenth century, although the debates over their existence subsided from public view. With the decrease in Louisiana's Indian population, the increase in the African Louisianian population, and the entrenchment of slavery, Euro-Louisianians shifted their concerns about métissage onto the licit and illicit relationships between white men and black women, ignoring those few Indian–Euro-Louisianian relationships that persevered.[135]

In their efforts to establish Louisiana as a French colony, French and Canadian administrators in Louisiana, both secular and religious, saw families and farms as the necessary foundation for the re-creation of a European society. They quickly realized that Louisiana's economy could not survive based on resource extraction since its furs and skins did not match the quantity or quality of those coming from New France, and Louisiana's oft-sought-after mines proved elusive to find. The shift in focus to agriculture brought about a particular political and economic stage that, in the eyes of Louisiana officials, necessitated the calls for European brides. Euro-Louisianian constructions of Indian sexuality and its perceived effects on marriage practices as well as racial, cultural, and property-based concerns over the children of such relationships made marriages between Indian women and Euro-Louisianian men an unsuitable path to the twin goals of families and farms.

NOTES

1. In French Louisiana the *commissaire ordonnateur*, or subintendant, held a position just below but not subordinate to the governor, and was responsible for the day-to-day management of the colony.

2. Jean-Baptiste Martin D'Artaguiette, "Memoir to Prevent Libertinism in Louisiana as Far as Possible" (Sept. 8, 1712), in *Mississippi Provincial Archives: French Dominion*, ed. Dunbar Rowland and A. G. Sanders, 3 vols. (Jackson: Press of the Mississippi Department of Archives and History, 1927–32), 2:72 (hereafter *MPAFD*). During the first thirty years of French colonization of Louisiana, the primary concerns of secular administrators were relationships with Indian nations and the establishment of a viable economic base (which included repetitive requests for African slaves). Discussions of Indian women–Frenchmen relationships, while of lesser importance, were a constant refrain. Religious officials were preoccupied by vice in general.

3. Tivas de Gourville, "On the Establishment of Louisiana and on the Advantages That Might Be Derived from the Products of this Colony" (June 1712), in *MPAFD*, 2: 68.

4. James Thomas McGowan, "Creation of a Slave Society: Louisiana Plantations in the Eighteenth Century" (Ph.D. diss., University of Rochester, 1976), 11–12.

5. Like indentured servants in the British North American colonies, *engagés* committed themselves to work for a particular length of time in exchange for passage to Louisiana, but were distinguished from their northern counterparts in that they received a salary during their term of service.

6. The term *métissage* comes from Ann Stoler, who uses it to refer to sexual relationships between individuals of different cultures in colonial Southeast Asia; I have adopted it to avoid the more problematic terms "miscegenation" and "interracial" relationships. See Stoler, "Sexual Affronts and Racial Frontiers: European Identities and the Cultural Politics of Exclusion in Colonial Southeast Asia," *Comparative Studies in Society and History* 34 (1992): 514–51.

7. See Gilberto Freyre, *The Masters and the Slaves: A Study in the Development of Brazilian Civilization*, trans. Samuel Putnam (1946; 2d English language ed., rev., New York:

Alfred A. Knopf, 1986); Magnus Mörner, *Race Mixture in the History of Latin America* (Boston: Little, Brown, 1967); Carl N. Degler, *Neither Black nor White: Slavery and Race Relations in Brazil and the United States* (New York: Macmillan, 1971); and Joel Williamson, *New People: Miscegenation and Mulattoes in the United States* (New York: Free Press, 1980).

8. See Sylvia Van Kirk, *Many Tender Ties: Women in Fur-Trade Society in Western Canada, 1670–1870* (Norman: University of Oklahoma Press, 1983), 10; W. J. Eccles, "Sexual Mores and Behavior: The French Colonies," in *Encyclopedia of the North American Colonies*, ed. Jacob Ernest Cooke (New York: Charles Scribner's Sons, 1993), 2:699; Gary Nash, *Red, White, and Black: The Peoples of Early America* (1974; 3d ed., Englewood Cliffs, N.J.: Prentice Hall, 1992), 280; Winthrop D. Jordan, *White over Black: American Attitudes toward the Negro, 1550–1812* (Chapel Hill: University of North Carolina Press, 1968), 136–78; and Eugene D. Genovese, "The Slave States of North America," in *Neither Slave nor Free: The Freedmen of African Descent in the Slave Societies of the New World*, ed. David W. Cohen and Jack P. Greene (Baltimore: Johns Hopkins University Press, 1972), 258–77.

9. B. W. Higman proposes a demographic argument but one that focuses on the gender ratios of Jamaica's black population, shifting away from the sexual choices of European men by granting some agency to the women involved in these relationships, even if this agency is still demographically determined. See Higman, *Slave Population and Economy in Jamaica, 1807–1834* (Cambridge: Cambridge University Press, 1976), 143ff.

10. On the role of sexuality in late nineteenth-century European colonialism in Africa and Asia, see Ann Laura Stoler, *Race and the Education of Desire: Foucault's* The History of Sexuality *and the Colonial Order of Things* (Durham: Duke University Press, 1995); Robert J. C. Young, *Colonial Desire: Hybridity in Theory, Culture, and Race* (New York: Routledge, 1995); and Anne McClintock, *Imperial Leather: Race, Gender, and Sexuality in the Colonial Context* (New York: Routledge, 1995).

11. Thomas Ingersoll argues that "interracial marriage was unknown [and] concubinage was uncommon" ("Old New Orleans: Race, Class, Sex, and Order in the Early Deep South, 1718–1819" [Ph.D. diss., University of California, Los Angeles, 1990], 374), as does McGowan ("Creation of a Slave Society"). For arguments that métissage—in the form of both concubinage and state-sanctioned marriages—was common in colonial Louisiana, see Carl A. Brasseaux, "The Moral Climate of French Colonial Louisiana, 1699–1763," *Louisiana History* 27 (1986): 27–41; Daniel H. Usner, Jr., *Indians, Settlers, and Slaves in a Frontier Exchange Economy: The Lower Mississippi Valley before 1783* (Chapel Hill: University of North Carolina Press, 1992), 50; and Paul F. Lachance, "The Formation of a Three-Caste Society: Evidence from Wills in Antebellum New Orleans," *Social Science History* 18 (1994): 211–42.

12. Stoler, *Race and the Education of Desire*, 97.

13. W. J. Eccles, *France in America* (rev. ed., East Lansing: Michigan State University Press, 1990), 167.

14. Light Townsend Cummins, "Colonial Louisiana," in *Louisiana: A History*, ed. Bennett H. Wall (Arlington Heights, Ill.: Forum Press, 1990), 3–38.

15. "Census of the Officers, Petty Officers, Sailors, Canadians, Freebooters, and Others Located at Biloxi" (May 25, 1700), in *The Census Tables for the French Colony of Louisiana from 1699 through 1732*, comp. and trans. Charles R. Maudell, Jr. (Baltimore: Genealogical Publishing Co., 1972), 4–7.

16. "Census of Louisiana, Fort St. Louis" (Aug. 31, 1704), and "Census of Louisiana" (Aug. 12, 1708), cited in McGowan, "Creation of a Slave Society," 7–8.

17. McGowan, "Creation of a Slave Society," 8–9. *Coureurs de bois* were fur traders who operated without licenses, living on the margins of society both legally and culturally.

18. Bienville to Pontchartrain, Oct. 12, 1708, *MPAFD*, 2:38; and Jean-Baptiste Martin d'Artaguiette, "Memoir on the Present Situation of the Colony of Louisiana" (May 12, 1712), in *MPAFD*, 2:61.

19. Cadillac to Pontchartrain, Oct. 26, 1713, *MPAFD*, 2:167. Cadillac was appointed governor in 1710 but did not arrive in Louisiana until 1713.

20. W. J. Eccles, *The Canadian Frontier, 1534–1760* (rev. ed., Albuquerque: University of New Mexico Press, 1983), 89.

21. See Richard White, *The Middle Ground: Indians, Empires, and Republics in the Great Lakes Region, 1650–1815* (New York: Cambridge University Press, 1991), 69; James Merrell, *The Indians' New World: Catawbas and Their Neighbors from European Contact through the Era of Removal* (New York: W. W. Norton, 1989); and Van Kirk, *Many Tender Ties*.

22. Bienville to Pontchartrain, July 28, 1706, *MPAFD*, 2:26.

23. See André Pénicaut, *Fleur de Lys and Calumet: Being the Pénicaut Narrative of French Adventure in Louisiana*, ed. Richebourg Gaillard McWilliams (1723; reprint, Tuscaloosa: University of Alabama Press, 1988), 25, 30, 67–68, 73–79; and Ingersoll, "Old New Orleans," 41–42.

24. McWilliams, editor's note, *Fleur de Lys*, 25 n. 13; and Bienville to Pontchartrain, Oct. 12, 1708, *MPAFD*, 2:41.

25. Joyce Marshall, introduction to *Word from New France: The Selected Letters of Marie de l'Incarnation*, ed. Joyce Marshall (Toronto: Oxford University Press, 1967), 48. See also Eccles, *France in America*, 8, 81.

26. See Marcel Giraud, "France and Louisiana in the Early Eighteenth Century," *Mississippi Valley Historical Review* 36 (1950): 657–74.

27. Pénicaut, *Fleur de Lys*, 105–16.

28. Duclos to Pontchartrain, July 10, 1713, *MPAFD*, 2:75.

29. Jean François Benjamin Dumont de Montigny, "History of Louisiana: Translated from the Historical Memoirs of M. Dumont" [1753?], in *Historical Collections of Louisiana, Embracing Translations of Many Rare and Valuable Documents Relating to the Natural, Civil, and Political History of That State*, ed. B. F. French (New York, 1852), 5:19–21.

30. Cadillac to Pontchartrain, Oct. 26, 1713, *MPAFD*, 2:168–69. Cadillac's complaints about the condition of the soldiers and officers were likely intended as a criticism aimed at his predecessor, Bienville.

31. Pénicaut, *Fleur de Lys*, 105–16.

32. Ibid., 108.

33. Antoine Simon Le Page du Pratz, *The History of Louisiana, or of the Western Parts of Virginia and Carolina: Containing a Description of the Countries That Lie on Both Sides of the River Mississippi: With an Account of the Settlements, Inhabitants, Soil, Climate, and Products* (1758; reprint, New Orleans: Pelican Press, [1947?]), 312.

34. See Kathleen M. Brown, "Brave New Worlds: Women's and Gender History," *William and Mary Quarterly*, 3d ser., 50 (1993): 311–29; and idem, "The Anglo-Algonquian Gender Frontier," in *Negotiators of Change: Historical Perspectives on Native American Women*, ed. Nancy Shoemaker (New York: Routledge, 1995), 26–48.

35. For attempts to understand Indian women's motives for participating in relationships with fur traders elsewhere in North America, see Van Kirk, *Many Tender Ties*, 75; and Eirlys M. Barker, "Princesses, Wives, and Wenches: White Perceptions of Southeastern Indian

Women to 1770," in *Women and Freedom in Early America*, ed. Larry D. Eldridge (New York: New York University Press, 1997). While Richard White and James Merrell do not explicitly speculate about women's motives, their works do reveal some possibilities. See White, *Middle Ground*, 64–75; and Merrell, *Indians' New World*, 30–31.

36. Father le Petit to Father d'Avaugour, July 12, 1730, in *The Jesuit Relations and Allied Documents: Travels and Explorations of the Jesuit Missionaries in New France, 1610–1719*, ed. Reuben Gold Thwaites, 73 vols. (Cleveland: Burrow Brothers, 1896–1901), 68:203 (hereafter *JR*).

37. Le Page du Pratz, *History of Louisiana*, 330. The historian Marcel Giraud claims that Le Page du Pratz did in fact father a child with a Natchez woman. *A History of French Louisiana, The Company of the Indies, 1723–1731*, trans. Brian Pearce (Baton Rouge: Louisiana State University Press, 1987), 5:393.

38. Le Page du Pratz, *History of Louisiana*, 18; see also Stanley Clisby Arthur's foreword.

39. "General Census of All Inhabitants of New Orleans and Environs" (Nov. 24, 1721), in Maudell, *Census Tables*, 17–22; and "General Census of Inhabitants in the Area of Biloxi and Mobile" (June 26, 1721), in Maudell, *Census Tables*, 23–27. On the Indian slave trade, see Giraud, *History of French Louisiana*, 5:316; and Brasseaux, "Moral Climate," 30.

40. Using letters and other incidental reports, the historian Marcel Giraud asserts that in the mid-1720s, most Indian slaves in New Orleans were women. *History of French Louisiana*, 5:316. The Spanish census of 1771, the first to distinguish Indian slaves by gender, lists seventy-seven Indian slave women and forty-three men in all of Louisiana, including forty-two women and nineteen men in New Orleans, "Census of Louisiana" (Sept. 2, 1771), in *Spain in the Mississippi Valley, 1765–1794: Translations of Materials from the Spanish Archives in the Bancroft Library*, ed. Lawrence Kinnaird (Washington, D.C.: U.S. Government Printing Office, 1945), pt. 1:196.

41. Cadillac to Pontchartrain, Oct. 26, 1713, *MPAFD*, 2:169.

42. Father Henry de la Vente, "Memoire sur la Conduite des François dans la Louisiane" (1713 or 1714), Archives Nationales, Archives des Colonies, series C13a, 3:390vo (hereafter AC, C13a), cited in Brasseaux, "Moral Climate," 30–31.

43. Sister Marie-Madeleine Hachard to her father, April 24, 1728, in *The Ursulines in New Orleans and Our Lady of Prompt Succor: A Record of Two Centuries, 1727–1925*, ed. Henry Churchill Semple (New York: P. J. Kenedy and Sons, 1925), 230.

44. Underlying this conflict was la Vente's accusation that Bienville had "a too great familiarity . . . with a woman which scandalized the entire colony," which Bienville dismissed as "false assertions." See la Vente to Pontchartrain, March 2, 1708, *MPAFD*, 2:30–31; and Bienville to Pontchartrain, Oct. 12, 1708, *MPAFD*, 2:41.

45. It is not clear from la Vente's correspondence whether he wanted to restrict these marriages to converted and baptized Indian women. Giraud asserted that missionaries insisted on the conversion of Indian women before they would perform Indian-French marriages. *History of French Louisiana*, 5:326, 456, 463.

46. La Vente, "Memoire sur la Conduite des François dans la Louisiane," 390vo.

47. Ingersoll, "Old New Orleans," 36; Cornelius J. Jaenen, "Interracial Societies: The French Colonies, Canada," in *Encyclopedia of the North American Colonies*, 2:170–71; and Eccles, *France in America*, 81.

48. Bienville to Pontchartrain, July 28, 1706, *MPAFD*, 2:27.

49. King Louis XIV, "Memoir from the King to Sieur de Muy, Governor of Louisiana, to Serve Him When He Arrives in That Country" (June 30, 1707), in *MPAFD*, 3:56.

50. Jaenen, "Interracial Societies," 171. Article 6 of the 1724 Code Noir prohibited marriages between "white subjects" and "blacks" as well as forbidding "white subjects and even

the manumitted or free born blacks, to live in a state of concubinage with slaves." Indians were not named in the Code Noir; thus Indian-European relationships occupied an ambiguous space. For the Code Noir, see Charles Gayarré, *History of Louisiana: With City and Topographical Maps of the State, Ancient and Modern,* 4 vols. (4th ed., New Orleans: Pelican, 1965), 1:531–32.

51. La Vente to Pontchartrain, March 2, 1708, *MPAFD,* 2:31.

52. Cadillac to Pontchartrain, Oct. 26, 1713, *MPAFD,* 2:169. In the same letter, however, he noted that he had "not been able to find any one who has been willing to take charge of the washing."

53. Bienville to Pontchartrain, Oct. 12, 1708, *MPAFD,* 2:43.

54. Duclos to Pontchartrain, Dec. 25, 1715, *MPAFD,* 2:207.

55. "The Iberville Journal" (1699), in *A Comparative View of French Louisiana, 1699 and 1762: The Journals of Pierre Le Moyne d'Iberville and Jean-Jacques-Blaise d'Abbadie,* ed. and trans. Carl A. Brasseaux, University of Southwestern Louisiana History Series, no. 13 (Lafayette: Center for Louisiana Studies, University of Southwestern Louisiana, 1979), 50.

56. *Pénicaut, Fleur de Lys,* 18.

57. In *White over Black,* Jordan outlines how, for Elizabethan Englishmen, African standards of "public attire" and matrimonial practices combined to indicate a "primitive" and "provocative" sexuality (39–40).

58. Bernard Diron D'Artaguiette, "Journal of Diron D'Artaguiette" (1722–23), in *Travels in the American Colonies,* ed. Newton D. Mereness (New York: Macmillan, 1916), 48. Diron D'Artaguiette referred to the Natchez as polygamous, but only men had multiple spouses, so the practice was polygyny rather than polygamy. For marriage practices among southeastern Indians, see John R. Swanton, *The Indians of the Southeastern United States* (1946; reprint, Washington, D.C.: Smithsonian Institution Press, 1979).

59. Duclos to Pontchartrain, Dec. 25, 1715, *MPAFD,* 2:207.

60. D'Artaguiette to Pontchartrain, June 20, 1710, *MPAFD,* 2:58.

61. Father le Petit to Father d'Avaugour, July 12, 1730, *JR,* 68:143.

62. Diron D'Artaguiette, "Journal," 73.

63. Pénicaut, *Fleur de Lys,* 87; and Diron D'Artaguiette, "Journal," 73, 48. While most French commentators claimed that, in Pénicaut's words, Indian "girls . . . love the French very much" (*Fleur de Lys,* 86), there were some Indian women who kept themselves away from Frenchmen. Diron d'Artaguiette noted in his journal, "I do not believe that there is a man in the colony who can boast of having had any gallant relations with any Arkansas girl or woman. The reason which is offered for this is rather curious, if one cares to believe the interpreters, who say that their men make them believe that they would die if they had the least intercourse with us" (58).

64. D'Artaguiette, "Memoir to Prevent Libertinism," 72.

65. Cadillac to Pontchartrain, Oct. 26, 1713, *MPAFD,* 2:167, 171.

66. De Gourville, "On the Establishment of Louisiana," 69.

67. Pontchartrain's comment appears in the margins of de Gourville's memoir, "On the Establishment of Louisiana," 68 n. 6.

68. Ann Stoler, "Carnal Knowledge and Imperial Power: Gender, Race and Morality in Colonial Asia," in *Gender at the Crossroads of Knowledge: Feminist Anthropology in the Postmodern Era,* ed. Micaela di Leonardo (Berkeley: University of California Press, 1991), 55.

69. La Chaise to the Directors of the Company of the Indies, Sept. 6 and 10, 1723, *MPAFD,* 2:306.

70. D'Artaguiette to Pontchartrain, June 20, 1710, *MPAFD*, 2:58.

71. Minutes of the Council, Sept. 1, 1716, *MPAFD*, 2:218.

72. La Vente to Pontchartrain, March 2, 1708, *MPAFD*, 2:31.

73. McGowan, "Creation of a Slave Society," 11–12.

74. Gayarré, *History of Louisiana*, 1:392–94. See also Giraud, *History of French Louisiana*, 5:464. French children were also appointed tutors but only if both parents had died. Frenchwomen, in France and Louisiana, were not appointed curates upon their husbands' deaths and enjoyed a great deal of discretion over their husbands' property, especially when compared to their counterparts in the British North American colonies. See Ingersoll, "Old New Orleans," 185, 174–76. On the independent legal capacity of widows in France, see James F. Traer, *Marriage and the Family in Eighteenth-Century France* (Ithaca: Cornell University Press, 1980), 139.

75. Duclos to Pontchartrain, Dec. 25, 1715, *MPAFD*, 2:207–08.

76. Minutes of the Council, Sept. 1, 1716, *MPAFD*, 2:218.

77. Le Page du Pratz, *History of Louisiana*, 76, 41.

78. Pénicaut, *Fleur de Lys*, 24.

79. Minutes of the Council, Sept. 1, 1716, *MPAFD*, 2:218.

80. Pénicaut, *Fleur de Lys*, 34.

81. Ibid., 110; emphasis added.

82. On the crucial role of aesthetic judgments in eighteenth- and nineteenth-century French racialist ideologies, see Tzvetan Todorov, *On Human Diversity: Nationalism, Racism, and Exoticism in French Thought* (Cambridge: Harvard University Press, 1993), 103–05.

83. Minutes of the Council, Sept. 1, 1716, *MPAFD*, 2:218 n. 2.

84. D'Artaguiette to Pontchartrain, Feb. 12, 1710, *MPAFD*, 2:53.

85. De Gourville, "On the Establishment of Louisiana," 68. British and Portuguese colonists in Virginia and Brazil, respectively, also actively sought to increase the numbers of marriageable European women in their colonies. See David R. Ransome, "Wives for Virginia, 1621," *William and Mary Quarterly*, 3d ser., 48 (1991): 3–18; and Stuart B. Schwartz, "The Formation of a Colonial Identity in Brazil," in *Colonial Identity in the Atlantic World, 1500–1800*, ed. Nicholas Canny and Anthony Pagden (Princeton: Princeton University Press, 1987), 21.

86. D'Artaguiette, "Memoir to Prevent Libertinism," 72. See also idem, "Memoir on the Present Situation," 64.

87. Mandeville, "Memoir on the Colony of Louisiana" (April 29, 1709), in *MPAFD*, 2:49.

88. D'Artaguiette to Pontchartrain, June 20, 1710, *MPAFD*, 2:57.

89. Yves Landry, "Gender Imbalance, Les Filles du Roi, and Choice of Spouse in New France," in *Canadian Family History: Selected Readings*, ed. Bettina Bradbury (Toronto: Copp Clark Pittman, 1992), quotation on 17.

90. Marie de l'Incarnation to her family, Oct. 18, 1667, in *Word from New France*, 330.

91. De Gourville, "On the Establishment of Louisiana," 70–71.

92. D'Artaguiette, "Memoir on the Present Situation," 62.

93. D'Artaguiette, "Memoir to Prevent Libertinism," 73.

94. Vaughan B. Baker, "Cherchez les Femmes: Some Glimpses of Women in Early Eighteenth-Century Louisiana," *Louisiana History* 31 (1990): appendix 2, 37.

95. D'Artaguiette to Pontchartrain, June 20, 1710, *MPAFD*, 2:57–58.

96. Pontchartrain to Bienville, Jan. 30, 1704, *MPAFD*, 3:15–16.

97. Baker, "Cherchez les Femmes," 26.

98. Pénicaut, *Fleur de Lys*, 144. According to Pénicaut there were twenty-five girls aboard this ship, but Cadillac reported twelve. Cadillac to Pontchartrain, Oct. 26, 1713, *MPAFD*, 2:184–85.

99. Ingersoll, "Old New Orleans," 23.

100. Gayarré, *History of Louisiana*, 1:390.

101. McWilliams, editor's note, *Fleur de Lys*, 240 n. 5. See also Mathé Allain, *"Not Worth a Straw": French Colonial Policy and the Early Years of Louisiana* (Lafayette: Center for Louisiana Studies, University of Southwestern Louisiana, 1988), 84; and Brasseaux, "Moral Climate," 30–31.

102. Joe Gray Taylor and Richebourg Gaillard McWilliams estimate that half of the 1,215 women who arrived between 1717 and 1721 were prostitutes; Carl Brasseaux puts the figure at 256, or roughly one-fifth. See Taylor, *Louisiana: A History* (New York: W. W. Norton, 1984), 10; McWilliams, editor's note, *Fleur de Lys*, 240 n. 5; and Brasseaux, "Moral Climate," 31.

103. Father du Poisson to unknown Father, Oct. 3, 1727, *JR*, 69:285.

104. Chassin to Father Bobé, July 1, 1722, *MPAFD*, 2:274–75.

105. Pontchartrain to Bienville, Jan. 30, 1704, *MPAFD*, 3:16.

106. Pénicaut, *Fleur de Lys*, 96–97.

107. Allain, *"Not Worth a Straw,"* 83.

108. Duclos to Ministry, 1713, cited in Charles Gayarré, *The Creoles of History and the Creoles of Romance: A Lecture (Delivered in the Hall of the Tulane University, New Orleans, by Hon. Charles Gayarré, on the 25th of April, 1885)* New Orleans: C. E. Hopkins, 1885), 5; and Cadillac to Pontchartrain, Oct. 26, 1713, *MPAFD*, 2:184–85.

109. Allain, *"Not Worth a Straw,"* 85.

110. Cadillac to Pontchartrain, Oct. 26, 1713, *MPAFD*, 2:184–85.

111. Cadillac, 1714, cited in Gayarré, *Creoles of History*, 5.

112. "List of Officers, Workers for the Company, Girls from the Poorhouse of La Rochelle, Soldiers, and Others Embarked on the *Maréchal de Villars* Commanded by M. Meschin Bound for Louisiana from La Rochelle" (Jan. 26, 1719), in *First Families of Louisiana*, trans. and comp. Glenn R. Conrad, 2 vols. (Baton Rouge: Claitor's, 1970), 1:29–32.

113. Pénicaut, *Fleur de Lys*, 249–50.

114. Gayarré, *History of Louisiana*, 1:390; Giraud, *History of French Louisiana*, 5:261; and Allain, *"Not Worth a Straw,"* 85.

115. "List of Private Passengers and Girls Embarked on the *Mutine* Commanded by M. de Marlonne and Bound for Louisiana" (1719), in Conrad *First Families*, 1:26–28; "List of Company Employees, Concessionaries, Private Passengers, Tobacco Smugglers, Illicit Salt Dealers, Vagabonds, Deserters, and Others Embarked on the *Deux Frères* Commanded by M. Ferret Bound for Louisiana from La Rochelle" (Aug. 16, 1719), in Conrad, *First Families*, 1:60–65; and "List of Concessionaries and Their People, Workers for the Company, Private Passengers, Soldiers, Illicit Salt Dealers, Tobacco Smugglers, Vagabonds, Deserters, and Others Embarked on the *Duc de Noailles* Commanded by Monsieur Couttant Departing from the Roadstead of Chef de Baye Bound for Louisiana" (Sept. 12, 1719), in Conrad, *First Families*, 1:66–70.

116. Ingersoll, "Old New Orleans," 113–16.

117. Dale Miquelon, "Repeopling the Land: The French Colonies," in *Encyclopedia of the North American Colonies*, 2:320.

118. Dumont de Montigny, "History of Louisiana," 15.

119. Pénicaut, *Fleur de Lys*, 250.

120. Dumont de Montigny, "History of Louisiana," 16.

121. Bienville to Pontchartrain, July 28, 1706, *MPAFD*, 2:28.

122. Louis XIV, "Memoir from the King," 58–59. Unfortunately, de Muy died during the voyage to Louisiana and the unnamed, unmarried woman is not referred to again. It is possible that she was either François Marie Anne de Boisrenaud or Gabrielle Bonet, both of whom appear on the "List of the Marriageable Girls Who Arrived Aboard the Pélican at Biloxi" (1704), in Maudell, *Census Tables*, 8, and then again in the 1706 census of Louisiana as women living alone in Mobile, "Census of Families and Habitants of Louisiana" (1706), in Maudell, *Census Tables*, 10.

123. Brasseaux, "Moral Climate," 31.

124. On the support promised to immigrating women, see Giraud, *History of French Louisiana*, 5:261.

125. Cadillac to Minister, Jan. 5, 1716, AC, C13a, 4:532vo, cited in Brasseaux, "Moral Climate," 31.

126. Périer and Salmon, March 29, 1732, *MPAFD*, 4:116–19.

127. La Chaise and the Councilors of Louisiana to the Council of the Company of the Indies, April 26-June 3, 1725, *MPAFD*, 2:462.

128. Council of Louisiana to the Directors of the Company of the Indies, Aug. 28, 1725, *MPAFD*, 2:494. Besides la Chaise's suggestion that forced male migrants be returned to France, no colonial official recommended that male Euro-Louisianians be exiled. Indeed, officials were more concerned with their desertion and worked hard to keep these men in the colony. The desire of colonial elites to expunge women of "bad character" was not restricted to Louisiana but was expressed throughout the North American colonies, especially in frontier-like situations. See James H. Merrell, "Shamokin, the Very Seat of the Prince of Darkness" (paper presented at the Colonial History Workshop, University of Minnesota, June 13, 1996), 15–16.

129. Périer and la Chaise to the Directors of the Company of the Indies, Nov. 2, 1727, *MPAFD*, 2:558–60.

130. Sister Marie-Madeleine Hachard to her father, Jan. 1, 1728, *Ursulines in New Orleans*, 199. On European women in nineteenth-century Dutch colonies and "issues of sexual management," see Stoler, *Race and the Education of Desire*, 40.

131. La Chaise to the Directors of the Company of the Indies, Sept. 6 and 10, 1723, *MPAFD*, 2:315.

132. Father Raphäel to Abbé Raguet, May 19, 1726, *MPAFD*, 2:521.

133. Petition of New Marriage Contract, Feb. 15–23, 1725, Records of the Superior Council, *Louisiana Historical Quarterly* 2 (1919): 110–11. The Franchommes were granted a new marriage certificate as the Superior Council deemed that their marriage had taken place and was legitimate.

134. Nuncupative Will of Charles Hegron, Surnamed Lamothe, March 18, 1745, Cabildo Archives, *Louisiana Historical Quarterly* 3 (1920): 564–66. See also Gwendolyn Midlo Hall, *Africans in Colonial Louisiana: The Development of Afro-Creole Culture in the Eighteenth Century* (Baton Rouge: Louisiana State University Press, 1992), 15.

135. Marriages between Indian women and Euro-Louisianian men continued to take place outside the purview of the Superior Council, especially in the more remote areas of the colony. In Natchitoches, for example, Jean Baptiste Brevel and Anne "of the Caddoes" were married in 1736, while in 1774 Pierre Raimond married Françoise, "a free Indian." See Elizabeth Shown Mills, comp., *Natchitoches, 1729–1803: Abstracts of the Catholic Church*

Registers of the French and Spanish Post of St. Jean Baptiste des Natchitoches in Louisiana (New Orleans: Polyanthos, 1977), 4, 126–27. For relationships between African women, both slave and free, and Euro-Louisianian men in French Louisiana, see Hall, *Africans in Colonial Louisiana;* Usner, *Indians, Settlers, and Slaves;* McGowan, "Creation of a Slave Society"; and Ingersoll, "Old New Orleans."

Chapter Three

The Pastor and the Prostitute

Sexual Power among African Americans and Germans in Colonial New York

Graham Russell Hodges

On March 23, 1745, Wilhelm Christoph Berkenmeyer, pastor of the Zion Loonenburg (now Athens), New York, Lutheran Church and superintendent of all Lutheran churches in the mid-Atlantic region, related to his church elders a "sorrowful but untruthful rumor spread by one of the descendants of Ham." Berkenmeyer explained that Margareta "Grit" Christiaan, a young woman of color, whom he had employed as his family servant from the time she was seven until she was twenty-one, when he discharged her, had accused him of fathering her yet unborn child. Local gossip forced Berkenmeyer to speak publicly about this charge. A week before, Grit had come to his home, announced that she was pregnant, and told Berkenmeyer that he was the father. When he angrily denounced her, Grit responded, "I shall make you all very sorry." She then told her story to Mother Betty Van Loon, the local midwife and the spouse of Albert Van Loon, Jr., the most prominent landowner in the village and a descendant of the man for whom Loonenburg was named. Word of the scandal spread quickly among church members. Other whites told the news to boatmen working on the Hudson River vessels going to New York City. As Berkenmeyer later noted, news of his disgrace soon "went the rounds of the Negroes in the form of the riddle." As public humiliation loomed, Berkenmeyer took the matter to his church elders and placed blame for the story on Satan. In the coming weeks pastor and prostitute—as she was frequently called—battled each other over the paternity of her child.[1]

Loonenburg was a small village southwest of Albany, New York, and on the west side of the Hudson River. Statistically, its importance is not large. About three hundred Lutherans lived there, a tiny fraction of the 10,600 souls enumerated in the 1749 census for Albany County, of which it was then a part; about 1,500 of this total were black, but most of them lived in Albany. Loonenburg's black population was quite small. As part of Livingston Manor, Loonenburg was not truly independent. But the dispute between Berkenmeyer and his former servant transcends local importance. Their clash illuminates little-understood sexual dynamics between black and white colonists in the North. For example, it is significant that none of the contestants were Anglo-American. Berkenmeyer was a native of Germany; Grit was a second-generation African American who probably spoke only Dutch and attended a German church. The most influential study of mixed-race relations in the American colonies, Winthrop Jordan's *White over Black*, discusses only Anglo-African ties, omitting contacts, for example, between African Americans and Germans.[2] This is also the story of shifting sexual and racial attitudes among white Lutherans toward interracial marriage and the inclusion of blacks in church. It uncovers the rising disaffection African Americans felt toward a denomination that had sheltered them over nearly a century. In this case, the participants used a language of increasing racial stridency. Grit received no tangible benefit from the case, and was repeatedly called a prostitute. Berkenmeyer, as shown below, commonly generalized all blacks from the example of Grit and her relatives.

Finally, dissecting the case adds greater breadth to discussion of the texture of interracial sex in the American colonies. Despite the animosities between Berkenmeyer and Grit, there were, as we shall see, examples of true love within Afro-Lutheran society. Winthrop Jordan's discussion of such unions in *White over Black* casts interracial relationships in highly negative terms. Marriages were extremely uncommon, Jordan contends, and white males dominated casual relationships, which developed only where there was a paucity of white females. Jordan argues that whites regarded such relationships with aversion, and that interracial sex took place primarily in tropical, staple-crop plantation colonies where white men exploited defenseless enslaved black women. Unions between black men and white women created such tensions that colonists related them to slave rebellions.[3] In contrast, among German Lutherans and African Americans, interracial sexual relations were peaceful mixtures that led to marriage and families and were sanctified in church rituals.

First let us consider the two principal actors in this drama. Pastor Berkenmeyer, considered by some to be the organizer of North American Lutheranism, had been expert at fending off controversy since his arrival at Loonenburg in 1725. For Protestant churches in colonial America, attracting ambitious, well-educated pastors like Berkenmeyer from Europe to serve in wilderness outposts was very difficult. Many rural parishes in stronger denominations such as the Church of England or the Reformed Church had to wait decades before securing a pastor knowledgeable about official theology. For the Lutherans, a minority denomination since the first European settlements, acquiring a cleric like Berkenmeyer to a tiny congregation like Loonenberg was a coup.

Even after he accepted the post, problems arose. While still in Europe, Berkenmeyer received a letter informing him that the church had chosen someone else. The Loonenburg congregation had selected a pietist tailor with no theological training but with a predilection to jump into unoccupied pulpits. He was so unorthodox in his beliefs that he could in fact fit into any denomination. To Berkenmeyer, with his solid education, staunch orthodoxy, and high conception of his office, no insult could have been more offensive. His appointment came from the church hierarchy in Europe, however, not from local members, and so he headed west to expel his rival. His was no easy assignment. Berkenmeyer was responsible for a number of churches, and the sacred tailor then dogged him from parish to parish, often preaching to a congregation as soon as Berkenmeyer departed.[4] This initial trouble epitomized the tensions between orthodox, European-trained pastors and colonial, pietist congregations. This was more true in rural areas than urban, where orthodoxy held sway, but it explains why his parish was not grateful for Berkenmeyer's appearance.

Still, Berkenmeyer was selected by the church leaders in Germany, so the Loonenburg congregation accepted him. To understand the gravity of Grit's charges, one must understand the significance of the pastor to a Lutheran community. Pastoral power paralleled and sometimes exceeded that of the civil magistrates. The pastor was always an outsider to the village, frequently came from a pastoral family, was educated at Latin schools, and trained at a university. His duties included keeping the church records, maintaining moral discipline in the community, administering the sacraments, and carrying out the various life-cycle rituals such as baptism, confirmation, marriage, and burial. He supervised the schoolmaster, who often doubled as choirmaster. The pastor also schooled his flock in politics; all new laws, edicts, and criminal indictments were read from the pulpit or outside after church. He was joined in these tasks by his consistory (church court), which was composed of the leading male members of the church. The pastor led the consistory in all proceedings and, in concert with the sheriff, maintained social and moral order in the community. In a village like Loonenburg, where the governing Livingston family had never bothered to create a civil government, Pastor Berkenmeyer ruled its Lutheran congregation directly.[5] In short, an attack on the pastor's moral reputation struck directly at the heart of the community. Grit Christiaan took a bold step when she accused Berkenmeyer.

This is not to say that the pastor was unassailable. His powers and demands often led to conflicts with his parishioners, particularly with prosperous members, upon whom the pastor leaned for support. Members of the Van Loon family, which employed the Christiaans, were great supporters of Berkenmeyer theologically, but clashed with him over such pedestrian issues as land use, firewood, and corn allotments. The pastor also had to intervene in regional disputes. Berkenmeyer and his protégé, Pastor Michael Christian Knoll, had to mediate a nasty wrangle caused by an incompetent Lutheran cleric named Wolf who upset his congregation in Bergen County, New Jersey, by his vitriolic accusations. Among the more sensational charges made by Wolf was that his wife, who had given him two children, had a third child by a "Negro slave." Berkenmeyer and Knoll were able to dismiss this allegation and eventually helped arrange a settlement by which Wolf returned alone to Germany. Still, it took eleven years to get rid of him.[6] In addition to these controversies, Berkenmeyer had some early successes. He consecrated a new church, Trinity Lutheran, in New York City in 1729. After several years of itinerant ministry, he divided his mission in half, taking the northern half of the Hudson Valley and giving the southern region to Knoll. Berkenmeyer then concentrated his efforts on Loonenburg.[7]

Opposing this august personage in the affair was a poor servant girl of mixed race. Grit's father was Pieter Christiaan, who was born in Madagascar about 1680. He was purchased but later freed by Jan Van Loon, Sr., a principal Lutheran landowner in Albany County and the father-in-law of Mother Betty. After receiving his freedom, Pieter Christiaan married Anna Barbara, a Palatine widow, in 1714. After Anna's death Christiaan married a second Palatine woman, Elisabeth Brandemoes, in 1716. Lutheran pastors officiated over both marriages. Pieter and Elisabeth Christiaan had eleven children. Margareta was the fifth, born around 1723. She went to work for Pastor Berkenmeyer in 1731 and remained with him and his wife, Benigna, until she was discharged in October 1744. Nine months later, she gave birth to a son.[8]

Grit's pregnancy was not the first such incident to trouble Berkenmeyer. Grit's mother, Elisabeth (known as Old Lies), had a child by a man who was not her husband. Anna Catharina Christiaan, Pieter and Lies's eldest daughter, was the mother of several illegitimate children. After the birth of Anna Catharina's third child in 1743, Berkenmeyer admitted her to communion over the objections of the church council and other members. Berkenmeyer defended his actions, arguing that lacking legal proof of her guilt, he could not bar her from the Lord's Supper. Pregnancies out of wedlock were still rare in Lutheran society and so admittance of adulterers to communion had long troubled Berkenmeyer; but in fairness, he was unwilling to take active measures to exclude them until a consistorial decision came from Germany. Berkenmeyer's determination steeled him against opposition from his angry white parishioners. His dedication acted as armor when Anna Catharina would later slander him. Anna Catharina was apparently so angered by the white congregants that she fled in exile to New York City. Before leaving, however, she defamed her benefactor by publicly circulating embarrassing gossip about Berkenmeyer. Her sister Grit had told her years before of an occasion when she had observed Berkenmeyer's sexual behavior with his wife. While there is no record of any unusual behavior by the pastor and his wife, public knowledge of their sexual habits certainly undercut his dignified position in the community. Anna Catharina swiftly spread this choice news about the pastor before departing for the big city. She later returned unrepentant.[9]

Such personal attacks did not turn Berkenmeyer against his mission to convert African Americans to Lutheranism. In this he had ample historical precedent. Virtually alone among early Protestant denominations in the colonial North, Lutherans defied convention by admitting African Americans freely to their congregations as full members, and, more amazingly, permitted and supported interracial marriages. This liberalism had been present since the 1660s. The Lutherans welcomed blacks when no other church would do so. For example, domines (ministers) in the Dutch Reformed Church, the strongest sect in the Hudson Valley, declared after the English conquest that they would no longer baptize blacks. Reformed domines contended that blacks were interested in Christianity only if it led to emancipation for their children. As enslavement became the primary status of blacks in New York by the turn of the eighteenth century, the gap between black aspirations for a nurturing Christianity and white suspicion meant that few African slaves received any instruction in Christ.

The Church of England's Society for the Propagation of the Gospel in Foreign Parts (SPG) mounted the most famous missions to enslaved blacks. Yet its efforts did not really begin until 1703, when Elias Neau opened his school for slaves in

New York City. In the countryside, Anglican power was weak. Lutherans became the church of choice for Africans seeking membership in a European creed. The remaining free blacks in colonial New York moved from the Dutch Reformed Church to the German denomination. Soon, Lutheran baptismal records listed the descendants of the seventeenth-century emancipated blacks who were formerly members of the Dutch Reformed Church. A fifty-year-old man named Emanuel became in 1669 the first black person baptized by the Lutherans. Before long, families whose children appear in church registers included the Matthys, Anthonys, Franciscos, and Petersons, whose ancestries are traceable to the first Angolan arrivals in New Netherlands in 1626.[10]

This cultural embrace continued into the early eighteenth century. Lutherans held marriage ceremonies for free black families around Hackensack, New Jersey. Ceremonies included the rites of the marriage of Willem Smidt and Barbara Franssen of Hackensack, and the marriage of Caspar Francis Van Sallee (the grandson of Anthony the Turk, another early free man of color) and Johanna Cromwell, a free black woman, at Hackensack in 1746. By performing such rites without requiring deep personal investment, the Lutherans showed far greater openness than any other denomination. The New York Lutheran synod performed numerous marriages in the late 1720s among slaves and between slaves and free blacks. For example, Tobyias, a baptized Negro, with consent of his master, and Marya, with her mistress's consent, married in Albany in 1729. The Lutherans also performed interracial marriages. On June 6, 1741, James Elsworth, an Englishman, and Mary Jorga, a "free Portuguese baptized negress who had received liberty of her mistress to marry," were joined in matrimony at the home of Nicolaus Emmings in Highland, New York.[11]

One African American became an important Lutheran leader. Arie Van Guinee, a native of Suriname, came to New York with his wife, Jora, in 1705 and joined the Lutheran church there. In 1712 the couple moved to the Raritan Valley in New Jersey and held the first Lutheran service in New Jersey at their home. (Later, Van Guinee donated the site where the first Lutheran church in New Jersey was constructed.) Van Guinee assisted in the baptisms of his niece and nephew. He and his family purchased sizable plots of land over the years, making Van Guinee a man of considerable means and influence in the church. After his first wife's death in 1735, Van Guinee married Mareetje Pietersen, granddaughter of Solomon Petersen, a free person of color present in the colony in the 1640s.[12]

When Berkenmeyer arrived in 1725, then, the Lutherans could claim three-quarters of a century of successful support of free and enslaved African Americans and of mixed marriages. Pastor Berkenmeyer concurred with the Lutheran position on slaves. He was also doubtless influenced by the missionary efforts of the SPG. He came to America, however, when European faiths were reevaluating their attitudes about proselytizing blacks. One chief dilemma was the issue of enslaving Christians. Fundamentalist Protestants in general, and rural members in particular, believed strongly that Christians should not be enslaved. As owners of slaves themselves, they felt that the best way to avoid such a contradiction was to deny enslaved people of African descent membership in the church. Pietists of all denominations were unconvinced by the New York colonial law of 1706, which specifically separated baptism from civil emancipation. In disagreements over such issues Berkenmeyer represented the orthodox or state position, while his congregation defended the pietist, more independent outlook. Berkenmeyer's congregants accepted his methods as long as black applicants for membership were deemed to be clean of any sin. The Christiaan family was far from pure.[13]

A second area of contention was the pastor's ownership of slaves. Like the Anglicans, Berkenmeyer saw no contradiction between catechizing African Americans and owning them. He owned at least three slaves and baptized them along with their children. He was unapologetic about this to his parishioners, who, like other rural pietists, regarded this contradiction with suspicion. Berkenmeyer defended his purchase of human chattel by noting that "I thank God, and I am not indebted to any of those who make trouble for my Negro, for one penney of what he has cost." He formulated the church constitution of 1735, which specified,

> In regard to the Negroes, a pastor shall previously ascertain that they do not intend to abuse their Christianity, to break the laws of the land, or to dissolve the ties of obedience; yea he must have a positive promise that Christianity will not only be entered upon, but that the same shall be practiced in life.

In so arguing, Berkenmeyer was much closer to the Anglican belief that Africans could be Christianized; his parishioners, on the other hand, doubted the wisdom of such attempts. This division would affect his later trials.[14]

By the time of Grit's pregnancy, all the elements were in place for a major scandal. Berkenmeyer, though widely respected, feuded with church members over issues great and small. The pastor personified the power of the state church while the congregation, living on the frontier, was becoming more pietist and independent.[15] The Van Loon family, though his closest neighbors and considered very loyal to the pastor, quarreled with him over land and fuel tithes. The Christiaan family included at least two daughters with questionable sexual mores and who displayed animus toward Berkenmeyer.

These attitudes became clear as Berkenmeyer tried to extricate himself from the scandal. Because church transcripts provide only the pastor's defense, we can only infer Grit's position through quotations attributed to her. The documents reveal that Berkenmeyer feared Grit and worried that the Christiaan family wanted revenge against him. In one memorial to church elders made a week after announcing Grit's accusations, Berkenmeyer noted that father Piet claimed that the pastor had impregnated his daughter, contending that Grit had so told him. Berkenmeyer then quoted Grit as saying that she would "make a song of [the scandal] to offend the Pastor's wife." Grit, according to Berkenmeyer, was urged on by her sister Anna Catharina to "revenge her Negro race by a vile slander on our whole congregation."

Succeeding testimony by Berkenmeyer indicates that although he was interested in squelching the rumors and hoped Grit would repent, he was not worried about losing his job. Removal could occur, he told the congregation, only with the approval of a consistory "in the fatherland, according to the church constitution, which may be quoted and read." Because a true consistory was impossible under the conditions, he proposed an ecclesiastical inquiry, which he as "the Shepherd" would lead, into the conduct of the "prostitute." As pastor, Berkenmeyer controlled the proceedings and their resolution completely. He made all the statements in this ecclesiastical trial by posing questions to which he supplied the answers.

The inquiry was short and predictable. First, Berkenmeyer described himself. He was fifty-eight years old, had been married eighteen years, and was childless. He knew that he was not guilty of conceiving an illegitimate child. He had never been drunk, insane, or unconscious as long as he had been in America. He added that he was praying daily for God's forgiveness of the "prostitute." Deeply troubled, the church nonetheless concluded the inquiry by declaring Berkenmeyer innocent of the charges and confirmed the "pleasure and satisfaction in granting to our Pastor, who had belonged to us for more than twenty years, this testimonial of his honor and truthfulness," adding, "The Lord is our sun and shield." The verdict, too, was predictable. The pastor was better educated and more skilled in debate than virtually anyone else in the county, let alone a young servant girl. He had had years to build up patronage networks, had the respect if not the affection of his parishioners, and held unassailable leadership and power. His accuser, by contrast, was from a poor, somewhat disreputable mixed-race family. The huge imbalance in their authority did not keep Berkenmeyer from pushing harder to eradicate any doubt about Grit's guilt and his innocence.[16]

Berkenmeyer's immense power was evident on the day of the child's birth. On June 9, 1745, Mother Betty, the midwife, was called out of church at the beginning of the afternoon service by a local black person, who asked her to come to the Christiaan home. Before helping Grit give birth, Mother Betty demanded that "the prostitute" identify the father of the child. Grit moaned and cried, "Oh, Mother Betty, I cannot say it." Putting duty above perceived morality, Mother Betty called in other women and delivered the illegitimate child. Asked by "Old Lies" (Elisabeth Brandemoes Christiaan) if the child was white, Mother Betty answered that she had never seen a blacker baby even among the blackest of Negroes. The room roiled with emotion. The new grandmother called out, "That Prostitute!" Piet Christiaan came yelling that the "prostitute should be whipped or hanged or burned." Asked again who the father was, Grit answered that "it must have happened when I was asleep." Her mother threatened to throw the child into the river. Terrified, Grit hid in shame under the blankets.

Three weeks later, Pastor Berkenmeyer related this sad account to his congregation. He was supported by prominent church members who, noting that Grit had never identified the father, claimed that "the finger of God . . . struck dumb the devil of slanders and took away his armor, that is, He nullified the prostitute's efforts." The leaders went on to say that the black skin and Negro head of the child betrayed the father and cleared the pastor. They affirmed that the "prostitute" had accepted her guilt and declared that her master had never touched her in a sexual manner as long as she lived at his house.

Using the approach any tyrant employs after the devastating defeat of an opponent, Berkenmeyer offered forgiveness to all who had slandered him. In addition to members of the Christiaan family, he absolved a black attorney who told Grit to stay with her story, and pardoned all those in taprooms and in houses of prostitution who had made merry over the pastor and said that he deserved this punishment for taking "too great pains in behalf of the blacks."

But Berkenmeyer then shifted ground. Having forgiven the Christiaans, he asked the church council to consider what punishment they should receive. Here his language becomes vengeful and filled with racial hatred. Berkenmeyer first forgave "the prostitute" and "all of her race" on condition that she never again cross the threshold of his house. Further, because Old Piet had spread this scandal and still dared to come to communion, Berkenmeyer declared that "it may be concluded from this that much evil is rooted in this race of Piet and also no good can come from, or make a lasting impression on them, especially since they misuse their coming to church as a cover for their evil and thus defy God and the people." Generalizing from this example, Berkenmeyer next asked the church to ban the Christiaan family and "all their followers" for a year and a month and to readmit them only when "each gives evidence of sufficient regret, repentance, and promise of improvement in the future, on penalty of being excluded from the congregation." Furthermore, though the illegitimate child had to be baptized, neither the mother nor any one of her family could be a sponsor. Nor could "the lying prostitute" name any man the father, "since she tells only lies to the whole world." Berkenmeyer insisted that if any of these conditions were violated, he would refuse to baptize the child. His council agreed.[17]

What is particularly striking about the pastor's injunctions is his expression of deep-seated anger. As noted, Berkenmeyer had expressed liberal ideas about black membership and remained unconcerned about racial mixture, in contrast to his Anglican colleagues around New York City, who mentioned it with disgust. Once her words were doubted, Grit had little power to topple the pastor. To refer to Grit as a "prostitute" was to expose her to public disgrace; to withhold her child's access to baptism was thereby to deny its humanity; and to denounce Piet and "all his race" either betrayed racism in Berkenmeyer (with which his council readily concurred) or perhaps hid a more sinister emotion, which could not be publicly revealed.

The ecclesiastical hearing seemed to repair the damage to Berkenmeyer and his church. But there was still the matter of the child's baptism. On July, 3, 1745, Mother Betty came unannounced to the pastor's home, asking about a baptism for Grit's baby. She relayed that the young mother was deeply ashamed, yet grateful that Berkenmeyer had not taken her to court in Albany, an act that could have resulted in her execution. In practice, in fact, Lutherans rarely used physical punishment against women in cases of illegitimacy, preferring to humiliate them publicly and ostracize them. Accordingly, Berkenmeyer responded that he wanted nothing more to do with the family. That, said Mother Betty, troubled the Christiaans deeply. Old Lies worried that she might never be able to come to church again in this life, while Grit felt that the punishment was much too harsh, as "she was accustomed to come to church regularly." Berkenmeyer, unmollified, answered that he was willing to baptize the child, but without any members of the family present. Mother Betty responded that she would relay those rules to the Christiaan family, but then asked if the pastor would give a name for the child. He answered: "What have I to do with the name-giving?" Rebuffed, Mother Betty declared she would name the baby after Andries, a local slave. The pastor demurred and said he would discuss the matter with his consistory. The pastor and the midwife agreed that if the child was at her house, but no one else from the family was present, he would come to baptize it. He also declared that he would wait until he discussed the issue of the baptism with his congregation. There was no baptism recorded in 1745 in the Loonenburg Lutheran Church for an African American infant, but a curious entry appears early the following year. In January 1746, months after the close of the scandalous accusations against him, Pastor Berkenmeyer documented a private baptism of Jurge, a slave child. Pastor Berkenmeyer named the child Jurge in memory of "my sainted father, who died in 1706—the God of my father be with this Jurge." Unlike two similar baptisms of black children in which Berkenmeyer used other family names, this entry listed no parents, no spouse, and no sponsors. Apparently no other church official was aware of this ritual.[18]

Was this a silent admission by the aged pastor of his paternity? The entry is not conclusive, but its distinctiveness from similar baptisms suggests how unusual it was. Baptisms were joyous, communal events in colonial churches, and witnesses not only were required by church law, but symbolized the support of the extended family and the community. Berkenmeyer had presided over many baptisms of illegitimate or abandoned children of both races. He had cheerfully accepted any explanation of paternity or often had not even required a statement about fatherhood. In his twenty-six years of service to the Loonenburg Lutheran Church, this is the sole entry without any other witnesses. Also to be considered is Mother Betty's suggestion that Berkenmeyer name the child. This could be taken as an act of charity, or it could have been a carefully veiled suggestion that, while the community was unwilling to fling its distinguished pastor into disgrace, there was still a lingering suspicion that he might be the father of the child. It is not possible to state conclusively that Berkenmeyer was the father of Jurge, although like similar situations involving a famous American political philosopher a half century later, the evidence points strongly to his paternity.[19]

What is clear is that the accusations hurt the pastor and his church terribly. Berkenmeyer threatened to resign from the church; its membership was forced to give him even more authority. Even so, younger pastors in the region, such as Henry Muhlenberg and John Christopher Hartwick, regarded Berkenmeyer as hopelessly dated. Attendance in the church dropped precipitously over the next few years, and by 1750 church officials in New York City declared the congregation "ruined." Berkenmeyer lived until 1751, but baptized only one more black infant, an illegitimate daughter of his own slave. After his death the church could not attract a pastor until after the American Revolution.

The furor over Grit's accusations against Pastor Berkenmeyer directly affected only one church, but it represented new, negative attitudes in church and society toward interracial unions. The contemptuous labels Berkenmeyer and his congregants used against Grit were part of a new perception of interracial sex as illicit.

Such younger Lutheran pastors as Muhlenberg and Hartwick failed to resume the church's historical mission to blacks. Perhaps Lutherans were stung by Benjamin Franklin's observations in his 1751 pamphlet, *Observations Concerning the Increase of Mankind*, that German Americans were more swarthy and less white than Anglo-Americans. At the same time, white North Americans were developing a racial ideology that portrayed black women as sexually savage and even bestial. The controversy over a servant girl's accusations helped construct what Mrs. Anne Grant, a Hudson Valley chronicler, noted forty years later as "the barrier, which it was in a high degree criminal and disgraceful to pass."[20]

African Americans responded in two ways to controversies such as the paternity of Grit's child. The fate of the Christiaan family's membership in the Loonenburg church illustrates the first path. The family's request to return to the church, reported in March 1749, was refused until the congregation perceived an improvement in their morals. Dejected by this exclusion, the Christiaan family along with other black families withdrew from the Lutheran Church and moved into Methodism, the rising new evangelical denomination, which tolerated black adherents. No other black family stepped forth to baptize their children at the Loonenburg church or in other regional Lutheran churches in the colonial era. The pall over the church, stemming from the dispute over Grit's child, revealed the fracturing alliance between African Americans and Lutherans, who had once given safe harbor to interracial families and opened the sanctuary of religion to them. Offended by worsening racism in North American denominations, African Americans left them entirely. Eventually, after the American Revolution, blacks opened their own churches, or, in the most extreme cases, went into exile in search of religious and civil equality elsewhere.[21]

NOTES

1. *The Albany Protocol: Wilhelm Christoph Berkenmeyer's Chronicle of Lutheran Affairs in New York Colony, 1731–1750*, trans. Simon Hart and Sibrandina Gertrude Hart-Runeman, ed. John P. Dern (Ann Arbor, Mich.: J. P. Dern, 1971), 439–41. On Van Loon, see *History of Greene County, New York with Biographical Sketches of Its Prominent Men* (New York: J. B. Beers, 1884), 152–54.

2. For population, see Robert V. Wells, *The Population of the British Colonies in America before 1776: A Survey of Census Data* (Princeton: Princeton University Press, 1975), 112; for Loonenburg, see Cynthia A. Kierner, *Traders and Gentlefolk: The Livingstons of New York, 1665–1790* (Ithaca: Cornell University Press, 1992), 108. On interracial marriage, see Winthrop D. Jordan, *White over Black: American Attitudes toward the Negro, 1550–1812* (Chapel Hill: University of North Carolina Press, 1968), 136–78.

3. Jordan, *White over Black*, 136–78. The most recent word on mixed marriages in America, though far more sympathetic than Jordan, still casts a negative light on their social reception. See Werner Sollors, *Neither Black nor White Yet Both: Thematic Explorations of Interracial Literatures* (New York: Oxford University Press, 1997), 286–355.

4. Harry J. Kreider, *Lutheranism in Colonial New York* (New York: Columbia University Press, 1941), 39–42.

5. David Warren Sabean, *Property, Production, and Family in Neckarhausen, 1700–1870* (New York: Cambridge University Press, 1990), 67–68; for lack of local government in Loonenburg, see Kierner, *Traders and Gentlefolk*, 109.

6. *The Journals of Henry Melchior Muhlenberg*, trans. Theodore G. Tappert and John W. Doberstein, 3 vols. (Philadelphia: Evangelical Lutheran Ministerium of Pennsylvania and Adjacent States and the Muhlenberg Press, 1953), 1: 185–88.

7. Kreider, *Lutheranism in Colonial New York*, 40.

8. *Albany Protocol*, 545.

9. For rarity of illegitimate children, see Sabean, *Property, Production, and Family*, 333–34. For slander, see *Albany Protocol*, 313–15. For baptisms, see *New York Genealogical and Biographical Record* 82, no. 1 (January 1951): 27, 88 (hereafter *NYGBR*).

10. Kreider, *Lutheranism in Colonial New York*, 55. Kenn Stryker-Rodda, ed., "Baptisms of the Lutheran Church of New York City," *NYGBR* 97–102 (1967–72); "First Communions in the Lutheran Church of New York City, 1704–1769," *NYGBR* 104 (1973): 111, 115, 183–85.

11. See "Some Early Records of the Lutheran Church of New York," in *Year Book of the Holland Society of New York, 1902* (New York: Holland Society, 1902), 8, 14–15, 17, 19, 20–22; *Olde Ulster* 3 (1907): 253; "New York Lutheran Church Book, 1704–1723," in *Holland Society Year Book, 1903* (New York: Holland Society, 1903), 6, 8, 15, 17, 20, 21. See also Joyce D. Goodfriend, *Before the Melting Pot: Society and Culture in Colonial New York City, 1664–1730* (Princeton: Princeton University Press, 1991), 126.

12. Kreider, *Lutheranism in Colonial New York*, 55. For Arie Van Guinee and his family, see Norman C. Williver, Jr., *The Faithful and the Bold: The Story of the First Service at the Zion Evangelical Lutheran Church, Oldwyck, New Jersey* (Oldwyck, N.J.: Zion Evangelical Lutheran Chuch, 1984), 8–9; *Year Book of the Holland Society of New York, 1903*, 40, 57; Simon Hart and Harry J. Kreider, *Protocol of the Lutheran Church of New York City, 1707–1750* (New York: Synod [United Lutheran Synod of New York and New England], 1958), 89n; Harry J. Kreider, *The History of the United Lutheran Synod of New York and New England (1786–1860)* (Philadelphia: Muhlenberg Press, 1954), 1:2–4; *Somerset County Historical Magazine* 2 (1913): 91. For a fascinating controversy between Van Guinee and a German pastor, see Simon Hart and Harry J. Kreider, trans., *Lutheran Church in New York and New Jersey, 1722–1760, Lutheran Records in the Ministerial Archives of the Staatsarchiv, Hamburg, Germany* (New York: United Lutheran Synod of New York and New England, 1962), 75–76, 137, 148, 163.

13. On reevaluation, see Larry E. Tise, *Proslavery: A History of the Defense of Slavery in America, 1701–1840* (Athens: University of Georgia Press, 1987), 21–25; for discussion of baptism and slavery, see Graham Russell Hodges, *Slavery and Freedom in the Rural North: African Americans in Monmouth County, New Jersey, 1665–1865* (Madison, Wisc.: Madison House Publishers, 1997).

14. For quotations, see Kreider, *Lutheranism in Colonial New York*, 56. For SPG, see Frank J. Klingberg, *Anglican Humanitarianism in Colonial New York* (Philadelphia: Church Historical Society, 1940), 176–78.

15. A. G. Roeber, *Palatines, Liberty, and Property: German Lutherans in Colonial British America* (Baltimore: Johns Hopkins University Press, 1993), 15.

16. *Albany Protocol*, 443–51.

17. Ibid., 459–62.

18. Ibid., 653–64. For baptism of Jurge, see *NYGBR* 83, no.2 (January 1952): 32. For other baptisms, see *NYGBR* 83, no. 2 (January 1952): 27, and 83, no.3 (April 1952): 114.

For Lutherans and illegitimacy, see Isabel V. Hull, *Sexuality, State, and Civil Society in Germany, 1700–1815* (Ithaca: Cornell University Press, 1996), 102–03.

19. For the latest word on Thomas Jefferson and his relationship with Sally Hemings, see Annette Gordon-Reed, *Thomas Jefferson and Sally Hemings: An American Controversy* (Charlottesville: University Press of Virginia, 1997).

20. For church problems, see *History of Greene County*, 170. On contemporary criticism of Berkenmeyer, see Kreider, *Lutheranism in Colonial New York*, 47. Benjamin Franklin and Mrs. Anne Grant are quoted in Jordan, *White over Black*, 143–44. For construction of racial ideology, see Jennifer L. Morgan, " 'Some Could Suckle over Their Shoulder': Male Travelers, Female Bodies, and the Gendering of Racial Ideology, 1500–1770," *William and Mary Quarterly* 54 (1997): 167–92.

21. *Albany Protocol*, 484–88, 503. For discussions of blacks leaving white churches because of insulting behavior, see Gary B. Nash, *Forging Freedom: The Formation of Philadelphia's Black Community, 1720–1840* (Cambridge: Harvard University Press, 1987); and Graham Russell Hodges, *Black Itinerants of the Gospel: The Narratives of George White and John Jea* (Madison, Wisc.: Madison House Books, 1993). On exile, see Graham Russell Hodges, ed., *The Black Loyalist Directory: African Americans in Exile after the American Revolution* (New York: Garland, 1996).

Chapter Four

The Saga of Sarah Muckamugg
Indian and African American Intermarriage in Colonial New England

Daniel R. Mandell

In 1728, at the home of William Page in Providence, Rhode Island, Sarah Mucka-mugg, a Nipmuc from Hassanamisco in Massachusetts, "solemnized" her union with Aaron, a slave of African ancestry. The two had at least one child, Joseph Aaron, before their union dissolved twelve years later. Sarah then returned to Hassanamisco (which had, during her absence, become the mostly Anglo-American town of Grafton) and became involved with another African, Fortune Burnee. In 1744 she bore a child from that union, also named Sarah. But her new relationship was also ill-fated: she became sick, was abandoned by Burnee, and died at the home of a white man in the summer of 1751.[1]

Sarah Muckamugg, her spouses, their relationships, and their "mixed" children represent the emerging trend of Indian-African intermarriage in late colonial New England. When we carefully place these few bits of direct evidence into the broader picture of Indians and African Americans in colonial New England, a penetrating view emerges of the causes and effects of the little-noted but increasingly common love and marriage across the line separating Natives from involuntary African immigrants. Sarah's relationships with Aaron and Fortune show how intermarriages developed out of the needs of Indians and blacks, who shared a marginal social status in New England. Her two marriages also highlight the two worlds in which Indians and Africans met and married: urban seaports where poor laborers of all races came together, and farm villages that had once been entirely Indian. At the same time, Sarah's problems with both of her husbands show how the different needs of individuals from the two groups, as well as the pressures generated by their shared condition, could shatter their marriages.

Finally, the different experiences of Sarah's two children from these marriages, Joseph Aaron and Sarah Burnee, highlight the ways in which the offspring of intermarriages raised issues of community membership and communal control of resources. Their lives also point to the widening gap between Native and Anglo-American identities and between Native and Anglo-American attitudes toward these "mixed" offspring.

*

Sarah Muckamugg may herself have been the product of a mixed marriage. Her father, Peter Muckamugg, was either a Narragansett or grew up among Narragansetts, having lived as a boy in or near Providence, Rhode Island. Her mother, Sarah Robbins, was a Nipmuc, the people who occupied central, inland Massachusetts.[2] In the wake of King Philip's War in 1675–76, Hassanamisco lay within a frontier where no English dared live, due to continuing conflicts with Abenakis and their French allies. Of approximately eight thousand Indians who remained in southern New England after the war, about five hundred, mostly Christianized Natives from "praying towns" who had been incarcerated by the English, resettled a few interior villages after the war, including Hassanamisco, Sarah Robbins's community. They fished, hunted, and grew crops—as had their aboriginal ancestors—but also traveled to work for English farmers or to trade furs, deerskins, and other produce with the colonists. And Natives no doubt visited with some of the Indians who were servants or slaves in the growing port towns. Hassanamisco lay where the path between Boston and Connecticut intersected with the Blackstone River, which ran down a wide valley to Providence and the Narragansett Bay, making an easy highway.[3] While we do not know where or when Peter Muckamugg and Sarah Robbins met and married, or when or where their daughter Sarah was born, they apparently traveled back and forth between Hassanamisco and Providence.

The 1713 Treaty of Utrecht ended British hostilities with the French and their Native allies, and reopened Nipmuc territory to eager colonists. Fifteen years later, colonists purchased the Hassanamisco reserve from the seven Indian families living there, including the Muckamuggs, in exchange for money, shares in the schoolhouse and church to be built by the colonists, and large allotments in the new town of Grafton. When Peter and Sarah Muckamugg returned to claim their allotments in May 1728, they left their daughter Sarah living in the Providence household of John Whipple, the eldest son of one of the most prestigious families in the town, apparently working as a domestic.[4] Like Sarah, a growing number of Indians were moving to New England port towns to find work as laborers, mariners, tavern help, and in other unskilled occupations. There they lived and worked alongside poor whites and freed and enslaved Africans, whom they often loved and married. One such relationship was "solemnized" about 1728, when "an Indian woman known by name of Indian Sarah, also called the daughter of Sarah Muckamaug was married to a Negro man named Aaron the servant of Col. Joseph Whipple of Providence."[5]

Only about a thousand Africans and their descendants—mostly enslaved but a few free—lived in New England in 1700, but their number rapidly increased to about eleven thousand by midcentury. Slaves in New England experienced a very different life than their contemporaries in the South and the West Indies. Most lived in port towns and performed tasks for which free labor was scarce: they worked as artisans' assistants, house servants, seamen, and in construction. The few slaves in rural villages usually served as status symbols as well as providing relatively inexpensive menial labor for the local elites, particularly ministers.

Like indentured servants and apprentices, slaves were considered part of the extended household, a situation that held both benefits and drawbacks. Individuals experienced a considerable lack of autonomy, and were expected to adopt the dominant culture quickly. On the other hand, blacks were allowed to participate in the larger community and its culture. Many were taught to read, for it was a Puritan duty to see that all could read and understand the Bible. They could hire themselves out to work for other employers, and even buy their own and their family's freedom. And slaves in New England port towns worked alongside free, apprenticed, and indentured laborers, and often caroused with them in pubs after work.[6]

Few Africans lived in Providence: only 7 of the 1,500 residents (0.5 percent) in 1708, rising to 225 of 3,177 (7 percent) in 1748. Even fewer Indians resided in that town: only fifty at midcentury. Aaron, Sarah, and other African Americans and Indians in Providence were set apart as the lowest social class in New England, and were subject to special laws designed to exert an extra measure of control over the potentially dangerous minority. In 1703 the Rhode Island Assembly required "any negroes, or Indians, either freemen, servants, or slaves" walking the streets after nine at night to carry "a certificate from their masters" or to be accompanied by "some English person of said family." Tavern keepers would be fined if they entertained servants, "either negroes or Indians, without leave of their masters or to whom they do belong," after nine. Similar restrictions existed in Massachusetts.

Africans and Indians were also barred, by law and custom, from joining with whites in socially sanctioned sex—that is, in marriage. Rhode Island forbade anyone to join in marriage "any white person with any Negro, Indian or mulatto, on the penalty of two hundred dollars"; all such marriages would be "absolutely null and void." In 1706 Massachusetts debated a bill designed to prevent "a Spurious and Mixt Issue" by criminalizing sexual relations or marriage between a European and an Indian, black, or mulatto. While the distinguished Reverend Samuel Sewall used all of his immense influence to remove Indians from the act, custom frowned on marriages between Indians and whites, and in 1786 the legislature added Indians to the ban. These measures clearly limited potential partners for both Indians and African Americans and, considering their small numbers, helped bring Aaron and Sarah Muckamugg together in the Anglo-American town of Providence.[7]

We do not know where or how Sarah and Aaron found each other and fell in love. Most likely they met when he went with Joseph Whipple on a visit to his master's eldest son, John, in whose house Sarah lived. Perhaps the two had their first romantic encounter in the kitchen, while John and Joseph played whist or discussed business or Joseph's medical problems in an adjoining room.[8] Their relationship could have blossomed in subsequent visits by Aaron to Sarah, alone or with Joseph Whipple. The couple may have also met for the first time in the marketplace, outside the church that their masters attended, or at one of the taverns kept by "free Negroes and Mulattoes" in Providence, where "servants and others" (of all colors?) socialized. In any case, their union was "solemnized" in the home of William and Mary Page.[9]

But was their union recognized as a marriage by others? The son and daughter of John Whipple, who claimed to have known both Sarah and Aaron quite well, were adamant that "we never understood that the said Aaron and Sarah were married together but on the contrary are almost certain that they never were married." The Providence town clerk testified that he could find no record of their marriage. Years later, several Anglo-American acquaintances claimed to know nothing of their being married.[10] In fact, the ceremony that joined Sarah and Aaron lay outside the scope of state-sanctioned marriages in New England. The midwife Hallelujah Olney, who assisted at the births of Sarah's children, first described "Sarah Aaron" as "the wife of a Negro man Aaron," and then three years later testified that she never knew that Aaron was married to Sarah "but frequently heard that they Cohabited together."[11]

Such "common-law" marriages remained normal for Indians and African Americans, dwellers on New England's margins, even as more whites sought the legal protection and legitimation of unions set in law. A two-tiered system of marriages emerged during the late colonial period, as legal forms and rituals became more prominent and prevalent in Anglo-American society, while folk customs continued among Indians, blacks, and poorer whites.[12] Such marriages were, as an Anglo-American minister noted, "performed by mutual consent without the blessings of the church," and the two partners could easily agree to break "by mutual consent their negro marriage."[13] And such marriages were rarely recorded—unfortunately for historians, for estimates of the number of Indian–African American unions are impossible.

Like most nonliterate individuals and laboring families, Sarah and Aaron left no traces except when social problems or tragedy drew the attention of the authorities or the lettered elite. We know from others that Sarah had at least four children while in Providence. The couple's circumstances were hardly conducive, however, to a long and happy marriage: not only did they live with the ongoing pressure of social and legal subordination, but they were unable even to live together under one roof as husband and wife, for Aaron remained Joseph Whipple's slave and Sarah remained in John Whipple's household. Around 1740 something snapped the fragile threads that bound them together—perhaps the birth of their last child, Joseph Aaron. Sarah probably had hoped that Aaron would be able to live with her and help support their children, and perhaps Aaron's reaction when Joseph arrived made the finality of their situation clear to her. Their relationship soured: they were frequently quarreling, and Aaron may have become abusive.[14]

Approximately a year after Joseph's birth, Sarah Muckamugg left Providence with several of her children, seemingly headed for Hassanamisco, now Grafton. Probably her relationship with Aaron had become unbearable, and she may have missed her aging parents. Her ability (and willingness) to leave Aaron and Providence on her own also points to the different customs of Indian women, who, since they traditionally held and worked land, could readily leave husbands. Sarah's route north through the Blackstone River valley took her past the Smithfield farm of a family named Wilkinson. There she stopped and obtained the Wilkinsons' permission to build a wigwam and live on their land. Their detailed recollections of Sarah hint that she may have helped around the Wilkinson home, as she did for the Whipples.

Aaron, who, like other bound Africans, could obtain his owner's permission to travel independently for short visits or other personal matters, soon made the short trip to the Wilkinson farm. Their reunion only widened the rupture between the African man and the Nipmuc woman, and generated an explosion that was noticed even by the master of the farm. Three decades later, Israel Wilkinson remembered that Aaron "had some Difference with her and I have heard her say that she was not married to the said Negro Man."[15] Sarah was far more forthcoming with Israel's wife, Mary (or perhaps Mary paid more attention to Sarah's words); the bond between these two women may have been deeper than their ethnic or racial divide. One day, when returning to the house—perhaps from the orchard or barn—Mary found Sarah crying bitterly. When asked, the Nipmuc woman sobbed out the bitter state of her relationship with her visitor. "She said that Aaron Sayeth that he never would Live with me any more neither would he help maintain the Children & I asked her wether they was ever marryed & she Said no & I asked what the Reason was & she Said that he promised to do well by me & further Said that She would then by [be] marr[ie]d but he w[o]uld not & further Sayeth that he had got another Squaw that he Lovd better."[16]

Sarah's words hint at a relationship that was split by gradually widening expectations that were impossible to reconcile. She had been happy, back in 1729, to bear his children after he had "promised to do well by me" when they formalized their union. But by 1740 Sarah wanted or needed more, for "She would then be married," perhaps because the legal status and future welfare of their children were in doubt, or more likely because she was weary of her dependence and near-servitude at the Whipples and wanted her family to live together. Unfortunately, Sarah lacked the money to buy her husband's freedom, as many Indian women would do for their African American spouses. Perhaps this was the wedge that had split Aaron from Sarah: he desperately wanted his freedom and abandoned her for another when it became clear that she could not fulfill that desire. And their conflict may have had a deeper complexity that reflected their different backgrounds. Did "Indian Sarah" (as some documents call her) want her children raised as Hassan-amisco Nipmucs, with roots in her clan and community? Aaron, on the other hand, would have seen far more opportunity, for himself as well as for their free children, in the expanding maritime town of Providence. Different customs in postmarital residence—Nipmuc matrilocality versus Anglo-American (and perhaps African) patrilocality—may also have underlain the friction between Sarah and Aaron.

On the other hand, the fate of their children points to different concerns in their relationship and the observance of customs that were quite different from Anglo-American ways. Apparently during her relationship with Aaron, Sarah bound three of her children—Abraham, Rhode, and Abigail—to a white family named Brown. Richard Brown and his son Richard were amazed to find that "Aaron had no concern about this," and saw the African man's failure to exercise patriarchal authority as casting doubt on Sarah and Aaron's marriage.[17] The Browns could not have been surprised that Sarah and Aaron's children were indentured; such arrangements were not unusual for Anglo-American children, particularly from poorer families, and were quite common for African American children. What surprised them was that, when Sarah took responsibility for her children's future, she displayed the familial authority that was exercised by the husband in the dominant culture and legal system. Sarah's actions, Aaron's apparent lack of "concern," and the Browns' surprise point to the different levels of authority that women and men held in Indian, African, and Anglo-American cultures. And while Sarah clearly claimed the authority due her within the matrilineal Nipmuc culture, and Aaron voiced no objections to observers, the two must have had conflicts that arose from their very different roots.[18]

Sarah Muckamugg did not remain long at her wigwam on the Wilkinson farm, but soon returned to her family in Grafton. By midcentury Grafton had become a typical New England farming village, with excellent pasture and cropland, not far from the growing regional center of Worcester. Few Nipmucs remained in the town, and few Anglo-American residents owned African slaves: a provincial census in 1764–65 found 7 Negroes, 14 Indians, and 742 whites. Sarah may have arrived in Grafton as early as January 1741, for town records show Thomas English, an Indian, marrying a Sarah Muckamugg on that date, but records do not make clear whether this was mother or daughter. Sarah Muckamugg had certainly returned by November 1744, when she bore a daughter, Sarah, to Fortune Burnee, a "free Negro."[19]

Burnee's background remains a mystery; nor do we know where and how they met. Perhaps they met while Sarah was living at the Wilkinsons' farm. Gideon Hawley, the white minister of the Indian enclave of Mashpee, noted to his dismay that "many of our women have found negroe husbands, as they were stroling in the country and bro't them home."[20] If Sarah had not been the Muckamugg who married English, perhaps she brought Fortune home to Hassanamisco. Or perhaps he was already living in or near Grafton. But clearly they were united by Sarah Burnee's birth in 1744.[21] Tragically, neither their relationship nor Sarah Muckamugg's life lasted long. She fell ill in late 1750 or early 1751. Fortune either abandoned Sarah or was physically unable to care for her, for she was placed by the town's selectmen in the home of an Anglo-American, Hezekiah Ward, where she died in the summer of 1751.[22]

By the time of Sarah Muckamugg's death, marriages between Indian women and African American men were becoming increasingly common in New England. Native enclaves suffered from a precipitous decline in the number of their men between 1740 and 1780. Many enthusiastically volunteered for and died in the militia during King George's War (1744–48) and the Seven Years' War (1754–60). Censuses from Massachusetts, Rhode Island, and Connecticut, taken between 1765 and 1774, show about 60 percent more women than men. Men were needed to father the next generation and to work the fields or to bring home income from the dominant world of the Anglo-American economy. Anglo-American prejudice against Indians meant that Native women were often able to meet their emotional, demographic, economic, and social needs only by marrying African American men—which also served to adopt the newcomers into family and community.[23]

Sarah Muckamugg's saga helps us translate these regional demographic trends into the experiences of individuals. Few Indians, but a growing number of blacks, lived in the small but vital port town of Providence, so while Sarah lived there she was far more likely to meet men of African descent. Upon her return to Grafton, Sarah found only eight adult Hassanamisco men, most of whom were already married; six soon died in the war. Other Hassanamisco women made similar choices. Abigail Printer, a daughter of Hassanamisco's foremost family, first married another Indian, Andrew Abraham, Jr., in 1739. But after his death during King George's War she married an African American, William Anthony, in 1752. Anthony died soon after their marriage, and in 1757 Abigail married Sarah Muckamugg's widower, Fortune Burnee. The two Lawrence sisters both married African Americans in the 1760s: Esther married Sharp Freeborn, one of the few blacks in Paxton, and moved to his farm, while Patience and Cesar Gimbee decided to stay on her family's land in Grafton. As Sarah Muckamugg demonstrated and Gideon Hawley noted, Native women peddling crafts or working as domestics often met black men in the bustling streets of Boston or the roads of rural New England. In addition, in the larger, coastal Indian groups, intermarriages often resulted when seamen brought "foreign" shipmates home on visits.[24]

Sarah may have had another reason, far more personal, elusive, and impossible to quantify, for seeking out and marrying African American men: a preference for a man from another culture, with different values, who would be willing and able to support her and her children in their changing world. She cried out to Mary Wilkinson, on that devastating day in Smithfield, that she had originally committed herself to Aaron because "he promised to do well by me," but that now he was not only refusing to live with her, but "neither would he help maintain the children."[25] Other Indian women demonstrated the desire for a decent living as defined by the dominant Anglo-American culture. Alice Prophetess, a Narragansett, bought an African American husband around 1770, according to family legend,

> in order to change her mode of living. It was customary for the woman to do all the drudgery and hard work in-doors and out. The Indian men thought it a disgrace for them to work; they thought they did their part by hunting and procuring game. The Indian women observing the colored men working for their wives, and living after the manner of white people, in comfortable homes, felt anxious to change their position in life.[26]

Of course, few Indian men in eighteenth-century southern New England subsisted by hunting and fishing; most labored on their own or others' farms or worked as sailors. But considering that so many Indian women married outsiders, perhaps Sarah, Alice, and others were indeed convinced that marrying black men provided the best opportunities in the changing world for themselves and their families.

During the colonial period, African American men married Indian women for many of the same reasons. The two peoples in fact experienced complementary demographic imbalances, for New England's demand for semiskilled laborers meant that most of the black slaves brought to the region were men. Although the percentage of native-born blacks grew throughout the eighteenth century, at midcentury the 2,700 adult African Americans in Massachusetts included 1.75 men for each woman. For men like Aaron in Providence in the 1720s or Fortune Burnee in

Grafton in the 1740s, an Indian may have been their only possible mate, given the lack of black women, their frequent isolation in otherwise all-white households and villages, and Anglo-American prejudices.[27]

African men also gained social and economic benefits from an Indian wife. Even if she could not purchase his freedom, their children would be born free. The husbands of Indian women like Sarah Muckamugg gained access to Native land and other resources. Last, but not least, an African man could gain a community with an Indian wife, for Native enclaves generally welcomed newcomers. Sarah's second husband, the appropriately named Fortune Burnee, is one of the best examples of the advantages that a man of African descent could gain. He obtained access to the Muckamugg land and annual interest receipts by marrying Sarah. After her death in 1751 he became the guardian of their young daughter, seemingly the only heir to the family property. But since much of Sarah's property was sold in May 1752 to pay her medical bills, six years later he married another Hassanamisco, Abigail Printer. After Abigail died in 1776, Fortune continued to use and profit from her land and annual interest income until his death in 1795. While Burnee was barred by Massachusetts law from selling his wife's lands without the General Court's permission, he held her property in all but title.[28]

Alice Prophetess's grandson believed that the desire of Indian women to marry African men caused Native men to have a "very bitter feeling" against blacks.[29] By the end of the century, gender conflicts erupted in a few Indian communities as some Native men came to believe that "their" women preferred African American husbands who had embraced Anglo-American ways. In 1788, thirty-one Mashpee men complained about "the coming of Negroes & English, who, unhappily, have planted themselves here, hath managed us, and it is to be feared, that they and their Children, unless they are removed, will get away our Lands & all our Privileges in a short time."[30] The white guardian of Chappaquiddick and Christiantown noted that "there were many disputes among them oweing to their Females Marrying Negroes whom they did not wish to have any right to their lands," and that Christiantown men filed at least two lawsuits between 1805 and 1811 to stop African American men from marrying into their community.[31] In 1859 a state commissioner found that the Indians of Gay Head were "jealous of the influence of [black] foreigners, having had much trouble with some of those who have intermarried with their women and settled amongst them."[32]

But such resistance did nothing to slow the rising tide of intermarriage, nor did it have much effect on how Native communities dealt with these "foreigners." Even before the mid-eighteenth century, the larger enclaves that continued to hold their lands and other resources in common, such as Mashpee and Gay Head, limited landholding to those born into the group. Newcomers could not vote in meetings or claim resources, although their "mixed" offspring would be full members of the community. These boundaries were porous enough, and the Native population inside was large enough, to bring in outsiders and to assimilate their children. On the other hand, Sarah Muckamugg's community, like other small inland villages that had developed close connections to the dominant economy and culture, and had been hammered by poverty, disease, and war, were quickly reshaped by intermar-

riage with blacks.[33] In a village like Hassanamisco, lacking a sizable Native population and strong community controls over resources, the ambitions of African
American spouses could wreak substantial damage. When Fortune Burnee married
again, following Abigail's death in 1776, it was, according to a guardian, to "an
old negro wench," not an Indian. And no doubt the Hassanamiscos as well as their
guardians were angered when he willed the Printer properties to a white lawyer,
including a third of the remaining Indians' shrinking funds.[34]

Yet at the same time, the Hassanamisco community survived in large part because of intermarriage. In 1762 Ezra Stiles, a prominent minister and scientist,
found in Grafton "not a Male Ind. in the Town, & perh. 5 Squaws who marry
Negroes," and one year later, apparently on another visit, noted four Indian families
in the enclave, including four men, five women, six boys, and seven girls.[35] While
white observers were confused about matters of ethnic identity, the contradictions
in their accounts point to the importance of intermarriage in Hassanamisco and
other Indian villages. About three generations later, state investigator John Earle
found that

> little trace of Indian descent is apparent in the members of this tribe. It is most marked
> in the few who have mixed chiefly with the whites. . . . The remainder of the tribe have
> the distinguishing marks of African descent and mixed African and white, of various
> grades . . . and, in every successive generation the slight remaining characteristics of
> the race become less apparent.[36]

Earle's observations also indicate that there was intermarriage between Indians
and whites. While white hostility generally barred such unions, which were legal
until the end of the colonial period, individuals did occasionally marry into Indian
communities. In addition to his description of Hassanamisco, Earle told the General
Court that since 1700 almost every marriage in the Yarmouth Indian community
on Cape Cod had been between whites and Indians, an astonishing but unfortunately brief observation.[37] A half century earlier, in 1798, Natick's Anglo-American
minister, Stephen Badger, noted that some of "his" Indians had married whites as
well as blacks.[38] And at about the same time, Gideon Hawley told a friend that,
besides blacks, some Englishmen and four Hessian deserters from Burgoyne's army
had married Mashpee women, "whereby we have a motley medley of characters
more heterogenous, if possible, and some of them not less turbulent, than the elements."[39] But while Indian-white unions were more frequent than town records
indicate, they were relatively rare due to Anglo-American prejudice against intermarriage.

More significant and potentially controversial than marriages between Indians and
African Americans were the offspring of those marriages. By the close of the colonial period, the children of mixed marriages personified the developing conflict
between the emerging African American culture, which embraced the dominant
society's patriarchy and individualism as the means for community cohesion and
respectability, and Native ways that gave a woman and her community greater
power. Indian and African American groups created different cultural "markers" to

limit their community boundaries. Native enclaves began to modify theirs early in the century, as their rural reserves were besieged by outsiders seeking scarce land and other resources. Birth, residence, and behavior became key: full members of the community included the descendants of those already recognized as Indians, those raised in any Indian enclave, and individuals who demonstrated their support for the community. The markers developed by African Americans are much more elusive, in large part because black churches, lodges, and charitable groups were organized only after the American Revolution, and only in cities with sufficient black populations. Those institutions, like Indian enclaves, created standards of behavior for their members—but standards that mirrored those of the Anglo-American elite: temperance, hard work, savings, and patriarchal families.[40]

The evolving boundaries of Indian groups and the challenge posed by "mixed" offspring can be seen in Sarah Muckamugg's children. Sarah Burnee, born in 1744, was seven when her mother died. One wonders how she felt about her father, who came from outside Hassanamisco, seemingly abandoned her mother to die in a stranger's house, and just six years later married Abigail Printer. Sarah apparently grew up in her late mother's house as her sole heir, serving as her father's entrée to the income from the Muckamugg family farm and annual Hassanamisco account receipts. She first appeared as an independent person in the community's records in 1768, reclaiming at the age of twenty-four her family's property and income.[41] Sarah may have followed in her mother's footsteps, marrying by April 1771, according to one document, "Prince Dam, a Negro man, belonging to Woodstock," in Smithfield—although in other records from the 1770s she is referred to as a "spinster."[42] In 1786 she married Boston Phillips, an African American, and before his death a decade later they had two children, a son named Ben and a daughter named Sarah. At least four generations of Hassanamisco women, beginning with the mother of Peter Muckamugg's wife, named their daughters Sarah, hinting at the persistence of Nipmuc matrilineage. In fact, Muckamugg's wife had also passed her family name, Robbins, on to her daughter, the mother of Sarah Burnee; and Burnee referred to herself in 1821, just before her death, as "Sarah Phillips, alias Muckamuk." Clearly, Sarah Burnee was acculturated into the Hassanamisco community from her birth and remained there until her death.[43]

Sarah's half-brother, Joseph Aaron, represents another path taken by the offspring of mixed marriage, and the conflicts and opportunities that such individuals posed to Indian families and communities. Like his brothers and sisters, and so many other Indian and black children, he was "bound and apprenticed at the age of 12 or 13 years."[44] We know little else of his life between his birth in 1740 and his arrival in Hassanamisco nearly thirty years later. Hallelujah Olney, who assisted at his birth, testified in 1768 that he had lived most of his life in Providence. There he probably would have lived as part of the undifferentiated "people of color," for no African American institutions existed in that town until the 1780s, and there is no evidence that he visited Grafton or had any connection to Hassanamisco until 1768. In that year he suddenly appeared in the Hassanamisco records, living with his half-sister Sarah, his Nipmuc ancestry reclaimed and recognized by the community's guardians, who gave him part of the group's annual receipts. Like so many others of his social class and ancestry, Aaron worked as a laborer in the rural community while farming his family's few acres.[45]

For several years the two siblings managed to live together. But in 1771 controversy tore the family apart. In May, the two petitioned to divide the 154-acre Muckamugg farm. Joseph may have demanded clear possession of part of the estate, perhaps driven by the acquisitive, masculine values learned during his apprenticeship. When a committee from the General Court made an initial division, Joseph "was much Dissatisfied" at his part and appealed to "his master" (probably the man with whom he had served his apprenticeship) for assistance, for they had given Sarah not only the house but "by far the Best part of the present profits and where Joseph has Bestowed his labour and as we understand have ordered Considerable part of the Grain to Sarah when Joseph had been at the Sole Cost of Raising whatever may grow [there] of that kind this year."[46] Anglo-Americans traditionally saw labor as giving value to "vacant" land, and assumed that since that labor was performed by the man, the land properly belonged to him. Aboriginals, by contrast, had seen the land as part of the community or clan, and women performed most of the agricultural labor. While Hassanamisco's culture had gone through massive changes, Joseph's complaint indicates that gender roles and community values were part of the conflict, and of course the Muckamugg farm had been wholly Sarah's before Joseph arrived.

Sarah apparently challenged Joseph's claim to shared ancestry and Hassanamisco identity. In March, April, and July 1771, a "Prince Paine"—perhaps the Prince Dam whom Sarah may have married that April—obtained depositions from people in Providence and Smithfield, testifying that Sarah Muckamugg was not married to Aaron Whipple.[47] But this attempt to disprove Joseph's claim to Muckamugg land and Hassanamisco ancestry was in vain, in large part because of the other documents that testified to Joseph Aaron's birth and the relationship between Aaron and Sarah Muckamugg, but also perhaps because Joseph *looked* "Indian." Decades after his death, whites remembered him (inaccurately) as "a full-blooded Indian, with long, straight hair."[48] And judging by his subsequent prominence in the Hassanamisco records, other Nipmuc descendants accepted Joseph Aaron as a full member of the community.

The conflict between Sarah's two children has many possible implications. It could be cast as a conflict between persistent Indian communalism and the American individualism embraced by many blacks, between a prominent role for women as leaders and landholders and a subordinate role for women. Such conflicts did erupt in some of the larger enclaves such as Mashpee in the mid-nineteenth century, as African American husbands saw more opportunity in the dominant political and legal system, and sought to gain control of their Native wives' land.[49] But in 1727 the Hassanamiscos had embraced landholding in severalty and participation in the dominant economy, and the contest between Joseph and Sarah was not over communal land but over family property. So was their wrangle simply one more example of the New England proclivity to war over inheritance and other family concerns, and was Prince Paine simply trying to cast doubt on Joseph's parentage and thus his right to a piece of that property? Perhaps. On the other hand, the Hassanamiscos did retain a valuable piece of communal property: the funds from the sale of their reserve, which provided annual interest payments to each adult member of the community. Once acknowledged as Hassanamisco by the guardians, Joseph was granted a share. And since all Hassanamisco land was owned in severalty, and ancestry was a key element in Indian ethnicity, a recognized claim to land owned by a Hassanamisco family must have been prima facie proof of membership in the community.

The potential effects of the rising tide of intermarriage on Indian ethnicity can be glimpsed in the conflict between Sarah Muckamugg's children. Joseph Aaron's childhood and adolescence in Providence must have provided little knowledge of Nipmuc traditions, and one must wonder what his intentions were when he claimed his mother's heritage and land, and how he might have affected the Hassanamisco community. He was clearly part of the evolving intersection between Anglo-American and Indian ways: like other Hassanamiscos, he worked the family farm before the conflict erupted, claimed his share of that property as an integral part of his Hassanamisco heritage through his mother, and was given an annual interest payment. And he demonstrated his regard for the community by joining a protest to the General Court in 1785 against the behavior of the Hassanamisco guardians. At the same time, Joseph showed his acceptance of Anglo-American gender roles, for he insisted on control of the family's crops (although he agreed to give a percentage of that year's harvest to Sarah) while not contesting his sister's retention of the family home.

While delineating membership was especially important for Indian groups that retained valuable communal property, the controversy over Joseph Aaron's ancestry shows that members of smaller communities shared similar standards. By the middle of the eighteenth century, New England Indian "markers" included communal resources, a distinct folklore, inclusive meetings, kinship ties to a recognized Indian, individual behavior (for example, how one made a living), social conduct, and perhaps most important, though difficult to document, the desire to make a legitimate claim to be Indian.[50] Exclusion also shaped Indian ethnic boundaries, for white perceptions of Indian behavior helped fashion cultural markers, and white prejudice against Indians and other people of color reinforced those boundaries.

Smaller groups that lacked numbers and retained few communal resources, such as the Nipmucs in Hassanamisco, depended on African American husbands for survival. Their social boundaries were therefore fairly permeable, consisting primarily of "ascription and identification" and invisible to almost all but members and outsiders wishing to join the group.[51] At the same time, those seemingly weak boundaries were reinforced, ironically, by the Anglo-American guardians who controlled the Indian groups' funds. Larger enclaves, such as Gay Head and Mashpee, had clearer rules on who could claim communal resources, and were somewhat less vulnerable to the machinations of their white guardians. But small and large groups alike saw marriage partners from the outside, such as Fortune Burnee, as not quite full members of the community. Their offspring, raised and acculturated into the group, were full members, regardless of skin or hair color or "blood quotient." The similarities in Hassanamisco and Mashpee membership, despite the enclaves' radically different circumstances, demonstrate how the emerging New England Indian ethnic identity focused on three points: where individuals lived, the origins of their parents, and whether their conduct demonstrated a proper regard for the group.[52]

Among African Americans in New England during the colonial period, by comparison, intermarriage and "mixed" offspring held no threat. Blacks had limited autonomy, were newcomers in a strange land, and lacked community institutions until after the Revolution. Most lived in Anglo-American–dominated urban seaports where mobility was high and social institutions were weak, and held neither political power nor communal property to defend. But as African Americans in New England gained their freedom between 1780 and 1820, they forged churches and charitable organizations that required members to follow codes of conduct that included most Anglo-American virtues: sobriety, punctuality, industry, and patriarchal families. And in the early nineteenth century, African Americans also adopted the emerging ideals of masculine "achievement, autonomy, and 'intensive competition for success in the marketplace.' "[53]

African Americans were not simply trying to emulate Anglo-American Protestant virtues, for blacks could not assume that they would soon be accepted as equal members of New England society. The creation of such organizations should be seen as part of the process of forming a free but separate community, with standards that could include all blacks, would allow them to enter as close an orbit as possible to the dominant culture, and would govern relations with whites. Few members were permanently cast out for breaking these rules, while blacks could use their respectability to forge beneficial patron-client relations with Anglo-American elites.[54] At the same time, these individualistic and evangelical Protestant standards represented the deepening divide between Indians and African Americans.

While individuals continued to cross this cultural gap, they posed new problems for Native groups. Unlike whites, Indians traditionally welcomed marriages with "foreigners" as a way to bring new skills and power into the community. But those thus "adopted" were likewise expected to adopt their new community, to meet certain standards of conduct, and to raise their children as members of the group. Gender was embedded in Indian boundaries: only those born into the community could represent their household in meetings and claim resources held in common— and, since newcomers were usually men, women served as the gatekeepers. The tensions that could erupt within mixed families would have been even more intense when the Indian daughters of an African American man reached the age when they could vote in community meetings and claim pieces of communal land, rights that the father was denied as a foreigner. In the outside world, of course, daughters and wives were subservient to the patriarchal head of the family.

By the close of the colonial period, the rising tide of intermarriage and "mixed" offspring posed new challenges to Indians. Native communities had to deal with the problem of individuals choosing between the different ethnic identities of their parents, and the need to maintain communal property and moral standards as children of mixed marriages moved between groups. The two sons of Cesar and Patience Gimbee, an African-Hassanamisco couple, moved to Worcester and in 1801 sought to sell all of the family's land in Grafton as they "consider[ed] themselves as having inheriting from their Father, who was not an Indian, all the rights of free Citizens among which that of disposing of their property is one."[55]

Indians were also handicapped by the inability of Anglo-Americans, who wrote and enforced legal standards and shaped the region's dominant culture, to understand mixed marriages and their offspring. Natives saw their community boundaries as quite clear and well-established, but many whites saw only "mulattoes," "mongrels," and vanishing Indians. The Natick minister Stephen Badger found it "almost impossible to come to any determination" of the Indian population in and near the town, for they "are intermarried with *blacks*, and some with whites; and the various shades between these, and those that are descended from them."[56] Thus the statistics assembled by whites on "people of color" (Indians, blacks, and mulattoes) are at best questionable and at worst racist distortions. Indeed, the federal census, beginning in 1790, identified whole households only as "white," "slave," or "all other free persons." The evolving ideology of race distorted even the most careful observations.

By the beginning of the nineteenth century, white observers began to notice and regret the disappearance of "true" Indians. Investigations of Indian groups after 1800 inevitably found few "pure bloods." At the same time, many white New Englanders, particularly the elite who benefited from early industrialization, were upset by the social changes that accompanied the new factory economy, and expressed regrets for their (rose-tinted) disappearing past. James Fenimore Cooper's *Last of the Mohicans*, published in 1826, popularized the emerging image of the noble savage, endowed with grace and unpolished intelligence. Indians were part of that past—but only Indians who looked and played their proper roles. Thus the emerging myth of the "vanishing Indian" in New England had its origins in the potent combination of racism and romanticism. Many towns have cherished legends of the "last Indian" from the early to mid-nineteenth century that feature one (and sometimes both) of the two classic images of Indians: the noble if pathetic woodsman who taught the town's boys to fish and hunt, or the lazy, somewhat threatening drunkard.[57]

Sarah Muckamugg's lineage has grown to this day, although by the middle of the nineteenth century white observers were unable or unwilling to find her descendants. John Milton Earle of Worcester, commissioned by the governor in 1858 to investigate the numbers and conditions of Indians in Massachusetts, found no Muckamuggs, Burnees, or Phillips. He and others observed the Indians' continuing high mortality, and believed that condition to be the tragic hallmark of the "vanishing race." But as Earle himself noted (while discussing the Natives' high mortality), the many generations and high rate of intermarriage between Indians and African Americans, and the migration of Indians to cities and other towns, made it impossible for him to render a complete census. Many chose to keep their ancestry and identity private.[58]

Indians and African Americans brought similar needs but different expectations and desires to marriages across their ethnic boundaries—boundaries that widened at the end of the colonial period. The two peoples shared a marginal position in New England society and complementary demographic imbalances. Many Indians, like Sarah Muckamugg of Hassanamisco, had no choice but to marry outsiders, the men they married, like Aaron of Providence or Fortune Burnee of Grafton, faced similar constraints. In many cases Indians and African Americans were each other's only potential spouses, offering the sole opportunity for companionship, support, and the perpetuation of their families and community. Some Indian women, like the Narragansett Alice Prophetess, would also benefit from the energy and abilities of their husbands.

Their relationships, unfortunately, would suffer from a host of problems, including, as with Sarah and Aaron, prolonged separations. Wives as well as husbands were often forced to find work far from home. Couples who remained in or moved to Native enclaves found that Indian traditions of female independence and authority and community management of property clashed with the patriarchal, market-oriented values adopted by African Americans. Indian groups were initially willing and able to accept the newcomers and to raise their children. But as more Indian women married black men, Indian men became resentful, and conflicts arose over rights to communal resources. While groups with valuable resources adopted new rules to manage immigrants, the boundaries of small enclaves such as Hassanamisco became more permeable.

The children of intermarriages were faced with difficult choices of identity and community, particularly when an African American community emerged in the region and embraced very different values. Initially most, such as Joseph Aaron and Sarah Burnee, seem to have embraced the ways of their mothers and the enclave in which they were raised. But as time went on, a growing number of "mixed" children in the smaller groups with weak boundaries, like the Gimbees of Hassanamisco, followed their fathers and found more opportunities in the outside world. At the same time, New England whites became less willing and able to distinguish Indians from African Americans. In these ways, intermarriage both literally and symbolically reshaped Native communities.

NOTES

Grey Osterud's editing, suggestions, and friendship have been extremely helpful. I also wish to thank the National Endowment for the Humanities, Massachusetts Historical Society, and Old Sturbridge Village for the fellowships that helped me research and write this essay.

1. Several witnesses who knew Aaron referred to him as "a servant" who "belonged to" John Whipple; depositions, box 1, folder 4, John Milton Earle Papers, American Antiquarian Society, Worcester, Mass. (hereafter Earle Papers). He may have been an indentured servant; some Africans in New England (particularly in the seventeenth century), like many English in colonial America, had limited terms of servitude. But as Lorenzo Greene pointed out in his landmark study, *The Negro in Colonial New England* (New York: Columbia University Press, 1942), "Negro 'slaves' were usually spoken of as servants in New England" (86 n. 62), and by the eighteenth century "unfree workers were chiefly Negro slaves" (75). See also Winthrop D. Jordan, *White over Black: American Attitudes toward the Negro, 1550–1812*

(Chapel Hill: University of North Carolina Press, 1968), 52–53, 66–71. I have therefore assumed that Aaron was enslaved rather than indentured; either way he was subject to the same legal and social disabilities. The precise year of Sarah and Aaron's wedding is unknown; William Page recalled only that the marriage occurred "about 23–24 years ago"; deposition, May 2, 1752, box 1, folder 4, Earle Papers. On Sarah's death, see Accounts of Hassanamisco Indian Trustees, 2:108, Earle Papers (hereafter Hassanamisco Accounts). I will refer to the Indian community as "Hassanamisco" throughout, although the village was called Hassanamissett (the Nipmuc word for "a place of small stones") by the colonists before 1700.

2. Two Peter Muckamuggs—"Senr" and "young"—appeared in Providence in 1708 and 1709; docs. nos. 16809, 16904, vol. 39a, Providence Town Papers, Rhode Island Historical Society, Providence. A Grafton historian, Frederick Pierce, wrote that Sarah Robbins was Peter Muckamugg's mother; Pierce, *History of Grafton* (Worcester: Chas. Hamilton, 1879), 28. But a number of documents in the Earle Papers make reference to Peter Muckamugg and his wife, Sarah Robbins.

3. On precontact Native cultures in southern New England, see Kathleen Bragdon, *Native People of Southern New England, 1500–1650* (Norman: University of Oklahoma Press, 1996). For developments between the arrival of the English and King Philip's War, see Alden Vaughan, *New England Frontier: Puritans and Indians 1620–1675*, 3d ed. (Norman: University of Oklahoma Press, 1995); and Francis Jennings, *The Invasion of America: Indians, Colonialism, and the Cant of Conquest* (Chapel Hill: University of North Carolina Press, 1975). On Indians in the region after King Philip's War, see Daniel Mandell, *Behind the Frontier: Indians in Eighteenth-Century Eastern Massachusetts* (Lincoln: University of Nebraska Press, 1996); and John Sainsbury, "Indian Labor in Early Rhode Island," *New England Quarterly* 48 (1975): 378–93.

4. Massachusetts colonial records, Massachusetts State Archives, Boston, 31:117–18, 120–21 (hereafter MCR); *The Acts and Resolves, Public and Private, of the Province of Massachusetts Bay, vol. 11, 1726–1733* (Boston: Wright and Potter, 1903), Resolves of 1727, chap. 88, June 28, 1727; Acts of 1727–28, chap. 36, Dec. 12, 1727, chap. 52, Dec. 19, 1727.

5. Page, deposition.

6. William D. Piersen, *Black Yankees: The Development of an Afro-American Subculture in Eighteenth-Century New England* (Amherst: University of Massachusetts Press, 1988), 14–16, 165; Robert J. Cottrol, *The Afro-Yankees: Providence's Black Community in the Antebellum Era* (Westport, Conn.: Greenwood, 1982), 5, 14–20, 29; James C. Garman, "Viewing the Color Line through the Material Culture of Death," *Historical Archaeology* 28 (1994): 77.

7. Piersen, *Black Yankees*, 165; John Barlett, Records of the *Colony of Rhode Island* (Providence, 1860), 5:270, 3:492–93; Acts and Resolves . . . of Massachusetts, vol. 13, 1741–1747 (Boston: Wright and Potter, 1905), Acts of 1744–45, chap. 176, Feb. 2, 1745; Greene, *Negro in Colonial New England*, 134–42; *Boston Selectmen's Minutes, 1736–1742* (Boston: Boston Record Commissioners, 1890), 241–42; *Boston Selectmen's Minutes, 1769–1775* (Boston: Boston Record Commissioners, 1892), 45; "An Act to Prevent Clandestine Marriages," section 5, *The Public Laws of the State of Rhode Island . . . January, 1798* (Providence, 1798); Act of June 22, 1786, in *Laws of the Commonwealth of Massachusetts, From November 28, 1780 . . . to February 28, 1807*, 3 vols. (Boston: Thomas and Andrews and Manning and Lorring, 1807), 1:324.

8. Colonel Joseph Whipple had twelve children; John, the first (1685–1769), was "a noted bone-setter." See Clair Newton, *Captain John Whipple, 1617–1685* (Naperville, Ill., 1946).

9. Colonial New Englanders of all classes and both genders met in taverns to socialize and transact business. Puritans had no problems with drinking in moderation; it was the disorder that followed excessive use of alcohol that was a sin. See David Conroy, *In Public Houses: Drink and the Revolution of Authority in Colonial Massachusetts* (Chapel Hill: University of North Carolina Press, 1995), 1–56. Provincial authorities were wary of taverns kept by Africans; see "An Act for breaking up disorderly Houses kept by free Negroes and Mulattoes," section 5, *Public Laws of the State of Rhode Island.*

10. Hezekiah Whipple and Ellen Crow, deposition, March 25, 1771; George Taylor, deposition, April 22, 1771; Richard Brown, deposition, July 4, 1771; Richard Brown, Jr., deposition, July 5, 1771; all box 1, folder 4, Earle Papers.

11. Hallelujah Olney, depositions, Oct. 19, 1768, and July 5, 1771, Earle Papers.

12. Ann Marie Plane, "Colonizing the Family: Marriage, Household, and Racial Boundaries in Southeastern New England to 1730" (Ph.D. dies., Brandeis University, 1994), 7, 134–92.

13. Quoted in Piersen, *Black Yankees*, 89.

14. Olney, depositions; Mary Wilkinson, deposition, July 24, 1771, Earle Papers. Wilkinson noted that Sarah "complained of [Aaron's] abuse to her I then asked if he was her Husband she answered he was none of her Husband Neither had she any thing to Do with him." While Sarah's outburst came after leaving Providence, her words indicate long-standing problems in their marriage.

15. Wilkinson, deposition; Israel Wilkinson, deposition, July 25, 1771, Earle Papers.

16. Mary Wilkinson, deposition. According to Richard Brown, Jr., after Aaron left Sarah he had children by Elisha Bowmans, "a Negro woman"; Richard Brown, Jr., deposition. While Sarah seemed to be saying that she and Aaron *had* lived together, other witnesses from Providence stressed that the two always lived apart. Either the other witnesses were wrong— perhaps John Whipple had allowed her to move in with Aaron—or she was saying that Aaron had denied her any hope of ever living together.

17. Richard Brown and Richard Brown, Jr., depositions.

18. Inland Native groups, such as the Nipmuc, had weaker hierarchies, were more dependent on female-dominated agriculture, and were likely matrilineal and matrilocal; see Bragdon, *Native People*, 52–53, 176–83.

19. J. H. Benton, *Early Census Making in Massachusetts, 1643–1765* (Boston: Goodspeed, 1905); *Vital Records of Grafton, Massachusetts, to the End of the Year 1849* (Worcester, Mass.: Franklin Rice, 1906), 255. Peter and Sarah Muckamugg both disappeared from the Hassanamisco account book after 1735; Hassanamisco Accounts.

20. Gideon Hawley to James Freeman, Nov. 2, 1802, Hawley Papers, Massachusetts Historical Society, Boston.

21. *Vital Records of Grafton.* These records show only that a daughter was born to "Forten Burnee and "Sarah (Indian)"; they do not specify Sarah Muckamugg. There is also no recorded marriage between Sarah and Fortune. But other records can be pieced together. A note in the Hassanamisco records names "Sarah Robbins" as the mother of Sarah Burnee (box 1, folder 1, Earle Papers). Fortune Burnee had only one daughter, named Sarah (Hassanamisco Accounts), and Sarah Burnee was Joseph Aaron's sister (box 1, folder 1, Earle Papers). These relationships are all possible only if Sarah Burnee's mother was Sarah Muckamugg, formerly Aaron Whipple's spouse. The records also indicate that Sarah Muckamugg was still, at times, using her mother's unmarried name.

22. MCR, 32:592–93.

23. Mandell, *Behind the Frontier*, 128–32; Benton, *Early Census Making*; "Number of Indians in Connecticut . . . January 1, 1774," *Massachusetts Historical Society Collections*

10 (1809): 117–18 (hereafter *MHSC*); "The Number of Indians in Rhode Island . . . Taken between the 4th of May and the 14th of June, 1774," *MHSC* 10 (1809): 119.

24. *Vital Records of Grafton*; Benjamin Heywood to Estes How, Jan. 16, 1812, box 1, folder 1, Earle Papers; Grafton, Mass., Town Records; Worcester County Probate Records no. 36457; Hassanamisco Accounts; unpassed Senate legislation, no. 1671, 1793, Massachusetts State Archives, Boston (hereafter MSA).

25. Mary Wilkinson, deposition.

26. William J. Brown, *The Life of William J. Brown* (Providence, R.I., 1883), 10–11.

27. Piersen, *Black Yankees*, 1–19, 59–61.

28. Edward Kendall, *Travels through the Northern Parts of the United States in the Years 1807 and 1808* (New York: I. Riley, 1809), 2:179; note on sale of Sarah Burnee's lands, May 5, 1752, in Hassanamisco Accounts, 2:66, Earle Papers; Benjamin Heywood on estate of Abigail Burnee, box 1, folder 1, Earle Papers; documents relating to Resolves of 1811, chap. 159, Feb. 28, 1812, MSA.

29. Brown, *Life of William J. Brown*, 10–11.

30. Mashpee petition to Massachusetts legislature, July 1788, in documents relating to Acts of 1788, chap. 38, Jan. 30, 1789, MSA.

31. Benjamin Allen, Christiantown guardian, to Massachusetts Legislature, in documents relating to unpassed Senate legislation, nos. 12207 (1846) and 13034 (1850), MSA.

32. John Milton Earle, "Report on Indians," Massachusetts *Senate Reports*, no. 96 (Boston, 1861), 32.

33. Mandell, *Behind the Frontier*, 192–93.

34. Heywood, statement of facts, Earle Papers. Indian property could not be transferred to non-Indian ownership without the General Court's permission, and after Fortune died in 1795 the Hassanamisco guardians refused to fulfill the will. But in 1811, after a lawsuit by the white man's heirs and a request by the town of Grafton for part of Burnee's estate to assist Indian paupers, the legislature ordered the funds to be divided between two claimants; documents relating to Resolves of 1811, chap. 159, MSA.

35. Franklin Dexter, ed., *Extracts from the Itineraries and Other Miscellanies of Ezra Stiles, 1755–1794* (New Haven: Yale University Press, 1916), 203, 262.

36. Earle, "Report on Indians," 101.

37. Ibid., 109.

38. Stephen Badger, "Historical and Characteristic Traits of the American Indians in General, and Those of Natick in Particular," *MHSC*, 1st ser., 5 (1798): 43.

39. Hawley to John Davis, Oct. 17, 1794, Savage Papers, 2:214, Massachusetts Historical Society.

40. Mandell, *Behind the Frontier*, 187–88; James O. Horton and Lois Horton, *Black Bostonians: Family Life and Community Struggle in the Antebellum North* (New York: Holmes and Meier, 1979); James Horton, "Freedom's Yoke: Gender Conventions among Free Blacks," in *Free People of Color: Inside the African American Community* (Washington, D.C.: Smithsonian Institution Press, 1993), 102–16.

41. Hassanamisco Accounts, 2:98.

42. Smithfield Justice of the Peace, April 20, 1771, box 1, folder 4, Earle Papers; this is either a marriage record from the town or a deposition taken on that date. For references to Burnee as a spinster, see box 1, folder 1, Earle Papers. Women called spinsters would not have been living in common-law marriages.

43. *Vital Records of Grafton*, 178; various documents in box 1, folder 1, Earle Papers; Sarah Phillips petition, documents relating to Resolves of 1821, chap. 14, June 13, 1821, MSA.

44. David Daniels et al. to the Hassanamisco guardians, May 28, 1771, box 1, folder 1, Earle Papers.

45. Olney, deposition, Oct. 19, 1768; Hassanamisco Accounts, 2:100; Daniels et al. to Hassanamisco guardians, box 1, folder 1, Earle Papers.

46. Deeds and related documents, May-June 1771, box 1, folder 1, Earle Papers; Daniels et al. to Hassanamisco guardians.

47. Sarah's objections are not recorded, although the depth of this conflict—the fact that it generated so many depositions—points to her feelings in the matter. Sarah must have realized that as a woman living in New England, she had little power to obtain the necessary evidence to nullify Joseph's claim. There are also no records of Joseph's reasons for dividing the farm. Box 1, folder 4, Earle Papers.

48. Harriette Merrifield Forbes, *The Hundredth Town: Glimpses of Life in Westborough, 1717–1817* (Boston, 1889), 170.

49. Legislative Committee on Indians, "Report on Mashpee Meeting," Massachusetts *House Report*, no. 502 (Boston, 1869).

50. Ann Marie Plane and Gregory Button, "The Massachusetts Indian Enfranchisement Act: Ethnic Contest in Historical Context, 1849–1869," *Ethnohistory* 40 (1993): 597.

51. Frederick Barth, introduction to *Ethnic Groups and Boundaries: The Social Organization of Cultural Difference* (Boston: Little, Brown, 1969), 10.

52. A strikingly similar pattern exists among the modern Lumbees of North Carolina; see Karen Blu, *The Lumbee Problem: The Making of an Indian People* (New York: Cambridge University Press, 1980).

53. James Horton and Lois Horton, "Violence, Protest, and Identity: Black Manhood in Antebellum America," in *Free People of Color*, 86; *Laws of the African Society, Instituted at Boston, Anno Domini, 1796* (Boston, 1802), 5–6.

54. Horton and Horton, *Black Bostonians*.

55. Cesear and Moses Gimbee, petition to the legislature, Jan. 19, 1801, in documents relating to Resolves of 1800, chap. 68, Jan. 17, 1801, MSA.

56. Badger, "Historical and Characteristic Traits," 43.

57. Legislative Committee on Indians in Massachusetts, "Report," March 1, 1827, *House Reports*, no. 68 (Boston, 1827); Commissioners Investigating the Condition of Indians in Massachusetts, "Report," Feb. 1849, *House Reports*, no. 46 (Boston, 1849); *Report of the Commissioner on the Narragansett Tribe of Indians, 1858* (Providence, R.I., 1858); *Report of the Commissioners on Distribution of Lands of the Mohegan Indians* (Hartford, Conn., 1861); John DeForest, *History of Indians of Connecticut from the Earliest Known Period to 1850* (Hartford, 1851), 443, 445, 488. For examples of "last Indian" stories, see Charles Brooks, *History of the Town of Medford* (Boston: James M. Usher, 1855), 80–81; Ledyard Bill, *The History of Paxton* (Worcester: Putnam, Davis, 1889), 45–46; Forbes, *Hundredth Town*, 170.

58. Earle, "Report on Indians," 7–8.

Chapter Five

Eroticizing the Middle Ground
Anglo-Indian Sexual Relations along the Eighteenth-Century Frontier

Richard Godbeer

John Lawson, English explorer and naturalist, traveled extensively through the Carolinas in 1700–1701, following a horseshoe-shaped course that took him deep into the backcountry. Several years later, after settling in North Carolina, Lawson published a vividly detailed journal of his experiences and observations during the expedition. A recurrent topic in his account was sexual contact between colonists and Indians. English traders who lived among the Indians, he observed, usually had "Indian wives," women who provided sexual companionship and domestic services for the duration of the traders' residence in the community. One trader pointed out to Lawson a "cabin" that belonged to his "father-in-law": "he called him so by reason the old man had given him a young Indian girl, that was his daughter, to lie with him, make bread, and to be necessary in what she was capable to assist him in, during his abode among them." Although traders generally envisaged that such relationships would last only until they moved on, some Englishmen who became "accustomed to the conversation of these savage women, and their way of living" were "so allured with that careless sort of life, as to be constant to their Indian wife," never returning to live "amongst the English." Alongside these relationships, temporary and lasting, casual sex between Englishmen and Indian women was also common, Lawson wrote. Some of these encounters he construed as involving sexual commerce: like many other eighteenth-century Europeans, Lawson characterized as prostitution exchanges that functioned for native Americans as a component of diplomatic, social, and economic reciprocity. Lawson lamented that promiscuous sex between Indians and Englishmen had led to the rampant circulation of venereal disease, another common theme in European writings about sexual contact with native Americans. Fortunately, he observed, Indians were well versed in a range of cures.[1]

Lawson's comments on Anglo-Indian sexual relations were not anomalous. Other eighteenth-century travelers in the southern backcountry noted the prevalence of both casual sex and domestic relationships between native Americans and Englishmen. This essay uses travel journals in conjunction with letters written by traders, colonial officials, and itinerant missionaries, as well as official records, to examine Anglo-Indian sexual relations along the southern frontier. The writers whose journals, letters, and reports provide the basis for what follows had their own preoccupations, biases, and ulterior motives in writing about Anglo-Indian relations. Their remarks about indigenous culture are most suspect, often revealing more of the authors' fantasies and fears than of the societies they purported to describe. Yet these accounts are remarkably consistent in asserting that Anglo-Indian sexual relations were common along the frontier, and their different perspectives on the subject are instructive when placed in counterpoint to one another. If read with great caution and in conjunction, they reveal not only the English male attitudes that they were designed to express, but also the cultural negotiations and compromises into which such men were drawn, often unwittingly; these accounts provide a valuable, albeit incomplete, body of information about the complex dynamics involved in erotic and romantic concourse across the racial divide.

What follows does not challenge the conventional wisdom that early colonists, and later those who lived within the established parameters of colonial society, were generally unwilling to countenance intermarriage with native Americans. It contends, however, that sex had an important role to play in Anglo-Indian relations along and beyond the edges of colonial settlement. As travelers, traders, soldiers, and diplomats dealt with native Americans on what one historian has called "the middle ground,"[2] their interactions, accommodations, cultural misunderstandings, and conflicts were as much sexual as they were economic, diplomatic, and military. That sexual middle ground bore witness to the many possibilities of intercultural contact: it embodied not only the violence of colonial appropriation but also the mutual and successful accommodation of different peoples.

Despite a shortage of women in the early English settlements, especially in the Chesapeake, male colonists were reluctant to take Indian women as wives. The settlers' aversion to Anglo-Indian marriage was based on a range of concerns, some ideological and others pragmatic. Most fundamental were biblical injunctions against marriage to non-Christians and English disdain for the Indians' "barbaric" way of life. Forced to rely on Indian food supplies and advice as they struggled to survive in a new environment, the colonists sought to shore up their battered sense of superiority by maintaining a self-conscious boundary between the "savage" natives and their "civilized" selves; Anglo-Indian marriage threatened that strategy both physically and symbolically. On a more practical level, colonists harbored suspicions that the Indians might use intermarriage as a way to infiltrate colonial settlements. They were also concerned that Anglo-Indian unions might give rise to native male jealousy. Those settlers who valued premarital chastity were shocked by the Indians' apparently permissive attitude toward sexual experimentation before marriage, while even those without such scruples worried about the alleged prevalence of syphillis among the Indians. Marriage to native women, then, endangered the colonists' sense of cultural supremacy as well as their mores, safety, and health.[3]

Perhaps the most eloquent expression of colonial discomfort with the idea of Anglo-Indian union was contained, ironically, within a marriage proposal. When John Rolfe petitioned to marry Pocahontas in 1614, he dwelt at length on possible

objections to their marriage and his own ambivalence toward the union.[4] Aware
that his "settled and long continued affection" for Pocahontas might be mistaken
for sexual desperation, Rolfe insisted that he could, if he wanted, find English
women to satisfy his "carnall" needs (albeit at the price of "a seared conscience")
and that he did not lack marital prospects back in England. He was driven by love,
"not any hungry appetite, to gorge myself with incontinency." But Rolfe's petition
expressed profound anxiety about cultural and spiritual contamination through
union with a "strange" and "barbarous" woman. In a "private controversy," Rolfe
had sought to justify his "affection" to himself as well as to others. He had recalled
"the heavie displeasure which almightie God conceived against the sonnes of Levie
and Israel for marrying strange wives," and had weighed the "inconveniences" of
uniting "in love with one whose education hath bin rude, her manners barbarous,
her generation accursed," and "discrepant in all nurtriture" from himself. Scriptural
injunctions, a fear of the "barbarous," and anxieties about sexual degeneration
combined with his suspicion that Satan himself had "hatched" his love for Pocahontas to form a lurid nightmare of self-destruction. Rolfe had finally convinced himself
that dedicating his marriage to the spiritual redemption of Pocahontas would enable
a triumph over "transitory pleasures and worldly vanities," a sanctification of the
flesh. Their union would justify itself not only as a political alliance, "for the good
of this plantation, for the honour of our country," but also and, indeed, primarily
as an evangelical enterprise, "for the converting to the true knowledge of God and
Jesus Christ an unbelieving creature, namely Pocahontas."

Rolfe's "private controversy" may have been partly, or even wholly, concocted
as a way to assure critics that he understood and even shared their objections to his
marriage proposal; but even if a tactical ploy, it remains helpful in conveying the
kind of nightmarish image that Rolfe believed intermarriage would provoke in his
fellow colonists. His more positive view of intermarriage as a happy and high-
minded conjunction of spiritual duty and romantic fulfilment was not widely shared
by his contemporaries. During the first decade of settlement in the Chesapeake,
English males had been drawn away to Indian communities by sheer hunger and an
equally desperate appetite for female companionship, but the union between Rolfe
and Pocahontas in 1614 did not lead to a spate of Anglo-Indian marriages. Not
only did English prejudice against such unions remain firmly in place, but Indian
women had little reason to choose as husbands men who were generally much less
adept at hunting, fishing, and other pertinent skills than prospective mates in their
own communities.[5] The greater availability of English women by the end of the
seventeenth century removed any practical justification for intermarriage, while the
growing population of slaves provided an outlet for planters' extramarital sexual
appetites. Throughout the colonial period, Anglo-Americans living in eastern settlements occasionally formed sexual and domestic relationships with Indians, but most
of those who did so seem to have been marginal figures.[6] Any English man or
woman who became sexually intimate with an Indian was liable to stigmatization
as "debased" or "defiled." For many members of colonial society, Anglo-Indian
sexual relations or marriages remained fundamentally problematic in their cultural
implications.[7]

There were individuals who saw the colonists' repudiation of intermarriage as a lost opportunity. Writing in the early eighteenth century, the Virginia planter William Byrd lamented the settlers' "squeamish" and "unreasonable" opposition to Anglo-Indian marriage, caused according to him by their "aversion to the copper complexion of the natives." Intermarriage, as John Rolfe had clearly understood, could be used as a tool of conversion: "a sprightly lover," Byrd wrote, "is the most prevailing missionary that can be sent amongst these or any other infidels." Furthermore, Anglo-Indian marriage could have prevented bloodshed by allowing the colonists to expand onto land deeded to them through dowry agreements: "the poor Indians would have had less reason to complain that the English took away their land if they had received it by way of a portion with their daughters." And finally, Byrd wrote, the predominantly male colonial population in the seventeenth-century Chesapeake would have grown much more rapidly had the men been willing to marry Indians. Native women, he wrote, would have proven "altogether as honest wives for the first planters" as the English "damsels" who crossed the Atlantic, many of whom were reputed to have shady pasts.

Byrd pointed out that the issue of color would have faded as the progeny of interracial marriages became paler with each passing generation: "if a Moor may be washed white in three generations, surely an Indian might have been blanched in two." By the early eighteenth century, there would have been no "reproach" attached to such a union because the physical signs of intermarriage would have disappeared. Besides, Byrd argued, the early colonists should have ignored superficial distinctions, focusing instead on underlying similarities and the Indians' potential for "improvement." Like James Harriot and John White, Byrd portrayed Indians as underdeveloped rather than intrinsically primitive: "All nations of men have the same natural dignity, and we all know that very bright talents may be lodged under a very dark skin. The principal difference between one people and another proceeds only from the different opportunities of improvement." Byrd's self-conscious magnanimity in no way compromised his sense of cultural superiority: like their land, the native inhabitants' "complexion" and "talents" could be "improved" by becoming anglicized.[8]

Robert Beverley, writing at the end of the seventeenth century, and Lawson both emphasized the practical advantages of intermarriage. Had such a strategy been pursued, Beverley argued, "the abundance of blood that was shed on both sides would have been saved" and "the colony, instead of all these losses of men on both sides, would have been increasing in children to its advantage."[9] Lawson advocated that "ordinary people, and those of a similar rank" be given financial incentives to marry Indians and bring them into English settlements. As a result, "the whole body of these people would arrive to the knowledge of our religion and customs, and become as one people with us." Intermarriage, Lawson argued, would prove a much more effective means to conversion "than to set up our Christian Banner in a field of blood." Anglo-Indian marriage would, moreover, give the English "a better understanding of the Indian tongue" and readier access to "all the Indians' skill in medicine and surgery," along with their knowledge of the regional topography.[10]

Yet such critiques are potentially misleading. Byrd's straightforward claim that

Virginia colonists were physically repelled by the Indians' "copper complexion" belied the more complex attitude toward Indians as aesthetic and sexual objects that emerges from early American writings, including Byrd's own. English culture did invest light-colored skin with connotations of virtue, cleanliness, and civilized beauty; migrants to North America proved themselves true Englishmen by expressing disdain for Indian (and, of course, African) complexions.[11] But cultural imperatives did not prevent English colonists from finding Indians with whom they interacted attractive and desirable: experience often conflicted with preconceptions. Furthermore, although Byrd and Lawson were doubtless correct in asserting that Anglo-Indian marriage was exceptional in colonial society, both men observed stable relationships, more temporary liaisons, and casual sexual contact between Englishmen and Indians along and beyond the frontier of colonial settlement. Indeed, it was their observation of Anglo-Indian unions in the backcountry that led them to advocate the practice further east.[12]

Explorers and early colonists had often commented on native beauty and provided those who followed with a tantalizing portrait of Indian sexual culture as uninhibited and permissive.[13] Eighteenth-century settlers and Europeans traveling in North America also commented on the beauty of Indian women, although usually framing their remarks with defensive caveats about the natives' dark color or lack of hygiene. Such remarks came overwhelmingly from genteel travelers and reflected a preoccupation with cleanliness and fashionable, leisured pallor (dark skin indicating the need to labor outside) that colonists outside the elite would most likely not have shared. Diron D'Artaguiette, a French official in Louisiana, wrote in the 1720s that the Natchez women's habit of blackening their teeth, "together with their tawney color," made them "rather disagreeable to those who are not prejudiced in their favor"; nevertheless, he conceded, they had "rather regular features" and were "fairly passable." Robert Hunter, a young merchant who traveled in North America during 1785–86 to collect debts owed to his father's firm in London, described Indian women as "handsome . . . notwithstanding their color." According to Luigi Castiglioni, a Milanese botanist traveling through the United States in 1785–87, Indian women were "very dirty and ill-smelling," but some "combine[d] a pretty figure with a vivacious face." Lawson declared much less grudgingly that Indian women were "as fine-shaped creatures (take them generally) as any in the universe . . . not so uncouth or unlikely, as we suppose them."[14]

Descriptions of Indian women were often at least implicitly pornographic, incorporating fantasies about scantily clad, innocent yet alluring, and apparently available women into narratives of sexual aggression. Byrd, writing about his travels through the backcountry as leader of a boundary commission, commented that native women had "an air of innocence and bashfulness that with a little less dirt would not fail to make them desireable." He then related, in an oblique yet prurient passage, the expedition chaplain's consternation on observing "that the ruffles of some of our fellow travelers were a little discoloured with puccoon [red dye], wherewith the good man had been told those ladies used to improve their invisible charms."[15]

William Bartram, a Philadelphia naturalist who traveled through the Carolinas,

Georgia, and Florida in 1773–77, provided a particularly redolent description of native beauty in a passage that used idyllic motifs to frame, and partly camouflage, an account of thwarted sexual assault. Bartram conjured for his readers an enticing image of "primitive innocence," discovered in "a vast expanse of green meadows and strawberry fields" by Bartram and his companions as they traveled through the South Carolina backcountry:

> companies of young, innocent Cherokee virgins, some busily gathering the rich fragrant fruit, others having already filled their baskets, lay reclined under the shade of floriferous and fragrant native bowers of Magnolia, Azalea, Philadelphus, perfumed Calycanthus, sweet Yellow Jessamine and cerulian Glycine frutescens, disclosing their beauties to the fluttering breeze, and bathing their limbs in the cool fleeting streams; while other parties, more gay and libertine, were yet collecting strawberries or wantonly chasing their companions, tantalising them, staining their lips and cheeks with the rich fruit.

The strangers' arrival threatened to transform this charming and sensual scene into one of sexual violence. The prospect of "sylvan nymphs," Bartram wrote, was "perhaps too enticing for hearty young men to continue idle speculators," and so they crept down toward the young women, determined "to have a more active part in their delicious sports." Bartram admitted that their interest in the "Cherokee virgins" was at least potentially sexual and predatory:

> although we meant no other than an innocent frolic with this gay assembly of hamadryades, we shall leave it to the person of feeling and sensibility to form an idea to what lengths our passions might have hurried us, thus warmed and excited, had it not been for the vigilance and care of some envious matrons who lay in ambush, and espying us gave the alarm, time enough for the nymphs to rally and assemble together.

The defensive maneuvers executed by the "matrons" and perhaps also a sudden realization that Indian men might be close at hand jolted the travelers into a more circumspect and gentlemanly comportment. Once Bartram and his companions convinced the "matrons" that they were willing to restrain themselves, tension dissipated and the strangers were invited to join them in eating some fruit, "encircled by the whole assembly of the innocently jocose sylvan nymphs." Bartram's account allowed readers to delight in visions of Edenic innocence while participating vicariously in the travelers' voyeurism as well as their barely contained lust for the native women. In doing so, he invited them to appropriate his own experiences and fantasies into a pornographic gaze upon the New World.[16]

Other eighteenth-century authors admitted that those who came into contact with native inhabitants were eager to sample "their favors," although they usually emphasized the Indian women's eagerness to oblige, given their allegedly permissive sexual mores.[17] Early observers of the Indians had sometimes reminded their readers that the indigenous peoples' apparently relaxed attitude toward sex should be understood as "rather a horrible licentiousness than a liberty," but travelers throughout the colonial period not infrequently welcomed the opportunity to enjoy a little sexual "liberty," or even "licentiousness."[18] In October 1711, for example, when Byrd took part in militia exercises just outside the Indian settlement at Nottoway

Town, he noted in his diary that he and other militiamen entertained themselves by cavorting with native women. One morning, they "rose about 6 o'clock and then took a walk about the town to see some Indian girls, with which [they] played the wag." In the evening of the following day, he wrote, "some of my troop went with me into the town to see the girls and kissed them without proceeding any further." The following night, "Jenny, an Indian girl, had got drunk and made us good sport." (It is not clear from Byrd's laconic entry how far the "sport" went and to what extent Jenny was a willing participant.)[19]

Two decades later, after leading an expedition to investigate the boundary between Virginia and North Carolina in 1728, Byrd recalled the sexual escapades between members of the commission and Indians they met in the backcountry. When the commissioners stayed overnight as the guests of an Indian tribe, he commented with more than a hint of pique that their hosts "offered us no bedfellows, according to the good Indian fashion, which we had reason to take unkindly." Some members of the expedition had no intention of allowing this lapse in "hospitality" to keep them away from the native women: William Dandridge and several other "gentlemen" went "hunting after" the "sad-coloured ladies" through the night; their dye-stained linen gave them away. Byrd sought to explain away Dandridge's behavior by suggesting that "curiosity made him try the difference between them and other women." He was less concerned that their subordinates had been frolicking with the native women, since these men were, after all, "not quite so nice [i.e., particular]." The next day, Byrd and Dandridge visited "most of the princesses at their own apartments," intending to admire their beauty at close quarters, "but the smoke was so great there, the fire being made in the middle of the cabins, that we were not able to see their charms." As with Bartram's description of his encounter with the "sylvan nymphs," Byrd's account combined voyeurism with the tantalizing possibility of sexual possession, providing salacious material for the reader's and his own imagination.[20]

Although, as we will see, sexual interest in native women sometimes took the form of violent assault, it would be wrong to assume that English advances were always unwelcome or that the advances always came from the English. Eighteenth-century observers noted with prurient fascination that young women in many Indian tribes were free to experiment sexually prior to marriage and eager to do so with white as well as native men. Some narratives made sweeping generalizations on this as on many aspects of Indian mores. "The 'Flos Virginis,' " wrote Lawson, "so much coveted by the Europeans, is never valued by these savages."[21] But other writers recognized that not all Indian nations had the same attitude and noted carefully for the benefit of prospective travelers which ones seemed to be sexually permissive. D'Artaguiette informed readers that young Illinois women were "the mistresses of their own bodies (to use their own expression)" and welcomed the attentions of European visitors, whereas Arkansas women were not available (their menfolk had convinced them, "if one cares to believe the interpreters," that they would die if they had sex with Europeans).[22] Thomas Nairne, a soldier and diplomat in South Carolina during the early eighteenth century, noted that Chickasaw mores forbade the sexual license allowed youngsters elsewhere: "[y]ou shall not see them ogle and splite glances as the other savages['] ladies usually do." Under the guise of praising such nations for preventing "scandalous liberties," such passages warned which Indian women the travelers could not approach without risking native anger and retribution.[23]

Europeans and colonists found that native women generally expected some kind of gift in exchange for a sexual encounter. Byrd wrote that Indian women were "a little mercenary in their amours and seldom bestow[ed] their favors out of stark love and kindness." When four Saponi women offered themselves to Byrd and his companions, "the price they set upon their charms" was "a pair of red stockings."[24] Travelers and writers assumed that such women were prostituting themselves, an interpretation that conveniently conflated native women with, and reduced them to, vendible goods, but Indians themselves would have perceived such encounters very differently. The notion of exchange lay at the very heart of native American culture, providing a fundamental structure with accompanying rituals of civility for any interaction, including courtship. Young women who asked for goods in exchange for sexual intimacy were insisting upon a social etiquette that Europeans frequently misinterpreted, blind as they were to the underlying cultural logic.

In some cases, native women may have used their bodies to procure goods of value to their kin network, cannily exploiting travelers' hunger for female companionship. Such goods as women were likely to demand in return for use of their bodies were also precious as commodities of exchange for food and other essentials. A "pretty young girl" whom one of Lawson's companions had procured for the night persuaded her prospective bedfellow to show her "all the treasure he was possessed of, as beads, red cadis [cheap serge], etc., which she liked very well, and permitted him to put them into his pocket again." Before morning, she disappeared with the entire contents of his pocket, and also his shoes. The travelers had intended to use some of these "treasures" to pay for their "victuals."[25]

Among the native peoples encountered by Lawson in the Carolinas, sexual commerce was highly organized, or so he perceived. Certain young women were "set apart" to be "trading girls." They had "a particular tonsure" by which they were distinguished from those women available for marriage. Most of their income went to "the king's purse." Lawson characterized the "king" as "the chief bawd, exercising his prerogative over all the stews of his nation, and his own cabin (very often) being the chiefest brothel-house." The "trading girls" apparently "led that course of life for several years," using abortive medicine to end any incidental conceptions; their marital prospects were not, so far as Lawson could discern, damaged by their "having been common to so many."[26]

From the Indians' perspective, "trading girls" may well have functioned not only as a commercial proposition but also as a component of diplomatic ritual. Since diplomacy and commerce were bound together in Indian exchange culture, it would not be surprising if sex as diplomatic courtesy and sex as trade were sometimes conflated. Lawson noted that when another of his companions refused a trading girl offered to him by a sachem, "his majesty flew into a violent passion, to be thus slighted, telling the Englishmen, they were good for nothing."[27] The sachem may well have been frustrated by his failure to extract goods from the traveler in return for the woman's services, but he may also have been enraged by the white man's lack of manners in rejecting a gesture of welcome. Byrd's reference to "the compliment of bedfellows" as customary Indian "hospitality" certainly points in that direction.[28]

English forts offered ample opportunities for Indians to deploy female bodies as a medium of exchange. Some women functioned as temporary companions to officers with the means to support them. Visiting Fort Niagara in 1785, Robert Hunter observed an "abundance of squaws" who were "mostly kept by the gentlemen who reside there." These "kept" women were "dressed remarkably well" and "living in the height of luxury." Nonetheless, Hunter noted disapprovingly, they would "immediately leave their keeper" if "any little quarrel" occurred and take up with someone else. Even while being "kept" they would, "before their keeper's face, go with anybody else who will offer them some rum, which they are extravagantly fond of." The women were willing to partner irrespective of English racial distinctions: "[e]verybody is alike indifferent to them, black, white, or Indian." The picture that emerges from Hunter's account is of a fluid and multiracial sexual marketplace in which native women provided services, apparently on their own terms, to the troops in residence, either in the form of brief encounters or as part of a temporary domestic relationship. Whether the initial decision to engage sexually with the fort's inhabitants had been made by the women themselves or by relatives is unclear (this presumably varied from nation to nation), but Hunter's description of the women's behavior at the fort suggests that they considered themselves free of English control and indeed empowered by demand for their services. The goods that they procured as a result of these sojourns would presumably make their way back to kin networks. Such women, then, acted as conduits for the acquisition of wealth and status.[29]

Sexual exchange could sometimes take a more inadvertent form. Travel narratives warned that venereal disease, "that hateful distemper," was "frequent in some of these nations."[30] As D'Artaguiette put it, "the malign influences of Venus are so common that those who are wisest restrain themselves and go bridle in hand." Images of alluring nymphs frolicking in Edenic landscapes were juxtaposed in European minds with fears of physical (as well as cultural) contamination. Fortunately, the Indians knew "how to cure all sorts of venereal diseases" and had "healed numerous Europeans."[31] Historians have long recognized that Indians passed on crucial agricultural expertise to colonists as they adapted to life in North America. For those who became sexually intimate with Indians while traveling or living in the backcountry, native ability to treat venereal disease was equally indispensable for their survival.[32]

Lawson blamed the prevalence of venereal disease among the Indians on "the English traders that use amongst them."[33] Traders, who spent most of their time traveling beyond the frontier and who often lived in native communities for prolonged periods, had by far the most sustained and intimate contact with Indians. Those among them who succeeded in establishing a cordial, trusting rapport with their hosts became valuable diplomatic as well as economic intermediaries between native and colonial societies. It was not unusual for traders to enter relationships with Indian women, which not only satisfied personal needs but also eased their acceptance into the local community. However, while some traders settled into at least temporarily stable relationships, others were notoriously promiscuous—thus Lawson's attribution of responsibility for the spread of venereal disease in many Indian communities. The traders who attracted most attention from colonial officials were those who treated the Indians with least respect. Their abusive and violent behavior, which often manifested itself in sexual form, could poison Indian attitudes not only toward the individual concerned but also toward Englishmen in general, undermining decades of patient diplomacy. Although it is clear that many traders dealt peaceably and respectfully with the native peoples among whom they lived, the outrages perpetrated by their colleagues often overshadowed the more constructive results of trading activity in both Indian and colonial minds.

Maverick and abusive sexual behavior toward neighboring Indians disturbed colonial officials and clerics for moral and practical reasons. Anglican missionaries touring the backcountry claimed that many of the traders were "utter strangers to the virtues of temperance and chastity."[34] Appalled by the traders' "notoriously lewd and immoral practices," they feared that the Indians would be discouraged from converting by the image of English Christianity that the traders presented.[35] Such concerns were not without foundation: in 1725 a Cherokee "priest" in conversation with the trader and interpreter Alexander Long expressed (presumably ironic) amazement that men with "such good priests and such knowledge as they have" could be so "debauched" and "wicked."[36] Those involved in colonial government lamented "the evil impressions which those savages are liable to receive from the rudest of mortals," and worried about the disruption of peaceful relations by the abusive and insulting behavior of the traders, some of whom were "more savage than them."[37] In letters of instruction that captured effectively the blend of ethical and pragmatic concerns that motivated colonial officials, the commissioners for Indian trade in South Carolina enjoined agents "to regulate the lives of the traders, so that they give not the Indians offence and scandal, against the Christian religion, and to bring them within the bounds of morality at least."[38]

The negative impact of the traders' "immoral practices" on diplomatic relations caused colonial officials grave concern. Informants in the backcountry kept members of the governing elite appraised of traders' sexual depredations. David Crawley, himself involved in trade along the frontier, devoted part of a 1715 letter to a forceful denunciation of South Carolina traders and, specifically, their behavior toward the Indians with whom they were staying: "when they had sent the [Indian] men away about their business or they were gone ahunting [I] have heard them brag to each other of debauching their [the Indians'] wives sumtime forc[ing] them and once s[aw] it myself in the day time."[39] William Byrd, to whom Crawley's letter was addressed, claimed that the misconduct of Carolina traders toward the Indians, "abusing their women and evil entreating their men," was "the true reason of the fatal war which the nations round about made upon Carolina in the year 1713."[40]

Rival colonial powers were eager to exploit the unsavory reputation that some traders earned as representatives of the English presence. In the late 1750s English officials in South Carolina learned that the French were trying to undermine their relations with the Cherokee by playing on fears that the English would, if given the chance, "debauch their women." The French, whose own behavior toward the Indians in neighboring Louisiana was hardly a model of sexual propriety, told the Chickasaws that English officers took Indian women into forts "before their husbands' faces" to be "used by the soldiers." Although English agents sought to persuade the Chickasaws that "it is all French lies," they were evidently none too sure of that: "I hope this is not true," one of them wrote.[41]

The Indians themselves were not reticent in expressing outrage when traders preyed on their women. In 1752 leaders of the Lower Creek nation met with the governor's agent and "complained very heavily of the white people in general for debauching their wives and mentioned several in particular that were found guilty, and said if his Excellency would not punish them for it, the injured persons would certainly put their own laws in execution."[42] At a 1765 meeting with representatives of the new English government in Louisiana, Choctaw chiefs protested "the behaviour of the traders towards our women," claiming that "often when the traders sent for a basket of bread and the generous Indian sent his own wife to supply their wants, instead of taking the bread out of the basket they put their hands upon the breast of their wives." The chiefs warned that such "indecent freedom" threatened to produce "very great disturbances."[43]

Additional tension was created by the presence of "idle vagrants" who, either unable or unwilling to support themselves in the backcountry, made their way out to native communities and then sought to coax their way into the Indians' favor and their women's beds. These "vagrants," wrote an agent for the South Carolina government in 1757, "frequently raise bad blood between the white people and Indians by telling them lies, and romancing stories to ingratiate themselves among the Indians to procure a livelihood and get an Indian wife which is all their desire, and frequently they take the better of them and defraud them, to the no small prejudice of our interest."[44] A few years earlier, traders with the Cherokee had met the governor of South Carolina and complained about "sole dissolute people, white men, who under the notion of traders, live a debauched and wicked life."[45] The Lower Creek nation demanded that "all the strolling white people that are not employed in the Indian trade may be ordered out of their nation" since "several" of them were notorious for "decoying" Indian wives from their husbands, "etc.," when out hunting with them.[46]

Yet while government officials focused their attention on the political damage wrought by "debauched" traders and other "dissolute people" who moved beyond the frontier, eighteenth-century travelers often encountered traders whose dealings with native peoples were peaceful and constructive. Those who lived in Indian communities for extended periods often established domestic relationships with native women for the duration of their stay. This kind of arrangement was compatible with the Indian view that marriage did not necessarily constitute a permanent bond.[47] In addition to functioning as "she-bed-fellow[s]," "dressing their victuals," and performing other domestic chores, native wives could help traders develop a closer "friendship with the savages," learn the local language more quickly, and become acquainted with "the affairs and customs of the country."[48] They could prove invaluable as intermediaries, sources of information about Indian movements, and fronts for illegal trade.[49]

Traders who became involved with Indian women were given privileges otherwise unavailable to outsiders. Bartram, for example, mentioned a man who, "being married to a Cherokee woman of family, was indulged to keep a stock of cattle." Indian women, Bartram wrote, were usually loyal and energetic in promoting the interests of "their temporary husbands": "they labour and watch constantly to promote their private interests, and detect and prevent any plots or evil designs which may threaten their persons, or operate against their trade or business." Should conflict arise between a trader and members of the community in which he was living, the kin associations he had acquired through his marriage could offer some measure of protection.[50] But traders did not take Indian wives simply because white women were unavailable and doing so benefited them commercially. Their attitude toward such relationships was clearly pragmatic but not necessarily cynical: as Bartram put it, although "fully sensible" of the advantages offered by such "affections and friendship in matters of trade and commerce," in many cases "their love and esteem" for each other were quite "sincere." As we will see, some Anglo-Indian unions developed into lasting and devoted marriages, causing Englishmen to settle permanently in native communities.[51]

From the perspective of Indian wives and their kinfolk, marriage to an English trader, whether temporary or lasting, had much to offer as they drew the Englishman, along with his goods, into the kinship orbit. Eighteenth-century observers paid little attention to the practical advantages that native women derived from such relationships, claiming that they were "prone to European attachments" because their own menfolk were "not so vigorous or impatient in their love as we are."[52] Like John Rolfe in his discussion of Pocahontas, later writers tended to gloss the complex political and economic considerations that underlay Indian attitudes toward intermarriage as a straightforward "love" for the English. Yet we may surmise that Indian women were drawn to traders as much by the attendant benefits as by English sexual enthusiasm. Such relationships conferred considerable status, given the important economic and diplomatic roles played by trader-husbands, and enabled women to gain access to valuable goods that they then passed on to their kin. This did not always sit well with other Indians interested in acquiring goods. In 1753 representatives of the Lower Creek nation complained that traders had inflated their prices in order to compensate for the expense of "giv[ing] away such quantities to their wives."[53]

As contemporary acounts occasionally recognized, "temporary husbands" could serve to further the interests of canny, sometimes ruthlessly ambitious women. Bartram related the trials of a susceptible trader from North Carolina living among the Seminoles who had apparently become the dupe of a "beautiful savage":

> Her features are beautiful, and manners engaging. Innocence, modesty, and love, appear to a stranger in every action and movement; and these powerful graces she has so artfully played upon her beguiled and vanquished lover, and unhappy slave, as to have already drained him of all his possessions, which she dishonestly distributes amongst her savage relations.

The trader was "now poor, emaciated, and half-distracted, often threatening to shoot her, and afterwards put an end to his own life." Yet he had "not resolution even to leave her," but instead "endeavour[ed] to drown and forget his sorrows, in deep draughts of brandy." The Seminole woman had used her "powerful graces" to invert the European male vision of domination that pervades Bartram's text. Bartram himself was careful to emphasize, ostensibly in deference to "the virtue and moral conduct of the Siminoles [*sic*], and American Aborigines in general," that her conduct was "condemned and detested by her own people, of both sexes."[54]

Just as traders who entered relationships with Indian women might find sexual dominion more elusive than they had anticipated, so individuals who violated Indian mores by, for example, bedding an Indian's wife, discovered that their lusts were subject to the conditions and boundaries laid down by the community in which they lived. The frontier and beyond did not, after all, constitute a sexual playing field without rules or restrictions; traders with maverick libidos found themselves in a highly vulnerable and dangerous position. Bartram was acquainted with a trader, referred to as Mr. T____y, who had married a chief's daughter in the Creek town of Muklasa, where he was living. He was subsequently "detected in an amorous intrigue" with the wife of another chief, who "with his friends and kindred resolved to exact legal satisfaction." The punishment for adultery in this nation was "cropping," the removal of both ears. The trader was seized, stripped, and beaten, but managed to escape before the cropping could take place. After hiding in a swamp, he "finally made a safe retreat to the house of his father-in-law," who "gave his word that he would do him all the favour that lay in his power." A "council of the chiefs of the town" decided "that he must loose his ears, or forfeit all his goods, which amounted to upwards of one thousand pounds sterling." The cuckolded chief still wanted his life. Bartram promised the trader that he would ask George Galphin, an influential and wealthy trader based at Silver Bluff, South Carolina, to intercede on his behalf. When he did so, Galphin remarked that the trader was "in a disagreeable predicament, and that he feared the worst, but said he would do all in his power to save him." (Unfortunately, Bartram's account ends with this ultimatum, probably because he did not know how the situation resolved itself.)[55]

The case of Mr. T____y served as a reminder to Europeans that those who passed through or lived in native communities did not enjoy sexual impunity. He who assumed otherwise did so at his peril. But most traders were committed to establishing and maintaining a peaceful coexistence with the native peoples among whom they lived, and behaved accordingly. They understood that obtaining sexual access to Indian women, whether through a relationship or as a casual encounter, was usually quite straightforward if they were willing to abide by native prohibitions and codes of reciprocity and courtesy.[56]

Although partnerships between traders and Indian women were often intended to last only for the duration of the Englishman's residence, some developed into lasting marriages. As Lawson acknowledged, it was not unusual for traders to settle permanently in native communities, drawn by their personal attachments to native women, as well as by the Indians' way of life:

we often find that Englishmen, and other Europeans that have been accustomed to the conversation of these savage women, and their way of living, have been so allured with that careless sort of life, as to be constant to their Indian wife, and her relations, as long as they lived, without ever desiring to return again amongst the English, although they had very fair opportunities of advantages amongst their countrymen; of which sort I have known several.[57]

Other colonists whose business took them westward sometimes found personal happiness and material opportunities among native peoples. At Pittsburgh the actor-manager John Bernard met a land surveyor named Wools, whose surveying "had led him among the Indians near the Mississippi, where he had married a king's daughter" and received "a tract of land which he soon contrived to convert into a handsome independence." Wools had married his wife in an Indian ceremony.[58] Englishmen who settled with Indian partners in Indian territory on Indian terms struck observers as bizarre and unsettling curiosities. Like Indian captives who refused to return to colonial society[59] and settlers in the backcountry who dressed and behaved "as Indians,"[60] they brought into question the resilience and superiority of English culture.[61]

The issue of cultural allegiance became most pressing when Englishmen had children with Indian women. Regardless of whether the context was a casual sexual liaison, a temporary relationship, or a lasting marriage, decisions had to be made about the children's upbringing. Lawson considered it a "great misfortune" that such children went to the mother by "rule and custom amongst all the savages of America," and so were raised "in a state of infidelity."[62] But this was clearly an unwarranted generalization. Nathaniel Osborne, an Anglican missionary, mentioned in a 1715 report that he had recently baptized five "mulatto children," the offspring of "our Indian traders, by Indian women during their abode amongst them."[63] Alexander Cameron, a British agent among the Cherokee from 1764 to 1781, married an Indian woman who resided with him at his plantation, Lochaber, and bore him three children, all of whom were later sent to England.[64] On a recruiting expedition in 1775, Bernard Elliott stayed as a houseguest with the trader George Galphin, whose daughters by an Indian woman were "politely enough educated with music, etc."[65] But most traders lacked the resources of Cameron or Galphin and were themselves no longer fully committed to an English way of life. Their children often built lives that straddled the physical and cultural frontier: by the middle of the eighteenth century, many of the traders were themselves offspring of Anglo-Indian relationships.[66]

The ritual through which a mixed couple formalized their marriage had far-reaching implications for cultural power in the relationship and could be fraught with anxieties for those involved. The trader James Adair mentioned an Englishman who married an Indian, Dark-Lanthorn, "according to the manner of the Cherokee," but then took her to an English settlement in order to remarry in an English ceremony, which involved having Dark-Lanthorn baptized. According to a Frenchman who traveled through North America in 1795–97, marrying according to Indian custom appealed to some European men because they could treat the ceremony as binding them no longer than they themselves chose.[67] But in this case the Englishman worried about the apparent transience of native marriages and the implications of the matriarchal system within which they were contracted:

> observing that marriages were commonly of a short duration in that wanton female government, he flattered himself of ingrossing her affections, could he be so happy as to get her sanctified by one of our own beloved men with a large quantity of holy water in baptism—and be taught the conjugal duty, by virtue of her new Christian name, when they were married anew.

The personal negotiations and educative process involved in preparing for a marriage of this sort must have been challenging, regardless of which culture predominated. Dark-Lanthorn became increasingly impatient as a minister subjected her to a detailed examination prior to the marriage ceremony. Her husband, acting as interpreter, "recommended to her a very strict chastity in the married state," the importance of which he clearly feared she did not appreciate. "Very well," Dark-Lanthorn replied, "that's a good speech, and fit for every woman alike, unless she is very old—But what says he now?" When the cleric continued to question her about religious doctrine and lectured her on the need for "a proper care in domestic life," she called him an "Evil Spirit" and instructed her husband to "[t]ell him his speech [was] troublesome and light."

Adair finished his account by noting sardonically that the minister later had to erase Dark-Lanthorn's name from his book of converts "on account of her adulteries." Adair gave no clue as to the circumstances under which these alleged "adulteries" took place. If, for example, Dark-Lanthorn left her husband without a formal divorce and then initiated a sexual relationship with another man, this would have counted as adultery from an English legal perspective, but not necessarily from an Indian perspective. Whatever the actual train of events, Adair saw the collapse of their marriage as a warning to those contemplating alliances to women from cultures not only "savage" but also subject to "wanton female government." Such marriages involved the risk that one's spouse might not prove susceptible to patriarchal structures, a particularly horrifying testimony to the backcountry's inversion of "civilized" norms and the potential cost of embracing the middle ground.[68]

Compromise, accommodation, confusion, tension, and fracture: all of these figured in the relationship between Dark-Lanthorn and her unnamed English husband. They also encapsulate more generally the range of dynamics produced by Anglo-Indian erotic and romantic relations. The surviving evidence suggests that sexual contact between Indians and Englishmen created a broad spectrum of intercultural scenarios, with violent coercion at one extreme and respectful coexistence at the other. Along and beyond the frontier, as Indians and Englishmen eroticized the middle ground between their cultures, they bore testimony together to the possibilities of their meeting as well as to its dangers and ultimate tragedy. Rape was doubtless more common and relations in general more contested than the extant sources, with all their biases, suggest; but we should not ignore evidence for more positive interactions. Indians and Englishmen could and sometimes did enjoy each other, love each other, and live together in peace.

Eighteenth-century commentators on Anglo-Indian relations reacted to interracial sex along the frontier with prurient ambivalence. Most of these writers adopted a tone that combined to varying degrees incomprehension, condescending humor, and disapproval, even as they reveled in the voyeuristic possibilities afforded by such interactions. Genteel travelers, including those who partook of Indian women, sought to distance themselves, at least rhetorically, from interracial familiarities. Their determination to sustain a sense of cultural difference and superiority demanded no less. Members of the southern elite invested heavily, both psychologically and economically, in their own gentility and worried about humiliating comparisons with their counterparts across the Atlantic.[69] The adoption by backcountry inhabitants of Indian customs and their occasional absorption into native communities, despite "fair opportunities of advantages amongst their countrymen," raised the specter of cultural degeneration and must have deepened the self-doubts of those southerners who aspired to gentility.

The southern gentry may have found sexual intimacy with Indians equally fascinating and disturbing because of its association in their minds with erotic relations between Englishmen and Africans. The dangers resulting from the sexual appropriation of Indian women perhaps resonated with the constant threat of violent retribution from slaves for abuse, sexual and otherwise, meted out by their masters.[70] Sexual relationships between common whites and Indians embodied an interracial subaltern familiarity akin to that between poorer English settlers and Africans, the dangers of which had motivated in part the fostering of racial contempt by the elite. Edmund Morgan has drawn our attention to the interplay between Anglo-Indian and Anglo-African relations in the development of southern racial consciousness. That close association may well have informed the ambiguities and tensions in eighteenth-century commentaries on sexual relations between native Americans and Englishmen.[71] Be that as it may, the southern gentry and their European guests clearly saw the eroticization of contact with Indians as alluring yet dangerous: those attracted sexually to Indians might be "beguiled and vanquished" in more ways than one.

NOTES

The research for this essay was made possible by support from the American Philosophical Society and the Academic Senate of the University of California, Riverside. The author wishes to thank Gene Anderson, Myra Anderson, Emory Elliott, Alan Karras, Rebecca Kugel, Christopher Ontiveros, Alan Taylor, and especially Ann Marie Plane for their comments and advice.

1. John Lawson, *A New Voyage to Carolina*, ed. Hugh Talmage Lefler (1708; reprint, Chapel Hill: University of North Carolina Press, 1967), 25–26, 29–30, 35–36, 41, 190–92, 194.

2. Richard White, *The Middle Ground: Indians, Empires, and Republics in the Great Lakes Region, 1650–1815* (New York: Cambridge University Press, 1991).

3. David D. Smits provides the most thorough examination of English attitudes toward intermarriage with native Americans in " 'Abominable Mixture': Toward the Repudiation of

Anglo-Indian Intermarriage in Seventeenth-Century Virginia," *Virginia Magazine of History and Biography* 95 (1987): 157–92. He cites other scholars who have discussed this issue in n. 3. See also Bernard W. Sheehan, *Savagism and Civility: Indians and Englishmen in Colonial Virginia* (New York: Cambridge University Press, 1980); and Edmund S. Morgan, *American Slavery, American Freedom: The Ordeal of Colonial Virginia* (New York: W. W. Norton, 1975), esp. 89–90.

4. John Rolfe to Sir Thomas Dale, April 1614, in *The Old Dominion in the Seventeenth Century: A Documentary History of Virginia, 1606–1689*, ed. Warren M. Billings (Chapel Hill: University of North Carolina Press, 1975), 216–19.

5. Smits, " 'Abominable Mixture,' " 168, 176. In New England, where the settlers' commitment to spiritual purity and social cohesion was more pronounced, not even Indian converts in the "praying towns" were deemed suitable partners for the English. See Smits, " 'We are Not to Grow Wild': Seventeenth-Century New England's Repudiation of Anglo-Indian Intermarriage," *American Indian Culture and Research Journal* 11 (1987): 1–31.

6. Much more common were marriages between Indians and African Americans; see Daniel R. Mandell, *Behind the Frontier: Indians in Eighteenth-Century Massachusetts* (Lincoln: University of Nebraska Press, 1996), chap. 6.

7. Smits, " 'Abominable Mixture,' " 188–89; J. Douglas Deal, *Race and Class in Colonial Virginia: Indians, Englishmen, and Africans on the Eastern Shore during the Seventeenth Century* (New York: Garland, 1993), 41–44; Ann Marie Plane, "Colonizing the Family: Marriage, Household, and Racial Boundaries in Southeastern New England to 1730" (Ph.D. diss., Brandeis University, 1995), 114–24; Mandell, *Behind the Frontier*, 186–87; and Cornelia Hughes Dayton, *Women before the Bar: Gender, Law, and Society in Connecticut, 1639–1789* (Chapel Hill: University of North Carolina Press, 1995), 242. In Massachusetts, suspicions that John Alden had "[lain] with Indian squaws, and [had] Indian papooses" figured in his identification as a witch. See Paul Boyer and Stephen Nissenbaum, eds., *The Salem Witchcraft Papers: Verbatim Transcripts of the Legal Documents of the Salem Witchcraft Outbreak* (New York: Da Capo, 1977), 1:52.

8. William Byrd, "History of the Dividing Line," in *The Prose Works of William Byrd of Westover*, ed. Louis B. Wright (Cambridge: Harvard University Press, 1966), 160–61, 221–22; Thomas Harriot, *A Briefe and True Report of the New Found Land of Virginia* (1590; reprint, New York: Dover, 1972).

9. Robert Beverley, *The History and Present State of Virginia*, ed. Louis B. Wright (1705; reprint, Chapel Hill: University of North Carolina Press, 1947), 38–39.

10. Lawson, *New Voyage to Carolina*, 244–45.

11. See Winthrop D. Jordan, *White over Black: American Attitudes toward the Negro, 1550–1812* (Chapel Hill: University of North Carolina Press, 1968), pt. 1.

12. Most of the Anglo-Indian liaisons mentioned in contemporary accounts were between English men and native women; for an exception, see William Bartram, *The Travels of William Bartram*, ed. Francis Harper (1791; reprint, New Haven: Yale University Press, 1958), 11.

13. Smits, " 'Abominable Mixture,' " esp. 158–60; Kathleen M. Brown, *Good Wives, Nasty Wenches, and Anxious Patriarchs: Gender, Race, and Power in Colonial Virginia* (Chapel Hill: University of North Carolina Press, 1996), 58–61.

14. Bernard Diron D'Artaguiette, "Journal of Diron D'Artaguiette," in *Travels in the American Colonies*, ed. Newton D. Mereness (New York: Antiquarian Press, 1961), 48; Robert Hunter, Jr., *Quebec to Carolina in 1785–1786, Being the Travel Diary and Observations of Robert Hunter, Jr., A Young Merchant of London*, ed. Louis B. Wright and Marion Tinling (San Marino: Huntington Library, 1943), 55; Luigi Castiglioni, *Luigi Castig-*

lioni's "Viaggio": Travels in the United States of North America, 1785–87, ed. and trans. Antonio Pace (1790; reprint, Syracuse: Syracuse University Press, 1983), 39; Lawson, *New Voyage to Carolina*, 189.

15. Byrd, "History of the Dividing Line," 218, 222.

16. Bartram, *Travels*, 225–26; see also 306–07.

17. Diron D'Artaguiette, "Journal," 48.

18. Richard Eden, preface to *The Decades of the New World* (London, 1555). Occasionally opportunities would arise well within English territory: Alexander Hamilton mentioned that one night at Huntington, Long Island, a traveler named Parker made "strenuous courtship" to "three buxom girls" serving them at supper, one of whom was "an Indian girl named Phoebe." See Alexander Hamilton, "The Itinerarium of Dr. Alexander Hamilton," in *Colonial American Travel Narratives*, ed. Wendy Martin (New York: Penguin, 1994), 244.

19. William Byrd, *The Secret Diary of William Byrd of Westover, 1709–12*, ed. Louis B. Wright and Marion Tinling (Richmond, Va.: Dietz Press, 1941), 423–25.

20. William Byrd, "The Secret History of the Line," in *Colonial American Travel Narratives*, ed. Martin, 113–14; idem, "History of the Dividing Line," 218, 222.

21. Lawson, *New Voyage to Carolina*, 41.

22. Diron D'Artaguiette, "Journal," 58, 73.

23. Thomas Nairne, *Nairne's Muskhogean Journals: The 1708 Expedition to the Mississippi River*, ed. Alexander Moore (Jackson: University Press of Mississippi, 1988), 44. For other accounts emphasizing native sexual freedom before marriage (and fidelity once married), see Ann Marie Plane, "Bringing Forth Bastards: Gender and Indian 'Fornication' in Colonial New England" (paper presented to Berkshire Conference on the History of Women, University of North Carolina, Chapel Hill, 1996), 7 n. 13. The Indians' reputed facility in dealing with unwanted pregnancies through abortion or infanticide must have reassured those contemplating "scandalous liberties." Plane, "Colonizing the Family," 387. Richard White points out that the apparently free sexual behavior of young women in some Indian societies was actually regulated by relatives in ways that Europeans would not have noticed or understood. White, *Middle Ground*, 64.

24. Byrd, "History of the Dividing Line," 218, 314. See also Castiglioni, *"Viaggio,"* 101.

25. Lawson, *New Voyage to Carolina*, 46–47.

26. Ibid., 41, 194.

27. Ibid., 50.

28. Byrd, "History of the Dividing Line," 218.

29. Hunter, *Quebec to Carolina*, 110–11.

30. Nairne, *Muskhogean Journals*, 44; Lawson, *New Voyage to Carolina*, 226.

31. Diron D'Artaguiette, "Journal," 48. See also Thomas Ashe, "Carolina, or A Description of the Present State of That Country" (1682), in *Narratives of Early Carolina*, ed. Alexander S. Salley (1911; reprint, New York: Barnes and Noble, 1953), 156; Maurice Mathews, "A Contemporary View of Carolina in 1680," *South Carolina Historical Magazine* 55 (1954): 157; Lawson, *New Voyage to Carolina*, 26, 226.

32. The problem had become so serious in French Louisiana by the early 1720s that a hospital was built specifically "for curing venereal diseases." Diron D'Artaguiette, "Journal," 91.

33. Lawson, *New Voyage to Carolina*, 25.

34. William Tredwell Bull to Secretary of Society for Propagation of Gospel, Aug. 10, 1715, *South Carolina Historical Magazine* 63 (1962): 25.

35. Robert Maule to Secretary of Society for Propagation of Gospel, Aug. 2, 1711, *South Carolina Historical Magazine* 61 (1960): 8–9. See also Commissary Gideon Johnston to Secretary of Society for Propagation of Gospel, July 5, 1710, in *Carolina Chronicle: The Papers of Commissary Gideon Johnston, 1707–1716*, ed. Frank J. Klingberg (Chapel Hill: University of North Carolina Press, 1946), 53.

36. Alexander Long, "A Small Postscript of the Ways and Manners of the Indians Called Cherokees" (1725), *Southern Indian Studies* 21 (1969): 20.

37. Governor Johnstone to Don Antonio D'Ullua, May 3, 1766, in *Mississippi Provincial Archives, 1763–1766: English Dominion*, ed. Dunbar Rowland (Nashville: Brandon, 1911), 312–13.

38. W. L. McDowell, ed., *Colonial Records of South Carolina: Journals of the Commissioners of the Indian Trade, 1710–1718* (Columbia: South Carolina Archives Department, 1955), 30, 34. See also idem, ed., *Colonial Records of South Carolina: Documents Relating to Indian Affairs, 1750–1754* (Columbia: South Carolina Archives Department, 1958), 81, 87–88, 135–36; and idem, ed., *Colonial Records of South Carolina: Documents Relating to Indian Affairs, 1754–1765* (Columbia: University of South Carolina Press, 1970), 560.

39. David Crawley to William Byrd, July 30, 1715, in *The Correspondence of the Three William Byrds of Westover, Virginia, 1684–1776*, ed. Marion Tinling (Charlottesville: Virginia Historical Society, 1977), 1:289.

40. Byrd, "History of the Dividing Line," 311.

41. McDowell, *Documents Relating to Indian Affairs, 1754–1765*, 265, 371.

42. McDowell, *Documents Relating to Indian Affairs, 1750–1754*, 306.

43. Rowland, *Mississippi Provincial Archives*, 238–39, 241.

44. McDowell, *Documents Relating to Indian Affairs, 1754–1765*, 355.

45. McDowell, *Documents Relating to Indian Affairs, 1750–1754*, 447.

46. Ibid., 306. According to Castiglioni, "the new pioneers" who "spread out into the interior" after the Revolutionary War were "for the most part a bad lot" who "enraged the Indians by stealing their canoes, molesting their wives, and intruding into territory not ceded to them, with the result that the natives very often avenged these injuries with the massacre of whole families." Castiglioni, *"Viaggio,"* 49.

47. It was also quite consistent with the widespread practice of serial monogamy among colonists in the backcountry, usually misunderstood by government and church officials as adultery and bigamy. I will be discussing this phenomenon and its misconstruction in a forthcoming book.

48. Lawson, *New Voyage to Carolina*, 29–30, 190–92.

49. "Journal of Colonel George Chicken's Mission from Charleston, South Carolina, to the Cherokees, 1726," in *Travels in the American Colonies*, ed. Mereness, 104; "David Taitt's Journal of a Journey through the Creek Country, 1772," in ibid., 512; McDowell, *Journals of the Commissioners of the Indian Trade, 1710–1718*, 17; idem, *Documents Relating to Indian Affairs, 1750–1754*, 70, 117; idem, *Documents Relating to Indian Affairs, 1754–1765*, 243–44, 247.

50. See, for example, the case of T___y, discussed below.

51. Bartram, *Travels*, 124, 221. See also Sylvia Van Kirk, *"Many Tender Ties": Women in Fur-Trade Society in Western Canada, 1670–1870* (Norman: University of Oklahoma Press, 1983), esp. 33.

52. Alexander Kellet, *A Pocket of Prose and Verse* (1778; reprint, New York: Garland, 1975), 20–21; Lawson, *New Voyage to Carolina*, 193. According to Lawson, "those Indian

girls that have conversed with the English and other Europeans, never care for the conversation of their own countrymen afterwards."

53. McDowell, *Documents Relating to Indian Affairs, 1750–1754,* 407. The emergence of substantial female majorities in many eighteenth-century Indian nations, resulting from an upsurge in warfare brought on by the increased Euro-American presence, may have softened objections to marriage with whites and highlighted the advantages. While a straightforward demographic explanation for Indian interest in intermarriage would be reductive, it may well have been part of the picture for at least some native peoples.

54. Bartram, *Travels,* 71–72.

55. Ibid., 283–84, 292.

56. There were, of course, exceptions. See, for example, McDowell, *Journals of the Commissioners of the Indian Trade, 1710–1718,* 4.

57. Lawson, *New Voyage to Carolina,* 192. See also Castiglioni, *"Viaggio,"* 83.

58. John Bernard, *Retrospections of America, 1797–1811* (New York: Harper and Brothers, 1887), 182.

59. See James Axtell, *The Invasion Within: The Contest of Cultures in Colonial North America* (New York: Oxford University Press, 1985), chap. 13; June Namias, *White Captives: Gender and Ethnicity on the American Frontier* (Chapel Hill: University of North Carolina Press, 1993); and John Demos, *The Unredeemed Captive: A Family Story from Early America* (New York: Vintage, 1994).

60. See Richard J. Hooker, ed., *The Carolina Backcountry on the Eve of the Revolution: The Journal and Other Writings of Charles Woodmason, Anglican Itinerant* (Chapel Hill: University of North Carolina Press, 1953), 121; and Tom Hatley, *The Dividing Paths: Cherokees and South Carolinians through the Revolutionary Era* (New York: Oxford University Press, 1995), 181–82.

61. During his residence with the Cherokee as a French agent, the infamous Christian Priber developed plans for a multicultural utopian community that would be sexually permissive in ways similar to Indian society as seen through European eyes. His plans aroused great interest and anxiety in South Carolina, partly because of their implications for cultural integrity. See *South Carolina Gazette,* Aug. 15, 1743; "Journal of Antoine Bonnefoy's Captivity among the Cherokee Indians, 1741–1742," in *Travels in the American Colonies,* ed. Mereness, 249; "Historical Relation of Facts Delivered by Ludovick Grant, Indian Trader, to His Excellency the Governor of South Carolina, 1756," *South Carolina Historical and Genealogical Magazine* 10 (1909): 59; Knox Mellon, Jr., "Christian Priber and the Jesuit Myth," *South Carolina Historical Magazine* 61 (1960): 75–81.

62. Lawson, *New Voyage to Carolina,* 192.

63. Nathaniel Osborne to Secretary of Society for Propagation of Gospel, March 1, 1715, *South Carolina Historical and Genealogical Magazine* 50 (1949): 175.

64. John L. Nichols, "Alexander Cameron, British Agent among the Cherokee, 1764–1781," *South Carolina Historical Magazine* 97 (1996): esp. 100.

65. "Bernard Elliott's Recruiting Journal, 1775," *South Carolina Historical and Genealogical Magazine* 17 (1916): 98–99.

66. Hatley, *Dividing Paths,* 60–62, 85.

67. Duc de la Rochefoucault-Liancourt, *Travels through the United States of North America, the Country of the Iroquois, and Upper Canada* (London, 1799), 1:167.

68. James Adair, *The History of the American Indians* (1775; reprint, New York: Promontory Press, 1973), 133–35.

69. See Kenneth Lockridge, *The Diary, and Life, of William Byrd II of Virginia, 1674–1744* (Chapel Hill: University of North Carolina Press, 1987).

70. See Gerald W. Mullin, *Flight and Rebellion: Slave Resistance in Eighteenth-Century Virginia* (New York: Oxford University Press, 1972).

71. Morgan, *American Slavery, American Freedom*, esp. chap. 16.

Chapter Six

"Shamefull Matches"
The Regulation of Interracial Sex and Marriage in the South before 1900

Peter W. Bardaglio

Few areas of the law provide a better window on the social construction of race in North America than the regulation of interracial sex and marriage.[1] Miscegenation, a term coined during the Civil War years, had a special significance for southerners who lived during slavery and its immediate aftermath, for strong links existed between attitudes toward race mixing, on the one hand, and the development of racial bondage and the drive to preserve white dominance following emancipation, on the other. Miscegenation laws, enforced from the 1660s to the 1960s, not only reflected but also shaped American racial attitudes. Because of the close interplay between illicit sexuality and ideas about race, miscegenation laws also offer an effective way to examine the impact of gender relations on the construction of race.

Contrary to some historians, who discount the value of statutes for revealing the character of society, this essay argues that statutory law is an important source of evidence for assessing white sexual anxiety about black men. When used to understand social behavior and conditions, statutes can be misleading; but statutory law does tell us a great deal about the hopes and fears of society, at least among those who have the power to influence and pass legislation. For example, when southern legislators prescribed castration or capital punishment for black males convicted of attempting to rape white women, the passage of these criminal statutes says something significant about the anxieties and fears of the white men who made the laws, especially in the context of other laws that imposed only a prison sentence on white males found guilty of committing the very same crime, and in the absence of any laws whatsoever that punished males for attempting sexual assaults on black women. Of course, rape statutes themselves reveal little if anything about the actual extent of interracial rape, and we cannot simply assume that the laws once on the books were systematically and effectively enforced. But we can safely conclude that somewhere in the legislative process white sexual anxiety about black men came into play and that the passage of these laws contributed to the formation of racial and gender norms.[2]

In seeking to reconstruct the past, we must not generalize on the basis of any one body of evidence; resort to other historical sources can minimize the limitations inherent in a particular kind of data. Judicial decisions, for example, can flesh out the reasoning behind the statutes, shedding light on the intentions of lawmakers. These decisions are also more useful than statutes in telling us about how people behaved, since this is what brought them into court. The following analysis of interracial marriage and sex will rely on both kinds of evidence in drawing conclusions about changing southern attitudes toward miscegenation.[3] What emerges from this analysis is a clear sense that white sexual anxiety about blacks was a persistent force under slavery, but it intensified dramatically with the end of bondage, acquiring a newly politicized status in the post-emancipation South.

The Slave South

The racial character of American slavery and the commitment to white supremacy fostered a widespread antipathy toward race mixture in southern society. Whites feared that sexual relations between blacks and whites, if not controlled, could undermine the institution of slavery and the racial order. Children of mixed European and African ancestry, in particular, blurred the sharply demarcated boundaries between the races essential to slavery in the South.[4]

The restrictive policy toward intermixture that emerged before the Civil War, however, was not all-encompassing. Miscegenation laws sought not so much to eliminate interracial sexual contacts as to channel them. Those in power employed these laws, as well as laws against fornication and adultery, mainly to keep white women and black men apart. The legal process exhibited a degree of toleration for white males who had sexual relations with black females, as long as the liaison was kept casual and discreet.[5] This sort of illicit intercourse—between men of the higher-status racial group and women of the lower—reinforced rather than challenged the existing system of group stratification in the South.

Southern elites tended to oppose sexual relations that implied either gender or racial equality, such as white female relations with black men or legal interracial marriages, although recent work has uncovered some instances of toleration even in these situations.[6] Overall, the twofold goal of miscegenation laws was to keep black men and women in their place and to protect the purity of white womanhood, a goal that reflected the degree to which the structure of power in the South rested on both gender and racial classifications. Significant regional variations existed in southern attitudes toward miscegenation, but generally speaking, only white men could cross the color line in the South without incurring severe social and legal penalties, and then only in certain circumstances.[7]

Although the early evidence of attitudes toward interracial sexual unions is ambiguous, southern authorities took a decisive stand against miscegenation following the legislative enactment of slavery in the late seventeenth century.[8] The rise of legal barriers to interracial sex and marriage was a notable exception to the general hesitancy about monitoring the private lives of individual whites. Indeed, miscegenation laws offered the strongest example of state intrusion in southern domestic life before the Civil War.[9]

The fact that white southerners—who usually opposed mobilizing the machinery of the state when matters of local morality were concerned—passed such legislation and reenacted it on a regular basis gives some indication of the depth of feeling against racial intermixture. The early passage of miscegenation laws underscores the central role of race and gender relations in prompting the expansion of public governance over the southern household. Lawmakers sought to preserve white dominance and stigmatize white women who had sexual relations with black men. The legacy of these early patterns left its imprint on nineteenth-century efforts to control miscegenation, and thus the colonial statutes require a closer look.

English settlers in North America especially frowned upon racial intermarriages, and such unions were relatively rare. Interracial sexual contacts outside marriage, however, occurred frequently, a fact underscored by the presence of large numbers of mixed-race offspring. This illicit intercourse usually took place between white men and black women, but ample evidence exists of sexual relations in the colonial era between white women and black men.

Although interracial sexual relations were extensive in colonial America, few whites thought that intermixture was a good thing. Public feeling about miscegenation was potent enough to make its way into the statute books of many colonies.[10] The development of these miscegenation statutes was an American legal innovation, for no such ban existed at common law or by statute in England at this time. The laws against miscegenation generally took two forms: those banning fornication between blacks and whites and those prohibiting marriage between these two groups.[11]

The Maryland and Virginia assemblies led the way in legislating against miscegenation, beginning in the 1660s. Maryland at first punished only interracial marriage, and Virginia only interracial fornication, but by the end of the seventeenth century the two colonies penalized both acts.[12] From the beginning, miscegenation legislation in Maryland manifested an intense concern with controlling the sexual behavior of white women. A 1664 law, for example, denounced "diverse freeborne Englishwomen [who were] forgetfull of their free Condition and to the disgrace of our Nation doe intermarry with Negro slaves." To discourage "such shamefull Matches," the statute stipulated that any white woman who married a black slave was to serve her husband's master until the slave died.[13] The Maryland assembly altered the penalties for mixed marriages in 1681, shifting the burden of punishment from the female servants to the masters who allowed marriages with black slaves to take place. The legislators disclosed their continuing anxiety about the sexual proclivities of white women, however, insisting that interracial marriages were "*always to the Satisfaction of their Lascivious & Lustfull desires.*"[14]

Eleven years later, Maryland lawmakers established a separate set of punishments for fornication between whites and blacks in the colony for the first time. The law provided that a white woman who had a bastard child was to serve for seven years, and if the black man was free, he also had to serve for seven years. Although the statute stated that white men who "begett with Child any negro woman" were subject to the same penalties as white women, this provision was tacked on almost as an afterthought.[15] Moreover, restrictions on the right of blacks and mulattoes to testify in court against whites hindered the successful prosecutions of white males who engaged in interracial sex.

Maryland's miscegenation law, in short, was directed primarily at white women, black men, and their mulatto offspring. Recognizing that only the reproduction of "pure white" children by white women could maintain the fiction of a biracial society, the legal system was particularly determined to keep white women from interracial sexual unions. This preoccupation, combined with the custom of lumping mulattoes and blacks into the same category, provides a crucial insight into the social and legal construction of reproduction. Under the social rules that operated in the South, a white woman could give birth to a black child—thus the need for strict legal regulation of her sexual behavior. But under the same rules, a black woman could not give birth to a white child. Such a construction of reproduction clearly served the interests of white men in the South, allowing them to roam sexually among women of any color without threatening the color line.[16]

A similar thrust characterized miscegenation legislation in Virginia. The colony's assembly decided in 1662 that interracial fornication demanded special penalties; the fine it imposed for this crime was twice that stipulated for illicit intercourse between persons of the same race. Legislators moved at the same time to clarify the status of mulatto offspring of interracial unions. Declaring that the child of a black woman by a white man would be "bound or free only according to the condition of the mother," the assembly broke with English common law, which stated that the status of a child followed that of the father. Virginia lawmakers thus ensured that the transgressions of white men would lead to an increase in the population of the slave labor force, providing a powerful economic incentive to engage in interracial sex even as criminal sanctions were imposed for such behavior. To say the least, this new legislation delivered a mixed message to white males.[17]

That the Virginia assembly was primarily concerned with regulating the sexual behavior of white women became apparent when it set out in 1691 to ban interracial marriage. Although the 1691 act prohibited mixed marriages involving white males as well as females, making any free white person who contracted such a union liable to permanent banishment from the colony, its stated purpose was to prevent "that abominable mixture and spurious issue which hereafter may encrease in this dominion, as well as by negroes, mulattoes, and Indians intermarrying with *English, or other white women*, as by their unlawfull accompanying with one another." The new legislation dropped the earlier sanctions against white males who indulged in interracial fornication, focusing its attention on the illicit relations of white women with black or mulatto men. Both white men and women were subject to punishment if they sought to legitimize their relationship with a black person by marriage. But the statute did not impose any penalties on a white man for having sexual relations with a black woman, and it was not a crime for a black woman to have a bastard child by a white man. Engaging in interracial sexual relations outside marriage became a crime only when a white woman had a black man's child.[18]

The other three plantation colonies also adopted some form of statutory prohibition against miscegenation, although South Carolina did not explicitly ban marriages between whites and blacks.[19] In contrast, only two northern colonies passed miscegenation legislation: Massachusetts in 1705 and Pennsylvania in 1725–26.[20] The lack of statutory bans against race mixture in other northern colonies did not necessarily indicate support for such practice, but rather a reliance on social custom and prejudice to maintain racial purity. The near uniformity of opinion among legislatures of the plantation colonies, however, suggests the more pronounced nature of southern opposition to miscegenation, opposition that exhibited a growing belief among southern whites in their racial superiority.

Statutory proclamations in the colonial South declaring that interracial sexual contacts were "shamefull" and would result in an "abominable mixture and spurious issue" reinforced as well as reflected white beliefs that blacks possessed a degraded nature. In the same way, sexual slander among whites upheld racial norms when it implied that interracial sex was somehow "unnatural." As Kathleen Brown observes, this process of "racializing sex" created new avenues for white elites to consolidate their power in a slave society.[21]

Besides helping to redefine and reinforce racial boundaries, the colonial bans on miscegenation aimed at strengthening white men's sexual control over women of both races. The patriarchal assumptions of those men who held power in southern society found expression in statutes prohibiting intermixture to the extent that these laws had the effect of retaining white women for the use of white men. Moreover, by winking at intercourse between male slaveholders and female slaves, miscegenation legislation provided masters with a key economic advantage. Most of the South by the early eighteenth century had followed Virginia, which adopted the legal doctrine that black and mulatto offspring inherited the mother's status, so that any children born of sexual encounters between white men and female slaves were potential additions to the labor force. These encounters also allowed slaveholders to further their social control of the slave community through sexual subjugation.[22]

The fact that mulatto children derived their status from their mother also helps to explain why southern lawmakers struggled to prevent sexual relations between white women and black men. Although mulatto children of black female slaves were subject to enslavement, mulatto offspring of white females could not be placed in slavery. These free mulattoes threatened the racial caste system ideologically, if not practically, because their presence could lead to the blurring of the distinction between slave and black, on the one hand, and free and white, on the other.[23]

Following the American Revolution, public control of intermixture in southern society became even more stringent. The growth of the free black population in the new nation and increasingly vehement attacks on slavery by northern abolitionists, beginning in the 1830s, convinced white southerners of the need to bolster the color barrier.[24] Despite the strictness of the ban against interracial sex, this behavior persisted. While the number of white females who violated the taboo was far from negligible,[25] most miscegenation occurred between white men and black women, much of it resulting from slaveholders and their sons, as well as overseers, taking sexual advantage of female slaves. Although some liaisons between white men and black women became enduring relationships based on mutual affection, female slaves confronted a limited choice in sexual matters involving their masters. The tremendous disparity between the social and legal position of white men and that of black women ensured that psychological, if not physical, coercion was a significant component of such encounters.[26]

The sexual abuse of female slaves generated much tension and conflict in southern households. Black women who were sexually exploited and black men who could not protect their women experienced the most pain and distress.[27] White women often resented mulatto offspring as reminders of their husbands' sexual infidelity, and miscegenation caused them profound anguish, too. The sexual exploitation of slaves thus disrupted the family life of both races, giving all women good reason to condemn this practice.[28]

Even white men in the antebellum South could not entirely escape the repercussions generated by their pursuit of interracial sex.[29] Of course, there were always white males who had sex with black women without feelings of affection or guilt. But the situation was not always so simple, and some white men found it difficult to manage their interracial affairs without becoming emotionally involved. In cases like this, sexuality that crossed social boundaries had the potential to undermine as much as reinforce the hierarchy of southern society.[30]

Those white men not afflicted by a sense of attachment to the black women with whom they had sex might still feel responsible for any children. The development of increasingly strict manumission laws during the antebellum period hindered the capacity of masters to free their slave mistresses and children, but many slaveowners made efforts to provide for their mulatto offspring.[31] Such efforts, sincere as they might have been, did not eliminate the contradiction that sexual exploitation of slave women posed to the paternalistic vision of those planters who argued that duty and responsibility, not abuse and avarice, linked master and slave. In an effort to excuse miscegenation, southern whites frequently cited the "natural lewdness of the negro" as the main cause of interracial sex. This attempt to place the responsibility for race mixing onto the shoulders of blacks, however, could not disguise the extent to which white men imposed their sexual desires on slave women.[32]

⌈Given the widespread indulgence of slaveholders in illicit intercourse with female slaves, the white wives and daughters of these slaveholders became the primary vehicle for the protection of racial purity. Placed on a pedestal, they found themselves honored for their moral virtue yet hemmed in by the severe constraints on their social and sexual behavior. They were the key point of vulnerability in the edifice erected to maintain the color line; they had to be protected from the danger of interracial intercourse at all costs.[33]⌉

Whereas elite white women were installed on a pedestal, mulattoes were commonly relegated to the status of blacks. Some white southerners actually argued that mulattoes were inferior to blacks of purely African heritage. Others demonstrated a pronounced pro-mulatto bias, asserting that the offspring of intermixture were more intelligent and responsible than blacks. However much antebellum whites might disagree about the superiority of mulattoes to blacks of purely African heritage, there was a solid consensus that too many individuals of a mixed racial background were slipping into the ranks of the white race. By using the law to classify the mulatto as "black," southern whites sought to prevent the breakdown of racial demarcations.

During the colonial period, there had been little preoccupation with the question of strictly defining who was a mulatto and therefore subject to the laws governing the conduct of slaves and free blacks. Only Virginia and North Carolina passed legislation establishing guidelines for racial identification. Both colonies decided that anyone with African ancestry within the last three generations should be lumped together with "negroes," although sometimes North Carolina stretched the definition to include four generations. Other colonies simply grouped mulattoes loosely with blacks without writing the custom into law. In all the colonies, legal definitions aside, anyone who displayed the physical characteristics of African ancestry was deemed black.[34]

An increased concern with strengthening the color barrier in the postrevolutionary era led most southern states to pass legislation setting the limits of blackness and whiteness. Although social custom decreed that any amount of African "blood" made one black, the law found the notion impossible to apply literally. Southern states needed some measurable standard in the courtroom in order to make racial background susceptible to proof. Consequently, by the early nineteenth century, various southern states applied one-fourth or one-eighth rules about African "blood" to determine one's legal color. This legislation, by establishing seemingly precise definitions of what constituted blackness, meant that some individuals with African ancestry slipped through the legal net, however fine the mesh. Virginia lawmakers proclaimed in 1785 that an individual with one African ancestor in the previous two generations was a mulatto and hence subject to laws regulating free blacks. This definition was subsequently adopted by Arkansas, Florida, and Mississippi. Alabama, Georgia, Tennessee, and Texas passed more restrictive legislation that pushed the line back three generations.[35]

These various legislative efforts to define racial boundaries in the slave South provide a striking example of the extent to which race is an ideological construct rather than a physical fact.[36] The attempt to establish a fractional definition of blackness for mulattoes accompanied the spread of statutory bans on intermarriage, making it easier for authorities to enforce these bans. The use of state power to regulate mixed unions stood in stark juxtaposition to other areas of antebellum marriage law in the North and South, which usually encouraged a hands-off approach to matrimony.[37]

The perceived need to clamp down on intermarriage in order to preserve racial distinctions prodded the overwhelming majority of states in the antebellum South to enact rigorous public controls. This new legislation made marriages between blacks and whites null and void rather than merely voidable. In addition, some of these states established special penalties for interracial couples who cohabited outside wedlock. Conviction for miscegenation could draw punishments of anywhere between a hundred-dollar fine in North Carolina to a jail sentence of two to five years in Texas.[38] Five states, moreover, imposed stiff fines on clerks who issued licenses for mixed marriages and officials who performed ceremonies for such unions.[39]

The proliferation of laws forbidding intermarriage, together with those setting the limits of blackness and whiteness, testifies to the deeply rooted commitment in the Old South to a racial caste system.[40] Yet not all southern states mounted such elaborate legal efforts to buttress the color barrier. The South Carolina legislature refused to impose a single standard for distinguishing the races. Afraid that a rigid definition of who was what might lead to an overly crude application of the color line, lawmakers left the problem of determining racial identification up to the courts.[41] In this way, judges and juries could weigh on a case-by-case basis factors such as social reputation as well as color and bloodline.[42]

South Carolina not only refused to establish strict definitions about who was white and who was black, it also did not implement any legal sanctions against intermarriage. In addition, Mississippi and Alabama lacked effective statutory measures to prevent interracial marital unions.[43] The less systematic nature of legal efforts in these three states to reinforce the boundary between the races reflected the somewhat different conditions that characterized portions of the lower South. Race relations in this area, including Louisiana, evolved in a pattern borrowed from the West Indies, one that tended to treat free mulattoes as a social group with special privileges and status. The influence of the West Indies, together with the high proportion of black slaves to the number of whites, predisposed many whites to perceive the mulattoes who made up the bulk of the free black population in the lower South as an intermediate element between the races. This more sophisticated system of race relations, with its keener awareness of the complexities of color, encouraged the development of a more porous racial boundary than elsewhere in the South, at least until the intensifying racism of the late antebellum era pushed free mulattoes downward toward the lower caste.[44]

The development of a distinctive attitude toward mulattoes, most evident in South Carolina and Louisiana, did not mean that intermarriage was common in the lower South. If anything, the tremendous social chasm between most whites and blacks made intermarriage so inconceivable that it did not have to be legislated against.[45] Support for this point of view can be found in the *Charleston Mercury*, which insisted in 1823 that "there is not a white person in the community who would hazard a defence of it [intermarriage between blacks and whites]. The feeling on this subject is universal. A white person so acting would be considered as degraded in society without a dissenting voice."[46]

Although there may have been little need for legal prohibitions against interracial marriage in South Carolina, the absence of any statutory ban left state judges in a quandary when faced with determining the validity of matrimony between blacks and whites. In 1842, for example, the South Carolina court considered a property dispute involving the legality of a union between an emancipated slave woman and a white man. The mulatto children of this marriage sought title to a tract of land that had been given to their deceased mother under the terms of her former owner's will. The lawyer for the children asserted that the mother's marriage was valid and therefore the offspring had inheritance rights to the property in question that must be recognized. Acknowledging the great hostility toward interracial unions, the attorney remarked that "such marriages are *revolting*, and justly regarded as *offensive to public decency*," but he held that they were "not contrary to *existing laws*." Because no ban on intermarriage existed at common law, he contended, only "*express statutory provisions*" could "make such marriages unlawful," and these provisions were absent from the lawbooks of South Carolina.[47]

The South Carolina court disagreed over the question of whether the black woman's marriage was valid. Admitting that the case involved "points that are not free from difficulty, and on which there might be some diversity of opinion," the majority of jurists opted to sidestep the question. Instead, they decided against the mulatto offspring on a technicality regarding the will left by the slaveholder who had emancipated their mother and given her the land. Two of the judges, however, issued dissenting opinions, claiming that the inheritance rights of the children could not be denied. Absent any legislative initiative, they agreed, marriage "was good and legal between a white person and a free negro."

Antebellum jurists in other southern states also maintained that the lack of common-law authority made it impossible to impose the restriction on intermarriage without a statutory ban.[48] Of course, most southern legislatures supplied the necessary statutes, and when such legislation existed, it won the wholehearted endorsement of the southern judiciary. Antebellum courts, in particular, firmly backed those laws making interracial unions null and void. The racial prohibition was "one eminently affecting the public order," announced the Louisiana Supreme Court in 1860. "Hence the *nullity* declared by the [statute] is absolute, and cannot be cured by ratification. The law is of that rigorous nature that it will not permit a marriage to exist between persons of two different races for a moment."[49]

Legislation making marriage between blacks and whites void was the most significant antebellum development in miscegenation law. Judicial endorsement of this legislation had several important consequences. First, it meant that when an interracial couple attempted to contract matrimony, the result was precisely the same as if no license had been obtained or ceremony performed and the parties had simply indulged in illicit sexual relations. As the North Carolina appellate court observed in 1852, the parties were thus subjected "to the risk of being indicted for fornication and adultery, as long as they continued to cohabit." In many cases this is exactly what happened.[50]

Furthermore, because a marriage violating the racial prohibition was void and of no legal effect, someone who was not a party to the marriage could attack it collaterally (as in an estate proceeding).[51] The possibility also existed that a couple who contracted matrimony in a jurisdiction where the union was not prohibited might find its validity challenged when they entered a state that banned intermarriage.[52] All in all, such judicial rulings made it nearly impossible for interracial couples who married to experience any peace of mind.

Southern law before the Civil War not only opposed interracial marriage but also continued to mirror fears concerning illicit sexual intercourse between the races. Public antagonism toward sexual relations between white women and black men had a noticeable impact on judicial policy, as two North Carolina cases demonstrated in 1832. In both appeals, Chief Justice Thomas Ruffin faced white men who sought divorces from their wives because these white women had given birth to mulatto children shortly after their marriages. The men, who admitted taking part in premarital sexual relations with their future spouses, charged nuptial fraud, each asserting that the woman he had married was not a fit marital partner because she had given herself to a black man.

In the first ruling, Ruffin refused to grant Marville Scroggins a divorce. The chief justice decided that he had no choice but to uphold the common-law principle that "persons who marry, agree to take each other *as they are.*" Reminding Scroggins that he knew his wife was not chaste at the time of their marriage, Ruffin admonished him, "He who marries a wanton [woman], knowing her true character, submits himself to the lowest degradation, and imposes on himself." The North Carolina judge was well aware of the powerful prejudices operating in this case, and he acknowledged that the sexual involvement of Scroggins's wife with a black man had made it difficult for him to deny the divorce: "The stigma in our state of society is so indelible, the degradation so absolute, and the abhorrence of the community against the offender, and contempt for the husband so marked and unextinguishable, that the court has not been able, without a struggle, to follow those rules which their dispassionate judgment sanctions."[53] Indeed, public revulsion against race mixture involving white women was so intense that in the second case it proved impossible to overcome.

In *Barden v. Barden*, Ruffin made it clear that his personal inclination was to issue the same verdict as in the *Scroggins* case. But the majority of the North Carolina court felt otherwise. Ruffin was compelled to modify his previous stand on the common-law rule of nuptial fraud, and he granted the divorce that Jesse Barden sought. Apparently, the public opposition generated by Ruffin's first opinion was enough to surmount the court's commitment to common-law tradition. As Ruffin frankly concluded, his decision to award the divorce was "a concession to the deep rooted and virtuous prejudices of the community" regarding miscegenation. The dramatic reversal of the North Carolina court in *Barden v. Barden* underscored the power of the community in southern society to mobilize state sanctions against racial intermixture, especially when it involved white women crossing the barrier of color.[54]

Emancipation and the Hardening of Racial Boundaries

The defeat of the Confederacy and the collapse of slavery prompted a reevaluation by southern courts of the legitimacy of the antebellum miscegenation bans. The outcome of this inquiry into the constitutionality of the legal prohibitions proved to be a fateful one for the history of race relations in the South. For this reason, the judicial findings deserve careful consideration. A close analysis of the appellate court decisions reveals a deepening racial hostility among southern judges that compelled them to resist the full-scale adoption of a contractual understanding of matrimony, despite the headway that the precepts of contract made in other areas of domestic relations law and labor law.[55]

Now that the protective barrier of bondage had collapsed, southern whites exhibited considerable apprehension about their ability to retain control over former slaves. Miscegenation quickly became one of the most volatile legal and social issues, as white anxiety over black male sexuality reached unprecedented heights. Feelings of insecurity about maintaining the racial and gender order provoked an intensified obsession with racial purity and led to the growing importance of rape and miscegenation in the political discourse of the post-war South.[56]

Playing upon white fears of miscegenation and black rape, northern and southern opponents of Republican race policies warned that they would lead directly to intermixture.[57] Despite Republican denials of any intention to legalize interracial marriages, southern critics of Reconstruction continued to make these charges. They did so in part because the miscegenation issue proved to be an effective way to split up white Republican support in the South and mobilize resistance to radical Reconstruction. At the same time, the rhetorical emphasis on racial purity had the advantage of obscuring the degree to which whites themselves were responsible for the extensive miscegenation that had already taken place.[58]

Following the reorganization of state governments under President Andrew Johnson's direction in 1865, southern legislatures moved rapidly to establish prohibitions against interracial marriage. The South Carolina Black Code, adopted in 1865, contained the first law ever enacted in the state barring marriage between whites and blacks.[59] In that same year, Alabama and Mississippi significantly bolstered their comparatively weak antebellum sanctions. Alabama included a provision in its new state constitution making interracial marriages null and void, and Mississippi's black code stipulated that any person convicted of intermarriage should be confined to the state penitentiary for life.[60] While southern legislatures instituted stern measures to prevent interracial marriage, several states did not take the trouble to make interracial sex outside marriage a separate crime. In these states, presumably, legislators believed that already existing statutes punishing fornication, cohabitation, and "lascivious and lewd" conduct sufficiently deterred interracial sexual behavior outside marriage.[61]

During the period of radical Republican dominance, several southern states (including Mississippi and South Carolina) temporarily abandoned the prohibition against miscegenation.[62] This move raised an outcry among conservative whites, who predicted that racial intermixture would bring about the "*extinction* of such descendants of whites and Africans."[63] With the overthrow of radical Reconstruction, resurgent white supremacists in the South reenacted antebellum measures or put new statutes on the books outlawing miscegenation. In addition, six southern states followed Alabama in prohibiting intermarriage by constitutional provision.[64]

As before the Civil War, these new laws usually pronounced interracial marriages void, making the parties to such marriages subject to prosecution for violation of the laws against fornication and cohabitation. Maximum terms of imprisonment under the miscegenation statutes ranged from six months in Georgia to ten years in Florida, Mississippi, and North Carolina. Only Alabama, Georgia, Tennessee, and Texas made it a separate crime for unmarried persons of different races to live together, but many states continued to punish anyone issuing a marriage license to an interracial couple or performing the ceremony for them.[65]

Outside the South the hardening of the color line in the late nineteenth century led to a new wave of legislation against interracial marriage, but this took place primarily in western states that entered the Union after the Civil War. The major innovation of the West during this period was to extend its ban to include the growing number of Asians in the region. In the North, most states continued to rely on customary rather than legal restraints to enforce the color line in matrimony. Four northern states even abolished the prohibition: Rhode Island (1881), Maine (1883), Michigan (1883), and Ohio (1887). By the end of the nineteenth century at least twenty-six states, mainly in the South and West, had laws forbidding interracial marriage.[66]

In the South, the revitalized effort during the late nineteenth century to prevent interracial marriage and cohabitation manifested itself not only in a new round of prohibitory legislation but also in the rigorous treatment that criminal prosecutions under this legislation received in the high courts. Those who sought to escape miscegenation convictions in the state supreme courts had little success. Indictments of individuals who intermarried made up 72 percent of the appellate cases involving miscegenation prosecutions between 1865 and 1899, and 24 percent concerned indictments of persons who violated statutes punishing interracial fornication or cohabitation.[67] The gender of the white and black partners made little difference in the rates of reversal, and southern appellate courts affirmed over two-thirds of the convictions.[68]

Defendants found guilty of violating the miscegenation statutes petitioned the appellate courts on a variety of technical grounds, including alleged flaws in the indictment process, insufficient or inadmissible evidence, improper instructions to the jury, and other procedural irregularities.[69] In the few reversals that did occur, the evidence regarding the racial identity of one or both of the parties was frequently in dispute.[70]

Although successful in the sense that they received a new trial, defendants in these appeals did not challenge the validity of the miscegenation statutes. Far more threatening were those cases that raised questions about the constitutionality of the bans on interracial marriage and sexual relations. In their responses to these challenges, southern judges usually expressed an unremitting opposition to liaisons between blacks and whites. "The laws of civilization demand that the races be kept apart in this country," said the Tennessee Supreme Court in 1871. "The progress of either does not depend upon an admixture of blood."[71]

Given the support for such views among southern jurists after the Civil War, it is not surprising that the judiciary was nearly unanimous in its endorsement of legal sanctions against miscegenation. As members of the North Carolina bench proclaimed in 1869, "Late events, and the emancipation of the slaves, have made no alteration in our policy, or in the sentiments of our people." According to the court, Reconstruction measures were "not intended to enforce social equality, but only civil and political rights. This is plain from their very terms; but if the terms were doubtful, the policy of prohibiting the intermarriage of the two races is so well established, and the wishes of both races so well known, that we should not hesitate to declare the policy paramount to any doubtful construction."[72]

Nonetheless, the expanded legal personality of African Americans brought about by civil rights legislation and constitutional amendments during Reconstruction compelled the courts to rethink the basis for the bans on miscegenation. Antebellum policies had been formulated when most blacks lived in the shadow of slavery and thus had few legal rights. The new political and civil rights of the freedpeople seriously undermined the old legal foundation, and in response, judges devised a more elaborate framework to uphold the color line in domestic affairs. The aim of this revised defense was to narrow the scope of black citizenship and resist the principle of equal rights. In doing so, southern judges employed the institution of marriage to place significant limits on federal interference in their states.[73]

The impact of Reconstruction race policy on the thinking of southern jurists could be seen most clearly in Alabama, where the prohibition against miscegenation became a source of conflict among appellate judges.[74] In 1872 the Republican-dominated state court drew on the Civil Rights Act of 1866 and the Fourteenth Amendment to strike down the sanctions against interracial marriage, making Alabama the only state before 1948 whose judiciary invalidated a miscegenation law. As the justices pointed out in *Burns v. State*, the granting of citizenship to blacks included the right to make and enforce contracts. Viewing marriage as "civil contract," the court maintained that the "same right to make a contract as is enjoyed by white citizens means the right to make any contract which a white citizen may make. The law intended to destroy the distinctions of race and color in respect to the rights secured by it." The Alabama judges dismissed the contention that the ban on intermarriage was nondiscriminatory because it applied equally to both races. As they put it, the Civil Rights Act "did not aim to create an equality of the races in reference to each other. If so, laws prohibiting the races from suing each other, giving evidence for or against, or dealing with one another, would be permissible. The very excess to which such a construction would lead is conclusive against it." Thus no restraints could be imposed on the ability of any citizen to contract matrimony with a person of a different race.[75]

The invalidation of the Alabama miscegenation laws proved to be short-lived. Five years later, following the fall of Reconstruction, a new court made up of Redeemers overturned the Republican ruling. Contrary to the *Burns* decision, the judges in *Green v. State* asserted that the racial prohibition did not discriminate against African Americans because both races were subject to the same criminal punishment under the law. Insisting that the Civil Rights Act of 1866 did not intend to legalize interracial marriage, the justices observed that many of the congressmen voting for the measure lived in states with similar laws on mixed marriages.[76]

Most important, the Alabama court relied on an increasingly accepted view of marriage as a legal status, rather than simply a contract, to uphold the power of each state to determine marital capacity. Rejecting the emphasis of their Republican predecessors on the contractual nature of marriage, the new judges stressed the peculiar character of matrimony and the "undoubted right" of each state to supervise it. The main advantage of this approach, of course, was that it kept the enlarged contractual capacities of blacks from threatening the validity of racial curbs. Indeed, the justices contended that the state had an obligation to shore up these barriers because interracial unions endangered the social order and family stability. Viewing homes as "the nurseries of States," the Alabama court asked, "Who can estimate the evil of introducing into their most intimate relations, elements so heterogeneous that they must naturally cause discord, shame, disruption of family circles and estrangement of kindred?"[77]

Interracial households made up of slaveowners and their slaves had formed the cornerstone of the Old South, but the destruction of slavery necessitated a bolstering of boundaries between whites and blacks. The judges concluded that marriage was a social right rather than a political or civil right, and as such, was subject to state intervention. In an age that increasingly endorsed the principles of the wage contract, the ability to enter into the marriage contract thus became hedged in by regulations and prohibitions.[78]

Other southern courts, seeking to defend prohibitions against interracial marriage, also emphasized the noncontractual character of matrimony. The Texas high court mounted this defense of the ban on intermarriage in 1877 when it heard the appeal of the white Charles Frasher, who had been indicted for entering into wedlock with an African American woman. Frasher claimed that the Reconstruction amendments and legislation at the federal level made the state's miscegenation statute unconstitutional because it imposed a penalty upon a white person who violated its provisions, but prescribed no punishment for the black partner. The Texas Court of Appeals, however, held that marriage was "not a contract protected by the Constitution of the United States, or within the meaning of the Civil Rights Bill." Instead, matrimony was a "civil *status*, left solely by the Federal Constitution and the law to the discretion of the states, under their general power to regulate their domestic affairs." Since the states had the authority to prohibit interracial marriages, the Texas jurists continued, "it therefore follows, as the night follows the day, that this state can enforce such laws as she may deem best in regard to the intermarriage of whites and negroes in Texas, provided the punishment for its violation is not cruel or unusual."[79]

Accompanying the redefinition of marriage carved out in late nineteenth-century decisions like the *Frasher* case was an increased propensity to defend miscegenation statutes on the grounds that interracial unions posed serious social and biological risks to society, and thus states had a responsibility to prevent such unions. The racial prohibition, from this perspective, was part of a broader judicial trend in the post-war period to promote more rigorous tests of marital fitness that supposedly protected the well-being and safety of the public. Included in this development were tightened marital restrictions dealing with age, kin ties, and mental and physical health.[80]

In formulating the social and biological argument, southern courts used pseudo-scientific findings drawn from a growing body of racial thinking that was characterized by its pessimistic views of heredity. During the late nineteenth century, most white southerners became convinced that not only were blacks racially inferior, but their extinction was all but certain in the struggle for existence.[81] It followed from such contentions that miscegenation would lead to the deterioration of the white race and that the preservation of racial purity was a legitimate object for the exercise of legislative power. As the Georgia Supreme Court insisted in 1869, "The amalgamation of the races is not only unnatural, but is always productive of deplorable results."[82]

The costs allegedly incurred when racial purity was not preserved led southern jurists to support not only the ban on intermarriage, but also laws against interracial sexual relations. In *Pace and Cox v. State* (1881), the Alabama appellate court affirmed the legality of imposing stricter penalties on interracial fornication or adultery than on illicit intercourse between members of the same race, pointing out that the penalties were applied equally to both races. "The discrimination is not directed against the person of any particular color or race," said the court, "but against the *offense*, the nature of which is *determined by the opposite color of the cohabiting parties*."[83]

Southern appellate jurists, then, developed a twofold defense of miscegenation statutes. On the one hand, they claimed that marriage was more of a legal status than a mere contract, allowing them to forestall the classification of marriage as a political rather than a social right. On the other hand, the judges cited the social and physiological consequences of racial intermixture to support the legitimacy of sanctions against both interracial marriages and sexual relations. Such sanctions were necessary, in their opinion, to protect the health and welfare of society. Similar arguments found their way into appellate opinions outside the South, but they were deployed most extensively in courts below the Mason-Dixon line.[84]

Having secured the constitutionality of the miscegenation laws, southern jurists set out to evaluate the ramifications of these laws. Judges in the late nineteenth century agreed with their antebellum predecessors that statutes making interracial marriages absolutely void necessitated treating the offending parties as unmarried persons. Consequently, the courts upheld the practice of prosecuting individuals of different races who married under the fornication and cohabitation laws.[85]

A simple declaration that a marriage between a white person and an African American was "null and void," however, did not settle the status of children born to parents of different races. Indeed, the issue was much debated at the appellate level in the post-war South. North Carolina was unusual in that its miscegenation statute explicitly prevented the father from legitimizing the offspring of a mixed marriage, so the courts there had little difficulty denying such children the right to inherit. In fact, the North Carolina Supreme Court did just this in an 1892 case.[86]

The situation was somewhat different in Virginia. The law in this state declared that children of a void marriage were legitimate, but members of the appellate bench could not agree about whether this provision applied to the offspring of an interracial couple. Although a majority of the jurists concluded that it did not, Justice Richardson sharply dissented, asserting that "the dominant white race has not yet struck, nor will it likely ever strike at the natural legal rights of unoffending children through the sins of their parents." "The idea of amalgamation is repugnant to the white race," Richardson observed, but this did not mean that "the blight and curse of bastardy" should be inflicted on those who were the product of intermixture.[87] Overall, as Mary Frances Berry shows, children of interracial relationships won at least twenty cases involving inheritance disputes in southern state supreme courts between 1868 and 1900, while it appears that they lost eight contests.[88]

Another thorny issue involved couples who contracted matrimony in a state where the marriage was not banned and later entered another state where it was. Mississippi, Texas, and Virginia had laws on the books after the Civil War that expressly condemned any effort to evade the prohibition against miscegenation by marrying out of the state and then returning to it.[89] Although statutes in the other southern states made no direct reference to this problem, post-war judges clearly agreed with the antebellum position that when an interracial couple left the state in which they resided solely for the purpose of dodging its ban on intermarriage and later returned to their domicile, the marriage was void.[90]

The application of rules regarding the conflict of laws became more complex when parties dwelling in a state whose laws allowed intermarriage later moved to another state that punished the practice. The record of southern jurists during the late nineteenth century on whether such marriages were valid is murky. In *State v. Bell* (1872), the Tennessee Supreme Court decided to nullify a marriage between a white man and a black woman who had contracted matrimony in Mississippi when interracial unions had been permitted there. According to the court, "Each State is sovereign, a government within, of, and for itself, with the inherent and reserve right to declare and maintain its own political economy for the good of its citizens, and cannot be subjected to the recognition of a fact or act contravening its public policy and against good morals, as lawful, because it was made or existed in a State having no prohibition against it or even permitting it."[91]

Not all southern jurists agreed with the emphasis of the Tennessee judiciary on state sovereignty. Although members of the North Carolina bench also denounced miscegenation as "immoral and opposed to public policy," they acknowledged the validity of unions involving interracial couples who moved to the state from other jurisdictions that allowed such marriages. In *State v. Ross* (1877), the appellate judges affirmed the legality of a marriage between a white woman and a black man that had been celebrated in South Carolina when interracial unions were not forbidden. Noting that the husband and wife had both established residence in South Carolina before entering into wedlock, the jurists concluded that the marriage "must be regarded as subsisting after their immigration here."[92]

Such findings affected only a small minority of interracial couples and did not in any way indicate support on the part of the North Carolina Supreme Court for the practice of intermarriage. Like their colleagues elsewhere in the South, North Carolina judges had no doubts that the state could prohibit interracial marriages within its own boundaries, and that residents could not elude this prohibition by marrying in another state and then returning to their domicile. Whatever minor disagreements existed over the consequences of miscegenation statutes, the southern judiciary in the late nineteenth century shared an unwavering commitment to the preservation of racial distinctions in matters involving marriage or sexual contact.

The changing arguments in support of the bans on miscegenation revealed a growing inclination among southern judges to enlarge state supervision of the household. Before the Civil War, although southern jurists firmly backed the legal effort to prevent miscegenation, they perceived the racial curbs as merely reinforcing the social controls provided by slavery. Following the defeat of the Confederacy, a rising concern about the impact of emancipation on private life and public order gave added significance to the racial restrictions and led to the forging of a sturdy new legal rationale for this prohibitory legislation. The expanded judicial justification for state intervention was so effective that the sanctions against interracial marriage and sexual relations remained on the statute books in the South until the late twentieth century.[93] The new reliance on the state to define and protect the public welfare, which fueled the revitalization of the racial prohibitions, eventually resulted in the legal transformation of the southern household.[94] In this way, persistent beliefs about race in the post-war South encountered changed circumstances and then adjusted to them through the mechanism of legal innovation, preserving the core of the beliefs—a commitment to white supremacy and racial purity—in the process.

APPENDIX: MISCEGENATION CASES IN THE
POST-WAR SOUTH

The following tables summarize information garnered from southern appellate court opinions dealing with miscegenation between 1865 and 1899. They have been constructed on the basis of all the relevant cases that could be discovered in the published appellate records. As such, they provide a helpful if somewhat crude guide to the contours of appellate behavior in the southern state courts, and the types of prosecutions that reached the high courts in this area of the law. They should not, however, be employed to make any generalizations about the workings

TABLE 6.1
*Prosecutions Involving Miscegenation before Southern High
Courts, 1865–1899*

Type of case	Number of cases	Percentage
Intermarriage	18	72
Interracial fornication	6	24
Performing illegal marriage	1	4
Total	25	100

NOTE: In the course of my research I uncovered six other appellate cases during the post-war period in which individuals were indicted for violating laws against illicit intercourse or cohabitation when the other party was of a different race. These cases are not included in table 6.1 because they did not involve prosecutions under miscegenation statutes. See *Richardson v. State,* 34 Tex. 142 (1871); *Kinard v. State,* 57 Miss. 132 (1879); *Scott v. Commonwealth,* 77 Va. 344 (1883); *Mulling v. State,* 74 Ga. 10 (1884); *Stewart v. State,* 64 Miss. 626 (1887); and *State v. Chancy,* 110 N.C. 507 (1892). Mary Frances Berry also has discovered two late nineteenth-century appeals from convictions for cohabitation, rather than miscegenation, that involved interracial couples: *Sullivan v. State,* 32 Ark. 187 (1877); and *Smelser v. State,* 31 Tex. 96 (1868). See Berry, "Judging Morality: Sexual Behavior and Legal Consequences in the Late Nineteenth-Century South," *Journal of American History* 78 (1991): 839 n. 14.

TABLE 6.2
*Appeals from Miscegenation Convictions before Southern High
Courts, 1865–1899*

Type of miscegenation	Number of cases	Reversals	Rate of reversal
White male/black female	7	2	29%
Black male/white female	13	4	31%
Total	20	6	30%

NOTE: One other appeal from conviction, *Burns v. State*, 48 Ala. 195 (1872), dealt with the indictment of a justice of the peace for performing an interracial marriage. Since the appellate opinion did not provide any information about the parties who contracted marriage, beyond the obvious fact that they were not of the same race, it is not included in table 6.2.

of the southern legal system as a whole because appellate cases are, by their very nature, inherently unrepresentative.

NOTES

1. The South is defined here as the eleven Confederate states, except in the discussion of colonial developments, which includes Maryland. On miscegenation law and the ideological construction of race, see Eva Saks, "Representing Miscegenation Law," *Raritan* 8 (1988): 39–69; and Peggy Pascoe, "Miscegenation Law, Court Cases, and Ideologies of 'Race' in Twentieth-Century America," in this volume.

2. See, for example, Diane Miller Sommerville, "Rape, Race, and Castration in Slave Law in the Colonial and Early South," in *The Devil's Lane: Sex and Race in the Early South*, ed. Catherine Clinton and Michele Gillespie (New York: Oxford University Press, 1997); Peter W. Bardaglio, "Rape and the Law in the Old South: 'Calculated to excite indignation in every heart,'" *Journal of Southern History* 60 (1994): 749–72. Somerville criticizes what she calls the "myopic reliance on southern rape statutes to gauge white sexual anxiety about blacks" (77). Given that my analysis of southern white attitudes toward interracial sexual relations, including rape, is based on several hundred appellate court cases as well as statutes, "myopic reliance" seems an unfair characterization of this work.

3. For a more detailed discussion of the advantages and disadvantages of state statutes and court decisions as historical sources, see Peter W. Bardaglio, *Reconstructing the Household: Families, Sex, and the Law in the Nineteenth-Century South* (Chapel Hill: University of North Carolina Press, 1995), xvi–xviii.

4. This essay adopts Martha Hodes's distinction between toleration and tolerance to describe white attitudes toward interracial sex. The former, she argues, "suggests a measure of forbearance for that which is not approved," while the latter "implies a liberal spirit toward those of a different mind." *White Women, Black Men: Illicit Sex in the Nineteenth-Century South* (New Haven: Yale University Press, 1997), 3.

5. John G. Mencke, *Mulattoes and Race Mixture: American Attitudes and Images, 1865–1918* (Ann Arbor: University of Michigan Press, 1979), 7–8; Winthrop D. Jordan, *White over Black: American Attitudes toward the Negro, 1550–1812* (Baltimore: Penguin Books, 1969), 136–38, 167–68, 178, 475; George M. Fredrickson, *White Supremacy: A Comparative Study in American and South African History* (New York: Oxford University Press, 1981), 95–99; Joel Williamson, *New People: Miscegenation and Mulattoes in the United States* (New York: Free Press, 1980), 63, 71, 73–75.

6. Bertram Wyatt-Brown, *Southern Honor: Ethics and Behavior in the Old South* (New York: Oxford University Press, 1982), 296–97, 307–08; Victoria E. Bynum, *Unruly Women: The Politics of Social and Sexual Control in the Old South* (Chapel Hill: University of North Carolina Press, 1992), 36–37, 96–98; Catherine Clinton, *The Plantation Mistress: Woman's World in the Old South* (New York: Pantheon, 1982), 204–05, 209–10; A. Leon Higginbotham, Jr., *In the Matter of Color: Race and the American Legal Process; The Colonial Period* (New York: Oxford University Press, 1978), 40–41; and Hodes, *White Women, Black Men*, chaps. 2–4.

7. On regional variations in southern attitudes toward miscegenation, see Williamson, *New People*, 14–24, 33–42; Jordan, *White over Black*, 144–50; and Gary B. Mills, "Miscegenation and the Free Negro in Antebellum 'Anglo' Alabama: A Reexamination of Southern Race Relations," *Journal of American History* 68 (1981): 16–34.

8. Winthrop D. Jordan, "Modern Tensions and the Origins of American Slavery," *Journal of Southern History* 28 (1962): 27–29; Edmund S. Morgan, *American Slavery, American Freedom: The Ordeal of Colonial Virginia* (New York: W. W. Norton, 1975), 333–34; Karen A. Getman, "Sexual Control in the Slaveholding South: The Implementation and Maintenance of a Racial Caste System," *Harvard Women's Law Journal* 7 (1984): 121–24; Williamson, *New People*, 7–8.

9. Bardaglio, *Reconstructing the Household*, chaps. 1–3.

10. James Hugo Johnston, *Race Relations in Virginia and Miscegenation in the South, 1776–1860* (Amherst: University of Massachusetts Press, 1970), 165–90; Julia Cherry Spruill, *Women's Life and Work in the Southern Colonies* (New York: W. W. Norton, 1972), 176–77; Jordan, *White over Black*, 138–39; Morgan, *American Slavery*, 334; Peter H. Wood, *Black Majority: Negroes in Colonial South Carolina from 1670 through the Stono Rebellion* (New York: W. W. Norton, 1974), 98–99, 233–36; T. H. Breen and Stephen Innes, *"Myne Owne Ground": Race and Freedom on Virginia's Eastern Shore, 1640–1676* (New York: Oxford University Press, 1980), 107.

11. Harvey M. Applebaum, "Miscegenation Statutes: A Constitutional and Social Problem," *Georgetown Law Journal* 53 (1964): 49–50; Michael Grossberg, "Guarding the Altar: Physiological Restrictions and the Rise of State Intervention in Matrimony," *American Journal of Legal History* 26 (1982): 200.

12. For more detailed discussions of miscegenation law in colonial Maryland and Virginia, see Fredrickson, *White Supremacy*, 101–07; Higginbotham, *In the Matter of Color*, 40–47; Getman, "Sexual Control," 125–31; A. Leon Higginbotham, Jr., and Barbara K. Kopytoff, "Racial Purity and Interracial Sex in the Law of Colonial and Antebellum Virginia," *Georgetown Law Journal* 77 (1989): 1989–2008; Kathleen M. Brown, *Good Wives, Nasty Wenches, and Anxious Patriarchs: Gender, Race, and Power in Colonial Virginia* (Chapel Hill: University of North Carolina Press, 1996), chap. 6; and Paul Finkelman, "Crimes of Love, Misdemeanors of Passion: The Regulation of Race and Sex in the Colonial South," in *Devil's Lane*, ed. Clinton and Gillespie.

13. The quotations from the act of 1664, as well as those from the acts of 1681 and 1692 in the following paragraphs, can be found in Jonathan L. Alpert, "The Origin of Slavery in the United States—The Maryland Precedent," *American Journal of Legal History* 14 (1970): 195, 209, 211.

14. The new act stipulated that any master who encouraged or permitted a white woman servant to marry a black slave would be fined, and the woman and her children immediately discharged from their indentures. In addition, any minister who performed such marriages was fined. See Getman, "Sexual Control," 129; and Alpert, "Origin of Slavery," 209–10.

15. The act of 1692 also revised the punishments for interracial marriage: any white woman who married a black man was subject to seven years of servitude; if she was a servant and the master had instigated the marriage, the woman was to be released from servitude. If the marriage took place "without the Connivance or procurement of her master," the female servant's indenture was increased by seven years. Alpert, 210.

16. Fredrickson, *White Supremacy*, 106; Barbara J. Fields, "Ideology and Race in American History," in *Region, Race, and Reconstruction: Essays in Honor of C. Vann Woodward*, ed. J. Morgan Kousser and James M. McPherson (New York: Oxford University Press, 1982), 149.

17. Virginia, *Statutes at Large* (Hening 1809–23), 2:170 (act of 1662); Finkelman, "Crimes of Love," 127–29; Brown, *Good Wives, Nasty Wenches*, 132–35.

18. Under the law of 1691, a free white woman who had an illegitimate child by a black or mulatto father was fined. If she could not pay, she was to be sold for a five-year term. The offspring, though free because its mother was free, was bound out until the age of thirty. If the woman was a servant, she was to serve her master an additional two years, as the law provided for servants having bastards, and then she was to be sold for another five years. Virginia, *Statutes at Large* (Hening 1809–23), 3:86–87 (act of 1691). Emphasis added in quotation.

19. North Carolina's act of 1715 banned intermarriage and punished white women who bore mulatto children. Georgia pronounced all interracial marriages "absolutely null and void" in 1750, when blacks were first admitted to the colony. While South Carolina did not act on the issue of intermarriage, it passed a statute in 1717 that exacted serious penalties for interracial fornication that ended in pregnancy. See North Carolina, *State Records* (Clark 1886–1907), 23:65 (act of 1715); Georgia, *Colonial Records* (Candler 1904–16), 1:59 (act of 1750); and South Carolina, *Statutes at Large* (Cooper and McCord 1836–41), 3:20 (act of 1717). Only North Carolina (and briefly Virginia) included Indians in its miscegenation legislation. See David D. Smits, " 'Abominable Mixture': Toward the Repudiation of Anglo-Indian Intermarriage in Seventeenth-Century Virginia," *Virginia Magazine of History and Biography* 95 (1987): 157–92.

20. Higginbotham, *In the Matter of Color*, 81, 285–86; Jordan, *White over Black*, 139; Fredrickson, *White Supremacy*, 101.

21. Kirsten Fischer, " 'False, Feigned, and Scandalous Words': Sexual Slander and Racial Ideology among Whites in Colonial North Carolina," in *Devil's Lane*, ed. Clinton and Gillespie; Brown, *Good Wives, Nasty Wenches*, 207–11.

22. Getman, "Sexual Control," 126; Higginbotham, *In the Matter of Color*, 44; Clinton, *Plantation Mistress*, 203; Jordan, *White over Black*, 141.

23. Morgan, *American Slavery*, 336; Joel Williamson, *The Crucible of Race: Black-White Relations in the American South since Emancipation* (New York: Oxford University Press, 1984), 32; Adele Logan Alexander, *Ambiguous Lives: Free Women of Color in Rural Georgia, 1789–1879* (Fayetteville: University of Arkansas Press, 1991), 36.

24. Ira Berlin, *Slaves without Masters: The Free Negro in the Antebellum South* (New York: Random House, 1974), 86–89; Eugene D. Genovese, *Roll, Jordan, Roll: The World the Slaves Made* (New York: Random House, 1974), 50–58; Williamson, *New People*, 13–14.

25. Genovese, *Roll, Jordan, Roll*, 422; Clinton, *Plantation Mistress*, 210; Bynum, *Unruly Women*, 41–45, 92–93; Hodes, *White Women, Black Men*, chaps. 3–4.

26. Kenneth Stampp, *The Peculiar Institution: Slavery in the Ante-Bellum South* (New York: Random House, 1956), 353–56; Genovese, *Roll, Jordan, Roll*, 418–19; Clinton, *Plantation Mistress*, 213–14; Alexander, *Ambiguous Lives*, 66.

27. John W. Blassingame, *The Slave Community: Plantation Life in the Antebellum South* (New York: Oxford University Press, 1972), 82–85; Stampp, *Peculiar Institution*, 359–61; Genovese, *Roll, Jordan, Roll*, 422, 428; Jacqueline Jones, *Labor of Love, Labor of Sorrow: Black Women, Work, and the Family from Slavery to the Present* (New York: Basic Books, 1985), 28, 37–38; Orville Vernon Burton, *In My Father's House Are Many Mansions: Family and Community in Edgefield, South Carolina* (Chapel Hill: University of North Carolina Press, 1985), 185–89; Melton A. McLaurin, *Celia, A Slave* (Athens: University of Georgia Press, 1991).

28. Catherine Clinton, "Caught in the Web of the Big House: Women and Slavery," in *The Web of Southern Social Relations: Women, Family, and Education*, ed. Walter J. Fraser, R. Frank Saunders, Jr., and Jon L. Wakelyn (Athens: University of Georgia Press, 1985), 28–32; Elizabeth Fox-Genovese, *Within the Plantation Household: Black and White Women of the Old South* (Chapel Hill: University of North Carolina Press, 1988), 325–26.

29. See, for example, Drew Gilpin Faust, *A Design for Mastery: James Henry Hammond and the Old South* (Baton Rouge: Louisiana State University Press, 1982), 314–20.

30. Perhaps one of the most remarkable instances of a long-term interracial relationship has been documented in Alexander, *Ambiguous Lives*, 80–87.

31. Stampp, *Peculiar Institution*, 357–59; Clinton, *Plantation Mistress*, 214–17; Genovese, *Roll, Jordan, Roll*, 15–16; Guion Griffis Johnson, *Ante-Bellum North Carolina: A Social History* (Chapel Hill: University of North Carolina Press, 1937), 591–92; Johnston, *Race Relations*, 17–36; Judith K. Schafer, " 'Open and Notorious Concubinage': The Emancipation of Slave Mistresses by Will and the Supreme Court in Antebellum Louisiana," *Louisiana History* 28 (1987): 115–82.

32. Thomas Virgil Peterson, *Ham and Japeth: The Mythic World of Whites in the Antebellum South* (Metuchen, N.J.: Scarecrow Press, 1978), 52–53, 76–77; Michael P. Johnson, "Planters and Patriarchy: Charleston, 1800–1860," *Journal of Southern History* 46 (1980): 70–71.

33. Ann Firor Scott, *The Southern Lady: From Pedestal to Politics, 1830–1930* (Chicago: University of Chicago Press, 1970), 4–21; Clinton, *Plantation Mistress*, 87–89, 93–94; Fox-Genovese, *Within the Plantation Household*, 196–97, 203; Hodes, *White Women, Black Men*, 4–5.

34. Mencke, *Mulattoes and Race Mixture*, 7–8; Berlin, *Slaves without Masters*, 97–99; Jordan, *White over Black*, 168–70; Robert Brent Toplin, "Between Black and White: Attitudes toward Southern Mulattoes, 1830–1861," *Journal of Southern History* 45 (1979): 185–200.

35. Virginia, *Statutes at Large* (Hening 1809–23), 12:184 (act of 1785); Berlin, *Slaves without Masters*, 161–62 n. 39. In North Carolina an individual with one African ancestor in the previous two generations was a mulatto, except for marriage to a white person, when the line was drawn at three generations.

36. On the importance of placing ideas about race in their historical context and not viewing race simply as a biological fact, see Fields, "Ideology and Race"; and Thomas C. Holt, "Marking: Race, Race-Making, and the Writing of History," *American Historical Review* 100 (1995): 1–20.

37. The most significant illustration of this overall commitment to free choice in marital matters was the broad acceptance of common-law marriage, in which unions were consummated without procedural formalities or state involvement of any kind. Grossberg, "Guarding the Altar," 200–201; Maxwell H. Bloomfield, *American Lawyers in a Changing Society, 1776–1876* (Cambridge: Harvard University Press, 1976), 104–09.

38. Following the American Revolution, the three states that had enacted colonial legislation prohibiting miscegenation—Virginia, North Carolina, and Georgia—amended their laws in several important respects. For the new penalties, see Virginia, *Statutes at Large* (Shepherd 1835–36), vol. 1, chap. 42, sec. 17, pp. 134–35; Virginia, *Code* (Patton and Robinson 1849), chap. 196, sec. 8, p. 740 and chap. 109, sec. 1, p. 471; North Carolina, *Revised Statutes* (Nash, Iredell, and Battle 1837), vol. 1, chap. 71, sec. 5, pp. 386–87; North Carolina, *Revised Code* (Moore and Biggs 1855), chap. 68, sec. 7, p. 391; and Georgia, *Code* (Clark, Cobb, and Irwin 1861), sec. 1664, p. 333; sec. 4445, p. 866; and sec. 4419, p. 860.

New legislation also appeared elsewhere in the South between the Revolution and the Civil War. For antebellum statutes prohibiting miscegenation, see Arkansas, *Revised Statutes* (Ball and Roane 1838), chap. 94, secs. 4 and 9, p. 536; Florida, *Compilation of the Public Acts* (Duval 1839), 88–89, 120; Louisiana, *Civil Code* (Upton and Jennings, 1838), title 4, chap. 2, art. 95, p. 17; Tennessee, *Compilation of the Statutes* (Caruthers and Nicholson 1836), chap. 19, secs. 1 and 3, p. 451; Texas, *Digest of the Laws* (Dallam 1845), 168; and Texas, *Digest of the General Statute Laws* (Oldham and White 1859), art. 386, p. 503; art. 395a, p. 504; and art. 392, p. 504.

39. The five states were Florida, North Carolina, Tennessee, Alabama, and Virginia. Florida, North Carolina, and Tennessee declared issuing a license or performing a ceremony that involved parties of different races a crime. See Florida, *Compilation* (1839), 89; North Carolina, *Revised Statutes* (1837), vol. 1, chap. 34, sec. 72, pp. 108–09; and Tennessee, *Code* (Meigs and Cooper 1858), secs. 4926–27, p. 880. Alabama and Virginia punished only the person who married an interracial couple, not the clerk who granted the license. See Alabama, *Code* (Ormand, Bagby, and Goldthwaite 1852), sec. 1956, p. 377; and Virginia, *Code* (1849), chap. 196, sec. 9, p. 740.

40. Between independence and the Civil War, several legislatures in the North and Midwest also implemented bans on intermarriage. A few northeastern states, however, turned back efforts to pass prohibitory legislation. Furthermore, Massachusetts in 1840, Iowa in 1851, and Kansas in 1857 repealed their statutes. See Applebaum, "Miscegenation Statutes," 50 n. 10; Jordan, *White over Black*, 471–72; and Michael Grossberg, "Law and the Family in Nineteenth Century America" (Ph.D. diss., Brandeis University, 1979), 141.

41. Berlin, *Slaves without Masters*, 163–65; Mencke, *Mulattoes and Race Mixture*, 11–13. On South Carolina, see Michael P. Johnson and James L. Roark, *Black Masters: A Free Family of Color in the Old South* (New York: W. W. Norton, 1984).

42. For examples, see *Johnson v. Boon*, 1 Spears 268 (S.C. 1843); and *State v. Hayes*, 1 Bailey 275 (S.C. 1829).

43. The only law in Mississippi that touched on this question before the Civil War was an 1822 act authorizing designated officials to "solemnize the rites of matrimony between any free white persons" who presented a valid license. The act implied that interracial marriages were illegal, but no explicit prohibition existed against blacks contracting matrimony with whites. Mississippi, *Revised Code* (Poindexter 1824), chap. 102, sec. 1, pp. 445–46.

In Alabama, an 1805 statute permitted unions "between any free persons," leaving open the possibility of marriage between whites and free blacks. This loophole was not closed until the 1852 code, which stated that "marriages may be solemnized between free white persons, or between free persons of color." The code also provided that any person who performed a marriage "when one of the parties is a negro and the other a white person" was guilty of a misdemeanor and subject to a minimum fine of a thousand dollars. Although Alabama law punished the individual who performed the ceremony, it did not pronounce interracial marriages null and void, and it established no penalty for those who intermarried. Alabama,

Digest (Toulmin 1823), 576; *Code* (1852), secs. 1946 and 1956, pp. 376-77. See also *Black v. Oliver*, 1 Ala. 449 (1840).

44. Williamson, *New People*, 2–3, 14–24; Berlin, *Slaves without Masters*, 196–99, 214–16, 343–80; Johnson and Roark, *Black Masters*, 160–68, 187–94, 236–48, 256–62. On Louisiana, see Virginia R. Domínguez, *White by Definition: Social Classification in Creole Louisiana* (New Brunswick: Rutgers University Press, 1986), esp. 23–26.

45. Marina Wikramanayake, *A World in Shadow: The Free Blacks in Ante-bellum South Carolina* (Columbia: University of South Carolina Press, 1973), 13, 176; Johnson and Roark, *Black Masters*, 53; Fredrickson, *White Supremacy*, 108.

46. See "Coloured Marriages," *Charleston Mercury*, Oct. 29, 1823, reprinted in *Carolina Law Journal* 1 (1830): 92–106 (quotation on p. 99).

47. *Bowers v. Newman*, 2 McMull. 472 (S.C. 1842), 481, 480.

48. Ibid. 486, 492. See also *Wells v. Thompson*, 13 Ala. 793 (1848), in which the Alabama Supreme Court upheld the validity of a marriage between a white man and a woman of "mixed white and Indian blood."

49. *Succession of Minvielle*, 15 La. An. 342 (1860), 342–43.

50. *State v. Melton*, 44 N.C. 49 (1852), 51. In this case, which involved a white woman and a man of Indian descent, the court found the defendants innocent of fornication because there was no clear proof that the husband fell within the statutory definition of an Indian. See also *State v. Fore*, 23 N.C. 378 (1841); *State v. Hooper*, 27 N.C. 201 (1844); and *State v. Brady*, 28 Tenn. 74 (1848). These three cases involved white women who married black men. Although the appellate judges found the white women guilty of illegal cohabitation, the Tennessee Supreme Court arrested judgment against the male defendant in *State v. Brady* on the grounds that blacks were not liable to indictment under the state's statute prohibiting intermarriage.

51. See, for example, *Succession of Minvielle*, 15 La. An. at 342.

52. In *Dupre v. Boulard*, 10 La. An. 411 (1855), the court denied the legality of an interracial marriage when the parties went to France to contract matrimony and then returned to Louisiana.

53. *Scroggins v. Scroggins*, 14 N.C. 535 (1832), 545, 546.

54. *Barden v. Barden*, 14 N.C. 548 (1832), 550. For other cases dealing with interracial fornication before the Civil War, see *Commonwealth v. Isaacs*, 5 Rand. 634 (Va. 1826); and *Commonwealth v. Jones*, 43 Va. 555 (1845). Both decisions involved indictments of white men for cohabiting with black women; in the first, the indictment was quashed on a technicality, and in the second, the conviction of the man was overturned because of procedural errors in the lower court trial. Apparently, southern judges saw no pressing need to override common-law traditions when interracial sex between white men and black women was involved.

55. On the growing importance of contract in postbellum law, see Bardaglio, *Reconstructing the Household*, chap. 5; and Amy Dru Stanley, "Conjugal Bonds and Wage Labor: Rights of Contract in the Age of Emancipation," *Journal of American History* 75 (1988): 471–500.

56. James L. Roark, *Masters without Slaves: Southern Planters in the Civil War and Reconstruction* (New York: W. W. Norton, 1977), 94–108; Leon F. Litwack, *Been in the Storm So Long: The Aftermath of Slavery* (New York: Random House, 1979), 265; Laura F. Edwards, "The Disappearance of Susan Daniel and Henderson Cooper: Gender and Narratives of Political Conflict in the Reconstruction-Era U.S. South," in this volume; Hodes, *White Women, Black Men*, chap. 7.

57. Forrest G. Wood, *Black Scare: The Racist Response to Emancipation and Recon-*

struction (Berkeley: University of California Press, 1968), 53–79, 148–52; George M. Fredrickson, *The Black Image in the White Mind: The Debate on Afro-American Character and Destiny, 1817–1914* (New York: Harper and Row, 1971), 171–93; Jean H. Baker, *Affairs of Party: The Political Culture of Northern Democrats in the Mid-Nineteenth Century* (Ithaca: Cornell University Press, 1983), 252–53.

58. Michael Grossberg, *Governing the Hearth: Law and the Family in Nineteenth-Century America* (Chapel Hill: University of North Carolina Press, 1985), 136; Alfred Avins, "Anti-Miscegenation Laws and the Fourteenth Amendment: The Original Intent," *Virginia Law Review* 52 (1966): 1227; Litwack, *Been in the Storm So Long*, 267.

59. Williamson, *New People*, 91–92.

60. Alaska, *Revised Code* (Walker 1867), 38 (Constitution of 1865, art. 4, sec. 31); Mississippi, *Session Laws* (1865), chap. 4, sec. 3, p. 82. See also Vernon L. Wharton, *The Negro in Mississippi, 1865–1890* (Chapel Hill: University of North Carolina Press, 1947), 227.

61. Mary Frances Berry, "Judging Morality: Sexual Behavior and Legal Consequences in the Late Nineteenth-Century South," *Journal of American History* 78 (1991): 839.

62. Arkansas, Florida, Louisiana, Mississippi, and South Carolina dispensed with the ban for varying periods of time during Reconstruction, but all five states reintroduced stringent prohibitions by the end of the nineteenth century. See Arkansas, *Digest of the Statutes* (Gantt 1874), in which the 1838 statute declaring interracial marriages illegal and void does not appear; and *Digest of the Statutes* (Mansfield 1884), sec. 4593, p. 911, which reaffirms the 1838 act. Florida, *Digest of Statute Law* (Bush 1872), 578 n. q notes that the "various provisions of the statutes in relation to marriages between white and colored persons are omitted out of deference to the opinion of those who think that they are opposed to our Constitution and to the legislation of Congress." New prohibitory legislation appeared, however, in *Digest of Laws* (McClellan 1881), chap. 59, sec. 13, p. 376. In addition, Louisiana was without a statutory ban on interracial marriages from 1870 to 1894, and Mississippi lacked such a ban between 1870 and 1880. For Louisiana, see Act 54 of 1894 in *Revised Civil Code* (Merrick 1900), title 4, chap. 2, art. 94, p. 23; and Harriet Spiller Dagget, "The Legal Aspect of Amalgamation in Louisiana," in *Legal Essays on Family Law* (Baton Rouge: Louisiana State University Press, 1935), 5. For Mississippi, see *Revised Code* (Campbell 1880), chap. 1147, p. 335; and Wharton, *Negro in Mississippi*, 228–29. Radical Republicans in South Carolina repealed the prohibition against intermarriage after they assumed power in 1868, but Redeemers enacted new legal sanctions in 1879. See Act of 1879 in South Carolina, *Revised Statutes* (Breazeale 1894), vol. 1, chap. 2163, p. 753; Joel Williamson, *After Slavery: The Negro in South Carolina during Reconstruction, 1861–1877* (New York: W. W. Norton, 1975), 297; and George B. Tindall, *South Carolina Negroes, 1877–1900* (Columbia: University of South Carolina Press, 1952), 296–97.

63. "The Negro Problem," *De Bow's Review* 38 (1868): 253.

64. The six states besides Alabama that prohibited intermarriage by constitutional provision were Florida, Georgia, Mississippi, North Carolina, South Carolina, and Tennessee. See Florida, *Revised Statutes* (Blount, Cooper, and Massey 1892), 69 (Constitution of 1885, art. 16, sec. 24); Georgia *Code* (Clark, Cobb, and Irwin 1867), 983 (Constitution of 1865, art. 5, sec. 1, par. 9); Mississippi, *Code* (Whitfield, Catchings, and Hardy 1906), 106 (Constitution of 1890, sec. 263); North Carolina, *Code* (Dortch, Manning, Henderson 1883), 2: 723 (Constitution of 1868, art. 14, sec. 8, 1875 provision); South Carolina, *Code* (Bethea 1912), 2:613–14 (Constitution of 1895, art. 3, sec. 33); and Tennessee, *Compilation of the Statute Laws* (Thompson and Steger 1873), 1:118 (Constitution of 1870, art. 11, sec. 14).

65. Consult the following for details of this late nineteenth-century legislation in the South: Alabama, *Revised Code* (1867), secs. 3602–3603, p. 690. Arkansas, *Digest* (1884), sec. 4593, p. 911; sec. 4601, p. 912; sec. 4617, p. 914. Florida, *Digest* (1881), chap. 59, sec. 13, p. 376; chap. 149, secs. 8–11, p. 753. Georgia, *Code* (1867), sec. 1707, p. 344; sec. 4483, p. 881; sec. 4487, p. 882. Louisiana, *Revised Civil Code* (1900), title 4, chap. 2, art. 94, p. 23. Mississippi, *Revised Code* (1880), sec. 1147, p. 335. North Carolina, *Code* (1883), vol. 1, secs. 1084–1085, pp. 437–38; sec. 1284, pp. 513–14. South Carolina, *Revised Statutes* (1894), vol. 1, sec. 2163, p. 753. Tennessee, *Compilation* (1873), vol. 1, secs. 2437a–2437b, p. 1097; secs. 2445–2447, p. 1098. Texas, *Digest of the Laws* (Paschal 1866), art. 2016, p. 429; art. 2026, p. 430; art. 4670, p. 783. Virginia, *Code* (Munford 1873), chap. 192, secs. 8–9, p. 1208.

66. Grossberg, "Law and the Family," 464–65; Fredrickson, *White Supremacy*, 130; Applebaum, "Miscegenation Statutes," 50 n. 10. In addition, Applebaum notes that Washington in 1867 and New Mexico in 1886 repealed their statutes prohibiting interracial marriages.

67. See table 6.1 in the appendix. Only one of the appellate cases pertained to the prosecution of an official who solemnized a mixed marriage. See *Burns v. State*, 48 Ala. 195 (1872). Nearly all these appeals reached the state supreme courts as the result of convictions handed down at the lower level. Two cases dealt with motions to quash indictments: *Robeson v. State*, 50 Tenn. 266 (1871); and *State v. Bell*, 66 Tenn. 9 (1872). Besides these two cases, *State v. Reinhardt*, 63 N.C. 547 (1869) and *State v. Ross*, 76 N.C. 242 (1877) concerned petitions by the state to overturn acquittals.

68. See table 6.2 in the appendix.

69. See, for example, *Linton v. State*, 88 Ala. 216 (1889); *Bell v. State*, 33 Tex. Cr. R. 163 (1894); and *Frasher v. State*, 3 Tex. App. 263 (1877).

70. Serious problems also existed with the evidence regarding the racial identities of the parties in *Moore v. State*, 7 Tex. App. 608 (1880); *McPherson v. Commonwealth*, 69 Va. 939 (1877); *Jones v. Commonwealth*, 79 Va. 213 (1884); and *Jones v. Commonwealth*, 80 Va. 538 (1885). For other reversals, see *Ellis v. State*, 42 Ala. 525 (1868) and *Frasher v. State*, 3 Tex. App. at 263.

71. *Lonas v. State*, 50 Tenn. 287 (1871), 310–11.

72. *State v. Hairston*, 63 N.C. 451 (1869), 452, 453. The North Carolina court upheld this decision in *State v. Reinhardt*, 63 N.C. at 547.

73. Grossberg, "Law and the Family," 448, 455–56; Morton Keller, *Affairs of State: Public Life in Late Nineteenth-Century America* (Cambridge: Harvard University Press, 1977), 149–50, 451–52.

74. Peter Wallenstein, "Race, Marriage, and the Law of Freedom: Alabama and Virginia, 1860s–1960s," *Chicago-Kent Law Review* 70 (1994): 374–87 provides a detailed examination of changes in Alabama's miscegenation policies during the post-war period.

75. *Burns v. State*, 48 Ala. at 197. The Alabama Supreme Court had outlawed interracial marriages before the Republicans took over. See *Ellis v. State*, 42 Ala. at 525. In *Ford v. State*, 53 Ala. 150 (1875), the court upheld the legality of the state's statute punishing whites and blacks who cohabited, arguing that the *Burns* decision covered only the unconstitutionality of laws prohibiting interracial marriage.

76. *Green v. State*, 58 Ala. 190 (1877), 192.

77. Ibid., 195, 194.

78. Stanley, "Conjugal Bonds and Wage Labor," 477, 480–81.

79. *Frasher v. State*, 3 Tex. App. at 276, 277. Despite this harsh and far-reaching opinion, Frasher escaped a four-year term in the penitentiary (at least temporarily) because the appel-

late judges found that the lower court had erred in its instructions to the jury, making a new trial necessary. The constitutionality of the state's miscegenation statute was affirmed in *Francois v. State*, 9 Tex. App. 144 (1880). The legislature, however, in 1879 extended criminal penalties to offenders of both races. See Texas, *Revised Penal Code* (1879), art. 326, p. 44. Other cases advancing the position that marriage was more than a civil contract and thus subject to state regulation include *Lonas v. State*, 50 Tenn. at 287; and *Dodson v. State*, 61 Ark. 57 (1895). As Mary Frances Berry points out, however, in an 1876 bigamy case involving whites, the Alabama Supreme Court referred repeatedly to marriage as a contract. See Berry, "Judging Morality," 840; and *Beggs v. State*, 55 Ala. 108 (1876).

80. Michael Grossberg discusses the development of this trend in both northern and southern courts in "Guarding the Altar," 206–26. For a striking example of pseudoscientific thinking, see *Scott v. State*, 39 Ga. 321 (1869), discussed below. See also *Kinney v. Commonwealth*, 71 Va. 858 (1878), 869.

81. A more paternalistic strain of thinking viewed blacks as inferior but capable of uplifting themselves. On developments in late nineteenth-century thinking about race, consult Mencke, *Mulattoes and Race Mixture*, 99–123; Fredrickson, *Black Image in the White Mind*, 198–255; Williamson, *Crucible of Race*, 85–139; and Ronald T. Takaki, *Iron Cages: Race and Culture in Nineteenth-Century America* (New York: Alfred A. Knopf, 1979), 194–214.

82. *Scott v. State*, 39 Ga. at 323.

83. *Pace and Cox v. State*, 69 Ala. 231 (1881), 232. The penalty for conviction of interracial fornication or adultery was imprisonment for two to seven years, while those convicted of illicit intercourse with a person of the same race were subject upon the first offense to a minimum fine of one hundred dollars and no more than six months in jail. See Alabama, *Revised Code* (1867), sec. 3598, p. 689, and sec. 3602, p. 690. The U.S. Supreme Court upheld the constitutionality of the state's miscegenation statute in *Pace v. Alabama*, 106 U.S. 583 (1883).

84. For miscegenation cases before state supreme courts outside the South, see Applebaum, "Miscegenation Statutes," 56–62; Grossberg, "Law and the Family," 458–61; and Keller, *Affairs of State*, 150, 451–52. See also Cyrus E. Phillips IV, "Miscegenation: The Courts and the Constitution," *William and Mary Law Review* 8 (1966): 135–39; and George Schuhmann, "Miscegenation: An Example of Judicial Recidivism," *Journal of Family Law* 8 (1968): 72–78.

85. *Hoover v. State*, 59 Ala. 57 (1877); *Kinney v. Commonwealth*, 71 Va. at 858. See also *Carter v. Montgomery*, 2 Tenn. Ch. 216 (1875), in which the Tennessee court held that an interracial marriage was void even though the statute simply prohibited the marriage and contained no nullifying clause. In Mississippi, the temporary lifting of the ban on intermarriage allowed a white man and a black woman to legalize their union. Although the couple commenced their cohabitation at a time when marriage between them was prohibited, the court decided in 1873 that the constitution in force removed all "former impediments to marriage between blacks and whites," and thus their cohabitation as husband and wife had consummated their marriage. Of course, the ban on intermarriages was reinstituted in 1880. See *Dickerson v. Brown*, 49 Miss. 357 (1873); and Wharton, *Negro in Mississippi*, 150, 228–29. Marriages between blacks and whites were void in Georgia, but the court maintained that a husband could not prevent his wife from suing him for alimony by raising questions about her racial background and thus challenging the legality of the marriage. See *Dillon v. Dillon*, 60 Ga. 204 (1878).

86. North Carolina, *Code* (1883), vol. 1, sec. 1284, pp. 513–14; *Hopkins v. Bowers*, 111 N.C. 175 (1892). See also Florida, *Digest* (1881), chap. 149, sec. 9, p. 753.

87. *Greenhow v. James' Ex'r*, 80 Va. 636 (1885), 648–49. The Georgia Supreme Court

agreed with Justice Richardson, arguing in 1887 that there was nothing in the state's law to prohibit David Dickson, a white man, from making provision in his will for the offspring of his cohabitation with Julia Frances Lewis, who had been his slave before emancipation. See *Smith v. DuBose*, 78 Ga. 413 (1887), 442; Alexander, *Ambiguous Lives*, 185–88; and Kent Anderson Leslie, *Woman of Color, Daughter of Privilege: Amanda America Dickson, 1849–1893* (Athens: University of Georgia Press, 1995).

88. Berry, "Judging Morality," 843 n. 26.

89. Mississippi, *Revised Code* (1880), sec. 1147, p. 335; Texas, *Revised Penal Code* (1879), art. 326, p. 44; Virginia, *Code* (Burks, Staples, and Riely 1887), sec. 3783, pp. 898–99.

90. *State v. Kennedy*, 76 N.C. 251 (1877); *Kinney v. Commonwealth*, 71 Va. at 858; *Greenhow v. James' Ex'r*, 80 Va. at 636. See also *Dupre v. Boulard*, 10 La. An. at 411.

91. *State v. Bell*, 66 Tenn. at 10–11.

92. *State v. Ross*, 76 N.C. at 244, 246, 247. See also *Succession of Caballero*, 24 La. An. 573 (1872).

93. In 1967 the U.S. Supreme Court declared Virginia's miscegenation statute unconstitutional in *Loving v. Virginia*, 388 U.S. 1 (1967). See Wallenstein, "Race, Marriage, and the Law of Freedom," 421–33.

94. Bardaglio, *Reconstructing the Household*, 222–28.

Part II

Early National and Antebellum Periods

Chapter Seven

Lines of Color, Sex, and Service
Comparative Sexual Coercion in Early America

Sharon Block

Rachel Davis was born a free white child in the Pennsylvania mountains in 1790. She was fourteen when she became an indentured servant to William and Becky Cress in Philadelphia County. By the time Rachel was fifteen, William had begun making sexual overtures toward her. After months of continuing sexual assaults, William's wife, Becky, suspected that her husband was having a sexual relationship with their servant. Ultimately, Becky demanded that Rachel be removed from the house. William continued to visit Rachel at her new home, again trying to have sex with her. In 1807 Rachel's father found out what had occurred and initiated a rape prosecution against William, who was found guilty and sentenced to ten years in prison.[1]

Harriet Jacobs was born an enslaved black child in Edenton, North Carolina, in 1813. In 1825 she became a slave in James and Mary Norcom's household. By the time Harriet was sixteen, James had begun making sexual overtures toward her. After months of continuing sexual assaults, James's wife, Mary, suspected that her husband was having a sexual relationship with their slave. Ultimately, Mary demanded that Harriet be removed from the house. James continued to visit Harriet at her new home, again trying to have sex with her. In 1835 Harriet became a runaway slave, and spent the next seven years a fugitive, hiding in her free grandmother's attic crawlspace.[2]

If we were to focus on the conclusions to these stories, we would frame a picture of the contrasting consequences for masters who sexually coerced black and white women: the master of the white servant was sent to prison, while the black slave imprisoned herself to escape her abuser. But these opposing ends tell only part of the story. Until their conclusions, both women engaged in nearly parallel struggles with masters, mistresses, and unwanted sexual overtures. This contrast between the laborers' similar experiences and their stories' opposing conclusions suggests that the practice of sexual coercion and the classification of the criminal act of rape were differently dependent on status and race: shared cultural scripts formed the mechanics of coercion long before a racially based legal system was expressly invoked. By not privileging a court "truth" over an autobiographical novel, we can compare how a black woman in slavery and a white woman in servitude each experienced and represented her white master's sexual liberties.[3]

To date, much of the historical research on the sexual exploitation of black women has examined them in isolation from white women. Because American slavery was a racially based system that created social, economic, and political segregation, many studies of African American women's sexuality focus primarily on enslaved women.[4] In comparison, because servitude was neither racially segregated from mastery nor a permanent condition, there have been far fewer social histories specifically about white servants' sexual experiences. General studies of early American servitude might comment briefly on women's vulnerability to sexual coercion, but spend little time analyzing the meanings or mechanisms of such acts.[5] Thus the sexual exploitation of African American enslaved women has received attention as a marker and means of their enslavement, while the sexual exploitation of white servant women has been unsystematically documented. In other words, racially based sexual exploitation has received attention that class-based sexual exploitation has not.

Modern regional and thematic specialization has further separated studies of the sexual coercion of enslaved black and free white women. While much of the work on black women's sexual exploitation focuses on the antebellum slave systems of the American South, many of the examinations of the crime of rape have been based on the extensive legal records in the North, where there were far fewer black women.[6] Cultural and legal histories of sexual violence in the South have often focused primarily on the prosecution and persecution of enslaved and African American men as rapists.[7] As in Harriet Jacobs's life, much of black women's experiences of sexual coercion was marked by an absence of legal intervention, so that criminal justice histories cannot do much more than note African American women's absences. Thus, as a result of source selection or conceptual boundaries, studies that have focused on "women's" sexual exploitation have often excluded black women, and studies of crime and slavery have focused largely on black men's crimes.[8] By tying some of these separate histories together with a purposefully comparative analysis, we can begin to explore more fully the effects of sexual color lines in early America.

Legally, the endings to Harriet Jacobs's and Rachel Davis's stories were foregone conclusions: Rachel had an opportunity for institutional intervention that was unequivocally denied to Harriet. Enslaved women in early America did not have access to legal redress against white men who raped them. While no colonial or early republican statute explicitly excluded enslaved women from being the victims of rape or attempted rape, many mid-Atlantic and southern legislatures passed statutes setting harsh punishments for black men's sexual assaults on white women, thus implicitly privileging white women as victims of rape.[9] At the same time, enslaved men and women could qualify as witnesses only in cases with nonwhite defendants, so an enslaved woman could not testify against a white man who had raped her.[10] Accordingly, no historian has recorded a conviction of a white man for the rape of a slave at any point from 1700 to the Civil War, let alone a conviction of a master for raping his own slave. Rape in early America was a crime whose definition was structured by race.[11]

Even though the early American legal system segregated Rachel Davis and Harriet Jacobs into incomparable categories, their own presentations told nearly parallel stories of sexual coercion. In both women's stories, the prerogatives of mastery went beyond their masters' abilities to force them physically into sexual intercourse. Instead, their masters attempted to control the parameters and definitions of sexual acts. Rather than directly ordering his dependent to have sexual relations with him, each master took advantage of the woman's status to create a situation in which her ability to consent or refuse had been whittled away. Rape in these situations was not just an act of power, it was also the power to define an act. By translating authority over a woman's labor into opportunities for sexual coercion, economic mastery created sexual mastery, allowing masters to manipulate forced sexual encounters into a mimicry of consensual ones. Servants and slaves could not only be forced *to* consent, but this force was refigured *as* consent.

At the same time, neither Harriet Jacobs nor Rachel Davis presented herself as an abject victim of her master's will. Each engaged in continual negotiations and interactive struggles with her master; as much as he attempted to control the terms of any sexual interactions, so too did she try to change his definitions. Harriet Jacobs's and Rachel Davis's resistance to and strategic manipulation of their masters formed a vital part of their stories.

Rather than making a clear demarcation between the rape of slaves and the rape of servants, these narratives suggest that black and white laboring women interpreted and experienced a master's sexual coercion in strikingly similar ways. The parallels in these two stories, however, stopped at the courtroom door, where a racially based legal system ended the women's comparable negotiations of personal interactions.[12]

Creating Mastery: The Process of Coercion

How did a master sexually coerce a servant or slave in early America? Unlike a surprise attack where an assailant might use explicit physical force, a master did not have to rely on physical abilities to force his dependents into a sexual act. Instead, he might use the power of his position to create opportunities for sexual coercion, backing a woman into a corner where capitulation was her best option. A servant or enslaved woman often recognized this manipulation and tried to negotiate her way around her master's overtures rather than confronting him with direct resistance. But that compromise came at a high price: when a dependent negotiated with a master, sexual coercion could be reformulated into a consensual relationship. Negotiation implied willingness, and a woman's willingness contrasted with the early American legal and social code that rape consisted of irresistible force. Despite its surface counterintuitiveness, it was precisely women's attempts to bargain their way out of sexual assaults that made these sexual encounters seem consensual.[13]

Both Harriet Jacobs and Rachel Davis drew direct links between their status and their masters' sexual assaults on them. Each explained how her master had forced her into situations where he could sexually coerce her without being discovered. Rachel described several such incidents in her courtroom testimony. First, William ordered her to hold the lantern for him one night in the stable, where he "tried to persuade me to something." While the two were alone measuring grain in the barn, "he caught hold of me & pulled me on the hay." And in the most blatantly contrived incident, when they were reaping in the meadow, William "handed me his sickle & bad me to lay it down. He saw where I put it."[14] Later that night, William asked Rachel

> where I put them sickles. I asked if he did not see—he said no, I must come & show him. I told him I cd go with my sister, or by myself. he said that was not as he bad me. I went. Before we got quite to sickles, he bad me stop—I told him I was partly to the sickles—he bad me stop—I did—he came up & threw me down. . . . I hallowed—he put his hand over my mouth . . . he pulled up my cloathes, & got upon me . . . he did penetrate my body. I was dreadfully injured.

According to Rachel's statement, William had forced her to accompany him into a dark field on a contrived search for a purposefully lost farm implement so that he could rape her. William's authority to control where she went and what she did was integral to his ability to force Rachel to have sex with him.

Harriet Jacobs was even more explicit about the connections between James Norcum's mastery and his ability to force her into sexually vulnerable positions. It seemed to Harriet that he followed her everywhere—in her words, "my master met me at every turn"—trying to force her to have sex with him. As William did with Rachel, James structured Harriet's work so that she was often alone with him. He ordered Harriet to bring his meals to him so that while she watched him eat, he could verbally torture her with the consequences of refusing his sexual overtures. Harriet further recalled that "when I succeeded in avoiding opportunities for him to talk to me at home, I was ordered to come to his office, to do some errand." Tiring of Harriet's continued resistance, James ordered his four-year-old daughter to sleep near him, thus requiring that Harriet also sleep in his room in case the child needed attention during the night. After his wife objected to that arrangement, James tried to make Harriet accompany him on a trip to Louisiana that he was taking without his wife. James repeatedly used his position as a master who controlled his slave's labor to manipulate Harriet into sexually vulnerable situations.[15]

Harriet and Rachel were not the only laborers to connect their masters' economic power over them to their vulnerability to sexual coercion. A servant named Unice Williamson told a New York City court in 1797 that her master "ordered her to go upstairs and make the bed," and while she was carrying out his orders he "put her on the floor and ravished her." In 1818, also in New York, thirteen-year-old Maria Forshee told a court that her master "sent her down Cellar to get some kindling wood to make a fire," followed her down there, seized her, and tried to rape her. In 1787 a Pennsylvania servant told a court that after her master had "called me up to help to fill a bag of Grain," he threw her down in the loft and sexually assaulted her. Whether in rural or urban settings, servants recounted their experiences of a master's sexual assault on them in the context of their role as his servant.[16]

Masters or overseers might use similar techniques to manipulate enslaved women into sexual acts. In Josiah Henson's recollection of the overseer who raped his mother in the 1790s, he explained that the overseer had "sent my mother away from the other field hands to a retired place" so that he could force himself on her. The ex-slave Lewis Clarke recalled that his sister's master "sent for her" repeatedly so that he could sexually assault her. Like Harriet Jacobs's and Rachel Davis's descriptions, these sexual assaults were enacted through the relationships of social and economic labor relations, not as random physical attacks. Controlling a woman's daily routine, her work requirements, and her physical presence—in other words, control over her labor and her body—gave men in positions of mastery access to a particular means of sexually coercive behavior.[17]

Neither Harriet nor Rachel immediately acknowledged certain defeat to her master's desires, but neither offered absolute resistance either. It was in both women's interests to maintain as productive a rapport with their masters as possible. Any relationship, even the incontrovertibly inequitable one of slavery, depended on both participants' negotiations over its terms. If avoiding their masters did not work, then Harriet and Rachel had to try to balance on the fine line between covert resistance and outright disobedience.

In commenting on the manipulative techniques that her master used to isolate her, each woman also recalled how she had challenged her master's right to force her into a sexual relationship. Rachel recounted how she had "resisted" and "cried" when William tried to pull her into a darkened bedroom after sending the rest of the servants to bed, and how she threatened to tell his wife what he was doing. When these forms of resistance did not end his overtures, Rachel tried to carry out her master's orders in ways that might prevent her own sexual vulnerability. Rachel's description of being raped in the dark field began with her recollection that she had suggested that William could find the sickle himself, and then offered to find it on her own or with her sister. Ultimately, William resorted to his position as a master—"he said that was not as he bad me"—and issued a direct order for Rachel to accompany him. Rachel portrayed an interactive relationship with William: she may not have been able to override her master's orders, but she forced him to change their content. Rather than submitting to sex in the bedroom while the other children slept and his wife was away, Rachel forced William to order her into the dark field, thereby disrupting his original attempts at a seamless consensual interaction.

Harriet Jacobs's story contained similar efforts to avoid her master's sexual overtures that forced him to refigure his behavior. When Mary Norcum's suspicions made her husband revert to physical gestures instead of words to convey his sexual desires to Harriet, Harriet responded by letting "them pass, as if I did not understand what he meant." When James realized that Harriet could read, he wrote her notes that expressed his sexual intentions. But Harriet repeatedly pretended that " 'I can't read them, sir.' " Overall, "by managing to keep within sight of people, as much as possible during the day time, I had hitherto succeeded in eluding my master. . . . At night I slept by the side of my great aunt, where I felt safe." Harriet forced James into baldly claiming his right for sexual access as a privilege of mastery: according to Harriet, James began constantly "reminding me that I belonged to him, and swearing by heaven and earth that he would compel me to submit to him" because "I was his property; that I must be subject to his will in all things." Like Rachel Davis, Harriet Jacobs engaged in an exchange of maneuvers with her master where each tried to foil the other's plans and counterplans. Despite her master's legal property in her body, Harriet did not portray herself as utterly powerless. By playing into his image of her as too stupid to understand his signs and too illiterate to read his notes, Harriet used her own position as a slave to avoid her master's sexual overtures, forcing him to raise the stakes of his desires for her.[18]

Even Harriet's choice to enter into a sexual relationship with another white man was a maneuver against her master because "I knew nothing would enrage [my master] so much as to know that I favored another; and it was something to triumph over my tyrant in that small way." Harriet did not stop with games of cunning and indirect noncompliance. She recalled that "sometimes I so openly expressed my contempt for him that he would become violently outraged." She recounted telling her master in a moment of anger, "you have no right to do as you like with me." Even to the extent of occasional outright disobedience, Harriet Jacobs employed an array of tactics to shape the terms of her relationship with her master.[19]

Because he did not receive unquestioned acquiescence from a servant or slave, a master had to create situations in which his laborers had little choice but to have sexual relations with him. Rachel's attempted refusal to go alone into a dark field with her master and Harriet's feigned ignorance of her master's intentions forced each man to modify his route to sexual interactions. By not consenting to a master's more subtle attempts at sexual relations, a servant or slave might force her master into more overtly coerced sexual acts. Ironically, this compelled a master to enact his laborer's interpretation of his overtures. The men were forced to use coercion, rather than the sexual offers they had first proposed, to carry out their sexual plans. Theoretically, a master could coerce through his physical prowess, but most masters did not have to rely exclusively on fists or whips to commit rape. Instead, they could rely on the strength of their mastery.

To what extent was sexual coercion a prerogative of the general authority attributed to white masculinity in early America, versus the literal mastery in these particular situations? Certainly there was some overlap—the sexual privileges of mastery spilled over to many powerful white men. But the specific methods of a master's sexual assaults on a female dependent were less effective when a man was not her legal master. For example, Rachel described how William continued to pursue her sexually after she had been sent to another household. When William "sent in for me" to bring him a drink, Rachel suspected that he was again trying to isolate her in a sexually vulnerable situation, so she "told Beck (the bound Girl) to carry him drink" instead of doing it herself. When Rachel was William's servant, her attempts to avoid being alone with him could be thwarted by William's direct orders to do as he told her. But once she was somebody else's servant, she had more leeway to avoid his manipulative requests.

Harriet Jacobs's master steadfastly refused to allow her sale, so we have no evidence how his sexual overtures might have failed after she belonged to someone else. But Harriet herself saw a distinction between her master's sexual pursuit of her and her choice to have sexual relations with another powerful white man. While Harriet recognized that her relationship with this white man was still an inequitable one, she purposely contrasted him with her master, stating that "there is something akin to freedom in having a lover who has no control over you, except that which he gains by kindness and attachment." Although her master also offered special gifts and promises, Harriet did not interpret these actions as kindnesses. Her white lover may have had many of the prerogatives attributed to wealthy white men in the antebellum South, but from her perspective, they did not include the specific powers of mastery over her. Harriet Jacobs emphasized the choice of a sexual partner as a marker of freedom.[20]

Unlike the archetypal early American rape, in which an unknown man physically threw himself upon a woman in an isolated location, beat and raped her, and escaped off into the night, the continuous sexual coercion of dependent women was marked by more subtle forms of control.[21] Beyond the unadorned physical power that could compel a woman into a sexual act, a master had an array of indirect means to force a dependent to have sex with him that simultaneously denied her resistance to him. While manipulation of their labor could force women into sexually vulnerable positions, further pressure was necessary to compel them into sexual acts; opportunity did not necessarily equal consummation. As might be expected, William and James sometimes used the threat of physical violence to coerce Rachel and Harriet, respectively, into sexual relations. Although Harriet repeatedly stated that James never beat or whipped her, she also mentioned that "a razor was often held to my throat to force me to" consent to sexual overtures.[22] Similarly, Rachel recounted that in the midst of one sexual struggle William "said, if I did not go to bed he'd pull that topnot of mine to the damndest." While both of these men might turn to the threat of physical assault to obtain their ends, their authority over their dependent laborers also allowed them to use less direct forms of coercion.

Harriet characterized her master as "a crafty man, [who] resorted to many means to accomplish his purposes. Sometimes he had stormy, terrific ways, that made his victims tremble; sometimes he assumed a gentleness that he thought must surely subdue." James promised Harriet that if she would give in to him sexually, "I would cherish you. I would make a lady of you." The possibility of a better life that transcended her racial and labor status was more than a bribe to induce Harriet's consent. It created a fiction that Harriet could voluntarily choose to have sexual relations with her master. By switching between the threats of physical harm and the gifts of courtship, James undercut the appearance of a forced sexual interaction. By theoretically allowing space for Harriet's consent to his sexual overtures, James was redefining coercion into consensual sexual relations.[23]

Similarly, William's verbal narration of consensual relations overlay his forceful attempts at sex. While he had Rachel trapped underneath his body, William told her that "he wd have the good will of me." William's modification of the classic legal description of rape as a man having carnal knowledge of a woman "*against her will*" verbally created a consensual act even as he used force to have sexual relations.[24] In the same incident, William called Rachel by her family nickname, telling her, "Nate you dear creature, I must fuck you." Even while forcing Rachel to have sex with him, William used terms of endearment toward her. This masquerade substituted William's will for Rachel's consent as his verbal intercourse of consensuality masked his actions of coercion. William's presentation of an affectionate and therefore consensual sexual relationship with Rachel differentiated his actions from the brutality that early Americans would most easily recognize as rape.

In the acts of sexual intimidation explored here, the process of master-servant and master-slave sexual coercion was not exclusively tied to racial boundaries. Harriet Jacobs's and Rachel Davis's similarly recounted experiences suggest that their sexual interactions were more directly shaped by lines of status and dependency. These patterns would be repeated as masters and their servants or slaves struggled to control public perceptions of what had occurred.

Creating Master Narratives: The Process of Publicity

The process of sexual coercion did not end with a master's attempts at sexual relations with his slave or servant. Just as masters and servants or slaves fought over sexual interactions, they also battled over public interpretations of those acts. Given these different versions of events, how did families, other household members, and communities interpret evidence of a possibly coercive sexual interaction? How did assaulted women portray what had happened to them? Harriet Jacobs's and Rachel Davis's narratives show that the process of publicizing a master's sexual overtures was again structured by the woman's position as his personally dependent laborer. Words—the power to speak them and the power to construct their meaning—became the prize in a struggle among masters, mistresses, and the assaulted servant or slave.

After attempting sexual overtures toward their laborers, masters had to contend with the possibility that the women would tell others about their masters' behavior. Harriet Jacobs's and Rachel Davis's masters attempted to threaten their laborers into silence about their sexual interactions. Harriet wrote that her master "swore he would kill me, if I was not as silent as the grave." On another occasion, she wrote, "He threatened me with death, and worse than death, if I made any complaint" of his treatment.[25] Similarly, William told Rachel that if she told "any body, he wd be the death of me." When Rachel threatened to tell his wife what William had been doing, "he sd if I did, I shd repent." By demanding her silence, each master tried to dictate the parameters of his sexual interactions with his servant or slave without outside interference that might contradict his interpretation or stop his sexual pursuit.

But each woman also believed that her master was afraid of the damage she could do by publicizing his sexual behavior. Besides making threats of physical violence, William promised Rachel a "gown if she would not tell" what he had done; on another occasion, he "begged [Rachel] not to tell" her new mistress because "it wd be the Ruin of him." Harriet similarly opined that her master "did not wish to have his villainy made public." Instead, he "deemed it prudent to keep up some outward show of decency." The masters' attempts to control the dissemination of information through the interchange of threats and promises mimicked their strategies for sexual coercion. From each woman's vantage point, then, her master's concern about his public image again allowed her some room for negotiation: he needed his servant or slave to conceal their sexual interactions. But by not telling anyone about her master's sexual assaults, a woman increased the likelihood that their sexual relationship would not appear to be a rape. This double-edged sword made the servant or slave an unwilling accomplice in the masking of her own sexual coercion.[26]

If pressuring his servant or slave into silence through bribes or threats did not silence her, a master might try to control her description of their sexual interaction. William Cress enacted an elaborate punishment scene that forced Rachel Davis to claim responsibility for anything that may have passed between them. After Rachel's complaints to her mistress prompted Mary to confront her husband about Rachel's allegations, William immediately challenged Rachel. " 'Well Rachael', William said, 'what are this you have been scraping up about me'?" Even in the formulation of his question he denied the possibility of his own misdeeds. When Rachel could not present a satisfactory answer, William employed the power of physical correction allowed to him as her master to reform her story. According to Rachel, he "whipt me dreadfully & he said . . . that he never had such a name before. . . . I fell down— he damned me, & bad me beg his pardon. I said I did not know how—he bad me go on my knees . . . he bad me go to house & tell" his wife that she (Rachel) had lied. By whipping Rachel, William attempted to disprove her story of sexual assault: his wife had said that if Rachel's assertions of sexual relations between herself and William "was lies" as William claimed, "he ought to whip" Rachel for her dishonesty. William used the acceptable force of mastery—punishing a disobedient servant—to deny the theoretically unacceptable power of a master to coerce sex from his servant.

This whipping was not just a punishment unfairly inflicted, it was a punishment that retroactively attempted to define the sexual interactions between a servant and a master. Once subjugated, Rachel was required to deny that William had forced her to have sex with him. Rachel's younger sister, also a servant to William, believed this new version of events: she admitted that "I do remember D[efendant] whipping my sister—it was for telling so many lies." William was using his position as master to rewrite the sexual act that had taken place between them.

Rachel ended her description of this incident by stating that after William had beaten her, "he went to church that day & I showed my back to [my] Sister." Those final words on her master's brutal punishment (a whipping with a stick as "thick as my middle finger" that prevented Rachel from lying on her side for three weeks) revealed the irony of the situation: while William continued to appear as a publicly reverent and virtuous patriarch, Rachel secretly bore the signs of his sins, visible only to those most intimate with her. In the process of sexual coercion, force did not have a solely physical purpose: masters also used force to create an image of consent.

Harriet Jacobs also noted the discrepancy between her master's public image and private behavior, telling her readers how he had preserved his image at her expense. When Harriet's mistress confronted Harriet with suspicions of her husband's sexual improprieties, Harriet swore on a Bible that she had not had a sexual relationship with her master. When Mary questioned her husband, however, James contradicted Harriet's statements. And just like Rachel's mistress, Harriet's mistress "would gladly have had me flogged for my supposed false oath." But unlike William Cress, James Norcum did not allow Harriet to be whipped because "the old sinner was politic. The application of the lash might have led to remarks that would have exposed him" to his family and community. Harriet did advance a rationale for her master's "false representation" of their sexual interactions. In her view, "it was to show me that I gained nothing in seeking the protection of my mistress; that the power was still in his own hands." James's contradiction of Harriet's denials (whether true or false) attempted to control the public image of his relationship with his slave.[27]

Unlike Rachel Davis, Harriet Jacobs did not report that she suffered beatings for telling others about her master's sexual overtures. However, she did recount one incident in which her master gave her a "stunning blow" when she expressed her love for another man. When James finally spoke to Harriet again weeks later, he "expressed regret for the blow he had given me, and reminded me that I myself was wholly to blame for it." Just as William had tried to make Rachel responsible for the whipping he gave her, James made Harriet to blame for his striking her. In both cases, masters denied the coercive powers of mastery by claiming that they had no choice but to react to their servant's or slave's improper behavior. Although William Cress's and James Norcum's motivations may have differed (William seemed more concerned with his wife's belief in his monogamy than was James), each man claimed the power to create the truth of his behavior toward his laborers.[28]

In Rachel's and Harriet's narratives, their mistresses—the wives of their abusers— played important roles in the categorization of the sexually abusive relationship. Each woman had to deal with a mistress who ultimately took her displeasure at her husband's sexual relationship out on her servant or slave. Each mistress also used her position of secondary mastery to create a temporary alliance with her servant or slave. Once this alliance outlived its usefulness, it became another tool with which the mistress could assist in redefining or denying the sexual relationship between the master and the slave or servant.

Harriet Jacobs had nearly uniformly harsh words for mistresses. She entitled one chapter "The Jealous Mistress" and complained that her own mistress was "totally deficient in energy" except when it came to ordering others to punish her slaves. She recounted stories of other slaves' interactions with wrathful mistresses that, like her own experiences, revolved around sexual triangles initiated by the master of the house. When a "young slave girl [was] dying soon after the birth of a child nearly white," her mistress "mocked at her like an incarnate fiend. 'You suffer, do you?' she exclaimed. 'I am glad of it. You deserve it all, and more too.' " In relation to her own master's sexual overtures toward her, Harriet opined that "the mistress, who ought to protect the helpless victim, has no other feelings toward her but those of jealousy and rage." Perhaps partly in hopes of bonding with northern abolitionist women, Harriet Jacobs portrayed slave mistresses and enslaved women as nearly universal antagonists to one another. But Harriet's own interactions with her mistress revealed a more complicated and nuanced relationship that closely paralleled the experiences noted by Rachel Davis.[29]

In both women's stories, the wives did not immediately take their hostility at their sexually aggressive husbands out on the objects of their husbands' overtures. When Rachel and William came back from retrieving the "lost" sickle, his wife, Becky, asked "where he had been—he said, after the sickles, with nate (so they called me in family) she sd it was very extraordinary, no body else could go." Perhaps Becky suspected some sort of sexual liaison between her husband and their servant, and her pointed questions let her husband know of her suspicions. When Becky heard William trying to kiss Rachel in the cellar, she "said she had caught him & he wd deceive her no longer," but William denied any wrongdoing and Becky left in tears. These verbal confrontations apparently did not alter William's behavior; he continued to force himself sexually upon Rachel. Finally, Rachel's mistress "saw something was the matter with me, & asked what it was. I told her." After questioning her husband had little visible effect, Becky turned to Rachel to find out about her husband's actions. This temporary alliance brought Rachel some protection from William's retribution, if not from his sexual overtures: when William heard that Rachel had told another relative some of what he had done to her, "he whipt me again, but not so bad—his wife wd not let him & said, he was in Fault."

Similarly, Harriet Jacobs believed that her mistress suspected James's illicit behavior: "She watched her husband with unceasing vigilance; but he was well practised in means to evade it." After Mary heard that her husband planned to have Harriet sleep in his room, she began questioning Harriet, who told her how James had been sexually harassing her. Harriet claimed that Mary, like most slave mistresses, "had no compassion for the poor victim of her husband's perfidy. She pitied herself as a martyr." But Harriet also admitted that Mary "spoke kindly, and promised to protect me," ordering Harriet to sleep with her rather than with James. This protective kindness also allowed Mary to try to obtain the "truth" of Harriet and James's relationship out of Harriet while Harriet slept: "she whispered in my ear, as though it was her husband who was speaking to me, and listened to hear what I would answer." When Harriet did not provide any self-incriminating information, Mary confronted her husband, but Mary's interventions did not end James's sexual overtures toward Harriet.[30]

If mistresses could not personally control their husbands' behavior, how could they stop the sexual relationship between master and laborer that was making a mockery of their marital vows? Theoretically, mistresses could turn to the legal system to petition for a divorce from their husbands. By the early nineteenth century, most states had divorce laws that allowed wives to apply for divorce on the grounds of their husbands' adultery, but women's petitions for divorce were more commonly based on charges of desertion.[31] Furthermore, proving adultery with a slave might be difficult without firsthand witnesses to the sexual interactions since the slave was limited in her ability to testify against the white man.[32] Married women also had a vested interest in their husbands' social and economic standing. Divorce or incarceration would most probably result in a woman's economic downturn from the loss of her husband's labor.

Besides the practical limitations on institutional remedies for misbehaving husbands, women were traditionally more accustomed to controlling and regulating other women's behavior than they were men's. Whether serving on matron's juries, as midwives testifying to the identity of a bastard's father, or extralegally enforcing sexual mores, early American women secured their own social respectability by policing others of their sex.[33]

In these particular cases, Mary Norcum and Becky Cress each attempted to use her laborer's body to turn her husband's immoral sexual acts into her laborer's misbehavior. By encouraging their husbands to whip their servant or slave, the mistresses tried to physically mark Harriet and Rachel as the guilty parties. Beyond simply proving that the laborer had lied, each mistress tried to force her husband to emphasize his connection to his wife at the expense of a servant or slave. Control over the public terms of the sexual acts became a three-way contest as mistresses tried to redefine their husbands' and laborers' sexual relations.

Ultimately, Rachel Davis's and Harriet Jacobs's mistresses concentrated their energies on removing their laborers from the household. Instead of bringing charges against her husband or applying for a divorce on the grounds of adultery, Becky Cress told Rachel Davis that she must "leave the house." Rachel recalled that "they then hired me out." Rachel's mistress may have ultimately recognized that her husband was (at best) complicit in his sexual relations with Rachel, but she also recognized that she, as his wife, was in a poor position to mandate a reform in his behavior. She could, however, as a mistress, remove the more disposable partner in the sexual relationship, and so she ordered Rachel to leave their home. Whether or not Becky believed Rachel's story of rape, she did not hold Rachel entirely innocent of wrongdoing. At the very least, she spread blame equally between her servant and her husband, with much of the resulting punishment falling on the more vulnerable of the two parties. As Rachel stated, "Before I was hired out, [my mistress] used me very bad & said she would knowck me down if I came to table to eat." Because William was a master—both of Rachel and of his household—his wife could enact only limited direct retribution against him. She could watch his behavior, confront him, and let him know her displeasure, but ultimately it was easier to remove the object of his overtures than publicly accuse him of wrongdoing.

Mary Norcum demanded that Harriet Jacobs leave the house once she learned that Harriet was pregnant, believing that conception was proof of their slave's sexual relationship with her husband. Harriet was not the only slave who was reputed to have been kicked out of her house because of a sexual relationship with the master. Recalling a story told to her by her grandmother about another slave,

Harriet wrote that "her mistress had that day seen her baby for the first time, and in the lineaments of its fair face she saw a likeness to her husband. She turned the bondswoman and her child out of doors, and forbade her ever to return." In both of these examples the mistress felt herself in sexual competition with the slave—even if the slave was not a willing competitor for the master's affections.[34]

While images of the competition between slaves and mistresses may be familiar from the abolitionist tracts and late antebellum diaries of plantation mistresses, similar conceptions of servants also existed in early America. A 1795 joke book told the story of "a certain lady, finding her husband somewhat too familiar with her chamber-maid, turned her away, saying '*Hussy, I have no occasion for such sluts as you, I hired you to do your own business, not mine.*' " This story set up a husband propositioning (physically coercing or not, we cannot tell) the chamber-maid, but the wife blamed the servant for encouraging the encounter. In Abigail Bailey's memoirs, first published in 1815, she recounted a similar sentiment when she noticed "very improper conduct" between her husband and a servant. Abigail pleaded with her husband to "consider the evil of his ways," but ultimately blamed the "rude" and "disagreeable" servant, and "prevailed to send the vile young woman from our family." In this memoir, as well as in Harriet's and Rachel's recollections, the mistress's reaction to the servant was not immediate; it was a secondary response when her husband proved unresponsive to her criticisms. These women could not easily punish their husbands, but they could justify punishing their servants and slaves for the sexual transgressions within their households. While a wife's place in the household hierarchy may have limited her options, it did not leave her entirely at her husband's mercy. Perhaps in return for her own public silence about the master-servant or master-slave sexual interactions, a wife had the leverage to demand the laborer's departure.[35]

Thus, by forcing her husband to prove his marital loyalty by whipping the laborer for telling untruths about his sexual conduct, each mistress tried to create her own version of household sexual alliances. When mistresses could not force husbands to modify their behavior, these wives turned to regulating their servant's or slave's actions: by first using her as the source of incriminating information, and later treating her as a problem that could be eliminated. Mistresses would not permanently join forces with slave or servant women to overthrow the household patriarch; they might want to change their husbands' behavior, but these wives did not wish publicly to condemn or disassociate themselves from their husbands through divorce or other legal action. Just as the abused woman did not find unequivocal support or protection from her mistress, she might receive similarly mixed messages from others to whom she turned for assistance.

Richard Dunn has called the history of labor in early America "the history of the inarticulate—laboring men and women who left few records or artifacts and who must be studied chiefly through the observations of their employers." Although Dunn was referring primarily to the lack of records left by slave and servant laborers, we might expand his meaning to examine the implications of a social system that denied a public, recorded voice to segments of the population: without a way to speak publicly, servants and slaves were made forcibly inarticulate, requiring that their masters spoke for them. In instances of sexual abuse where there was often a contest over whose classification of the sexual act would be believed, this had significant effects on the public image of a master's sexual behavior.[36]

The silencing of sexual coercion was more profound in Harriet Jacobs's autobiography than it was in Rachel Davis's court-ordered testimony specifically about rape. Harriet's representation of her conflict with her master centered on the power to create a singular version of reality through the privilege of public speech. Throughout her narrative, Harriet insisted that her master sexually assaulted her only with words, never with his body. She wrote that he "tried his utmost to corrupt the pure principles my grandmother had instilled. He peopled my mind with unclean images." Harriet silenced her own description of her master's actions by calling the sexual degradation of slavery "more than I can describe." Harriet's versions of her master's verbal actions may have stood in for the literally unspeakable physical sexual abuse she suffered at his hands. By describing only James's speech, Harriet turned his possibly physical assaults on her into verbal assaults that no reader could expect her to control. In so doing, she implicitly absolved herself of any willing collusion with his sexual desires because she could not avoid listening to her master's verbal attacks.[37]

In a personal letter written a few years before the publication of *Incidents in the Life of a Slave Girl* in 1861, Harriet hinted that she had indeed concealed the extent of James's actions. While she had tried to give a "true and just" account of her life in slavery, she admitted that "there are somethings I might have made plainer I know—Woman can whisper—her cruel wrongs into the ear of a very dear friend—much easier than she can record them for the world to read." In this passage, Jacobs drew a distinction between the private version of her pain and the version she chose to present for public consumption. Victorian womanhood's emphasis on modesty and respectability as well as the established genre of sexual euphemism popularized in sentimental novels probably encouraged Harriet Jacobs to present a sanitized version of her master's assaults on her. But her decision may also have reflected a personal need to distance herself from painful events, and a difficulty in telling others about her suffering that was shared by other victims—black and white—of a master's sexual harassment. Harriet Jacobs did not write that being an ex-slave made it difficult for her to commit the details of sexual abuse to public view; she located this hesitance in non–race-specific womanhood.[38]

Both Harriet and Rachel first told those closest to them about their masters' unwelcome sexual overtures. Harriet originally hesitated to tell Molly Horniblow, her grandmother and closest living relative, how James was treating her. Harriet "would have given the world to have laid my head on my grandmother's faithful bosom, and told her all my troubles," but both James's threats and her own fear of her grandmother's reaction made her stay silent. When Harriet eventually did talk to her grandmother, she told her only some of her difficulties: "I talked with my grandmother about it, and partly told her my fears. I did not dare to tell her the worst." Harriet also told her uncle about some of her suffering. He told another relative that "you don't know what a life they lead her. She has told me something about it, and I wish [her master] was dead, or a better man." Harriet's recollection of interactions with her grandmother and her uncle emphasized that neither relative knew the entire story of her master's abuses. Just as the reader was given a sanitized version in the public transcript of Harriet's life, her hesitancy to confess the full extent of sexual coercion was reiterated in Harriet's personal interactions. Her inability to confess "the worst" of her experiences may have maintained Harriet's image of sexual purity and self-identity, but it was at the cost of denying the full spectrum of her master's assaults on her.[39]

Similarly, Rachel eventually told people close to her—one of her sisters (a servant in another household), her aunt, and her new mistress—about what William was doing to her. She recounted that she was hesitant to tell the whole story even to them. Rachel told her new mistress "something of what passed in the meadow, but not the worst of it. I told my sister Becky . . . the whole of it." Like Harriet's claim that it was easier to tell a close friend than to proclaim one's victimization publicly, Rachel had an easier time confessing her problems to her sister than to her new mistress. When Rachel spoke with her aunt, Elizabeth Ashton, she again refrained from disclosing the full extent of William's coercion. Elizabeth told the court that Rachel had explained how William had isolated her in the cellar, had told her to go to bed with him when his wife was away, had cornered her in the barn, and had forced her to go with him to retrieve the sickle in the meadow. But Rachel stopped short of telling her aunt that William had succeeded in raping her, that his manipulative maneuvers had led to forced sexual intercourse. Elizabeth specified under cross-examination that "*I did not understand from her that he had fully effected his purpose in the meadow.*"[40] By minimizing the extent of her master's abuse of her, Rachel created a public version of her master's actions that denied that she had been raped.

The victims of sexual coercion were not the only people who purposefully avoided discussions of sexual assaults. Elizabeth Ashton did not know that William had raped Rachel partly because, as she told the court, "I did not enquire whether he obtained his will in the meadow." When Rachel's sister told her own mistress that "Mr Cress wanted to be gret [great] with her sister Rachael," the mistress replied, "I wanted to hear no more." When this sister eventually told their father what had happened, Jacob Davis recalled that she "did not tell me directly, she did not tell me the worst—I did not think it was so bad." A voluntary conspiracy of silence—from the servant who had difficulty discussing what had happened, to the other women who wanted neither to hear nor to tell the full extent of William's abuse of Rachel—worked together to deny the sexual coercion that William committed on his servant.

Likewise, Harriet Jacobs's fellow slaves were hesitant to volunteer verbal or physical assistance to her. Harriet believed that while her friends and relatives knew that she was being sexually abused, they were unable to speak of it. Harriet recalled that "the other slaves in my master's house noticed" her changed behavior as a result of her master's treatment of her, but "none dared to ask the cause. . . . They knew too well the guilty practices under that roof; and they were aware that to speak of them was an offence that never went unpunished." Harriet's fellow slaves' silence, necessary for their own self-preservation, limited their ability to help Harriet resist their master's overtures. By controlling potential allies, a master enmeshed his original acts of sexual coercion in an ever widening coercive web that structured his victim's possibilities for support or redress.[41]

By not telling others what had happened to her, Harriet was at the mercy of other people's versions of events. James's wife, Mary, went to the house of Harriet's free grandmother to tell her that Harriet was pregnant with James's baby. Molly Horniblow then turned on Harriet, presumably believing Mary's story that Harriet had consented to the relationship: " 'I had rather see you dead than to see you as you now are,' " she told her granddaughter. " 'You are a disgrace to your dead mother. . . . Go away . . . and never come to my house, again.' " Because Harriet had consistently denied or played down her master's sexual attempts on her, her grandmother believed Mary's story that Harriet had voluntarily had sexual relations with James. Later, Harriet's grandmother learned that Harriet had chosen to become pregnant with another man's baby to try to force her sexually abusive master to leave her alone or sell her. Once her grandmother understood "the real state of the case, and all I had been bearing for years. . . . She laid her old hand gently on my head, and murmured, 'Poor child! Poor child!' " Harriet's inability to speak about her master's sexual coercion temporarily isolated Harriet from the woman who was most able to support her. When Harriet ultimately received her grandmother's forgiveness, she also gained an ally in her fight against her master's sexual demands.[42]

Both Harriet and Rachel believed that an independently powerful figure outside the household could counterbalance their masters' attempts at dominance. When Rachel's aunt questioned "why she did not go to a Squire to complain" about her master's sexual assaults, Rachel replied that "she did not dare—she a bound girl & her father absent." After telling her sister what had happened, her sister "advised her to stay there & be a good girl. . . . I thought nothing could be done, as my father was away." Rachel herself told the court that "I did not know if I went to a Justice, he wd take notice of it. Enough people knew it, but waited till my Father came back." Without a patriarchal figure beside her, Rachel would not directly confront her master, and did not believe herself entitled to legal justice, a belief encouraged (or at least not contradicted) by the women in whom she confided. For Rachel, her father's support was crucial to her ability to receive public redress for her master's sexual assaults on her.

Enslaved women ordinarily did not have access to the protection offered by a patriarchal figure. Harriet Jacobs's often quoted line opined that enslaved men "strive to protect wives and daughter from the insults of their masters. . . . [but] Some poor creatures have been so brutalized by the lash that they will sneak out of the way to give their masters free access to their wives and daughters." Although Harriet Jacobs did not have a waiting patriarchal figure to whom she could turn for protection, supporters outside the household were still crucial to her limited redress. Harriet repeatedly spoke of her grandmother's respect in the community, of how James "dreaded" this woman's "scorching rebuke," so that "her presence in the neighborhood was some protection to me." Ultimately, her grandmother's home became a partial refuge from James's pursuit. Harriet also spoke of her white lover's assistance in combating her master's "persecutions" of her through his "wish to aid me." Harriet partly justified her decision to have sexual relations with this man (pseudonymously referred to as Mr. Sands), because she was "sure my friend, Mr. Sands, would buy me . . . and I thought my freedom could be easily obtained from him." While Harriet could not hope for institutional retribution against her master, she could hope that her new lover would help provide freedom from her master.[43]

Both Harriet Jacobs and Rachel Davis fought similar battles against the veil of silence surrounding their masters' treatment of them. Both were confronted by relatives and neighbors who had limited authority over another household's problems. Both women turned to another powerful figure—father or free grandmother and elite white lover, respectively—to rescue them from their masters' sexual abuse. When Rachel finally told her father about her master's sexual assaults, Jacob Davis successfully encouraged the local legal system to begin a criminal prosecution. But neither Harriet Jacobs's ultimate confession to her grandmother nor her involvement with a white lover could lead to legal intervention. The legal system marked an irreversible disjuncture in the two women's experiences.

Epilogue: Creating Rape: The Legal Process

Following the process of sexual coercion has led us back to this essay's opening, as Harriet Jacobs's and Rachel Davis's parallel stories reach diametrically opposed conclusions: while Rachel's master was convicted of rape and served a substantial jail sentence, there is no evidence that Harriet's master ever suffered criminal repercussions for his behavior. The privileges of whiteness allowed masters of both servants and slaves to enact particular forms of sexual coercion. But only servants were eligible for the legal privilege afforded to their status as free and white laborers.[44]

The similar strategies of interaction and negotiation that so characterized Harriet Jacobs's and Rachel Davis's relations with their masters fell victim to early America's legal attempts to distinguish free from enslaved and white from black. When a master tried to define coercive sex as consensual sex, servants and slaves could negotiate with his terms and battle against his actions. But when the legal system defined enslaved women outside the judicial parameters of rape, there was little room for negotiation. The parallels in Harriet Jacobs's and Rachel Davis's stories ended with the legal distinction of criminal behavior. A legal system that erased the social persona of enslaved women created a sexual system that elided their resistance by negating the power of their words.

By moving beyond a single focus on the criminal justice system, we can begin to unravel the multiple strategies and meanings of sexual coercion in early America. We need to understand not only the legal history of rape, but the social history of sexual coercion. For instance, one historian of slavery in the Chesapeake has written that some masters "raped black women, and others established longer relationships with them."[45] This statement suggests a distinction between rape as a one-time act of pure physical domination and the quasi-consensual ongoing master-slave sexual "relationships." While masters may have had nominally consensual relationships with their slaves or servants, they were also able to sexually coerce these women into long-term abusive sexual interactions. If we do not recognize that the very definition of ongoing sexual abuse as a "relationship" springs from a master's profound power to define the terms of sexual acts, the more subtle—but nonetheless coercive—powers of mastery remain hidden. Under a master's power, rape became sex, resistance became consent, and women's desires and pains became irrelevant.

By taking seriously the possibility that white and black women in early America could have some experiences in common, we can begin to reassemble the complicated interactions of race, gender, and social and economic status in American history. Nell Painter has urged historians not to "see race as an opaque barrier to feminist investigation," because while "southern history must take race very seriously, southern history must not stop with race." By enlarging Painter's suggestion to employ a comparative analysis that questions lines of geography, race, and type of servitude, we can better understand the range of sexual interactions in early America. By expanding our comparisons to look at women in potentially parallel situations throughout regions, across racial lines, and beyond our own preconceptions, we can also sharpen our understanding of a historicized category of race.[46]

Certainly the comparative possibilities are not exhausted with these two stories. Historians could compare the sexual experiences of free and enslaved African American women or white and black free servants to ask whether the mechanics of coercion discussed here were specific to legal mastery. Were similar strategies used outside of households, in any relationship between a powerful man and a less powerful woman? In all of these comparisons, we should think carefully about how sex was coerced and how the crime of rape was defined. If we frame our investigations using solely the legal judgment of rape, we not only miss much of the story, we again replace women's experiences—much as their coercers had tried to do—with external categorizations. Instead, by interrogating the multiple and contested meanings of sexual coercion, we can better understand the historical relationships of social and sexual power.

NOTES

Thanks to Martha Hodes, Walter Johnson, Leisa Meyer, Fredrika J. Teute, the OIEAHC Colloquium, and the Southern California Early Americanist Colloquium for their comments on various drafts of this essay.

1. Commonwealth v. William Cress, Feb. 1808, Pennsylvania Court Papers, 1807-1809, Historical Society of Pennsylvania, Philadelphia. Unless otherwise noted, all quotations regarding Rachel Davis are from these documents. For the criminal prosecution of William Cress, see Commonwealth v. William Cress, Philadelphia, Feb. 15, 1808, Pennsylvania Oyer and Terminer Docket, 1778–1827, 261, 262, 263, 265, Pennsylvania Historical and Museum Commission, Harrisburg.

Throughout this essay, I have chosen to use first names for all the actors in incidents of sexual coercion because first names more easily distinguish men from women and eliminate confusion in identifying members of the same family.

2. Harriet Jacobs, *Incidents in the Life of a Slave Girl Written by Herself*, ed. Jean Fagan Yellin (1861; reprint, Cambridge: Harvard University Press, 1987).

3. On the meanings of authorship and the production of Jacobs's text, see Betsy Erkkila, "Ethnicity, Literary Theory, and the Grounds of Resistance," *American Quarterly* 47 (1995): esp. 574–83; Deborah M. Garfield and Rafia Zafar, eds., *Harriet Jacobs and* Incidents in the Life of a Slave Girl: *New Critical Essays* (New York: Cambridge University Press, 1996).

On the (mostly civil trials') meanings of truth in the eighteenth-century English context, see James Oldham, "Truth-Telling in the Eighteenth-Century English Courtroom," *Law and History Review* 12 (1994): 95–121. On legal storytelling in modern contexts, see Gerald Torres and Kathryn Milun, "Translating Yonondio by Precedent and Evidence: The Mashpee Indian Case," in *Critical Race Theory: The Cutting Edge*, ed. Richard Delgado (Philadelphia: Temple University Press, 1995), 49–55; Alan M. Dershowitz, "Life is Not a Dramatic Narrative," in *Law's Stories: Narrative and Rhetoric in the Law*, ed. Peter Brooks and Paul Gerwitz (New Haven: Yale University Press, 1996), 99–105. For a compelling fictional exploration of twentieth-century household sexual coercion, see J. M. Redmann's three-book series culminating in *The Intersection of Law and Desire* (New York: W. W. Norton, 1995).

4. On enslaved African American women's sexual relations with white men, see Catherine Clinton, " 'Southern Dishonor': Flesh, Blood, Race, and Bondage," in *In Joy and in Sorrow: Women, Family, and Marriage in the Victorian South, 1830–1900*, ed. Carol Bleser (New York: Oxford University Press, 1991), 52–68; Thelma Jennings, " 'Us Colored Women Had to Go Through a Plenty': Sexual Exploitation of African American Slave Women," *Journal of Women's History* 1 (1990): 45–74; Hélène Lecaudey, "Behind the Mask: Ex-Slave Women and Interracial Sexual Relations," in *Discovering the Women in Slavery: Emancipating Perspectives on the American Past*, ed. Patricia Morton (Athens: University of Georgia Press, 1996), 260–77; Melton McLaurin, Celia: *A Slave* (Athens: University of Georgia Press, 1991). For a more general examination of African American women's sexuality, see Rennie Simson, "The Afro-American Female: The Historical Context of the Construction of Sexual Identity," in *Powers of Desire: The Politics of Sexuality*, ed. Ann Snitow, Christine Stansell, and Sharon Thompson (New York: Monthly Review Press, 1983), 229–35. On race and rape in another racially segregated society, see Patricia Scully, "Rape, Race, and Colonial Culture: The Sexual Politics of Identity in the Nineteenth-Century Cape Colony, South Africa," *American Historical Review* 100 (1995): 335–59.

5. On indentured servants in Pennsylvania, see Sharon V. Salinger, *"To Serve Well and Faithfully": Labor and Indentured Servants in Pennsylvania, 1682–1800* (Cambridge: Cambridge University Press, 1987), esp. 112. On nineteenth-century servitude, see Faye Dudden, *Serving Women: Household Service in Nineteenth-Century America* (Middletown, Conn: Wesleyan University Press, 1983), esp. 215; Christine Stansell, *City of Women: Sex and Class in New York, 1789–1860* (Urbana: University of Illinois Press, 1987), esp. 155–68.

6. See, for example, Cornelia Hughes Dayton, *Women before the Bar: Gender, Law, and Society in Connecticut, 1639–1789* (Chapel Hill: IEAHC at University of North Carolina Press, 1995), chap. 5; Marybeth Hamilton Arnold, " 'The Life of a Citizen in the Hands of a Woman': Sexual Assault in New York City, 1790–1820," in *Passion and Power: Sexuality in History*, ed. Kathy Peiss and Christina Simmons with Robert A. Padgug (Philadelphia: Temple University Press, 1989); Barbara Lindemann, " 'To Ravish and Carnally Know': Rape in Eighteenth-Century Massachusetts," *Signs* 10 (1984): 63–82. For one of the few pieces that explicitly explore comparative sexual history, see Nell Irvin Painter, "Three Southern Women and Freud: A Non-Exceptionalist Approach to Race, Class, and Gender in the Slave South," in *Feminists Revision History*, ed. Ann-Louise Shapiro (New Brunswick: Rutgers University Press, 1994), 195–216.

7. Jacquelyn Dowd Hall, " 'The Mind That Burns in Each Body': Women, Rape, and Racial Violence," in *Powers of Desire*, ed. Snitow, Stansell, and Thompson, 328–49; Martha Hodes, "The Sexualization of Reconstruction Politics: White Women and Black Men in the South after the Civil War," *Journal of the History of Sexuality* 3 (1993): 402–17; Thomas D. Morris, *Southern Slavery and the Law, 1619–1860* (Chapel Hill: University of North Carolina Press, 1996), chap. 14; Philip Schwarz, *Twice Condemned: Slaves and the Criminal Laws of Virginia, 1705–1865* (Baton Rouge: Louisiana State University Press, 1988), 155–64, 205–10; Diane Miller Sommerville, "The Rape Myth in the Old South Reconsidered," *Journal of Southern History* 61 (1995): 481–518.

8. On the scholarly othering of African American women, see Ann duCille, "The Occult of True Black Womanhood: Critical Demeanor and Black Feminist Studies," *Signs* 19 (1994): 591–629. On the exclusion of black women from the category of women, see Gloria Hull, Patricia Bell-Scott, and Barbara Smith, eds., *All the Women Are White, All the Blacks Are Men, but Some of Us Are Brave* (Old Westbury, N.Y.: Feminist Press, 1982).

9. For examples of statutes specifying the crime of black-on-white rape, see John D. Cushing, ed., *The Earliest Printed Laws of Pennsylvania, 1681–1713* (Wilmington, Del.: Michael Glazier, 1978), 69; B. W. Leigh, ed., *The Revised Code of the Laws of Virginia* (n.p., 1819), 585–86; Lamar Lucius, *A Compilation of the Laws of the State of Georgia, 1810–1819* (Augusta, Ga., 1821), 804–05; Harry Toulmin and James Blair, *A Review of the Criminal Law of the Commonwealth of Kentucky* (Frankfort, Ky., 1806), 1:129–30. In the later antebellum period, southern states used statutes or precedents explicitly to deny enslaved women protection from rape. See Morris, *Southern Slavery and the Law*, 305–07; Peter Bardaglio, "Rape and the Law in the Old South: 'Calculated to excite indignation in every heart,' " *Journal of Southern History* 60 (1994): 756–58.

10. For examples of statutes that denied slaves the ability to testify against whites in criminal cases, see William Waller Hening, *The Statutes at Large, Being a Collection of All the Laws of Virginia* (Richmond, 1923), 4:327 [1732]; Horatio Marbury and William H. Crawford, A Compilation of the Laws of the State of Georgia, 1755–1800 (Savannah, 1802), 429 [1770]. See also Thomas D. Morris, "Slaves and the Rules of Evidence in Criminal Trials," *Chicago-Kent Law Review* 68 (1993): 1209–39. Even if Harriet Jacobs had been a slave in early nineteenth-century Pennsylvania, the 1780 act for the gradual abolition of slavery would have prevented her from testifying against her white master. See John D. Cushing, *The First Laws of the Commonwealth of Pennsylvania* (Wilmington, Del.: Michael Glazier, 1984), 284.

11. In an extensive survey of criminal court records from 1700 through 1820, I found only one instance of a white man charged with raping a slave. It occurred in 1717 in Massachusetts, and the man died before the trial. *The Diary of Samuel Sewall, 1674–1729*, ed. M. Halsey Thomas (New York: Farrar, Straus, and Giroux, 1973), 2:853. For further discussion of the cultural definitions of rape in early America, see Sharon Block, *He Said I Must: Coerced Sex in Early America* (Chapel Hill: OIEAHC at University of North Carolina Press, forthcoming).

12. The legal system also might have difficulties enforcing theoretically absolute divisions between black and white, slave and free, as evidenced in the many antebellum trials focusing on an individual's racial or slave status. For an examination of one such case, see Walter Johnson, "Slavery, Whiteness, and the Market: The Strange Story of Alexina Morrison" (paper presented at the Wesleyan Center for the Humanities, Wesleyan University, Middletown, Conn., 1996).

13. On the modern "seemingly unshakable association of rape with physically violent misconduct," see Stephen J. Shulhofer, "Taking Sexual Autonomy Seriously: Rape Law and

Beyond," *Law and Philosophy: Philosophical Issues in Rape Law* 11 (1992): 35–94. Much of the following discussion about resistance's reformulation into consent was inspired by Ellen Rooney, " 'A Little More Than Persuading': Tess and the Subject of Sexual Violence," in *Rape and Representation*, ed. Lynn A. Higgins and Brenda R. Silver (New York: Columbia University Press, 1991), 87–114.

14. Punctuation added.

15. Jacobs, *Incidents*, 28, 27, 31–32, 41.

16. *The Trial of Nathaniel Price, for committing a rape on the body of Unice Williamson* . . . (New York, 1797), 2–3; People v. Thomas Conlen, March 4, 1818, New York County Court of General Sessions Indictment Papers, New York City Municipal Archives; Respublica v. David Robb, April 20, 1787, Yeates Legal Papers (March-April 1789), folio 2, Historical Society of Pennsylvania, Philadelphia.

17. Josiah Henson, *Truth Stranger Than Fiction: Father Henson's Story of His Own Life* (Boston, 1858), 3; Lewis Clarke, "Leaves from a Slave's Journal of Life," in *Slave Testimony: Two Centuries of Letters, Speeches, Interviews, and Autobiographies*, ed. John Blassingame (Baton Rouge: Louisiana State University Press, 1977), 156.

18. Jacobs, *Incidents*, 31, 32, 28, 27. Whether Harriet Jacobs was ultimately forced into acts of sexual intercourse with her master or whether she avoided all but his verbal sexual assaults is an unanswerable question, and for my purposes not directly relevant; in either case, James's treatment of Harriet was sexually abusive.

19. Ibid., 55, 32, 39.

20. Ibid., 55.

21. Such "stranger-rapes" were the type of sexual assault most likely to be prosecuted, and prosecuted successfully. For instance, of 491 charges of rape with a recorded verdict between 1700 and 1820, close to two-thirds of the men were found guilty overall, but in the 43 cases where the defendants knew their victims, only 42 percent resulted in a guilty verdict. Of eighty charges of rape where the verdict and location of the attack are known, three-quarters of those that occurred in an isolated outdoor location resulted in a guilty verdict, compared to fewer than half of those that occurred at the victim's home. For a fuller explanation of these statistics, see Sharon Block, "Coerced Sex in British North America, 1700–1820" (Ph.D, diss., Princeton University, 1995), chap. 5.

22. Jacobs, *Incidents*, 32.

23. Ibid., 27, 35.

24. Emphasis added. For the British standard of this classic legal formulation, see William Hawkins, *A Treatise of the Pleas of the Crown* (1724–26; reprint, New York: Arno Press, 1972), 1:108; Giles Jacob, *The Modern Justice* (London, 1720), 350. For American references, see Richard Starke, *The Office and Authority of a Justice of Peace* (Williamsburg, 1774), 292; *A New Conductor Generalis* (Albany, 1803), 388; John Elihu Hall, *The Office and Authority of a Justice of the Peace in . . . Maryland* (Baltimore, 1815), 172; C. J. Tilghman, "Definition of Crimes in 1806 or After," Pennsylvania Court Papers (box 6: Tyson-Yard and Miscellaneous Papers), 8, Historical Society of Pennsylvania, Philadelphia.

25. Jacobs, *Incidents*, 28, 32.

26. Ibid., 29.

27. Ibid., 35, 34.

28. Ibid., 39.

29. Ibid., 31, 12, 13, 27–28.

30. Ibid., 31, 33, 34.

31. Cornelia Dayton found that between 1711 and 1789, only 14 percent of women filing for divorce claimed adultery as the sole grounds for their petitions. Dayton, *Women before*

the Bar, 135. Marylynn Salmon found that charges of cruelty, desertion, or nonsupport were more common justifications for granting women divorce decrees than was adultery. Salmon, *Women and the Law of Property in Early America* (Chapel Hill: University of North Carolina Press, 1986), 58–80, esp. 63. Of sixty-five divorce petitions begun by wives in Davidson County, Tennessee Circuit Court between 1809 and 1849, only twelve (18 percent) were on the grounds of adultery. Lawrence B. Goodheart, Neil Hanks, and Elizabeth Johnson, " 'An Act for the Relief of Females . . . ': Divorce and the Changing Legal Status of Women in Tennessee, 1796–1860," pts. 1 and 2, in *Domestic Relations and Law*, vol. 3 of *History of Women in the United States: Historical Articles on Women's Lives and Activities*, ed. Nancy Cott (New York: K. G. Saur, 1992), 80–116, esp. 113.

On divorce in the antebellum South, see Jane Turner Censer, " 'Smiling Through Her Tears': Ante-bellum Southern Women and Divorce," *American Journal of Legal History* 25 (1981): 24–47; for Pennsylvania, see Merril D. Smith, *Breaking the Bonds: Marital Discord in Pennsylvania, 1730–1830* (New York: New York University Press, 1991); Thomas Meehan, " 'Not Made out of Levity': Evolution of Divorce in Early Pennsylvania," *Pennsylvania Magazine of History and Biography* 92 (1968): 441–64.

32. Though difficult, divorce based partly on a husband's sexual relations with his slave was not impossible. For such a case, see Goodheart, Hanks, and Johnson, " 'An Act for the Relief,' " 94. In this case, witnesses testified to the husband's open cohabitation and sexual acts with the enslaved woman.

33. On women's roles as midwives, see Laurel Thatcher Ulrich, *A Midwife's Tale: The Life of Martha Ballard Based on Her Diary, 1785–1812* (New York: Alfred A. Knopf, 1990). For the point that "good wives" partly secured their position by differentiating themselves from "nasty wenches," see Kathleen M. Brown, *Good Wives, Nasty Wenches, and Anxious Patriarchs: Gender, Race, and Power in Colonial Virginia* (Chapel Hill: IEAHC at University of North Carolina Press, 1996), esp. 75–104.

34. Jacobs, *Incidents*, 59, 122. In this case, as in Harriet's own circumstances, proof of pregnancy eclipsed the question of rape. On the trope of the mother in slave narratives, see Joanne M. Braxton, "Outraged Mother and Articulate Heroine: Linda Brent and the Slave Narrative Genre," in *Black Women Writing Autobiography: A Tradition within a Tradition* (Philadelphia: Temple University Press, 1989), 18–38.

35. *Feast of Merriment: A New American Jester* (Burlington, 1795), 33, emphasis in original. *Religion and Domestic Violence in Early New England: The Memoirs of Abigail Abbot Bailey*, ed. Ann Taves (Bloomington: University of Illinois Press, 1989), 58–59.

36. Richard S. Dunn, "Servants and Slaves: The Recruitment and Employment of Labor," in *Colonial British America: Essays in the New History of the Early Modern Era*, ed. Jack Greene and J. R. Pole (Baltimore: Johns Hopkins University Press, 1984), 157. For a discussion of the general silencing of African American women's history, see Darlene Clark Hine, "Lifting the Veil, Shattering the Silence: Black Women's History in Slavery and Freedom," in *The State of Afro-American History: Past, Present, and Future*, ed. Darlene Clark Hine (Baton Rouge: Louisiana State University Press, 1986), 223–49.

37. Jacobs, *Incidents*, 27–28. On the "multiple and interrelated dimensions of silence" in this book, see Joanne M. Braxton and Sharon Zuber, "Silences in Harriet 'Linda Brent' Jacobs's *Incidents in the Life of a Slave Girl*," in *Listening to Silences: New Essays in Feminist Criticism*, ed. Elaine Hedges and Shelley Fisher Fishkin (New York: Oxford University Press, 1994), 146–55. On silenced rape in a more modern narrative, see Jenny Sharpe, "The Unspeakable Limits of Rape: Colonial Violence and Counter-Insurgency," in *Colonial Discourse and Post-Colonial Theory: A Reader*, ed. Patrick Williams and Laura Chrisman (New York: Columbia University Press, 1994), 221–43.

38. Harriet Jacobs to Amy Post, June 21, 1857, in Jacobs, *Incidents*, 242. For a discussion of African American women's psychological reactions to systemic sexual exploitation, see Darlene Clark Hine, "Rape and the Inner Lives of Black Women in the Middle West: Preliminary Thoughts on the Culture of Dissemblance," *Signs* 14 (1989): 265–77.

39. Jacobs, *Incidents*, 28, 38, 25.

40. Emphasis in original.

41. Jacobs, *Incidents*, 28.

42. Ibid., 56, 57.

43. Ibid., 29, 54–55.

44. Free servants had significant advantages over enslaved women, but servants still did not have easy access to criminal justice when they were sexually coerced. Even though Rachel Davis's master was ultimately convicted of rape, this occurred several years after he had first assaulted her.

45. Allan Kulikoff, *Tobacco and Slaves: The Development of Southern Cultures in the Chesapeake, 1680–1800* (Chapel Hill: IEAHC at University of North Carolina Press, 1986), 386.

46. Painter, "Three Southern Women and Freud," 195, 213.

Chapter Eight

Unfixing Race

Class, Power, and Identity in an Interracial Family

Thomas E. Buckley, S. J.

In November 1816 Robert Wright, a slaveholding farmer from Campbell County in the Virginia Piedmont, petitioned the General Assembly for a divorce. Because the state courts lacked jurisdiction over divorce in the early nineteenth century, the legislators regularly considered such requests. Wright's petition, however, was unlike any other the assembly had ever received. According to Wright's account, his marriage to Mary Godsey in 1806 had been a happy one. Describing his behavior toward her as "kind and affectionate," Wright acknowledged that Mary had brought him "great domestic comfort, and felicity" until 1814, when William Arthur "by his artful, and insidious attentions" replaced Wright "in her affections." The couple eloped in January 1815, taking with them some of Wright's property, including a female slave, but were caught in neighboring Bedford County. Wright reclaimed his possessions, and Mary consented "to return to the Home, and the Husband she had so ungratefully, and cruelly abandoned." Despite her infidelity, Wright maintained that he had again treated his wife with affection, hoping "time . . . would reconcile her to her situation and restore her to Happiness." His hopes proved illusory. Ten months later, Mary and William ran off to Tennessee. Charging her with desertion and adultery, Wright asked the assembly to pass a law ending their marriage.

Thus far the case was familiar. Tales of infidelity, desertion, and scorned love the legislators had heard before. What made Wright's petition unique was his frank admission that as "a free man of color" he had married a white woman and so violated Virginia's law forbidding interracial marriage. While avoiding a rhetorical style that was either defiant or obsequious, Wright defended the validity of his union and presented his case in matter-of-fact fashion. His free status apparently empowered him with a sense of personal worth and dignity and a claim to equal treatment that he was unafraid to assert publicly. Equally noteworthy were the affidavits submitted with the memorial. Defying the mores historians commonly ascribe to white southerners, more than fifty white citizens of Campbell County ignored Wright's miscegenation, endorsed his request for a divorce, and testified to his good standing in their community.[1]

Wright's legislative petition and the accompanying documents are remarkable on several counts. First, they introduce us to the power relationships and the interaction of race and class, both within an interracial family and between that family and the local community, that operated as discursive processes in constructing the shifting identities of Robert Wright and his family.[2] Second, they suggest a level of openness in interracial sexual relationships and a degree of white acceptance of miscegenation that challenge historical generalizations and traditional stereotypes of both free blacks and the slaveholding society of the early nineteenth-century South.[3] Finally, they contest the commonly accepted view that free blacks operated cautiously on the fringes of southern society. This essay does not argue that the situation of Robert Wright and his family was typical, even of free blacks who held land and slaves, but rather, as Ira Berlin pointed out, that historians must pay attention to exceptions.[4] A scrutiny of Wright's background and his family and community connections demonstrates the complexity of antebellum race relations while simultaneously dramatizing the importance of studying the free black experience in terms of individual, family, and local histories at a time when slavery was vigorously expanding.[5]

In a burst of uncharacteristic liberalism, Virginia legalized manumission by deed or will in 1782. Early in the next decade, however, the Old Dominion retreated from emancipation when a new codification of laws concerning slaves spelled out their status as chattels and forbade free Negroes from entering the state. The revelation of Gabriel's plot in 1800 increased the outcry for harsher laws that would further restrict the activities of both slaves and free Negroes, prevent any more manumissions, and remove the free black population. The assembly responded by requiring newly emancipated slaves to leave Virginia and encouraging the various African colonization societies that sprang up in the next decade.[6] Meanwhile, by the end of the Revolution, the Piedmont held more slaves than the Tidewater. During the next three decades, the state's slave population doubled, while more and more whites joined the slaveholder ranks.[7] Richard R. Beeman has documented the expansion of slavery, with its concomitant commitment to agrarianism, into Lunenburg County and asserted that by 1830 the peculiar institution provided "the central point of definition for the Southside's white citizens."[8]

In nearby Campbell County, the same social and economic system provided the context for the Wright family. Fortunately, an abundance of sources makes it possible to reconstruct the interplay between family members. In addition to the divorce petition and the data available from deeds, wills, and census and tax records, a series of legal battles after Robert Wright's death left a rich deposit of court papers detailing his economic affairs as well as family and community relationships. A few years ago Michael P. Johnson and James L. Roark demonstrated the usefulness of family papers in tracing the experience of free African Americans in the antebellum South.[9] A reconstruction of the history of the Wright family indicates the wealth of information available in legislative petition collections and legal files squirreled away in state archives and county courthouses.[10]

Thomas Wright, a white man from a large family in Prince Edward County, bought an extensive plantation in Bedford County from Charles and Sarah Caffrey

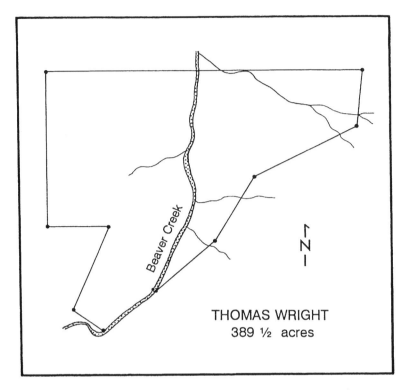

THOMAS WRIGHT
389 ½ acres

Fig. 8.1 In July 1779 Thomas Wright purchased a 389.5-acre plantation in Bedford County from Charles and Sarah Caffrey. This plat of the property on Beaver Creek is derived from the Campbell County Surveyor's Book, 1827–1924.

in July 1779 for 1,500 pounds of tobacco. Amounting to 389½ acres of prime farmland, the property straddled Beaver Creek just a few miles before the stream flows into the James River. Two years later that section of Bedford became part of newly established Campbell County, and in 1784 the town of Lynchburg was founded up the James River, a few miles southwest of Wright's plantation.[11] While struggling to establish himself financially during these years, Wright became estranged from his brothers and sisters. Shortly before he purchased the farm, his father, John Wright, had died, leaving a wife and at least seven children. His will details an extensive estate with bequests of varying sizes. Thomas was assigned one of the smallest portions, a monetary gift of £30 to be paid by his brother James within five years. This legacy was only a pittance, given the financial outlay required to purchase the land on Beaver Creek, but evidently he never received it. Later, in "his drinking fits," a resentful Thomas Wright swore that none of his relatives would ever inherit his property and vowed that he would rather give it to one of his neighbors or the county poor.[12]

Instead of these potential beneficiaries, however, Wright ultimately switched his attention and affection to the mulatto family he established along Beaver Creek. To his new home, Wright had brought several slaves, including a young woman, Sylvia, and her two children, Prudence and Anna, whom he had purchased from the Cabell estate four or five years before.[13] Sylvia was apparently of full African descent, because someone who knew her well later described her as "very black." At the time of her purchase, she was pregnant again and in 1775 gave birth to a son, James. Sometime during the following years, Thomas Wright began to cohabitate with her. On June 30, 1780, almost a year after they moved to the Beaver Creek plantation, she bore a mulatto son, Robert, and over the next decade and a half came three mulatto daughters: Betsy, Mary, and Eliza. Although Thomas Wright never formally married the mother of his children, they "lived together as man and wife." They also prospered. Within the economic ranks of Campbell County, Wright could be considered at least a modest planter. Nor did his miscegenous relationship with Sylvia injure his standing in the community. Rather than censuring or fining him, the county court periodically assigned him to survey roads and serve on juries, and he numbered among his friends some of the most important men in the community.[14]

As the years passed, Thomas Wright took increasing interest in his family and particularly his son. On September 1, 1791, when Robert was eleven years old, Thomas escorted the boy he called "his Robin" to the Campbell courthouse and recorded his manumission, which was to become effective on his twenty-first birthday in 1801.[15] The timing of this civil declaration was crucial in Robert's development. He was old enough to grasp the importance of the status being conferred on him, and the public nature of the announcement must have reinforced his own feelings of self-worth while giving him a keen appreciation of the value of his freedom and a profound gratitude toward his father, qualities that would mark his adult life. About this time, Thomas Wright began telling his friends that Robert would be his heir. Thus, the boy grew up with the sense of entitlement that came from being the only son of a well-to-do and doting father. Far from treating him as a slave, Thomas kept Robert in his home, carefully saw to his education in business as well as academic subjects, and gave him a horse to ride to school. His classroom companions and playmates at home were white boys such as William Hawkins and Stephen and William Perrow, whose fathers also possessed good-sized farms and slaves. Described variously as "light" and as a "bright" mulatto, Robert basked in the approval of a father who proudly pointed him out as one of the "strongest negro fellows" in the county.[16]

Eventually, Thomas Wright also provided for the freedom of his other children. On April 14, 1800, he filed papers for the manumission of his three daughters: Betsy, sixteen, Mary, fourteen, and Eliza, seven, as well as for Maria, three, the daughter of Anna, who was part of Sylvia's first family. Each girl would become free at the age of eighteen. The next February, Wright also manumitted Anna, twenty-eight, and James, twenty-six, "being fully persuaded that freedom is the natural right of all mankind." His belief in natural rights, however, did not induce him to liberate all his slaves. At his death Wright still owned at least five.[17]

In reality, he may well have freed Anna, James, and Maria because of his devotion to Sylvia and her influence over him. The provisions of his will indicate the

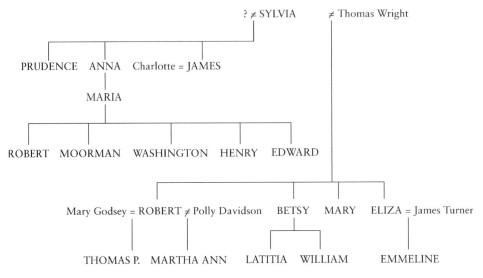

Fig. 8.2 Descendants of Sylvia Wright

nature of their relationship as well as his love for both Sylvia and their son. Accord-ing to reliable witnesses, Wright originally planned to leave the bulk of his estate to Sylvia for the rest of her life. Robert and several of the senior Wright's friends, however, persuaded him that Sylvia would be incapable of managing the property and was not interested in the land. It would be far better, they argued, to leave most of the estate in Robert's hands with the understanding that he would provide finan-cially for his mother's comfort as well as for the rest of the family. Thomas Wright concurred with this paternalism. As one of his closest associates and neighbors, Colonel Daniel B. Perrow, later attested, although Wright was "much attached" to Sylvia and extremely solicitous for her care, he also "had great Confidence in Robert before and at the time of his Death."[18]

When Thomas Wright died in late 1805, he left "the sole and exclusive use and enjoyment" of his plantation house and two acres around it to "Sylvee a woman of colour formerly my slave but since emancipated and with whom I have had chil-dren." She also received as her "absolute property forever" all furniture in the house, two milk cows of her own choosing, and whatever money Thomas possessed at the time of his death. The will further specified that Anna's daughter, Maria, should serve Sylvia until she became free at the age of eighteen. To his "natural son Robert Wright," Thomas gave the plantation land, slaves, stock, and equipment, as well as any other real estate or personal property he owned. Moreover, the house and acres in Sylvia's possession would revert to Robert after his mother's death. Apart from the land, the personal estate in the house and on the farm was appraised at almost £500.[19] Wright chose his executors carefully. Undoubtedly, he realized the unusual nature of his will, and he knew his white brothers and sisters and their descendants expected to claim his property. Three "trusty friends," Daniel B. Per-row, Charles Gilliam, and Lawrence McGeorge, served as his executors. Perrow was especially prominent in the county, which he represented for eleven terms in the state assembly, and later served as sheriff.[20] He and the other executors ensured that Sylvia and Robert took uncontested possession of the estate.

Thus, with his father's considerable assistance and the approval of the white elite, Robert Wright gained entry into Campbell County society and acquired an identity constructed by economic class rather than race. Almost a year later he displayed and reinforced his position when he married Mary Godsey, a white woman. Because Mary was underage, her mother gave her consent for the marriage license in October 1806, though the county clerk never recorded the marriage.[21] It is not difficult to imagine the minister arriving for the wedding only to discover that the bride and groom were an interracial couple, performing the ceremony under the social constraints of the occasion, and then covering himself with the law by destroying the certificate. If miscegenation under any circumstances had been unacceptable in Campbell County, Wright's neighbors should have demonstrated their disapproval by haling the couple before the county court for violating the law, or at least shunned them. In all the abundant legal records, however, no evidence exists that either then or later anyone publicly objected to their marriage.[22]

Robert brought his wife to a house located close by his mother's, and the next seven or eight years were probably the happiest of his life. An energetic worker like his father, he was adept at farming. Judging from the tax assessments and the comments of overseers, his acreage ranked among the best in the county. The plantation produced substantial crops of wheat, tobacco, oats, hay, and corn, along with burnt lime. The work was sufficient for seven laborers, most of whom were apparently slaves. Wright fit easily into the slaveholding ranks and seemingly was not troubled by owning slaves or purchasing them as he thought necessary.[23] His tastes were those of his class and age. In his free time he hunted in the nearby hills or gambled at cards with his friends. Like his father and many other Virginians of the day, he had a penchant for the bottle and drank freely and often. George MacKey, a white stonemason who boarded with him, considered Wright "industrious" around the farm but also noted that he indulged in "frequent Frolicks."[24]

Fulfilling the promises he had made to his father, Robert assumed responsibility for the care of his mother and siblings. Sylvia Wright provided the most difficult challenge. When she discovered that Thomas had altered his original will and given the plantation directly to Robert, she was upset. Evidently, she wanted her economic independence and resented his intervention in the matter of the will and subsequent financial control, which effectively undercut the identity she had constructed as the "wife" of the deceased Thomas. Neighbors noticed that mother and son had "frequent misunderstandings," but Sylvia later admitted that Robert had "honestly fulfilled his agreement" with his father and given her a "decent Support."[25]

Another change in the will may also have displeased Sylvia. At one time Thomas Wright had considered leaving fifty acres of his plantation to James, her elder son, whom he had also freed. But Robert dissuaded his father from breaking up the tract on Beaver Creek and promised that he would purchase land elsewhere for James. A few months after his father's death, he bought fifty-six acres in neighboring Bedford County for his half brother to farm but retained the deed himself to ensure that no one would "cheet [James] out of the land." Robert's half sister Anna had died some time earlier, and when her daughter, Maria, received her freedom at the age of eighteen, Robert sent her to live with her uncle James in Bedford and provided money for her support.[26] Robert also took responsibility for his mulatto sisters and met their needs as best he could. Betsy, the eldest, was raised in Lynchburg, mainly under the supervision of Sarah Winston Cabell, and later had two children, Latitia and William, without benefit of marriage. Although accused of being a drunkard and a "notorious prostitute," Betsy Wright would be a force to be reckoned with in the family and the courts for years to come. Betsy's reputation for loose conduct may have been the reason Sylvia kept her two youngest daughters at home. Mary died unmarried before her mother, while Eliza married James Turner, a free black shoemaker.[27]

By all accounts, Robert Wright played the role of gentleman farmer and *paterfamilias* well. His father had trained him for that position, and apparently he enjoyed it. After eight years of marriage, his wife gave birth in December 1814. Robert proudly named his son Thomas Pryor Wright, thus identifying him with his own father and his father's family. Within a few weeks, however, Mary rejected both her husband and their mulatto child and ran away with William Arthur. Though she initially returned home in response to her husband's pleading, Mary's elopement at the end of 1815 left Robert "very much exasperated against her" and plunged him into a bitterness from which he never recovered.[28] The cuckolded husband acted out his anger and humiliation. Convinced that his neighbors had assisted in the escape, he confronted Catherine Stockton, who deposed that Wright had threatened her "with a gun to make me talk and drew his fist to break my head." She finally went to court to make Wright "keep the peace." His suspicions were confirmed, however, when he discovered that James Wiley, one of his old gambling companions, had helped the couple elope. Robert cursed him soundly and repeatedly.[29]

The mulatto farmer soon formed a liaison with another white woman. In the fall of 1816 Polly Davidson moved into his home with the cordial approval of her father and other members of her family. George MacKey, who "lifted her off of her horse" the night she arrived, testified later that her father on his visits "never" expressed any reservations about the relationship his daughter had formed. Robert Wright himself told Catherine Stockton "that all the relatives of . . . Polly were pleased at her living with him." For the Davidsons, who owned no slaves and little property, this association meant an economic boost. To facilitate the new relationship, Wright also used raw economic power. On the day Polly moved into his house, Robert gave her a bond for one thousand dollars and, according to some sources, promised her half of his property if she bore his children. Her brother William became Wright's overseer on the plantation, and her clergyman brother may even have performed an informal marriage ceremony without benefit of license.[30]

Although Wright's divorce petition did not mention Polly Davidson, it indicates the depth of his feelings and the need to reassert his own self-worth and the identity constructed through bonding with his father and affiliation with the white, land-owning, slaveholding class in the county. Wright presented himself to the General Assembly as "a free man of color," his wife as "a free white woman," and Arthur as "a free white man." In stressing the eloping couple's free status, Wright emphasized the importance of his own. Freedom was the common denominator that made him their equal, while his wife's desertion and adultery without provocation on his part made Wright more sinned against than sinning. The Wrights had obtained a proper marriage license, and an authorized clergyman, William Heath, had officiated at the ceremony. Although admitting that the minister who performed an interracial marriage and the white party who contracted it could be punished under the law, Wright argued confidently that the wedding had been "to all intents and purposes valid and binding between the parties," because such penalties did not render it null and void. Given these circumstances, he wanted a divorce.[31]

The request in itself was unusual, for legislative divorces were extremely rare. Few Virginians applied, and far fewer had their appeals granted. Out of 107 divorce petitions between 1786 and 1815, the assembly acted affirmatively on only fifteen. Ironically in the case of Robert Wright, the most compelling reason a white husband could offer for a divorce in 1816 was proof through the birth of a mulatto child that his wife had been sexually involved with a Negro.[32] By acknowledging that his marriage had been interracial, Wright may have hoped to assure a divorce.

In a ringing endorsement of his request, the local white community rallied behind Wright and testified to his honorable position in their society. Lewis Franklin, Charles Gilliam, and Stephen Perrow, respectable farmers and slaveholders, signed their names at the bottom of his petition and, in a separate affidavit, asserted that as Wright's neighbors they had known him well for a long time. He behaved "with propriety," they told the legislature. Vouching for the accuracy of his statements, they asserted that he had "allways treated his wife with kindness." In still another petition, more than fifty other men testified to the General Assembly that they "have been well acquainted with Robert Wright ... for many years past, and do with pleasure certify that we consider him an honest, upright man, and good citizen." From the "information" they had gathered about his marital problems, they believed that his petition was a truthful account. Most of these men were middling farmers, but a few possessed extensive plantations of more than a thousand acres. About half owned slaves, and at least two were justices of the county court.[33] In short, they were broadly representative of the local community that regarded Wright as one of its own.

The scene is easily imagined. The men gathered outside the buildings at the county seat on one of the autumn court days. Franklin, Gilliam, and Perrow were well-known, respected members of the community. Perhaps one of them read Wright's petition aloud, noted their own endorsements, and encouraged the other men to sign the briefer statement. They could explain to those who were unfamiliar with his marital situation what his wife had done. The three were credible witnesses. Wright himself may well have appeared, as he did at court days. His economic status in the community, his capable management of the property he had inherited from his father, and the way he conducted himself in their society had helped the mulatto farmer forge strong relationships with his white neighbors. They gave him and his cause their public support.

Despite the widespread local approval, however, the House of Delegates rejected Wright's divorce petition out of hand without even referring it to committee.[34]

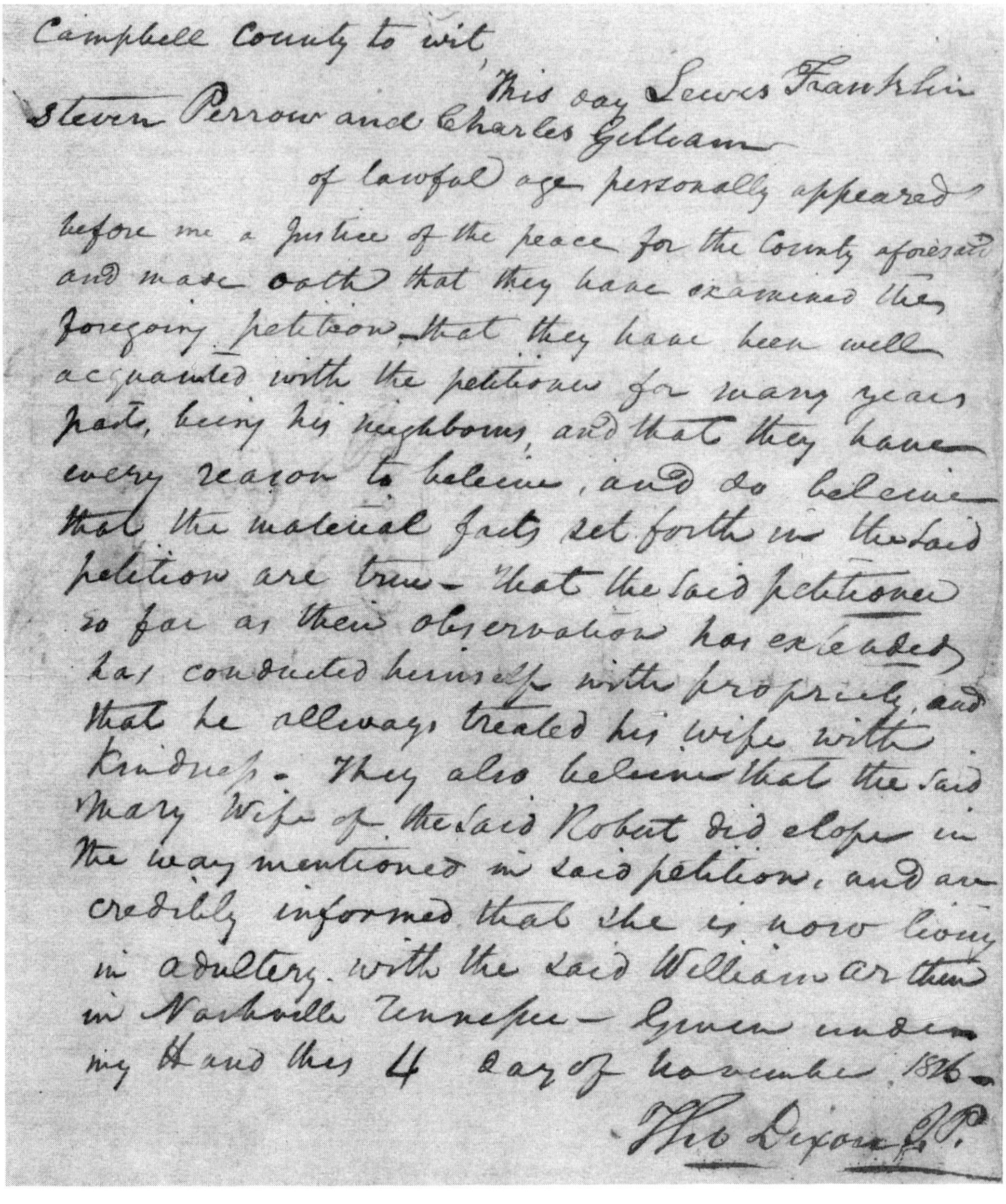

Campbell County to wit,

This day Lewis Franklin
Steven Perrow and Charles Gilliam
of lawful age personally appeared
before me a Justice of the peace for the County aforesaid
and made oath that they have examined the
foregoing petition, that they have been well
acquainted with the petitioner for many years
past, being his neighbours, and that they have
every reason to believe, and do believe
that the material facts set forth in the said
petition are true — that the said petitioner
so far as their observation has extended
has conducted himself with propriety, and
that he allways treated his wife with
kindness. They also believe that the said
Mary wife of the said Robert did elope in
the way mentioned in said petition, and are
credibly informed that she is now living
in adultery with the said William Ar then
in Nashville Tennessee — Given under
my Hand this 4 day of November 1816.

Tho Dixon J.P.

Fig. 8.3 In an affidavit sworn before Thomas Dixon on November 4, 1816, Lewis Franklin, Stephen Perrow, and Charles Gilliam supported Robert Wright's divorce petition and affirmed that Wright had "allways treated his wife with kindness." Legislative Petitions, Virginia State Library and Archives.

Affidavits and testimonials from western Campbell County counted for little in Richmond. Although Wright could be married to a white woman in his community, he could not be married to her in law.

Neither of the supporting documents that accompanied the petition mentioned race, yet both Wright and the local community were fully aware of his racial iden-

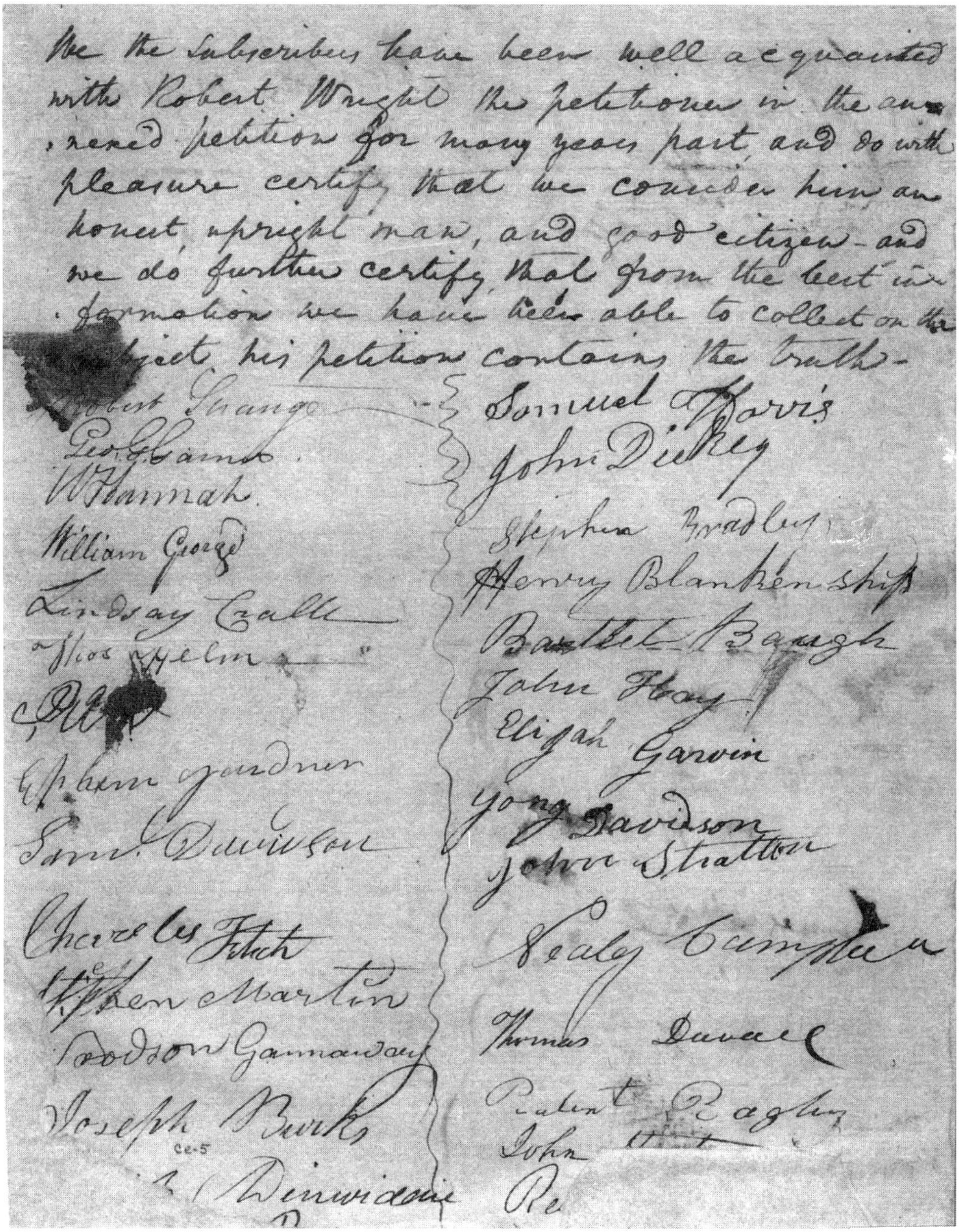
We the Subscribers have been well acquainted with Robert Wright the petitioner in the annexed petition for many years past and do with pleasure certify that we consider him an honest, upright man, and good citizen - and we do further certify that from the best information we have been able to collect on the subject his petition contains the truth -

William George
Saml. Davidson
Charles Fitch
Joseph Burks
Samuel Harris
John Dickey
Stephen Bradley
Henry Blankenship
Elijah Garvin
John Stratton
Thomas Duvall

Fig. 8.4 More than fifty men, most of them middling farmers and half of them slaveholders, subscribed their names to a petition in support of Robert Wright's request for a divorce. Wright's Campbell County neighbors testified that "we consider him an honest, upright man, and good citizen." Legislative Petitions, Virginia State Library and Archives.

tity. All the legal documents drafted after his death repeatedly labeled him "coloured" or "black" or "negro." County records do not indicate that he ever held any civil position or served on a jury. When he traveled outside Virginia, he was careful to carry on his person a certified copy of his emancipation papers.[35] Yet Robert Wright was in fact a split subject. For many if not most important purposes, class and economic condition, rather than race, constructed his identity. The tax records provide one significant index. The personal property tax list from his section of the county in 1816 counted 2,171 slaves over twelve years of age and seventy-two free Negroes over sixteen. Wright was not included, however, as either a free black or a mulatto in 1816 or in any preceding year. For tax purposes, he was considered to be white. Only in 1817 and 1818, after the divorce petition and during the last two years of his life, did the tax assessor write an *M*, for mulatto, next to his name.[36]

That change may have occurred because a new person filled the assessor's office; but it also may represent Wright's altered position in the neighborhood. When he and Mary Godsey had married, the local community had ignored their violation of the law against miscegenation. At least some in the county, however, disapproved of his public adultery with Polly Davidson. One of Wright's boarders recounted that the couple lived together "as though they had been man & wife in the utmost harmony." Polly was in full charge of the "Domestick affairs" in the home.[37] Although certain neighbors were sympathetic to Robert's plight and accepted this relationship, referring to Polly as his "wife" and as "Polly Wright," others condemned her character and insisted that her position as Robert's "concubine" rendered her "notorious in the neighbourhood."[38] Wright's strained relations at this time with his father's old friend and executor, Daniel Perrow, probably resulted from the latter's open disapproval of such "cohabitation." Though Robert had once sought the elderly colonel's advice and consulted with him on business, he no longer did so.[39] Indeed, Robert may well have expected the assembly to reject his petition but hoped that a good-faith attempt to obtain a divorce would gain community acceptance for the relationship he and Polly had formed. Polly may also have wanted the divorce in order to legitimize her position as Robert's wife.

In this uneasy atmosphere created by both Robert's continuing bitterness over Mary's desertion and the hostility of at least a portion of the community, a misunderstanding arose in the spring of 1818 between Robert and his closest friend, Stephen Perrow. Raised on neighboring farms, the two had played and gone to school together and had inherited their fathers' plantations about the same time. Though Robert was older by perhaps as much as seven years, one of the boarders in his home thought that the two men "appeared as greate as Brothers."[40] Perrow had strongly supported the divorce petition and, after Robert's death, would serve as Polly's closest adviser; but in early 1818 a slave told him and Fleming Duncan that Robert had cursed them for letting their hogs run wild in the woods and called them "no better than theives." Duncan wanted to confront Wright, but Perrow persuaded him that because this tale was simply "negro's news, Robin would deny it—that he knew Robin better than he did, & to let him alone." The incident, however, was repeated around the neighborhood. Ultimately someone informed an "astonished, and distressed" Wright during the April court days that Stephen Perrow and others among his peers no longer considered him a friend. Although Robert acknowledged the "dispute" between himself and Daniel Perrow, he was unaware of any other hostile neighbors and was particularly upset by the report that Stephen Perrow was "unfriendly to him." Unwilling to believe it, Wright immediately sought out Perrow and happily reported to Gilliam the next day "that everything was perfectly explained . . . and they were on the most friendly terms."[41]

Yet Wright's emotional distress was evident to his friends. Lewis Franklin witnessed Robert's crying when he and Perrow were discussing Robert's affairs at the courthouse in September.[42] The reason for Wright's unhappiness was probably not a business matter, because his economic status at this time was excellent. Stephen Perrow may have been warning his friend that he was in danger of being presented to the county court for adultery. Evidently Colonel Daniel Perrow, Campbell's recently retired sheriff, had seriously considered such an action. He later testified that Stephen Perrow had told him he might do so himself, but the colonel thought the younger man had made this statement just to keep him from taking that step. The emotional pressure intensified. Although his neighbors thought Wright was in good health, he began to have premonitions of approaching death. While staying overnight with Franklin, he remarked on the sickness in his family and stated "that he should die before long." He expressed the same belief to another old family friend, John Gardner. Both men later testified that Wright had also told them he had made his will, and Gardner added that Wright had named Stephen Perrow and Arthur Litchfield as his executors.[43]

Less than a month later, on October 14, 1818, Robert Wright died. He left a sizable estate in land, slaves, and crops with a promise of another plantation home, farm animals, and additional property to go to his heirs after the death of his mother.[44] A series of legal battles and appeals to the General Assembly ensued that embroiled the entire Wright family—white, black, and mulatto—involved the conflicting testimony of numerous friends, neighbors, and acquaintances, and employed a flock of lawyers off and on for more than fifty years. These conflicts revolving around the Wrights further demonstrate the status and treatment of a free black family and the way in which its members asserted their rights, used the law, and interacted with one another and the white members of an antebellum Virginia community.

On the evening before Wright died, his home was crowded with family members and friends. As Robert lay unconscious in his bedroom, Stephen Perrow showed a will in Robert's handwriting to several people who later said they had read it.[45] According to most versions of the testimony, Wright had planned to divide his property. His infant son, Thomas P. Wright, would receive the larger section of land on the north side of Beaver Creek; the property on the south side, where his home was located, would go to Polly during her lifetime and then to any child she might have within nine months of his death. If she did not bear his child, then when she died the house and land would revert to his son.[46] After Robert's death, however, the will could not be located, and Polly Davidson maintained that Robert's sister

Betsy had destroyed it. She explained that while Robert was dying, Betsy had come to her in another room and "asked for the keys to the Beaureau where the will & other Papers were Kept in the Room in which Robert lay & went directly & opened or unlocked the same." Later, Polly discovered that "the will & one hundred Dollars in money were missing & she thought Betsy Wright had taken them."[47] In support of Polly's story, Catherine Stockton swore that shortly after Robert's death, she had been on a road outside Lynchburg and heard Betsy boast to several other blacks that she "had stolen . . . Robert's will, and all the money he had and had conquered all the white folks."[48] A month after Robert's death, the county court sent Betsy, her daughter Latitia, and brother-in-law James Turner to jail until they produced the will, but later ordered their release.[49]

In the spring of 1819, Robert's putative will became the subject of a lawsuit filed by Polly Davidson against Samuel Fleming, whom the county court had appointed temporary curator of Wright's estate until the will was settled.[50] For more than a year both sides gathered affidavits from family members and neighbors. Stephen Perrow led the struggle to establish Polly Davidson's claim, while Fleming assembled witnesses who tried to throw doubt on Polly's credibility and Stephen Perrow's friendship with Robert Wright. As accusations of lying and deceit were hurled back and forth, the neighborhood along Beaver Creek became badly fractured. Members of the Perrow family, for example, wound up on opposing sides. Daniel Perrow, whose wife was Elizabeth Fleming, supported Samuel Fleming's case against his cousin Stephen Perrow.[51] Sylvia, Betsy, and the rest of Robert's black and mulatto family supported Fleming. Certainly they stood to gain if Thomas P. Wright inherited all of his father's property immediately. Betsy in particular took a hand in guiding affairs. Fleming and *"Relatives Interested"* paid their lawyer, James B. Risque, fifty dollars in advance and promised him another three hundred dollars if he won the suit.[52]

Before the case could be settled, however, the white members of the Wright family filed a cross suit in April 1820 charging that Robert Wright had never been legally emancipated and was therefore a slave and incapable of inheriting any property from his father in 1805. Because Thomas Wright had never married, they asserted that his legal heirs were his brothers and sisters and their descendants. They asked the court to set aside Thomas Wright's will and give them his property.[53] Even though the county clerk maintained that he could not find any evidence of Robert Wright's manumission, the court decided the statement in Thomas Wright's will that "he had '*duly emancipated*' him" was sufficient evidence of Robert's freedom and therefore his capacity to inherit his father's property. His white cousins wound up paying court costs.[54] They then appealed twice to the legislature to award them the property on the grounds that Robert had died "Intestate and unmarried." Both times the assembly turned them down.[55]

While these appeals were still in process, Polly Davidson lost her lawsuit. In *Davidson v. Wright*, a Bedford County court ruled "that Robert Wright did not make or execute such will as alleged," and the Lynchburg Superior Court of Chancery then awarded the entire estate to Thomas P. Wright.[56] After almost seven years of litigation, Samuel Fleming and Robert Wright's mother and siblings had emerged triumphant. Meanwhile, Fleming had been systematically robbing the estate and adding to his own personal wealth.[57] Wright had left extensive holdings in land, slaves, horses, stock, plantation equipment, and "a most excellent crop" in his fields and barns, as well as money and bonds worth as much as five hundred dollars. As Stephen Perrow later testified, Wright had been a capable manager with few debts. Soon after taking over the property, however, Fleming told Perrow that even though the estate had "a Balance of upwards of $500 . . . it made no difference as the estate was going to hell and he might as well have it as any one else."[58]

As curator, Fleming hired a succession of overseers to manage the Wright plantation. Their affidavits testify both to the excellent quality of the farm and its yield as well as the various ways in which the curator bilked the estate. Fleming regularly sold or took home for himself crops, lamb, pork, wool, cows, horses, beds, and other movable property, but revenues rarely appeared on the balance sheet. He also charged the estate one dollar for each trip he made to the plantation, while bragging to the overseer that he made such charges even when he did not appear.[59] Although Sylvia and Betsy Wright would later prove keen enough to defend their own interests in court, no complaints came either from them or from any other member of the Wright family. Fleming may well have been buying them off. Certainly he used estate funds to support Sylvia and the other Wrights, including Betsy's daughter, Latitia, who took care of young Thomas. They continued living in the old plantation house.[60]

Fleming's temporary curatorship ended with the conclusion of the suits over the will in 1825. In what was later proven to be an extraordinary fraud, he drew up a claim against the estate of $726.72, which he transferred jointly to German Jordan, a local tavern keeper, and Richard G. Haden, a deputy sheriff. Then, after selling his own plantation on Beaver Creek, Fleming pocketed his gains both legal and criminal and moved to Tennessee.[61] The county court next designated William Thompson, Jr., as curator, but when he discovered that Betsy Wright objected to his appointment, Thompson did not apply for the papers.[62] Instead, toward the end of 1825, Jordan had himself appointed first the estate's administrator and then Thomas P. Wright's guardian. The boy was eleven years old.[63]

If Fleming had swindled the estate, Jordan wasted it. After renting out the land and the slaves, he auctioned off the stock, crops, and other movable property. He also accepted without challenge several claims against the estate, including one by Haden of six hundred dollars. Asserting insufficient funds to settle the estate's debts, Jordan then sold the slaves over a three-year period between 1826 and 1829, some for a price far below market value.[64]

Complaints from his securities eventually spurred the court to relieve Jordan of his control over the estate. At young Thomas Wright's request, William Gough, who had recently purchased a large plantation next to the Wright property, became the boy's guardian. Gough retained Samuel and Maurice H. Garland, two prominent Lynchburg attorneys, and the next year brought suit in Lynchburg's Superior Court of Law and Chancery against Fleming, Jordan, and their securities. The inventory made shortly after Jordan became administrator had listed eleven slaves, horses, stock, crops, plantation utensils, and furniture worth $3,667. With the exception of Suckey, an old slave woman valued at nothing, it was *"all gone."* The attorneys blistered Jordan and Haden for their "high handed frauds & speculations." Jordan, they asserted, had "cheated the child out of all his estate but the land, and it's God mercy" that had not been sold also.[65]

After detailing the defendants' misdeeds, the Garland brothers suggested that "perhaps" Sylvia Wright and Jordan had shared "a secret understanding." In proposing that Sylvia had a hand in looting her grandson's property, the two lawyers spoke from firsthand knowledge, for they had represented her in two successful claims against the estate after Jordan became administrator. Sylvia had first sued Jordan in March 1826, demanding that he support her out of the estate. She claimed an annuity on the basis of her relationship with Thomas Wright and promises made after his death. Without mentioning that she had been a slave and that no marriage had taken place, Sylvia asserted that "in early life she associated herself with Thomas Wright . . . and until his death they lived together in harmony as man and Wife." Sylvia depicted their relationship as a partnership. Although initially "they were both porre, having no property," by their own "industry and economy they had acquired a considerable real and personal estate." After Thomas's death, first Robert Wright and then Samuel Fleming had fulfilled her expectations, but Jordan had reduced her to "a helpless and distressed Condition for the Ordinary Comfort of life and dependant upon Charity." She asked for "support for life" and threatened that without it "she must become chargeable upon the county."[66]

In his response as defendant, Jordan did not appeal to the provisions of Thomas Wright's will, challenge Sylvia's interpretation of events, or note her original status as Wright's slave. Nor did he mention that just a few months earlier, she had purchased furniture and stock at the estate auction. In short, Sylvia was no pauper; but because Jordan offered no contest, the court ordered him to pay her from estate revenues one hundred dollars a year in quarterly installments.[67] She took him to court the following year, charging that Robert had borrowed a sizable sum in 1806 and never repaid it, "altho' often required." Jordan did not even appear, and an estate slave was sold to satisfy her claim.[68]

Jordan's failure to defend his ward's estate was not the result of incompetence. In caring for his own interests, he was extremely astute and fast becoming a wealthy man. The case against him proceeded through several sessions until, after evaluating the commissioner's reports on the estate and the affidavits, the court held Jordan responsible "for the fair cash value of the slaves" who had been "improperly sold." This sum, together with the claims against his guardian accounts, amounted to $2,340.41, which he paid to the estate in March 1833. Even this sizable amount, however, did not seriously cut into his holdings.[69]

Meanwhile, Thomas P. Wright approached his majority. Although his early education had been intermittent, he later attended a school conducted by Thomas and Bartlett Baugh. The boy had bills for books as well as "slate, paper and inkpowder" and pocket money "to buy [a] Knife" and "sundries for Christmas." Sometimes he boarded at school, but his guardian also paid Sylvia "for boarding, washing and mending" and Latitia for "making Clothes."[70] When he became twenty-one on December 17, 1835, Gough paid him in cash $2,540.17, a hefty sum, which with the farmland he inherited might be expected to offer bright prospects.[71] Unfortunately, the young man was enmeshed in debts as well as in another lawsuit, brought by his grandmother against the estate for the annuities that Gough had ceased paying. His guardian had been fending her off for several years, and it must have been with great relief that Gough signed off that responsibility and removed himself from the Wright family affairs. In order to gain his inheritance, however, the grandson had to assume the lawsuit. He made a deed of trust with Charles Mosby and Maurice Garland, selling them the land he had inherited on the understanding that he could continue to reside there and take the profits as long as he paid his grandmother's past and current annuities. If they were not forthcoming, then the trustees could seize and sell his land.[72]

There were other debts, both large and small, so Wright formed a series of eight more deeds of trust with Mosby and Garland to pay a total of $2,361.91. Finally, he agreed that the trustees could auction the land, and Edward Hunter purchased the Wright plantation in 1836 for almost $4,000. Hunter's deed stipulated "that Sylvia Wright the grand mother of Thomas P. is to retain the house" together with the lot and rights to water from the spring and "sufficient wood to burn and timber to repair the house and keep up her fences." After she died, Hunter would receive the house and acres around it.[73]

Thomas Wright had other problems as well. Evidently he was something of a hell-raiser. In August 1835, before he turned twenty-one, he was presented in the Lynchburg Hustings Court for "swearing Twenty profane oaths" and fined $16.60. The next month he appeared before the same court for a breach of the peace, and in November the Campbell court prosecuted him for "beating" another man. Meanwhile, he continued to pile up debts of various sizes, possibly from gambling. In June 1836 the county authorities jailed him as an "insolvent debtor."[74]

Sylvia Wright died in January 1838. Despite the years she had spent with lawyers and lawsuits, she left no will. Betsy and Thomas both filed deeds turning over their share of her estate to Betsy's daughter, Latitia. Thomas Wright explained that his cousin had "rendered . . . important services in his infancy and childhood which have never been paid to her, and which [he] is now desirous to make good."[75] He also may have been trying to keep his creditors from swallowing up whatever he inherited from Sylvia's estate. The court named Allen L. Wyllie as administrator, but before the estate could be divided, Latitia died. Because Thomas had already yielded his claim, Betsy and her son, William, filed a lawsuit maintaining that they and Emmeline Turner, the daughter of Betsy's deceased sister Eliza, were the only three living descendants entitled to Sylvia Wright's estate. They asked the court to order a sale of Sylvia's slaves and a tripartite division of her property. Wyllie and the court concurred, and the three shares each amounted to about six hundred dollars.[76]

During the following summer, however, in neighboring Bedford County, James and Maria Wright, another son and granddaughter of Sylvia Wright, learned of Sylvia's death and came forward to assert their rights.[77] When Betsy denied any relationship to them, James and Maria explained the existence of Sylvia's first family before her sale to Thomas Wright and the provision that Robert Wright had made for them. Betsy's son, William, took exception to James Wright's affidavit in the case not only because James was "a party to the suit" but also because he was "a negro." Affidavits by white men in Bedford County, however, supported James and Maria's story. John Overstreet, for example, recalled how Robert had called James his "half Brother" and remembered "too yellow women at James Wrights on visits & said James was their brother." More witnesses came forward, including Stephen Perrow, who supported James and Maria's claims.[78] A court commissioner ultimately concluded that Sylvia had seven children: the first three were "of a black complection," while the last four possessed "a light complection, born whilst she and her master Thomas Wright, cohabited as man & wife, and recognized by him as his children." In 1852 the court eventually ordered a division of Sylvia's estate into five equal shares for Betsy, James, Maria, and William Wright and Emmeline Turner.[79]

Responding to this decree, Betsy reappeared in court. The previous decade and a half had been traumatic for the almost seventy-year-old woman. According to several neighbors, she had been badly burned in a fire in the early 1840s and spent almost two years confined to a rented, unfurnished home in Lynchburg, where her bed was "a parcel of rags." Frequently freezing in the winter's cold without wood for a fire and lacking even basic necessities, she existed on whatever food her friends and son, William, brought her. Then William had died, leaving her even more alone. By the end of the decade, Betsy resided in Lynchburg's poorhouse.[80] Despite her problems, however, Betsy's amended bill of complaint showed an extraordinary capacity for deception. Although still denying that James and Maria were her half brother and niece, she accepted the court's verdict that they were her relatives and thus claimed their estates. According to her story, they had both died unmarried and childless, as had her son, William, and her niece Emmeline Turner. Thomas P. Wright had died as well. Announcing that she was "the sole survivor of the whole family, and sole heir of all the rest," Betsy demanded "full and complete justice." Moreover, she hounded the court to act "*speedily* (for she is a tenant of the Poor house and with her just rights involved in this case, could be made comfortable, if not happy, the remnant of her days)."[81] Her persistence paid off. Although not entitled to the legacies of either James or Maria—James had lived with a woman he acknowledged as his wife, and Maria had five living children—Betsy received $450 from Wyllie in 1853 and several lesser amounts in later years. Although probably never finding either comfort or happiness and evidently remaining a "pauper," she certainly enjoyed longevity. When the last case was settled and the court accepted the final report of its commissioner in 1873, Betsy was almost ninety years old.[82]

The saga of the Wright family, however pathetic in its denouement, provides a valuable opportunity to examine the personal, social, and economic changes within an interracial family over three generations; the interaction of white, mulatto, and black relatives; and their relationships with the local white community. The most immediately arresting reality is that race did not fix identities. Indeed, the incidence of miscegenation on the part of men and women of both races met a tolerant, even

Fig. 8.5 When Robert Wright died on October 14, 1818, he left extensive holdings in land, slaves, horses, stock, plantation equipment, and "a most excellent crop" in his fields and barns, as well as money and bonds worth as much as five hundred dollars. His estate was subsequently squandered by curators and eaten up in lawsuits. This modern photograph shows Campbell County farmland once owned by the Wrights. Beaver Creek runs along the line of trees in the background.

supportive, reaction from one slaveholding Virginia community. Neither white father nor mulatto son felt compelled to disguise or deny the intimate liaisons they formed across the color line. For more than a quarter century, Thomas Wright lived with Sylvia out of wedlock; yet in conversation with friends and through his will, he made clear his love for the mother of his children and the happiness their union had brought him. As best he could, he constructed for her the identity of a wife. In her later years Sylvia treated their relationship as if it had been in fact a legitimate marriage and an economic partnership. For both, it obviously meant much more than the mating of a white master and a black slave.

Nor did Thomas Wright's open concubinage with Sylvia diminish his stature in the local community. Moreover, he successfully transferred his respected position in society to his son, who then reached beyond his parents to marry a white woman and live with her as his wife for ten years. So integral was this marriage to his identity that neither in his reported exchanges with his neighbors nor in his petition to the General Assembly did he ever apologize for his conduct, display embarrassment, or express remorse for violating a supposed taboo. Mary Godsey and Polly Davidson also crossed the racial line publicly and did so with the consent and even approval of their families. Moreover, all evidence indicates that the local community accepted the match between Robert and Mary. In short, everyone immediately concerned and their white neighbors behaved as if interracial marriage was normal and that the legislation prohibiting miscegenation in Virginia did not or should not exist.

Why did this happen—both for father and son? Most obviously, the respectable positions both men occupied in Campbell County were related to their economic standing as prosperous slaveholding farmers as well as to their public behavior. Class status was directly related to wealth in land and slaves. For this place and time in the culture of patriarchy, money counted far more than race in fixing social position. As a member of the planter class and the beneficiary of his father's transference of power, Robert Wright could openly defy even such a potentially explosive prohibition as that against interracial sexual intercourse and still find acceptance in his local community. Although his neighbors clearly knew Robert was a mulatto, they chose not to construct his identity primarily on that basis.

The role he assumed within the family after his father's death fit the patriarchal model he undoubtedly imbibed from Thomas Wright's example and tutelage and reinforced his identity. He fulfilled what was expected of the male head of the household. He supported his mother and provided for his black and mulatto siblings and their children. Thomas Wright also trained his son for the position he would fill in the neighborhood. He bequeathed to him not only his estate but also the patronage of powerful friends in the white community. They ensured that Robert inherited the property without challenge. White men of similar social and economic standing became his closest friends and associates. Slaveholders and lesser planters like himself, some had been schoolmates and boyhood companions. In addition to doing business with one another, they hunted, gambled, and drank together. As he shared their values, the mulatto farmer moved easily and naturally in their society. He ate at their tables and spent nights in their homes, and when his wife abandoned him, he turned to them for the assistance and support they readily provided. Only when he openly introduced Polly Davidson into his home and began living with her as his wife did a portion of the community recoil in disapproval. But the opprobrium resulted from the couple's public adultery, not from their miscegenation. Even then, Stephen Perrow and other close friends continued to sustain him.

Robert Wright's sense of entitlement to move freely and openly in white society was not unique in his family. Nor perhaps was it entirely a result of his father's training or genes. As the legal records make evident, both black and mulatto members of his family displayed a tough assertiveness in confronting members of the white community as well as one another. Undeterred by considerations of race or gender, Sylvia and her daughter Betsy did not hesitate to use the court system to demand what they claimed as their rights. Their legal opponents were usually white males. In case after case throughout the antebellum period, the two women pushed and shoved to advance their interests. Hiring the best lawyers in Lynchburg, they won more often than they lost. Indeed, they sometimes appear greedy. In the struggle to enhance her own economic security after Robert's death, Sylvia played into the hands of Samuel Fleming and German Jordan and thus jeopardized the inheritance of her grandson. Then again, watching the young Thomas P. Wright grow to maturity, she may have recognized his weaknesses and foreseen his inability to maintain his affairs.

Together with her son, William, Betsy turned repeatedly to the courts to secure her claims. Described by one of their securities as "idle, dissolute, & extravagant as far as they could obtain either credit or means to be so," the mother and son were continually in debt despite the money they received. Even with her later physical and financial problems, Betsy emerges as the least appealing family member, particularly in her attempt to deny her free black relatives their right to share in Sylvia's estate. Her defeat in that case was a result of the sturdy resistance offered by James and Maria Wright in concert with their white supporters. But that was the only court fight Betsy lost. In substantial measure, her frequent successes depended on her determined persistence. An exhausted Allen Wyllie, appointed by the court in 1838 to administer Sylvia's estate, wrote twenty years later that he had paid more money than he should have to settle the matter and satisfy "my anxiety to be cleared of the Wright[s]."[83]

The legal battles of Sylvia and Betsy Wright reinforce the inescapable conclusions drawn from Robert Wright's life: that emancipated slaves and free blacks did not necessarily live circumspectly on the margins of southern society, and that identities for southern blacks before emancipation could be constructed on bases other than race. Indeed, the story of the Wright family exemplifies the variety and complexity that underlay the status and position of free blacks in the South in the generations before the Civil War.

NOTES

The author wishes to thank Martha Hodes, Susan Miller, Joseph Tiedemann, and the outside readers at the *Virginia Magazine* for their comments and suggestions on earlier drafts of this essay. A Loyola Marymount University Research Grant and an Andrew W. Mellon Fellowship from the Virginia Historical Society supported the research for this project.

1. Petition of Robert Wright, 16 Nov. 1816, Campbell County, Legislative Petitions, Records of the General Assembly, Record Group 78, Virginia State Library and Archives, Richmond (hereafter cited as Vi). For the pertinent law of 1792, see Samuel Shepherd, ed., *The Statutes at Large of Virginia, 1792–1806: Being a Continuation of Hening*, 3 vols. (Richmond, 1835–36), 1:134–35. Catherine Clinton provides a typical perspective on pre–Civil War southern attitudes toward interracial sexual relations in " 'Southern Dishonor': Flesh, Blood, Race, and Bondage," in Carol Bleser, ed., *In Joy and in Sorrow: Women, Family, and Marriage in the Victorian South* (New York, 1991), 52–68. See also Sally G. McMillen, *Southern Women: Black and White in the Old South* (Arlington Heights, Ill., 1992), 27. Martha Hodes challenges this view in *White Women, Black Men: Illicit Sex in the Nineteenth-Century South* (New Haven, 1997).

2. For an explanation of this use of the documents, see Joan W. Scott, "The Evidence of Experience," *Critical Inquiry* 17 (1991): 773–97. The author is indebted to Susan Miller for suggesting this line of investigation and pointing out this article.

3. Extensive discussions of interracial sexual relationships may be found in A. Leon Higginbotham, Jr., and Barbara K. Kopytoff, "Racial Purity and Interracial Sex in the Law of Colonial and Antebellum Virginia," *Georgetown Law Journal* 77 (1989): 1967–2029; Joel Williamson, *New People: Miscegenation and Mulattoes in the United States* (New York,

1980); David H. Fowler, *Northern Attitudes towards Interracial Marriage: Legislation and Public Opinion in the Middle Atlantic and the States of the Old Northwest, 1780–1930* (New York, 1987); and Bertram Wyatt-Brown, *Southern Honor: Ethics and Behavior in the Old South* (New York, 1982), 307–24. See also Thomas Brown, "The Miscegenation of Richard Mentor Johnson as an Issue in the National Election Campaign of 1835–1836," *Civil War History* 39 (1993): 5–30.

Until recently, historians have tended to ignore or minimize the incidence of miscegenation on the part of white women. See, for example, Catherine Clinton, *The Plantation Mistress: Woman's World in the Old South* (New York, 1982), 209–22; Karen A. Getman, "Sexual Control in the Slaveholding South," *Harvard Women's Law Journal* 7 (1984): 115–52. For a contrasting view, see Eugene D. Genovese, *Roll, Jordan, Roll: The World the Slaves Made* (New York, 1972), 422; Herbert G. Gutman, *The Black Family in Slavery and Freedom, 1750–1925* (New York, 1976), 82, 389, 614–16; Gary B. Mills, "Miscegenation and the Free Negro in Antebellum 'Anglo' Alabama: A Reexamination of Southern Race Relations," *Journal of American History* 68 (1981–82): 16–34; and Hodes, *White Women, Black, Men*.

4. Ira Berlin, *Slaves without Masters: The Free Negro in the Antebellum South* (New York, 1974), xvii. Berlin's work remains the premier study of southern free blacks between the Revolution and the Civil War, although Wright's case challenges several of his conclusions about their status and treatment. See also Loren Schweninger, *Black Property Owners in the South, 1790–1915* (Urbana, 1990); A. Leon Higginbotham, Jr., and Greer C. Bosworth, " 'Rather Than the Free': Free Blacks in Colonial and Antebellum Virginia," *Harvard Civil Rights-Civil Liberties Law Review* 26 (1991): 17–66. Older, though still useful, are John Henderson Russell, *The Free Negro in Virginia, 1619–1865* (1913; New York, 1960); and Luther Porter Jackson, *Free Negro Labor and Property Holding in Virginia, 1830–1860* (New York, 1942).

5. Though some of their conclusions are not applicable to the situation of Robert Wright and his family, Michael P. Johnson and James L. Roark have produced a model study in *Black Masters: A Free Family of Color in the Old South* (New York, 1984). See also their essay, "Strategies of Survival: Free Negro Families and the Problem of Slavery," in Bleser, ed., *In Joy and in Sorrow*, 88–102. For the use of the terms *black, mulatto,* and *Negro,* see Johnson and Roark, *Black Masters*, xv–xvi.

Other recent family and local studies include T. O. Madden, Jr., *We Were Always Free: The Maddens of Culpeper County, Virginia: A 200-Year Family History* (New York, 1992); Lee H. Warner, *Free Men in an Age of Servitude: Three Generations of a Black Family* (Lexington, Ky., 1992); and Thomas N. Ingersoll, "Free Blacks in a Slave Society: New Orleans, 1718–1812," *William and Mary Quarterly*, 3d ser., 48 (1991): 173–200. For a collection of older local histories, see Elinor Miller and Eugene D. Genovese, eds., *Plantation, Town, and County: Essays on the Local History of American Slave Society* (Urbana, 1974).

6. William Waller Hening, ed., *The Statutes at Large; Being a Collection of All the Laws of Virginia . . . ,* 13 vols. (Richmond, 1809–23), 11:39; Shepherd, ed., *Statutes at Large,* 1: 122, 239; Robert McColley, *Slavery and Jeffersonian Virginia,* 2d ed. (Urbana, 1973), 71–72; Douglas R. Egerton, *Gabriel's Rebellion: The Virginia Slave Conspiracies of 1800 and 1802* (Chapel Hill, 1993).

7. Richard S. Dunn, "Black Society in the Chesapeake, 1776–1810," in Ira Berlin and Ronald Hoffman, eds., *Slavery and Freedom in the Age of the American Revolution* (Charlottesville, 1983), 49–82. See also Philip D. Morgan and Michael L. Nicholls, "Slaves in Piedmont Virginia, 1720–1790," *William and Mary Quarterly*, 3d ser., 46 (1989): 211–51; Peter J. Albert, "The Protean Institution: The Geography, Economy, and Ideology of Slavery in Post-Revolutionary Virginia" (Ph.D. diss., University of Maryland, 1976).

8. Richard R. Beeman, *The Evolution of the Southern Backcountry: A Case Study of Lunenburg County, Virginia, 1746–1832* (Philadelphia, 1984), 218.

9. Johnson and Roark, *Black Masters*; Michael P. Johnson and James L. Roark, eds., *No Chariot Let Down: Charleston's Free People of Color on the Eve of the Civil War* (Chapel Hill, 1984).

10. The petition collections have only begun to be tapped. For examples of their use for the eighteenth century, see Raymond C. Bailey, *Popular Influence upon Public Policy: Petitioning in Eighteenth Century Virginia* (Westport, Conn., 1979); and Ruth Bogin, "Petitioning and the New Moral Economy of Post-Revolutionary America," *William and Mary Quarterly*, 3d ser., 45 (1988): 391–425. In his published dissertation, *Race Relations in Virginia and Miscegenation in the South, 1776–1860* (Amherst, Mass., 1970), James Hugo Johnston quoted extensively from petition collections, but this work must be used with care, because it contains numerous inaccuracies.

11. Indenture between "Charles Caffrey and Sarah his wife . . . and Thomas Wright," dated 2 July 1779, recorded 26 July 1779, Bedford County Deed Book 6, pp. 253–56 (microfilm), Vi (unless otherwise noted, all county and tax records are at the Virginia State Library and Archives, Richmond). The amount was initially judged to be 370 acres, but a later survey raised that estimate (Campbell County Surveyor's Book, 1827–1924, 27 Mar., 3 Apr. 1828, p. 13 [microfilm]).

12. Will of John Wright, 18 Mar. 1775, Prince Edward County Will Book 1, pp. 218–19 (microfilm); inventory of the estate of John Wright, 19 June 1779, Prince Edward County Will Book 1, p. 226 (microfilm); affidavit of Daniel B. Perrow, 5 Feb. 1821, in *Wright v. Wright* [Fleming], Superior Court of Chancery (see Circuit Superior Court of Law and Chancery), Lynchburg District, file 525, Vi; affidavit of John Gardner, 5 Feb. 1821, in "Davidson v. Wright [Fleming]," Superior Court of Chancery (see Circuit Superior Court of Law and Chancery), Lynchburg District, file 578, Vi. These two cases were so closely related that many of the papers from the second case, file 578, are found in file 525.

13. Answer of James Wright, 9 June 1840, affidavit of Stephen Perrow, 21 Sept. 1841, in *Wright v. Wright*, Circuit Superior Court of Law and Chancery, Lynchburg District, file 1886, Vi. Their previous owner was probably Dr. William Cabell, who had died in 1774 and left almost his entire estate to his son, Nicholas. Alexander Brown, *The Cabells and Their Kin* (Boston, 1895), 62, 64. On an issue arising out of his father's estate, Nicholas Cabell brought suit against Thomas Wright in November 1785 (Campbell County Order Book 2, 1785–86, p. 232).

14. Affidavit of William Hawkins, 6 July 1840, answer of James Wright, 9 June 1840, affidavit of Stephen Perrow, 21 Sept. 1841, commissioner's report in *Wright v. Wright*, affidavit of John Overstreet, 13 Apr. 1841, file 1886; Campbell County Order Book 1, 1782–88, pp. 247, 255; Campbell County Order Book 2, 1785–86, p. 63; Campbell County Order Book 3, 1786–91, p. 64; Campbell County Order Book 7, 1801–4, p. 7.

15. Affidavit of John Gardner, 5 Feb. 1821, file 578; Campbell County Deed Book 3, p. 110 (microfilm).

16. Affidavit of John Gardner, 5 Feb. 1821, file 578; affidavit of Stephen Perrow, 8 Sept. 1831, in *Wright v. Jordan*, Circuit Superior Court of Law and Chancery, Lynchburg District, file 1174, Vi; affidavit of William B. Perrow, 6 Oct. 1820, file 525; affidavit of William Hawkins, 6 July 1840, affidavit of James Turner, 1 Mar. 1842, file 1886; affidavit of Jesse Thornhill, 29 Aug. 1821, file 578.

17. Campbell County Deed Book 5, 14 Apr. 1800, 9 Feb. 1801, pp. 85, 240 (microfilm); Campbell County Personal Property Tax Records, 1805 (microfilm). Sylvia's eldest child, Prudence, had injured her knee; Wright sent her to a doctor in New London to be healed.

During her recovery, Prudence married a slave of Nathan Reid and, because she refused to be separated from her husband, Wright sold her to Reid. Thus, Prudence was the only one of Sylvia's seven children who remained in slavery (answer of James Wright, 9 June 1840, affidavit of James Wright, 2 June 1840, file 1886).

18. Bill of Sylva Wright, Copy [of] Record, *Sylva Wright v. Wrights Adm.*, file 1174; affidavits of Elizabeth Gilliam, 11 Dec. 1825, and Daniel B. Perrow, 14 Mar. 1826, Copy [of] Record, file 1174. Thomas Wright's father had made a similar provision for his wife (will of John Wright, Prince Edward County Will Book 1, p. 218).

19. Will of Thomas Wright, signed 24 Oct. 1805, proved 9 Dec. 1805, Campbell County Will Book 2, pp. 226–27 (microfilm); inventory of the estate of Thomas Wright, 14 Apr. 1806, Campbell County Will Book 2, pp. 265–68.

20. Campbell County Will Book 2, p. 226; Ruth Hairston Early, *Campbell Chronicles and Family Sketches: Embracing the History of Campbell County, Virginia, 1782–1926* (1927; Baltimore, 1978), 480–81.

21. Petition of Robert Wright, 16 Nov. 1816, Campbell County, Legislative Petitions, Records of the General Assembly, RG 78. The marriage bond was dated 9 October 1806. The bride is named Polley Godsey on the license (Campbell County Marriage Bonds and Consents, 1782–1853, 9 Oct. 1806 [microfilm]). See also Shepherd, ed., *Statutes at Large*, 1: 132, 134–35. In a later court case, the clerk testified that the certificate had never been returned (affidavit of John Alexander, 28 Dec. 1828, Campbell County, Legislative Petitions, Records of the General Assembly, RG 78).

22. Robert Wright's "light" or "bright" appearance may have made the marriage more acceptable, at least to some.

23. Campbell County Land Tax Records, 1806–18 (microfilm); report, 24 Mar. 1832, in *Wright v. Jordan*, file 1174; affidavits of Robert Walthall and James Daniel, 8 Sept. 1831, file 1174; affidavit of Elizabeth Gilliam, Copy [of] Record, file 1174. Wright owned between six and eight slaves over twelve years of age (Campbell County Personal Property Tax Records, 1806–18 [microfilm]). For slaveholding among Virginia's free black population, see Philip J. Schwarz, "Emancipators, Protectors, and Anomalies: Free Black Slaveowners in Virginia," *Virginia Magazine of History and Biography* 95 (1987): 317–38.

24. Affidavit of Daniel B. Perrow, 7 Oct. 1820, file 578; affidavit of George MacKey, 1 May 1821, file 525. For MacKey's occupation, see affidavit of Samuel Fleming for continuation, 18 Oct. 1820, file 525.

25. Affidavit of William B. Perrow, 6 Oct. 1820, file 525; affidavit of Elizabeth Gilliam, 11 Dec. 1825, bill of Sylva Wright, Copy [of] Record, *Sylva Wright v. Wrights Adm.*, file 1174. For examples of free black women who did control property, see Loren Schweninger, "Property Owning Free African-American Women in the South, 1800–1870," *Journal of Women's History* 1 (1990): 13–44.

26. Bedford County Deed Book 12, pp. 92–93 (microfilm); affidavits of John Overstreet and William Hawkins, 6 July 1840, affidavit of James Wright, 2 June 1840, file 1886. Both remained in Bedford County. The lack of a firm title did not keep James from remaining on the property after Robert's death, and when James died years later, his widow, Charlotte, rented out the land. They had no children. Maria had five sons and named her eldest Robert (answer of John C. Noell, 11 Nov. 1853, file 1886).

27. Affidavit of James Turner, 1 Mar. 1842, file 1886; affidavit of Patterson Gilliam, 8 Oct. 1820, file 525; Campbell County Marriage Bonds and Consents, 1782–1853, 31 May 1809 (microfilm); *Recognizance, Comm. v. Davidson etc.*, 13 July 1832, Old Suits, Campbell County Courthouse, Rustburg, Va.

28. Affidavit of William B. Perrow, 6 Oct. 1820, file 525. Thomas P. Wright's date of

birth can be gauged by a deed he made on 17 December 1835 when he reached twenty-one (Campbell County Deed Book 20, pp. 159–60 [microfilm]). His mother, Mary Godsey Wright, married William Arthur in Tennessee, and the couple eventually settled near Knoxville and lived to an old age. William farmed and later became a miller (affidavit of Betsy Wright, Apr. 1822, in *Davidson v. Wright*, Judgments, 1825, Bedford County Courthouse, Bedford, Va.; U.S. Census Bureau, Seventh Census, 1850, Anderson County, Tenn.; U.S. Census Bureau, Eighth Census, 1860, Knox County, Tenn. [microfilm]).

29. Affidavit of George MacKey, 1 May 1821, affidavit of Catherine Stockton, 7 Oct. 1820, file 525.

30. Affidavit of George MacKey, 1 May 1821, affidavit of Catherine Stockton, 7 Oct. 1820, affidavit of William B. Perrow, 6 Oct. 1820, file 525; statement of Richard Stratham, 14 June 1819, file 1174; Campbell County Personal and Land Taxes, 1816 (microfilm). A Reverend Samuel Davidson appears on the tax rolls for Campbell County that year, and Samuel Davidson was one of the signers of the divorce petition. Robert Wright must have remained on good terms with Polly's family, because the three witnesses to his purported will were Polly's father, brother, and brother-in-law: James Davidson, William Davidson, and Charles Caffrey (deposition of James Williams, 24 Dec. 1819, file 525).

31. Petition of Robert Wright, 16 Nov. 1816, Campbell County, Legislative Petitions, Records of the General Assembly, RG 78. On the issue of validity, see Higginbotham and Kopytoff, "Racial Purity and Interracial Sex," 2007. For Wright's use of the term *man of color*, see Berlin, *Slaves without Masters*, 180–81. Berlin asserts that the term was "rarely" used in the Upper South.

32. These petitions and legislative action on them are in the *Journals of the House of Delegates of Virginia* (Richmond, 1827–28), 1786–1815. The texts and accompanying documents of most of these petitions are available by county and date in the collection of Legislative Petitions, Records of the General Assembly, RG 78. If the assembly passed a divorce bill or provided for another venue for the petitioner, those laws are in Hening, ed., *Statutes at Large*; Shepherd, ed., *Statutes at Large*; and, for bills passed after 1806, the annual *Virginia Acts of Assembly*.

33. Petition of Robert Wright, 16 Nov. 1816, Campbell County, Legislative Petitions, Records of the General Assembly, RG 78; Campbell County Personal Property and Land Tax Records, 1815–17 (microfilm); Early, *Campbell Chronicles*, 412–13, 480–81.

34. *Journal of the House of Delegates*, 16 Nov. 1816, 26.

35. Affidavit of John Gardner, 5 Feb. 1821, file 578.

36. Campbell County Personal Property Taxes, 1806–18 (microfilm). It is intriguing that tax records in the 1830s also fail to list Sylvia Wright as a free Negro or Thomas P. Wright as a free mulatto. Nor did the federal census of 1850 tag Betsy Wright with the telltale *M, B,* or *FN* next to her name. These sources do identify other persons as such, and the tax records also total the number of free blacks. Perhaps in some parts of the South people of color who owned or had owned a significant amount of property were not ordinarily labeled by race, because their economic status placed them in a higher stratum of society. If so, the identification of wealth among free African Americans in the pre–Civil War South becomes a much more complicated task (Campbell County Personal Property Taxes, 1831–38 [microfilm]; U.S. Census Bureau, Seventh Census, 1850, Campbell County [Lynchburg], Va., p. 97 [microfilm]).

37. Affidavit of John Hoar, 9 Oct. 1820, file 525.

38. Affidavit of John McAllister, Jr., 9 Oct. 1820, affidavit of William Thompson, 6 Oct. 1821, affidavit of Predhem Moore, 7 Apr. 1820, affidavit of William B. Perrow, 6 Oct. 1820, file 525.

39. Affidavit of Daniel B. Perrow, 5 Feb. 1821, affidavits of Patterson Gilliam, 1 Apr., 8 Oct. 1820, file 525.

40. Affidavit of George MacKey, 1 May 1821, file 525. The census of 1850 lists Stephen Perrow's age as sixty-three. If this figure is accurate, he was born about 1787 (U.S. Census Bureau, Seventh Census, 1850, Campbell County, Va., p. 204 [microfilm]).

41. Affidavit of Jared Gilliam, 7 Oct. 1820, affidavit of Patterson Gilliam, 1 Apr. 1820, file 525.

42. Affidavit of Lewis Franklin, 19 Feb. 1820, file 578.

43. Ibid.; affidavit of John Gardner, 19 Feb. 1820, file 578.

44. The date of his death is stated in the bill of complaint of Polly Davidson, file 525. An inventory of his estate in 1826 listed eleven slaves, three of them children. The total value, not including the land, was $3,667 (inventory of the estate of Robert Wright, Campbell County Will Book 5, p. 22 [microfilm]). Sylvia lived on almost twenty years after her son's death. Her estate was not probated until February 1838. Its value, apart from the house, was $738.49 (estate of Sylvia Wright, Campbell County Order Book 23, p. 7 [microfilm]; inventory of the estate of Sylvia Wright, Campbell County Will Book 8, p. 190 [microfilm]).

45. Affidavit of James Williams, 4 Dec. 1819, affidavit of Nancy Caffrey, 19 Feb. 1820, file 525; affidavit of William Davidson, 19 Feb. 1820, file 578.

46. Bill of complaint of Polly Davidson, affidavit of Predhem Moore, 7 Apr. 1820, file 525; affidavit of John Gardner, 19 Feb. 1820, affidavit of Lewis Franklin, 19 Feb. 1820, file 578; affidavit of George MacKey, 1 May 1821, file 525. At the time of Robert's death, Polly was in fact far advanced in pregnancy and within a few days gave birth to a daughter, Martha Ann, who died while still a baby.

47. Affidavit of Arthur Litchfield, 1 Apr. 1820, file 525. In her formal statement, which she drafted in 1821, Polly said the will disappeared "by means unknown" (bill of complaint of Polly Davidson, file 525).

48. Affidavit of Catherine Stockton, 7 Oct. 1820, file 525.

49. Campbell County Order Book 13, pp. 165, 176 (microfilm); *Risque v. Wright's Estate*, file 1174. The records do not state the reason for their release.

50. Curator's bond, 9 Nov. 1818, *Wright v. Jordan*, file 1174. A hearing is recounted in the affidavit of William B. Perrow, 6 Oct. 1820, file 525.

51. Answer, 13 Sept. 1819, file 525; affidavit of Daniel B. Perrow, 7 Oct. 1820, file 578; affidavit of William B. Perrow, 6 Oct. 1820, file 525; Early, *Campbell Chronicles*, 480–81. When the case initially appeared in Bedford County, Polly Davidson was suing with her "next friend Stephen Perrow," while Daniel B. Perrow and William Perrow were listed as defendants after Samuel Fleming (Common Law Order Book 3, 15 Apr. 1824, p. 100, Bedford County Courthouse, Bedford, Va.).

52. "The Estate of Robert Wright to J. B. Risque Due," file 1174.

53. Bill of complaint, 10 Dec. 1828, Campbell County, Legislative Petitions, Records of the General Assembly, RG 78. See also "Rough, Wright v. Fleming," file 525; answer of S. Fleming, 10 May 1820, answer of Polly Davidson alias Polly Wright, 9 Oct. 1820, file 578.

54. *Davidson v. Wright* and *Wright v. Fleming*, 10 Dec. 1828, Campbell County, Legislative Petitions, Records of the General Assembly, RG 78. Apparently the clerk neglected to consult Campbell County Deed Book 3, p. 110 (microfilm).

55. Petition of Samuel Wright and others, 6 Dec. 1827, 28 Dec. 1828, Campbell County, Legislative Petitions, Records of the General Assembly, RG 78.

56. Verdict, 14 Apr. 1825, notes of plaintiff's counsel, 20 Oct. 1825, notes of defendant's counsel, n.d., in *Davidson v. Wright*, file 578.

57. Note the increase in Fleming's personal property between 1818 and 1825 in Campbell County Personal Property Taxes, 1818–25 (microfilm).

58. Affidavit of Stephen Perrow, 8 Sept. 1831, file 1174.

59. Affidavits of John Akers, 14 Nov. 1831, James Daniel, 8 Sept. 1831, Mary K. Smith, 4 Mar. 1832, Pleasant Bagby, 14 Nov. 1831, George Byrd, 4 Mar. 1832, Robert Walthall, 8 Sept. 1831, John Jones, 17 Sept. 1831, file 1174.

60. Some of Fleming's accounts are in Campbell County Will Book 4, p. 361 (microfilm). The accounts do not mention Sylvia Wright, but in her later suit against German Jordan, she stated that Fleming paid her an allowance (bill of Sylva Wright, Copy [of] Record, *Sylva Wright v. Wrights Adm.*, file 1174; Campbell County Deed Book 21, p. 392 [microfilm]).

61. Assignment of claims, file 1174; Campbell County Deed Book 15, 5 Oct. 1825, pp. 198–201 (microfilm). Stephen Perrow maintained that Fleming offered to transfer the account to him "for a Negro Girl worth at that time about $200," but Perrow "refused to trade for it because I did not believe it just" (affidavit of Stephen Perrow, 17 Sept. 1831, file 1174).

62. Campbell County Will Book 5, 14 Aug. 1826, p. 346 (microfilm); affidavit of William Thompson, Jr., 14 Nov. 1831, file 1174.

63. Administrator's bond, 18 Nov. 1825, bill of complaint, 18 May 1830, *Wright v. Jordan*, file 1174. In December 1825 Jordan transferred his share of Fleming's claim to Haden. Despite earlier warnings from Perrow and Robert Walthall, the last overseer, that "the claim was unjust," Jordan paid Haden the full amount that Fleming maintained the estate owed him (affidavits of Stephen Perrow and Robert Walthall, 8 Sept. 1831, bill, 18 May 1830, file 1174). Responding to the bill of complaint, Jordan stated that he learned there were questions about the claims only after he had paid them (answer of German Jordan, file 1174).

64. Notes and account of sale, affidavit of Allen L. Wyllie, 16 Feb. 1832, affidavit of Stephen Perrow, 22 Sept. 1832, file 1174.

65. Campbell County Order Book 17, p. 358 (microfilm); "Inventory . . . of the Estate of Robert Wright Decd," file 1174 (also in Campbell County Will Book 5, p. 277 [microfilm]). This estimate, of course, did not include the value of the land and buildings, or the home and property of Sylvia Wright. See notes of plaintiff's counsel, June 1832, file 1174.

66. Notes of plaintiff's counsel, June 1832, file 1174; bill of Sylva Wright, Copy [of] Record, *Sylva Wright v. Wrights Adm.*, file 1174.

67. Order of Campbell County March Court, 1826, amount of sale, receipts, Silvey Wright, 29 Nov. 1826, 14 Jan. 1828, file 1174. When Jordan failed to pay the annuity in 1829, she took him back to court (Campbell County Order Book 19, 14 Sept. 1829, p. 44 [microfilm]).

68. Copy [of] Silvry Wright's record, *Wright v. Jordan*, file 1174.

69. Decree of court, 22 June 1832, file 1174; [Chancery] Execution Book, 1831–51, Circuit Superior Court of Law and Chancery, Lynchburg City Records, p. 21, Vi; guardian account, 9 Dec. 1833, Campbell County Will Book 7, pp. 234–35 (microfilm). Tax records show that Jordan steadily accumulated both land and slaves. By 1836 he owned seven lots at the courthouse, 1,154 acres of land, and nineteen slaves over the age of twelve. In 1850 his real estate was valued at $15,000 (Campbell County Land and Personal Property Taxes, 1825–50 [microfilm]; U.S. Census Bureau, Seventh Census, 1850, Campbell County, Va., p. 166 [microfilm]).

70. Receipts for tuition and boarding, 8 Apr., 14 May 1825, 9 Dec. 1826, [9] Dec. 1827, file 1174; Campbell County Will Book 6, pp. 462–63; Campbell County Will Book 7, pp. 151, 234 (microfilm).

71. Campbell County Will Book 7, pp. 399–400; Campbell County Order Book 21, p. 262 (microfilm).

72. Campbell County Deed Book 20, 17 Dec. 1835, pp. 159–60 (microfilm).

73. Indentures, 22 Dec. 1835, 5, 13 Jan., 2, 9, 10, 24 Feb. 1836, Campbell County Deed Book 20, pp. 161–63, 179–80, 189–90, 194–97, 210–11, 236–37; Charles Mosby and Maurice Garland to Edward Hunter, deed, 15 May 1836, Campbell County Deed Book 21, pp. 16–17 (microfilm); "Land for Sale," *Lynchburg Virginian*, 31 Mar. 1836, 4.

74. Chancery and Law Order Book, Lynchburg Hustings Court, 1835–38, 18 Aug., 23 Sept. 1835, pp. 18, 23, Lynchburg Courthouse, Lynchburg, Va.; Campbell County Order Book 21, 9 Nov. 1835, June 1836, pp. 248, 325, 326 (microfilm).

75. Campbell County Deed Book 21, 23 Jan. 1838, pp. 392, 410 (microfilm).

76. Bill of complaint, answer of Allen L. Wyllie, file 1886; Campbell County Order Book 23, p. 122 (microfilm); advertisement of "Slaves for sale," file 1886; inventory of the estate of Sylvia Wright, Campbell County Will Book 8, p. 190 (microfilm); report of the commissioner, filed May Court 1839, file 1886. Because Emmeline Turner was a person "of unsound mind," the county court appointed Wyllie to administer her affairs, a task he later said gave him "a great deal of Trouble" (Allen L. Wyllie to C. Dabney, 16 June 1838, file 1886).

77. Appointment, 31 Aug. 1839, *Wright v. Wright*, file 1886; petition of James Wright (signed also by Maria Wright), Sept. 1839, file 1886.

78. "The amended bill of complaint of . . . Betsey Wright and William Wright," [12 Nov. 1839], answer of James Wright, 9 June 1840, answer of Maria Wright, 9 June 1840, affidavit of James Wright, 2 June 1840, affidavits of John Overstreet, 6 July 1840, 13 Apr. 1841, affidavit of William Hawkins, 14 Apr. 1841, affidavit of Stephen Perrow, 21 Sept. 1841, file 1886. Two affidavits supported the story of Betsy and William Wright (see the affidavits of James Turner and Lavina Baker, 1 Mar. 1842, file 1886). Turner was Betsy Wright's brother-in-law.

79. Commissioner's report, [9 Sept. 1845], order, Circuit Court for the Corporation of Lynchburg, 17 Nov. 1852, file 1886; Circuit Superior Court of Law and Chancery Order Book 7, p. 341 (microfilm).

80. Affidavits of Samuel Pleasants, W. V. Millspaugh, and Adeline Dorsey, 27 Sept. 1853, file 1886; U.S. Census Bureau, Seventh Census, 1850, Campbell County [Lynchburg], Va., p. 97 (microfilm).

81. Second amended bill, 2 Feb. 1853, *Wright v. Wright et al.*, file 1886.

82. Answer of John C. Noell, 11 Nov. 1853, affidavits of Nicholas W. Owen and Lucy Tanner, 31 Oct. 1854, memo in *Wright v. Wright*, 10 May 1858, report of the commissioner, 24 May 1873, final decree, June Term, 1873, file 1886.

83. The separate answer of Timothy Fletcher, [27 Apr. 1853], Allen L. Wyllie to C. Dabney, 16 June 1858, file 1886.

Chapter Nine

From Abolitionist Amalgamators to "Rulers of the Five Points"

The Discourse of Interracial Sex and Reform in Antebellum New York City

Leslie M. Harris

Black-white interracial sex in nineteenth-century U.S. history is traditionally a story of the southern states. Historians have focused on the "myth of the black rapist" of the post-Reconstruction South and the coerced relationships between masters and slave women.[1] In this essay I move away from the increasingly familiar southern terrain to explore the cultural and political meanings of interracial socializing and sex, or "amalgamation," in nineteenth-century New York City. As in the nineteenth-and twentieth-century South, interracial social and sexual relationships between blacks and whites were mythologized, feared, and demonized by whites who opposed the struggle to end slavery and achieve equality for blacks. As New Yorkers debated radical abolition and black equality in the 1830s, and urban poverty and Irish immigration in the 1840s and 1850s, proslavery New York journalists and conservative religious reformers insisted that interracial sex was central to these issues and was a major threat to New York's racial and social order. Unlike the debate in the nineteenth-century South, however, the discourse about interracial sex in New York City largely referred to consensual sex between blacks and whites.

Central to this discussion is the word "amalgamation." Unlike the word "miscegenation," which was invented in 1863 for the express purpose of demonizing black-white relationships, the word "amalgamation" has a longer history. In Europe and the United States, amalgamation described the blending of any two or more distinct groups of people through intermarriage or nonsexual cultural exchanges. In England in 1775 amalgamation was used to describe the mixture of Normans and Saxons. In the United States in 1811 the emperor of Russia asked John Quincy Adams whether immigrants to the United States "all amalgamate well together." But by the mid-1830s in the United States, "amalgamation" connoted negative attitudes about black-white sexual and social relationships.[2] These relationships ranged from intermarriage to casual sex to dancing and other forms of socializing; and the offspring of interracial sexual relationships were also held up to negative scrutiny.[3]

A confluence of events led to the emergence of "amalgamation" as an important element in New Yorkers' political discourse. In the late 1820s and early 1830s, sexuality became a weapon wielded by a new group of moral reformers, many of whom allied themselves with the radical abolition movement. Radical abolitionists criticized the sexuality of northern anti-abolition and anti-moral reform elites, as well as interracial sex mores, North and South. Further, the radical abolitionists were the first interracial political coalition in which whites and blacks attempted to work together as equal partners. For anti-abolition and anti-moral reform whites, the actions of abolitionists disrupted New York's racial, social, and economic order. In the 1830s one element of New York's anti-abolition and anti-moral reform rhetoric focused on the power blacks might achieve through one form of amalgamation, intermarriage with white abolitionists. Although there were no cases of intermarriage among black and white abolitionists, newspaper editors and others used accusations of intermarriage to limit the attempts of New York's abolitionist coalition to achieve equality for New York's blacks.

By the 1840s a new group of urban reformers deployed the discourse of amalgamation in the struggle against the allegedly increasing poverty and immorality of New York City. A group of native-born, white, middle-class writers and reformers first laid the blame for this poverty at the feet of blacks, and then blamed new Irish immigrants. Irish immigrants moved into neighborhoods populated by poor blacks, particularly the Five Points, a historically black neighborhood. Initially, some Irish socialized and intermarried with their black neighbors. In this case, however, no one believed that interracial sex and socializing would give political or social power to these powerless groups. In giving eyewitness accounts of interracial dance halls, sexual relationships, and children born out of wedlock, some reformers stated that "amalgamation" reinforced the degeneracy of the Irish. And for a few reformers, amalgamation with the Irish threatened blacks' attempts to achieve moral equality. Although not the only factor, the critique of amalgamation by journalists and moral reformers may have led to the breakdown in Irish-black relations by the time of the Civil War.

New York's antebellum discourse on amalgamation forms an important precursor to the invention of the word "miscegenation" in 1863. Concerns about "miscegenation" did not spring simply from the South, but from the history of blacks, native-born whites, and Irish in the North as well.

White New Yorkers did not discuss interracial sex as a major threat to the social order until the rise of radical abolitionism in the early 1830s. In 1785 a legislative attempt to forbid intermarriage as a condition of emancipation failed, albeit by a narrow margin.[4] In the early 1800s, as New York City experienced gradual emancipation, attitudes toward interracial relationships remained relatively fluid. This lack of alarm over interracial sex reflected the degree to which white New Yorkers viewed emancipation as a smooth process. New York's gradual emancipation, enacted by law in 1799, had occurred not through black rebellion or civil war, but through the guidance of trusted elites such as John Jay, Alexander Hamilton, and the socially conservative Quakers who founded the New York Manumission Society. Further, by the completion of gradual emancipation in 1827, the position of New York's blacks at the lower end of the social order, a part of the working classes, yet distinct from white workers, had been established. The New York legislature had effectively disfranchised the vast majority of black men while giving the franchise to all white men. White workers and employers who refused to work alongside or hire free blacks stripped the population of the skilled positions they had held while enslaved, relegating most to unskilled manual labor in freedom. By 1829 New York Manumission Society members, blacks' major allies in New York City during the emancipation years, supported the goal of the American Colonization Society to remove blacks to Africa, despite the opposition of the majority of New York's blacks to such a scheme.[5]

By the 1830s, however, a new coalition of blacks and whites, the radical abolitionists, threatened to push for equal rights for blacks in a new way. They brought to the city not only a new chapter in race relations, but also a new type of moral reform. "Amalgamation" became a concern for New Yorkers as part of a new public discussion of sex, race, and morality in New York, at the center of which were the wealthy New York merchants Arthur and Lewis Tappan.[6] The Tappans came from the new middle class, who represented a new economic regime and attempted to impose a set of moral concerns that made many white New Yorkers uneasy. Migrants from New England, the Tappan brothers became among the most visible of the new generation of moral reformers in New York City, whose concerns ranged from eradication of prostitution in northern urban centers to the immediate abolition of slavery in the South.

Arthur Tappan's leadership of the Magdalen Society in 1831 highlighted sexuality as a flashpoint in New York's politics. Initially, the Magdalen Society, an organization intended to reform prostitutes, gained the support of a range of the city's religious, social, and political leaders.[7] Under Arthur Tappan's presidency, however, the society's efforts to reform prostitution became a discussion of the moral standards not only of wayward women, but also of some members of the city's elite. In its first report in 1831 the Magdalen Society charged that there were ten thousand prostitutes in New York City, and that the clients of prostitutes belonged to some of the city's most prominent and respectable families. Some New Yorkers were outraged at what they felt to be the exaggerated numbers, as well as the slandering of New York's best families by an upstart group of New England reformers.

Other New Yorkers were more directly affected by the Magdalen Society charges. Some members of New York's elite families were not only clients, but were actually entrepreneurs in the business of brothels. John Livingston, the brother of founding father Robert R. Livingston, was one of the most successful landlords in New York and built his wealth through brothels. John Delaplaine, an importer; George Lorillard, a tobacco entrepreneur; and Matthew Davis, an early Tammany Hall politician, all profited from prostitution. In fact, repeated proposals before New York's Common Council to raze houses of prostitution in the Five Points were defeated through a coalition of these wealthy and politically powerful men.[8]

The response to the Magdalen Society's pamphlet was swift. City elites such as former mayor Philip Hone and General Robert Bogardus, Manhattan's wealthiest real estate speculator, held anti-Magdalen meetings, railing against the "social influ-ence of New Englanders in the City." Newspapermen and Tammany leaders James Watson Webb, editor of the *Morning Courier and New-York Enquirer*, and Mor-decai Noah fanned the flames against the Magdalen Society and Arthur Tappan.[9] Arthur Tappan was denounced, and he and his house were threatened with vio-lence. Surprised and fearful of the repercussions of his activism, Tappan quickly withdrew from the society.[10]

The Magdalen Society controversy did not explicitly touch on issues of interracial sex. Two years later, however, the Tappans' embrace of radical abolition, and the formation of the American Anti-Slavery Society (AASS), resulted in the centering of "amalgamation" in New Yorkers' political landscape. Until 1833 Arthur and Lewis Tappan had been strong supporters of gradual measures of emancipation and col-onization of blacks in Africa. But in 1833 the Tappans were the most visible and wealthy defectors from the colonizationists, and others followed suit throughout the 1830s.[11] The Tappans' defection marked their final break with the old New York antislavery activists and with more conservative social reformers generally. As the anti-abolitionist David Meredith Reece said of the radical abolitionists, they were "not the creed and practice of Jefferson, Franklin, Rush, and John Jay, of the old school, for those laboured for *gradual* abolition, and were clearly right."[12] In New York, more conservative antislavery activists and proslavery supporters viewed the goals of immediate emancipation and racial equality as particularly threatening to the social order. The rise of radical abolition gave blacks economically and socially powerful new allies.

Abolitionists demonstrated that political tactics previously deemed fit only for whites could in fact be used by blacks also. The abolitionists presented forums in which black men and women spoke as political equals with white men and women. Abolitionists' political tactics and goals flew in the face of the attempt by some whites to remove blacks from politics by denying them the vote. In their actions and words, abolitionists expanded the meaning of politics by relying on moral suasion and by implicitly questioning universal white manhood suffrage and even the Constitution as the best examples of democracy and equality. Some white abo-litionists, of whom William Lloyd Garrison of Boston was the most radical, actively blurred racial caste lines. When visiting black organizations, Garrison often said that he visited "as a black man," or spoke to blacks "as one of you."[13] Such iden-tification did not simply place Garrison on the social or political level of blacks, but also raised the possibility of black equality with whites. To some New Yorkers, such rhetoric was practically amalgamation itself.

Although abolitionists did not intermarry, some did attempt to redefine public attitudes toward interracial sex in two major areas. They favored consensual inter-racial unions, as might occur among free blacks and whites in the North; and they opposed those that were coerced, as among southern slaves and slaveholders. In Boston in 1832 the white abolitionists William Lloyd Garrison and Lydia Maria Child began a highly public campaign to repeal the Massachusetts law that forbade interracial marriage. In Child's words, "The government ought not to be invested with power to control the affections, any more than the consciences of citizens."[14]

Few abolitionists sustained as strong a commitment to interracial marriage as did Child and Garrison. In New York City, black abolitionists denied that respectable blacks would wish to marry whites or participate in other forms of interracial socializing, but admitted that "dissolute" blacks were indeed guilty as charged. In an article in New York's *Freedom's Journal*, the nation's first black newspaper, a writer calling himself "Mordecai" stated, "I am not covetous of sitting at the table of Mr. N____, to hold [him] by his arm in the streets,—to marry his daughter, should he ever have one—nor to sleep in his bed—neither should I think myself honoured in the possession of all these favours."[15] Samuel Cornish and John Russwurm, the founders of *Freedom's Journal* and prominent black abolitionists and reformers, acknowledged the existence of interracial socializing, but blamed whites for initiating the contact by frequenting black neighborhoods: "Our streets and places of public amusement are nightly crowded," they wrote, with young white men and white prostitutes.[16]

Abolitionists also offered a direct critique of coerced sexual relationships between masters and slaves in the South. Lydia Maria Child, in her 1833 *Appeal in Favor of That Class of Americans Called Africans*, was the first abolitionist to denounce in print the rape of slave women by masters. Other abolitionists followed suit. At the first anniversary meeting of the American Anti-Slavery Society, held at the Chatham Street Chapel in New York in 1834, delegate James Thome of Kentucky related his observations of the "Young men of talents and respectability, fathers, professors of religion, ministers—all classes!" who consorted with slave women and contributed to the "overwhelming pollution!" of the South.[17]

Attitudes of abolitionists toward interracial socializing, sex, and marriage were thus far from simple approval.[18] But abolition's opponents, many of whom had earlier opposed the Magdalen Society, redefined the issue of antislavery and black equality as the desire of abolitionists to encourage amalgamation in New York City. Although there were other issues raised by the abolitionist coalition (such as their connection to British abolitionists and their advocacy of temperance and Sabbath reforms), amalgamation became the rallying cry for anti-abolitionists, leading in 1834 to one of the most violent riots in antebellum New York City. The amalgamation crises of 1830s New York City did not reflect actual instances of interracial sex between blacks and whites, but rather mythical relationships between black and white abolitionists. For supporters of slavery, racial conservatives, and some members of the white working class, amalgamation represented not simply the assimilation of blacks as equals in American society, but the potential for blacks to move into the middle classes and gain political and economic power through an abolitionist coalition. The charge of amalgamation became a means to discredit the ways in which abolitionists demanded inclusion of blacks in the political sphere.

Following Arthur Tappan's defection to the abolitionists in 1833, white New Yorkers who supported colonization of blacks were quick to attack the emerging abolitionist coalition. In October 1833 a mob encouraged and led by *Courier and Enquirer* editor James Watson Webb attempted to disrupt the organizational meeting of the New York City Anti-Slavery Society, a precursor of the American Anti-Slavery Society. The abolitionists, fearing such activities, had vacated Clinton Hall early. The rioters held a mock meeting in which they seized an elderly black man, named him Arthur Tappan, and forced him to preside over the meeting and make a speech. When the man stated, "I am a poor, ignorant man . . . but I have heard of the Declaration of Independence, and have read the Bible. The Declaration says all men are created equal, and the Bible says God has made us all of one blood. I think . . . we are entitled to good treatment, that it is wrong to hold men in slavery,"[19] the mob interrupted him and denounced immediate emancipation and "immediate amalgamation" before dispersing. The incident was only the first in a series of public altercations linking immediate emancipation, racial equality, and amalgamation. Throughout early 1834 New York newspapers printed numerous articles about the "fanatical" abolitionists and their opposition to colonization, and white editors frequently linked the abolitionists' goal of immediate emancipation to amalgamation.

James Watson Webb's *Courier and Enquirer* led the attack on the abolitionist coalition. During the annual meeting of the American Anti-Slavery Society, held in New York in May 1834, Webb and other anti-abolitionist newspaper editors raised the possibility of black equality and amalgamation as a reason to support the colonization of blacks and denounce immediate abolition. As "Quo" wrote in the *New York Journal of Commerce* (which ironically had once been owned by the Tappans), slavery in the United States could end only in "Colonization, Amalgamation, or Annihilation" of black people. Annihilation would occur after full emancipation because "the free blacks do not increase at all; on the contrary, they dwindle away. . . . They have not within them that stirring spirit which stimulates the white sons . . . to penetrate the West, and . . . people the world with intelligence and enterprise." Of amalgamation, this writer stated, "There will never be an honorable and virtuous amalgamation of the races. . . . A deluge of pollution must engulf our country, at the thought of which the heart sickens."[20] Webb's *Courier and Enquirer* stated more pointedly that abolitionists "enticed" blacks to stay in the United States with "the prospect of being speedily admitted to a social equality with the whites." Abolitionists, the paper commented,

> invite the blacks to dine with them; send their children to school with them; and, what we know to be a fact, invite and encourage them to seat themselves in the same pews with white ladies; to thrust themselves into their places in steamboats, and to obtrude their aromatic persons in places whence the customs of society, and, let us add, the instincts of nature, have hitherto banished them.[21]

In the weeks leading up to the full-scale rioting in July, the issues of blacks' political power, access to public spaces, and mixture with whites were hotly contested in the pages of New York's newspapers.[22]

The July riots began with mob harassment of black and white abolitionists by a crowd of "hundreds of young men," who disrupted the abolitionist celebration of the Fourth of July, held in Chatham Street Chapel. On July 7 a celebration of New York's Emancipation Day by blacks in the same chapel was disrupted by members of the Sacred Music Society, who claimed they had rented the chapel for the same night. The interruption ended with blacks routing the musicians from the church, amid epithets and broken furniture. News of the incident spread on July 8, and between July 9 and 12, whites rioted, destroying the homes of the white abolitionist Arthur Tappan, the homes and churches of the black Episcopalian minister Peter Williams, the white Presbyterian minister Samuel Cox, and the white minister Henry G. Ludlow of the Spring Street Church, as well as homes and businesses of blacks who lived in the interracial Five Points area.[23]

Although blacks had been the victims of mob violence before, this was the first time that the issue of amalgamation was the explicit concern and rallying cry. Further, the three days of violence constituted the largest riot in antebellum New York. The riots were so violent because amalgamation was an issue against which members of all classes of white New Yorkers united. As Leonard Richards has noted, because working-class blacks and whites shared neighborhoods, particularly in the Five Points area where much of the disturbance was centered, the meanings of black citizenship and amalgamation were of particular concern to working-class whites. Further, as Sean Wilentz has shown, many of the rioters were skilled workers who feared the economic as much as the social effects of the new regime represented by the Tappans. Rioting by the working classes against blacks continued with the approval of newspaper editors, police, and elites. The union of these groups with the white working classes allowed an intense level of destruction.[24]

Amalgamation was the focus of the rioters' hostility. But the charge of amalgamation both concealed and revealed fears of increasing black political and economic power. Rioters destroyed Arthur Tappan's house because allegedly he had entertained blacks there. Peter Williams's and Henry Ludlow's churches were attacked because it was rumored that their ministers had performed interracial marriages. Rioters attacked Samuel Cox's church twice during the riots for his denunciation of the practice of segregating blacks in "negro pews," and for his description of Jesus Christ as a dark-skinned man. Mobs attacked black residences in the interracial Five Points area fairly indiscriminately, but some more affluent blacks were singled out for special harassment. Isaiah Emory, a shopkeeper, received a threatening note. Another storekeeper feared that two brick houses he owned would be destroyed. One black-owned barbershop was destroyed and another black barber was assaulted.[25] Thus, the working-class white mob displayed a mixture of fear over interracial sex, resentment at sharing neighborhood space with blacks of any class, and particular resentment of attempts to elevate blacks to equal standing either with themselves or with middle-class white abolitionists, whether through intermarriage, through rhetoric, or through the efforts of blacks themselves.

New York City's abolitionists were unprepared for the violence with which black citizenship rights and interracial sexuality would be linked and denounced in the 1834 abolition riots. The mob actions of white New Yorkers against the abolitionist coalition resulted in a shift in emphasis among New York's abolitionist-reformers regarding the importance of the struggle for black equality. The charge of amalgamation was successfully used by anti-abolition New Yorkers to slow down abolitionist efforts to achieve black equality.

The abolitionist response to the riots was immediate. On Saturday, July 12, following the dispersal of the rioters, the white abolitionists Arthur Tappan and

John Rankin, on behalf of the executive committee of the American Anti-Slavery Society, posted handbills throughout the city that stated, among other points, "We entirely disclaim any desire to promote or encourage intermarriages between white and colored citizens."[26] On July 14, the black Episcopalian minister Peter Williams was ordered by the white Episcopalian Bishop Benjamin Onderdonk to step down from the AASS or resign his position as minister. Williams not only left the society, but denied that he had played an active role there. Although elected to the board of managers at the society's inaugural meeting, Williams claimed to have "never met with that Board but for a few moments at the close of their sessions, and then without uttering a word." When elected to the executive committee at the AASS meeting held in New York in May 1834, Williams claimed that he had "replied that I could not attend to it, and have never attended but on one occasion." Williams's retreat was published "with unfeigned pleasure" in the pro-colonization newspapers of the city.[27] His defection reflected the ambivalence black abolitionists had always felt about interracial sex and socializing as a measure of racial equality. Further, Williams revealed ambivalence among some blacks toward the abolitionists' radical tactics. By the time of the riots of 1834, it was clear that not only accusations of amalgamation but the abolitionist movement itself might place blacks and their white allies in physical danger.

Soon after the riots, it became increasingly clear that white abolitionists were also beating a fast retreat on the issues of amalgamation and black equality. On July 17 Tappan and Rankin were joined by the white abolitionists Lewis Tappan, Elizur Wright, Jr., Joshua Leavitt, and William Goodell and the black abolitionist Samuel Cornish in sending a letter to Mayor Cornelius Lawrence, in which they again stated their opposition to interracial marriage and other forms of black-white interaction: "[We] affirm that the stories in circulation about individuals adopting colored children, ministers uniting white and colored persons in marriage, abolitionists encouraging intermarriages, exciting the people of color to assume airs, &c. &c. are wholly unfounded."[28] And one month later in the *Emancipator*, black and white New York abolitionists published yet another appeal, denying that abolitionists encouraged intermarriage. In this two-page appeal, however, abolitionists also defined additional limits of action for the cause of black citizenship and equality, in particular retreating from a defense of black use of public space: "It is not true . . . that abolitionists encouraged colored men to ride up and down Broadway on horse back," they wrote, "or otherwise put themselves forward in public parades."[29] This statement was even stronger than the earlier objections of the black reformers Samuel Cornish and Peter Williams to black parades in 1827. Cornish had attempted to stop the parades, but had also upheld black rights to parade in celebration of Emancipation Day, "in common with the rest of the community."[30] By 1834 such public parades had become even more threatening to whites who feared black equality. A second rumor put forth during the riots charged that " 'fifty of those' colored lads 'who belonged to a Sabbath school before the abolition measures commenced,' deserted it and went 'parading the street with their canes and dandy dress, seeking white wives.' "[31] Female relatives of members of the New York Manumission Society were largely responsible for instituting "Sabbath schools" for the benefit of the black community during the emancipation years. These rumors highlighted the distinctions between older methods of social reform for blacks and the new radicalism of the abolitionists, and invoked sexuality to provoke fear of the new movement. Black and white abolitionists, however, largely retreated from defenses of black public displays, and thus effectively gave over the streets to whites.

The abolitionist response to the riots confirmed the power of the mob and the weakness of black claims to middle-class standing and political power within and outside the abolitionist movement. In strongly rejecting interracial marriage, New York's black and white abolitionists implicitly dissociated themselves from William Lloyd Garrison's continuing campaign to repeal the Massachusetts law against interracial marriage.[32] Abolitionists through the Civil War drew a distinction between their own personal actions and their opposition to legal restrictions on interracial marriage.[33] However, in the wake of the 1834 riots, the Tappans and other New York abolitionists, both black and white, did not risk such a complex statement, instead rejecting such possibilities completely.

Further, white abolitionists, with the possible exception of William Lloyd Garrison, began to draw distinctions between blacks and whites that depicted blacks as uneducated laborers, even as white abolitionists continued to associate with educated, middle-class blacks in their organizations. They drew such distinctions in order to define the limits of black equality, as well as the limits of the abolitionists' role in helping blacks achieve equality. As the Bostonian Lydia Maria Child wrote in 1834, "On the subject of equality, the principles of the abolitionists have been misrepresented. They have not the slightest wish to do violence to the distinctions of society by forcing the rude and illiterate into the presence of the learned and refined." Abolitionists wished only to give blacks the same rights enjoyed by "the lowest and most ignorant white man in America."[34] But the "lowest" white people increasingly saw themselves as by definition above the level of blacks.[35] Child's statement further implied that all blacks, to a degree, were "rude and illiterate." The views of Child and other white abolitionists, as George M. Fredrickson has noted, "could be used to reinforce the unfavorable free-Negro stereotype that was promulgated by colonizationists and defenders of slavery."[36] Thus, because white abolitionists themselves reinforced views of blacks as inferior, their attempts to grant social and economic equality to New York's blacks were in disarray.

After the 1834 riots, black and white abolitionists continued to play a pivotal role in the cultural discussion of amalgamation, but largely only as critics of southern slaveholders. Particularly in New York City, which in the 1840s became home to the more conservative arm of the abolitionist movement, the American and Foreign Anti-Slavery Society, defenders of interracial social contact between blacks and whites were few. Black and white abolitionists instead focused on other measures of equality: education, the vote, and freeing southern slaves. Arguably, separation of blacks and whites in social settings became a marker of middle-class respectability.[37]

After the retreat of black and white middle-class abolitionists from charges of fostering intermarriage, newspaper editors, travel writers, and finally reformers linked interracial sex with New York's working classes. Unlike the abolitionist controversy, accounts of amalgamation among New York's workers were more based in reality. Social and sexual relationships between New York's black and white workers had existed since slavery. During moments of crisis, such as the 1741 slave plot or the 1818 Rose Butler arson trial, reformers, judges, slave owners, and others concerned about the potential disruption to the social order held up these interracial relationships for public scrutiny.[38] But the word "amalgamation," with its increasingly negative connotations, was used in relationship with the working classes only after the 1834 riots.

Immediately after the 1834 riots, the penny press took over discussions of incidences of working-class amalgamation in New York City. The *New York Transcript* regularly published accounts of and conflicts over interracial socializing and sex taken from police reports and court cases. These ranged from accounts of prostitution, to conflicts between interracial couples, to conflicts over dancing between blacks and whites. Such accounts reveal the continuation of interracial sexual encounters even after the violence of July 1834. In November of that year, fourteen black and white women were arrested for prostitution by "the indefatigable inspector of the Sixth Ward, M'Grath." The women allegedly spent their time together "enticing sailors into their haunt" in the Five Points, "making them drunk, and robbing them." During a night of escapades, the white workers Samuel Dunn and Dan Turner supposedly began their evening by "blackguarding some black beauties whom chance placed in their path." John Curry, a sailor accused of "striking a female with his fist," defended himself by saying that women "black or white, red or brown, I love 'em all; and with they'd all only get one mouth, and I had the kissing on't." Two white women were arrested and convicted for "assaulting a black man and trying to kiss him."[39]

These and other descriptions of "amalgamators" were often more concerned with the actions of whites than of blacks, and sought to demonstrate that whites who socialized with blacks or intermarried were morally weak. In such stories, black partners were either morally upright or silent. Charles Albraith was "a dapper little tailor from Philadelphia" who "became enamoured of a *black* woman," Mary Brown, the owner of an oyster cellar. Soon after their engagement, however, Albraith became so drunk, "riotous and noisy" that Mary became angry. He responded by striking her, and she broke off the engagement and had him arrested. The court withheld a conviction of assault on the condition that Albraith return to Philadelphia. In this instance, Albraith's descent into interracial marriage proved his damaged masculinity: he wanted to marry a black woman, he drank excessively, and he assaulted a woman. Mary's actions, including her decision to break off the engagement, displayed her moral uprightness and her role in restoring racial order to this small segment of New York City.[40]

The danger of interracial sexual contacts to single white women was the theme of a complicated account reprinted in the *New York Transcript* in September 1835. Elias Kent met the chambermaid Mary Ann Markey in Albany, New York. The white couple soon moved to New York City and married. Within two weeks of the wedding, the new bride discovered what an "infernal scoundrel" her husband was.

"A *coloured girl* called at the house of her father," and stated that Kent had been married to her for over three years, that she had had two children with him, and that she had come to claim her husband. Mary Ann's father "was so enraged to think that she had married such a fellow upon six weeks acquaintance, that he turned her out of doors."[41] This story provided a racial twist to reformers' fears of the consequences resulting from the lives that single white working-class women were developing independently of their families during the early 1830s. Mary Ann was a chambermaid in Albany, on her own and far from the guidance of her father, when she met Elias.[42]

In the stories of Charles Albraith and Mary Ann Markey, the adjective "black" was italicized as if to note that the writer (and reader) were surprised at such contact. After the riots of 1834 it was increasingly expected that whites would reject black-white socializing. Clearly, some working-class blacks and whites rebelled against these norms by embracing a more fluid set of race relations. But journalists were quick to play up instances in which whites upheld the color line. In October 1834 a black boatman, Michael Cracken, was walking past a house where a party was being held by recent German immigrants. When he joined in, "the Germans very naturally and very properly ejected him." Cracken then fetched a number of his friends "to retaliate for the insult which he conceived had been put upon him." He and his friends threw brickbats at the house until the watchman came and dispersed the "rioters," managing to arrest three of them, who were ordered to pay five hundred dollars bail or go to jail.[43]

Such newspaper accounts demonstrated that not all working-class blacks, immigrants, and native-born whites agreed so easily to the separation of the races. But from the 1840s through the Civil War, middle-class journalists and reformers linked amalgamation, first between blacks and native-born whites and then between blacks and Irish, to their allegations of the increasing poverty and crime in New York City. By the mid-1840s stories of amalgamation in New York City were associated with poverty and urban decay. The Sixth Ward in lower Manhattan, and particularly the Five Points area, became the focus of accounts of black-white interracial sex. The Five Points (named for the intersection of five streets) was the geographic center of the first free black settlements in the city during the emancipation years. By the mid-1830s the Sixth Ward had the largest concentration of blacks in New York. During the same time, it became one of the leading centers of prostitution in the city, containing 31 percent of the city's brothels.[44] And after the mid-1840s the Sixth Ward also became known as the "Irish ward" because of the large numbers of Irish immigrants who made their homes there.

Middle-class writers and reformers in the 1840s and 1850s emphasized a discourse of sexuality, race, and criminality that focused on the relationship between the black and Irish communities of the Five Points district. The Five Points consisted of only five city blocks, but to white middle-class New Yorkers it was the center of a maelstrom of prostitution, interracial sex, murder, and theft that threatened to engulf the city. The proximity of the Five Points to the center of the city and to Broadway, which was experiencing middle-class flight as wealthier New Yorkers moved farther north, further fueled middle-class anxiety. Writers and reformers documented the changes there and reflected the concerns of white New Yorkers over the changing ethnic and geographic nature of poverty; at the same time, they helped to shape white New Yorkers' attitudes toward those changes.

The changing nature of the Broadway area and the Five Points had been outlined in the police and court sections of the *New York Transcript* and other penny newspapers in the 1830s. But the publication of Charles Dickens's *American Notes for General Circulation* in 1842 fixed a geographic specificity to concerns about the connections between amalgamation and poverty in New York City, and shaped the ways in which middle-class New York writers and reformers would view the Five Points and interracial working-class contacts. Although Dickens did not refer explicitly to amalgamation in his descriptions of the neighborhood, his *American Notes* was the starting point for travel writers and reformers for the next two decades of descriptions and discussions of interracial poverty.

Unlike the earlier *New York Transcript* descriptions, Dickens's descriptions were not taken from police reports or court transcripts, but from his own explorations of the Five Points. In what would become formula for travel writers and reformers after 1840, Dickens described his visits to the homes of some of the poor who lived in the Five Points. At his initial "descent" into the neighborhood, Dickens described the blacks he met there in animalistic terms: "Many . . . pigs live here. Do they ever wonder why their masters walk upright in lieu of going on all-fours? and why they talk instead of grunting?"[45] At the same time, Dickens also elevated the district as a central site of New York black cultural activity. With his trip to Almack's, a black-owned dance hall, Dickens catapulted the owner and black dancing to international fame. Dickens was clearly awestruck by the skill of the dancers there:

> But the dance commences. . . . Single shuffle, double shuffle, cut and cross-cut: snapping his fingers, rolling his eyes, turning in his knees, presenting the backs of his legs in front, spinning about on his toes and heels like nothing. . . . And in what walk of life, or dance of life, does man ever get such stimulating applause as thunders about him, when, having danced his partner off her feet . . . he finishes by leaping glouriously on the bar-counter . . . with the chuckle of a million of counterfeit Jim Crows, in one inimitable sound![46]

Similar to the minstrel performers of the period, Dickens combined disgust and admiration in his depictions of black life and culture. Indeed, Dickens viewed the dancing through the caricatures of minstrelsy itself: "rolling his eyes," "chuckle of . . . Jim Crows."[47]

Unlike other places in the United States, particularly the South, where Dickens's writings were seen as too critical of American customs, New York writers saw the work as too positive in its depiction of the Five Points. Dickens described no prostitution or danger to himself, no fighting or riots. The freewheeling sexuality for which the Points had been and would continue to be famous was largely absent from his account, and only the presence of several "mulatto" women at Almack's hinted at the interracial sex that the *New York Transcript* had already located in the district. Dickens described no interracial dancing or sharing of housing.

In response, white middle-class journalists such as Nathaniel Parker Willis and

George Foster, and reformers such as Louis M. Pease and Samuel Halliday both capitalized on the popularity of *American Notes* and explicitly challenged what they saw as a romanticized depiction of life in the Five Points. Using *American Notes* as a starting point, travel writers and reformers through the Civil War reconstructed the neighborhood in their descriptions, focusing on poverty and interracial sex and in the process creating a geography of alleged vice in Manhattan's Five Points area. Within a year of the publication of *American Notes*, Willis retraced Dickens's steps, publishing his accounts in New York newspapers. Having at first glance seen "well-dressed and well-mannered people" at Almack's, on second look he noticed "a few 'young men about town,' mixed up with the blacks; and altogether it was a picture of 'amalgamation,' such as I had never before seen," and which the "superficial eye" of Dickens had turned into "the merriest quarter of New York." Willis established the connection between amalgamation and crime when one of his companions discovered that his pocket had been picked.[48]

Willis's account reflected his view of the changing geography of poverty and race in New York. Before venturing to "Dickens' Hole," he "had had an idea that this celebrated spot was on the eastern limit of the city, at the end of one of the omnibus-routes." But to his surprise, poor blacks and interracial vice had shifted from their location in the 1820s, on the docks at the edge of the city, to "not more than three minutes' walk from Broadway, and in full view from one of the fashionable corners." Willis's account of the Five Points ended with a cry for the reclamation of the Points and the areas around it from blacks: "We should like to know, among other things, why the broadest, most accessible, most convenient street in New York, the noble avenue of WEST BROADWAY, is entirely given up to negroes?" Thus, Willis ultimately laid the blame for amalgamation and the degradation of the city at the feet of blacks alone, ignoring white consumers and participants. In an early move against flight to more suburban locales, he stated, "The *rage* is to move up town," and called for the white middle class to stay and hold out against the allegedly encroaching black poverty.[49]

In 1850 George Foster, one of the most popular of this genre of writers, published *New York by Gas-Light*, which sold 200,000 copies.[50] Foster's essays also weighed in against Dickens's glorified account of the Five Points. Foster expanded on the themes of interracial sex and criminality, also casting blacks as owners of the major establishments, responsible economically and culturally for the character of the Five Points. On the one hand, he acknowledged the achievement of some black men in being able to "scrape together a good deal of money." On the other hand, however, Foster believed that black men used this economic power to gain "white wives or white mistresses," to "associate upon at least equal terms with the men and women of the parish," and to be "regarded as desirable companions and lovers by the 'girls.' " But according to Foster, black men's humanity was irredeemable: "They are savage, sullen, reckless dogs, and are continually promoting some 'muss' or other, which not unfrequently leads to absolute riot."[51]

Foster and other writers reserved special scorn for the most successful of the black dance hall owners, Peter Williams. Acknowledging that "Pete Williams, Esq." had "made an immense amount of money from the profits of his dance-house,"

Foster judged him for "regularly [gambling the money] away at the sweat-cloth or the roulette-table as fast as it comes in."[52] Describing a cultural rather than sexual amalgamation, another writer described Williams as "in complexion and features . . . thoroughly African, [but] in his business tact and intuitive knowledge of men and things, he was decidedly Yankee."[53]

Thus, for many white journalists in the 1840s and 1850s, blacks were "the rulers of the Five Points," as the white South Carolina travel writer William Bobo dubbed them in his critical view of New York City.[54] They blamed amalgamation on blacks, largely ignoring the fact that most blacks in the Five Points rented from whites, and that the dance halls and brothels established by blacks catered to native-born, middle-class whites as well as to working-class whites and blacks. None of these writers focused on the Irish as central to the "problem" of amalgamation.

By the late 1840s, however, with the increased presence of immigrant Irish in the Five Points area, some reformers began to raise questions as to who were the "rulers of the Five Points"—blacks or Irish. Although the increase in Irish immigration began in the 1830s, the 1840s and 1850s saw the greatest expansion in numbers of Irish in New York City. Largely poor and confined to low-wage, unskilled jobs, the Irish competed with blacks for jobs as waiters, domestics, and unskilled laborers. Increasingly in the 1850s, the Irish were winning the battle. But such success came at a price. Occupying jobs that had formerly been the domain of blacks and that signified servility and dependence in republican discourse, the Irish experienced a prejudice akin to that experienced by blacks for so long.

The increasing numbers of Irish immigrants in New York City raised the issue of racial status. Although in Europe the Irish had been considered a different, inferior race from the English, in the United States, with the presence of black slaves as the ultimate symbol of dependence and degradation, the position of the Irish was up for grabs. Did the Irish have the potential to become "white"? Should "whites" embrace them and reshape them into "whites," thus lifting them above blacks? Or were blacks in fact morally, and thus racially, superior to the Irish? Thus, although some called the Irish "white niggers," others used the words "white" and "Irish" almost interchangeably in their descriptions of these immigrants.[55]

Regardless of the racial standing of the Irish, middle-class reformers saw the amalgamation of blacks and Irish as threatening to the social order. Both the increase in the Irish population and the journalists' depictions of the Five Points spurred a group of New York City's non-abolitionist reformers to action. In 1848 the Ladies' Home Missionary Society of the Methodist Episcopal Church turned to the Five Points as a place to begin a city mission. As Carroll Smith-Rosenberg has shown, the Five Points "was for them a most grievous example of the evil afflicting American society."[56] By 1850 they had obtained a board of trustees composed of wealthy men, hired Louis M. Pease as their first missionary, and established the Five Points Mission in the heart of the slum. Within a year, Pease expanded the mission's work in its chapel and day school to include job training, housing, and employment. Assistance was granted on the condition that Five Points residents live at the mission. By February 1851 Pease had rented an adjoining building and moved himself and his family into a house in the district. However, the women who had begun the mission objected to Pease's materialist bent, and by 1852 Pease's mission had split off from the more religiously oriented women. In 1854 Pease's Five Points House of Industry was separately incorporated. Through the Civil War, Pease and his successors ran one of the largest and most well-known missions in New York City.[57]

In their separate endeavors, both Pease and the Ladies' Home Missionary Society established themselves as a new type of observer-participant in the life of the Five Points. They utilized the sensationalist tactics begun with Dickens, but set themselves above the population as reformers rather than as mere critics. From 1848 through the Civil War, the missionaries printed accounts of the neighborhood in reform journals, annual reports, and published memoirs that depicted the Points residents and the missionaries' efforts to change them. These accounts demonstrated their belief that the presence of both blacks and immigrants was central to the slum conditions that prevailed in the area. For example, the Ladies' Home Missionary Society presented the black presence as one that had disturbed an earlier, healthier Five Points that had consisted of ponds, creeks, and meadows.[58] This bucolic scene ended with "the first records of human history, [which] in this place are stained with blood"—a reference to the Negro Plot of 1741, a slave uprising, following which thirteen blacks were burned at the stake, and twenty more hanged in chains on an island in the neighborhood's Fresh Water Pond.[59] Further, although the majority of residents were white immigrants by the mid-1850s, the women quoted Dickens's description of blacks verbatim, a description in which they found "the details that make the *tout ensemble* of horrors."[60] By 1854, then, not only the "immorality" of the present but the early history of the Five Points was inextricably linked to images of violent, degraded, immoral blacks.

But the increase in Irish immigration at this time also led these and other reformers to point to Irish and native-born whites as part of the problem. Concern about the "Irish problem" in New York reached the state capital in Albany, where the state legislature established a Special Committee on Tenement Houses in New-York and Brooklyn. This committee visited the Five Points district and found "the Irish . . . predominant, as occupants" of "hundreds of dilapidated, dirty and densely populated old structures." In a rare attack on German as well as Irish immigrants, the committee noted that

> in some of the better class of houses built for the tenantry, negroes have been preferred as occupants to Irish or German poor; the incentive of possessing comparatively decent quarters appearing to inspire the colored residents with more desire for personal cleanliness and regard for property than is impressed upon the whites of their own condition.[61]

The worst fate of the city, however, was not in the presence of one or the other group, but in the mixture of blacks and Irish. The fate against which the reformers were working was clearly spelled out in a visit to the Points conducted by the missionary Benjamin Barlow and a policeman for the benefit of readers of the *Independent* newspaper in 1861. In a garret, adjacent to an apartment where only recently "a millionaire's beautiful daughter" was found "lying on the bare floor with a drunken negro," Barlow and the policeman supposedly came across old Sambo over his brazier of coals, toasting his hands, and in the corner of the den is a long pile of rags. . . . It moves at one end; and an Irish woman lifts her tangled mop of a head out of the heap, and with a jolly voice, bids us "good evenin'." "Look here, gentlemen, look at this little codfish;" and with this she lifts out from beneath the rags a diminutive mulatto child of a few weeks old, to the great delight of Sambo, who reveals all his ivory.[62]

According to the reformers, the fate of such a child would be to have "rum its first medicine, theft its first lesson, a prison its first house, and the Potter's Field its final resting-place."[63]

Although the reformers, like the sensational journalists, linked interracial sexuality with crime, the reformers differed on an important point. Whereas in the journalists' accounts the fault for amalgamation lay largely with blacks, in the reformers' writings the Irish were an equal, if not more blameworthy, influence. Separation of the races, and particularly of blacks from Irish, was crucial to the uplift of the Five Points, for "where the blacks were found by themselves, we generally encountered tidiness, and some sincere attempt at industry and honest self-support." As one reformer noted, "the negroes of the Five Points are fifty per cent in advance of the Irish as to sobriety and decency."[64] Second, according to the missionaries, there were few instances of white men consorting with black women. "In nearly every garret we entered," one report stated, "the same practical amalgamation was in fashion; but in each case a black Othello had won a fair Desdemona—not one white man was found with a colored wife."[65] Whether such a shift was one of perception or reality remains unclear. The apparently casual nature of the relationships depicted appears to have prevented their documentation in the census records of the 1840s and 1850s, which might have provided a clue to the actual number of interracial households.[66]

Reformers' visits "under the crust" of New York marked the beginning of a new intimacy in the accounts of the Five Points. During and after the Civil War, middle-class men and women entered the Points and other slums not simply as voyeurs, but as resident activists. The missionaries' interactions in the day-to-day lives of the Five Points' residents may have influenced the attitudes of working-class whites and immigrants who sought to achieve political and social equality by distinguishing themselves from their black neighbors.

The success of the reformers' vision of interracial relations as degrading to native-born white and immigrant New Yorkers can be measured in the degree to which anti-amalgamation violence was a part of the 1863 New York City draft riots.[67] Although the draft riots began as a protest against the unfairness of the conscription laws, and then quickly became an effort to remove blacks from the city, one element of the violence was against alleged amalgamators. The rioters, chiefly Irish, attacked anyone who crossed the color line, from middle-class abolitionists to working people. The home of Abby Hopper Gibbons, a prison reformer and the daughter of the white abolitionist Isaac Hopper, was destroyed by rioters. Ann Derrickson and Ann Martin, two white women married to black men, and Mary Burke, a white prostitute who catered to black men, were harassed. But rioters saved their most savage attacks for black men, making a sport of mutilating their dead bodies, sometimes sexually. Ann Derrickson's son was saved from lynching only through the intercession of her neighbors. In another instance, a dead black man was dragged through the streets by his genitals. The riots indicate the degree to which the association of blacks by antebellum journalists and reformers with illicit sexuality and poverty affected all classes of whites. The violence was an attempt by white workers to dissociate themselves from blacks. For some, the act of the rioting may also have released guilt over former interracial pleasures.[68]

Ironically, the Five Points was one area of the city in which blacks and whites banded together against the rioters. No brothels there were attacked, nor were blacks killed within its borders. When the black drugstore owner Philip White was threatened by a mob in his store at the corner of Gold and Frankfurt Streets, his Irish neighbors drove the mob away, for he had often generously given credit to them. And when rioters invaded Hart's Alley and became trapped at its dead end, the black and white residents of the alley together leaned out of their windows and poured hot starch on them, driving them from the neighborhood. The neighborhood depicted as the center of amalgamation, and thus degradation, was saved from destruction through interracial cooperation.[69]

By the time of the Civil War, the meaning of "amalgamation" for New Yorkers had undergone several transformations. Prior to the 1830s "amalgamation" referred to both sexual and nonsexual interactions among different groups. These could include various Europeans, as well as blacks or whites in the United States. In the 1830s anti-abolitionist New Yorkers deployed the term "amalgamation" against the interracial radical abolitionist coalition. Amalgamation represented in the minds of anti-abolition New Yorkers the culmination of a range of activities from dancing to politics that involved blacks and whites and threatened to overturn the racial hierarchy. Amalgamation ideology sexualized all types of black-white interactions, and became a way to attempt to prevent black-white cooperation even on the most basic neighborly levels. As New York's middle-class black and white abolitionists retreated from the discourse of northern interracial sex in the wake of the 1834 riots, however, accusations of amalgamation were launched against poor blacks and whites.

The working class continued to socialize, cooperate, and marry across racial lines throughout the antebellum period. But around them, journalists and reformers depicted these cross-race interactions as distasteful and damaging to the city. Although Irish and blacks shared geographic, social, economic, and cultural space in New York City in the 1840s and 1850s, Irish workers increasingly adopted the mores of the reformers as the best way to achieve equality for themselves. The Civil War draft riots of 1863 and the violence, often sexualized, of Irish workers against blacks revealed the extent to which the fear of amalgamation had influenced some of the Irish community. Fears of amalgamation became part of the constellation of forces that made the city, once viewed as a haven, increasingly dangerous for blacks, and particularly black workers, on the eve of the Civil War.

The draft riots were perhaps the last instance in which the word "amalgamation" would alone be used to describe interracial sexual relations. Later that same year, the Democratic Party politicians David Croly and George Wakeman published a pseudoscientific pamphlet entitled *Miscegenation: The Theory of the Blending of the Races, Applied to the American White Man and Negro.* Croly and Wakeman invented the word "miscegenation" from the Latin *miscere,* to mix, and *genus,* race. Although the pamphlet was an elaborate hoax designed to discredit the Republican Party, one element of the pamphlet rings true. Croly and Wakeman claimed there was a need for a new word to describe interracial sex, for "amalgamation" was a "poor word" since it referred to the "union of metals . . . and was in fact only borrowed for an emergency."[70] Despite the ultimate discrediting of the pamphlet, the word "miscegenation" took root. Its adoption and usage into the twentieth century in the United States embody the triumph of racist attitudes toward interracial sex.

NOTES

Part of this essay was presented at the 1997 American Historical Association conference in New York City as " 'Rulers of the Five Points': Interracial Sex and Class in Antebellum New York." I would like to thank Cynthia Blair, Elizabeth Clements, Karen Dunn-Haley, Ariela Gross, Wendy Lynch, Kathy Peiss, Renee Romano, Wendy Wall, and Alice Yang-Murray for comments on early drafts of this essay. Mary Odem and Martha Hodes provided crucial comments and suggestions on later drafts. Writing of this essay was supported in part by an Emory College Faculty Development Award.

1. For a summary of the literature on interracial sex in the South, see John D'Emilio and Estelle B. Freedman, *Intimate Matters: A History of Sexuality in America* (New York: Harper and Row, 1988), 93–108; and Catherine Clinton, "Caught in the Web of the Big House: Women and Slavery," in *The Web of Southern Social Relations: Women, Family and Education,* ed. Walter J. Fraser, Jr., et al. (Athens: University of Georgia Press, 1985). See also Nell Irvin Painter, "Of *Lily,* Linda Brent, and Freud: A Non-Exceptionalist Approach to Race, Class, and Gender in the Slave South," *Georgia Historical Quarterly* 86 (1992): 241–59; Joel Williamson, *New People: Miscegenation and Mulattoes in the United States* (New York: Free Press, 1980); Melton A. McLaurin, *Celia, A Slave* (Athens: University of Georgia Press, 1991); Darlene Clark Hine, "Rape and the Inner Lives of Black Women in the Middle West," in *Unequal Sisters,* ed. Ellen Carol DuBois and Vicki L. Ruiz (New York: Routledge, 1990), 292–97. George M. Fredrickson and Winthrop D. Jordan examine both northern and southern thought about interracial sex. Fredrickson, *The Black Image in the White Mind: The Debate on Afro-American Character and Destiny, 1817–1914* (Middletown, Conn.: Wesleyan University Press, 1971), esp. 117–24; and Jordan, *White over Black: American Attitudes toward the Negro, 1550–1812* (1968; reprint, New York: W. W. Norton, 1977), esp. 469–75, 542–69. Work on consensual relationships between black and white southerners includes Martha Hodes, *White Women, Black Men: Illicit Sex in the Nineteenth-Century South* (New Haven: Yale University Press, 1997). For a useful overview of interracial relationships and the law, see Peggy Pascoe, "Miscegenation Law, Court Cases, and Ideologies of 'Race' in Twentieth-Century America," in this volume.

2. *Oxford English Dictionary*; Richard H. Thornton, *An American Glossary: Being an Attempt to Illustrate Certain Americanisms upon Historical Principles* (New York: Frederick Ungar, 1962), 1:13. William A. Craigie and James R. Hulbert, *A Dictionary of American*

English on Historical Principles (Chicago: University of Chicago Press, 1938), 37. "Amalgamation" also referred to the mixing of metals.

3. Peggy Pascoe's "Miscegenation Law," although about post–Civil War miscegenation, is useful in delineating the various levels of interracial relationships encapsulated in the word "miscegenation." A similar process occurred with "amalgamation" in the antebellum era.

4. Jordan, *White over Black*, 471–72.

5. See Leslie M. Harris, "Creating the African-American Working Class: Black and White Workers, Abolitionists and Reformers in New York City, 1785–1863" (Ph.D. diss., Stanford University, 1995).

6. See Timothy J. Gilfoyle, *City of Eros: New York City, Prostitution, and the Commercialization of Sex, 1790–1920* (New York: W. W. Norton, 1992), 17–22, 29; and Carroll Smith-Rosenberg, *Religion and the Rise of the American City: The New York City Mission Movement, 1812–1870* (Ithaca: Cornell University Press, 1971), 98–100.

7. Smith-Rosenberg, *Religion*, 98–100.

8. Gilfoyle, *City of Eros*, 42–46.

9. Bertram Wyatt-Brown, *Lewis Tappan and the Evangelical War against Slavery* (Cleveland: Case Western Reserve University Press, 1969), 68–70; quotation from Barnabas Bates, *An Address Delivered at a General Meeting of the Citizens of the City of New-York*, in Wyatt-Brown, 68. Bogardus is not identified as a brothel landlord in Gilfoyle's *City of Eros*.

10. Smith-Rosenberg, *Religion*, 100–101; Lewis Tappan, *Life of Arthur Tappan* (New York: Hurd and Houghton, 1870), 113, 116; Gilfoyle, *City of Eros*, 43–46.

11. See Sean Wilentz, *Chants Democratic: New York City and the Rise of the American Working Class, 1789–1850* (New York: Oxford University Press, 1984), 260–66, for working-class attitudes toward abolitionists. For the tensions caused by the increasing power of abolitionists and the decreasing power of the colonizationists, see Leonard L. Richards, *"Gentlemen of Property and Standing": Anti-Abolition Mobs in Jacksonian America* (New York: Oxford University Press, 1970), 24–25, 30–31, 48–49, 168.

12. David Meredith Reese, *Humbugs of New York* (1838; reprint, Freeport, N.Y.: Books for Libraries, 1971), 143.

13. *Emancipator and Republican*, Dec. 15, 1836.

14. Lydia Maria Child, *An Appeal in Favor of That Class of Americans Called Africans* (1836; reprint, Salem, N. H.: Ayer, 1994), 196.

15. *Freedom's Journal*, Aug. 17, 1827. The pseudonymous Mordecai is not to be confused with the anti-abolitionist Mordecai Noah mentioned above. The *Freedom's Journal* writer may have taken the name Mordecai as a counterpoint to Noah's tendency to criticize blacks in mainstream New York newspapers.

16. *Freedom's Journal*, Aug. 24, 1827.

17. *First Annual Report of the American Anti-Slavery Society; with the Speeches Delivered at the Anniversary Meeting, Held in Chatham-Street Chapel, in the city of New-York, on the sixth day of May, 1834* . . . (1834; reprint, New York: Kraus Reprint Co., 1972), 8–9.

18. See also Ronald G. Walters, "The Erotic South: Civilization and Sexuality in American Abolitionism," *American Quarterly* 35 (1973): 177–201.

19. Quoted in Tappan, *Life of Arthur Tappan*, 171–72.

20. *New York Journal of Commerce*, April 30, 1834.

21. "The Fanatics," *Morning Courier and New-York Enquirer*, June 23, 1834.

22. Primary accounts of the riots can be found in Tappan, *Life of Arthur Tappan*, and in various New York newspapers. Secondary source accounts include Linda K. Kerber,

"Abolitionists and Amalgamators: The New York City Race Riots of 1834," *New York History* 48 (1967): 28–39; Richards, *"Gentlemen of Property and Standing"*; Paul A. Gilje, *The Road to Mobocracy: Popular Disorder in New York City, 1763–1834* (Chapel Hill: University of North Carolina Press, 1987), 162–70; and Wilentz, *Chants Democratic*, 264–66.

23. Tappan, *Life of Arthur Tappan*, 203–04.

24. Richards, *"Gentlemen of Property and Standing,"* 150–53; Wilentz, *Chants Democratic*, 264–66.

25. Examples of affluent blacks are taken from Gilje, *Road to Mobocracy*, 166, and from *Mercantile Advertiser and New York Advocate*, July 14, 1834.

26. Tappan, *Life of Arthur Tappan*, 215–16.

27. See, for example, *New York Commercial Advertiser*, July 15, 1834; and the American Colonization Society's *African Repository and Colonial Journal*, Aug. 1834.

28. *New York Commercial Advertiser*, July 18, 1834.

29. "An Appeal of the American Anti-Slavery Society to the People of the City of New-York," *Emancipator*, Aug. 19, 1834.

30. *Freedom's Journal*, June 29, 1827. On black parades, see Shane White, " 'It Was a Proud Day': African-Americans, Festivals, and Parades," *Journal of American History* 81 (1994): 13–50.

31. Rumor repeated in "An Appeal of the American Anti-Slavery Society."

32. The Massachusetts law was not repealed until 1841.

33. See Fredrickson, *Black Image*, 122–23, for the attitudes of abolitionists toward amalgamation.

34. Child quoted in Fredrickson, *Black Image*, 37.

35. David R. Roediger, *The Wages of Whiteness: Race and the Making of the American Working Class* (London: Verso, 1991).

36. Fredrickson, *Black Image*, 37.

37. The most significant exception to this pattern would be the black abolitionist Frederick Douglass, who from the 1850s until the end of his life flouted these evolving racial standards of middle-class practice.

38. For the 1741 slave plot, see Thomas J. Davis, *A Rumor of Revolt: The "Great Negro Plot" in Colonial New York* (New York: Free Press, 1985), 4–5, 7, 75, 105–06. For the Rose Butler case, see Harris, "Creating the African-American Working Class," 40–46.

39. "A Large Haul," *New York Transcript*, Nov. 13, 1834; "Police Office," *New York Transcript*, March 11, 15, 27, 1835. Although blackguarding has many definitions, here it probably means making remarks of a sexual or seductive nature.

40. "Practical Amalgamation," *New York Transcript*, July 24, 1835; and "Special Sessions—Yesterday," *New York Transcript*, July 25, 1835.

41. "Police Office: Othello Travestie," *New York Transcript*, Sept. 8, 1835.

42. See Christine Stansell, *City of Women: Sex and Class in New York, 1789–1860* (1986; reprint, Urbana: University of Illinois Press, 1987), 89–91.

43. "Police Office," *New York Transcript*, Oct. 16, 1834.

44. Robert Ernst, *Immigrant Life in New York City, 1825–1863* (New York: King's Crown Press, 1949), 41; Gilfoyle, *City of Eros*, 34.

45. Charles Dickens, *Pictures from Italy: American Notes for General Circulation* (1842; reprint, London: Chapman and Hall, n.d.), 272.

46. Ibid., 274–75.

47. Eric Lott, *Love and Theft: Blackface Minstrelsy and the American Working Class* (New York: Oxford University Press, 1995). *American Notes* sold fifty thousand copies in

three days, and newspapers across the country reprinted excerpts. Kris Lackey, "Eighteenth-Century Aesthetic Theory and the Nineteenth-Century Traveler in Trans-Allegheny America: F. Trollope, Dickens, Irving and Parkman," *American Studies* 32 (1991): 34.

48. Nathaniel Parker Willis, *The Complete Works of Nathaniel Parker Willis* (New York: J. S. Redfield, 1846), in [I. N. Phelps Stokes], "New York City Slums. Notes taken for I. N. Phelps Stokes in preparation of the book, *The Iconography of Manhattan Island* (New York, Robert H. Dodd, 1915-1928)," typed manuscript, Rare Book and Manuscript Room, New York Public Library, New York, N.Y., 670.

49. Willis, *Complete Works*, 668, 672.

50. Stuart M. Blumin, introduction to *New York by Gaslight and Other Urban Sketches by George G. Foster* (Berkeley: University of California Press, 1990), 38.

51. George G. Foster, *New York by Gas-Light, with Here and There a Streak of Sunshine* (1850; reprint: *New York by Gas-Light and Other Urban Sketches by George G. Foster*, ed. Stuart M. Blumin [Berkeley: University of California Press, 1990]), 124.

52. Ibid., 145-46.

53. "Dance Houses of the Five Points," *Monthly Record of the Five Points House of Industry* 1 (October 1857): 149.

54. William M. Bobo, *Glimpses of New-York City, by a South Carolinian (Who Had Nothing Else to Do)* (Charleston: J. J. McCarter, 1852), 95-97.

55. See David Roediger's excellent analysis of the cultural relationship between blacks and Irish in *Wages of Whiteness*, 133-63. See also Noel Ignatiev, *How the Irish Became White* (New York: Routledge, 1995), esp. 76, 87, 140-44; and Graham Hodges, " 'Desirable Companions and Lovers': Irish and African Americans in the Sixth Ward, 1830-1870," in *The New York Irish*, ed. Ronald H. Bayor and Timothy J. Meagher (Baltimore: Johns Hopkins University Press, 1995).

56. Smith-Rosenberg, *Religion*, 226.

57. Account of the Five Points Mission taken from Smith-Rosenberg, *Religion*, 225-35; and Herbert Asbury, *The Gangs of New York: An Informal History of the Underworld* (New York: Alfred A. Knopf, 1928), 16-19.

58. [Five Points Mission], *The Old Brewery and the New Mission House at the Five Points. By the Ladies of the Mission* (New York: Stringer and Townsend, 1854), 15-16.

59. Ibid.

60. Ibid.

61. *Documents of the Assembly of the State of New-York. Eighteenth Session.—1857*, in Stokes, "New York City Slums Collection," 784-85.

62. "(From the Independent) A Peep into Cut-Throat Alley. By Rev. Theodore L. Cuyler," *Monthly Record of the Five Points House of Industry* 4 (April 1861): 266.

63. Ibid.

64. Ibid., 267-68.

65. Ibid., 267.

66. Graham Hodges implicitly argues that black-Irish relationships predominantly involved black men and Irish women. However, given the number of white, and possibly Irish, men who were observed with black women in earlier journalists' and travelers' accounts, the assumption that the predominant pairing was between Irish women and black men may be problematic. See Hodges, " 'Desirable Companions and Lovers,' " esp. 107, 123.

67. The best historical account of the draft riots is Iver Bernstein, *The New York City Draft Riots: Their Significance for American Society and Politics in the Age of the Civil War* (New York: Oxford University Press, 1990).

68. Details of the draft riots are from Bernstein, *Draft Riots*, 25-37. See Roediger, *Wages*

of Whiteness, 150–56 for a discussion of blacks as representative of preindustrial guilty pleasures to the Irish; and Lott, *Love and Theft*.

69. Harry A. Williamson, "Folks in Old New York and Brooklyn," typed manuscript, 1953, Library, New-York Historical Society, New York, N.Y., 2–5.

70. For the fullest discussion of Croly and Wakeman's pamphlet, see Sidney Kaplan, "The Miscegenation Issue in the Election of 1864," *Journal of Negro History* 34 (1949): 274–343. Quotation from 278n. See also Roediger, *Wages of Whiteness*, 154–56; and Fredrickson, *Black Image*, 171–74.

Chapter Ten

White Pain Pollen
An Elite Biracial Daughter's Quandary

Josephine Boyd Bradley and Kent Anderson Leslie

> White faces, pain pollen, settle downward through
> cane-sweet mist and touch the ovaries of yellow flowers.
> —Jean Toomer, *Cane*[1]

In a world where the ruling race justified selling human beings by depicting them as absolutely "other," what emotions and actions could be categorized as love? Could a white father love his mulatto daughter across these boundaries and not socialize her to be aware that, to the outside white world, she was the "other"? The story of Amanda America Dickson of Hancock County, Georgia, gives us some insight into these provocative questions.

White antebellum southerners realized the conflict between the ideology of racial slavery and their use of the metaphor of the family to organize social relationships. In 1864 Judge C. J. Lumpkin of Georgia commented, "Which of us has not narrowly escaped petting one of the pretty little mulattoes belonging to our neighbor as one of the family?" Herein lay a terrible dilemma. These "pretty little mulattoes belonging to our neighbor" were sometimes members of the family. On an ideological level, these walking contradictions might be explained away as the products of the "lustful entrapments" of black women, as the "frolics of the lower classes," or as frail creatures who would die out as a result of natural selection. In reality, however, individuals had to deal with each other on a personal level. It was on this level that the conflict between the ideology of race and the ideology of the family caused human anguish. As E. Franklin Frazier observed, "Neither color caste nor the law of slavery could resist altogether the corrosive influences of human feeling and sentiment generated in these lawless families."[2] The boundaries of race were unsustainable. Antebellum southerners never resolved this dilemma. They simply declared "race" an absolute in the abstract and maintained a semblance of order at the expense of both logic and feelings. The story of Amanda America Dickson, an elite biracial lady, demonstrates that, for some, that price was simply too high to pay.

One day in the middle of February 1849, David Dickson rode across his fallow fields. A wealthy white man of forty, large and heavyset, he wore his long black hair straight, Indian-style. As he rode, he spotted a young slave playing in a field. Dickson knew the slave. She was, in fact, a "great pet" of his mother's. Deliberately he rode up beside the slave child, reached down, and swung her up behind him on his saddle; as a member of her African American family would remember 140 years later, "that was the end of that." The slave's childhood ended as Amanda America Dickson's life began on that day when her father raped her mother. This act of violence created a child who was not supposed to be recognized, who was not supposed to inherit wealth, a child who was supposed to be denied by her white father.

Sources of information about Amanda America Dickson's life include the African American Dickson Family Oral History (which her granddaughter related to her own grandchildren and great-grandchildren), legal records housed at the Hancock County Courthouse in middle Georgia, and newspaper articles describing the trial over her father's controversial will leaving his enormous estate to his mulatto daughter. The Dickson Family Oral History paints a picture of an elite mulatto "lady." According to these sources, Amanda Dickson spent her infancy, childhood, and young adulthood in her white father's and grandmother's household, as a privileged daughter. She married a white Civil War veteran and had children of her own before returning to her father's home. She inherited her father's enormous estate and eventually moved to Augusta, Georgia, where she died amid luxury, at home in the wealthiest section of the city.[3]

If we explore Amanda America Dickson's life by paying close attention to her connections with her slave mother (Julia Frances Lewis Dickson), her white grandmother (Elizabeth Dickson), and her white father (David Dickson), is it possible to describe reciprocal relationships that involved affection—that is, love? What of the mother's relationship to Amanda's father? As members of a dominant elite, David and Elizabeth were able to collapse the category of race into the categories of daughter and grandchild. However, Julia Frances Lewis Dickson, as a slave and servant, was denied the role of authoritative mother, denied the opportunity to teach her daughter the survival skills necessary to cope if Amanda were ever forced to define herself as an African American woman in the world outside the Dickson plantation and the community surrounding it. If it is true that public sentiment, not abstract ideology, controlled the amount of miscegenation that took place in the nineteenth-century South, then what factors combined to create a place where an elite white male could rape a slave child and raise the offspring of that act of violence in his own household, as his daughter?[4] A partial answer lies in the geography, history, and social and economic arrangements that evolved in Amanda America Dickson's place, a place where she was both protected and trapped.

Amanda America Dickson's birthplace, Hancock County, Georgia, is located in the fertile Black Belt of the state, 125 miles south and east of Atlanta, between the pre–Civil War capital of Milledgeville and the river port city of Augusta. Between the establishment of Hancock County by the state of Georgia in 1793 and the official end of Indian-white hostilities in 1838, the county emerged from its frontier status and became a place where poor-to-middling settlers congregated, waiting to move on to land in the middle and western parts of the state. Farmers who had accumulated a surplus of capital bought up the fertile bottomlands of the county and stayed put. The white population of the area reached 9,605 in 1800 and steadily declined thereafter, with only a slight variation in the trend for the next 150 years. Conversely, the slave population increased from 4,855 souls in 1800 to 8,137 in 1860.[5]

The process of "civilizing" its inhabitants and the evolution of a plantation regime took place at the same time in Hancock County. Some individuals and families became wealthy at the expense of others. Between 1802 and 1860 the total number of slaveholders in the county declined from 819 to 410. By 1860 the leading fifty-six planter families, or five percent of the families in Hancock County, owned more than half the land and 40 percent of those who were enslaved. The average value of their real and personal property was approximately seventy thousand dollars. At the end of the antebellum period, based on income per capita—and excluding the enslaved—Georgia was the richest state in the Union, Hancock County was one of its richest counties, and David Dickson was Hancock's richest citizen.[6] This, then, was Amanda America Dickson's place, a relatively isolated county where the enslaved outnumbered free citizens by almost two to one; a place where education, culture, and even luxury were available to a small minority of the ruling race; a place where enough was available for everybody to subsist; a place where people had often known each other all their lives.

Elizabeth, David, Julia Frances, and Amanda Dickson's stories represent threads that intertwine to form a pattern distorted by tensions between racial ideology and the family, between paternalism and exploitation. Amanda America Dickson's life unfolded within the boundaries of her grandmother's and father's social and economic power, her mother's conflicting loyalties, and her own evolving sense of self.

At the time Amanda America Dickson was conceived, her mother, Julia Frances Lewis Dickson, was twelve years old and her father, David, was forty. Julia was a slave who belonged to David's mother.[7] David knew who she was; the rape was not a random act of violence. The fact that Julia was a "great pet" of Elizabeth Dickson did not protect her from the domination of David. It may even have made her the target of David's violence.

Julia is remembered in the African American Dickson Family Oral History as a small, copper-colored person with soft hair and beautiful teeth, a woman who was "very temperamental and high strung." At the time of the rape, Julia lived in the Dickson's yard with her own mother, Rose, who was also a Dickson slave. Julia's two brothers, Seab and John, also lived on the Dickson plantation. We do not know what reactions the violence of Amanda America Dickson's conception evoked, what the slave community thought, or what David's mother thought. According to the Dickson Family Oral History, Julia never forgave David for forcing her to have sex when she was so young, and it was she who lived to tell the story from her own perspective.

We do not know whether Amanda America Dickson was born in the Dickson home place or in Julia Dickson's house in the yard. Nor did anyone record her naming. America is certainly a patriotic, and consequently ironic, name for an en-slaved person. It does not seem likely that Julia Frances named her daughter Amanda America. Perhaps her father or grandmother gave her the name. Perhaps they were expressing their own patriotic view of the sectional conflict that raged over slavery in the territories at that time. Were they expressing their belief that this child could be brought into their family in spite of her color, that she could be rescued from slavery and racial categories by their individual wills, that a safe space could be created for her, even in the American South?

After Amanda America was weaned, she was taken from her mother, another act of violence against Julia Dickson as tragic as the rape itself. Thereafter the child lived in her white grandmother's room, sleeping in a trundle bed that Elizabeth Dickson had made especially for her. She lived in that same room in the Dickson household until her grandmother's death in 1864. Later in his life David Dickson reflected on the decision to bring Amanda America into the Dickson household, declaring that it was his duty to care for his daughter, and that he wanted her to be with him. Perhaps these feelings had prompted Dickson to take the infant into his household. Perhaps Elizabeth Dickson had made the decision to separate Amanda America from her mother in an effort to make amends for her son's loss of control, or perhaps she simply wanted the company of her grandchild. Years later, one of Elizabeth's grandsons commented that he had "never seen a man in all his life who was as kind to his mother as he [David] was; I have never seen any person any kinder; there was nothing he could do for her but what he was ready to do it." Perhaps David and Elizabeth made the decision together to create a "family" that excluded the enslaved mother.[8]

When Amanda America was born, the white Dickson household was composed of older, widowed, or never-married white people. Elizabeth Dickson was seventy-two when her granddaughter was born. David was forty, a sister was forty-three, and a brother was thirty-five. The Dickson Family Oral History and the court transcript from the trial over David Dickson's will reveal that this nuclear family treated Amanda America like "any other child" and as a member of the family. To be white, Amanda America had to remain chosen by her white family and their community. To be black, she would have had to choose that category and accept the consequences. Instead she chose to endeavor to create a racial category that was neither black nor white.

In the antebellum South, it was not unusual for a master or mistress to bring a slave into a white household. According to Mary Chesnut, her mother-in-law slept with two servants in the same room, in case she needed attention in the night, and two servants in the next room as guards, which implies that the elder Chesnut had absolute faith in these particular enslaved people. In the case of slave children, it was widely believed that the best way to socialize house servants was to raise them in the master's or mistress's household. Ella Gertrude Clanton Thomas observed in her diary that a slave child, whom she knew, was "a bright, quick child and who raised in our family could have become a good servant," adding, "As it is she will be under her mother's influence and run wild in the street." In the case of Amanda

America, the servant was an infant. For a time at least, she would be the one who would have to be cared for in a family of older white people.[9]

From her birth in 1849 until her grandmother's death in 1864, Amanda America Dickson remained legally a slave. During this time, it would have been virtually impossible for Elizabeth or David to free Amanda and to keep her with them in Georgia. As early as 1801 Georgia had outlawed manumission within the state, except by petitioning the legislature, a process that became more and more restrictive over time. Amanda Dickson could have been freed in another state, but she could not have legally returned as a free person of color. In order for Elizabeth and David to keep Amanda America with them on the Dickson home place, the child had to remain enslaved and continually at risk, vulnerable to her grandmother's and her father's mortality.[10] They were not willing to send her away to freedom. They did not love her enough to part with her.

According to both the Dickson Family Oral History and white observers, Amanda America spent most of her childhood and youth in her grandmother's room. Julia Frances Dickson observed that Amanda stayed there night and day, studying her books and doing "whatever she was told to do." Dr. E. W. Alfriend, the Dickson family doctor, observed that Amanda America was "very devoted" to her grandmother and "very comfortably situated" in her grandmother's room.[11] Was it love that prompted the grandmother to keep Amanda America in her bedroom? Was Elizabeth Dickson trying to protect the child?

Some evidence exists that at times Amanda was treated like "any other child" by her white relatives. When asked what Amanda did, one of David Dickson's nephews commented that "she was about the house like any other child would be; helped at sweeping the floor and such as that." However, when asked what the feelings of Elizabeth Dickson were toward Amanda, the same relative responded that she "had the kindest feelings towards Amanda."[12] Yet for her entire childhood, Amanda America was legally an enslaved person.

While she may have performed some duties that would typically be performed by "any other child," the evidence also suggests that some of the individuals in the white Dickson household treated Amanda America as they would a pet, as someone to spoil. According to the Dickson Family Oral History, Amanda America was the "darling of David Dickson's heart." He "adored her" and "gave her everything that she wanted." He had her "bathed in sweet milk to lighten her skin." He "allowed her to claim newborn slaves as her own and name them whatever she liked." Everyone on the plantation called her "Miss Mandy," including her father and, one would presume, her own mother. According to this oral history, "She was his pampered darling." Amanda America Dickson was being socialized as a member of a white family, a person who expected to be obeyed without question, a raceless little princess being raised in a make-believe world.[13] David and Elizabth did not seem to realize that as an adult Amanda America Dickson would have to face the barriers of race. Was this denial an act of authentic love for this child or an act of arrogance? Curiously, the African American Dickson Family Oral History records this situation not with regret but with pride.[14]

Some evidence suggests that the white Dickson household did indeed provide for Amanda America Dickson as though she were a member of the family. Amanda America learned to read and write, which was certainly a luxury for any girl child of the time and forbidden by law for slaves. Elizabeth and Julia were both illiterate, while David was not. Perhaps Amanda America learned to read and write from her father. The Dickson Family Oral History states that "Old Dr. Porter" came out to the plantation to teach Amanda.[15] During the trial over the validity of David Dickson's will, it became evident that Amanda shared many of her father's characteristics. Judge J. C. Simmons commented that Amanda America "favored Mr. Dickson in her personal appearance, her manner of speech, and general management of business." Her father taught her to manage her own business affairs. While residing within the boundaries of the white Dickson household, Amanda America learned the skills and manners appropriate to her white family's class. She learned to play the piano, to dress with subdued elegance, including the display of jewelry, and to behave like a "lady." She learned to act white, which placed her outside the categories of house slave and field hand and precariously inside the category of family.

We do not know who Amanda America Dickson's friends were in her childhood or adulthood. We do not know if or how the family of Elizabeth, David, and Amanda protected themselves, especially Amanda, from chance encounters with individuals who were not aware of their unorthodox arrangements. And we do not know how Julia Frances Dickson reacted to having her daughter raised to be a mulatto princess who was addressed by everyone, including her mother and white father, as "Miss Amanda" or "Miss Mandy."

While Amanda America was growing up and spending most of her time reading in the "big house," her mother lived a very different sort of life. Julia Frances Lewis Dickson began her life as a slave living in a "nigger" house in the yard with the other servants. It was a large frame building, two stories high, with three to five rooms. By 1857 Julia Dickson was living in another house on the edge of the yard that was "a little better furnished." Julia lived upstairs in this second house, in a room partitioned off from the other servants. Her mother, Rose, had an adjoining room separated from Julia's space by a door.[16] From these residences, Julia Frances Dickson moved in and out of the white Dickson household as a slave with a privileged position. Yet that privileged position did not separate her from the black enslaved community.

The psychological space Julia Frances Dickson inhabited was profoundly affected by the fact that she was raped at the age of twelve and continued to live in the household of her rapist. This space denied her the role of woman, mother, lover, and wife. Julia's response to these distorted relationships was to "rule David Dickson with an iron hand" and control the keys to the plantation, a recognized symbol of authority.[17] Julia's freedom was a result of her ability to invert love and guilt.

Between 1849 and 1863 David Dickson prospered. His labor force grew from 53 to 160 slaves. All of these individuals had to be housed, fed, and clothed, and Julia Dickson was part of the great organic structure that made this possible. One of David Dickson's nephews remembered that Julia "waited in the house and minded the table, and so on." He added that "after the child [Amanda] was born,

[Julia], was confined a good deal nursing the child and while she was nursing the child she did a good deal of sewing; after that period ceased she was active about the house under the direction of my grandmother like any other slave would be." Julia Dickson described her own work as follows: "I assisted in making up the beds; swept the yards and did everything else about the house, worked in the garden."[18]

During the trial over David Dickson's will, several witnesses were called on to testify about David and Julia's relationship. Two witnesses testified that Julia wielded some influence over David Dickson. W. H. Matthews, a crippled Civil War veteran who used to fish in the Dickson ponds just after the war, was asked whether he had "any transaction with Mr. Dickson which was attended to by Julia?" Matthews answered, "I would catch the fish and carry them up and he would tell me to deliver them to Julia and she would pay me; he never paid me a nickel in his life, she always paid me. . . . Well, I think this woman had a great deal of influence over Mr. Dickson." Matthews also stated that Julia was "in charge" of "household matters," that Dickson paid the "most regard" to Julia's suggestions, and that he himself had seen David Dickson kiss Julia "several times."[19] Yet upon cross-examination, Matthews also admitted that he had never seen Julia Dickson "exercise any control" over David Dickson outside household matters. Was David Dickson unduly influenced if that influence was exercised only in the domestic sphere?

James M. Eubanks, one of David Dickson's nephews and a business associate who had lived on the Dickson home place from 1855 to 1862, stated that Julia Dickson "exercised more influence over David Dickson than anybody else."[20] Although under cross-examination Eubanks testified that Julia exercised no control over David Dickson's business affairs, Eubanks continued to argue that Julia Dickson did indeed have undue influence over David Dickson because David treated Julia as a wife rather than a servant. "Dickson didn't direct her like a servant," Eubanks declared, "he directed her like a wife; like a man would direct his wife; he didn't speak harsh to her like a servant."[21] The other witnesses for the caveators claimed that David Dickson did not treat Julia Dickson like a servant, but they would not conclude that she had undue influence over him. Joe Brookens, one of David Dickson's former slaves and the father of Julia Dickson's second child, stated that Julia had as much control in household matters as any man's wife. However, under cross-examination, Brookens admitted that "she [Julia] was under him [David] and had to obey him; they all had to obey him. . . . he had it all in his hands and did as he pleased."[22]

The white relatives endeavored to demonstrate that Julia exercised undue influence over David Dickson because of his affection for her. James M. Dickson, who stated at the trial that he had known David Dickson "ever since childhood," reported that when he visited the Dickson home place as a little boy he had seen Green Dickson, David's brother, threaten to kill David "because he (David) had put this nigger (Julia) over their mother."[23] S. D. Rogers, Dickson's nephew, stated that he had known David Dickson since "his first recollection" and that he had lived at the Dickson home place off and on as a boy. When the court asked Rogers whether he ever saw David Dickson oppose Julia in "any of her wishes," he recounted this story from his childhood:

I never knew of any clashing but once; when I was a boy several years before the war, I was down there on a visit, and he (David Dickson) had a housegirl by the name of Lett, and she made a complaint to him that some articles that he had given her had been destroyed; they were some articles of dress trimming; they all started a search for it, Lett and some other girls he had about the house there, and I think Lett called his attention to the back door where Julia was standing, cutting up this trimming; he asked her what she was doing and she made no reply at all, and he hit her with a cowhide, and I think she hit him, anyway they had a lively little scuffle.

The exchange then proceeded as follows:

Q: State what she did.
A: She jumped on him.
Q: Tried to whip him? Did he strike her more than one lick?
A: Only one lick. I was satisfied that he regretted that he had struck her.
Q: How long before they made it up?
A: Not before the next morning. I was there and saw her and she seemed to be in a good humor.
Q: What was Julia's condition at that time?
A: She was a slave.
Q: I will ask you to state whether or not the relation between Mr. Dickson and Julia was that of a master and slave or was it more like the relation between a man and his sweetheart?
A: It was much more like a man and his sweetheart or a husband and wife, something of that sort.[24]

How shall we interpret this encounter? If Julia felt threatened by David's attention to Lett, then she knew how to defy David and put Lett in her place.

Other witnesses testified that David Dickson exhibited affection for Julia. William S. Dickson, another witness for the caveators, stated that he had talked to Tyler Harrison, a black man who worked on the Dickson place after the war, and that Harrison had told him that on one occasion Julia had threatened to leave David Dickson. In response, Dickson had "looked like he was most crazy . . . cried and took on about it."[25] In addition, four hostile witnesses said that they had seen David Dickson kiss Julia.[26] Of these witnesses, Matthew Dickson and Joe Brookens had been Dickson slaves, and Washington Printup had worked on the Dickson home place after the war. The fourth was the white W. H. Matthews, who traded with David Dickson.[27]

During the decade before the Civil War, Julia Dickson gave birth to two more children by different fathers. In 1853, when Julia Dickson was seventeen, she delivered Julianna, whose father was another Dickson slave, Joe Brookens the wagoner. Thirteen months later, at eighteen, she gave birth to Lola, whose father was "Doc Eubanks," a white man. Lola died as a small child. These early pregnancies compromised Julia Dickson's health. E. W. Alfriend, the Dickson family doctor from 1854 to 1861, remembered that he "never missed a year that I didn't attend [Julia] in some sickness."[28]

In addition to these sexual encounters, Julia also maintained an intimate relationship with David Dickson that was more than sexual. During the trial, when Julia

Dickson was asked by the attorneys for the caveators about these multiple sexual relationships, the following exchange took place:

> Q: Did anybody else have anything to do with you [sexually] except the men who were the father[s] of these children?
> A: No sir.
> Q: You say it mighty weak? Julia?
> A: I can say it strong.
> Q: You just confined your favors to these three?
> A: To those three.
> Q: And to Joe Brookens?
> A: I don't know anything about confining myself: I was not a bad woman.[29]

After the birth of Julia Dickson's three daughters, Elizabeth Dickson became more and more infirmed, and the younger woman assumed control of the household. Along with another mulatto slave, Lucy, Julia stood guard over the keys to the plantation and presided over the kitchen. In essence, Julia became David Dickson's housekeeper. In this role she was described by Dr. E. W. Alfriend as "a very attentive business woman about the house." In fact, said Dr. Alfriend, "I became very much attached to the woman."[30]

Anne Goodwyn Jones has observed that there existed a role for a black woman in white antebellum southern homes as "mammy," an individual who "became the nurturing, all-giving mother figure, beloved because she threatened the hierarchy of neither race nor sex." In the white Dickson household, Julia Frances Dickson was, in certain respects, the antithesis to Jones's ideal "mammy." She "attentively" controlled the domestic sphere of David Dickson's domain while maintaining an intimate relationship with the master. She was, in Deborah Gray White's terms, both the mammy, serving as surrogate mother to her own child, and the Jezebel, serving as the mistress of the master.[31] Did this arrangement threaten labor management on the Dickson plantation, where Julia controlled the access of her own kin to both the necessities of life and the few luxuries that were available? How did this arrangement affect whites who transacted business through Julia Frances Dickson? Viewed as political acts, these arrangements threatened some of the essential myths of the racial hierarchy of chattel slavery.

In 1861, when the war erupted, Amanda America Dickson was twelve years old. At the time, her household consisted of her grandmother, who was eighty-four, and her father, who was fifty-two. At the age of twelve, Amanda may have been unaware of the impending crisis. After all, she lived in the household of a powerful patriarch-paternalist, a man who had protected her from other ambiguities and anxieties. But by the end of the war in 1865, at the age of sixteen, Amanda America must have been aware of her uncertain future.

What Julia Frances Dickson thought about the impending crisis is unclear. She was a twenty-five-year-old slave when the Civil War broke out. One of her living daughters had been taken from her and benefited materially from the slave system while the other, Julianna Youngblood, had not. In fact Julianna, Julia's mother,

Rose, and her brothers, John C. (Lewis), and Seab (Lewis), were Dickson slaves. Julia's privileged position as the Dicksons' housekeeper rested on David Dickson's wealth, which rested on the backs of his slave labor force, Julia Dickson's kin.

In 1865 Julia Frances Dickson was twenty-nine and a free woman. She was free to leave the Dickson home place, free to leave her position as "housekeeper," and free to terminate her sexual relationship with David Dickson. No mention is made in the African American Dickson Family Oral History, of which Julia Frances Dickson is the primary source, of Julia's feelings toward David, except that she never forgave him for forcing her to have sex with him at such a tender age and that she "ruled David Dickson with an iron hand." According to what the family chose to remember, control in the domestic sphere constituted Julia Dickson's revenge.

Julia Frances Dickson chose to stay on the Dickson plantation after the war. Perhaps she was reluctant to leave the place where she had grown up. Perhaps Julia Dickson stayed because of her responsibility in the operation of the Dickson plantation. Perhaps she stayed because David would not allow Amanda America to leave or because Amanda America would not leave. Perhaps she stayed because she did not want to leave David Dickson.

In 1865 Amanda America Dickson was sixteen. Her white grandmother had been dead a year. Her father's empire lay in ruins, and she faced the possibility of being insecure for the first time in her life. She had always been treated as essentially free from slavery, but she was also trapped in the domain of her white family. The material privileges that she enjoyed were the result of the enslavement of other people of African descent. She may have been afraid of those others. She may have been afraid of poverty. Or she may have put her trust in the belief that her father was still in control.

With the end of the war, another segment of Hancock County's population was free: Confederate soldiers were free to come home. Among the returning soldiers was Charles Eubanks, David Dickson's nephew. Eubanks enlisted in the Hancock Confederate Guards and fought until April 1865. Eubanks had been born in Georgia in 1836 and had lived all his life in Hancock County. There is some evidence that he spent a good deal of time on the Dickson plantation. In 1865 Charles Eubanks was twenty-nine, the same age as Julia Frances Dickson. Sometime in 1865 Amanda America Dickson began an intimate sexual relationship with Charles Eubanks, a relationship that was not remembered in the Dickson Family Oral History as "forced." By choosing to "marry" her first cousin, Amanda America abandoned the slave-sanctioned preference for endogomous marriages and adopted the white convention of consanguine marriages. She also chose to defy the law against miscegenation. Was this an act of defiance against both the black and white communities or simply a manifestation of Amanda America's belief that rules of any sort did not apply to her? By May of 1865 Amanda America Dickson Eubanks was pregnant with her first child, Julian Henry, born in 1866.[32]

Because of existing antimiscegenation laws, Charles Eubanks and Amanda America Dickson could not legally marry in the state of Georgia. One of the first laws passed by the Georgia legislature after the Civil War reinstated a prohibition against "interracial" marriage. The Dickson Family Oral History records that David Dickson took the couple to Baltimore to be married.[33] According to that same source, David Dickson gave the couple a plantation on the banks of the Oostanaula River in Floyd County, Georgia. In fact, in 1866 Charles H. Eubanks purchased 17.7 acres of land on the Oostanaula for six hundred dollars. In 1870 the couple had a second son, Charles Green. African American "Aunt Mary Long," Amanda America Dickson Eubanks's personal servant, remembered seeing Amanda and Charles Eubanks with their small sons and their nurses crossing the river on a ferry as they left to go live on their own "plantation."[34]

As Amanda America attempted to establish an existence independent of her father, David Dickson began the process of financial recovery. Initially, Dickson lamented that he was planting "cautiously, not caring to save money until we had a government that would protect us in person and property." On September 4, 1865, David Dickson begged the pardon of the United States with these words: "I am now satisfied [that] the rebellion is at an end and that slavery is forever gone. I propose to come back to the old government, if permitted."[35] This action was necessary for Dickson to regain control of his property, excluding his slaves, and to be able to vote or run for public office.

According to the Dickson Family Oral History, shortly after the birth of her second child, Amanda America and the two children returned to the Dickson plantation. Amanda explained the situation to her father with the comment, "I want to live with you, Pappy." Charles Eubanks, who attempted to retrieve his wife and children, was met with a "stormy" reply and "never came back." Were Amanda's emotions an expression of the love of a daughter for a father, or a form of dependence? As a result of her privileged childhood, was Amanda America unable to fulfill the role of wife and mother, just as her father had been unable to fulfill the role of husband? The census of 1870 lists Eubanks as living with his mother, Elizabeth Eubanks.[36]

Nevertheless, according to Julia Frances Dickson, after the separation the "boys" remained close to their white grandmother and went to visit the Eubanks's home in Hancock County. No mention is made of divorce.[37] David Dickson arranged for Amanda and her sons to take the Dickson surname. David Dickson then took them to New Orleans and "had them declared white." The remembering of these events illustrates the conviction by the African American branch of the Dickson family that David Dickson could transform his mulatto daughter and his mulatto grandchildren into a white daughter and white grandchildren, and then return to a community that knew of their racially mixed heritage. The only way this family could have escaped the public stigma of race would have been to abandon their home place.

According to the Dickson Family Oral History, David Dickson loved the little boys, called them "my little men," and slept with them. Dickson "never wanted them to do anything but ride over the plantation with him and see what was going on. He indulged them all." When visitors came to the plantation they sometimes asked whether they had to eat with Amanda and the children, to which David would reply, "By God, yes, if you eat here you will."[38]

During the trial over David Dickson's will, the excluded white relatives argued that David Dickson's behavior toward Amanda and her children illustrated that he had been "unduly influenced"; he treated them as if they were members of a *real* family. At home Amanda called him "Pappy" and her children called him "Grand-papa."[39] The boys ate at the table with David Dickson and hopped up next to him on the sofa when white people were present.[40] W. S. Lozier, one of David Dickson's employees, commented that David acted toward the boys "pretty much like I would towards my children," while J. M. Eubanks, David's nephew, observed that David "talked to them kindly as he would his own children." Rebecca Latimer Felton, Georgia's own racist suffragist, described the situation in the Dickson household as follows:

> I remember well a noted home in Middle Georgia where a rich man lived in open alliance with a colored woman and where Governors and Congressmen were often invited to dine and where they were glad to go. These visitors understood conditions in the Dickson home. They knew there were children there born of a slave mother and the law of Georgia forbade such miscegenation.[41]

Sometime in 1870 or 1871 David Dickson began construction of a "new house" for Julia, Amanda America, and the children. David built the house approximately three hundred yards from the Dickson home place, on a crest of the sloping land-scape that made up the Dickson plantation. When the house was completed, it was "a very respectable," "comfortable," two-story home, with "a nice room for a parlor." The parlor contained a piano and "had everything that usually constitutes the furniture in that kind of room. . . . Everything was nice and kept in nice order." When W. S. Lozier was asked which was the best of the two houses, the Dickson home place or the new house, he replied that the new house was "a good deal the best house. I would rather have had it at the time."[42]

On October 2, 1871, David Dickson drew up a deed selling "the new house" and 210 acres of land, "more or less, with a right of way consisting of twenty feet the whole distance between the house lot and [the] John R. Latimore place." Amanda America Dickson purchased a seven-eighths interest in the property for $1,000, and Julia Frances Dickson purchased a one-eighth interest for $125.[43] One wonders where Amanda America and Julia got the funds to make such an agree-ment. This transaction appears to be another form of protection. If Amanda Amer-ica and Julia paid a significant amount for their house, then they would legally own it. Was this an act of love on David's part, an act of defiance, or an act motivated by guilt?

After completing the new house and moving his "outside" family into that com-fortable dwelling, David Dickson did something that must have been universally shocking. He married the white Clara Harris on October 3, 1871. At that time Clara Harris was twenty-five, three years older than Amanda America and thirty-seven years younger than David. Clara Harris had been born in Hancock County in 1846, the second daughter in a prominent family whose history in the county stretched back to 1800. Clara's father had been a member of the secession conven-tion, had been captain of the Hancock Mounted Rifles, and had served on the staff of Governor Brown through the Civil War. Both of Clara's parents were younger than David Dickson and probably had known his family all their lives.[44]

We do not know how David Dickson met Clara or what their courtship was like. Why would David become romantically involved at the age of sixty-two? Why would Clara Harris consent to marry a man who was older than both her parents and who lived out in the country in a simple house, surrounded by his tenants? David Dickson was wealthy, and he was famous. He had a reputation for being both generous and hospitable, at least to his good friends and the agricultural community at large. And what of David Dickson's "outside" family?

What did Julia Frances Dickson think about the match? Much later, during the trial over David Dickson's will, when she was asked when she had ceased to have a sexual relationship with David, Julia Dickson replied "we separated before he ever married or thought about it, I reckon." This marriage was not included in the African American Dickson Family Oral History. Julia Dickson erased it as she retold the family story. She exerted her power to decide what would be remembered.[45]

Amanda America Dickson and her sons might also have felt threatened by the arrival of Clara Harris Dickson. The two women were about the same age. They lived three hundred yards apart in the Dickson compound. Perhaps Amanda America Dickson felt secure enough in her relationship with her father to be civil to Clara at a distance, or simply to ignore her. As for Clara, she entered into an established set of relationships and consequently was at the greatest disadvantage.

After their wedding, David and Clara Dickson traveled north on a wedding trip for a few weeks and then returned to Sparta. Clara Dickson stayed there a few days with her family and then proceeded to the Dickson home place to settle down as the wife of a country squire, a role that proved to be exceedingly complicated. In order to take her rightful place on the Dickson plantation, Clara Dickson would have to displace Julia Dickson. The ornamental aspect of being a lady probably appealed more to Clara than the prospect of taking charge of a complex agricultural household guarded by a formidable older black woman. W. S. Lozier, the carpenter who thought the new house was superior to the home place, described Clara Harris's presence on the Dickson plantation as follows: "while she was about there, I never saw her take hold of any business, but she seemed to be like someone on a visit."[46]

With regard to the presence of David Dickson's "outside family," it appears that Clara Harris Dickson took offense and tried to have the offenders removed from the plantation. S. D. Rogers remembered a conversation that he had had with his uncle, David Dickson. Dickson, he recounted, "mentioned to me in the presence of my wife that his wife [Clara] had requested him to send Julia and Amanda away from there, and he told her he wasn't going to do any such thing. He said that Julia and Amanda were there when she came there and that they would have to stay."[47]

After the first year of David and Clara's marriage, Clara went into Sparta to visit her mother more and more often and stayed away for longer periods of time, a reaction that Deborah Gray White has noted was not unusual for plantation mistresses who were caught between the necessity of ignoring "outside" families and the difficulty of obtaining a divorce. In July 1873 Clara became seriously ill and died a month later. David Dickson was not present when she died. B. H. Sasnett, Clara Harris Dickson's cousin, described the scene: "I saw [David Dickson] come in when his wife was in her coffin. He was not a demonstrative man; he was a purely unemotional man; and I saw no evidence of any emotion. He seemed embarrassed in company generally—a very awkward man; he showed that awkwardness on that occasion, but I didn't see any emotion."[48] Clara Harris was not buried with her mother and father in the Sparta cemetery. Legend has it that David Dickson had a rock hollowed out and buried her inside it, but no one remembers where.[49]

Ironically, on July 31, 1871, one day before Clara died, Amanda America's husband, Charles Eubanks, had died. In his will Eubanks directed his executors, David Dickson and T. J. Warthen (Dickson's nephew), to keep his estate intact until "my children, Julian Henry Dickson and Charles Green Dickson arrive at years of maturity." Eubanks did not use the legal term "natural children," a term that would indicate the children had been born out of wedlock. Eubanks charged his executors to maintain and educate his sons and support his mother, Elizabeth Eubanks. Even with the latter provision, Elizabeth and her other son, James M. Eubanks, objected to the will on the grounds that it was improperly executed, that it was obtained by fraud, and that the two children were "born of a Negro." The Eubankses withdrew their objections after David Dickson removed himself as executor.[50]

Shortly after the deaths of Clara Harris Dickson and Charles Eubanks, T. J. Warthen moved into the Dickson household "to look over the plantation and the lots." At the time, Warthen was thirty-five, and he too had been a frequent visitor on the Dickson plantation in his youth. From 1867 to 1873 Warthen came to visit his uncle every week "as business required." In 1873 Amanda Dickson was twenty-four, a widow with two small children. Sometime during this period, Amanda America Dickson and T. J. Warthen entered into a sexual relationship that Warthen later described in court as occurring "a few times."[51] Scholars have described serial sexual relationships between mulatto women and prominent white men—men who were related by blood. When Julia Frances Lewis Dickson described her own serial sexual relationships with David Dickson (white), "Doc" Eubanks (white), and Joe Brookens (black), she declared that "I was not a bad woman."[52]

After Clara Harris Dickson's death, David Dickson continued to care for Amanda America and her children. In late 1873 he deeded 1,560 acres of land to Amanda America.[53] Here David Dickson referred to Amanda America's children using the legal term "natural children," meaning children born out of wedlock. During this same era, Julia Frances Lewis Dickson "spent most of her time at the meeting house."[54] Indeed, Julia was active in the life of her church and the school that it supported. In 1874, as a concession to Julia, David Dickson signed an indenture between himself and John C. Lewis, Julia Frances Dickson's brother, Gilbert Castleberry, Boston Dickson, Washington Warthen, and Julia Dickson, all trustees for the Cherry Hill Church and School of the Methodist Episcopal Church South. For five dollars he agreed to sell three acres of land to the Cherry Hill Church. The trustees were to hold the land as a place of worship and for a schoolhouse and keep the roads in good repair; otherwise the land would revert back to David Dickson. Through this agreement Julia Frances secured the future of her church and school against the possibility that David might marry again, and David made sure that the use of the land was limited.[55]

Not long after David Dickson deeded the land surrounding the Cherry Hill School to its African American trustees, an event occurred that illustrates how carefully Dickson maintained the precarious balance between his "outside" family and his white kin. In August 1874 David Dickson's nieces Mary and Sallie had "some trouble" with their brother and turned to their uncle for help. Dickson sent them on to the home of B. F. Riley, his neighbor. As Riley explained,

> Well, I went down there [to David Dickson's plantation] and he asked me if Mary and Sallie had been to see me. I told him that they had; he asked me if they told me who sent them. He then told me, says he, "Now, I reckon you think it strange of me for sending those girls to your house when I am their uncle."

According to Riley, Dickson then explained his actions by saying, "Amanda is my child and I want Amanda and her children around me; it might be unpleasant to Mary and Sallie to be there and will be unpleasant to their company." Riley continued, "Therefore he had sent them to my house. He told me that he would see that I got money to pay for their board and to charge them enough to cover all their expenses down at my house. He told me that I shouldn't lose anything by it."[56] Although David Dickson was sensitive to the needs of his nieces, he did not want to change his living arrangement for their benefit, and he knew how to make other acceptable arrangements.

During the 1870s and early 1880s Julia Frances Dickson continued to be David Dickson's housekeeper and to trade in Sparta. According to an 1885 article in the *Sparta Ishmaelite*, Julia Dickson was perceived by the people of that town as a "very quiet, inoffensive woman" whose role in the Dickson home was to wait on guests. In this role, according to the reporter, she "never put herself forward." When Julia Dickson visited Sparta to trade, she brought "things" to David Dickson's friends, and when they would invite her to dinner, "she would always prefer having her dinner sent to the kitchen, where she would eat with the other servants."[57] Ironically, this report indicates that white citizens of Sparta who were friends of David Dickson invited Julia to eat with them in the dining room, another inversion of southern manners.

On February 18, 1885, David Dickson died at the age of seventy-six. According to the African American Dickson Family Oral History, Amanda America's reaction was to cling to David Dickson's body and repeat, "Now I am an orphan; now I am an orphan." Amanda America was an orphan only if she defined herself as a member of a family composed of herself and her white father. Her mother was alive. Nevertheless, Amanda America Dickson defined herself as an orphan, with neither black relatives nor white relatives. Amanda America Dickson chose to define herself as a kinless "no nation."[58]

In March 1887 David Dickson's will entered the public domain when the executors, T. J. Warthen and Dickson's "personal friend" and lawyer, Charles W. Dubose, submitted the document to the Court of Ordinary of Hancock County. Like a clap of thunder this event shattered the agreed-upon silence that had separated David Dickson's private life from his public life. David Dickson made his mulatto daughter and her children the largest property owners in Hancock County, Georgia.[59]

Scholars have argued that while the power of the master constituted the linchpin of slavery as a social system, no one satisfactorily defined the limits of that power.[60] Theoretically, this tension was resolved with the determination that "the collective conscience of the ruling class must prevail over the individual interests constituting that class."[61] This does not appear to have been the case with David Dickson in that this master and father both raised his mulatto daughter inside the boundaries of his family and legally appointed her his successor, making her, in some sense, an oxymoronic member of the ruling class, a wealthy black "lady." Dickson left the administration of his estate to the "sound judgment and unlimited discretion" of Amanda America Dickson "without interference from any quarter," including "any husband which she may have."[62]

In bequeathing his estate to Amanda America and bringing his relationship with her into the public domain of the law, David Dickson made it impossible for his community to continue to practice what John Blassingame has called "selective inattention," or an agreed-upon fiction not to notice this relationship as a political act with, one would assume, dangerous implications.[63] Everyone knew that everyone else knew. David Dickson had made several assumptions: that he could trust his good friend and lawyer, Charles Dubose, to shepherd the will through the courts; that his will would eventually be upheld; and that no one would be so outraged as to resort to violence. In essence, David Dickson assumed that his power to exercise his right to appoint his successor would transcend his own mortality.

In his will, David Dickson charged Amanda America to support and educate her children, "their support to be ample but not extravagant, their education to be the best that can be procured for them with a proper regard to economy," all of which was left to "the sound judgment and discretion of the said Amanda Dickson." When Amanda America died, the remains of the estate were to be inherited by her children.[64]

After the Superior Court of Hancock County ruled in favor of David Dickson's will in November 1885, and before the Georgia Supreme Court upheld that ruling in June 1887, Amanda America Dickson began preparing to leave Hancock County for good. In 1886 she purchased a large brick house at 452 Telfair Street in Augusta, Georgia, for $6,098. An *Atlanta Constitution* reporter described the house as "quite a large, double brick house, three stories high, containing some twelve to fifteen rooms, shaded in front by three mammoth oaks, surrounded by a large yard; all in all, a most desirable residence."[65] Because of the attention the Dickson will had received in the newspapers of the state, we can safely assume that Amanda Dickson's fame preceded her to the city of Augusta. The *Sparta Ishmaelite* of March 18, 1885, reported that

> Amanda A. Dickson, the $400,000 heiress from Hancock, went to Augusta last Friday. Everyone on the trains was anxious to see the richest colored woman in the United States. She created about as much of a sensation as did Henry Ward Beecher when he traveled through the South. She was dressed in deep mourning and had her mother and her youngest boy with her.

The general populace there would know that she was wealthy, illegitimate, and a woman of color.[66]

On July 14, 1892, Amanda America married Nathan Toomer of Perry, Georgia. Toomer was also a "wealthy and highly educated" mulatto. The *Houston Home Journal*, Toomer's hometown newspaper, stated at the time that Toomer, "the esteemed colored farmer," had married the "richest Negress in Georgia" and that he "has [had] many white friends in Houston County who will cordially congratulate him."[67] The marriage lasted less than a year. Amanda America Dickson died on June 11, 1893. Her death certificate listed the cause as "complications of diseases." Haggie Brothers Funeral Home was called to Telfair Street to prepare Amanda America Dickson for burial. They embalmed her body and dressed it in the wedding gown that Amanda had worn when she married Nathan. The body was placed in an expensive copper-lined casket with rose-colored, plush cushioning. It was described by the *Milledgeville Union Recorder* as the "handsomest casket ever brought into that city [Augusta]." One hearse and six carriages were ordered for the funeral.[68]

Amanda America Dickson's funeral took place in the Trinity Colored Methodist Episcopal Church. According to a tribute written for the *Augusta Chronicle* by "A Friend," the funeral was attended by "a very large and respectful gathering of friends and acquaintances." Three ministers of the gospel "officiated" and paid tribute to Amanda America's "Christian life and character, her exemplary worth, her unostentatious charities, and the beauty of her home life." Scripture passages that she had marked in her own Bible were read, and the service ended with a song that Amanda had requested to be sung on that occasion, "Shall We Meet beyond the River," which "moved to tears almost the entire audience." The body was buried in the Toomer plot of the Colored Cedar Grove Cemetery in Augusta, behind the Magnolia Cemetery for whites. The tombstone, erected later by Nathan Toomer, is the largest in the Cedar Grove Cemetery and bears the inscription

> Sacred to the Memory of
> Amanda Dickson Toomer
> Wife of Nathan Toomer
> Born November 20, 1849
> Died June 11, 1893
> A True Christian a Loving
> Wife a Devoted Mother
> and Daughter
> May her Soul Be at Rest.[69]

Amanda America Dickson's obituaries in white newspapers described her as the "wealthiest colored woman in the world," "the wealthiest Negro in the United States," and "one of the wealthiest, if not the wealthiest negro woman in the state."[70] Without exception, these obituaries add that Amanda America inherited her wealth from her father, David Dickson, one of the wealthiest planters in Hancock County. The black *Savannah Tribune*'s obituary described Amanda America Toomer "née Dickson," but with no mention of David, as "one of the richest persons in the state."[71] Nathan Toomer was mentioned in the newspaper obituaries as a "lawyer from Perry," wealthy and highly educated, or as one who was "immensely rich."[72]

The *Sparta Ishmaelite* did not mention Amanda America Dickson Toomer's death until 1895. In an article entitled "Her Last Resting Place," the editor noted that a tombstone was being prepared in Augusta: "There are very few of our readers who are not perfectly familiar with the name, Amanda Eubanks, the colored woman who was so liberally remembered in the distribution of the immense fortune of the late David Dickson, of Hancock County."[73] The *Ishmaelite* continued, "She was the richest colored woman in the south, her portion of the estate being about $400,000." With a consoling tone, the editor continued: "In the marble yard of Theo. Markwalter, Augusta, Georgia, stands a beautiful monument cut from Georgia granite which will soon be placed in position to mark her last resting place. It is a fine piece of art, and speaks well for the affectionate remembrance of her people."[74]

Amanda America's tributes and obituaries reveal something about the way she was perceived by the black and white communities in which she lived. She was described in the *Atlanta Constitution* as "modest, generous, and benevolent, a woman who enjoyed her fortune"; "others shared her pleasure." The article continues, "She was kindhearted and in no way pompous or assuming on account of her wealth."[75] In a tribute by "A Friend," we learn that "to her mother she was all that a dutiful, loving child should be. As she lived, so she died, a gentle, sweet spirit."[76] The last thing in the world Amanda America Dickson needed to be in an increasingly racist public space was a "gentle, sweet spirit," but then, she had been socialized to be a lady.

The lives of the actors in this narrative are so intertwined that it is difficult to determine where one life begins and another ends. The complex motivations of the white Dicksons required a set of contradictory behaviors. As a grandmother, Elizabeth took Amanda, who was defined by a dominant ideology as the "other," into her room, her family, and her circle of love. David defied the very social structure that gave him power by endowing Amanda America with wealth and privilege, instead of denying her place as a daughter. In his relationship with Julia, David circumvented the possibility of love between equals by resorting to violence. Unfortunately for David, Julia did not exhibit the stereotypical behavior of the rape victim. She never allowed herself to be erased. She did not die nor did she go away, she was not sold off nor did she run away. She chose to stay, even after emancipation, keeping the memory of the rape alive through her presence, and living to tell the story.

NOTES

1. Jean Toomer, *Cane* (New York: Liveright, 1975), 106. Jean Toomer went to Sparta, Georgia, in the summer of 1921 to teach school and to search for his father's, Nathan Toomer's, family. Ironically, what Jean Toomer found was the source of his father's wealth, Amanda America Dickson's estate. The elusive father was from Perry, Georgia.

2. Judge C. J. Lumpkin in *Bryan v. Walton*, 33 Georgia 11 (1864); William Harper, "Harper's Memoir on Slavery," in Chancellor Harper, Governor Hammond, Dr. Sims, and Professor Dew, *The Proslavery Argument as Maintained by the Most Distinguished*

Writers of the Southern States . . . (Philadelphia: Lippincott, Gambo, 1853), 40; Louis Wirth and Herbert Goldhamer, "The Hybrid and the Problem of Miscegenation," in *Characteristics of the American Negro*, ed. Otto Klineberg (New York: Harper and Brothers, 1944), 249–365; Robert Brent Toplin, "Between Black and White: Attitudes toward Southern Mulattoes, 1830–1861," *Journal of Southern History* 45 (1979): 179–80; E. Franklin Frazier, *The Negro Family in the United States* (Chicago: University of Chicago Press, 1966), 69.

3. For a more complete discussion of the life of Amanda America Dickson, see Kent Anderson Leslie, *Woman of Color, Daughter of Privilege: Amanda America Dickson* (Athens: University of Georgia Press, 1995).

4. Elizabeth Fox-Genovese, *Within the Plantation Household: Black and White Women of the Old South* (Chapel Hill: University of North Carolina Press, 1988), 326.

5. John Rozier, *Black Boss: Political Revolution in a Georgia County* (Athens: University of Georgia Press, 1982), 197.

6. James C. Bonner, "Profile of a Late Antebellum Community," *American Historical Review* 49 (1944): 663–80.

7. Testimony of Augustus E. Eubanks, *Dickson Will Case Transcript* (hereafter *Transcript*), *Smith v. Dubose*, Hancock County Superior Court, Georgia Department of Archives and History, Atlanta, 147.

8. *Transcript*, Henry Harris, 90; Augustus E. Eubanks, 147.

9. *Mary Chesnut's Civil War*, ed. C. Vann Woodward (New Haven: Yale University Press, 1981), 202; Fox-Genovese, *Within the Plantation Household*, 163; Ella Gertrude Clanton Thomas, *The Secret Eye: The Journal of Ella Gertrude Clanton Thomas, 1848–1889*, ed. Virginia Ingraham Burr (Chapel Hill: University of North Carolina Press, 1990), 268.

10. Oliver O. Prince, ed., *A Digest of Laws of the State of Georgia* (Athens: University of Georgia Press, 1837), 787; Lucius Q. C. Lamar, ed., *A Compilation of the Laws of the State of Georgia, 1810–1819* (Augusta, 1821), 811–12.

11. *Transcript*, Julia Frances Dickson, 161; Dr. E. W. Alfriend, 129.

12. *Transcript*, Augustus E. Eubanks, 148.

13. See W. E. B. Du Bois, "Princess of the Hinterland," in *Darkwater: Voices from within the Veil* (New York: Schocken, 1969); African American Dickson Family Oral History, in Leslie, *Woman of Color, Daughter of Privilege*, appendix A, 135–39, original in the possession of the author.

14. Jane Turner Censer, *North Carolina Planters and Their Children, 1800–1860* (Baton Rouge:Louisiana State University Press, 1984), 135; Du Bois, "Princess of the Hinterland"; African American Dickson Family Oral History.

15. African American Dickson Family Oral History.

16. *Transcript*, James M. Eubanks, 57–58.

17. African American Dickson Family Oral History.

18. *Transcript*, Augustus E. Eubanks, 147; Julia Frances Dickson, 160.

19. *Transcript*, W. H. Matthews, 37–38.

20. *Transcript*, James M. Eubanks, 57.

21. Ibid., 59.

22. *Transcript*, Joe Brookens, 47.

23. *Transcript*, James M. Dickson, 50.

24. *Transcript*, S. D. Rogers, 62–63.

25. *Transcript*, W. S. Dickson, 53.

26. *Transcript*, Matthews, 37; Washington Printup, 40; Brookens, 44; Matthew Dickson, 72.

27. *Transcript*, Matthews, 37.

28. *Transcript*, Alfriend, 130.

29. *Transcript*, Julia Frances Dickson, 165.

30. Lucy Dickson is listed in the U.S. census of 1880 as a mulatto female, twenty-seven years old, living in the house with David Dickson and T. J. Warthen (David's nephew) as a servant. Lucy Dickson is mentioned in the *Transcript* as "the most important servant" (Harris, 91). She died on June 19, 1884. John C. Lewis, Julia's brother, was the administrator of the estate; *Transcript*, W. S. Lozier, 20, 29; Printup, 41; J. T. Barry, 85; Harris, 91; Alfriend, 130.

31. Anne Goodwyn Jones, *Tomorrow Is Another Day: The Woman Writer in the South, 1859–1939* (Baton Rouge: Louisiana State University Press, 1981), 12; Deborah Gray White, *Ar'n't I a Woman? Female Slaves in the Plantation South* (New York: W. W. Norton, 1985), 29, 49.

32. Herbert G. Gutman, *The Black Family in Slavery and Freedom, 1750–1925* (New York: Vintage, 1976), 88; Censer, *North Carolina Planters*, 7; Lillian Henderson, comp., *Roster of the Confederate Soldiers of Georgia, 1861–1865* (Hapeville, Ga.: Longino and Porter, 1959), 2: 476.

33. There are no records of the marriage in the Maryland State Archives under the names Eubanks and Dickson. A newspaper account, published after David Dickson's death, states that the marriage took place in Boston; however, there are no existing records there either for Eubanks or Dickson; African American Dickson Family Oral History; Marriage Records, Maryland State Archives, Annapolis; Marriage Records, Massachusetts State Archives, Boston.

34. African American Dickson Family Oral History; Floyd County Courthouse, Rome, Ga., Deeds, between S. C. Johnson and Charles H. Eubanks.

35. David Dickson, *A Practical Treaties on Agriculture to Which Is Added the Author's Published Letters* (Macon, Ga: Burke, 1870), 242; Pardon, a "Special Pardon" by Andrew Johnson, petitioned for on August 9, 1865, Record Group 59: General Records of the Department of State, Amnesty Oaths, Individual, Georgia Civil War Papers, National Archives and Records Service, Washington, D.C.

36. U.S. Census for Hancock County, Ga., 1870, African American Dickson Family Oral History.

37. African American Dickson Family Oral History.

38. Ibid.

39. *Transcript*, Brookens, 44; Lozier, 19.

40. *Transcript*, Lozier, 19–20.

41. *Transcript*, Lozier, 19–20; James M. Eubanks, 57. Rebecca Latimer Felton quoted in Sylvia Hoffert, "This One Great Evil: The Sexual Practice That Northern Abolitionists Exploited, Southern White Men Concealed, and Proper Ladies Never Discussed," *American History Illustrated* 12 (1977): 38.

42. *Transcript*, Lozier, 19; Brookens, 44; Lozier, 20; Lozier, 19; James M. Eubanks, 57; Lozier, 18–19.

43. This deed was not recorded until June 11, 1885, Deed Book W, 298–99, Clerk of the Superior Court, Hancock County Courthouse, Sparta, Ga.

44. Marriage Certificate, Hancock County Courthouse, Marriage Records, no. 106, 1871; Elizabeth Wiley Smith, *History of Hancock County, Georgia* (Washington, Ga.: Wilkes, 1974), 2: 69, 70, 83, 85, 128; Historical Activities Committee, National Society of Colonial Dames of America in the State of Georgia, comp., *Early Georgia Portraits, 1718–1870* (Athens: University of Georgia Press, 1975), 92–93.

45. *Transcript*, Julia Frances Dickson, 162.

46. *Transcript*, B. H. Sasnett, 67; Printup, 41; Lozier, 37; James M. Dickson, 48; Lozier, 16; James M. Eubanks, 55; Lozier, 20.

47. *Transcript*, Rogers, 66.

48. White, *Ar'n't I a Woman?* 41; *Union and Recorder*, Aug. 6, 1873, 2; *Transcript*, Sasnett, 68–69.

49. Interview with the owner of the Exxon filling station on the road to Hamburg that runs by David Dickson's plantation.

50. Estate records and will of Charles H. Eubanks, Judge of Probate Office, Hancock County Courthouse, Sparta, Ga.

51. *Transcript*, T. J. Warthen, 154–58.

52. *Transcript*, Julia Frances Dickson, cross-examination, 160–66; R. Ridley Torrence, *The Story of John Hope* (New York: Macmillan, 1948); Adele Logan Alexander, *Ambiguous Lives: Free Women of Color in Middle Georgia* (Fayetteville: University of Arkansas Press, 1991). John Hope's grandmother Althea was from Hancock County.

53. Hancock County Courthouse, Deed Book U, 137–38.

54. *Transcript*, Lozier, 17.

55. Hancock County Courthouse, Deed Book U, 595–96.

56. *Transcript*, B. F. Riley, 101.

57. *Sparta Ishmaelite*, Aug. 1, 1885, 1.

58. African American Dickson Family Oral History; James Kinney, *Amalgamation: Race, Sex, and Rhetoric in the Nineteenth-Century American Novel* (London: Greenwood, 1970), 100.

59. David Dickson's Will, March 2, 1885, Probate Court Records, Drawer D, Hancock County Courthouse, Sparta, Ga.; Tax Digest for Hancock County, Ga., 1885, Georgia Department of Archives and History, Atlanta.

60. Fox-Genovese, *Within the Plantation Household*, 326.

61. Eugene D. Genovese, *The World the Slaveholders Made* (New York: Vintage, 1971), 213.

62. David Dickson's Will.

63. John W. Blassingame, *Black New Orleans, 1860–1880* (Chicago: University of Chicago Press, 1973), 209.

64. David Dickson's Will.

65. *Atlanta Constitution*, July 19, 1887, 6.

66. *Sparta Ishmaelite*, March 18, 1885, 3. Deposition of Dr. W. H. Foster, a prominent doctor in Augusta who lived near Amanda America Dickson at 320 Greene Street, BC Court of Common Pleas (Court Papers) *Nathan Toomer v. the Pullman Palace Car Co.*, 1893, Box 153, 3-2-10-40; Maryland State Archives, Annapolis.

67. *Houston Home Journal*, July 21, 1892, 2.

68. Amanda America Dickson Toomer's death certificate stated that she was forty-three years old, "colored," born in Georgia, that she was a housewife, and that she was married; *Toomer v. the Pullman Palace Car Co.*, evidence used in the lawsuit; *Union Recorder*, June 20, 1893; bill from the Haggie Brothers Funeral Home. Cost of the casket was five hundred dollars.

69. *Atlanta Constitution*, June 12, 1893, 2. Tribute paid by "A Friend," *Augusta Chronicle*, June 13, 1893, 2. I am grateful to Gordon B. Smith for this reference. The entrance to the Cedar Grove Cemetery is located on Watkins Street in Augusta. According to the *Savannah Morning News*, "Amanda Toomer (or Dickson), the wealthy colored woman who was buried in the colored cemetery of Augusta last week was buried with some valuable jewelry

on her person. A policeman is guarding the grave to prevent robbery." *Savannah Morning News*, June 19, 1893, 6.

70. *Houston Home Journal*, June 15, 1893, 2; *Atlanta Constitution*, June 2, 1893; *Savannah Morning News*, June 13, 1893.

71. *Savannah Tribune*, June 17, 1893, 2.

72. *Atlanta Constitution*, June 12, 1893; *Savannah Morning News*, June 13, 1893; *Savannah Tribune*, June 17, 1893.

73. In all the newspaper articles there is great confusion about the size of David Dickson's bequest. Estimates range from $250,000 to $1 million. Because Charles DuBose had recorded the inventory of the estate in the Sparta Courthouse as a public record, the estimate in the *Sparta Ishmaelite* of $400,000 is probably the most accurate.

74. *Sparta Ishmaelite*, Jan. 18, 1895.

75. *Atlanta Constitution*, June 12, 1893, 2; *Augusta Chronicle*, June 13, 1893, 2.

76. "In Memorium," *Augusta Chronicle*, June 13, 1893.

Part III

Civil War and Reconstruction

Chapter Eleven

Misshapen Identity
Memory, Folklore, and the Legend of Rachel Knight

Victoria E. Bynum

In December 1948 the Jones County Circuit Court of Ellisville, Mississippi, debated the identity of Rachel Knight, a woman who had been dead for fifty-nine years. At stake was the fate of her twenty-four-year-old great-grandson, Davis Knight, who was on trial for the crime of miscegenation. Davis, in physical appearance a white man, had married Junie Lee Spradley, a white woman, on April 18, 1946. Whether Davis was white or black, and therefore innocent or guilty of marrying across the color line, hinged on the racial identity of a distant ancestor whom he had never met, but who still excited the memories of the older citizens of Jones, Jasper, and Covington Counties in southeastern Mississippi.[1]

For four days in the Ellisville courthouse, Davis Knight's neighbors and relatives argued whether Rachel Knight was a Creole, an Indian, or "just an old Negro." Of special interest to the court was Rachel's relationship to Newton Knight, the legendary leader of Mississippi's most notorious band of deserters during the Civil War. In 1948, however, the state of Mississippi expressed no interest in Newton Knight's Civil War exploits, only in the intermarriages of his daughter Molly and son Mat with Rachel's son Jeff and daughter Fannie. These marriages, contracted around 1878, began the mixed-race community of "white Negroes" into which Davis Knight was born; thus, both Newton Knight and Rachel Knight were his ancestors.[2]

Several witnesses testified at Davis Knight's trial that Newton Knight, his wife, Serena, and their children Molly and Mat were of the "pure white race." Indeed, the state's major witness at the trial was Newton's and Serena's "pure white" son Tom, who had published a sympathetic account of his father's Civil War activities two years earlier. The witnesses hotly debated, however, Rachel's racial identity and her relationship to the white Knight family.[3]

Long before and after their deaths, Rachel and Newton Knight captured the attention of southern Mississippians. Gossipmongers speculated that Rachel, the former slave of Newton's grandfather, had been more than simply Newton's accomplice in his actions against the Confederacy, that the two had been lovers and had produced mixed-race children.[4] After all, Rachel shared Newton's surname, property, and, in death, his private cemetery.

In the increasingly segregated postbellum South, such intimacy aroused suspi-

Fig. 11.1 *Left:* Reputed to be Rachel Knight (1840–1889). Undated. Reprinted from a tintype found in the Bible of Anna Knight, Rachel's granddaughter, after her death in 1972. Courtesy of Dorothy Marsh, Anna Knight Papers, Washington, D.C.

Fig. 11.2 *Right:* Newton Knight (1837–1922). Undated. Courtesy of Earle Knight, Laurel, Mississippi.

cions of forbidden sexual behavior. Indeed, Jacquelyn Dowd Hall argues that by the 1920s the public's obsession with interracial sexual relations amounted to a well-entrenched "folk pornography" that underwrote violent systems of racial and sexual domination. Between 1890 and 1920 white southern literature—especially newspapers—commonly portrayed interracial sexual relations as the result of sex-crazed black "fiends" ravishing innocent, virginal blondes, rather than white men raping black women, or blacks and whites participating in consensual sexual relations.[5] For defeated white Confederates who began their return to power during Reconstruction, the alleged lust of black men for white women provided a further pretext to impose racial segregation and restrict the political and social rights of African Americans.[6] Most whites were too horrified by tales of racial violence and lust to question their veracity, and most blacks did not dare to challenge the source of such stories. Those southerners who dared campaign for laws against lynching, however, understood that the "protection" white lynch mobs provided white women against supposed ravishment by black men served a larger purpose. Such was the case of the black feminist Ida Wells-Barnett and her white counterpart Jessie Daniel Ames. They recognized that lynch mob protection controlled African Americans through terror and white women through enforced helplessness.[7]

Newton Knight died in 1922, in the midst of rigid racial segregation. Despite Mississippi's five decades of pro-Confederate, white supremacy campaigns, he died an unrepentant foe of "Johnny Reb," surrounded, as he had been since 1880, by his mixed-race kin. In his obituary the *Ellisville Progressive* lamented that he had "ruined his life and future by marrying a negro woman," although no proof of such a marriage existed.[8]

By the time Newton died, Rachel had been dead for thirty-three years. Then in 1948, twenty-six years after Newton's death, the marriage of Davis Knight and Junie Lee Spradley revived the old rumors and scandals that had long plagued the numerous branches of the Knight family. The jury of the Jones County Circuit Court decided that Davis Knight's descent from Rachel Knight did indeed make him a Negro, and it accordingly convicted him of miscegenation. The judge sentenced him to five years imprisonment in the state penitentiary.[9] In November 1949, however, the Mississippi Supreme Court reversed the lower court's decision, ruling that it had failed "to prove beyond all reasonable doubt that the defendant had one-eighth or more negro blood." Since Mississippi law held that one-eighth or more African ancestry made one a Negro, Rachel would had to have been of full African ancestry—something no witness could prove and several effectively disputed—in order for Davis to be an African American. The high court thus proclaimed Davis Knight legally white.[10]

The customary method of defining one's race differed, however, from the legal one. To most white Mississippians, many of whom believed a blood test could determine the proportions of one's African or European ancestry, a single drop of "tainted" African "blood" sufficed to make one black. Many whites considered even living among African Americans grounds for being socially defined as one.[11] Thus, although Davis Knight's legal ordeal was over, the local debate over the "purity" of the Knight family's blood raged on.

Two years after the state supreme court's decision, a grandniece of Newton Knight, Ethel Knight, published *The Echo of the Black Horn*, a sensationalized "history" of Newton Knight that thinly disguised her effort to discredit Newton Knight's anti-Confederate uprising and rid the white branches of the Knight family of the taint of miscegenation. Touting her book as "an authentic tale" of "the free state of Jones," she dedicated it to "the memory of the Noble Confederates who lived and died for Jones County."[12] Her version of Jones County's Civil War uprising displaced Tom Knight's earlier *Life and Activities of Captain Newton Knight and His Company and the "Free State of Jones County"* (1946) as the "true" story of Newton Knight.

Ethel Knight cleverly gained Tom Knight's endorsement of her version of his father's life by showcasing Tom's bitter denunciation of his father's interracial relations on the dust jacket of *The Echo of the Black Horn*. The former storekeeper was over ninety years old and reduced to peddling pencils, chewing gum, candy bars, and copies of his book on the streets of Laurel.[13] By the mid-1950s his scraggly appearance frightened children, including mixed-race kin, who passed by him. Yet Tom Knight reportedly told Ethel that through God's help he had lived down "the disgrace and the shame that my father heaped upon me when he went to the Niggers!" Since he was "soon to die," he allegedly authorized her "to tell it all, the whole truth about my father." Presumably, Tom had omitted Rachel Knight from his own book out of shame, but the public trial of Davis Knight had exposed this shame. The truth must now be told. Even old Tom agreed.[14]

Ethel conceded that interracial marriages occurred between the children of Newton Knight and the children of Rachel Knight, but she seized the opportunity to shape the events that preceded and followed these marriages. In her hands, Rachel became a cunning, seductive, mulatto "Jezebel" who could not identify the fathers of her several white-skinned children.[15] Unlike Tom Knight, whose book portrayed his father as a principled Robin Hood, Ethel portrayed Newton as a murderous Civil War outlaw whose wrongheaded rebellion against the Confederacy alienated all but a few of his neighbors and relatives. According to Ethel, it was his increasing isolation from respectable society that pushed him ever closer to Rachel, who had provided him crucial aid in resisting the Confederacy. After the Civil War, she revealed, the two outcast Knight families, white and black, lived together on Newton's land. The children of Rachel and Newton later intermarried, thus laying the mixed-race foundations for Davis Knight's later miscegenation trial.[16]

Ethel Knight's fantastic "history" is a tangle of family memories, oral and documentary history, and the racist catechism taught to New South schoolchildren during her girlhood.[17] She set out to dissociate those branches of the Knight family descended from Newton's brothers and cousins from those descended from the children of Newton and Rachel Knight. Indeed, to further quash rumors of the Knight family's "impure blood," Ethel claimed that except for Davis Knight the descendants of the mixed-race couples had "all left the country and moved where they were not known, and married white." She assured her readers that "there are no mixed people living today [in Jones, Covington, and Jasper Counties] who have in them Knight blood." In other words, with the exception of Davis Knight, the family's blood was "pure."[18]

Unwittingly, Ethel Knight breathed life into the long-buried story of Rachel Knight. The Newton Knight rebellion has been told in histories, folklore, fiction, and film, but all have erased Rachel from the drama. Early chroniclers of the legend practiced a genteel silence in regard to this tale of interracial intimacy in the slave-holding and segregated South. More recent historians, who have viewed the uprising mainly through the narrow lens of battles and conflicts between white men, probably concluded that Rachel was irrelevant to the "real" story of the Piney Woods uprising.

Rachel, like so many southern women who participated directly in the Civil War, must be included in the war's narratives. As historians increasingly focus their research on the home front rather than the battlefield, on intraregional conflicts rather than just the conflict between the Union and the Confederacy, women like Rachel emerge center stage, vitally engaged in the struggles of war.[19] In her effort to defuse an old scandal brought to life by Davis Knight's trial, Ethel Knight not only restored Rachel's historical role, but unveiled a powerful, larger-than-life woman who had endured slavery, sexual exploitation, the Civil War, Reconstruction, and Mississippi's mounting campaign for white supremacy and racial segregation. Most strikingly, Rachel Knight seemed to have had as much impact on the world around her as it did on her.

Unfortunately, Rachel's historical reemergence was guided by the pen of a white segregationist whose own Knight ancestors fought and died for the Confederacy. Ethel Knight constructed a woman whose behavior and very existence embodied the lessons that she insisted the white South must learn once and for all: that the invading North's abolition of slavery destroyed the happiness of both blacks and whites in the South, and that Reconstruction under northern Republicans had brought ten years of ignorant "Negro rule" to Mississippi. In Ethel's view, racial integration defied the biblical word of God.[20]

Until we reimagine Ethel's narrative from the perspective of her subject, Rachel's life will remain defined by the inheritors of the very world she defied. Ethel's versions of events during the Civil War and Reconstruction are rooted in the Myth of the Lost Cause that she so revered, and in her commitment to maintaining white supremacy in the 1950s South.[21] As Natalie Zemon Davis argues, the historian must address the "competing moral positions" of participants in past events, particularly when one of them—or, in this case, one of their descendants—is telling the story of the other.[22]

At present, intriguing mysteries surround Rachel's very identity. One white descendant of the Knight family claimed that Rachel could hardly speak English when brought from Georgia to Mississippi, suggesting she came from the coastal Sea Islands. Ethel Knight's descriptions of Rachel suggest the same. She portrayed Rachel as a conjure woman who prepared "magic potions" for Newton and told fortunes for the community by reading coffee grounds. To protect herself and her family from evil spirits, Rachel allegedly placed a whittled cedar pinwheel at the gate to her home.[23] Witnesses at Davis Knight's trial variously described Rachel as Creole, Cherokee, Choctaw, or South African. Newton Knight's son Tom swore that she was "just an old Negro woman," with the "kinky hair," "flat nose," and "big thick lips" of an African. In contrast, Dr. J. W. Stringer and Wiley W. Jackson, both white men, and Henry Knight, Rachel's grandson, remembered a "gingercake colored" woman who had long, curly black hair that "swung across her shoulders," and who looked more Indian than African. Their memories suggest a striking-looking woman likely of European, Native American, and African heritage.[24]

Although Rachel died eighteen years before Ethel Knight was born, Ethel confidently described her as "an unusual mulatto, almost beautiful," with "blue-green eyes" and hair that "hung down to her waist in waves of shining chestnut . . . only a shade darker than her smooth face." Thus, Ethel confirmed—even exaggerated—the descriptions provided by Stringer, Jackson, and Henry Knight. She, like the judges of the high court, concluded that Tom Knight was too embittered by his siblings' interracial marriages to provide an honest description of the woman he held responsible for his family's shame.[25] Besides that, for Ethel's purpose, an "almost beautiful" green-eyed mulatto fit perfectly the tales of feminine wiles, seduction, and forbidden sex that enlivened the pages of *The Echo of the Black Horn.*

Records confirm that Rachel was the slave of Newton's grandfather. According to Ethel Knight, John "Jackie" Knight purchased her in the U.S. Land Office town of Augusta, Mississippi, "the only sizable town north of Mobile," in April 1856. Jackie Knight, a former Georgian who moved to Mississippi in the 1820s, was one of Covington and Jones Counties' wealthiest men. Although most of his neighbors were self-sufficient farmers or herders who owned few if any slaves, by 1850 he owned twenty-two slaves and several tracts of land in both counties. Despite some descendants' and a former slave's claim that he trafficked in slaves, Ethel emphatically denied it. She insisted that he was simply a softhearted horse trader who had a penchant for buying slaves in order to ameliorate their condition.[26]

Ethel portrayed Jackie Knight as the quintessential paternalistic gentleman who "had as carefully reared his slaves as he had his own children."[27] Such a man could not be a slave trader, for Ethel blamed all the evils that plagued the institution of slavery on this class. Slave traders, she explained, were social outcasts who obtained "filthy money by traffic[king] in human life." Men like Jackie Knight did not deserve this stigma because they spent money to buy slaves in order to "save" them from traders. They then treated the slaves like family members.[28] Ethel blamed slave traders for the beating of slaves (which she erroneously claimed was against the law) and for miscegenation. "From this type of men sprang the first Mulattoes," she declared. "In many instances, the females, were bred, unwillingly, like beasts."[29] In her Old South, however, white gentlemen like Jackie Knight did not debauch defenseless slave women. Like the antebellum defenders of plantation slavery, she described a benevolent institution in which masters cared for and civilized a race "whose ancestors boiled and ate their sons."[30]

Despite Ethel's defense of slavery, she did not deny that Rachel had been debauched by a white man, and that this probably accounted for her being sold on the auction block. According to Ethel, Rachel identified her first two children's father as the "handsome, blond" son of her rich master.[31] Although Rachel was only sixteen in 1856, the year Jackie Knight allegedly bought her, she was already the mother of one-year-old Georgeanne (whom Jackie also purchased) and possibly pregnant with her first son, Jeffrey. The white appearances of both children indicated the mixed ancestry of their mother and their almost certainly white father or fathers.[32]

For all her identification with the South's white master class, as a woman Ethel deplored the rape of black women by white men. In writing the story of Rachel, she struggled to reconcile her defense of slavery with her awareness of black women's sexual vulnerability. In self-conscious prose, Ethel wrote that "sometimes even the best master would be forced to sell off a slave for an objectionable reason. . . . Many of the objectionable instances were never mentioned, such as rape." She denounced this "practice" as "horrible, since these unfortunate people were victims of circumstance, treated without any consideration whatsoever." Perhaps because she was close to admitting that slaveholders, too, molested slave women, Ethel turned abruptly to describing the horrors that awaited slaves at the hands of the evil slave traders. As always, they, not the institution itself, debased otherwise contented slaves.[33]

Ethel did not consider that Jackie Knight might have purchased Rachel for economic and perhaps sexual purposes. She claimed that Jackie bought Rachel solely to prevent her separation from her children. At this point Ethel added a strange twist to the story. She described how yet another daughter of Rachel, Rosette, scrambled up on the auction block just as Jackie Knight made his purchase, thus forcing the softhearted planter to buy her, too. Ethel claimed that Rosette lived well into adulthood, but there is no evidence that such a person ever existed.[34]

Rosette's appearance in *The Echo of the Black Horn* is even more curious, since she is the only child of Rachel described by Ethel as having black skin. Ethel may have sought to establish Rachel's Africanness as negatively as possible through this daughter. She described Rosette's father, for example, as "a full-blooded, blue-gummed African" from whom Rosette "inherited her negroid characteristics . . . even to that little odor peculiar to the full-blooded black race." Ethel's description of Rosette conjured up the demeaning images of black children popularized by various white media during the first half of the twentieth century. In Ethel's literary imagination, Rosette was a "banjo-bellied, spindle-legged waif" who "rolled her big eyes, and scratched her kinky head."[35]

These cruel caricatures revealed Ethel's revulsion for African Americans, notwithstanding her honeyed praise for those who "loved their white folks and were in turn loved by them, as members of families."[36] When viewed in conjunction with Rosette's questionable authenticity, these caricatures suggest that Ethel manufactured or embellished the images of Rosette and her father in order to discourage her white readers from sympathizing with the green-eyed Rachel and her white-skinned progeny. Ethel's version of Rachel's history, a version that included a sexual relationship with a "blue-gummed African" and a black-skinned, kinky-haired child who was a product of that liaison, sealed Rachel's debasement. White Mississippians bred on vitriolic racist dogma no doubt recoiled in disgust at Rachel's doubly "polluted"

Fig. 11.3 Left to right: Grace Knight (1891–1966), Lessie Knight
(1894–?), Georgeanne Knight (1856–1922). Georgeanne Knight was
the oldest child of Rachel Knight. Many people believe that her
daughters Grace and Lessie, shown here, were fathered by Newton
Knight. Courtesy of Dorothy Marsh, Anna Knight Papers, Washington, D.C.

sexual history. Through Rosette, Ethel sought to remind readers that the beautiful
Rachel and her white-skinned children were, after all, "just another Negro family."[37]

Ethel Knight abhorred interracial sexual intimacy yet displayed a lurid fascination with it. She described Rachel's nights with Newton Knight's band of deserters
in erotic, if horrified, detail.

> Orgies [occurred], ghastly in obscenity, where Rachel and another black slave woman
> writhed and twisted their naked bodies in eerie dances, to the applause of the Deserters.
> Where fiddling and dancing went on for hours, undisturbed . . . where there was feast-
> ing, drinking and pleasure. Where booze-crazed, prurient, sex-mad men indulged in
> fornication, and evil pleasures of a hideous nature.[38]

Rachel became the female counterpart of the beastly black male rapist of white
southern lore, the "Jezebel" who reduced white men to their basest instincts. Thus,
Ethel and her white readers could simultaneously deplore and wallow in the forbidden sexual behavior of society's black and white "outlaws."

Rachel was indeed a sexually active woman who, between 1855 and 1875, gave
birth to perhaps nine children without ever marrying.[39] Ethel's explanation for this
was quite simple. She linked such promiscuity to Rachel's roots in Africa, where
"parentage was as varied and uncertain as that of the beasts of the forests." "It was

the custom," she claimed, "for slave women to bear children of different fathers." Rachel simply continued that "custom" after gaining her freedom.[40] According to Ethel, Rachel became such a "strumpet" during the war that she could not even identify which of the 125 followers of Newton Knight fathered her white-skinned daughter Fannie. Although others gossiped that Fannie's father was Newton, Ethel preferred to think of Rachel as "satisfy[ing] the evil pleasures" of all 125 of Newton's men rather than having a single sexual partner.[41]

It is highly misleading to discuss Rachel's sexual activity without viewing it in the historical context of slavery. While an enslaved teenaged woman, Rachel was impregnated by a white man. While still a teenager, and perhaps pregnant again, she and her child were sold and transported from Georgia to Mississippi, presumably severing whatever other kinships or friendships she had.[42] She arrived in the Piney Woods of Covington County, Mississippi, powerless and alone except for her child. Light-skinned and physically very attractive, she was the sort of slave after whom many white men lusted. The fact that she had a white-skinned daughter conveyed to interested men that she had already been "initiated" into the world of interracial sexual relations.

Rachel gave birth to another child, Edmund, about two years after giving birth to Jeffrey. Two years later, she gave birth to Fannie, the last of her children to be born into slavery. Until the Civil War erupted, she had no reason to anticipate that she or her children would ever live their lives as other than slaves.[43] Her participation, however, in the uprising led by Newton Knight catapulted her into the most powerful role she had ever known. Whether fact or fantasy, the campfire orgies described by Ethel Knight pale in comparison to the fantasies of freedom that the Civil War and Newton Knight's rebellion must have triggered for Rachel.

Ethel's account of Rachel's wartime behavior, though laden with racial invective and criticism of those who opposed the Confederacy, is filled with intriguing snapshots of a very dynamic Rachel. In fact, these snapshots reveal a much more complex portrait than the "Jezebel" image that Ethel so assiduously cultivated. For example, to explain how Rachel came to assist Newton Knight, Ethel said that Newton first learned from other slaves that Rachel possessed "great powers" as a conjure woman. Concluding that such a woman might be useful, he initiated their first meeting. They allegedly struck a bargain whereby Rachel promised to supply the deserters with food in return for Newton's promise to work for the liberation of all African Americans.[44]

Unlike other accounts of Newton Knight's rebellion that do not even mention Rachel, *The Echo of the Black Horn* has contributed significantly to our understanding of the wider role of women in the rebellion. Newton, shortly before his death in 1922, described the vital participation of women in his movement. In an interview with Meigs Frost of the *New Orleans Item*, he described how women poisoned the bloodhounds of the Confederate cavalry sent into Jones County to arrest deserters. "Yes," Newton grinned and recalled, "Those ladies sure helped us a lot. . . . They had 44 blood-hounds after us, those boys and General Robert Lowry's men. But 42 of them hounds just naturally died. They'd get hungry and some of the ladies, friends of ours would feed 'em. And they'd die. Strange, wasn't it?" Newton further described how the women sprinkled polecat musk and red pepper on the trails leading to the deserters' hideout.[45]

Ethel Knight claimed that Rachel had taught this trick to white women in the movement, that she had learned it while participating in the Underground Railroad of fugitive slaves. Rachel allegedly told Newton and his men to rub the musk, red pepper, and garlic on the bottoms of their shoes; the garlic would confuse the hounds, while the pepper would make them cough and sneeze. Soon after, wrote Ethel, the women friendly to the deserters were supplying them with dried, powdered red pepper.[46] Ethel gave no source to document this story, but it is likely that a slave woman would know better than a white farmwife how to throw off the scent of bloodhounds. This story may well have originated in oral accounts of the uprising passed down through the generations. Perhaps Rachel was omitted in later written accounts because the authors, particularly Newton's son Tom, wanted her role expunged from the record in order to bury the scandal of miscegenation. The gospel of racial segregation in the New South condemned Rachel to historical oblivion.

Ethel described several more instances during the Civil War in which Rachel aided Newton Knight, none of which can be substantiated, but all of which seem plausible. When Colonel Lowry's men murdered Newton's cousin Ben in the mistaken notion that they had at last captured the elusive Newton Knight, Rachel reportedly brought the news to Newton, who in turn summoned his men by blowing his infamous black horn. Rachel further warned him that the cavalry would be returning to the deserters' swamp the next day, and thus enabled him to ambush the cavalry at another location. Finally, in Newton's closest brush with death following a shoot-out, Ethel described how a doctor, brought to the deserters' hideout at gunpoint to tend Newton's wounds, was surprised to find "a pale ginger Mulatto" woman—presumably Rachel—already nursing him.[47]

Ethel may have exaggerated Rachel's contributions to the Jones County uprising in order to "blacken" Newton's reputation. The lifelong connections of the couple and the intermarriages of their children, however, suggest that she did not exaggerate Rachel's role. Ethel apparently reported every tale she had ever heard about Rachel and Newton's Civil War exploits in order to denigrate both of them in the harshest terms possible. To this end, she told her stories carefully, though without regard for documentable fact, embellishing them whenever it served her needs.[48] Ethel was determined that Newton would never again be perceived as the courageous leader of a principled rebellion against the Confederacy. Adding Rachel to the story contributed to this goal, but required that she break the Knight family's code of silence about the "white Negroes" who shared their blood. What had long been gossip was now part of the written record.[49]

Despite Ethel's pretensions, *The Echo of the Black Horn* is not historical scholarship. As folklore and folktales committed to print, however, it is invaluable. The best-known and most frequently read work on "the free state of Jones" in the entire state, it provides a window on the popular beliefs that it has helped to shape. "Miss Ethel" is an icon among many local people, and the book recently received its sixth printing. "I believe Miss Ethel is closer than anyone to the truth," one descendant

Fig. 11.4 Grace Knight (1891–1966). Undated. Daughter of Georgeanne Knight; granddaughter of Rachel Knight. Rumored to be the daughter of Newton Knight. Courtesy of Dorothy Marsh, Anna Knight Papers, Washington, D.C.

of Newton Knight's Civil War associates concluded. "That Rachel, she was a beautiful animal—but she hoodooed Newton."[50]

From her modest white frame home, located on the edge of the Leaf River woods where Jones, Jasper, and Covington Counties intersect, and where Newton, Rachel, and the band of deserters evaded Confederate capture, Ethel Knight stands guard over her version of the story of their lives. Indeed, she has become as much a part of the area's living and volatile past as the people and events she chronicled.

More than simply a "version" of the past, however, her book embodies continued domination of whites over blacks and conventional authority over dissent, in its imprisonment of Rachel and Newton within a "New South" glorification of the Old South's prerogatives of race and class. Rachel, resuscitated by Ethel on the one hand, is reenslaved by her caricatures on the other. Once the racial, class, and gendered discourses of *The Echo of the Black Horn* are deconstructed, however, Rachel's remarkable life and the sheer force of her personality captivate us. In fact, in many ways she has become the captor, not the prisoner, of her biographer. Rachel appears to have "hoodooed" Ethel Knight and her readers into a never-ending fascination with her memory.

NOTES

Research for this article was funded by a Research Enhancement Grant from the Office of Research and Sponsored Programs, Southwest Texas State University. I wish to give special thanks to Winona Knight Hudson of Fresno, California, and Florence Blaylock of Soso, Mississippi, for arranging for me to interview the kinfolk of Rachel Knight, and to Dorothy Marsh of Washington, D.C., for sharing with me the papers of Rachel's granddaughter Anna Knight. Thanks also to Earle Knight, who arranged my visit to the Newton Knight cemetery, to Gregg Andrews for his editorial assistance, and to Shearer Davis Bowman for his helpful comments at the 1994 convention of the Texas State Historical Association.

1. *State of Mississippi v. Davis Knight*, Dec. 13, 1948, case no. 646, court transcripts of the Circuit Court, Jones County, Miss., Clerk's Office, Mississippi Supreme Court.

2. Ibid. Molly Knight's proper name was Martha Ann Eliza Knight; Jeffrey's was Jeffrey Early; Mat's was George Mathew; Fannie was listed as Frances in the 1900 Federal Manuscript Census. Family records and censuses indicate that the marriages took place in 1878, although Ethel Knight claimed that both couples were married on Christmas Eve, 1884. U.S. Federal Manuscript Censuses, 1880, 1900, Jasper County, Miss.; Jan Sumrall and Kenneth Welch, *The Knights and Related Families* (Denham Springs, La.: n.p., 1985), 12; Ethel Knight, *The Echo of the Black Horn* (n.p., 1951), 298.

3. *State v. Knight*, court transcript; Thomas J. Knight, *The Life and Activities of Captain Newton Knight and His Company and the Free State of Jones County* (n.p., 1946). A copy of an almost identical manuscript, dated 1934 and entitled "Intimate Sketch of Activities of Newton Knight and 'Free State of Jones County,' " is contained in the Special Collections of the Mississippi Department of Archives and History, Jackson.

4. The debate over whether Newton Knight and Rachel Knight produced children together continues among local residents today. Ethel Knight claimed that they did not (*Echo of the Black Horn,* 264). The tradition among descendants of Rachel, however, is that several of Rachel's youngest children were fathered by Newton. Olga Watts, a granddaughter of Augusta Ann Knight Watts, was told by her father that Augusta Ann and her brothers, John Madison ("Hinchie") and Stewart, were the children of Rachel and Newton. Olga Watts, interview by Victoria Bynum, July 22, 1996, Soso, Miss. Audrey Knight Crosby, the oldest living child of Hinchie Knight, stated emphatically that her father was the son of Newton and Rachel. Audrey Knight, interview by Victoria Bynum, July 23, 1996, Soso, Miss. Although the descendants of Rachel do not always agree on which of Rachel's nine children were fathered by Newton, most would agree with Annette Knight's general statement that Rachel had "lots of babies" by him. Annette Knight, interview by Florence Blaylock, June 29, 1996, Soso, Miss.

After Rachel's death in 1889, Newton may have become sexually involved with her oldest daughter, Georgeanne. In 1926 B. D. Graves, a lifelong associate of Newton, told a community gathering that Newton "took a negro woman [Georgeanne] as his wife." From "Addresses Delivered at Hebron Community Meeting" (prepared and presented to the Eastman Memorial Foundation Library by the First National Bank of Laurel, June 17, 1926), Lauren Rogers Museum of Art, Laurel, Miss. In 1934 Martha Wheeler, a former slave of the Knight family, told a WPA interviewer that "Rachel was considered his [Newton's] woman." After Rachel's death, she claimed, Georgeanne "took her place." Sometime between 1880 and 1900, Serena Knight moved out of Newton's household. George P. Rawick, ed., *The American Slave: A Composite Autobiography Supplement*, series 1, vol. 10, pt. 5, p. 2268; Federal

Manuscript Censuses, 1880, 1890, Jasper County, Miss. For further corroboration, see Sumrall and Welch, *Knights and Related Families*, 161.

5. Jacquelyn Dowd Hall, " 'The Mind that Burns in Each Body': Women, Rape, and Racial Violence," in *Powers of Desire: The Politics of Sexuality*, ed. Ann Snitow, Christine Stansell, and Sharon Thompson (New York: Monthly Review Press, 1983). For an analysis of how dominant beliefs about appropriate race, class, and gender behavior converged to ignite mass hysteria and violence, see Nancy McLean, "The Leo Frank Case Reconsidered: Gender and Sexual Politics in the Making of Reactionary Populism," *Journal of American History* 78 (1991): 917–48. Elizabeth Young presents an analysis of the 1935 film *Bride of Frankenstein* as a "racist American discourse of the 1930s on masculinity, femininity, rape, and lynching," in "Here Comes the Bride: Wedding, Gender, and Race in *Bride of Frankenstein*," *Feminist Studies* 17 (1991): 403–37. For more comprehensive analyses of race relations during this era, see Joel Williamson, *Crucible of Race: Black-White Relations in the American South since Emancipation* (New York: Oxford University Press, 1984), 111–323; and Neil McMillen, *Dark Journey: Black Mississippians in the Age of Jim Crow* (Urbana: University of Illinois Press, 1989), 8–114.

6. William Gillette, *Retreat from Reconstruction, 1869–1879* (Baton Rouge: Louisiana State University Press, 1979), 166–235. Still useful on Mississippi is Vernon Lane Wharton, *The Negro in Mississippi, 1865–1890* (Chapel Hill: University of North Carolina Press, 1947). On southern law, race, and sexual relations, see Peter W. Bardaglio, *Reconstructing the Household: Families, Sex, and the Law in the Nineteenth-Century South* (Chapel Hill: University of North Carolina Press, 1995); and Mary Frances Berry, "Judging Morality: Sexual Behavior and Legal Consequences in the Late Nineteenth-Century South," *Journal of American History* 78 (1991): 835–56. For a comprehensive overview of the era, see Eric Foner, *Reconstruction: America's Unfinished Revolution, 1863–1877* (New York: Harper and Row, 1988).

7. Paula Giddings, *When and Where I Enter: The Impact of Black Women on Race and Sex in America* (New York: Bantam, 1985), 17–31; Jacquelyn Dowd Hall, *Revolt against Chivalry: Jessie Daniel Ames and the Women's Campaign against Lynching* (New York: 1979; rev. ed., Columbia University Press, 1993).

8. *New Orleans Item*, March 20, 1921. Knight's death was reported in the *Ellisville Progressive* on March 16, 1922. The "Negro wife" referred to by the editor was probably Georgeanne Knight. In 1920 Newton Knight lived in a household that included his white daughter Cora and his three white grandchildren. In the next household was Otho Knight, the mulatto son of Newton's daughter Molly and Rachel's son Jeffrey. In yet another household was Georgeanne, Rachel's oldest daughter, and Georgeanne's daughter Grace. The former slave Martha Wheeler claimed that Grace was Newton's daughter. U.S. Federal Manuscript Censuses, 1880, 1900, 1910, 1920, Jasper County, Miss.; Rawick, *American Slave*, vol. 10, pt. 5, p. 2268. According to Jeannette Smith, a granddaughter of Hinchie Knight, Newton had three wives during his lifetime—Serena, Rachel, and Georgeanne—and did not treat any of them as simply concubines or lovers, despite the illegality of the last two relationships. Jeannette Smith, Sandra Shaw, and Flo Wyatt, interview by Victoria Bynum, July 24, 1996, Soso, Miss.

Nor, according to several descendants of Hinchie Knight, did Newton deny his relationship to his mixed-race children and grandchildren. Annette Knight, Yvonne Bevins, and Anita Williams recalled being told that Newton treated all his black and white children equally; Bevins and Williams heard from elders that he would gather them all together at Christmas.

Annette Knight, interview; Yvonne Bevins and Anita Williams, interview by Florence Blaylock, July 4, 1996, Soso, Miss. Audrey Knight Crosby, seven years old at the time of Newton's death, remembered his bringing apples in a wagon to her father, Hinchie's, farm. Audrey Knight Crosby, interview.

9. *State v. Knight*, court transcript.

10. *Knight v. State*, 207 Miss. 564 (1949).

11. In 1900 a census enumerator for Jasper County classified Newton Knight, Serena Knight, Molly Knight, and various children of Newton and Serena as black, presumably because they were living among their mixed-race kin. Similarly, Ethel Knight alleged that Tom Knight told his mother, Serena, that "people who live with Negroes are no more than Negroes." *State v. Knight*, court transcript; Federal Manuscript Census, 1900, Jasper County, Miss.; Knight, *Echo of the Black Horn*, 310. On the classification of misbehaving whites as blacks, see Williamson, *Crucible of Race*, 467.

12. Knight, *Echo of the Black Horn*, frontispiece and dedication page. Ethel, whose maiden name was Boykin, claims descent through her mother from James Knight, a brother of Newton. Her husband, Sidney Knight, was descended from Daniel Knight, an uncle of Newton. Both ancestors served and died for the Confederacy. Ethel Knight, interview by Victoria Bynum, Aug. 10, 1993, Covington County, Miss. See also Winnie Knight Thomas, Earle W. Knight, Lavada Knight Dykes, and Martha Kaye Dykes Lowery, *The Family of John "Jackie" Knight and Keziah Davis Knight, 1773–1985* (Magee, Miss.: Robert and DeLores Knight Vinson, 1985), 25, 30.

13. Tom Knight was listed as the owner of a Laurel grocery store in the 1920 Federal Manuscript Census for Jones County, Miss. He was described as a peddler in the *Laurel Leader Call*'s Dec. 19, 1951, review of *Echo of the Black Horn*. Earle Knight, the grandson of Newton Knight's cousin and fellow unionist, William Martin ("Dickie") Knight, remembered that Tom had once owned a store but in later years had operated a street stand. Earle Knight, interview by Victoria Bynum, July 28, 1994, Laurel, Miss.

14. Quoted from the dustjacket of Knight, *Echo of the Black Horn*. According to Ethel, Tom Knight sold her his manuscript materials and copyright shortly after the Davis Knight trial. Though Tom presumably agreed that Ethel Knight should tell the story of Rachel, his cousin Earle Knight stated that Tom was unaware that his father's political principles and goals would be recast as well. Flo Wyatt remembered being frightened as a child by the sight of Tom Knight on the streets of Laurel. Ethel Knight, interview; Earle Knight, interview; Wyatt, interview.

15. The image of the lascivious, cunning mulatto "Jezebel" was well entrenched by the time Ethel Knight employed it. For a historical overview of literary images of African American women, see Patricia Morton, *Disfigured Images: The Historical Assault on Afro-American Women* (Westport, Conn.: Greenwood, 1991). On black women as "Jezebels," see especially Deborah Gray White, *Ar'n't I a Woman? Female Slaves in the Plantation South* (New York: W. W. Norton, 1985), 27–61; see also Victoria E. Bynum, *Unruly Women: The Politics of Social and Sexual Control in the Old South* (Chapel Hill: University of North Carolina Press, 1992), 36–40; and Elizabeth Fox-Genovese, *Within the Plantation Household: Black and White Women of the Old South* (Chapel Hill: University of North Carolina Press, 1988), 292.

16. Knight, *Echo of the Black Horn*, 253–58, 289–90, 300.

17. On the literature of this era, see Williamson, *Crucible of Race*, 140–76. For an overview of the content of New South textbooks, see Carl Degler, "The South in Southern Textbooks," *Journal of Southern History* 30 (1964): 52–63.

18. Knight, *Echo of the Black Horn*, 279–314.

19. The author James Street, whose novel *Tap Roots* (Garden City, N Y · Sun Dial Press, 1943) formed the basis of the 1948 movie of the same name, created the mixed-race character of Kyd, a member of the story's main family. In addition to the works of Thomas J. Knight and Ethel Knight, the most important histories include Rudy H. Leverett, *Legend of the Free State of Jones* (Jackson: University Press of Mississippi, 1984); Goode Montgomery, "Alleged Secession of Jones County," *Publications of the Mississippi Historical Society* 8 (1904): 13–22; G. Norton Galloway, "A Confederacy within a Confederacy," *Magazine of American History* 8 (1886): 387–90. Recent works that highlight southern women's participation in the Civil War include Drew Gilpin Faust, *Mothers of Invention: Women of the Slaveholding South in the American Civil War* (Chapel Hill: University of North Carolina Press, 1996); LeeAnn Whites, *The Civil War as a Crisis in Gender: Augusta, Georgia, 1861–1865* (Athens: University of Georgia Press, 1995); Catherine Clinton and Nina Silber, eds., *Divided Houses: Gender and the Civil War* (New York: Oxford University Press, 1992); Bynum, *Unruly Women*, 111–50; George C. Rable, *Civil Wars: Women and the Crisis of Southern Nationalism* (Urbana: University of Illinois Press, 1989); Philip Shaw Paludan, *Victims: A True Story of the Civil War* (Knoxville: University of Tennessee Press, 1981).

20. These themes run throughout *Echo of the Black Horn*, but see especially page 19.

21. The most comprehensive revisions of New South history are Edward L. Ayers, *The Promise of the New South: Life after Reconstruction* (New York: Oxford University Press, 1992); and C. Vann Woodward, *Origins of the New South, 1877–1913* (Baton Rouge: Louisiana State University Press, 1951). On the creation of the "Lost Cause" myth in Georgia, see Whites, *Civil War as a Crisis in Gender*. For an early review of Lost Cause historiography, see Bernard A. Weisberger, "The Dark and Bloody Ground of Reconstruction Historiography," *Journal of Southern History* 25 (1959): 427–47. The continued popularity of Ethel Knight's work in Mississippi is testimony that the Lost Cause version of southern history is still embraced by much of the nonacademic community.

22. Natalie Zemon Davis, "On the Lame," *American Historical Review* 93 (1988): 599.

23. Earle Knight, interview; Federal Manuscript Censuses, 1870, 1880, Jasper County, Miss.; Knight, *Echo of the Black Horn*, 258, 263–64. On the language of Sea Island blacks, see Lawrence W. Levine, *Black Culture and Black Consciousness: Afro-American Folk Thought from Slavery to Freedom* (New York: Oxford University Press, 1978), 144–49; on the importance of conjuring, witchcraft, and carved wooden charms, see Georgia Writers' Project, Works Projects Administration, *Drums and Shadows: Survival Studies among the Georgia Coastal Negroes* (1940; reprint, Athens: University of Georgia Press, 1986).

24. Existing photographs of Rachel's descendants, especially those of her daughter Augusta Ann Watts and granddaughters Anna and Grace Knight, indicate both Indian and European heritage. Curtis Watts, the son of Augusta Ann, told his niece Olga Watts that Rachel was a Creek Indian. Olga Watts, interview. The only witness who corroborated Tom Knight's testimony that Rachel looked like an African was D. H. Valentine. The state supreme court discounted Valentine's testimony because although he was born one year after Rachel Knight's death, he claimed to have seen her several times as a child. *State v. Knight*, court transcript.

25. Knight, *Echo of the Black Horn*, 34, 312.

26. Jackie Knight married Keziah Davis in Columbia County, Georgia, on November 5, 1798. By the 1820s the couple lived in Covington County, Mississippi. In 1860 Jackie Knight owned real estate valued at $3,000 and personal property valued at $23,000. Federal Manuscript Censuses and Slave Schedules, 1860, Covington County, Miss. According to the

Federal Agricultural Census for Covington County for that year, he owned 680 acres of land (200 of which was under cultivation) and livestock valued at $1,200. He produced two thousand pounds of rice, one thousand bushels of corn, and fourteen bales of ginned cotton. Although his descendant Earle Knight contends that he bought and sold slaves, I found no documentation of this. Knight, *Echo of the Black Horn*, 27–37; Thomas et al., *Family of John "Jackie" Knight*, 320, 340–43; Earle Knight, interview; "Legends of Ghosts, Treasures," *Laurel Leader Call*, Jan. 18, 1993; Rawick, *American Slave*, vol. 10, pt. 5, p. 2267; Natchez Trace Slaves and Slavery Collection, 1793–1864, Center for American History, University of Texas, Austin.

27. Knight, *Echo of the Black Horn*, 24. Ethel's description of Jackie Knight's paternalism is corroborated by the former slave Martha Wheeler's description of him as "good and kind" and his slaves as "wellfed and clothed." Rawick, *American Slave*, vol. 10, pt. 5, pp. 2264–67.

28. Knight, *Echo of the Black Horn*, 29–30.

29. Ibid., 29–31.

30. Ibid., 250.

31. Ibid., 284.

32. Ibid., 34–37. The inscription on Georgeanne's tombstone lists her birthdate as October 14, 1855; this would make her less than a year old when Jackie Knight purchased her and her mother.

33. Knight, *Echo of the Black Horn*, 31. Three particularly fascinating studies of the tangled web of kinships created by interracial relationships in the South are Kent Anderson Leslie, *Woman of Color, Daughter of Privilege: Amanda America Dickson, 1849–1893* (Athens: University of Georgia Press, 1995); Adele Logan Alexander, *Ambiguous Lives: Free Women of Color in Rural Georgia, 1789–1879* (Fayetteville: University of Arkansas Press, 1991); and Pauli Murray, *Proud Shoes: The Story of an American Family* (New York: Harper and Row, 1956).

34. Knight, *Echo of the Black Horn*, 34–37. No Rosette Knight appears in the Federal Manuscript Censuses for Jasper, Jones, or Covington Counties, Miss., between 1860 and 1920, nor is one mentioned in John Knight's will. Although several witnesses at Davis Knight's trial recalled the names of various children of Rachel, not one mentioned a Rosette. Nor has a single Knight descendant interviewed by myself or Florence Blaylock offered evidence that this Rosette Knight existed.

35. Knight, *Echo of the Black Horn*, 37, 262–63. The documentary film *Ethnic Notions* (San Francisco: Resolution Inc./California Newsreel, 1987) provides an excellent overview of negative media stereotypes of African American adults and children.

36. Knight, *Echo of the Black Horn*, 30.

37. Ibid., 262–63.

38. Ibid., 283–84.

39. The 1870 Federal Manuscript Census listed six children in Rachel's household: Georgeanne, Jeffrey, Edmund, Fannie, Marsha [Martha Ann], and Stewart. In 1880 Edmund was gone but three more children were listed: Floyd, A. A. [Augusta Ann], and Henchy [John Madison]. Federal Manuscript Censuses, 1870, 1880, 1900, Jasper County, Miss.

40. Knight, *Echo of the Black Horn*, 250, 261.

41. Ibid., 253, 260. According to the 1900 Federal Manuscript Census for Jasper County, Fannie Knight was born in March 1864.

42. According to her granddaughter Anna Knight, Rachel was born in Macon, Georgia. Anna Knight's papers indicate that Rachel's daughter Georgeanne was born Oct. 14, 1855, when Rachel was fifteen. Although Ethel Knight claimed that Rachel was pregnant with

Jeffrey when Jackie Knight bought her, the 1900 Federal Manuscript Census, Jasper County, Miss., gives Jeffrey's birthdate as March 1860, some four years after Ethel alleged that Jackie purchased her. Anna Knight, *Mississippi Girl* (Nashville: Southern Publishing Association, 1952); Anna Knight Collection, courtesy of Dorothy Marsh, Washington D.C.; Knight, *Echo of the Black Horn*, 37.

43. It is difficult to determine exactly when Rachel's children were born because census data vary significantly between decades. In 1870, for example, the census enumerator for Jasper County indicated that Georgeanne's birth year was 1853 and Jeffrey's was 1855, while the 1880 enumerator indicated that Georgeanne's was 1855 and Jeffrey's was 1859. In the 1900 census, in which actual months and years of birth were given, Georgeanne's birthdate was given as October 1856, while Jeffrey's birthdate was given as March 1860. Federal Manuscript Censuses, 1870, 1880, 1900, Jasper County, Miss.

44. Knight, *Echo of the Black Horn*, 73–75, 122.

45. *New Orleans Item*, March 20, 1921. Newton Knight referred to Robert Lowry as "General," but Lowry was still a colonel at the time their battles occurred. Tom Knight expanded on his father's accounts of women's participation. See *Life and Activities of Captain Newton Knight*, 33, 71. Colonel Robert Lowry and his men were ordered into Jones County by T. M. Jack, an assistant adjutant-general. See Special Order no. 80, Headquarters, Demopolis, Ala., March 20, 1864, *Official Records of the War of the Rebellion* (Washington, D.C.: Government Printing Office, 1891), series 1, vol. 32, pt. 3, p. 662.

46. Knight, *Echo of the Black Horn*, 173–74.

47. Ibid., 193.

48. Shortly before his death at age one hundred in 1952, Newton's first cousin George Knight (nicknamed "Clean Neck") insisted that Ethel's book was filled with distortions and lies. Earle Knight, interview.

49. Ethel Knight was particularly galled by James Street's portrayal of *Tap Roots*'s protagonist Hoab Dabney as a highly principled unionist because she believed that Street based this character on Newton Knight. Nevertheless, many members of the Knight family were upset when Ethel Knight not only vilified Newton Knight, but told the story of Rachel. Not surprisingly, mixed-race Knights and other African Americans objected to the manner in which she told the story. Ethel Knight, interview.

50. Julius Huff, interview, by Victoria Bynum, Aug. 8, 1993, Covington County, Miss.

Chapter Twelve

Still Waiting

Intermarriage in White Women's Civil War Novels

Lyde Cullen Sizer

In *Playing in the Dark: Whiteness and the Literary Imagination*, Toni Morrison focuses on seemingly subsidiary black characters in the novels of whites to suggest both their necessity to the plot and their suggestiveness about the nature of white fear and desire. She makes her case by using the work of Herman Melville, Willa Cather, William Faulkner, Gertrude Stein, and other major canonical writers, but it is clear that her insights can be—indeed, have been—applied more broadly. In one sense they are especially applicable to the fiction of white women abolitionists in the early Reconstruction period.

This is true despite the differences between these novels and those that Morrison studies. First, in a number of these novels, black characters are not simply subsidiary, but absolutely central. Second, love and marriage between white and black characters—a latent if ever-conscious theme of much earlier white fiction—are explicit. The intertwined lives of black and white people become political messages about the failures and possibilities of national reunion and repair. Largely overlooked by political historians, these texts provide a glimpse into the tangled and contradictory ways that antislavery white women imagined themselves and others in a nation rebuilding itself.

In this sense Morrison's insights reveal the schism at the center of these political visions. "The fabrication of an Africanist persona is reflexive," she argues, "an extraordinary meditation on the self; a powerful exploration of the fears and desires that reside in the writerly conscious. It is an astonishing revelation of longing, of terror, of perplexity, of shame, of magnanimity."[1] In this case, the Africanist presence reflects not only a meditation on the self, but a meditation on a nation rebuilding, a nation filled with "fears and desires." The efforts of these activists was to create a moral whiteness through stories of black Americans struggling to be free in the aftermath of the Civil War. One of the most common strategies in creating moral whiteness was the creation of literal "whiteness" in the black characters. While "passing" characters already had a significant presence in the work of both black and white authors by the post-war period, its use here had multiple meanings, suggesting solutions to the seeming dilemma of national rupture.

Three novelists in particular directly confronted the fears of the post-war period with novels about the war. Each had a different relationship to abolitionism and each advocated a different form of cultural and political work during Reconstruction. Lydia Maria Child had struggled and sacrificed for the fight against slavery for over thirty years in 1865; her *Romance of the Republic* (1867) suggested that intermarriage and personal efforts at education would successfully integrate blacks into white society. Anna Dickinson, a virtual newcomer to antislavery compared to Child, argued in *What Answer?* (1868) not so much for intermarriage—her lovers are literally killed by prejudice—as for black suffrage. And Rebecca Harding Davis, who struggled to illuminate the complexities of the Civil War to her readers, suggested in *Waiting for the Verdict* (1868) the most idealistic solution of all: that right-thinking white individuals and families adopt the fortunes of less fortunate black families, living side by side in communitarian relationships. Her depiction of love relationships between the races, however, was more realistic: they failed because of deeply embedded and lasting racial prejudice.

These white women had divergent visions of the post-war social and political world, but they shared an underlying strategy of imagining post-war life through romantic love between blacks and whites. For Child, Dickinson, and Davis, Reconstruction had metaphorical possibilities with pointed political implications. Such unusual messages had unusually qualified messengers: Lydia Maria Child, a longtime abolitionist and political gadfly; Anna Dickinson, who lectured in the House of Representatives in front of an assembled Congress and President Lincoln himself; and Rebecca Harding Davis, who had won two kinds of audiences: a serious literary one, with *Life in the Iron Mills* (1860) in the *Atlantic Monthly*, and a more middle-class one with her stories and sketches in *Peterson's Lady's Magazine* and *Harper's New Monthly Magazine*.

These women used history and criticism more directly than numerous other post-war white women novelists.[2] As the historian Martha Hodes would note later, they understood "how sex between white women and black men [and marriage between white men and black women] came to be a deeply political issue connected directly to the maintenance of racial hierarchy from emancipation forward."[3] They knew that the end of the war marked only the beginning of a social revolution still largely to be achieved in race relations, and the fight over civil rights and voting legislation formed the backdrop for their writings. In many ways this work was more honest, bracing, and effective than that of later writers, yet it also revealed the difficulty of translating abstract abolitionist pieties into a workable post-war program. They took what Morrison would call Cather's "dangerous journey" to view the "void of racism," but like Cather, they did not arrive safely.[4]

The volatility of the issue of intermarriage at the time these three authors first conceptualized and then published their works can be dramatized by the struggle over a pamphlet published in 1863. In an effort to scare voters away from President Lincoln, and in the wake of the Emancipation Proclamation, Democrats artfully constructed *Miscegenation: The Theory of the Blending of the Races, Applied to the American White Man and Negro*.[5] In *Miscegenation*, where the word was coined, the ostensibly abolitionist authors argued that intermarriage would solve the nation's racial problems by producing a better breed of children.[6] They declared that "whereas, the result of the last Presidential election has given the colored race on this continent its freedom, the next Presidential election should secure to every black man and woman the rest of their social and political rights; that the progressive party must rise to the height of the great argument, and not flinch from the conclusions to which they are brought by their own principles."[7]

Significantly, the pamphlet included "testimonies" from prominent abolitionists in an appendix gleaned from their work. Harriet Beecher Stowe's novel *Dred* was among these, including quoted descriptions of her mulatto characters. For these political writers, the choices made even by women novelists were telling. The abolitionist community largely *did* flinch at "the conclusions to which they are brought by their own principles," however; they rejected the pamphlet in some cases wholeheartedly, and in others, partially.[8]

In 1867 and 1868 some of the reforms Child, Dickinson, and Davis called for were already being implemented. Andrew Johnson's presidential Reconstruction, an abysmal failure in terms of justice to freedpeople, had ended. The program of the radical Republicans, strongest in these years, had begun with the Reconstruction acts and the Fourteenth Amendment, which promised more protection for freedpeople from the Ku Klux Klan (formed in 1866) and dismantled Black Codes that had curtailed the personal and legal freedom of southern blacks. The Fifteenth Amendment, for which Dickinson specifically called, was a year away in Congress and would be ratified in 1870.

Yet despite the very real hope of these years, there was still much to fear in 1867 and 1868. Redistribution of land had proven an elusive dream for the freedpeople, and the system of sharecropping, which promised freedom from daily direction from whites, caught many in a spiraling trap of fraud and debt. And if freedpeople looked to political change to solve many of their nation's ills, the results of the 1868 elections would give them pause. General Ulysses S. Grant won the presidency, but with the support of moderate rather than radical Republicans, as the political tide began to shift. "The Radical generation was passing," the historian Eric Foner argues, "eclipsed by politicos who believed the 'struggle over the Negro' must give way to economic concerns."[9]

That whites' economic concerns trumped their moral ones during Reconstruction made the arguments of these white women writers less persuasive. Caught in a liminal time, between the powerful reaction to white southern resistance in 1866 and the shifting of attention away from freedpeople beginning in 1868, these novels were reminiscent of the political strategies of the pre-war period, but their content was more radical than what even the more progressive legislators were willing to accept, and well beyond the racial beliefs of much of white America.

Most of the northern women writing novels about the war in the post-war period condemned slavery and celebrated its demise. In many cases, such condemnations and celebrations were made by white characters, which suggested that the hero or heroine saw God's will in the whirlwind before the nation did. "A.O.W.," author of *Eyewitness*, a novel written to record the efforts of white southerners loyal to the

Union, had her heroine say to her cousin, " 'O Harry, what greater evil could be visited upon man than slavery? . . . God grant, if this war must be, that it may ultimately and completely do away with slavery.' "[10] Another southern Unionist, from Bella Z. Spencer's *Tried and True*, was equally convinced of slavery's wrongs, but before the war despaired of change: " 'It is like attempting to overturn the world, for one woman to put her small strength against so mighty an evil as this evil of slavery.' " During the war she was forced to abandon home and child because of these views and her aid to a fugitive slave; she then turned her efforts to nursing the wounded near southwestern battlefields.[11]

Other novelists used white male characters to express their antislavery views, perhaps thus making political statements more acceptable. Louisa May Alcott commented on the evil effects that slavery had on whites through a fictional soldier impelled to heroism by his love for a good white woman. Once a Confederate, her hero was now a Unionist, and told his fellow soldiers on the picket line, " 'Have I not cause to dare much?—for in owning many slaves, I too became a slave; in helping to make many freemen, I liberate myself.' "[12] In Mary J. Holmes's novel *Rose Mather*, a white boy with southern sympathies made the author's condemnation of slavery complete. He fled the South with his Unionist sister and was dying of disease, confused and upset at the outcome of the war. He told his sister,

> I get terribly perplexed thinking it all over, and how it has turned out. I think—yes, I know I am glad the Negroes are free. We never abused them. Uncle Paul never abused them. But there were those who did; and if slavery is a Divine institution as we are taught to believe, it was a broken-down and badly-conducted institution, and not at all as He meant it to be managed.[13]

By choosing a character with southern loyalties to make this statement—understated as it is—Holmes stressed that even slaveholders themselves could admit the wrong they perpetrated.

The position that many of these novels establish allows for an embrace of the lost white South. If wrong, as it surely was, the South was inhabited by valiant and true Unionists—many of them white women—who through love and influence would change the rest. And, as in Holmes's novel, this position accepted the moderate southern view of simply a "broken-down" institution, not "as He meant it to be managed." Here, then, was a redeemable white South, and black characters are generally left comfortably in the background, distanced by the perceived needs of northern white writers to forgive and forget.

In this context, it was rather startling for white women writers to have black characters express their arguments. Even more startling was the fact that many of these characters were involved in interracial relationships. Child, Dickinson, and Davis went beyond what the historian George Fredrickson considers a "viable abolitionist position" on miscegenation in the post-war period (that is, looking the other way when blacks and whites fell in love and married) and crossed the line into having their characters consciously contemplate such a course.[14] During the war, as well, the American Freedmen's Inquiry Commission suppressed testimony about liaisons between white women and black men out of fear that such information would threaten the goal of emancipation.[15] Although sexual and marital unions between blacks and whites had been a public subject to varying degrees in the antebellum North, the issue had been framed within a critique of slavery, and centered around black women's vulnerability and resistance to rape by white men. Here, however, blacks were depicted as legal and social equals.

The specter of consensual unions between blacks and whites had been present since the announcement of emancipation, and had been discomfiting even to whites who considered themselves antislavery. Not surprisingly, such unions were especially frightening for white men, because they potentially undercut control over the bodies of women, both black and white. As the historian Deborah Gray White observes about an earlier period, "Women and blacks were the foundation on which southern white males built their patriarchal regime. If, as seemed to be happening in the North during the 1830s, blacks and women conspired to be other than what white males wanted them to be, the regime would topple."[16]

Of the three novels, Lydia Maria Child's *Romance of the Republic* had the most conservative implications. The plot concerned two "octoroons" who until they were orphaned lived in ignorance of their racial background. Most of the novel focused on their growing awareness of the difficulties of maintaining sexual purity and respectability while slaves, even ostensibly protected ones. By the end of the novel both had married white northerners, and the problems of slavery were largely solved by the Civil War.

The complacency and underlying racial hierarchy that informed the novel seem unlike Child, whose letters sounded a far more rigorously critical tone concerning racial prejudice. What emerges is the sense that Child, for all her thirty years of work, including a history of religious beliefs that refused to exalt Christianity at the expense of other faiths, retained a sense that New England white culture was preferable to all others: for blacks to enter white society as equals, they must become white.

The issue of intermarriage revealed both Child's hopes for an end to racial prejudice and her own unquestioned sense of cultural and racial hierarchy. Her two heroines were unintellectual, named for flowers (Rosa and Floracita) and surrounded by them, and had to be saved by men. In the one case where a secondary white character (who believed he was black) married a dark-skinned woman, she was quickly taught how to act white. Child's central characters, two (appropriately) cultured African American sisters, drew this woman, Harriet, into their circle in order to teach her to become a lady lest she hold her husband back. Harriet learned how to sew and copy in an elegant hand, for "belonging to an imitative race, she readily adopted the language and manners of those around her." Falling into yet another racial stereotype, Child described her as failing to be truly beautiful because of "too crisp" hair: "Her features were not handsome, with the exception of her dark, liquid-looking eyes; and her black hair was too crisp to make a soft shading for her brown forehead. But there was a winning expression of gentleness in her countenance, and a pleasing degree of modest ease in her demeanor."[17] One of the white male characters, returning home from the war, asked to see the extent of the women's influence in effecting Harriet's transformation. After she left the room, he said paternally, "Really, this is encouraging," adding, "If half a century of just treatment and free schools can bring them all up to this level, our battles will not be in vain, and we shall deserve to rank among the best benefactors of the country; to say nothing of a corresponding improvement in the white population."[18] "They," it seems, needed to have their culture and their traditions trained out of "them," since "they" were an "imitative" race, and "they" soon adopted the appropriate styles of middle-class whites and light-skinned blacks. The irony, of course, is clear: his fellow civilizers were actually among "them."

Child used these fictional marriages to refute the argument that whites and blacks naturally repelled each other as love objects. With them she directly challenged northern white resistance to the effects of African American freedom on white society. And yet Child—and Dickinson and Davis—constructed African American characters as special, odd, exceptional. Lydia Maria Child's "octoroon" pair, Rosa and Floracita, talked in light, flowery phrases interspersed with words in French and Spanish. They were adept at music and art but unable to take up sterner courses of study. They were remarkably naive and had to be helped out of their difficulties by others (darker black servants, a white woman from the North, white men). Child's heroines lacked the backbone of Dickinson's and Davis's, and instead embodied the ideal of dependent, submissive, pious, true women. They were clearly victims—and clearly exceptions. And yet their final marriages to white northern men were constructed as a positive good, rather than the tragic mistakes these unions became for Dickinson and Davis.

Anna Dickinson's 1868 novel *What Answer?* followed Harriet Beecher Stowe's tradition of providing evidence to support her story, with the addition of a bibliographic note at the end of the text. However, Dickinson's tale of the tragic marriage of a wealthy white-skinned black Philadelphian and a Civil War officer ended in a significantly different way than most midcentury domestic novels. The lovers were brutally murdered in the New York City riot of 1863 by unrepentant Irish racists (the wealthy white lover's British father was equally racist). They died holding each other; his head, "from which streamed golden hair, dabbled and blood-stained," rested "upon her faithful heart."[19]

In *What Answer?* Dickinson focused on intermarriage as a way to make a larger point about both northern racism and social justice. Yet if her Francesca Ercildoune had the backbone that Rosa and Floracita lacked, she too was portrayed as an exception. She was so beautiful that when the Anglo-Saxon William Surrey saw her out of his window he chased after her down the street to meet her. Her courageous brother Robert earned the praise of even previously racist white men as he carried the flag in battle while suffering two wounds. (A member of the Massachusetts Fifty-fourth, Robert was an example of the careful research that Dickinson gave to her war plot.)

Their marriage, ironically, was most faithfully defended by Jim Given, a white working-class character who labored in Surrey's factory and served under him during the war. In her portrayal of this character (and Given's sweetheart, Sallie), Dickinson complicated stereotypical renderings of a racist, urban working class. By depicting loyal working people, Dickinson suggested both that New York City working men did fight for the Union and that racism was not confined to the lower classes, who were subject to reeducation through interaction with (good) black characters. Thus, Given strenuously argued with another soldier on the picket line when he heard of the marriage. Nature placed a barrier between blacks and whites, the soldier said. Not true, Given countered, pointing to mulattoes.

> 'T wan't the abolitionists; 't was the slaveholders and their friends that made a race of half-breeds all over the country; but, slavery or no slavery, they showed nature hadn't put any barriers between them,—and it seems to me an enough sight decenter and more respectable plan to marry fair and square than to sell your own children and the mother that bore them. Come now, ain't it?[20]

In any case, he continued, Ercildoune wasn't really African American, just as his friend wasn't Indian, despite his Indian ancestor. If the Anglo-Saxon race was the master race, he suggested, wasn't Francesca's seven-eighths white blood master over her one-eighth Negro blood? Slavery, then, continued; one blood had "mastery" over the others.

After the lovers died, the novel continued for another three chapters, which suggested that the real solution to racial prejudice was not so much intermarriage as politics. The darker brother of the near-white heroine was permanently maimed in the war, yet despite this mark of his patriotism, he was still taunted by whites when he went to the polls. Looking at his white companion and friend, he asked, "1860 or 1865?—is the war ended?" "No!" his friend told him, taking his arm. How it will end, he said, "is for the loyal people of America to decide." The suggestion was clear: African American men deserved the vote, and this was the answer "loyal people" should give.[21] That the vote would not include women, black or white, and that it alone would not solve a racial prejudice so deep that it pulled apart families and felled good people was never addressed. A lecturer and not a novelist, Dickinson wrote a complicated novel meant to speak to one issue.

Rebecca Harding Davis's novel was far more complex than either Child's or Dickinson's. Davis told the story of two families, white and black, whose lives were entwined. What emerged were three story lines, all entangled. In one, a northern white working-class woman named Rosslyn married Garrick Randolph, a southern aristocrat. Rosslyn—a virtuous and religious woman—had to remake Garrick, who in an act of selfishness and cruelty sold Hugh, a faithful slave and the head of the second family of the novel, in order to silence him about a family secret. In order for Garrick to retain Rosslyn's affections, however, he had to undo the evil he had caused, and he made a pilgrimage south both to reconnect the family he had broken and to tell the secret. The relatives of Hugh, in a parallel story, struggled to reunite during the war despite terrible odds (like Eliza in *Uncle Tom's Cabin*, a young mother escaped slavery and walked for miles carrying her son). In the end, Rosslyn offered a home and land for all three generations—Hugh, his son Nathan, Nathan's wife, Anny, and their small boy, Tom—as a kind of retributive act of justice.

It is the friendship between Rossyln and Anny that seems, ultimately, to suggest the way of social revolution. When the two women were together discussing their children, it was the African American character who gave the novel its title. She questioned whether her son would get the birthright of freedom and opportunity he deserved.

> I'm not ungrateful, God knows. . . . Freedom and clo's, and a home of our own, is much. But it's not all. Forgive me. A mudder kerries her chile's life on her heart when he's a man, jes as before he was born; you know dat. I wondered what was my boy's birthright in dis country. . . . Dar's four millions of his people like him; waitin' for de whites to say which dey shall be—men or beasts. Waitin' for the verdict, madam.[22]

Davis wondered whether the spiritual hunger of African Americans would be fulfilled with material comforts alone. Her political solution—to provide a home for those in one's backyard—was based on a pre-war hope for individual perfectionism. Yet if it shared the adage "forty acres and a mule," it still relied on black submission—being grateful—and white action—"waitin' for de whites"—rather than African American agency.

Davis plumbed questions of class, together with those of race, in *Waiting for the Verdict*, and she held out far more hope in the war's transformative power over particular characters. Her novel was meant to change the minds of her readers by soothing their fears. Rosslyn explained these racist fears to Anny:

> "I think," Ross hesitated, "one reason for the coolness with which the whites listen to your cry for help is, the dislike to the thoughts of intermarriage."
>
> "Dar's no danger of many marriages," said Anny, gravely and significantly; "an' as for mixin' de blood, it's been the fault ob de whites when dat eber was done. Dar'll be less of it when cullored women is larned to respect themselves. O, Missus! dat talk of marryin' is sech a fur-off shadder! But the ignorance an' disgrace ob my people is no shadder!"[23]

If Davis brought black characters forward in her text and gave them dignity in a way many of her contemporaries did not, she still mixed her messages, either out of her own racial prejudice or out of some sense of what her audience would bear. If "it's been the fault ob de whites when dat eber was done," still, Anny added, "Dar'll be less of it when cullored women is larned to respect themselves," a contradiction. And Anny still did not call her friend "Rosslyn," but rather "Missus"; if the women lived side by side, if the implication was a kind of social equality, the depiction contained another message.

Intermarriage as a "fur-off shadder" was depicted earlier in Davis's story, with John Broderip (Hugh's son "Sap" renamed in order to pass) and the resolutely Anglo-Saxon Margaret Conrad, and represented the third strand of her plot. Davis allowed Broderip to "pass" not only in the novel's story but to the reader as well, until a climactic scene. Broderip, a surgeon of considerable skill, was drawn as an eccentric, moody yet endearing man, and the profound, critical, and highly intelligent Conrad fell in love with him.[24] When Broderip's darker brother Nathan escaped from slavery after risking his life to save Rosslyn's grandfather and came to find his brother "Sap" (John Broderip), the reader became privy to Broderip's deep ambivalence: should he continue to pass in order to win the love of Margaret and thus forsake both his family and his race?

Here Davis used the sympathy toward Broderip she created in her readers to stress the nature of his struggle with prejudice. If Broderip recognized Nathan, he lost everything he owned—his social standing, his lover. If he did not, he rejected family, honesty, honor. He was not a pure hero; he struggled with this question. In attending to his brother's wounded arm, Broderip pondered briefly the possibility of letting his scalpel slip and "accidentally" kill Nathan, thus avoiding having to admit his race to the world. Margaret was waiting outside, and Broderip had finally determined to ask her to marry him before Nathan arrived. Margaret's subsequent refusal to consider marriage with the man she loved because of his race becomes all the more disappointing. Significantly, her blind father was supportive of the match, even after Broderip revealed himself: here, it was the white woman who sustained racial prejudice.

By the end of the novel, after Broderip's heroic death (also with the Massachusetts Fifty-fourth), Margaret conquered much of her destructive prejudice, and despite the love of an honorable white man, waited only to join Broderip in heaven. Davis suggested here, through love between black and white, that Margaret's refusal to acknowledge her love was the "unnatural" act. By leading white readers to identify with and feel affection for Broderip, she worked more subtly to force them to confront their prejudices.

Like the antislavery authors of the late war, Child, Dickinson, and Davis depicted active and honorable black men in order to counter white fears about the future of freedpeople. These men earned their rights as citizens, and thus justified the war's outcome. Rather than creating frightening portrayals of justified anger, these novelists created men who resisted the forces that oppressed them in "honorable" ways—going to fight for the Union forces or aiding Union soldiers behind the lines. Their anger was channeled in socially acceptable ways. The writers stressed that these black men fought like white men, earned their freedom, and subscribed to familiar conventional values (men go off to battle, and women, when they can, stay home). These men seemed conscious counterimages to the growing white southern myth of the black rapist.

Yet it is significant that when all three novelists treated the theme of intermarriage, it was rarely black men who figured in that portrait; in most instances white men fell in love with black women. To return to Morrison, black characters were used as means to express ideas about whiteness. In most interracial relationships, white authors reinscribed a kind of social order: white men still had their choice of women, black and white, and black women were allowed to be "true women" by virtue of white desire to continue marking them as malleable, domestic, and passive. But if black men aspired to white women, these acceptable markers of social status shifted: black men were thus sexualized, active, and assumed to be able to protect white women. To soften such a dramatic shift, then, Davis made Broderip effeminate and Margaret masculine, and yet their final images reverse this: he became a brave soldier, she a chastened teacher and mother-figure. Yet their union could not thrive except in heaven.

For each of these writers their novels were something of a turning point in their careers. Lydia Maria Child put a great deal of hope and energy into a post-war novel meant to address persistent racial prejudice, North and South. The antislavery struggle had been her life's work, and although she sympathized with suffragists, Child felt she had "fought through a somewhat long campaign" against slavery, and had "little energy for enlisting in a new war."[25] *A Romance of the Republic* was to be her last major effort for freedpeople, even though she continued to write editorials for political newspapers. Exceptional by any standard of persistence and passion for social justice and activism, Child was representative of a generation of white antislavery reformers whose energies waned after the war's end, even as they continued to hope for and work for the millennium they increasingly felt would never quite come.[26]

Anna Dickinson, nineteen when the war began, became an influential lecturer during the war years, considering both national issues and narrower partisan ones, peaking in her 1864 lecture to Congress. Her style was passionate and inspirational, and it drew huge crowds of both men and women. Throughout the war, newspapers debated the propriety of her place behind the lectern even as they announced her next engagement. The journalist Fanny Fern celebrated Dickinson's work and its larger meaning for women in the *New York Ledger* on more than one occasion, suggesting at the same time that it had been bitterly criticized.[27] *What Answer?* was considerably less successful than Dickinson's lectures, given its largely negative critical reception and the fact that it was published in only a single edition.

"Peace must have put a sudden barrier in the way of many women's new found careers," Rebecca Harding Davis wrote to Annie Fields in 1866, musing that she had not seen any work from Louisa May Alcott recently.[28] Certainly her own career demonstrated a similar brief decline as she recovered from the birth of her second son and negotiated with James Fields of the *Atlantic* over what seemed a breach of contract.[29] In this period of personal turmoil, however, Davis began work on what was her most ambitious novel to date, one that questioned the progress of Reconstruction, touched upon the thorny issue of miscegenation, presented an unvarnished working-class heroine, and eschewed the "painted" histories of the Civil War for one less sentimental and more complex.[30] "The subject [of Civil War and Reconstruction] is one which has interested me more than any other and I wish to put whatever strength I have into that book and make it, if possible, different from anything which I have yet been able to do," Davis wrote of *Waiting for the Verdict* to the editors of the new magazine the *Galaxy*.[31]

For each of these writers, then, fiction became a political vehicle through which to move the nation forward. Lydia Maria Child hoped to put the form of novel writing to as good use as had her friend Harriet Beecher Stowe. In her typically astute fashion she summed up the political intent of her novel to an African American correspondent and antislavery compatriot, the Philadelphian Robert Purvis, who had written to praise it. "In these days of novel-reading, I thought a Romance would take more hold of the public mind than the most elaborate arguments; and having fought against Slavery, till the monster is *legally* dead, I was desirous to do what I could to undermine Prejudice," she wrote.[32] Her letter to Purvis sounded an optimistic note, but it preceded and followed others with a far more cynical and despairing tone. Yet the novel's unenthusiastic reception by white critics was daunting for Child, sapping her energy for writing another. "[T]he apathy of my friends" for her novel "took all the life out of me, and has made me feel as if I never wanted to put pen to paper again," she confessed. In all, the work brought "a great deal of disappointment and humiliation" and little income, largely, her biographer surmises, because of the subject of intermarriage.[33]

Anna Dickinson's novel involving an interracial couple was also rejected by the white press, if acclaimed by an important few. Harriet Beecher Stowe praised the work, and wrote to Dickinson as a member of an older generation passing the torch of social reform to a new one. "I lay on my sofa all alone on Saturday night and read your book all through, and when I got through I rose up mentally and fell on your neck and said, Well done, good and faithful Anna—daughter of my soul," Stowe exclaimed. "Your poor old grandma in this work rejoices to find it in your brave young hands." Later she added, "Don't mind what anybody says about it as a work of art. Works of art be hanged! You had a braver thought than that." The response of the *Nation* was more typical. "Whatever a novel should have, it lacks," the reviewer asserted, "and whatever a novel should not be it is. A thoroughly bad novel."[34]

The white response to Rebecca Harding Davis's novel was equally mixed, although seemingly treated with a bit more respect by her reviewers. Her biographer argues that her labors were not wholly in vain, for "*Waiting for the Verdict* is one of her best novels and, as an epic of the Civil War and its aftermath, an important literary document of the period."[35] Contemporaries disagreed. Harriet Beecher Stowe wrote in favor; the *Nation* reviewer, in this case (as perhaps with Dickinson), Henry James, Jr., dismissed it with contempt. James found her use of working-class and black characters curious and her clear-eyed realism distasteful. Yet James's distaste gave Stowe the determination to write to Davis and thus began their acquaintance. "*The Nation* has no sympathy with any deep and high moral movement—no pity for human infirmity," she wrote. "It is a sneering respectable middle aged skeptic who says I take my two glasses and cigar daily." As with Dickinson, Stowe saw in Davis's work her political viewpoint, and deeply sympathized with it. Rather than creating elite literature, Stowe rightly saw Davis as engaged in reform through her writing, and she told her frankly never to expect sympathy from the *Nation* for "any attempt to help the weak & sinning & suffering."[36]

In courageously attempting to work against the grain of popular white opinion—an opinion that would subsequently harden—Child, Dickinson, and Davis perhaps not surprisingly failed to see the contradictory stances embedded in their own work. Child's cultural elitism, Dickinson's unrealistic faith in partisan politics, Davis's depiction of white benevolence and black gratitude—each represented a clinging to some sort of racial order, even while conceding much more than their audience might allow. The use of characters that "passed" into white society heightened that contradictory quality. Meant to suggest the common humanity that bound the races together—the elusiveness of difference—passing also valorized white beauty at the expense of black. It suggested, ultimately, that the work that intermarriage could do in Reconstruction was erasure. Tangled with the bodies of their black and white characters, then, were Child, Dickinson, and Davis's racial beliefs, drawn out and sustained by their imagining of African Americans.

NOTES

The author would like to thank the members of Sarah Lawrence College's Faculty Writing Workshop: Bob Desjarlais, Musifiky Mwanasali, Chikwenye Ogunyemi, Mary Porter, Sandra Robinson, and Komozi Woodard for their help and encouragement; my students Christina Saraceno and Michelle Erfer for generously reading and commenting on my work; editor Martha Hodes for insightful and precise editing; and Jim Cullen for everything.

1. Toni Morrison, *Playing in the Dark: Whiteness and the Literary Imagination* (New York: Vintage Books, 1993), 17.

2. Frances Ellen Watkins Harper wrote the only nineteenth-century Civil War novel published by an African American woman, *Iola Leroy* (1892), which was produced in and reacted to an entirely different—and even grimmer—political and social context.

3. Martha Hodes, "Wartime Dialogues on Illicit Sex," in *Divided Houses: Gender and the Civil War*, ed. Catherine Clinton and Nina Silber (New York: Oxford University Press, 1992), 242.

4. Morrison, *Playing in the Dark*, 28.

5. George M. Fredrickson, *The Black Image in the White Mind: The Debate on Afro-American Character and Destiny, 1817–1914* (New York: Harper Torchbooks, 1971), 171–74; James M. McPherson, *Ordeal by Fire: The Civil War and Reconstruction*, 2d ed. (New York: McGraw-Hill, 1992), 449.

6. Hodes, "Wartime Dialogues," 230.

7. [David Goodman Croly and George Wakeman], *Miscegenation: The Theory of the Blending of the Races, Applied to the American White Man and Negro* (New York: H. Dexter, Hamilton, [1863]), 65.

8. Fredrickson, *Black Image*, 172.

9. Eric Foner, *A Short History of Reconstruction, 1863–1877* (New York: Harper and Row, 1990), 147.

10. A. O. W. [A. O. Wheeler], *Eyewitness; or, Life Scenes in the Old North State, Depicting the Trials and Sufferings of the Unionists during the Rebellion* (Boston: B. B. Russell, 1865), 104.

11. Bella Spencer, *Tried and True; or Love and Loyalty: A Story of the Great Rebellion* (Springfield, Mass.: W. J. Holland, 1867), 282–83.

12. Louisa May Alcott, *On Picket Duty, and Other Tales* (Boston: James Redpath, 1864), 30.

13. Mary J. Holmes, *Rose Mather: A Tale* (New York: G. W. Carleton, 1868), 302–03.

14. Fredrickson, *Black Image*, 171.

15. Hodes, "Wartime Dialogues," 240.

16. Deborah Gray White, *Ar'n't I a Woman? Female Slaves in the Plantation South* (New York: W. W. Norton, 1985), 58.

17. Lydia Maria Child, *A Romance of the Republic* (Boston: Ticknor and Fields, 1867) 433.

18. Ibid., 434.

19. Anna Dickinson, *What Answer?* (Boston: Ticknor and Fields, 1868) 267.

20. Ibid., 195.

21. Ibid., 297.

22. Rebecca Harding Davis, *Waiting for the Verdict* (New York: Sheldon, 1868), 354–55.

23. Ibid., 354.

24. Here, as elsewhere, I refer to the characters as the authors do. Davis, particularly, always referred to her female characters by their first names, and her male characters by their last. The exceptions to this rule were Davis's black characters, who always went by first names unless they "passed" like Broderip. Nathan, for example, was always just Nathan.

25. Milton Meltzer and Patricia G. Holland, eds., *Lydia Maria Child: Selected Letters, 1817–1880* (Amherst: University of Massachusetts Press, 1982), 467.

26. Some antislavery reformers, like William Lloyd Garrison, felt that emancipation marked the end of the struggle. Others argued that Reconstruction was crucial in securing the war's promise, and continued their work. In any case there was a palpable sense of an era's end, and many writers in the antislavery community celebrated this with memoirs and collective biographies of the war's greatest soldiers.

27. Fanny Fern, for example, wrote two columns on women lecturers, most likely in response to the fervor Dickinson was causing. See Fanny Fern, "Women Lecturers," *New York Ledger* 19, no. 12 (May 23, 1863): 8; idem, "Woman on the Platform," *New York Ledger* 20, no. 2 (March 12, 1864): 8.

28. Quoted in Sharon M. Harris, *Rebecca Harding Davis and American Realism* (Philadelphia: University of Pennsylvania Press, 1991), 128.

29. For an analysis of their dispute, see ibid., 126–27.

30. Davis called many of the post–Civil War histories of the conflict "painted," see her autobiography, *Bits of Gossip* (Boston: Houghton Mifflin, 1904), 138.

31. In the end, however, Davis was not able to write the exact book she desired, as the editors of *Galaxy* became impatient with the length of *Waiting for the Verdict*. See also Jane Atteridge Rose, *Rebecca Harding Davis* (New York: Twayne, 1993).

32. Meltzer and Holland, *Lydia Maria Child*, 482–83.

33. Quoted in Deborah Pickman Clifford, *Crusader for Freedom: A Life of Lydia Maria Child* (Boston: Beacon Press, 1992), 281.

34. Quoted in Giraud Chester, *Embattled Maiden: The Life of Anna Dickinson* (New York: G. P. Putnam's Sons, 1951), 106.

35. Harris, *Rebecca Harding Davis*, 132.

36. Quoted in ibid., 137. On this same page Harris refers to Henry James, Jr., as the correspondent of Gail Hamilton when it was his father, Henry James, Sr. Her point about James, Sr.'s gender politics, however, is equally applicable to his son.

Chapter Thirteen

"Not That Sort of Women"
Race, Gender, and Sexual Violence during the Memphis Riot of 1866

Hannah Rosen

On June 1, 1866, in the Gayoso House hotel in downtown Memphis, Tennessee, a former slave named Frances Thompson spoke before a congressional committee investigating the riot that had occurred in that city one month earlier. Thompson informed the committee that seven white rioters broke into the house that she shared with another former slave, Lucy Smith. Thompson recounted her efforts to resist the demand for "some woman to sleep with" made by these men. "I said that we were not that sort of women, and they must go." Yet her refusal to have sex proved unacceptable to the intruders. Thompson described to the committee how both she and Lucy Smith were raped.[1]

Frances Thompson was among five freedwomen who recounted being subject to sexual violence during what became known as the Memphis Riot.[2] This attack on recently emancipated slaves commenced in the late afternoon of May 1, 1866, and persisted for three days. It took place primarily in the neighborhood of South Memphis, where the freed community of the city was concentrated. The assailants were mostly city police and other lower-middle-class white men, many of whom lived in the same neighborhood with the riot's victims.[3] The riot represented the culmination of increasing tensions between a growing freed community and white Memphians, above all between African American Union soldiers stationed at the federal army's Fort Pickering in South Memphis and the city's white police force. During the riot at least forty-eight African Americans were killed and between seventy and eighty were wounded.[4] Rioters set fire to ninety-one houses and cabins, four churches, and twelve schools, robbed one hundred freedpeople, and destroyed approximately $127,000 worth of property.[5] Rioters also raped at least five freedwomen.[6] Freedwomen's testimony about these sexual attacks reveals the ways that gender and sexuality became key sites for waging battles over race after emancipation, as rioters struggled to reclaim privileges as white men, and black women struggled to be free.

For African American women to testify in a legal forum about sexual violence was itself a dramatic political act in the battles of Reconstruction. Prior to emancipation, one demonstration of white male dominance of southern society had been the virtual legal impunity with which white men sexually abused African American women. Antebellum laws in the southern states generally excluded female slaves from the legal definition of those who could be raped, and did not recognize their abuse as a crime.[7] This exclusion was justified in the law by the absence of legal sanction for marriage between slaves and thus the lack of patriarchal rights that could be violated by coerced sexual intercourse outside marriage.[8] This logic dovetailed with widespread imagery representing black women as sexually indiscriminate, consenting to and even pursuing sexual activity with white men, and thus lacking feminine "virtue."[9] It was this quality of "virtue," along with patriarchal rights, that was imagined to be injured in the crime of rape. Thus freedwomen declaring publicly that the violence they had suffered constituted rape, that they were the "sort of women" who could be violated and who deserved legal protection from sexual abuse, represented a radical reversal of both antebellum legal notions and white constructions of black womanhood.

Historians of the Memphis Riot have often pointed to the occurrence of rape to highlight the atrocities and terror that freedpeople suffered over those tumultuous three days.[10] Yet the significance of the specifically sexual form of this violence has not been explored.[11] Sexual violence in the midst of a race riot reveals more than simply extreme brutality. The instances where rioters raped freedwomen reflect the nexus of race, gender, and sexuality within the overall power struggles gripping the post–Civil War South. I will explore this nexus by examining the ways in which post-emancipation struggles over racial relations and identities in Memphis were fought out on the ground of gender and sexuality.[12] Gendered constructions of race emerged in the everyday political conflicts in Memphis in the time leading up to the riot, particularly in contests over the meaning and significance of race transpiring in various arenas of the city's public space. Strikingly similar gendered constructions of race were invoked by rioters when they sexually assaulted black women. This discursive convergence sheds light on the historical meaning of the sexual violence that occurred during the Memphis Riot. As white southern men struggled to reclaim the power and privilege that white manhood had signified in a slave society, they turned to black women's gender and sexuality as a site for reenacting and reproducing racial inequality and subordination. This politicization of gender and sexuality shaped the perilous terrain upon which freedwomen struggled to render freedom meaningful for themselves and their communities.

Complicating a reading of the sexual violence that occurred during the Memphis Riot is the riot's unexpected postscript. Ten years after testifying before the congressional committee about having been raped, Frances Thompson was arrested for being a man dressed in women's clothing. Thompson's transvestism raises important questions about the form and meaning of the sexual violence that occurred during the Memphis Riot, the full implications of which cannot be explored within the confines of this article.[13] I will, though, discuss the propagandistic use made of Frances Thompson's cross-dressing by conservatives in their efforts to discredit all the women who testified that they had been raped and in general to oppose Reconstruction in Memphis. The newspaper coverage that followed Thompson's exposure as a cross-dresser reveals again the central role that gender and sexuality played in contests over race in the post-emancipation South.

*

Prior to the Civil War, Memphis's black population had been relatively small: 3,882 people, or 17 percent of the city's inhabitants in 1860. Ninety-five percent of this group were slaves whose public conduct was strictly regulated by city ordinances.[14] Although laws prohibiting slaves' travel through the city without a pass, hiring out their own time, residing away from their owner, or congregating for social or political activities were never fully enforced, city police were empowered to interfere with and constrain the actions of African Americans in the city at all times.[15] Moving about the streets of antebellum Memphis, white and black people observed and experienced racial difference in their everyday lives in part through inequalities in the power to utilize the city's public spaces.

The Civil War permanently altered these racial dynamics in Memphis, where public space was transformed by the resultant change in status and dramatic increase in number of African Americans. The occupation of the city by the Union army in June 1862 brought thousands of African American migrants to the city. Regiments of black troops were stationed at Fort Pickering, located at the southern edge of the city.[16] Following these troops came their family members and other fugitive slaves seeking the protection of the Union forces. By 1865 these migrants together with African Americans already living in Memphis constituted 40 percent of the city's total population, or just under eleven thousand people, an increase to the antebellum black population of 275 percent.[17] The significance of this migration for social relations and public activity in Memphis lay not only in its size. In the past, African Americans had been brought to Memphis by force, to be sold in slave markets and to labor in white-owned businesses and homes; after the Union occupation, they entered Memphis as a "city of refuge," a space in which they would be free.[18]

During the Civil War and Reconstruction years, refugees from slavery forcefully entered public spaces in Memphis—the streets, markets, saloons, and other visible spaces of labor and leisure; public sites of legal authority, such as police stations, the Freedmen's Bureau, and courtrooms; civil institutions such as schools, churches, and benevolent societies; and realms of public discourse such as speaking events, parades, and the Republican press—in anticipation of new rights and freedoms.[19] The political status of these new public actors in Memphis was uncertain. They were no longer slaves, yet they had no formal political rights. Until the Civil Rights Act was passed in April 1866, African Americans were denied even the most nominal legal recognition as citizens.[20] Nonetheless, freedpeople made use of the limited power available to them to claim many aspects of citizenship. They began their lives in Memphis with expectations for freedom that included the ability to enjoy free movement, social life, and family in an urban community of their own choosing, to be compensated for their labor, and to have these rights protected by law in the form of the Freedmen's Bureau and the police power of the occupying Union army. They expected to be citizens of the city. The reaction of many whites illustrates how powerfully African Americans' public activities in Memphis disrupted whites' previous norms of racial difference rooted in slavery and adumbrated a new nonracialized citizenship. A conflict over public space ensued, as white Memphians sought therein to redraw racial boundaries, delegitimate black people's public presence, and oppose the new power differentials embodied in what they observed around them.

African American women were central actors in the process of laying claim to a new urban citizenship in ways that dramatically transformed public life in Memphis. Women constituted a sizable proportion of those former slaves who made their way to Memphis both during and after the Civil War.[21] White Memphians quickly experienced the reality of emancipation and the changed meaning of race through these women's movement through public space and their use of public authority in the form of the Freedmen's Bureau Court and the police protection of the Union army.[22] Some whites responded by attempting to cast black women's new public presence in a disparaging light.[23] Both white police officers and newspaper editors from the city's conservative press, in their conduct toward and representation of freedwomen in the city's public spaces, enlisted gendered constructions of race, specifically a discourse representing all black women as "unvirtuous" or "bad," and often as prostitutes, to depict black women as unworthy of citizenship.[24] These representations were echoed in the words and actions of rioters who raped black women during the Memphis Riot, suggesting how this violence reflected the confluence of race, gender, and sexuality that structured everyday political conflict in the post-emancipation South.

It was specifically to realize their freedom that African American women migrated to Memphis after the end of the Civil War. Freedwomen fled conditions reminiscent of slavery in the countryside—physical violence, work with no pay, forced separation from family—and came to the city to seek assistance and protection made available by the power of African American Union soldiers and the federal authority of the Bureau.[25] Some came specifically to join, and seek support from, male family members in the Union army.[26] Many women enlisted the aid of soldiers in order to claim possessions, children, and compensation owed them for past labor from abusive employers on the plantations from which they had fled.[27] Thus black women came to Memphis to assert new rights of citizenship—motherhood, property ownership, rights as free laborers—that were guaranteed by state power in the hands of armed black men.

In the city, black women secured other profound, if less tangible, liberties previously reserved for whites. For instance, they fashioned social lives and urban communities that revolved around the grocery-saloons and street corners of South Memphis. In these spaces, freedwomen gathered, danced, and drank with black soldiers, often into the morning hours.[28] Freedwomen also helped build independent black churches in Memphis, such as the Methodist Episcopal Church and various Baptist churches.[29] Former slave women were the backbone of these institutions. They sponsored picnics, fairs, and other public events to raise funds for new church buildings and organized mutual aid societies for the support of church members.[30]

Black women further undermined whites' prior monopoly on public life, and exclusive claims to citizenship, by utilizing the Freedmen's Bureau Court to secure their rights. Freedwomen pressed charges against whites to claim unpaid wages and to protest violent assaults.[31] The impact of legal action at times spilled over from the court into the streets, when whites resisted verdicts and clashed with soldiers making arrests, collecting fines, and confiscating property.[32] Even when cases did not lead to convictions, freedwomen's actions brought charges of white abuse against blacks, and evidence of the new rights and powers of former slaves, prominently into the public eye.[33] Overall, black women's actions after emancipation left indelible marks on Memphis's landscape, changing the city materially and redrawing the racial boundaries around citizenship and freedom symbolized by activities in its public space.

When the presence of freedwomen in Memphis was noted by the conservative press of the city, it was never in reference to victims or opponents of exploitation and abuse. Nor were black women represented as "respectable" church women or "ladies" participating in the civic life of their community. Rather, the rhetoric of newspaper editors and the focus of most reporting suggest efforts to denigrate the public activities of freedwomen in the city by insinuating connections between their presence and an alleged increase in crime and disorder, specifically of "lewd women" or prostitutes, supposedly threatening white Memphians in the city's streets and alleys.[34] Onto the real activities of women in public, in all their variety and unpredictability, was imposed a bifurcated concept of womanhood. As was common in nineteenth-century depictions of urban life in the United States in general, women were represented as inhabiting one of two opposing realities: the delicate, chaste, and virtuous "lady" or the vicious, rude "public woman," or prostitute, the former being the woman whom society must protect, the latter by whom society was threatened.[35] In post-emancipation Memphis, this binary imagery operated along racial lines. Representations of African American women in the conservative press implied their essential relation to the latter category. Depictions were not consistent; the negative characteristics associated with freedwomen were presented at times as menacing and at other times as comical. Together these images appearing throughout commentary on local affairs elaborated the racial power and privilege of whites in Memphis by gendering black women as "bad" women, and often as sexually "dangerous." Newspaper reports labeled black women's presence in the city's public spaces illegitimate and thus challenged their claim to identities as citizens.

For instance, Neely Hunt, a freedwoman, with the assistance of a squad of black Union soldiers, forcibly entered and searched the house of a white family where she believed her child was being held. For this action she was punished not only by the Freedmen's Bureau, which had her arrested, but also by negative characterizations of her in the *Memphis Daily Appeal*. This paper described Hunt as a "negress," who was "enraged," "raving," "threatening," and "us[ing] very abusive and insulting language," in contrast to "the ladies of the house," whose delicate constitutions were allegedly unsettled by this confrontation. The *Appeal* labeled Hunt a liar and suggested that her deceitful and disreputable character was generalizable to all freedwomen.[36] By identifying assertive black women acting in the public of Memphis with terms such as "negress," the press avoided describing them as "women," distancing them from images of respectable womanhood and associating them with disrepute. Newspaper editors often combined this strategy with other insulting labels, such as when the *Appeal* reported the charge of theft of a pistol made against "an ugly looking negress."[37] Another news item repeatedly used "wench," a term meaning "young female" that also had implications of servitude and sexual wantonness, to describe a black woman charged with drunk and disorderly conduct.[38] Another reported the arrest of five "female roughs of African descent" for disorderly conduct and speculated about the origins of black women's alleged misbehavior: "Freedom seems to have an intoxicating effect on colored females."[39] And the report of a robbery by three black men who supposedly stole a number of hoopskirts editorialized that the skirts were intended as gifts for "some of their dark paramours."[40] Through an assertion of both theft and illicit sexual relations, this report questioned the legitimacy and honor of freedwomen appearing in public in fine clothes.

Images associating black women in Memphis with disrepute and sexual promiscuity circulating in the city's conservative press were reinforced by police action against freedwomen, such as frequent arrests for "lewdness," "vagrancy," and "drunk and disorderly conduct." These arrests, often under false charges and amounting to harassment of black women by police, were then highlighted and exaggerated in newspaper accounts. Some reports implied that a specific incident indicated an epidemic of black prostitution, such as the following: "Six more negro prostitutes were yesterday arrested and brought before the officers of the Freedmen's Bureau, who sent them out to work on different farms in the country."[41] Others used arrests of black women for charges that may or may not have been associated with prostitution simply to assert that those arrested were prostitutes: "Three colored prostitutes were arrested, charged with vagrancy, and were hired out to contractors to go into the country and work," and "Viney Springer, Mary Jane Springer, and Sarah Parker, colored nymphs *du pave*, were arrested for disorderly conduct and incarcerated."[42] These reports make clear the high price freedwomen paid for these arrests, being either imprisoned in the city jail or forced to leave the city and labor on plantations. Although some black women may have been engaged in prostitution or criminal activity, there is evidence that many of these arrests were fraudulent and abusive. A "prominent citizen" reported one such case to the city's Republican newspaper. He had witnessed a white man "kicking a colored woman, who was calling loudly for a 'watch.' Soon a well known officer came running to the rescue, and without asking her for explanations, seized the woman, threw her down, slapped her in the face, dragged her on the ground and finally took her to the station-house and locked her up for disorderly conduct."[43] Other officers, similarly "well known," made a practice of harassing, insulting, and abusing freedwomen. These same officers would be recognized by freedpeople among the Memphis rioters.

One such policeman harassed Amanda Olden, a freedwoman living in South Memphis, with a false charge related to prostitution just days before the riot. Olden was not intimidated by this officer's particular extortion scheme and took her charges to the Freedmen's Bureau. There she recounted that "one Carol or Carrol, a city policeman, came to my house, and compelled me to give him twenty-two dollars at the same time falsely charging me with keeping a house of ill-fame." Carroll told Olden that this money would cover her fine for the charged offense.

However, when she went to the Recorder of the Police Court the next morning, "ready for an investigation of these false charges . . . this policeman did not appear, nor had he made any report of this action in my case to his proper officer."[44] Through false charges against African American women, city police not only contributed to the representation of freedwomen as "unvirtuous" in Memphis's public, they also attempted to use those representations to exploit individual women in ways that could be hidden from the public under the cloak of that same imagery.

The actions of Officers Welch and Sweatt, the latter of whom was also later identified among the rioters, offer further evidence of police using arrests to denigrate the activities of black women in the public spaces of Memphis rather than to punish real offenders.[45] According to a complaint filed with the Freedmen's Bureau by three black men who had attended a "negro ball," the two police officers intruded into the party and "proceeded to arrest some two or three of the ladies" in attendance. These policemen thus imputed a disreputable character to black women enjoying the privileges of "ladies" in public. Men from the party intervened and forcibly prevented the police from taking the women away. Welch and Sweatt retreated, but soon returned with several armed white firemen, who "cocking their weapons demanded a surrender" and "behaved in a very rough and boisterous manner, crying 'shoot the damned niggers.' "[46] That the men and women attending this ball were apparently members of the city's small African American elite seems to have prevented violent incident and allowed the African Americans involved to reassert respectable gender identities as ladies and gentlemen. They received an apology from the firemen, who explained that Welch and Sweatt had "misrepresented the affair," and from the mayor, responding to the provost marshal's complaint that such incidents were "becoming so frequent as to demand attention."[47]

Although most freedwomen did not receive apologies for police misconduct, they did pursue retribution through the courts of the Bureau to defend, and to construct, their rights to enjoy free movement, work, and leisure in the public spaces of Memphis. Certain whites, such as police and newspaper editors, contested those rights as they sought to reassert their control over public space, and over the meanings of race signified by a free black presence in public. The conduct of the Memphis Riot suggests that those three days of violence represented a similar attempt to eviscerate the meaning of African American citizenship and freedom.

It was not surprising that the Memphis Riot began as a clash between black Union soldiers and city police. Since the initial occupation of the city by the federal army, the police force and black troops had been the front lines in an ongoing battle between civilian and military authorities over governance of the city. When their paths crossed in the streets, they often taunted each other, using "very hard language . . . daring each other to fight," concluding at times in serious physical violence.[48] Many observers believed that the police were often the instigators, insulting, shoving, and threatening black men in uniform, and often arresting soldiers under unspecified or fabricated charges and beating soldiers in custody.[49] In the days before the riot, two cases of severe beatings by police led to calls from soldiers for vengeance if such practices were repeated.[50] Given escalating tensions, it would seem not to be a coincidence that several policemen waited until May 1, 1866, the day after most black soldiers had been mustered out of service and forced to turn in their army weapons, to provoke the conflict that began the riot.[51] On this day, the police knew that they now had the upper hand.

Nor was it surprising that the riot began as a clash over freedpeople's activities in public space, in this case a visible and festive gathering of African Americans on a main thoroughfare of South Memphis. On Tuesday afternoon a group of police officers interrupted an impromptu street party on South Street, in which freed-women, children, and soldiers were "laughing and shouting and making considerable noise."[52] "Some of them [were] hallooing 'Hurrah for Abe Lincoln,' and so on," recalled Tony Cherry, a discharged soldier and participant. "A policeman came along and told them to hush, and not to be hallooing in that way, and another policeman said, 'Your old father, Abe Lincoln, is dead and damned.' "[53] The police sought to silence this defiant tribute to emancipation by arresting some of the soldiers. As the police began to retreat with two soldiers in custody, other soldiers fired pistols in the air or perhaps at the police.[54] On hearing these gunshots and seeing one police officer fall (he apparently slipped and shot himself in the leg with his own gun), the police turned and began shooting indiscriminately into the crowd.[55] Although those few soldiers with weapons fired back, they were overpowered; few white men were injured in the fighting.[56]

Rumors of an uprising of African American soldiers spread through the city, bringing other white men from South Memphis and surrounding areas into the riot. After several hours of what was termed by one observer "an indiscriminate slaughter" of freedpeople by police and white civilians,[57] Union army officers from Fort Pickering arrived to quell the disturbance, forcibly dispersing the crowds and marshaling most black soldiers into the fort. Here soldiers were held over the next few days against their will and despite the efforts of many to leave, rendered powerless to protect their families from the violence that ensued.[58] Around ten o'clock that night, a large crowd of police and white civilians spread throughout South Memphis. Under the pretense of searching for weapons to stop the alleged uprising, rioters intruded into freedpeople's houses and brutalized residents, beginning the looting, assault, murder, arson, and rape that would continue until Thursday evening.

The Memphis Riot was one episode in an ongoing battle over race, citizenship, and rule in the post-emancipation public of Memphis. The riot was a protest among certain lower-middle-class white men against the power freedpeople exercised in public space, and the nonracialized citizenship this power signified. In that sense it was a violent continuation of the efforts of many white Memphians to reclaim privileges for whiteness and to counter new identities and powers for African Americans that challenged white dominance. The freedwoman Hannah Robinson remembered hearing one rioter declare, "It is white man's day now."[59] Throughout the process of reclaiming the "day" for white men, rioters would employ constructions of gender as weapons in efforts to resignify racial difference and inequality.

Rioters acted out meanings of white manhood and insisted on "unworthy" gender identities for African Americans through violence against black women. This can be seen, first, in how certain black women became targets of rioters' violence. Ann Freeman recounted that the party of white men who broke into her home declared that "they were going to kill all the women they caught with soldiers or with soldiers' things."[60] Directing violence against black women because of their relationship to black Union soldiers was made particularly evident in the case of rape. Four of the survivors of rape during the riot were connected to soldiers in ways that figured prominently in the women's recollections of what they had suffered.

Lucy Tibbs was about twenty-one when she came to Memphis from Arkansas soon after the Civil War broke out. She came to the city with her husband, who by 1866 had found work on a steamboat and was away from home much of the time. She lived in South Memphis with her two small children, and was nearly five months pregnant with her third. On May 1 she was outside when the fighting began. She screamed in outrage as "they broke and run in every direction, boys and men, with pistols, firing at every black man and boy they could see." After observing the shooting death of two soldiers and seeing rioters "going from house to house," she understood that all black soldiers were in danger. She thus encouraged her older brother, Bob Taylor, who had been a member of the Fifty-ninth U.S. Colored Infantry stationed in Memphis, to flee. He ran, but was found dead the next morning near the bayou in back of Tibbs's house. Later that night, a crowd of men broke into her home and stole three hundred dollars. One of these men raped her while "the other men were plundering the house." She later speculated that her home had not been randomly chosen for attack: "I think they were folks who knew all about me, who knew that my brother had not long been out of the army and had money."[61]

Harriet Armour came to Memphis as a slave before the Civil War began. Later she married an African American Union soldier, who was in Fort Pickering during the riots. She lived around the corner from Lucy Tibbs, and she too watched the initial clashes and killings of Tuesday evening. Early Wednesday morning, two men carrying revolvers came to her room.[62] Molly Hayes, a white woman who lived in the adjacent house, overheard these men confronting Armour: "There were two men who came there and asked her where her husband was. She said he was in the fort. They said, 'Is he a soldier?' She said, 'Yes.' . . . The last word I heard him say was, 'Shut the door.'"[63] Armour testified that after they barred her door shut, they both raped her: "[One of the men] had to do with me twice and the other man once, which was the same as three."[64]

Sixteen-year-old Lucy Smith had been raised in slavery in Memphis. Frances Thompson, who was somewhat older, had been a slave in Maryland. At the time of the riot, Smith and Thompson shared a South Memphis home, supporting themselves by taking in sewing, washing, and ironing. Late Tuesday night, seven white men, two of whom were police officers, came to their house and stayed for close to four hours, during which time they robbed Smith and Thompson of many of their possessions and all of their money and food. The rioters threatened to shoot them and set fire to their house. Smith testified that one of these men also choked and then raped her, and that another attempted to rape her. Thompson recounted being beaten by one of the rioters and raped by four. Thompson and Smith also both remembered that the rioters demanded to know why there were red, white, and blue quilts in the house. Thompson later testified, "When we told them we made them for the soldiers they swore at us, and said the soldiers would never have them on their beds, and they took them away with the rest of the things." They also noticed pictures of Union army officers in the room, and as Smith later remembered, "they said they would not have hurt us so bad if it had not been for these pictures."[65]

By raping women associated with black Union soldiers, white men reclaimed their power over representatives of black masculinity, of freedpeople's power and protection in public space, and of federal and military power in Memphis.[66] Rioters demonstrated that black soldiers, now decommissioned, disarmed, and absent, were unable to protect freedwomen from violence. Yet it was not only as women related to soldiers that freedwomen were attacked. Equally important to understanding the sexual form of violence during the Memphis Riot is an analysis of the ways in which rioters enacted particular relations with freedwomen themselves. Through acts of rape, rioters physically overpowered black women. In the process, they also used language and acted in a manner that identified these women as "unvirtuous" or "lewd," in ways reminiscent of the representations of African American woman-hood circulating in the conservative press in Memphis prior to the riot. That discourse had offered all white men identities as superior and worthy of power through the denigration of African American women. However, these identities were not necessarily realized in the lives of many white men, whose power was frequently challenged in their everyday interactions with freedpeople. The language rioters used and the scenes they staged around rape reveal how white men attempted to realize that discourse in a tangible way in their own conflicts with freedwomen, and thus attempted to experience for themselves a white manhood that rested on the dishonor of black women.

During the riot, men initiated rape with casual requests for sex and other patterns of behavior that invoked imagery of black women as sexually available to white men. Recall the dialogue described to the congressional investigating committee by Frances Thompson. The seven men who broke into her and Lucy Smith's home in the middle of the night treated their residence as if it were a brothel and demanded that Thompson and Smith act out roles as servants and prostitutes. The men first insisted that they be served supper. Thompson remembered the rioters saying, "they must have some eggs, and ham, and biscuit. I made them some biscuit and strong coffee, and they all sat down and ate."[67] Lucy Smith similarly testified, "They told us to get up and get some supper for them. We got up, and made a fire and got them supper."[68] When finished eating, the intruders announced that "they wanted some woman to sleep with." Thompson recounted that it was when she insisted that she and Smith "were not that sort of women" that the men physically attacked her, asserting that Thompson's claim "didn't make a damned bit of difference."[69] Smith also refused the rioters' demand and the identity they imputed to her. She testified that when "they tried to take advantage of me . . . I told them that I did not do such things, and would not." In response, one of the men "choked me by the neck" and "said he would make me."[70] It was then that these men "drew their pistols and said they would shoot us and fire the house if we did not let them have their way with us."[71]

On the night of May 2, the words and actions of the rioters who assaulted two freedwomen living in adjoining rooms similarly identified these women as "unvirtuous" and sexually available to white men. Elvira Walker described to the congressional committee the following scene: "I was entirely alone; some men came and knocked at my door. They came in, and said they were hunting for weapons. . . . One of them put his hands into my bosom. I tried to stop him, and he knocked down my hands with his pistol, and did it again." This man forcibly touched Walker's body in ways that implied that in his eyes she was not a respectable woman. He then further insulted her. "He . . . said there was $5 forfeit money, and that I must come to the station-house with him." This demand for cash was strikingly similar to Officer Carroll's attempted extortion from Amanda Olden a few days earlier. It suggests that this man was a member of the police force and that he intended to identify Walker with illicit sexual activity.[72]

This theme was continued when the same group of rioters entered the room next door, where Peter and Rebecca Ann Bloom were sleeping. The rioters forcibly removed Peter Bloom from the room, demanding that he obtain the five dollars needed to avoid Walker's arrest.[73] One rioter remained behind. As Rebecca Ann Bloom recounted, "He wanted to know if I had anything to do with white men. I said no. He held a knife in his hand, and said that he would kill me if I did not let him do as he wanted to. I refused. He said, 'By God, you must,' and then he got into bed with me, and violated my person, him still holding the knife."[74] The man who raped Bloom, like those who attacked Thompson and Smith, first solicited her for sex and then employed force when his request was rejected. "Having to do with," a phrase also repeated by Harriet Armour and Frances Thompson in their testimony, referred to sexual intercourse. By asking Bloom whether she had intercourse with white men, this rioter forced her to engage in a dialogue that positioned her as an "unvirtuous" woman. In drawing attention to his whiteness, his words identified her blackness. He simultaneously refused to recognize her identity as a wife, though her husband had just been dragged from the bed in which she still lay. Instead of the respect in theory attributed to married women, the rioter invoked myths of black women seeking sexual relations with white men. When Bloom refused to participate in his fantasy, he forced her under threat of deadly violence.

These sexual assaults, then, were not spontaneous acts of sexual aggression released from "normal" restraints in the pandemonium of a riot. They were, rather, elaborate and, in a sense, "scripted" enactments of fantasies of racial superiority and domination that operated around gendered constructions of racial difference and concluded in rape. In lengthy encounters, assailants employed words and violence to position freedwomen in previously constructed "scripts" that placed them in the role of being "that sort of women" who could not or would not refuse the sexual advances of a white man. In these "scripts," white men demanded sex, black women acquiesced, and white men experienced their dominance and superiority through black women's subservience.[75] In this sense, these men attempted to make meaningful to themselves and their audience of other rioters the racist discourses on black women's gender and sexuality circulating in Memphis at the time. Through rape, rioters acted out identities as superior and powerful white men by refusing any recognition of "virtue" and rights to "protection" for African American women. In freedwomen's testimony, there is evidence of their refusal of rioters' "scripts," of their articulation of a gendered identity different from the one white men were attempting to impose. When freedwomen rejected the scenes set up by the attackers, the men imposed them with threats or physical force. With their violence, rapists struggled to stage events that "proved"—in a type of causally backward logic—freedwomen's lack of "virtue" by forcing their participation in "dishonorable" acts.

There was a contradiction inherent in these scenes: black women were not in fact consenting, and thus proving their own lack of "virtue"; rather, white men were engaging in extremely "unvirtuous" conduct, forcing women to participate in sexual acts against their will. Rioters contained this contradiction through conduct that erased black women's agency and cloaked white men's force. Through their demands for food followed by sex, or inquiries about freedwomen's sexual partners, rioters invoked antebellum racist imagery of black women as sexually promiscuous and always available for sexual relations with white men, simulating an air of everyday, casual, and consensual sex that belied the terror and violent coercion involved in their actions.[76] Other aspects of assailants' language further denied that they acted against the will of the women they attacked. Harriet Armour remembered as particularly painful that one of the men who raped her questioned her reason for crying. This man tried to force her to perform fellatio. "Then [he] tried to make me suck him. I cried. He asked what I was crying about, and tried to make me suck it."[77] This rioter's question dismissed the possibility that his actions could cause Armour pain, that she had will or "virtue" that could be violated by such an act. In Lucy Tibbs's case, one of the rioters objected to the conduct of the man who raped her on the grounds of Tibbs's pregnancy. Yet this man's words only further denied the possibility of committing rape against a black woman. Tibbs remembered his saying, "Let that woman alone—that she was not in any situation to be doing that." Although this suggests the perhaps common contradiction between white imagery of black women as sexually "loose" and the reality of white men's interactions with specific black women, his words also implied that had she not been pregnant, she would have been available for sex. As well, his choice of the active voice to describe Tibbs in this moment—"*she* was not in any situation to be *doing* that"—shows a refusal to recognize her lack of consent to sexual intercourse.[78]

That some of the rapes that occurred during the riot took place within a discourse simulating scenes of promiscuous black women willingly engaging in sex with white men did not prevent the attackers from inflicting extreme violence. For instance, Lucy Smith described the violence she suffered:

> One of them . . . choked me by the neck. My neck was swollen up next day, and for two weeks I could not talk to anyone. After the first man had connexion with me, another got hold of me and tried to violate me, but I was so bad he did not. He gave

me a lick with his fist and said I was so damned near dead he would not have anything to do with me. . . . I bled from what the first man had done to me. I was injured right smart. . . . They were in the house a good while after they hurt me, but I lay down on the bed, for I thought they had killed me. . . . I was in bed two weeks after.[79]

The women surviving rape during the Memphis Riot experienced prolonged physical pain and terror. Each rape was ultimately carried out through violence or threats of death that belied the casual scenes that the perpetrators sought to stage.

Placing this reading of sexual violence in the context of the conflicts over public space leading up to the Memphis Riot reveals another layer to the political meaning of rioters' rape "scripts." By dishonoring black women, white men contested the power these women exercised in the public spaces of Memphis. To identify black women as "loose" women or prostitutes was to imply that they were the "sort of women" who endangered the community if free and unrestrained in public. Through their violence, rioters attacked the citizenship freedwomen had exercised in public by attacking their identities as respectable women. This is not to suggest that this was a consciously designed strategy. The relationship between gendered constructions of racial difference and contests over citizenship was deeply embedded in the discourse circulating among white opponents of Reconstruction in Memphis. The white men who raped freedwomen during the Memphis Riot enacted a fantasy of social subordination that drew on an existing gendered discourse of racial inequality, one that had already politicized gender identities in contests over race, power, and citizenship in post-emancipation Memphis.

The Memphis Riot came to an end on Thursday, May 3, when federal troops spread throughout the city.[80] By that time the murderous events of the past three days had drawn the attention of Republicans in Washington, D.C. On May 14, 1866 Congressman Thaddeus Stevens proposed that a congressional committee travel to Memphis to investigate "the recent bloody riots in that city."[81] Radical Republicans looked to this investigation to provide support for their position that stronger federal intervention into the affairs of southern states was necessary to protect the rights and lives of freedpeople.[82]

Stevens's plan was adopted. A House select committee composed of three congressmen—Elihu B. Washburne of Illinois and John M. Broomall of Pennsylvania, both Republicans, and George S. Shanklin of Kentucky, a Democrat—arrived in Memphis on May 22. Sixty-six African Americans came before the committee to testify.[83] For the freedwomen who testified about sexual violence, the committee created a forum of unprecedented state power in which they articulated new public identities as citizens and contested racist constructions of black womanhood. For African American women, to testify that they had been raped was a radical act in the context of southern state law and tradition. A legal and cultural refusal to recognize black women's accounts of rape had served a dominant white discourse of racial inequality that bolstered slavery in the antebellum South. Post-emancipation imagery of freedwomen as "unvirtuous" drew on this pre-war exclusion of black women from the category of "women" who could be raped. The rioters who raped freedwomen had expressed these same meanings to contest the power that freedwomen were exercising as citizens of Memphis. When black women represented their experience of coerced sexual intercourse with white men as a violation of their will, they asserted a claim to the status of "woman" and "citizen." In the process, they would also counter conventional discourses on womanhood, rape, and "virtue."

Freedwomen employed language of violation and harm in order to identify assailants' actions as rape rather than illicit sex. Rebecca Ann Bloom maintained before the Freedmen's Bureau that the man who got into bed with her had "violated my person, by having connexion with me."[84] Before the congressional committee, Frances Thompson affirmed that she and Lucy Smith were "violated" by the men who intruded into their home.[85] Lucy Smith chose similar words to describe rioters' actions: they "tried to violate me . . . [and] they hurt me."[86] When asked by Congressman Washburne whether the men who plundered her home had hurt her, Lucy Tibbs responded, "they done a very bad act," and then confirmed Washburne's assumption that by this she meant they had "ravish[ed]" her.[87] Stressing that rioters' actions were imposed against their will, freedwomen refuted the contrary image that rioters had sought to create in the scenes surrounding the actual rapes, namely that the women's experiences were evidence of their own lack of "virtue." Freedwomen further confuted rioters' "scripts" that had denied black women's agency and suffering by recounting the terror they had experienced. Harriet Armour recalled how she cried but was too terrified to call for help.[88] Lucy Smith believed that there were seven men who came into her house on the night she was raped, but "I was so scared I could not be certain."[89] Lucy Tibbs recounted that "I was so scared I could not tell whether they were policemen or not," and described begging her assailants to leave her and her children in peace.[90] This testimony resisted the meanings that assailants had attempted to stage during the riot.

Some of the women who testified had to defend their honor in the face of hostile and insinuating questioning from members of the committee. After answering in the affirmative the chair's question, "Did they ravish you?," Lucy Tibbs still had to contend with the committee's apparent doubt. Washburne continued, "Did they violate your person against your consent?" to which Tibbs again insisted, "Yes Sir. I had just to give up to them. They said they would kill me if I did not." Washburne again suggested the possibility that the attack was somehow a product of Tibbs's own conduct: "Were you dressed or undressed when these men came to you?" She stated that she was dressed. "Did you make any resistance?" the chair then asked. Tibbs responded by sharing with him the information she had used to calculate her safest course of action: "No sir; the house was full of men. I thought they would kill me; they had stabbed a woman near by the night before." Tibbs had heard others report that this same woman had also been raped.[91] Believing that resistance might result in her own death, Tibbs surrendered to the assailant physically. But here, in the committee's hearing room, she resisted both the rioters' and the congressmen's implications that what had happened in some way reflected shame on herself.

Harriet Armour also came under challenging questioning from the committee.

She recounted that she had seen no possibility of escape from the men who attacked her, because one of them had barred her door shut. Washburne then asked, "What did he do with the window?" Armour explained that she could not have fled through the window because two slats were nailed across it. "And you made no resistance?" he asked. "No," she answered, repeating that "they had barred the door. I could not get out, and I could not help myself." Yet the suspicions persisted. "Did I understand you that you did not try to prevent them from doing these things to you?" Congressman Broomall asked in disbelief. "Could not the people outside have come to help you?" Armour tried again to explain her strategy to survive the attack:

> No, sir; I did not know what to do. I was there alone, was weak and sick, and thought I would rather let them do it than to be hurt or punished. . . . I should have been afraid to call [for help]. . . . I thought I had just better give up freely; I did not like to do it, but I thought it would be best for me.[92]

Both Armour and Tibbs had yielded to the rioters' demands in order to prevent further violence, and in the case of Tibbs perhaps to protect her children. Yet their judgment of what to do in such a situation did not conform to the patriarchal framework within which the elite white men on the committee appear to have imagined rape. The congressmen's questioning implied that even under the threat of potentially deadly force, anything but ceaseless resistance to sexual violation raised questions about a woman's "virtue."

Washburne and Broomall may have sincerely doubted Armour's and Tibbs's testimony that they had been raped, because it seemed to these men that the women had not resisted enough. It is also possible that the Republican congressmen's questions were intended to elicit further details so as to shape the testimony in ways that would best represent the women's claims before a national audience.[93] In either case, when faced with the congressmen's apparent uneasiness about their testimony, Armour and Tibbs defended their actions. They made clear that, as much as they had suffered from the rapes they experienced, they did not share the assumption that rape would damage them in ways worth risking death to prevent. Nor did they accept the implications of the rioters, that their submission implied that they were "unvirtuous" women. Armour and Tibbs both firmly maintained that despite physical acquiescence, the sex occurred against their will. To defend their honor and represent the events as violation, the women struggled to make intelligible to the committee a perspective that grew out of their experiences during the riot, and perhaps out of their experiences as slaves. They had recently lived under a system of slavery in which many women faced the grim choice between submitting to forced sexual intercourse with white men or risking other physical harm to themselves and their loved ones. These women's testimony then implicitly shifted the parameters of patriarchal discourse on rape. By inserting black women's experiences and perspectives into a public discussion of sexual violence, they presented alternative constructions of honorable womanhood. To them, in this context, honor depended more on surviving and protesting injustice than on privileging and protecting a patriarchal notion of women's sexual "virtue."

Perhaps Armour's persistence in demonstrating, under a barrage of hostile insinuation, that her strategy for survival in no way reflected her own dishonor stemmed from the fact that she had already suffered from another's sense that she was less valuable as a woman because of the attack. Cynthia Townsend, a freedwoman and neighbor of Armour, testified that "When [Armour's husband] came out of the fort, and found what had been done, he said he would not have anything to do with her any more." It was clear that Armour suffered enormously from her husband's rejection. "She has sometimes been a little deranged since then," Townsend explained.[94] In her testimony, Armour moved from subject to subject quickly, suggesting that recounting these stories may have been particularly difficult for her, more so than was apparent in other freedwomen's accounts. She segued directly from her description of one man's efforts to force her to perform fellatio to, "I have not got well since my husband went away," thereby connecting the attack with her husband's departure.[95] Armour was the only woman testifying to indicate any ostracism by a member of her community as a result of rape. It is possible that Armour's experience was exacerbated by the fact that she was attacked in daylight and thus suspected that others were aware of what was being done to her ("It was an open shanty, and they could see right in").[96] Any observers were doubtless powerless to stop the attack. Nonetheless, the fact that she understood her ordeal to have been a public spectacle of sorts may have been a factor in her devastation; it may have alienated her from her community, and contributed to her husband's rejection.

What is striking, then, is Armour's courage in coming forward to tell this story again in another public setting, that of the congressional hearing. There was no practical need for Armour or other women to discuss sexual assaults in order to condemn the rioters. When Armour, Lucy Tibbs, Lucy Smith, and Frances Thompson testified before this committee, they all reported other crimes and forms of violence in addition to rape, namely, theft and battery. That they chose to recount having suffered sexual violence, despite the risks involved, suggests that this testimony served ends important to them: the public condemnation of and protest against these acts as violation, and the implicit affirmation of their identities as free women with the will to choose or refuse sexual relations and with the right to be protected by law. Given the conservative pre-riot discourse that imputed dishonorable gendered identities to African American women, and the police harassment of black women in Memphis, both of which were efforts to limit black women's power as citizens, these women's portrayals of themselves as survivors of rape appear as important political acts in African Americans' overall struggle to realize their freedom.[97]

The courage the freedwomen showed in making their suffering public garnered the support of the Republican majority of the congressional investigating committee. Despite the committee's hostile questioning, freedwomen's narratives served Republican interests in representing southern white men as "unreconstructed" and thus unprepared for self-rule. The committee majority's final report highlighted the rape of African American women to depict the white rioters as uncivilized and dishonorable men. Eleven thousand copies of the report were printed, and it was excerpted in newspapers across the country.[98] Describing the riot as "an organized and bloody massacre of the colored people of Memphis," this report stated,

> The crowning acts of atrocity and diabolism committed during these terrible nights were the ravishing of five different colored women by these fiends in human shape. . . . It is a singular fact, that while this mob was breathing vengeance against the negroes and shooting them down like dogs, yet when they found unprotected colored women they at once "conquered their prejudices," and proceeded to violate them under circumstances of the most licentious brutality.[99]

To bolster this representation of the rape of black women as the ultimate atrocity of the riot, the authors assured readers that Lucy Smith was "a girl of modest demeanor and highly respectable in appearance." They similarly noted that both Harriet Armour and Lucy Tibbs were married—and thus legitimate—women, and that Tibbs had two young children and was pregnant with her third.[100] Through these images of female respectability, the committee's majority sought to preempt accusations of the "dishonorable" character of the women and therefore doubts about their legitimacy as victims of sexual assault.

Images of feminine "virtue" rooted in modesty and submission within marriage had not been part of freedwomen's self-representations when they defended their honor before the congressional committee. In general, freedwomen in Memphis had not shown their definitions of womanhood to depend upon notions of "proper" and submissive femininity. Rather, through their own forceful presence in the city's public spaces, they had claimed identities as women who were active, outspoken, and assertive with regard to their own and their community's rights to live freely as citizens. Yet once freedwomen's narratives concerning rape entered into the arena of national politics, their words were forced into a discourse of womanhood and "virtue" not of their own making.[101] When the congressional committee portrayed freedwomen as victims of rape, they drew on the same opposition between "virtuous" and "unvirtuous" women that conservatives had manipulated prior to the riot in order to reject black women's claims to full citizenship. And, as we will see, this same binary discourse of "virtue" and "vice" would ultimately help conservatives to discredit black women's testimony on sexual violence.

After the congressional investigation, no rioters were arrested or charged with any crimes. Freedwomen's testimony, though, did help to promote several state and national measures that extended greater protection and political power to African Americans during Reconstruction.[102] And the conservative press in Memphis was silenced by the overwhelming evidence of violence enacted by white men presented by the committee's report. The conservative *Appeal*, earlier full of condemnations of black women as deceitful, disreputable, and depraved, offered no immediate critique of the freedwomen who testified that they had been raped.[103]

Ten years later, however, conservatives in Memphis stumbled upon their chance to vindicate white men from charges made in the congressional report and to dismiss the freedwomen's testimony about rape. In 1876 Frances Thompson was arrested for "being a man and wearing women's clothing."[104] Because Thompson's testimony had occupied a prominent place in the congressional committee's report, her arrest for cross-dressing—an incident that might have received only passing mention in the local press under different circumstances—filled the city columns for days. Her arrest also served the interests of conservatives-turned-Democrats in the 1876 presidential election campaign, which would ultimately mark the end of Reconstruction at the national level and return control over the southern states to white southerners. In this context, the conservative newspapers contended that Thompson's transvestism proved her testimony about rape to have been a lie.[105]

Thompson herself paid dearly for her supposed crime. After her arrest she was placed on the city's chain gang, where she was forced to wear men's clothing and suffered constant ridicule and harassment from crowds drawn to the scene by mocking press reports.[106] Soon after she completed her prison term of one hundred days, she was discovered alone and seriously ill in a cabin in North Memphis. Members of the freed community moved her to the city hospital, where she died on November 1, 1876.[107] The coroner's report of her death recorded that she was indeed anatomically male.[108]

What can we make of the fact that Thompson—with a woman's identity and a male body—testified that she had been raped during the Memphis Riot? Was she drawing on Lucy Smith's experience of rape to perform for the committee that she too was a woman?[109] Or had she in fact been raped? Had the rioters been shocked when they discovered the "truth" about her anatomy? Or were they aware in advance that she was anatomically male? Did they attack her because of that fact? Was the materiality of bodies irrelevant, superseded by a "script" of black women's sexual wantonness that mattered most? Unfortunately, there are no sources with which to answer these questions.

There is evidence, though, of a campaign of vilification against Thompson in the conservative press, one designed to refute charges of white southern brutality against African Americans and to oppose Reconstruction policies supported by Republicans. Similar to the disparagement of black women prior to the riot, newspaper editors described Thompson as "lewd," associated her with prostitution, and portrayed her as the epitome of "unvirtuous" gender and sexuality. They attributed to her "vile habits and corruptions," decried her "utter depravity," and accused her of using her "guise" as a woman to facilitate her supposed role as "wholesale debaucher" and "procuress" of numberless young women for prostitution.[110] The papers then used these charges to condemn their Republican opponents, reminding their readers that the Republican Party—now referred to as "the Frances Thompson Radical party"—had relied upon Thompson's "perjurous evidence" to condemn white men in Memphis for violence and brutality.[111]

The conservative press alleged that Thompson's testimony was merely a charade to discredit the words of all the black women who testified that they had been raped during the Memphis Riot. The *Memphis Daily Appeal* criticized Lucy Smith for her corroboration of Thompson's testimony, which was now dismissed as "utterly at variance with the truth." The paper also mocked Smith's claim that she herself had been "violated." The *Appeal* insinuated that Smith did not possess the "virtue" supposedly needed for a woman to protest rape, because—and this they asserted with no evidence—Smith had been "occupying the same bed with Thompson" prior to the riot.[112] The other women who testified were not mentioned by name, but the conservative papers implied that Thompson's transvestism exposed the entire congressional report as "vile slander," manufactured by Republicans solely for political gain. With no new information other than Thomson's cross-dressing, one conservative paper denounced the report: "The evidence of the vilest wretches was received and worded in smooth phrase and published to the world to prove that the Southern people were a set of barbarians and assassins."[113] The *Appeal* went further, enlisting Thompson's image to vindicate all white southerners from accusations of racist violence during Reconstruction:

> Whenever you hear Radicals talking of the persecutions of the black race in the south, ask them what they think of Frances Thompson and the outrages committed on her by the Irish of this city during the celebrated riots. These pretended outrages in the south are all of a piece with this Frances Thompson affair. It is out of such material as this that all their blood-and-thunder stories are manufactured.[114]

Critics of Reconstruction attempted to supplant recognition of African American women's experiences of sexual violence—now mere "pretended outrages"—with the image of Thompson's allegedly "deviant" and "depraved," cross-dressing male body. Ultimately, Thompson's transvestism was such a powerful tool for conservatives not because Thompson was represented as bizarre or unique, but rather because her image resonated so strongly with the pre-existing conservative discourse attributing dishonorable gender and sexuality to all African American women. It was but a small step from images of women who were "unvirtuous" to images of women who were so "unvirtuous" that they were not women at all.

This postscript to the history of freedwomen's testimony about rape during the Memphis Riot suggests once again how discourses of gender and sexuality played a central role in political struggles over race, following emancipation. Former slaves in Memphis had insisted on their right as citizens to move, live, and work freely in the public spaces of the city. Their actions adumbrated a new social order that challenged the racial hierarchy of the antebellum South. White city police and conservative newspaper editors responded to African Americans' entry into public life in Memphis, among other ways, by condemning black women in public as prostitutes and by depicting them overall as the "sort of women" who were not "virtuous" and therefore not worthy of citizenship. In this way, gender served as a metaphor for racial difference. When emancipation threatened to efface racial inequality, racial difference was reinscribed through the misrepresentation and stigmatization of black women's gender and sexuality.

I have tried to show how the rapes that occurred during the Memphis Riot formed part of this same discourse of racialized gender. Rioters who raped freedwomen sought to reassert racial inequality and the privileges of white manhood by enacting antebellum fantasies of black women's sexual subservience and lack of feminine "virtue." During the rapes themselves, and indeed simply by testifying to having been raped, African American women rejected these scripts. Political contests over African American citizenship and freedom following emancipation were partly fought out through battles over gendered constructions of racial difference, battles that included elaborate and contested scenes of horrific sexual domination and violence. Analyzing incidents of rape, particularly in moments of violent political conflict, as part of discourse allows us to begin to understand the multiple historical forces and ideas that have given shape to this form of violence.

NOTES

I thank Cindy Aron, Leora Auslander, Cynthia Blair, Antoinette Burton, George Chauncey, Laura Edwards, Thomas Holt, Pradeep Jeganathan, Linda Kerber, Ann Lane, and particpants in the University of Chicago's Gender and Society Workshop for their invaluable comments on versions of this essay, and especially Martha Hodes and Richard Turits for their extensive input. The research was generously funded by the American Historical Association and the Carter G. Woodson Institute for Afro-American and African Studies at the University of Virginia.

1. Testimony of Frances Thompson, in *Memphis Riots and Massacres*, 39th Cong., 1st sess., 1865–66, H. Rept. 101, 196–97 (hereafter *MR&M*).

2. See also testimony of Lucy Smith, 197; Harriet Armour, 176–77; Lucy Tibbs, 160–62; and affidavit of Rebecca Ann Bloom, Affidavits Taken before Commission Organized by the Freedmen's Bureau (hereafter FBC), 351, all in *MR&M*. For further information on the rapes reported by these women, see testimony of Cynthia Townsend, 162–63; Henry Porter, 167–68; Molly Hayes, 186; Elvira Walker, 193–94; and affidavit of Peter Bloom, FBC, 348, all in *MR&M*.

3. Altina Waller, "Community, Class and Race in the Memphis Riot of 1866," *Journal of Social History* 18 (1984): 235. Police and firemen made up the largest occupational grouping of those men identified by Waller as being among the rioters, 34 percent. The next largest category consisted of small business owners, most of whom ran grocery-saloons.

4. Actual casualties may have been much higher. See Report, *MR&M*, 34. See also Richard Banks, "In the Heat of the Night," *Memphis* 15 (1990): 71–72.

5. Report, *MR&M*, 34–36.

6. For the possibility that other women were raped or molested, see testimony of Lucy Tibbs, 161; and Mary Grady, 187, *MR&M*.

7. Hannah Rosen, "Rape as Reality, Rape as Fiction: Rape Law and Ideology in the Antebellum South" (unpublished paper, 1989); Jennifer Wriggins, "Rape, Racism, and the Law," *Harvard Women's Law Journal* 6 (1983): 103–41; Melton A. McLaurin, *Celia, a Slave* (Athens: University of Georgia Press, 1991), esp. chap. 6; Deborah Gray White, *Ar'n't I a Woman? Female Slaves in the Plantation South* (New York: W. W. Norton, 1985), 152–53, 164–65; and Evelyn Brooks Higginbotham, "African-American Women's History and the Metalanguage of Race," *Signs* 17 (1992): 262–64. See also Diane Miller Sommerville, "The Rape Myth in the Old South Reconsidered," *Journal of Southern History* 61 (1995): 493 n. 34.

8. For instance, lawyers John D. Freeman in *George (a slave) v. State*, 37 Mississippi 317 (October 1859), and B. F. Trimble in *Alfred (a slave) v. State of Mississippi*, 37 Mississippi 307–08 (October 1859).

9. See, for instance, Winthrop D. Jordan, *White over Black: American Attitudes toward the Negro, 1550–1812* (Baltimore: Penguin Books, 1969), 151; and White, *Ar'n't I a Woman?* 27–61.

10. For reference to rape during the riot, see Kevin R. Hardwick, " 'Your Old Father Abe Lincoln Is Dead and Damned': Black Soldiers and the Memphis Race Riot of 1866," *Journal of Social History* 27 (1993): 109, 122; Waller, "Community, Class and Race," 234–35; Bobby L. Lovett, "Memphis Riots: White Reaction to Blacks in Memphis, May 1865–July 1866," *Tennessee Historical Quarterly* 37 (1979): 23; James Gilbert Ryan, "The Memphis Riot of 1866: Terror in a Black Community during Reconstruction," *Journal of Negro History* 62 (1977): 243; Jack D. L. Holmes, "Underlying Causes of the Memphis Race Riot of 1866," *Tennessee Historical Quarterly* 17 (1958): 195, 220; Eric Foner, *Reconstruction: America's Unfinished Revolution, 1863–1877* (New York: Harper and Row, 1988), 262; William S. McFeely, *Yankee Stepfather: General O. O. Howard and the Freedmen* (1968; reprint, New York: W. W. Norton, 1994), 277; Herbert G. Gutman, *The Black Family in Slavery and Freedom, 1750–1925* (New York: Vintage Books, 1976), 25–28; and George C. Rable, *But There Was No Peace: The Role of Violence in the Politics of Reconstruction* (Athens: University of Georgia Press, 1984), 39.

11. One exception is Beverly Greene Bond, " 'Till Fair Aurora Rise': African-American Women in Memphis, Tennessee, 1840–1915" (Ph.D. diss., University of Memphis, 1996), 96–103.

12. See also Catherine Clinton, "Reconstructing Freedwomen," in *Divided Houses: Gender and the Civil War*, ed. Catherine Clinton and Nina Silber (New York: Oxford University Press, 1992), 306–19; idem, " 'Bloody Terrain': Freedwomen, Sexuality, and Violence during Reconstruction," *Georgia Historical Quarterly* 76 (1992): 310–32; Laura F. Edwards, "Sexual Violence, Gender, Reconstruction, and the Extension of Patriarchy in Granville County, North Carolina," *North Carolina Historical Review* 48 (1991): 237–60; idem, "The Disappearance of Susan Daniel and Henderson Cooper: Gender and Narratives of Political Conflict in the Reconstruction-Era U.S. South," in this volume; and idem, *Gendered Strife and Confusion: The Political Culture of Reconstruction* (Urbana: University of Illinois Press, 1997).

13. I am currently working on a separate essay on Frances Thompson. For the purposes of this article, I approach Thompson as a witness to and survivor of sexual assault aimed at African American women. I continue to refer to Thompson as a woman and with feminine pronouns because that is how she identified and chose to live her life.

14. Gerald M. Capers, Jr., *The Biography of a River Town: Memphis: Its Heroic Age* (Chapel Hill: University of North Carolina Press, 1939), 107–08, 110, 164; Kathleen C. Berkeley, " 'Like a Plague of Locust': Immigration and Social Change in Memphis, Tennessee, 1850–1880" (Ph.D. diss., University of California, Los Angeles, 1980), 47–48; and Armstead Robinson, "In the Aftermath of Slavery: Blacks and Reconstruction in Memphis, 1865–1870" (thesis presented to the Scholars of the House Faculty of Yale College, May 1969), 26–28. I owe special thanks to the late Professor Robinson for sharing this invaluable study of Reconstruction-era Memphis with me. To compare Memphis's African American population statistics with those of other southern cities for 1860, see Richard Wade, *Slavery in the Cities: The South, 1820–1860* (New York: Oxford University Press, 1964), 326–27.

15. *A Digest of the Ordinances of the City Council of Memphis, from the Year 1826 to 1857: Together with All Acts of the Legislature of Tennessee Which Relate Exclusively to the City of Memphis*, prepared by L. J. DuPree, 1857, 122–26; *Digest of the Charters and Ordinances of the City of Memphis, from 1826 to 1860, Inclusive, Together with the Acts of the Legislature Relating to the City, and Municipal Corporations Generally*, 1860, 85–91,

269, 276, 361–67. Kathleen Berkeley presents evidence of more rigid control of slaves in Memphis than Richard Wade found in his study of slavery in other southern cities. See Wade, *Slavery in the Cities*; and Berkeley, " 'Like a Plague of Locust,' " 47–48.

16. Seven black regiments were stationed at Fort Pickering. Arthur L. Webb, "Black Soldiers of Civil War Left Impact on City," *Commercial Appeal*, February (n.d.), 1989. I am indebted to Mr. Webb for a copy of this article.

17. See Robinson, "In the Aftermath of Slavery," 67–68; Berkeley, " 'Like a Plague of Locust,' " 168–69; *Census of the City of Memphis, Taken by Joe Bledsoe, under a Resolution of the City Council, Passed April 25, 1865*, Memphis and Shelby County Room, History Department, Memphis Main Public Library; and Ernest Walter Hooper, "Memphis, Tennessee: Federal Occupation and Reconstruction, 1862–1870" (Ph.D. diss., University of North Carolina, Chapel Hill, 1957), 132.

18. Quotation from Louis Hughes, *Thirty Years a Slave: From Bondage to Freedom. The Institution of Slavery as Seen on the Plantation and in the Home of the Planter. Autobiography of Louis Hughes* (1897; reprint, New York: Negro Universities Press, 1969), 187.

19. For feminist conceptualizations of public space and the "public sphere," see, for example, Elsa Barkley Brown, "Negotiating and Transforming the Public Sphere: African American Political Life in the Transition from Slavery to Freedom," *Public Culture* 7 (1994): 107–46; Nancy Fraser, "What's Critical about Critical Theory? The Case of Habermas and Gender," in *Unruly Practices: Power, Discourse and Gender in Contemporary Social Theory* (Minneapolis: University of Minnesota Press, 1989), 113–43; Evelyn Brooks Higginbotham, *Righteous Discontent: The Women's Movement in the Black Baptist Church, 1880–1920* (Cambridge: Harvard University Press, 1993); and Mary Ryan, *Women in Public: Between Banners and Ballots, 1825–1880* (Baltimore: Johns Hopkins University Press, 1990). The Republican *Memphis Daily Post* reported the community activities of freedpeople in Memphis. There was no newspaper published by African Americans in Memphis at this time.

20. Foner, *Reconstruction*, 250–51.

21. In 1863 women made up over 40 percent of the 535 adults in a contraband camp in Memphis. John Eaton to Prof. Henry Cowles, March 13, 1863, document H8832, microfilm reel 193, American Missionary Association Archives (hereafter AMA). In 1865 a Freedmen's Bureau census found that women were 59 percent of the 16,509 freedpeople in Memphis and its surrounding areas; see Bond, " 'Till Fair Aurora Rise,' " 77.

22. The Freedmen's Bureau established the Freedmen's Court in 1865 to address the exclusion of African Americans from the right to testify in state courts. The Freedmen's Court held legal jurisdiction in all cases involving black people and was presided over by the provost marshal of freedmen. See Board of Mayor and Aldermen, Minutes, book 11, July 21, 1865, 695–97, Memphis and Shelby County Archives, Cossitt Library, Memphis (hereafter MSCA).

23. White Memphians responded with equal hostility to the presence of African American men in the city, particularly black Union soldiers. For the disparaging portrayals of black men in Memphis by white conservatives, see Hannah Rosen, "The Gender of Reconstruction: Rape, Race, and Citizenship in the Postemancipation South" (Ph.D. diss., University of Chicago, forthcoming), chap. 1.

24. By "conservative press," I am referring to the partisan newspapers that opposed Reconstruction policies of the Republican Party after the war. For this essay, I use evidence drawn primarily from the *Memphis Daily Appeal*. This paper, despite its somewhat more moderate rhetorical style relative to other conservative papers in Memphis at the time, still frequently misrepresented black women in its local reporting.

25. See, for instance, statements of Lizzie Howard, July 26, 1865; Ellen Clifton, Aug. 3,

1865; Eliza Jane House, Aug. 15, 1865; Mary Rodgers, Aug. 15, 1865; and Jane Coleman, Aug. 26, 1865; entry 3545, Records of the Bureau of Refugees, Freedmen, and Abandoned Lands, RG 105, National Archives and Records Administration, Washington, D.C. (hereafter BRFAL).

26. See statements of Mary Ann, July 31, 1865; Lizzie Howard, July 26, 1865; Elizabeth Jones, July 27, 1865; Hannah Biby, Aug. 2, 1865; Sophia Morton, July 10, 1865; Abraham Taylor, Aug. 1, 1865; Amy Covington, Aug. 10, 1865; Betsy Robinson, Aug. 3, 1865; and Mary Davis, Dec. 13, 1865, entry 3545, BRFAL.

27. See statements of Ellen Clifton, Aug. 3, 1865; Mary Rodgers, Aug. 15, 1865; Elizabeth Jones, July 27, 1865; and Lucy Williams, Aug. 9, 1865, entry 3545, BRFAL.

28. See testimony of A. N. Edmunds, 140; and Tony Cherry, 184, *MR&M*. See also testimony of David T. Egbert, 122; Mary Grady, 187–88; Captain A. W. Allyn, 245; and exhibit no. 2, 358, *MR&M*.

29. See David Tucker, *Black Pastors and Leaders: Memphis, 1819–1972* (Memphis: Memphis State University Press, 1975), 6–8; and Ewing O. Tade to Corresponding Secretary, Aug. 1, 1865, document H8965, microfilm reel 193, AMA.

30. Tucker, *Black Pastors and Leaders*, 8; Kathleen C. Berkeley, " 'Colored Ladies Also Contributed': Black Women's Activities from Benevolence to Social Welfare, 1866–1896," in *The Web of Southern Social Relations: Women, Family, and Education*, ed. Walter J. Fraser, Jr., R. Frank Saunders, Jr., and Jon L. Wakelyn (Athens: University of Georgia Press, 1985), 182, 193–94.

31. Statement of Catherine Martin, July 31, 1865, entry 3545, BRFAL; Salena Jones v. Gustavis Fisher, Aug. 1, 1865; and Susan Hill v. H. B. C. Miles, Dec. 1, 1865, Docket Freedmen's Court, entry 3544, BRFAL.

32. Michael Walsh to Ira Moore, June 11, 1866; and Michael Walsh to David Ingram, June 5, 1866, entry 3541, BRFAL. Lieutenant S. S. Garrett to Lieutenant J. S. Turner, Feb. 23, 1866; and statement of Betty Maywell, Dec. 5, 1865, entry 3545, BRFAL. See also "The Negro Again," *Memphis Daily Appeal*, March 3, 1866.

33. See, for example, statement of Elizabeth Burns, Feb. 9, 1866, entry 3545, BRFAL; and from the *Memphis Daily Appeal*, "Cruel Treatment," Feb. 15, 1866, p. 3, col. 1; and "Cruel Treatment," Feb. 23, 1866, p. 3, cols. 1–2.

34. For a discussion of how press accounts of freedpeople in Memphis were interwoven with public conversation about danger in the city, see Rosen, "Gender of Reconstruction" chap. 1. See also Clinton, "Reconstructing Freedwomen," 313–14.

35. Ryan, *Women in Public*, esp. 73, 76–92.

36. "The Negro Again,"20*Memphis Daily Appeal*, March 3, 1866; Provost Marshal of Freedmen to George R. Rutter, March 3, 1866, entry 3541, BRFAL.

37. "Freedmen's Court," *Memphis Daily Appeal*, Nov. 26, 1865, p. 3, col. 2.

38. "Sharp Wench," *Memphis Daily Appeal*, March 2, 1866, p. 3, col. 2.

39. "Female Roughs," *Memphis Daily Appeal*, March 2, 1866.

40. "Robbery," *Memphis Daily Appeal*, Nov. 17, 1865.

41. "Freedmen's Bureau," *Memphis Daily Appeal*, Nov. 11, 1865, p. 3, col. 1.

42. From *Memphis Daily Appeal*, "Freedmen's Court," Nov. 29, 1865, p. 3, col. 1; and "Police Arrests Friday Night," April 8, 1866, p. 3, col. 1. *Nymph du pave* was a euphemism for prostitute; see *The Compact Oxford English Dictionary*, 2d ed. (Oxford: Clarendon Press, 1991), 1191.

43. "Police Protection," *Memphis Morning Post*, June 7, 1866, p. 8, col. 2.

44. Statement of Amanda Olden, April 30, 1866, entry 3545, BRFAL. For the participation of a policeman named Carroll in the Memphis Riot, see testimony of Margaret Gardner,

98; Adam Lock, 115–16; and Dr. Robert McGowan, 126, *MR&M*. For a similar case, see bond for John Egan, April 17, 1866, entry 3545, BRFAL; testimony of Mollie Davis, 200; Ellen Brown, 200; and Mat. Wardlaw, 234, *MR&M*; and "The Riot—Continued," *Memphis Daily Post*, May 4, 1866, p. 8, cols. 2–4.

45. Affidavit of Lemuel (Samuel) Premier, FBC, *MR&M*, 338, identified Sweatt as one of the rioters.

46. Statement of C. C. Swears, Robert Church, and John Gains, Feb. 17, 1866, entry 3545, BRFAL.

47. Ibid.; S. S. Garrett to Major William L. Porter, Feb. 17, 1866; and endorsement from Mayor John Park, Feb. 22, 1866, entry 3545, BRFAL.

48. Testimony of Rachel Dilts, *MR&M*, 67. See also testimony of P. G. Marsh, 169; and James H. Swan, 178, *MR&M*.

49. See Benjamin P. Runkle, "Report Concerning the Late Riots at Memphis, Tenn.," in entry 3529, BRFAL; and "Report," 6; testimony of Dr. J. N. Sharp, 154, 156; Dr. D. P. Beecher, 145; James E. Donahue, 199; and William H. Pearce, 218, all in *MR&M*.

50. Testimony of Dr. J. N. Sharp, 157; Margaret Gardner, 98; Ellen Dilts, 64; Rachel Dilts, 67; Andrew Reyyonco, 169; and "Report," 6, all in *MR&M*. See also Runkle, "Report."

51. See report of Captain A. W. Allyn, exhibit 2, p. 358; and testimony of Thomas Durnin, 223, *MR&M*.

52. Benjamin P. Runkle to C. B. Fisk, May 23, 1866, entry 3529, BRFAL. Alex McQuarters noted that there were more women on the street than men. Testimony Taken before Military Commission Organized by General George Stoneman (hereafter MC), *MR&M*, 317. Quotation from affidavit of Albert Butcher, FBC, *MR&M*, 346. See also testimony of Adam Lock, 115–16; J. S. Chapin, 192; and James Finn, MC, 332, *MR&M*.

53. Testimony of Tony Cherry, *MR&M*, 182.

54. Witnesses differed as to where soldiers aimed their initial shots. See testimony of Adam Lock, 116; William Wheedon, 320; Abram Means, 173; C. H. Bowman, 324; Margaret Gardner, 98; and affidavits of Albert Butcher, FBC, 346; and Patzy Tolliver, 351, all in *MR&M*.

55. See Report, 7; testimony of Tony Cherry, 182; Dr. R. W. Creighton, 124–25; Dr. William F. Irwin, 131; and Dr. J. M. Keller, 133–34, all in *MR&M*.

56. See testimony of James Carroll Mitchell, 308–09; and Report, 7–8, *MR&M*.

57. Testimony of Dr. Robert McGowan, *MR&M*, 126.

58. See testimony of George Hogan, 149; Tony Cherry, 185–86; S. S. Garrett, 203–04; Frederick Hastings, 205–08; James Helm, 217; Thomas Durnin, 223–25; and Captain A. W. Allyn, 247, all in *MR&M*.

59. Testimony of Hannah Robinson, *MR&M*, 193.

60. Statement of Ann Freeman, May 22, 1866, entry 3545, BRFAL.

61. Testimony of Lucy Tibbs, *MR&M*, 160–62.

62. Testimony of Harriet Armour, *MR&M*, 177.

63. Testimony of Molly Hayes, *MR&M*, 186.

64. Testimony of Harriet Armour, *MR&M*, 176–77.

65. Testimony of Frances Thompson and Lucy Smith, *MR&M*, 196–97.

66. See also Hardwick, " 'Your Old Father Abe Lincoln Is Dead and Damned.' "

67. Testimony of Frances Thompson, *MR&M*, 196.

68. Testimony of Lucy Smith, *MR&M*, 197.

69. Testimony of Frances Thompson, *MR&M*, 196–97.

70. Testimony of Lucy Smith, *MR&M*, 197.

71. Testimony of Frances Thompson, *MR&M*, 196.

72. Testimony of Elvira Walker, *MR&M*, 194.

73. Ibid.; cf. affidavits of Rebecca Ann Bloom and Peter Bloom, FBC, *MR&M*, 351, 348.

74. Affidavit of Rebecca Ann Bloom, FBC, *MR&M*, 351.

75. "Rape scripts" is Sharon Marcus's term in "Fighting Bodies, Fighting Words: A Theory and Politics of Rape Prevention," in *Feminists Theorize the Political*, ed. Judith Butler and Joan W. Scott (New York: Routledge, 1992), 385–403. The classic reading of the rape of female slaves by white slave owners as an effort to impose a submissive gender on black women is Angela Davis, "Reflections on the Black Woman's Role in the Community of Slaves," *Black Scholar* 3 (1971): 3–15.

76. See also Marybeth Hamilton Arnold, " 'The Life of a Citizen in the Hands of a Woman': Sexual Assault in New York City, 1790 to 1820," in *Passion and Power: Sexuality in History*, ed. Kathy Peiss and Christina Simmons (Philadelphia: Temple University Press, 1989), 39.

77. Testimony of Harriet Armour, *MR&M*, 176.

78. Testimony of Lucy Tibbs, *MR&M*, 161.

79. Testimony of Lucy Smith, *MR&M*, 197.

80. See Report, *MR&M*, 3.

81. On the political context of this proposal, see Foner, *Reconstruction*, 243–61. For Stevens's motion in the House, see "Journal," *MR&M*, 45.

82. Rable, *But There Was No Peace*, 41.

83. The committee also appended to its report additional testimony collected by the Freedmen's Bureau and a military commission. See *MR&M*, 313–58.

84. Affidavit of Rebecca Ann Bloom, FBC, *MR&M*, 351. Bloom did not testify before the congressional committee; perhaps, like many freedpeople, she and her husband left the city after the riot. See Report, *MR&M*, 2; *Memphis Daily Avalanche*, May 5, 1866, reprinted in MC, *MR&M*, 334; "The Riot—Continued," *Memphis Daily Post*, May 4, 1866, p. 8, cols. 2–4.

85. Testimony of Frances Thompson, *MR&M*, 196.

86. Testimony of Lucy Smith, *MR&M*, 197.

87. Testimony of Lucy Tibbs, *MR&M*, 161.

88. Testimony of Harriet Armour, *MR&M*, 176.

89. Testimony of Lucy Smith, *MR&M*, 197.

90. Testimony of Lucy Tibbs, *MR&M*, 161.

91. Ibid.

92. Testimony of Harriet Armour, *MR&M*, 176.

93. This is suggested by the fact that the hostile questioning came from the two Republican members of the committee, while Shanklin, the committee's minority Democrat, who showed frequent support for white southerners during his questioning of witnesses, did not ask any questions about rape.

94. Testimony of Cynthia Townsend, *MR&M*, 163.

95. Testimony of Harriet Armour, *MR&M*, 176.

96. Ibid., 177; Cynthia Townsend, 163; Molly Hayes, 186; and Henry Porter, 168, all in *MR&M*.

97. See also Edwards, "Sexual Violence, Gender, Reconstruction"; idem, "The Disappearance of Susan Daniel and Henderson Cooper"; and idem, *Gendered Strife and Confusion*, 198–210.

98. See, for example, "Report of the Committee of Investigation on the Memphis Riots," *New York Times*, July 16, 1866, 1; Rable, *But There Was No Peace*, 41.

99. Report, *MR&M*, 5, 13. Did the authors of this report in fact perceive irony in men acting with "licentious brutality" toward those whom they constructed as inferior others? Or do the quotation marks around the phrase "conquered their prejudices" indicate a recognition that "prejudice" can have a role in, rather than be an obstacle to, fantasies of sexual domination?

100. Report, *MR&M*, 13–15.

101. Laura Edwards argues that this discourse, rather than empowering all women to resist sexual violence, marked only those who remained subservient to patriarchal dictates for women's appropriate behavior as deserving of protection. See Edwards, "Sexual Violence, Gender, Reconstruction." See also idem, *Gendered Strife and Confusion*, 210–13.

102. In addition to expediting the passage of Reconstruction acts in Congress, the congressional committee's report on the Memphis Riot provided the final evidence needed to pass the Metropolitan Police Bill in the Tennessee state legislature. This act, placing control of the city's police force in the hands of a commission appointed by the governor, led to the dismissal of the force that had instigated the riot. See "Metropolitan Police," *Memphis Daily Appeal*, May 1, 1866, p. 2, col. 1. From the *Memphis Daily Argus*, see "The Metropolitan Police Bill," p. 2, col. 1; and "Important Document," p. 3, cols. 3–5, both April 29, 1866; "The Memphis Riots: What Gen. Runkle of the Freedmen's Bureau Thinks about Them," May 12, 1866, p. 1, col. 8; and "The Police 'Head Center,' " May 29, 1866, p. 2, col. 1.

103. Cf. Rable, *But There Was No Peace*, 41.

104. See "A Mask Lifted," *Public Ledger*, July 11, 1876, p. 3, col. 4; "Local Paragraphs," *Memphis Daily Appeal*, July 11, 1876, p. 4, col. 2; and "Local Paragraphs," *Memphis Daily Appeal*, July 14, 1876. See also Elizabeth Meriwether, *Recollections of Ninety-Two Years, 1824–1916* (Nashville: Tennessee Historical Commission, 1958), 180. I thank Gerald Smith for directing me to this source.

105. See, for instance, "Under False Colors," *Memphis Daily Avalanche*, July 12, 1876, p. 4, col. 2; and "Thompson," *Memphis Daily Appeal*, July 13, 1876, p. 4, col. 4.

106. See "Local Paragraphs," *Memphis Daily Appeal*, Nov. 4, 1876, p. 4, col. 2; from the *Memphis Daily Avalanche*, July 18, 1876, p. 4, col. 2; July 19, 1876, p. 4, col. 2; July 20, 1876, p. 4, col. 2; and July 21, 1876, p. 4, col. 1; and from the *Public Ledger*; "Ledger Lines," July 13, 1876, p. 3, col. 3; and July 17, 1876, p. 3, col. 4.

107. "Frances Thompson Dead," *Weekly Public Ledger*, Nov. 7, 1876, p. 3, col. 1.

108. Register of Deaths, Memphis and Shelby County Health Department, 1876–1884, p. 24, MSCA.

109. Thompson appears on a list of freedpeople reporting violence to the Freedmen's Bureau in the days just after the riot. Next to Thompson's name, this list states that Lucy Smith had been raped. See "Report of Casualties and Property Destroyed during the Memphis riots," entry 3529, BRFAL. The entry is ambiguous. It seems to indicate that at this time Thompson did not tell the Bureau that she herself had been sexually assaulted. Even if this were certain, it would not prove that her testimony was fabricated.

110. See in the *Memphis Daily Appeal*, "Thompson," July 13, 1876, p. 4, col. 4; "Frances Thompson," July 14, 1876, p. 4, col. 4; and "Local Paragraphs," July 18, 1876, p. 4, col. 2; in the *Public Ledger*, "A Mask Lifted," July 11, 1876, p. 3, col. 4, and "That Man-Woman," July 12, 1876, p. 3, col. 5; and in the *Weekly Public Ledger*, "Frances Thompson Dead," November 7, 1876, p. 3, col. 1. Meriwether remembers that Thompson was "discovered" as a result of the accusation by a "respectable negro woman" that her daughter, working as Thompson's house maid, had become pregnant by Thompson (*Ninety-Two Years Recollected*, 180). I found no evidence to confirm this.

111. "Frances Thompson," *Memphis Daily Appeal*, July 14, 1876, p. 4, col. 4; and "Ledger Lines," *Public Ledger*, July 17, 1876, p. 3, col. 3. See also "Ledger Lines," *Public Ledger*, July 14, 1876, p. 3, col. 4.

112. "Thompson," *Memphis Daily Appeal*, July 13, 1876, p. 4, col. 4.

113. "Time Makes All Things Even At Last," *Public Ledger*, July 19, 1876, p. 2, cols. 2–3.

114. *Memphis Daily Appeal*, July 16, 1876, p. 2, col. 1.

Chapter Fourteen

The Disappearance of Susan Daniel and Henderson Cooper

Gender and Narratives of Political Conflict in the Reconstruction-Era U.S. South

Laura F. Edwards

Late in 1864 Susan Daniel, the wife of a landless white man, accused two slaves, William and Henderson Cooper, of rape. A few months later, on the eve of southern surrender, the Granville (N.C.) County Superior Court convicted and sentenced both men to death. Only William Cooper, however, was hanged. Henderson escaped and fled to Washington, D.C., where he lived until the fall of 1866, when Granville officials captured him and brought him back to the county. Although the court then affirmed his sentence and rescheduled his hanging, the execution never took place. At the eleventh hour, the Freedmen's Bureau intervened, declaring the sentence void, because it had been rendered by a Confederate court not recognized by the U.S. government. The bureau then directed the case to a court of inquiry for further investigation. Citing evidence that Susan Daniel had consented to the act and pointing out that Henderson Cooper was charged only with aiding and abetting, the court concluded that he had committed a crime but not one that merited death. Based on this report, a U.S. military tribunal then tried Henderson Cooper, found him guilty, and, ignoring the court of inquiry's recommendation, sentenced him to death. But Cooper's luck held. At this point, the Freedmen's Bureau's assistant commissioner declared this death sentence void and ordered the prisoner to be tried on a new indictment by local authorities. The decision could have resulted in Henderson Cooper's release, because he had been tried and convicted on the same charge once already. This time, however, fortune failed Henderson Cooper. In 1867, as he awaited his trial and possible acquittal, a fire burned the jail to the ground. None of the prisoners survived.[1]

The Cooper-Daniel rape case, which ultimately became a political issue in both Granville County and the state of North Carolina, provides a fascinating perspective on the connection between rape and politics during Reconstruction. Untangling this connection, so as to understand why political conflict so often crystallized around rape at this juncture in southern history, is one of the goals of this article. The other is to explore the ways gender functioned in narratives of the case to shape the political terrain at that time and, ultimately, our historical understanding of political conflict as well.

Documentation of the case comes from two elite white men—the conservative governor, Jonathan Worth, and a northern-born Freedmen's Bureau agent, Robert Avery. Predictably, they placed their own concerns at the center of their accounts. For Avery, the case symbolized the systemic corruption of a society organized around slavery. Worth, by contrast, saw it as yet another example of the threat northern policies posed to the South's social and political order. Despite these differences, both men depicted Susan Daniel and Henderson Cooper as empty, one-dimensional images. Their personae changed, chameleon-like, depending on the author. But their role as passive figures, incapable of fully participating in the events unfolding around them, did not. Herein lie the contradictions in Worth's and Avery's accounts. Their political parables depended on the actions of Susan Daniel and Henderson Cooper, a white woman and a black man. Yet they not only denied the agency of these two central actors but eliminated all women and all African American men from their narratives as well.

The Cooper-Daniel case carries important lessons for the ways historians use concepts of gender and position marginalized people in their own analyses. As a central component of power, gender can obscure as much about racial and class conflicts as it can reveal—particularly when historians rely on only one side of the story.[2] Both Governor Worth and Robert Avery worked from an understanding of power in which the gendered lines of authority within households provided the foundations for public power, thus casting propertied white men as society's proper guardians. In their telling of the Cooper-Daniel case, they actively sought to maintain this gendered political vision by containing the field of political conflict and eliminating certain people as political actors. Neither Governor Worth nor Robert Avery was entirely successful. Even in their written accounts, the two men found it difficult to make people like Henderson Cooper and Susan Daniel disappear completely. Outside the confines of paper and pen, it was virtually impossible. In fact, the meanings Worth and Avery attached to the case made sense only in relation to the actions of the people they were trying to erase from their narratives. Most immediately, the political conflicts the two men enacted through the case depended on the presence of Susan Daniel and Henderson Cooper. More broadly, the case became a political issue precisely because scores of women and men of both races refused to fill the roles allotted to them by men like Governor Worth and Robert Avery. In this way, Worth's and Avery's narratives suggest other sides to the history of Reconstruction and the value of understanding gender as a multisided power relationship defined through continual contest—one that necessarily includes people whose defeat in no way implied their absence from or unimportance to the whole process.

Power and politics suffused the Cooper-Daniel case from the very beginning. In 1864, long before Jonathan Worth even became aware of the case, conservative white leaders in Granville County seized on the case in a desperate bid to shore up their hold on an increasingly unruly population. By convicting and hanging two black men for the rape of a white woman, local authorities could address the racial fears of many white residents and demonstrate their ability to maintain antebellum racial hierarchies even as the institution of slavery was crumbling around them. Understood in this context, it is not surprising that these same conservative officials resurrected the case by capturing Henderson Cooper in Washington, D.C., in 1866, when the implications of the Confederacy's surrender were still unclear.[3] At this time, wealthy whites in the county faced the defiance of African Americans, who were trying to establish the terms of their newfound freedom. They also faced the resentment of many poor whites, who were painfully putting their lives back together after a war they had never been enthusiastic about in the first place. Hanging Cooper would send a strong message to all Granville County residents about who held power. A black man dead at the end of a rope warned all African Americans not to push the limits of their freedom too far. Cooper's execution would deliver a different message to whites. Because this particular case involved a poor white woman, conservative authorities could use it to ease the resentment among those whites who shared Susan Daniel's poverty and to affirm their own place as the legitimate representatives of all white residents. But the attempt to use the capture and execution of Henderson Cooper as a demonstration of the power and competence of conservative rule failed miserably. When the Freedmen's Bureau took Cooper into custody the day before his hanging, it summarily stripped county officials of their authority much as an errant son might be disciplined by his father. With conservatives left standing open-mouthed and empty-handed on the courthouse steps, their handling of the case appeared as little more than hollow posturing.

At this point, Jonathan Worth entered the conflict. Although a unionist and a former Whig, Worth stubbornly resisted any change to the racial and class hierarchies that had structured slave society. He only dug in his heels further as President Andrew Johnson's conservative Reconstruction plan lost credibility with Congress and his own term as governor of North Carolina drew to a close. Embittered and embattled, Worth saw in the Cooper-Daniel case all the dangers he believed federal policies posed to the people and the state of North Carolina. Supporting Granville authorities, he tried to influence the Freedmen's Bureau's treatment of the case. Later, he used it as a central piece of evidence in a series of articles exposing what he considered to be the atrocities of northern occupation.[4]

Governor Worth equated the Cooper-Daniel case with the public power of propertied white men and the disastrous consequences that would result if these men no longer stood at the apex of power. But why did he seize on a rape case to symbolize these fears? Although rape often becomes a metaphor for power relations of all kinds, its representative capacity is far from transcendent. The act and symbol of rape acquire meaning in particular social contexts. In the post-emancipation South, rape was more than just an expedient means of fanning racial fears and consolidating support for the state's conservative leaders. Its meaning was rooted deeply within the structures of southern society, namely, the household.

In the antebellum South, the household legally marked the boundaries between private and public space. It also linked these two spheres in the figure of a white head of household. Before emancipation, white heads of household assumed economic, legal, and moral responsibility for a range of dependents, who included

African American slaves as well as white women and children. Private authority translated directly into public power for household heads, giving them the right to represent their dependents' political interests. By contrast, law and social convention denied both private and public power to dependents—to wives, slaves, and children. Of course, these groups occupied distinctly different positions. Equating the subordination of slaves, which was absolute, with the subordination of white women and children in slaveholding families would constitute a serious misrepresentation of southern society. Still, the status of these groups overlapped in the sense that they could not claim the requisite civil and political rights that would allow them to assume the same independent public personae as white male household heads.[5]

The figure of a household head was an adult, white, propertied male. But white men claimed power through their ability to fulfill the duties of household head, not on the ascriptive basis of their race and sex alone. Not everyone measured up. Dependency tainted even white men who lacked sufficient property to control their own labor and maintain households of their own. Nevertheless, the position of propertyless white men was always different from that of white women and African Americans, who could step out of their proper place and even step into the role of household head, but could never fully embody the power of that role.[6]

The anomalous position of unmarried white women and free black women and men in the antebellum period suggests how strongly gender and race shaped notions of independence and dependence. Even when they headed their own households, the residues of dependency that clung to these people made it difficult for them to fulfill their duties. None could participate directly in politics. Beyond that, free black women and men faced legal and customary restrictions that denied them a whole range of civil rights and economic opportunities and, as a result, made it that much more difficult to maintain independent households. Unmarried free women, both black and white, did exercise rights in the status of *feme sole*, but individual rights to contract and own property did not mean that women could comfortably assume a place at the head of a household. Because southern law defined parental rights as the rights of fathers, mothers had only tenuous claims to their children. Without parental rights, women, particularly propertyless women, struggled against great odds to keep their families together. The task was almost impossible for unmarried free black women, whose children were routinely apprenticed as soon as they were old enough to be separated from their mothers and to carry on meaningful labor. All these barriers meant that neither free women, white or black, nor free black men could ever be a household head in the fullest sense of that term.[7]

War and emancipation shook the antebellum household to its foundations, destabilizing the configuration of private and public power it supported. Freed from their dependent position as slaves, African American men could, theoretically, take on the role of household head with all its private and public privileges. Although African American women would find it difficult to claim the same rights as their menfolk, they might well demand privileges previously reserved for white women as dependent wives and daughters. At the same time, many white men faced the loss of their property and, in the case of slaveholders, most of their dependents as well.

Not only did the borders of their households shrink, but the very basis of their mastery there was called into question, a situation that also undermined their exclusive claims to public power. Thus, the household, in both its private and public forms, became a highly contested political issue. After all, political and civil rights still hinged on how a household was defined, who qualified as a household head, and what rights they and their dependents could exercise. As early as 1864, at the time of Henderson and William Cooper's first trial, the answers to these questions were open to redefinition and contest in a way they had never been during slavery.

It was in this particular context that Susan Daniel's rape charge acquired such political resonance. Rape disrupted relationships within the household's borders. Both law and social convention defined the act as the raw exercise of power by a man over a woman. At the same time, rape was also an exercise of power by a man over another man, because the woman in question was assumed to be a dependent wife or daughter within a household headed by a white propertied man. In one sense, rapists committed a crime against property, by violently taking a woman's sexuality—that which she exchanged with men for material support and emotional companionship and which was, by law, her husband's or father's possession. Beyond that, rape cut through the web of social relations that knit family members together. A household head's authority over his dependents rested on his duty to provide and protect. In exchange, women surrendered themselves and their offspring to their husbands and male kinfolk. By compromising the ability of both the women and men involved to fulfill their appointed social roles, rape shattered this entire arrangement.[8]

But the implications of rape were not confined within the household's borders. Both the act and its legal treatment reflected and reinforced the racial and class dynamics that determined which people could claim civil rights and political power. In the antebellum period, neither southern law nor most whites recognized the rape of female slaves as a crime. As property, they could not be raped, or so the logic went. Similarly, law and white social conventions did not consider rape to be a crime against a slave woman's menfolk. As property and as dependents who could never form households of their own, slave men did not have the same rights to women as men who were white and free. In practice, this legal fiction condoned not only the rape of slave women but also the hierarchies of power that subordinated all African Americans within slavery. The act of rape dramatized the gender oppression that made slave women vulnerable to sexual exploitation, while it simultaneously affirmed the racial and class hierarchies that defined all African Americans as slaves, not women and men.[9]

Slavery, however, was not the only divide in southern society. Even though southern law privileged all white people, not all whites received equal treatment. The law included poor white women in the definition of rape, but in practice the courts often ignored their experiences with rape. Unlike elite white women, those who were poor had to prove themselves worthy before the court accepted their charges, not an easy job given the class bias of elite court officials. For poor white women, then, rape revealed gender and class hierarchies that made them far more vulnerable to sexual attack than elite white women. It also underscored the class subordination of poor white men, whose poverty and relative powerlessness made them less able than elite white men to protect their womenfolk from outside threats. Yet, because the legal denial of the experience of rape to poor white women occurred on a case-by-case basis, it appeared that decisions were made in terms of the character of individual women. The results upheld the fiction that all whites were equal under the law, just as they reproduced the class hierarchies that actually structured southern society.[10]

Poised between the private and public spheres, rape carried the potential to confirm or destabilize both simultaneously. But it entered political discourse only at moments of change and uncertainty. Reconstruction was just such a time. To be sure, propertied white men in the antebellum period had considered black-male-on-white-female rape a serious offense that challenged larger social relations. But as long as the hierarchies of southern society were firmly grounded by the institution of slavery, rape did not seem to be as great a threat as it would be after emancipation and the Confederacy's defeat. It was then that the Cooper-Daniel case moved over the boundary separating private disputes from public conflicts.[11]

Governor Worth interpreted the Cooper-Daniel case against this backdrop. Moving seamlessly between the rape and his concerns about the state's public institutions, he rarely bothered to distinguish between the two. In one passage, he graphically depicted the act itself: "This was a rape of peculiar atrocity. Two strong negroes enter the house of a poor but worthy woman and in the presence of her little daughter each of them commits a rape upon her. . . . " Then, without ending the sentence, he jumped from the dwelling where the rape was committed to the statehouse: "[and the federal government] interposes its shield and allows one of the monsters to go unpunished. . . . If alienation to the government in this state is on the increase, as is often alleged to our prejudice, is it to be wondered at?"[12] The vulnerability of Susan Daniel became the vulnerability of the people of North Carolina, and the illegitimate power of Henderson Cooper became the illegitimate power of northern officials who meddled in state government. As long as the state's rightful leaders remained hamstrung by these interlopers, the people of North Carolina, like Susan Daniel, had no recourse. They could only hope that justice would prevail. No doubt, conservative leaders within Granville County agreed.[13]

Governor Worth was so convinced that the interests of the state's propertied white men represented those of the population as a whole that it never occurred to him that African Americans might need the intervention of the federal government to protect their interests. The very idea was anathema to him, because he believed that African Americans had no political concerns or public existence in their own right. In fact, for Worth, any independent action on the part of those he considered dependents was subversive. Their proper place was within a household, the interests of which were represented by a white propertied man. He was also deeply suspicious of poor white men, whose lack of property signaled dependence and whom he termed "white negroes." These people were a threat. But then Governor Worth believed unruliness to be part of their nature.[14] In his eyes, the new crisis and the real problem were northern policies that upset the southern social and political order. Consequently, he saw the Cooper-Daniel case not as a political conflict that involved poor whites and African Americans but one that centered on the interests of elite white men, northern and southern. In his writings about the case, he accentuated the strength of Henderson and William Cooper, but it was power of a particular kind. Drawing on racial beliefs that emphasized African American men's uncontrollable hypersexuality, he described their power as the undirected rage of "monsters." This destructive power could be contained only if society was structured appropriately—that is, according to Worth's ideas of appropriate social relations, in which black men remained under the direct control of propertied white men. In his view, the power to direct events, shape policy, and create the conditions in which men like the Coopers could go unpunished rested solely in the hands of white northern leaders. Conservative officials within Granville County shared this perspective. Frustrated in their attempts to control the outcome of the Cooper-Daniel case or the political conflict that followed in its wake, they, like Governor Worth, could only think to blame the Freedmen's Bureau officials.[15]

Robert Avery's reports provide a counterpoint to Governor Worth's version of the Cooper-Daniel case to some extent. He, too, represented the case as the inversion of legitimate power relations. But unlike Governor Worth or Granville's conservative leaders, Avery identified the crux of the problem as a corrupt society dominated by slavery and the interests of slaveholders. Questioning Henderson Cooper in his investigation, he heard a very different story than the one in the official court record. Cooper maintained that Susan Daniel had consented to sexual relations, a line of defense that local authorities silenced. Given the "popular feeling which then longed for the conviction" of the two accused men, no white witnesses had come forward to substantiate the story or attack the character of Susan Daniel. Even two years after the trial, witnesses, both black and white, still feared retaliation. Based on this information, Avery determined the Coopers' trial to be little more than a cruel charade and questioned the ability of local authorities to uphold the rule of law: "[Henderson Cooper] was tried during a period of intense excitement, on him all the feelings of his times were enlisted against him." Agreeing with Avery's interpretation, the Freedmen's Bureau followed up on his recommendation and took the case into its own hands.[16]

Yet for all the differences, Jonathan Worth's and Robert Avery's versions of the case shared a great deal in common. Where Worth supported local authorities and the antebellum social order, Robert Avery criticized both and worked to realize civil and political rights for African Americans. Nonetheless, Avery still envisioned the conflict as one between white northerners and elite white southerners, just as Worth did. In his account, Henderson Cooper in particular and African Americans in general appear as worthy but passive recipients of the privileges of citizenship, which had been denied them by white southerners until white northerners arrived on the scene to correct matters. This view of African Americans conformed to the racial ideology of many white northerners. At its best, as with Robert Avery, it took the form of a responsibility to bring the ways of free labor and political democracy to an oppressed people. At its worst, it took the form of a racism that rivaled any southern variety in its virulence. Although there is a considerable difference between the two extremes, neither cast African Americans as political actors in their own right.[17]

Images of Susan Daniel restricted the public arena still further, eliminating women from its borders as well. For Governor Worth, Daniel was a gentle mother and a loyal Confederate wife. To Robert Avery, she was an evil seductress, whose conscious debauchery represented the corruption that permeated private life and public institutions across the entire South. Yet the double-sided image of Susan Daniel stemmed less from divisions between North and South than from a bifurcated view of women common to both regions. From this perspective, women were either virtuous or not. Virtue, moreover, obtained its meaning in reference to racial and class assumptions that characterized poor white and black women as innately depraved and their elite counterparts as morally principled. Indeed, some wealthy whites in Granville County, including Henderson Cooper's former master, agreed with Robert Avery, believing Susan Daniel to be little more than a common prostitute. Whether pure or corrupt, her presence symbolized the disruption of public space in both Worth's and Avery's accounts. Indeed, she was the only woman who appeared in any public role at all. Women, from this perspective, belonged within the private sphere. Once they ventured outside and intruded in the public arena, they too would become unwitting pawns in conflicts beyond their control. Those judged "virtuous" deserved rescue. Everyone else would be left to reap the whirlwind.[18]

But even as Worth and Avery rhetorically moved Susan Daniel and Henderson Cooper to the margins, people like them kept challenging their position there. As Cooper sat in jail awaiting his execution for the second time, Republicans in Washington, D.C., upped the political stakes by passing the Reconstruction Acts, which, among other things, increased the power of the Freedmen's Bureau and made ratification of the Fourteenth Amendment and its guarantee of African American male suffrage mandatory for readmission into the Union. Back in North Carolina, the fledgling Republican Party prepared for action, African Americans became ever more vocal in their political demands, and the opposition began its reign of terror. Granville County was no exception. Violence there soon escalated into a pitched battle for political power.[19]

In 1867 the situation was already so volatile that a group of the "most respectable citizens," as they called themselves, approached the local Freedmen's Bureau agent for help. In a request buried amidst the local agent's correspondence and apparently ignored by Worth and higher-level bureau agents, these "most respectable citizens" asked for a squad of U.S. soldiers to keep the peace at Henderson Cooper's execution. Noting that there had already been one attempt to rescue Henderson Cooper, they felt that federal troops would have a "wholesome effect on the Freedmen, and others, showing that the U.S. Authorities will sustain all efforts of the Civil Authorities to suppress and punish crime." Apparently, Henderson Cooper's recapture and resentencing had mobilized those, both black and white, who opposed the political domination of the conservative local elite.[20] It was an interesting request, considering the attitude of most elite white southerners toward the presence of federal troops. It also reveals the inability of Granville's conservative elite to control emerging political conflicts, as "the Freedmen and others" defiantly demonstrated their unwillingness to remain on the margins. The Freedmen's Bureau may have intervened on Henderson Cooper's behalf at an opportune time. But it was "the Freedmen and others" who drew the bureau's attention to the case and who drove the "respectable citizens" of Granville County to request federal intervention to prop up their own increasingly shaky position.[21]

Like those who rallied on his behalf, Henderson Cooper refused to accept a passive role in the events unfolding around him. Awaiting retrial after the bureau returned him to local authorities, he took fate into his hands and, in the company of his fellow prisoner, set fire to the jail in an attempt to break out. All the evidence suggests they were unsuccessful, but doubts lingered. The heat from the blaze had been so intense that only a few bones remained, none of which were readily identifiable. Given the testimony at the inquest, it appears that some African Americans and poor whites believed that Henderson Cooper had finally made his way to freedom. Needless to say, this interpretation carried a very different political lesson than that of either Worth or the Freedmen's Bureau.[22]

Appropriately enough, Cooper's fiery finale destroyed the jail, a building that symbolized to many the inequities of a political system designed to protect the power of a few. The jail—or rather the absence of one—soon became the source of acute embarrassment to the county's conservative leaders, who could not afford to rebuild it. Predictably, they blamed the Freedmen's Bureau. Because the bureau's prisoner had burned the jail down, they reasoned, the bureau should pay for a new one. The Freedmen's Bureau, however, unceremoniously declined, maintaining that Henderson Cooper was not its responsibility. No doubt Henderson Cooper would have added that he was not anyone's responsibility—or anyone's dependent. He acted as his own person. So did those around him who resisted conservative rule. These people were not provoked or duped by white northerners as Jonathan Worth and local officials believed; nor were their actions irrational outbursts, as the northern bureau agents thought. To the contrary, the "Freedmen and others" held their own visions of public life.[23]

Women stood among the "Freedmen and others," despite Governor Worth's and Robert Avery's attempts to deny their presence there. Even their descriptions of Susan Daniel suggest as much. If Worth managed to transform her into the flower of southern womanhood, he did so only with great difficulty. In fact, he could maintain the image only by writing the actual woman out of the story altogether. Not coincidentally, Worth rarely even bothered to mention her by name.[24] Although not the chaste figure of Worth's imagination, neither was Susan Daniel the epitome of moral corruption, as Avery made her out to be. Instead, she lived in a world where poverty and necessity shaped the meaning of virtue and where the boundaries between black and white overlapped considerably. When her husband was conscripted into the Confederate army, she was left to fend for herself and her young daughter as best she could. Like other poor women in her situation, she probably pieced together a subsistence through a combination of wage work, occasional prostitution, foraging, stealing, and the charity of family and neighbors. The Freedmen's

Bureau's reports provide what few facts there are about her life at this time. Daniel continued to live on J. C. Cooper's plantation, where her husband had worked as an overseer and where William and Henderson Cooper were enslaved. While there, she maintained close ties with several slaves and with William Cooper in particular. Whatever the nature of these relationships, they were not all that uncommon. In Granville County, free blacks, poor whites, and slaves often mixed, sexually and otherwise. Whites tolerated such behavior but only as long as it did not become too blatant. Apparently Susan Daniel crossed over that fine line. According to one bureau report, J. C. Cooper turned her out because she was too "familiar" with his slaves and thought her a bad influence on them.[25]

Sometime after that, Daniel charged William and Henderson Cooper with burglary and rape. That her husband was the former overseer, that he was fighting in the Confederate army, and that Daniel had continued to live on the plantation by herself raises a range of possible motives and explanations for whatever happened that night. Susan Daniel may have been caught up in an ongoing conflict between her husband (the overseer) and the slaves. Perhaps the alleged attack had something to do with her husband's or her own Confederate loyalties. Maybe Susan Daniel had taken advantage of opportunities opened up by her husband's absence. She may have become involved in the extralegal trade networks among slaves, free blacks, and poor whites that flourished in the county at the time. If so, conflicts may have grown out of her participation in them. She and William Cooper may have become lovers. Perhaps they had a falling out and this was her way of punishing him. Had she been engaged in prostitution, she may have been retaliating for lost compensation. If her relationship had become too flagrant for whites in the community, she may have been covering her tracks and trying to get back in the good graces of J. C. Cooper. Or there may have been a rape. Ultimately, however, the evidence does not reveal what happened that night. Nor will we ever know why Susan Daniel filed charges or what she thought of the case's subsequent trajectory, because her voice was so effectively excluded from the proceedings. She may have approved of the way local officials and Jonathan Worth handled the case. But even if she did, it is equally likely that she attached different meanings to the proceedings than did Worth, the Freedmen's Bureau, or county officials. For historians, the danger lies in letting the silent female figure of this particular case stand in for all women.[26]

There is no need to heroize Susan Daniel, whose actions not only played into conservative hands but also resulted in the deaths of two black men. Nonetheless, the complexity of her story suggests how hard Worth, Avery, and local officials had to work to keep women outside the public arena. Their success in this one instance was anything but representative of what would follow. Women formed a loud, visible, and vigorous public presence both during and after the Civil War. Political battles in fact unfolded within the homes of African American women, as the Klan and other white vigilante groups burned their houses, stole their possessions, mutilated their bodies, and even took their lives. Black women also assumed public roles themselves, running to Union lines, working in army camps, participating in political meetings, and pressing for recognition of their legal rights. White women entered the political arena as well. Some provided crucial service to the Confederate war effort on the home front and supported Democratic rule afterward. Others actively opposed the Confederacy, waging small-scale riots, taking food and goods from their wealthier neighbors, hiding deserters, and pressuring male kin to come home. Afterward, they loudly opposed the reconstruction of a social and political order that had so recently failed them.[27]

Even as Governor Worth and the Freedmen's Bureau were battling over the disposition of the Cooper-Daniel case, women began filling local courts with cases of rape and sexual assault. In so doing, they countered the political meanings that Worth and the Freedmen's Bureau gave to the Cooper-Daniel case. These women were more like the actual Susan Daniel than the symbolic one. Although not all white, they were poor women who did not meet elite white standards of womanhood, who had been denied legal protection in rape cases before the war, and who did not appear in Worth's or Avery's discussion of the Cooper-Daniel case. After southern surrender, conservatives like Worth enacted a Black Code, a series of laws designed to limit the civil rights of freedpeople in the same way those of free blacks had been before emancipation. Even before the code was formally abolished, African Americans were already undermining its intent by making use of the Freedmen's Bureau's judicial powers. Then in 1868, when the Republicans gained political control, they restructured the state courts. The new constitution swept away the impediments that kept African Americans from enjoying the same legal rights, under the law, as whites, and it also made key positions of magistrate and judge elective. All these changes bolstered confidence in the legal system among African Americans and poor whites, who began to bring their complaints to local courts with some expectation of an equitable settlement.[28] Women were prominent among those who made use of this opening in the legal system. In the first twenty years following the war, the Granville County courts tried twenty-four sexual violence cases, almost evenly divided between black and poor white women. Women in other counties did the same. They were most successful in prosecuting men of similar racial and class backgrounds. Nonetheless, these sexual assault cases still represent a significant departure from the past, when African American women had no legal recourse at all and poor white women faced barriers that made prosecution difficult at best. Insisting on recognition of their legal rights, these women openly challenged an assumption deeply embedded in both Worth's and Avery's telling of the Cooper-Daniel case: that the privileges of womanhood went only to "respectable" women who were, not coincidentally, white dependents of white propertied men.[29]

These cases also unmasked the fiction of black-male-on-white-female rape. Emancipation did not invert the social hierarchy: white men were not reduced to abject powerlessness, nor were their womenfolk indefensibly exposed to sexually predatory black men. If anything, emancipation heightened the vulnerability of African American women to violence at the hands of white men, who used rape and other ritualized forms of sexual abuse to limit black women's freedom and to reinscribe antebellum racial hierarchies. Poor white women were less vulnerable than black women. But they did not enjoy the privileged position that Worth extended to all white women in his telling of the Cooper-Daniel case. In Granville County, none of the other cases involving poor white women came close to generating the public outrage that Susan Daniel's did. Even when the alleged aggressor was black, most cases went quietly through the courts, received little or no notice in the local press, and resulted in minor prison terms for the convicted men.[30]

African American and poor white women's voices provided a counterpoint to the images of womanhood presented by Governor Worth and Robert Avery in other ways as well. Worth and Avery not only viewed rape through the prism of concerns over the distribution of power among men but also obscured other forms of violence against women by privileging rape. Neither did they see violence against women as a political issue in its own right or acknowledge that women might have political interests separate from those of their menfolk.[31] African American women and poor white women disagreed. They prosecuted not just sexual assault but physical assaults generally. They also charged a wide range of people, from employers and Klan marauders to men within their own families and communities. Unwilling to accept men's unlimited power as the price of protection, these women tried to set limits on that power. They also insisted that their concerns, as women, deserved a public hearing.[32]

But even when women challenged the men close to them, their actions were still connected to larger struggles for power in their communities. Poor white and African American women did not battle against violence by themselves. They were joined by other male relatives and community members, who often supported their legal efforts and initiated suits on their behalf. Injustice against women was injustice against them all, especially given the patriarchal values that framed social relations. Moreover, both women and men shared the restrictions of race and class. If black and poor white women could be abused because of their race and class, so could their menfolk. In his telling of the Cooper-Daniel case, for instance, Governor Worth did not just leave black women outside the bounds of womanhood. He depicted African American men as unruly minors who posed a serious threat to the families of responsible white men and society generally. And he erased poor white women and men from his narrative by ignoring the specific class barriers they faced. African Americans and poor whites in Granville County challenged these long-standing assumptions when they prosecuted violence against the women in their own families and communities.

In fact, the actions of these women and men supported each other. African American and poorer white men engaged in a range of political activities comparable to those of their womenfolk. But where women claimed the right to public respect and protection from abuse, men claimed the right to defend and protect their families and communities. Such claims marked a particularly dramatic change for African American men, who had been denied the privilege of presiding over their own households and the public power that came with that position. Their post-war assertions of these rights acquire much more significance given the obstacles they faced in order to make them a reality. African American men not only challenged violence against their womenfolk, but they also reclaimed apprenticed children, sued their employers for unpaid wages, and protected their property and homes. In the company of poor white men in the Republican Party, they demanded the legal rights and the political representation necessary to protect the interests of those who lived with them. In all these ways, these men buttressed their claims to public power by affirming their right to the position of household head, a position previously reserved for propertied white men and one that provided the foundation and justification for the exercise of political power not just in the South but in the nation as a whole.[33]

Considering the actions of these women and men, both Jonathan Worth and the Freedmen's Bureau had to fight hard to contain the political meanings of the Cooper-Daniel case. Their descriptions, which sought to define the issues and the terrain of political struggle, were central to their battles. The women and men they sought to define and control were at the short end of an unequal power relationship and were unable to shape the political terrain in the same way as Worth or the Freedmen's Bureau. But they did have their own ideas about how they might alter the basic landscape. Here, understanding the central role of gender in Worth's and the bureau's narratives is crucial. From this perspective we see new political issues, we see old ones in a new light, and we also see new arenas of political struggle. Without these insights, women would remain invisible, and poor white and African American men would figure less prominently. Nonetheless, conflict and contest are missing from the accounts of Worth and the bureau; so are the African American and poor white women and men who engaged in these conflicts, and so are their political visions. But then that was part of Worth's and the bureau's point. If we accept Worth's and the bureau's readings of the case uncritically, we have only part of the picture. We also run the risk of affirming their vision in our scholarship and duplicating it in our politics. I suspect that was part of their point as well.

NOTES

While revising this essay for publication, I received support through a Monticello College Foundation Fellowship at the Newberry Library. In addition to the reviewers for *Feminist Studies*, I would like to thank the following friends and colleagues for their comments and suggestions on various drafts of this essay: Jim Anderson, Noralee Frankel, Jim Grossman, Jacquelyn Hall, Nancy Hewitt, Bob Ingalls, Linda Kerber, John McAllister, Nell Painter, Kathleen Paul, Hannah Rosen, Anne Scott, and Amy Dru Stanley. I first presented this material as "Sexual Violence and Political Struggle: Finding Women in Reconstruction Politics," Berkshire Conference on the History of Women, Poughkeepsie, New York, June 1993, and at Sangamon State University, Springfield, Illinois, May 1993. I would like to thank the participants at these sessions for their comments.

1. The court of inquiry did not name the crime it suspected Henderson Cooper had committed, although it tried him on two counts, assault and battery with intent to commit rape and aiding and abetting the commission of rape. Documentation of the case comes from two main sources, the Freedmen's Bureau and the correspondence of Governor Jonathan Worth. See Robert Avery to James V. Bomford, 27 Mar. 1867; William W. Jones to M. Cogswell, 16 Mar. 1867; both in Letters Received, Second Military District, U.S. Army Continental Commands, RG 393, National Archives (NA). William W. Jones to the Assistant Commissioner, 28 Mar. 1867, Letters Received, North Carolina Assistant Commissioner's

Records, Bureau of Refugees, Freedmen, and Abandoned Lands (BRFAL), National Archives Microfilm Publications. Worth to William A. Philpott, 16 Oct. 1866, 231; Worth to the Governor of Virginia, 16 Oct. 1866, 234; James V. Bomford to J. M. Clous (a copy was forwarded to Worth), 22 Apr. 1867, 471–72; Worth to Maj. Gen. Sickles, 21 May 1867, 472–73; William A. Philpott to Worth, 8 Oct. 1867, 608; Worth to Robert Avery, 10 Oct. 1867, 607; all in Worth Letter Book, 1865–1867 (bound volume of correspondence), North Carolina Division of Archives and History (NCDAH), Raleigh. Worth to Andrew Johnson, 31 Dec. 1867, 5–9; E. W. Dennis to Louis V. Cazario (a copy was forwarded to Worth), 26 Mar. 1868, 111–15; both in Worth Letter Book, 1867–1868 (bound volume of correspondence), NCDAH. Worth's letter books contain copies of articles published in North Carolina newspapers. Some of Worth's correspondence has also been published: Robert Gilliam to Worth, 22 Nov. 1866, 2:844–45; Worth to Thomas Settle, 20 May 1867, 2:959–60; Worth to William A. Philpott, 18 Dec. 1867, 2:1089; Worth to W. A. Graham, 10 Jan. 1868, 2: 1128–31; Worth to Lewis Hanes, 17 Jan. 1869, 2:1265–67; all in J. G. de Roulhac Hamilton, ed., *The Correspondence of Jonathan Worth* (Raleigh: North Carolina Historical Commission; Edwards and Broughton, 1909). In *Reconstruction in North Carolina* (New York: Columbia University Press, 1914), 229–30, Hamilton also gives a summary of the case. Besides some of the orders and reports of the Freedmen's Bureau, the local court records contain only documentation of the formal proceedings of the case, such as the complaint, indictment, and order of execution: *State v. William and Henderson Cooper*, 1864–1867, Criminal Actions Concerning Slaves and Free Persons of Color, Granville County, NCDAH.

2. For discussions about gender and women's agency, see Judith M. Bennett, "Feminism and History," *Gender and History* 1 (autumn 1989): 251–72; Gisela Bock, "Women's History and Gender History," *Gender and History* 1 (spring 1989): 7–30; Elsa Barkley Brown, "Womanist Consciousness: Maggie Lena Walker and the Independent Order of Saint Luke," *Signs* 14 (spring 1989): 610–33; idem, "Polyrhythms and Improvisations: Lessons for Women's History," *History Workshop Journal* 31 (1991): 85–90; Jacquelyn Dowd Hall, "Partial Truths," *Signs* 14 (summer 1989): 902–11; Nancy A. Hewitt, "Reflections from a Departing Editor: Recasting Issues of Marginality," *Gender and History* 4 (spring 1992): 3–9; idem, "Compounding Differences," in "Intersections and Collision Courses: Women, Blacks, and Workers Confront Gender, Race, and Class: A Symposium," *Feminist Studies* 18 (summer 1992): 313–26; Evelyn Brooks Higginbotham, "African American Women's History and the Metalanguage of Race," *Signs* 17 (winter 1992): 251–74; Frances E. Mascia-Lees, Patricia Sharpe, and Colleen Ballerina Cohen, "The Postmodernist Turn in Anthropology: Cautions from a Feminist Perspective," *Signs* 15 (autumn 1989): 7–33; Louise Newman, Joan Williams, Lise Vogel, and Judith Newton, "Theoretical and Methodological Dialogue on the Writing of Women's History," *Journal of Women's History* 2 (winter 1991): 58–108; and Linda Nicholson and Nancy Fraser, "Social Criticism without Philosophy: An Encounter between Feminism and Postmodernism," in *Feminism/Postmodernism*, ed. Linda Nicholson (New York: Routledge, 1990).

3. See Avery to Bomford, 27 Mar. 1867; Worth to Philpott, 16 Oct. 1866, 231. Perhaps local authorities simply felt it was their duty to close the case and to bring Henderson Cooper to justice. Yet, judging from the crowded court docket, they clearly had enough to occupy their attention at home without embarking on a long and costly interstate manhunt. There were hundreds of cases before the local courts at this same time; see Criminal Action Papers, 1865–67, Granville County, NCDAH. The attention lavished on this particular case suggests that it was important in ways that the others were not.

4. Worth signed the papers necessary to secure Henderson Cooper's capture in 1866, but

he did not become actively involved in the case until 1867. Worth to Philpott, 16 Oct. 1866; Worth to the Governor of Virginia, 16 Oct. 1866. For the correspondence that includes his articles and discussions of them, see Worth to Graham, 10 Jan. 1868, 2:1128–31; Worth to Hanes, 17 Jan. 1869, 2:1265–67.

5. For discussions of the social and political importance of households, see Peter Bardaglio, *Reconstructing the Household: Families, Sex, and the Law in the Nineteenth-Century South* (Chapel Hill: University of North Carolina Press, 1995); Nancy Bercaw, "The Politics of Household: Domestic Battlegrounds in the Transition from Slavery to Freedom in the Yazoo-Mississippi Delta, 1850–1860" (Ph.D. diss., University of Pennsylvania, 1995); Elizabeth Fox-Genovese, *Within the Plantation Household: Black and White Women of the Old South* (Chapel Hill: University of North Carolina Press, 1988); Stephanie McCurry, *Masters of Small Worlds: Yeoman Households, Gender Relations, and the Political Culture of the Antebellum South Carolina Low Country* (New York: Oxford University Press, 1995); and LeeAnn Whites, *The Civil War as a Crisis in Gender: Augusta, Georgia, 1860–1890* (Athens: University of Georgia Press, 1995).

6. For a discussion of propertyless white men and dependence, see Laura F. Edwards, *Gendered Strife and Confusion: The Political Culture of Reconstruction* (Urbana: University of Illinois Press, 1997). Also see Robert J. Steinfeld, *The Invention of Free Labor: The Employment Relation in English and American Law and Culture, 1350–1870* (Chapel Hill: University of North Carolina Press, 1991).

7. For the work outlining the difficulties experienced by free women, white and black, in assuming the position of household head, see Victoria Bynum, *Unruly Women: The Politics of Social and Sexual Control in the Old South* (Chapel Hill: University of North Carolina Press, 1992); Drew Faust, " 'Trying to Do a Man's Business': Slavery, Violence, and Gender in the American Civil War," *Gender and History* 4 (summer 1992): 197–214; Suzanne Lebsock, *The Free Women of Petersburg: Status and Culture in a Southern Town, 1784–1860* (New York: W. W. Norton, 1984). For free blacks, also see Ira Berlin, *Slaves without Masters: The Free Negro in the Antebellum South* (New York: Pantheon, 1974); John Hope Franklin, *The Free Negro in North Carolina, 1790–1860* (1943; reprint, New York: Russell and Russell, 1969). Southern courts continued to define parental rights primarily as paternal rights, but they began to view the claims of mothers to their children more favorably toward the end of the antebellum period, a change that brought them more in line with northern patterns. Even then, custody was given at the discretion of the court. See Bardaglio, *Reconstructing the Household*, 100–101, 164.

8. Peter Bardaglio, "Rape and the Law in the Old South: 'Calculated to Excite Indignation in Every Heart,' " *Journal of Southern History* 60 (November 1994): 749–72; Jacquelyn Dowd Hall, " 'The Mind That Burns in Each Body': Women, Rape, and Racial Violence," in *Powers of Desire: The Politics of Sexuality*, ed. Ann Snitow, Christine Stansell, and Sharon Thompson (New York: Monthly Review Press, 1983); Martha Hodes, "The Sexualization of Reconstruction Politics: White Women and Black Men in the South after the Civil War," *Journal of the History of Sexuality* 3 (January 1993): 402–17.

9. Bardaglio, "Rape and the Law in the Old South"; Bynum, 36–39, 109–10; Catherine Clinton, "Bloody Terrain: Freedwomen, Sexuality, and Violence during Reconstruction," *Georgia Historical Quarterly* 76 (summer 1992): 310–32; Angela Davis, "Reflections on the Black Woman's Role in the Community of Slaves," *Black Scholar* 3 (December 1981): 3–15; Higginbotham; Darlene Clark Hine, "Rape and the Inner Lives of Black Women in the Middle West," *Signs* 14 (summer 1989): 912–20; Melton McLaurin, *Celia, a Slave* (Athens: University of Georgia Press, 1991); Hannah Rosen, "Struggles over 'Freedom': Sexual Violence during the Memphis Riot of 1866" (paper presented at the Berkshire Conference of

Women Historians, Poughkeepsie, New York, June 1993); Deborah Gray White, *Ar'n't I a Woman? Female Slaves in the Plantation South* (New York: W. W. Norton, 1985); and Jennifer Wriggins, "Rape, Racism, and the Law," *Harvard Women's Law Journal* 6 (spring 1983): 103–41.

10. Bardaglio, "Rape and the Law in the Old South"; Bynum, 109–10, 117–18; Laura F. Edwards, "Sexual Violence, Gender, Reconstruction, and the Extension of Patriarchy in Granville County, North Carolina," *North Carolina Historical Review* 68 (July 1991): 237–60. For the ways that the treatment of rape revealed class divisions in the North, see Christine Stansell, *City of Women: Sex and Class in New York, 1789–1860* (Urbana: University of Illinois Press, 1987), 23–28.

11. Recently some historians have argued that white southerners began to construe black-male-on-white-female rape as problematic only after the Civil War. See Hodes, "Sexualization of Reconstruction Politics"; and Diane Miller Sommerville, "The Rape Myth in the Old South Reconsidered," *Journal of Southern History* 61 (August 1995): 481–518. Other work, however, has shown that white southerners had always tied racial power to sexualized images, including black-male-on-white-female rape. The classic statement is Winthrop Jordan, *White over Black: American Attitudes toward the Negro, 1550–1812* (Chapel Hill: University of North Carolina Press, 1968). Indeed, as Bardaglio has argued in "Rape and the Law in the Old South," judicial decisions in antebellum rape cases reveal the complex play of race, class, and gender as well as the connection of rape to larger structures of power. It was this connection that made rape such a potent symbol in the social and political upheavals of the post-war years.

12. Worth to Johnson, 31 Dec. 1867, 8–9.

13. For parallels with the political rhetoric in antebellum South Carolina during the nullification crisis, see McCurry, *Masters of Small Worlds*, 260–76.

14. Worth feared the political power of poor whites as well as blacks. Without the guidance of the "better class," the "masses" could easily degenerate into "a great mob ruled by the will of the hour." See, for instance, Worth to W. F. Leak, 5 Jan. 1867, 2:860. For racialized references to whites, see Hamilton, 2:1004, 1048, 1215. For an expanded discussion of the views of conservative white elites in North Carolina, see Paul D. Escott, *Many Excellent People: Power and Privilege in North Carolina, 1850–1900* (Chapel Hill: University of North Carolina Press, 1985), 85–135.

15. Worth's obsession with the Freedmen's Bureau and its interference with the governance of the state pervades his correspondence. For the blame Granville officials placed on the Freedmen's Bureau, see Dennis to Cazario, 26 Mar. 1868, 111–15.

16. Avery to Bomford, 27 Mar. 1867; also see Bomford to Clous, 22 Apr. 1867, 471–72.

17. William W. Jones, the local Freedmen's Bureau agent in Granville County, worked from similar assumptions. An abolitionist and a strong defender of equal civil and political rights for freedpeople, Jones had initially asked the bureau to investigate the case because he suspected that the ruling of the Confederate court that had sentenced Henderson Cooper might not be valid in the eyes of the U.S. government. But when local white residents—the "most respectable citizens"—approached him to request federal troops to keep order at Henderson Cooper's execution, he was inclined to support their request. Apparently, he too saw the actions of the "Freedmen and others" as an inappropriate circumvention of the rule of law. See Jones to Cogswell, 16 Mar. 1867; and Jones to the Assistant Commissioner, 28 Mar. 1867. For Jones's abolitionism, see William W. Jones to Jordan Chambers, 20 Apr. 1869, Governor's Papers, Holden, NCDAH. For the ways northern racial ideology developed within the context of emancipation in the South, see Barbara J. Fields, "Ideology and Race

in American History," and Thomas C. Holt, " 'An Empire over the Mind': Emancipation, Race, and Ideology in the British West Indies and the American South," both in *Region, Race, and Reconstruction: Essays in Honor of C. Vann Woodward*, ed. J. Morgan Kousser and James M. McPherson (New York: Oxford University Press, 1982).

18. For Worth's view of Susan Daniel, see Worth to Johnson, 31 Dec. 1867, 5–9; Worth to Graham, 10 Jan. 1868, 2:1128–31. For the bureau's view, see Avery to Bomford, 27 Mar. 1867; Bomford to Clous, 22 Apr. 1867, 471–72. Many women's historians have discussed the racial and class dimensions of this bifurcated view of women. See, for instance, Bynum; Carol F. Karlson, *The Devil in the Shape of a Woman: Witchcraft in Colonial New England* (New York: W. W. Norton, 1987); Stansell; and White, 27–61.

19. See Escott, *Many Excellent People*, 103–04, 136–70; Hodes, "Sexualization of Reconstruction Politics"; Otto H. Olsen, *A Carpetbagger's Crusade: The Life of Albion Winegar Tourgée* (Baltimore: Johns Hopkins University Press, 1965); Allen Trelease, *White Terror: The Ku Klux Klan Conspiracy and Southern Reconstruction* (New York: Harper and Row, 1971). Also see Albion W. Tourgée, *A Fool's Errand* (1879; reprint, New York: Harper and Row, 1966). Political conflict in Granville County remained heated throughout the 1870s but was particularly intense in the 1860s. See Silas Curtis and others to William W. Holden, 11 Oct. 1868; Moses M. Hester, Joseph Coly, and Jacob Winston to William W. Holden, 9 Oct. 1868, Governor's Papers, Holden, NCDAH.

20. Jones to the Assistant Commissioner, 28 Mar. 1867.

21. It was the local Freedmen's Bureau agent, William W. Jones, who brought the Cooper-Daniel case to the attention of his superiors, when he wrote to the headquarters of the Second Military District asking whether "this sentence should be executed without approval of the President of the United States" because Cooper had been tried in a Confederate court (Jones to Cogswell, 16 Mar. 1867). Nonetheless, it would be a mistake to divorce Jones's interest in the case from the turmoil and conflict surrounding it. Although local white residents requested his aid in obtaining the presence of federal troops, it was Jones's own sense of the potential for violence and disorder that prompted him to forward the request to his superiors. Similarly, Jones probably would never have written his first letter inquiring about the legal status of Henderson Cooper's imminent execution if he had not known about the conflicts surrounding the case and the position of those who doubted Henderson Cooper's guilt.

22. Dennis to Cazario, 26 Mar. 1868, 111–15.

23. Ibid.

24. Worth gave lengthy descriptions of the case without naming Susan Daniel. See, for instance, Worth to Sickles, 21 May 1867, 472–73.

25. Bomford to Clous, 22 Apr. 1867, 471–72. For interracial relationships in the South, see Bynum, 88–110, 122–23, 152–53; Martha Hodes, *White Women, Black Men: Illicit Sex in the Nineteenth-Century South* (New Haven: Yale University Press, 1997). For the problems of white women during the Civil War, see Bynum, 111–50; Paul D. Escott, "Poverty and Governmental Aid for the Poor in Confederate North Carolina," *North Carolina Historical Review* 61 (October 1984): 462–80.

26. Women's historians have long noted the vast gulf that can exist between representations of women and real women's lives. Moreover, as recent work has shown, images do more than misrepresent women's lives, they also reaffirm particular perspectives of historical events by hiding conflict and contradiction. See, in particular, Jacquelyn Dowd Hall, "Private Eyes, Public Women: Images of Class and Sex in the Urban South, Atlanta, Georgia, 1913–1915," in *Work Engendered: Toward a New History of American Labor*, ed. Ava Baron (Ithaca: Cornell University Press, 1991); Elizabeth Faue, *Community of Suffering and Strug-*

gle: Women, Men, and the Labor Movement in Minneapolis, 1915–1945 (Chapel Hill: University of North Carolina Press, 1991).

27. Elsa Barkley Brown, "To Catch a Vision of Freedom" (paper presented at the Social History Seminar, Newberry Library, Chicago, October 1991); Bynum, 130–50; Faust, " 'Trying to Do a Man's Business' "; idem, "Altars of Sacrifice: Confederate Women and the Narratives of War," *Journal of American History* 76 (March 1990): 1200–1228; Noralee Frankel, *Freedom's Women: Black Women and Families in Civil War Era Mississippi* (Bloomington: Indiana University Press, 1999); Jacqueline Jones, *Labor of Love, Labor of Sorrow: Black Women, Work, and the Family from Slavery to the Present* (New York: Basic Books, 1985); George Rable, *Civil Wars: Women and the Crisis of Southern Nationalism* (Urbana: University of Illinois Press, 1989); Leslie Ann Schwalm, "The Meaning of Freedom: African-American Women and Their Transition from Slavery to Freedom in Low Country South Carolina" (Ph.D. diss., University of Wisconsin, 1991); and Whites.

28. Escott, *Many Excellent People*; Eric Foner, *Reconstruction: America's Unfinished Revolution* (New York: Harper and Row, 1988), 362–64; Donald Nieman, "Black Political Power and Criminal Justice: Washington County, Texas, 1868–1884," *Journal of Southern History* 55 (August 1989): 391–420.

29. For sexual violence cases in Granville County, see Edwards, "Sexual Violence, Gender, Reconstruction." Local courts elsewhere duplicated the pattern. See Criminal Action Papers, 1865–1890, Edgecombe County, NCDAH; Criminal Action Papers, 1865–1890, Orange County, NCDAH. These cases, moreover, underrepresent resistance to sexual assault, because they include only those in which the official charge was rape or attempted rape or where sexual assault was specifically mentioned in the complaint or testimony. They do not include cases dismissed by justices or those that involved sexual assault but were tried as simple assault. No doubt, poor white and black women hesitated to submit to the ordeal of trial, where their actions and intentions would be treated with skepticism, if not open hostility. Some may have preferred to resolve the matter within their communities, without state interference. For a discussion of this point, see Sara Rapport, "The Freedmen's Bureau as a Legal Agent for Black Men and Women in Georgia, 1865–1868," *Georgia Historical Quarterly* 73 (spring 1989): 39–41. Women could not prosecute either husbands or fathers. Marital rape was unheard of, and North Carolina did not pass a law prohibiting incest until 1879. See Peter Bardaglio, " 'An Outrage upon Nature': Incest and the Law in the Nineteenth-Century South," in *In Joy and in Sorrow: Women, Family, and Marriage in the Victorian South, 1830–1900*, ed. Carol Bleser (New York: Oxford University Press, 1991). For the rarity of rape cases in the antebellum period in North Carolina, see Bynum, 117.

30. Edwards, "Sexual Violence, Gender, Reconstruction." For black women's vulnerability, see Hannah Rosen, "Interracial Rape and the Politics of Reconstruction" (paper presented at the National Graduate Women's Studies Conference, Ann Arbor, Michigan, 1990); Clinton, "Bloody Terrain." For unpublicized black-male-on-white-female rape cases in addition to those in Granville County, see *State v. Elias*, 1865, Criminal Action Papers, Orange County; and *State v. McMinn* (documents forwarded to Gov. Worth in a pardon request), 9 June 1866, Governor's Papers, Worth, NCDAH.

31. I am also indebted to conversations with Hannah Rosen on this topic. Also Jacquelyn Dowd Hall makes this point in *Revolt against Chivalry: Jessie Daniel Ames and the Women's Campaign against Lynching*, rev. ed. (New York: Columbia University Press, 1993), xv–xxxviii.

32. In Granville County between 1865 and 1886 there were records of fifty-two cases involving male-on-female violence and twenty-four recorded cases of domestic disputes, involving physical abuse, abandonment, and bigamy; Criminal Action Papers, Granville

County. In many years, there were more cases involving women than those with just men. Other counties yield similar patterns. See Criminal Action Papers, 1865–1890, Edgecombe County; Criminal Action Papers, 1865–1890, Orange County, all in NCDAH. Frankel also points out that African American women rejected violence against them and often aggressively defended themselves, arguing that conflicts within families did not necessarily divide women and men within the community but often reinforced familial and community ties.

33. For an expanded discussion of this process, see Edwards, *Gendered Strife and Confusion.* Also see Jeanne Boydston, *Home and Work: Housework, Wages, and the Ideology of Labor in the Early Republic* (New York: Oxford University Press, 1990); Linda K. Kerber, "The Paradox of Women's Citizenship in the Early Republic: The Case of *Martin v. Massachusetts*, 1805," *American Historical Review* 97 (April 1992): 349–78; and Whites.

Chapter Fifteen

Livestock, Boundaries, and Public Space in Spartanburg
African American Men, Elite White Women, and the Spectacle of Conjugal Relations

Scott Nelson

A survey of the sexual landscape of the Spartanburg region in the post-war period must start with the history of livestock: cows, sheep, pigs, and horses.[1] Before the Civil War, large farm animals outnumbered people in this South Carolina county by almost four to one. Their history of the coming of war, the human pilgrimages across the state, and the emergence of the most violent Klan in the South would likely be very different from the history we have received from scholars who rely on human records. But I cannot provide that story. I lack facility with archaeological records, and would find working through the remains of nineteenth-century livestock a daunting and smelly task. Nevertheless I will risk anthropomorphism in an effort to describe the way in which these mute animals may give us another way into post-war Spartanburg—if not their perspective, then perhaps their place, in the reshaping of race, class, and gender boundaries in bloody Spartanburg.

In a certain sense, I am being contrary here. When I talk about livestock, I am talking about them as capital resources, as consumers of land, and as goods in a capitalist market. That the counties around Spartanburg relied on the raising and selling of livestock meant that conflicts after the war were not the familiar southern conflicts over who worked in cotton or tobacco fields, the portions divided in sharecrops, or the market price of fertilizer. Rather, Spartanburg's position in the livestock trade made economic conflicts in the region much more complex and, I would argue, left the roles of those who managed, rode, and sold livestock open to constant, bitter renegotiations. The borders between men and women, and between blacks and whites, remained unstable in post-war Spartanburg because the economic resources connected to livestock—the land they needed and the cost of the corn they consumed—were drastically altered first by the Civil War and then again by the emergence of an interstate railway system. Where previously every member of the community had a more or less established position in relation to beasts and to each other—for example, a different job when it came to pigs, depending on race, class, and gender—these broader economic changes in the wake of the war reshuffled everyone's position. White conservatives' anxieties about this reshuffling became increasingly fixed on the image of an intermingling of white female and black male bodies.[2]

This anxiety did not spring entirely from white imaginations. In some important cases, Klansmen targeted domestic arrangements between black men and white women that the spatial and economic disruptions in Spartanburg made possible. New kinds of domestic arrangements with black men allowed elite white women to trade their animals and to postpone decisions about marriage. These domestic re-arrangements, which let women turn livestock into commodities, provoked a mas-sive response. By 1870 a community of white men joined an organization called the Council of Safety, donned cloth masks, loaded up repeating rifles, and began a campaign of terror to put a stop to these changes.

Where was Spartanburg and why was livestock so important to its boundaries? The rolling hills of the Carolina upcountry were hundreds of miles from the nearest city port. The "rapid-flowing stream and magnificent shoals" of the Tyger River made Spartanburg County look like "a wild and romantic country," as one observer put it, but the wildness of the river also prevented water-borne navigation to the city centers.[3] Before the Civil War, some plantations grew cotton, but largely for local spinning, as the value of a cotton bale would be lost in the price of wagoning it thirty or forty miles to the Broad River.[4] Only in the bellies, breasts, and haunches of pigs and cattle could Spartanburg's bounty be transported out of the county and sold for a profit. Animals were instruments—they made corn fodder mobile and concentrated corn's protein into living tissue and fat. Spartanburg drovers moved animals down to plantations and cities on the Carolina coast, where they were added to the otherwise protein-deficient diet of slaves. South Carolina slaves in turn produced the consummate food crop for European markets: rice. Thus the pigs and cows of Spartanburg acted as the first link in a labor and food chain that finished, as rice, on the dinner tables of iron workers in the Ruhr valley and factory workers in Manchester.[5]

The South Carolina upcountry has been discussed largely from the perspective of those who rode horses: the heads of households. But Spartanburg's position in southern trade was more complex than the view from that height might suggest. The region was not remote enough from markets to be the self-sufficient world of sturdy yeomen, their wives, and a small number of slaves that Steven Hahn de-scribes in the Georgia upcountry.[6] In fact, one-third of Spartanburg County resi-dents were slaves, and their labor made lowcountry rice plantations work efficiently and cheaply. Neither was it a region dominated by would-be planters, as Lacy K. Ford, Jr., and James Oakes would have us believe.[7] White men did indeed leave the region to build plantations in Texas and Louisiana, but the story of the diverse collection of men and women who stayed behind—farmers, drovers, mothers, and coachmen—needs fuller explanation. To that end, the world of wool and meat that was formed before the war needs fuller scrutiny.

The Carolina upcountry near antebellum Spartanburg moved to the rhythms of the buying, selling, slaughtering, and shearing of animals. In this sparsely settled state there was no system for formally incorporating towns; collections of people and animals converged in loosely drawn "settlements." When pigs and horses congregated, so did white men. On "sale days," held once a month in upcountry districts, men came together to buy, sell, and mostly trade horses, cattle, and sheep.[8]

On sale days, trade and barter were carried on in concentric rings of racial and ethnic communities. The center of Spartanburg County had a courthouse around which the white men gathered. This, too, was where politics took place. White men heard speeches, listened to public notices, and gossiped about affairs in Columbia, Charleston, and Washington. Around the margins of the courthouse lay a second ring of less formal trade, in which drovers, horse traders, and local men could buy food and drink from shopkeepers, itinerant peddlers, and tinkers. This ring of trade was regulated by city ordinances. To prevent bitter arguments among wagoners and horse traders from becoming too dangerous, city officials prohibited peddlers from selling alcohol on a sale day.[9] (Tinkers, especially, were renowned for drinking a dram and then challenging all comers to a fight.)[10] Finally, very informal trade—the so-called black market—lay around the farthest boundaries of Spartanburg. Many slave families had gardens they worked on Saturdays and Sundays. Slave women sold these garden crops on public highways, work that was critical to the life of the community.[11] Slave women, too, traded herbs such as "life everlasting," "rabbit tobacco," and "spice bush bark" as medical remedies.[12] More disturbing to white authorities was the "black market" trading of chickens, possums, and whiskey engaged in by slave men and poor whites, often near stables, usually at the margins of upcountry towns.[13]

These boundaries and rings that divided men and women, white and black, were of course weakened by the very process of trading. Unlike markets in cotton and rice—which were highly organized and managed by factors who lived in port cities—horse and cattle trading was a face-to-face encounter. The people who could circulate in all of these communities were white men. Following the anthropologist Benedict Anderson, I argue that those who can journey from one community to another can also interpret and describe those communities, navigating not just streets but relationships. As translators, they can more easily become legislators or managers of these communities.[14] These secular pilgrims, as I will call them, could journey from one kind of economy to another—from formal and legal to informal and illegal. The pilgrimage itself is part of what gave white masters their power. They could move among these realms and also attend to political events in Washington; follow gossip in town; and catch rumors of slave mistreatment, conjure, and revolt. Horses provided the means by which these secular pilgrims navigated the landscape of Spartanburg. No one else could make this pilgrimage: law and propriety prevented white women from moving through these circuits. "Patrollers," white men who patrolled a fixed area or "beat," prevented black men and women from making the journey.[15]

Those white men who could negotiate these circuits of trade could draw from each of them. The ex-slave Peter Arthur recalled that his former owner, "the youngest Scott boy," took his horses and buggy into town once a year. The buggy had "a long hind end to fetch things to and fro in." Arthur recalled that "Marse Scott" would stay for two weeks to "have a little 'joyment befo' he come back home."[16]

As a planter's son, Scott could travel through each ring of trade. In part he had to, in order to buy goods unavailable elsewhere. Because local ordinances prohibited liquor from being sold in town on sale days, Scott would have bought brandied fruit from peddlers on the outskirts of town. Such fruit was neither forbidden nor fully legal, but since it worked like liquor if you drank up the juices, it became the favorite lunch of horse traders in the upcountry.[17] Perhaps, too, Scott's "little 'joyment" included time at a brothel near the edge of town.

One community missing from these racialized and gendered rings of trade was elite white women. After the war, some observers saw yeomen wives and daughters on sale days, often with corncob pipes and homespun dresses, but elite white women were conspicuously absent from community trade.[18] White women's absence from trade before the war should be even less surprising. Under South Carolina common law, white women underwent "civil death" when they married and were thus technically not allowed to hold, manage, or dispose of property, livestock included. When they married, unless it was arranged otherwise in a prenuptial agreement, their property was turned over to their husbands.[19] Emily Harris, the wife of a Piedmont yeoman farmer, remarked on this isolation when writing in her diary about how infuriating and distracting it was to have seven children: "[I] ask myself what I should do with them when the school was out, and then what I should do with myself if I had no children."[20] Women partly made up for the closed nature of public trading by gathering outside church after services, followed by rounds of "visiting." Micajah Clark, a visitor to upcountry Anderson County in 1857, found it possible to invade the "host of find [sic] looking Young Ladies there." As an interloper into the women's circles in front of the church, he remarked that he "saw many a strange eye among the Ladies wandering towards me."[21] White women met white men in situations that were simultaneously like and unlike the public trade of the courthouse. Men sought wives not at the center of town, but at barn dances called cotillions. A cow or a pig would be killed and smoked for a barbecue. Young men and women gathered to dance and to order themselves into couples. Potential wives would be swung from arm to arm for inspection. Men later made offers of marriage to fathers, at which time dowries of land, cattle, and slaves would be decided upon.[22]

Male and female slaves paired up at frolics, occasions quite unlike cotillions. "Mad" Griffin recalled that "Conjin Doc" would put a spell on their master Glenn, steal a pig on a Saturday night, and repair to a huge gully or hollow near the plantation for "our lil' mite o' fun." The pig would be "dressed and barbecued," then eaten by their "lil' gang." On Sunday morning, when the master asked where they had been, they would claim to have been at a church society meeting. The master believed these stories until some time later when the spell was mysteriously broken and he counted his pigs.[23] Other dances were arranged publicly for holidays, also in barns. White men were often allowed at these functions, presumably because access to black women could not be denied to them.[24] Here again they acted as secular pilgrims, reporting back on the "habits" of slaves. In other cases, black men and women met at corn shuckings. Men would line up and compete at shucking corn for the corn crib. The fastest shucker would be the one to find the single red ear, which could be traded for whiskey.[25]

Such events kept race and gender carefully ordered at the same time that infiltration and movement were possible. While the white barn dance operated something like a stockyard for choosing wives, it was officiated by black men who "called cotillion" with fiddles and pipes made of cane.[26] Geographically, the corn shuckings operated as nearly the reverse of livestock sales at the courthouse. Black men at the center shucked corn. Black women cheered them on in a circle around the men. White men and women watched the singing, shucking, and cheering from a respectable distance, eating dinner inside before the slaves ate dinner in the yard.[27] Perhaps because of the seemingly permeable boundaries between blacks and whites that upcountry trade and sociability made possible, free blacks were almost nonexistent in Spartanburg County, constituting two-thirds of one percent of Spartanburg's African American community in 1850.[28]

This whole edifice of transport and trade in human and animal flesh—carefully balanced inside these ambiguous cordons of race, class, and gender—would be drastically transformed by events between 1859 and 1868. The first event was cause for celebration among white Spartanburgers. The Spartanburg and Union Railroad connected the hill country to Charleston in 1859, allowing freight to be shipped down the state over the rickety track that crossed the Carolina swamps.[29] According to a local historian, dozens of cattle were killed for a massive barbecue, and slaveholders declared a "holiday for the colored people." Thousands turned out for the arrival of the train and "the devouring of the barbecued beef and loaves of bread which had been provided in sufficient plentifulness to feed the multitude." The celebrations finished that night with a ball, probably for white residents.[30]

In 1861 white men gathered around the Spartanburg courthouse again—this time not to trade, but to organize into Confederate militias. White men drilled with neighbors on the mustering grounds of the Enoree River, which bordered Spartanburg. Most white Spartanburgers joined "Big-eyed Bill" Smith in the Holcombe Legion.[31] Some black men and women crossed state lines to follow federal troops; others joined the Union army as soldiers; still others became "Pioneers"—soldiers who built and reconstructed railway lines for Union troops. Yet most of Spartanburg's African American population was too remote to join federal armies. Some who stayed behind helpfully pointed out where their masters had hidden or buried the meat when Wheeler's Confederate cavalry came through the county.[32]

Replacing the black and white men who left the county were coastal slaveholders escaping from federal forces on the coast. These migrants brought tools, bandboxes, and coffles of lowcountry slaves up into the hills and valleys along the swiftly flowing Pacolet, Tyger, and Broad Rivers.[33] Part of the appeal of the upcountry was its store of livestock, which might feed a large population longer than lowcountry rice fields. From the perspective of livestock, the Civil War was a deliberate and carefully organized carnage. Everyone—Confederate quartermasters, former planters, hungry families cut off by federal gunboats—wanted a piece. Throughout the upcountry, cattle were killed in huge quantities. For middling and smaller white farmers, animals were the closest thing they had to savings, and the loss of livestock effectively impoverished the region for decades.[34]

The Confederacy brought even more changes to Spartanburg's location in the geography of southern trade. One of Jefferson Davis's first acts as president was to provide for the construction of an inland railroad system to bind the southern states together. By offering exemptions from Confederate service to contractors and by drafting slaves for construction, Davis was able to put together a system of railroads from Richmond, Virginia, through Charlotte, North Carolina, past Spartanburg's neighboring York County, and on toward Augusta, Georgia.[35] The Confederacy gave with one hand and took away with the other, for Spartanburg was joined to the Richmond trunk line with track that had once tied Spartanburg to Charleston. By 1865 the Spartanburg region was a few miles from the backbone of an interstate southern railroad system that terminated in the massive deepwater port of Nor-folk.[36]

But the consequences of Spartanburg's new position in the geography of trade became most apparent after the abolition of slavery and the work of Reconstruction had begun.[37] In Spartanburg County, land became available in large quantities, corn became cheap, and widows could separate their property from the debts of their husbands. If livestock was rare in post-war Spartanburg, land was plentiful. The South Carolina Manufacturing Company (SCMC) was primarily responsible for this fact. Before the war, company-owned slave mechanics had made iron for the foundry using an antiquated charcoal method that required hundreds of acres of trees. Thus the SCMC foundries were stoked with twenty-five thousand acres of company-owned iron range and forest in Spartanburg County.[38] After the war, the SCMC's newly freed workers were determined to work five, rather than seven, days a week. The principal owner fired all his freed workers and tried to bring in white workers from North Carolina to replace them. He gave up when his chief iron founder requested higher wages.[39] The failure of the company thus made thousands of acres available for sale. As there was little local capital available for purchase, hundreds of valuable acres in Spartanburg were bought by the state for redistribution to former slaves. The land rapidly increased in value in the short time that state buyers held it, bringing cries of corruption from the county.[40] The fears of white farmers, however, were more concrete, for if freed workers had their own land they would grow their own corn, keep their own cattle, and never work on shares for white landowners.

The end of the war also undermined existing corn markets. Corn prices in up-country towns dropped precipitously as black and white families began buying barrels of cheap, bleached flour from stores near railroad centers rather than buying their corn in town.[41] This was largely a question of price, as cheap midwestern wheat flooded railway trunk lines.[42] Farmers rued that corn was at least "a good thing in a family." With few pigs and cattle to process the corn, farmers more often converted it to whiskey and sold it outside town illegally, usually cribbed away in cane brakes near the river. Many farmers were forced by the poor prices for corn

to sell out, and the Spartanburg newspaper did a thriving business in ads for sheriff's sales.[43]

This change in prices collapsed the older racial geography of trade. Now the
center of town was not where white men gathered to sell their cattle, but where the
sheriff sold off family land. The "black market" area around the outskirts of town
was no longer black, but a place where white men tried to sell off their distilled
crops without paying taxes. It was not so much that "the bottom rail was on top,"
a reference to the clean top and dirty bottom of a fence that white contemporaries
used to describe Reconstruction; in Spartanburg County the entire fence had completely shifted and no longer penned in its previous inhabitants. Those male slaves
who had been kept out of the courthouse grounds could now buy land as free men;
those white planters who had sold their animals with their coats on were now
rolling up their sleeves and selling corn liquor in the cane brakes.

Women stood to benefit from this redrawing of gender and racial boundaries in
Spartanburg. The new constitution drawn up by radical Republicans in 1868 eliminated the common-law restrictions on female property ownership. Married women
could now own their own land, have their property freed from the debts of their
husbands, and enter into contracts on their own account.[44] Thus Confederate widows could take over the land of their former husbands, and clear the land of its
former debts by advertising publicly in a local newspaper.[45]

The way in which white men and women met each other also changed, much to
the chagrin of the men who remembered the barn dances. More often after the war,
elite white men and women met at ice cream socials put on by the local Baptist
churches.[46] In such an environment white women were probably able to gather into
groups and talk with one another rather than with a male dance partner. The
Carolina Spartan noted the change in an editorial entitled "A Nice Girl":

> Though that class of girls is by no means extinct, still they are not so numerous as
> might be wished. . . . A nice girl is not the languishing beauty, drawing on the sofa,
> and discussing the latest novel, or opera, or the giraffeing like creature sweeping ma-
> jestically through the drawing room. . . . She is not given to sensitive novels, she is too
> busy. . . . Who makes the toast and the tea, and buttons the boy's shirts, and waters
> the flowers, and feeds the chickens, and brightens up the parlor, and sitting-room? Is
> it the languisher, or the giraffee, or the "elegante?" Not a bit of it; it's the nice young
> girl.[47]

Women's ability to "giraffe"—to peer around and inspect, rather than simply being
inspected—was precisely the problem in the eyes of white men. One could argue
that wartime losses reduced the number of marriageable men, but the fact that elite
white women could take their time choosing a white man, or not choose one at all,
was a source of considerable anxiety. With potential economic resources now sep-
arable from a husband, widows and daughters were also freed from the pen. Some
could even take their resources out of the state and marry north of the Mason-
Dixon line.[48] Where their next step would take them was likely on everyone's mind.

Some landowning white men adapted more quickly to the changes that trade and freedom brought to Spartanburg. Some enterprising property owners shifted from cattle and pork to cotton. Dr. John Winsmith, who had served in the state legislature during the war and thus avoided Confederate service, became by 1871 the largest private landholder in Spartanburg County. Winsmith's land was near the Confederate-built system that connected eastern Virginia to Columbia, and thus his land near the Glen Springs resort would increase in value when the newly proposed railroad between Charlotte and Atlanta was built. Winsmith and a few others had learned that such railroad systems provided cheap, phosphate fertilizer and direct access to national and international markets.[49] Around 1868 Winsmith declared himself a Republican and attracted freedpeople to his place by making book-schooling available to all tenants.[50] But Winsmith paid a price for his moving between communities of freedmen and planters; he nearly died in a gunfight with Klansmen on his property.[51]

Most former planters opposed Reconstruction, but none so violently nor so persistently as those in the counties around Spartanburg. Before and shortly after the elections of 1868, an organization calling itself the Ku Klux Klan began a concerted campaign of violence and murder throughout the South. While many southern "outrages" were sporadic—lynch mobs, riots of white men, gun battles in town—President Ulysses S. Grant learned from governors and the War Department that the South Carolina upcountry was the most consistently violent, even after federal troops were brought in. The president delayed action at first. Outrages subsided after his inauguration, but when violence flared up again after the Senate and state elections of 1870, Grant sent a message to Congress relaying the many instances of violence in the Carolinas.[52] Congress sent a joint committee into the South to interview both Democrats and Republicans to determine whether the attacks were sporadic, local, and designed to enforce caste distinctions (the Democratic claim) or organized, regional, and designed to intimidate voters (the Republican claim). The South Carolina upcountry was the most investigated region in the South, and it was only here that Grant declared certain counties in insurrection, suspended the writ of habeas corpus, and rounded up Klansmen for trials.[53]

The trials show a varied collection of pretexts for Klan violence. In South Carolina, black militias were called up in 1869 to put down violence that had started in 1868. This in particular seemed to enrage white conservatives and gave the Klan considerable local legitimacy among whites. While Klansmen paraded freely, hundreds of other white men stood in waiting to declare alibis if they were arrested. Complicity with the Klan went from the local sheriff to the local magistrates, from a circuit court judge who invalidated their arrests to the newspaper that publicly printed all their pronouncements.[54] The Klan's success in the Spartanburg region can best be understood in the context of the reshuffling of markets and masculinity there.

The most arresting fact about these attacks is that some of the most notorious ones were directed at black sharecroppers or coachmen who worked for white women. White landowning women were never attacked, but they seem to have been a key absent figure in many of these cases. The first important case here is that of the widow Whittemore. As the widow of a plantation owner, she could have taken her land from her husband's estate directly after 1868. Mrs. Whittemore had moved from outside the county in 1870, bought a plantation eight miles outside town, and a house in town. She had two horses that she wanted to sell off, but because it would have been improper for a woman to trade her horses in town, she had the coachman who lived out on her plantation, Samuel Simmons, trade for her. " 'Sam,' " she said " 'I will give you this horse in your hands, and the first time you can get a good trade take it; but I will not take less than $80 for him; but if you can make a good swap for him, make it.' "[55] Simmons apparently got an excellent trade for the horse, receiving a good mule from one Mr. Beloue for one of the horses. Two days later, Beloue determined that Simmons had indeed gotten the better deal, stopped Simmons and Mrs. Whittemore on the highway into Spartanburg, and demanded his mule back. Or, more succinctly, he said, " 'I am going to have my mule or blow your God damned brains out.' " When Simmons and Whittemore refused, Beloue became enraged. As Beloue told Mrs. Whittemore, " 'I will put six balls through your boy or have him back.' " When she refused, Beloue responded to Simmons, " 'If you don't give me back my critter I will bring the Ku-Klux on you, and swing you to a limb until you are dead, by God.' " Simmons told investigators that Mrs. Whittemore was worried for him, but that he was unafraid. Two or three weeks later, Klansmen broke into Simmons's house on the Whittemore plantation, searched for weapons, and told Simmons that they were soldiers who had died in 1862 and come from the graves to protect their grandchildren. They then showed him the horns on their heads, and how one had been bent in his coming out of his grave. Finally, they pulled Simmons's shirt over his head and whipped him thirteen times.[56]

Daniel Lipscomb, also of Spartanburg, had been the coachman for the white Linder family as a slave. Though he was seventy-five years old he was given a plot of land after the war because, as he remarked, he was "a favorite servant." Lipscomb, too, regularly made the circuit from the outskirts of the county to town in Spartanburg for marketing. He was also an important political organizer for the Republican Party in the region, connected with the supervisor for elections in the district. Around 1869 a white man in his township, Perry McArthur, asked Lipscomb to "electioneer" for him with the "young mistress" of the Linder family. Perry McArthur's intentions were romantic, and because the young mistress seldom got out of the house, Lipscomb, pilgrim between white and black, was the only man who could act as intermediary between McArthur and the object of his desire. When the mistress heard about McArthur's intentions, she gave the coachman a terse reply for her erstwhile suitor, " 'Uncle, I wouldn't notice him any more than I would a cat.' " When McArthur got the message from Lipscomb (which Lipscomb may well have repeated throughout the settlement), McArthur became enraged. McArthur, with some property but without an elder white man to act as his intermediary, turned to Klan violence to avenge the slights for which he felt Lipscomb was responsible. He and his friends dressed up in sheets, called Lipscomb out of his house, denounced him as a Republican "rattler," and whipped him five hundred times on the back with a riding crop about the width of a finger. Lipscomb barely survived the attack.[57]

The community of black men who gave testimony to these Klan outrages were mostly known to one another. Word of Klan attacks got around at the brush arbor churches, on the lines of railroads that were being built through the town, and at the steps of the courthouse where freedmen traded horses, heard political speeches, and gossiped about politics. What had happened in the face-to-face world of the drovers and traders of Spartanburg was a thorough transformation of racial and gender boundaries that could not be erased easily. During the years of presidential Reconstruction (1865–1867), white conservatives tried to require that freedmen carry licenses to trade in the towns of South Carolina. When Congress determined in March 1867 (during so-called radical Reconstruction) that state governments were in the hands of former Confederates, they called for states to be reorganized, this time giving Republican provisional governors the right to decide whom to enfranchise. In South Carolina, freedmen reconstituted the state with, again, capacious rights for white and black women to own property. The new governments also nullified the legislation that required black men to have licenses to trade. The freedmen in the best position to take advantage of this transformation were former coachmen, men like Simmons and Lipscomb. During Reconstruction they replaced white planters as the secular pilgrims among the racial and gender communities of Spartanburg. They knew the intimate details of the lives of folks on their plantations, and possessed a much wider knowledge of Spartanburg's African American community.[58] Lipscomb had a different last name from his former owners, suggesting that he was related to, or had been owned by, William Smith Lipscomb, the white hotelkeeper in Spartanburg.[59] These new men made the circuit from city to the outskirts of the county and were in a position to act both as formal representatives of the community in politics and as informal representatives in relaying news and gossip. What better people to target with Klan violence than black men who made the pilgrimage between public and private?

The coachmen crossed boundaries of race and community in another way as well. Many upcountry coachmen were mulatto, and their pilgrimages between worlds were an awkward and unacknowledged fact. Many mulatto men and women interviewed in the upcountry during the 1930s drew their lineage back to coachmen and house servants. What better community to operate between the worlds of black and white than people who were both and neither? Many recalled rumors that their fathers had been prominent white men in the community, but in one case in nearby Fairfield County, John C. Brown, who called himself an "altogether yellow" man, knew that all relationships were not between black women and white men: his mother was a white woman who had visited the plantation where his father, Sheton Brown, was a carriage driver and "ginger-bread colored man."[60]

However much coachmen might have acted as pilgrims between black and white communities before the war, they clearly did so after the war. Mulatto men who operated these new cotton plantations while their owners lived in town, or men who guarded white women from the romantic overtures of white men constituted a new kind of threat to the color line so carefully drawn before the war. Samuel Simmons may have been little more than an employee, entrusted with livestock that the widow could not sell herself. The elderly Daniel Lipscomb may not have been the confidante of the "young mistress," but he stood between her and Perry Mc-Arthur much as a brother or uncle might have. Elite white women could neverthe-less make use of these secular pilgrims as their intercessors in the public world of commerce and trade. Klansmen doubtless reworked the process in their own heads: connection, junction, union, coupling—how far did this relationship extend? These domestic arrangements seem to have increased the anxiety of Spartanburg Klans-men.

None of this, of course, explains the peculiar extralegal force that was employed to attack men like Simmons and Lipscomb. In part Klansmen's anger was simply public and political, as their victims were Republican activists. But the violence drew upon images that were private and unmentionable: Simmons was called "your boy," threatened with a piercing by balls, and prevented from putting on his pants when he was whipped. Lipscomb was called a "rattler" and whipped with an unusually wide strand of leather. Klansmen plumbed their imaginations when they attacked these black pilgrims, dramatically replaying connections into a spectacle of conjugal relations. A death threat addressed to Francis and Pink Johnston told them, " 'we no you have fed of the meat-houses of upper york & Gaston county, & fatened of the coten farms in the Clay Hill Neigher hood, & them principally of widow ladies at that.' "[61] The Johnsons, Klansmen claimed, preyed on white widows. Klansmen had little difficulty turning social contact into rape. One York County man was killed after Klansmen circulated the story that he made " 'threats of what he would do to white girls if he had the power to do it.' "[62]

But why did the Spartanburg region have such a large Klan? Why did they persist in the violence after ugly publicity, federal troops, and mass arrests? Mulatto men who managed property and households were likely common throughout the Recon-struction South. Why Spartanburg? Why then?

It is here, I think, that we must return to the animals and trade that made Spartanburg so different. Elsewhere in the South, cotton gins were owned by the largest planters, who refused to take cotton directly from freedmen (planters claimed that freedmen stole it from landowners). Freedmen elsewhere were forced to find a patron—a landowner—to trade their labor in international markets.[63] But in Spartanburg, where pigs were widely spread and cotton thinly spread before the war, the task of ginning was left to coachmen, who had mechanical skills.[64] Further, the layoffs from the South Carolina Manufacturing Company meant that many more blacks than whites had the mechanical skills to operate heavy machinery. The instability of Spartanburg's new location in the geography of trade allowed freed-men to insert themselves into the center of the economy, a transformation that white men found unsettling. Men of color not only penetrated the center of the regional economy, they also penetrated the public sphere in Spartanburg. Voting could not be publicly denied them after 1867, and common trading could not be denied them after 1868. Black militias formed and marched through town after 1868, led by men like Simmons and Lipscomb, who as officers and coachmen surely rode in on horseback.[65]

Before the war, when white landowners had policed the borders of this imagined community themselves, they may have imagined that their mastery over men and women was as natural as their mastery over the beasts that they traded in the center of town. But as the boundaries burst, white landowners surely felt that nature had failed them. The previously private and informal sphere of black trade, traffic, and gossip that had surrounded the city of Spartanburg was now within city borders. White men who had previously traded pigs, horses, and sheep in the center of town had to embrace the private (or "black") market, and sell their whiskey on the town's margins. The center of Spartanburg trade and politics was no longer white, and its periphery was no longer black. The world that whites had considered black and private (plantation, garden crops, black people) had penetrated the world they considered white and public (voting, bartering, gossiping, white people).

In their proclamations and attacks, Klansmen merged public and private. Klansmen imagined the abstract transformation they saw—the merging of public, informal, and private spheres—as a concrete one. They reimagined pubic penetration of the courthouse as pubic penetration of white womanhood. White women and black men were not simply conspiring to gain access to the public sphere of courthouse and public trade, they were in bed together. Indeed, turning this abstract crossing of boundaries into a physical mingling of bodies displaced the more embarrassing personal slights that Klan leaders themselves had faced. Perry McArthur or Mr. Beloue could protest their displacement (being ignored by the young mistress or getting cheated on a deal) without showing their faces. In their robes they could demonstrate the power they believed belonged to them as white men, and leave that power as a mark on the bodies of the men who had replaced them as secular pilgrims. And they theatrically staged this displacement as the grandest drama. McArthur, Beloue, and their friends dressed up as Confederate ghosts, wore the horns of a cuckold, and presented their personal and political grievances as the wrath of specters, unnaturally white.

NOTES

The author would like to thank Sharon Block, Chandos Brown, Leon Fink, Robert Gross, Grey Gundaker, Martha Hodes, Arthur Knight, Kate McPherson, Leisa Meyer, Cassandra Newby, Nell Irvin Painter, Adele Perry, and Leslie Rowland for their comments and criticism.

1. After the war, the principal divisions in South Carolina were changed from districts to counties; after 1880 the boundaries of these upcountry counties also changed. I use the term "Spartanburg region" here to encompass the area around Spartanburg, within the older boundaries of Spartanburg, northern Union, and western York Counties. Under the present county boundaries, the area discussed here is embraced largely by Spartanburg and Cherokee Counties.

2. Jacquelyn Dowd Hall, " 'The Mind That Burns in Each Body': Women, Rape and Racial Violence," in *Powers of Desire: The Politics of Sexuality*, ed. Ann Snitow, Christine Stansell, and Sharon Thompson (New York: Monthy Review Press, 1983); Martha Hodes, "The Sexualization of Reconstruction Politics: White Women and Black Men in the South after the Civil War," in *American Sexual Politics: Sex, Gender and Race since the Civil War*, ed. John C. Fout and Maura Shaw Tantillo (Chicago: University of Chicago Press, 1993).

3. J. B. O. Landrum, *History of Spartanburg County* (Atlanta: Franklin Printing and Publishing Co., 1900), 158; the nearest point of access was the Broad River along Union County's eastern border, but its rapids made cotton shipping a treacherous business. See Dick "Look-Up," in *The American Slave: A Composite Autobiography*, ed. George Rawick (1941; reprint, Westport, Conn.: Greenwood, 1972), vol. 3, pt. 1, 63–71.

4. On the Broad River, see also "Granny" Cain's reminiscences in *American Slave*, ed. Rawick, vol. 2, pt. 1, 166, and Bouregard Corry in vol. 2, pt. 1, 227–28. On the poor quality of antebellum roads, see Landrum, *History of Spartanburg*, 160; and Dorothy Lambright told to her by "Uncle Peter" Arthur in *American Slave*, ed. Rawick, vol. 2, pt. 1, 19. On the limited production of cotton in Spartanburg County, see U.S. Census Bureau, *Statistical View of the [1850] Census*. On the home spinning of cotton and wool, see John Boyd's account of neighboring Union County in *American Slave*, ed. Rawick, vol. 2, pt. 1, 70–73.

5. U.S. Census Bureau, *Statistical View of the [1850] Census*; Franklin H. Elmore Papers, *Records of Antebellum Southern Plantations from the Revolution to the Civil War* (Bethesda, Md.: University Microfilms International), series C, pt. 2, reels 2–5. On rice consumption, see Peter Coclanis, *The Shadow of a Dream: Economic Life and Death in the South Carolina Lowcountry, 1670–1920* (New York: Oxford University Press, 1989).

6. Steven Hahn, *The Roots of Southern Populism: Yeomen Farmers and the Transformation of the Georgia Upcountry* (New York: Oxford University Press, 1983).

7. Lacy K. Ford, Jr., *Origins of Southern Radicalism: The South Carolina Upcountry, 1800–1860* (New York: Oxford University Press, 1988); James Oakes, *The Ruling Race: A History of American Slaveholders* (New York: Alfred A. Knopf, 1982). Many social historians of the South have stressed the importance of class accommodation between yeomen and planters outside the upcountry. See Stephanie McCurry, *Masters of Small Worlds: Yeoman Households, Gender Relations, and the Political Culture of the Antebellum South Carolina Low County* (New York: Oxford University Press, 1995); and Joseph Reidy, *From Slavery to Agrarian Capitalism in the Cotton Plantation South: Central Georgia, 1800–1880* (Chapel Hill: University of North Carolina Press, 1992).

8. See Caleb Craig's account in *American Slave*, ed. Rawick, vol. 2, pt. 1, 229–33. Craig said that drovers passed through Blackstock, the stagecoach stop between Charlotte and Columbia, to sell slaves, mules, and hogs on days other than sale days.

9. John Paterson Green, *Recollections of the Inhabitants, Localities, Superstitions and Kuklux Outrages of the Carolinas* [Cleveland], 1880), 13–15; John William De Forest, *A Union Officer in the Reconstruction* (New Haven: Yale University Press, 1948), 54, 58. For wagoner battles, see *American Slave*, ed. Rawick, vol. 11, 297–99.

10. Green, *Recollections*, 14–15, 27.

11. John Campbell, " 'As a Kind of Freeman'? Slaves' Market-Related Activities in the South Carolina Upcountry, 1800–1860," in *The Slaves' Economy: Independent Production by Slaves in the Americas*, ed. Ira Berlin and Philip D. Morgan (Portland, Ore.: Frank Cass, 1991).

12. *American Slave*, ed. Rawick, vol. 3, pt. 3, 57; vol. 2, pt. 1, 241–42.

13. De Forest, *Union Officer*, 53, 93.

14. Benedict Anderson, *Imagined Communities: Reflections on the Origin and Spread of Nationalism* (New York: Verso, 1983), 55–56; Zygmunt Bauman, *Legislators and Interpreters: On Modernity, Post-Modernity and Intellectuals* (Ithaca: Cornell University Press, 1987), 1–7, 21–80.

15. *American Slave*, ed. Rawick, vol. 3, pt. 3, 57.

16. Ibid., vol. 2, pt. 1, 19.

17. Green, *Recollections*, 15.

18. De Forest, *Union Officer*, 50–52, 54.

19. Joan Hoff-Wilson, *Law, Gender, and Injustice: A Legal History of U.S. Women* (New York: New York University Press, 1990), 119, 381; on such agreements in the early national period, see Marylynn Salmon, "Women and Property in South Carolina: The Evidence from Marriage Settlements, 1730 to 1830," *William and Mary Quarterly*, 3d. ser., 39 (1982): 655–85.

20. Philip N. Racine, "Emily Lyles Harris, a Piedmont Farmer during the Civil War," in *The Lives They Lived: A Look at Women in the History of Spartanburg*, ed. Linda Powers Bilanchone (Spartanburg, S.C.: Spartanburg Sesquicentennial Focus on Women Committee, 1981), 15.

21. Anne King Gregorie, ed., "Micajah Adolphus Clark's Visit to South Carolina," *South Carolina Historical Magazine* 54 (1953): 26–27.

22. Burt Haygood, in *American Slave*, ed. Rawick, vol. 11, 186.

23. Mrs. M. E. Abrams, told to her by "Mad" Griffin, in *American Slave*, ed. Rawick, vol. 2., pt. 1, 1–4.

24. George Fleming, in *American Slave*, ed. Rawick, vol. 2, pt. 1, 128.

25. John N. Davenport [outside Newberry County], in *American Slave*, ed. Rawick, vol. 2, pt. 1, 241; Nellie Boyd, in vol. 11, 63; George Fleming, in vol. 11, 126–29.

26. Burt Haygood, in *American Slave*, ed. Rawick, vol. 11, 186; C. B. Burton, in vol. 2, pt. 1, 152.

27. On corn shucking, see Roger D. Abrahams, *Singing the Master: The Emergence of African American Culture in the Plantation South* (New York: Pantheon, 1992); on corn shucking in the South Carolina upcountry, see *American Slave*, ed. Rawick, vol. 11, 57.

28. U.S. Census Bureau, *Statistical View of the [1850] Census*.

29. On freight rates, see "Report of the Special Joint Commission Appointed to Investigate and Report as to Complaints in Regard to Railroads, and Other Matters Concerning the Same," in Charlotte and South Carolina Railroad, *Annual Report*, 1868, p. 4; Rates of Transportation from Meeting, March 10, 1851, in Richmond and Danville Railroad, "Minute Books of the Board of Directors," p. 21, both at Special Collections, Virginia Polytechnic Institute and State University.

30. Landrum, *History of Spartanburg*, 40ff.

31. George Briggs's account, in *American Slave*, ed. Rawick, vol. 2, pt. 1, 89–92; Landrum, *History of Spartanburg*, 213, 705–14.

32. John Boyd, in *American Slave*, ed. Rawick, vol. 2, pt. 1, 70–73.

33. *U.S. Census*, 1870, vol. 1, *Population*, 370; 42d Cong., 2d sess., House Rpt. 22 (Washington, D.C.: U.S. Government Printing Office, 1871), South Carolina, 34 (hereafter *KKK Report*).

34. Hahn, *Roots of Southern Populism*; Ford, *Origins of Southern Radicalism*; *American Slave*, ed. Rawick, vol. 2, pt. 1, 43.

35. Scott Nelson, "Public Fictions: The Southern Railway and the Construction of the South, 1848–1885" (Ph.D. diss., University of North Carolina, Chapel Hill, 1994), chap. 2.

36. Ibid., chap. 3.

37. On the conflicts between communities of former slaves and former masters throughout South Carolina, see Julie Saville, *The Work of Reconstruction: From Slave to Wage Laborer in South Carolina, 1860–1870* (New York: Cambridge University Press, 1994).

38. Spartanburg is roughly 875 square miles, or 560,000 acres. This makes it four percent of the land mass in the county.

39. Testimony of Simpson Bobo, *KKK Report*, South Carolina, 797.

40. For notice of sheriff's sales of land, see *Carolina Spartan*, 1868–70; *KKK Report*, South Carolina, 775, 813–15, 823–24.

41. For advertisements for "Brooks' Superfine Flour" at ten dollars a barrel, see *Carolina Spartan*, March 17, 1870.

42. Midwestern railroad competition and technological advances in the storing and for-warding of grain in the Midwest drastically lowered wheat and flour prices in the late 1860s. George Hall Miller, *Railroads and the Granger Law* (Madison: University of Wisconsin Press, 1971), chap. 1; Murray Rothstein, "Antebellum Wheat and Cotton Exports: A Contrast in Marketing Organization and Economic Development," *Agricultural History* 40 (1966): 91–100.

43. *Carolina Spartan*, July 13, 1871; *American Slave*, ed. Rawick, vol. 11, 244–45; *KKK Report*, South Carolina, 192–94; see *Carolina Spartan*, various issues in 1869–70 for sheriff's sales at the courthouse.

44. Hoff-Wilson, *Law, Gender, and Injustice*, appendix 1.

45. See *Carolina Spartan*, 1866–70, for numerous instances of debt-clearing of estates.

46. De Forest, *Union Officer*, 47.

47. "A Nice Girl," *Carolina Spartan*, Sept. 28, 1871.

48. Nina Silber, *The Romance of Reunion: Northerners and the South, 1865–1900* (Chapel Hill: University of North Carolina Press, 1993), chap. 3.

49. For new phosphate sales, see *Carolina Spartan*, March 17, 1870; Landrum, *History of Spartanburg*, 325.

50. *KKK Report*, South Carolina, 29–30, 99–100; Landrum, *History of Spartanburg*, 209.

51. *KKK Report*, South Carolina, 29–30, 99.

52. "Message of the President of the United States Communicating in Further Compliance with the Resolution of the Senate of the 16th of December, 1870, Information in Relation to Outrages Committed by Disloyal Persons in North Carolina, and other Southern States," U.S. Congress, 41st Cong., 3d sess., Ex. Doc. 16, pt. 1.

53. Allen W. Trelease, *White Terror: The Ku Klux Klan Conspiracy and Southern Reconstruction* (New York: Oxford University Press, 1971), chap. 24.

54. Landrum, *History of Spartanburg*, 316; "Ku Klux Klan Manifesto," *Carolina Spartan*, March 16, 1871.

55. *KKK Report*, South Carolina, 402–07.

56. Ibid.

57. Ibid., 427–28.

58. Ibid., 380–82, 413–14, 547, 806.

59. Landrum, *History of Spartanburg*, 375.

60. *American Slave*, ed. Rawick, vol. 2., pt. 1, 128.

61. *KKK Report*, South Carolina, 1403.

62. Ibid., 1365.

63. Ibid., 41–47.

64. *American Slave*, ed. Rawick, vol. 2., pt. 1, 128.

65. *KKK Report*, South Carolina, 227, 239–41, 759, 1386.

Part IV

Turn of the Century

Chapter Sixteen

Accomplished Ladies and *Coyotes*
Marriage, Power, and Straying from the Flock in Territorial New Mexico, 1880–1920

Pablo Mitchell

On June 24, 1919, while under observation in a Colorado Springs hospital room, Grover Harrison calmly announced to officers that he was almost finished getting dressed. He would be ready for his appointment with the sanity commission in a moment, he told them. The Harvard graduate, former minister, and thirty-two-year-old New Mexico native then proceeded to climb atop a chair in his room and hang himself with his underwear from a pipe running along the ceiling. The officers, according to newspaper reports, "heard a gurgling sound and [attempted] to get into the room by the use of a ladder and an ax."[1] But by the time they cut him down, Grover Harrison was dead. In a brief suicide note, Harrison proclaimed his weariness after "nearly ten years of an ugly litigation suit" and expressed his desire to "go home," where he would once again be reunited with the mother he had lost as a child. The note ended with an appropriately Dickensian literary flourish: "the rest that I go to is far, far better than I have ever known. No wonder then that I greet the unseen with a cheer."[2] Grover was referring to a suit he had brought against his father, the Albuquerque physician George Harrison, over the young man's inheritance from his mother, Guadalupe Perea. Five years earlier, in 1914, Grover had won the case and been awarded more than one hundred thousand dollars. In a bitter and pained last testament, Grover gave kindly to friends and institutions, and offered a total of one dollar to his father, stepmother, and their children.[3]

Grover Harrison's death was only one of many bizarre twists in an inheritance battle stretching over half a century. In the middle of the nineteenth century, Grover's stepgrandfather, and as it turned out the first husband of his mother, José Leandro Perea, was easily one of New Mexico's richest and most powerful men.[4] Perea was born in 1822 to an elite Hispano family, and in 1842 married into a similarly influential family with his wedding to Dolores Chávez (see fig. 16.1). Making their home in the village of Bernalillo in central New Mexico, the Pereas had nearly a dozen children before Dolores died in 1877 at the age of fifty-one. In 1878 José Leandro Perea married Guadalupe Perea, the eventual mother of the ill-fated Grover Harrison. When José Leandro Perea died in 1883, he divided his estate

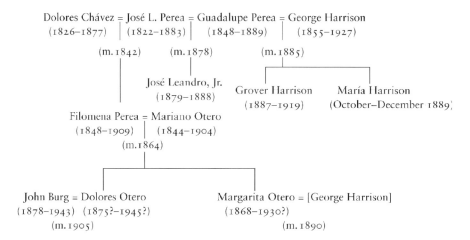

Fig. 16.1 Perea-Otero-Harrison Family Genealogy

among his wife, Guadalupe Perea, and his numerous children. Two years later, Guadalupe Perea married George Harrison, an Anglo physician from Missouri and the father of Grover Harrison. When Guadalupe died in 1889, she bequeathed a large portion of her estate, formerly the estate of José Leandro Perea, to her son Grover. Guadalupe's widowed husband, George Harrison, subsequently remarried soon afterward, to none other than Margarita Otero, a granddaughter of the aforementioned José Leandro Perea and Dolores Chávez. In a further crucial intermarriage, another granddaughter of José Leandro Perea, Dolores Otero, in 1905 became the wife of John Burg, a skillful and, as we shall see, fortunate lawyer. Thus, when Grover Harrison killed himself in a Colorado Springs hospital room in 1919, he left behind a deeply tangled estate, what would turn out to be more than two dozen heirs, and a complex family lineage stretching back some half a century.

The death of Grover Harrison ultimately illustrates far more, however, than a colorful family squabble over heirlooms. Indeed, the four decades between the marriage of José Leandro Perea and Guadalupe Perea in 1878, and the death of Grover Harrison in 1919, coincide with a remarkable period in the region's history. The transcontinental railroad entered New Mexico in 1880, carrying with it a host of dramatic transformations. Prior to 1880, according to one historian, "the framework of Hispanic culture was kept intact and continued to serve as the principal point of reference by which the people viewed their present and measured the future."[5] Although Anglo trappers, traders, Civil War soldiers, and merchants had settled in New Mexico throughout the nineteenth century, the structure of power in the territory continued to be based on centuries-old Spanish and Mexican patterns of dominance, including control of property and water rights through royal and governmental decrees, and the violent subjugation of New Mexico's Native populations.[6] Even well into the nineteenth century, Pueblos, Navajos, Apaches, and Utes continued to be excluded from significant power, and many were held in quasi-slavery. Lower-class Hispanos suffered as well, often struggling mightily to make a living as subsistence farmers, artisans, and peons. Those in power, New Mexico's elites, relied on informal and widely understood traditions, often governing through a combination of local custom and military might. Far from the administrative centers of successive Spanish, Mexican, and then American rulers, such elites, members of leading families such as the Armijos, Pereas, and Oteros, could exercise a level of control reminiscent of European feudal lordships and Latin American *patrones*. As we shall see, gender and sexuality, especially the crucial use of strategic marriage and intermarriage, were indispensable aspects of this long-standing regime.

In 1880 a new era dawned in New Mexico with the arrival of the transcontinental railroad. Richard White has noted that by 1900 the American West "depended on outside markets, outside capital, and most often skills and technologies imported from the outside," and New Mexico was no exception.[7] The arrival of the railroad carried in its wake significant changes, including increased integration into national markets and an unprecedented flow of mostly Anglo immigrants to the territory from throughout the United States and Europe. While older leading families scrambled to maintain their status, new elites rose to prominence in the growing towns of New Albuquerque, Las Vegas, and Santa Fe. These emergent elites, mostly Anglo but with a sprinkling of Hispanos, utilized new techniques and strategies in the consolidation of power. Increasingly, the informal, mostly Hispano-Native traditions governing interpersonal relationships, land use, and the transfer of property gave way to more formal, rationalized methods of interaction and control.[8] This transition, actually the emergence of a modern New Mexico, appeared in countless guises, from the meticulous surveying and distribution of the land to the explicit regulation of personal behavior.

As this essay will demonstrate, elites and aspiring elites also turned to the territorial courts and legislature. Although previous elites had certainly not shied away from using the legal system to acquire and consolidate their power, the extent of the reliance on law and the courts, including the use of newly educated lawyers and professionals from outside the territory, reached an unprecedented level after 1880.[9] As had occurred before 1880, Anglo and Hispano elites frequently formed coalitions with each other, often in an effort to continue the exclusion of Native Americans and poor Hispanos and whites from significant power in the region. In large measure, then, lawyers and judges in New Mexico came to occupy the positions once held by merchants and ranchers at the highest levels of society. In the half century after the arrival of the railroad in 1880, New Mexico thus balanced precipitously between two worlds: the premodern land of custom, informality, and tradition and the modern domain of legal codes, explicit property rights, and systematized cultural and cross-cultural interaction.

Nevertheless, amidst these momentous changes in New Mexico, certain aspects of the region remained much the same. Strategic marriages and the careful policing of elite boundaries had for centuries served well the interests of Spanish and then Mexican ruling elites. Marriage and sexuality, as Ramón Gutiérrez has demonstrated, were central features in the creation and sustenance of elite control in New Mexico prior to American conquest. Gutiérrez uses Pueblo and Spanish sources from colonial New Mexico to demonstrate, as he argues, that in New Mexico "marriage historically has structured inequality."[10] Even after the imposition of

American rule in 1848, the politics of gender and sexuality continued to play a critical role in the governing of the territory. Deena González has noted that in Santa Fe, intermarriages between Anglo men and Spanish-Mexican women were a crucial aspect in the transition from Mexican to American government and rule. "Spanish-Mexican women," González notes, "brought Euro-American men into their communities, their homes and their lives."[11] On a more individual level, several of midcentury New Mexico's most prominent Anglo leaders, such as Kit Carson, Governor Charles (Carlos) Bent, and Governor Henry (Enrique) Connelly, had married wealthy Hispanas of influential New Mexican families. Furthermore, scores of marriages between Hispano families, despite their fair share of love and affection, undoubtedly also served strategic ends.

The outlines of this deeply embedded sexual system endured well after 1880 in New Mexico, and, indeed, as a glance at the genealogies of contemporary elites will reveal, the pattern seems even to stretch into the present. Emergent elites post-1880, though anxious to wrap themselves in the formal and systematized garb of modernism, were hardly so uptown as to turn up their noses at the successful strategies of their predecessors. Equipped with new and improved techniques of rule, elites and striving elites also turned with striking frequency to the marriage altar as a strategic location in the consolidation of power. Increasingly well versed in the formal elements of law and the control of territorial courts, Anglo and Hispano elites alike nevertheless followed the grand New Mexican tradition of strategic marriage. It is thus my contention that sex across racial boundaries helped bridge the considerable gap separating the New Mexico territory of *patrones*, slaves, and serfs and the New Mexico state of lawyers, judges, and wage laborers. This enduring significance of intermarriage and interracial sexuality is especially evident in the history of the Perea-Otero-Harrison family and the particular life stories of Guadalupe Perea and her son Grover Harrison.

To illustrate my argument, I will follow one of the more prominent narrative threads holding together this story of intermarriage and intrigue in New Mexico: the money, specifically the vast estate left by José Leandro Perea after his death in 1883. Of a much larger original estate, some one hundred thousand dollars passed from Perea to his wife, Guadalupe, and subsequently to her son Grover, over the four decades between José Leandro's death and the suicide of his stepgrandson. This sum was hardly an undisputed legacy, as other, more prominent members of the Perea family fought in court for generations to obtain the inheritance. As quasi-illegitimate members of New Mexico's elite, Grover and Guadalupe nonetheless fought back. Though a Native American woman of servant status, Guadalupe passed on her portion of the estate not to other members of the Perea family but to Grover, her son by a second marriage. For his part, Grover, a "mestizo" likewise excluded from New Mexico high society, struggled first to recover and then to distribute after his death his share of his mother's fortune. Both Guadalupe and Grover utilized the courts, and implicitly challenged the legitimacy of the emergent Anglo-Hispano elite. It is this tension, lasting nearly forty years and pitting one proper, respectable Anglo-Hispano section of a family against another less respectable, Native-Hispano-Anglo side that drives this narrative.

The story begins in 1878 with the marriage of José Leandro Perea and Bibiana Guadalupe Perea. José Leandro, a widower of barely a year, was fifty-six when he married the thirty-year-old Guadalupe. He was already the father of nearly a dozen children by his first wife, Dolores Chávez, six of whom were older than his new wife. The life of José Leandro Perea is the stuff of New Mexico legend. For decades in the nineteenth century, he dominated the politics and economy of the village of Bernalillo and much of central New Mexico. When he died, his estate was estimated in the hundreds of thousands of dollars, including extensive property and livestock holdings. In 1860 he was one of only a handful of families in Bernalillo to be able to afford domestic servants, of which he had seven.[12] In 1877 he is reputed to have sold seventeen thousand sheep in one sale.[13] Another story of his life is likely apocryphal. According to the historian Marc Simmons, when the railroad was winding its way south along the Rio Grande, A.T.& S.F. engineers searched for a site to cross the river and begin the westward path to the coast. Bernalillo at the time was the likely choice, with Albuquerque a distant second. Don José Leandro owned much of the land the railroad would need to set up its thoroughfare, yet the old *patron* refused to sell at the rock-bottom prices the railroad demanded. Consequently, the railroad moved to the cheaper land south in Albuquerque, and, but for a lone depot, the transcontinental railroad effectively bypassed Bernalillo. In the hands of historians like Simmons, José Leandro Perea is fashioned a romantic, if naive, holdover from a bygone era, a feudal lord about to be eclipsed by "the clarion notes of progress."[14]

In certain ways, the life of Don José does indeed seem that of the archetypal pre-railroad New Mexican elite. As mentioned, Perea was one of the few men in his village, indeed probably throughout the Middle Rio Grande Valley, to be able to afford domestic servants. The seven servants listed in his household in 1860 had been preceded by three servants a decade earlier in 1850. In 1870 Guadalupe Perea and two other domestic servants appeared in the census, and in 1880 the family was listed with five servants.[15] Domestic servants were not the only factor defining elite status in nineteenth-century New Mexico. Upper-class New Mexicans also served as witnesses and godparents in marriages and baptisms. In the winter of 1846 José Leandro and his wife, Dolores, were listed as *padrinos*, or godparents, to one of the betrothed in the marriage of Juan Montoya and María Petra Perea. Ten years later, José and Dolores were again *padrinos*, this time in the marriage of Sydney Hubbell and María Ygnacia Perea.[16] A final indication of José Leandro's role as a New Mexico *patron* and quasi-feudal lord rests in the names of his domestic servants. Between 1850 and 1880 some fifteen servants lived with the Perea family. Without exception, each of the family's servants, whether male or female, young or old, "Indian" or "mestizo," was listed with the surname Perea, as sure a sign as any that Don José Leandro took quite seriously his role as standard-bearer of upper-class New Mexico society in the nineteenth century.[17]

José Leandro's marriage to Dolores Chávez, a member of an even more prominent New Mexican family, further highlights Perea's position as a traditional New Mexican elite. Their marriage also, of course, points to the significance of gender and sexuality in the pre-1880 consolidation of elite control. Dolores Chávez's father, Francisco Xavier Chávez, was, like José Leandro, a wealthy rancher and businessman in the Middle Rio Grande Valley.[18] Unlike Perea, however, Chávez had achieved high political office. In fact, he had been the last governor of New Mexico under Spanish rule, and reportedly had at one time owned 300,000 head of sheep. According to one historian, after his death at the age of ninety, his wealth was divided evenly among his eleven sons and daughters.[19] Thus it is quite likely that a fair portion of the wealth accumulated by the Perea family entered the family through either the dowry or the inheritance of Dolores Chávez, yet another indication of the snug relations between the institution of marriage and elite status and power in nineteenth-century New Mexico. Other examples of the strategic use of marriage and intermarriage in the Perea family are close at hand. One of José Leandro Perea's sisters, Dolores Lauvinia Perea, married Henry Connelly, the governor of the territory of New Mexico. One of José Leandro's daughters, Cesaria, married Sydney Hubbell, a district judge, while another married W. W. Lewis, an Anglo merchant. A son of Dolores and José Leandro, Mariano, married another member of the Hubbell family, Nina. Other daughters married prominent Hispanos such as Mariano Otero and Jacobo Yrisarri. In their vast wealth, social status as community leaders, and strategic marriages, José Leandro Perea and Dolores Chávez lived exemplary lives as representative New Mexican elites of the nineteenth century.

The Pereas' grasp on power, however, began to unravel, if only in the slightest of ways, with the death of Dolores in 1877 and José Leandro's marriage to Guadalupe Perea a year later. Unlike Dolores Chávez, who entered the Perea family with elite status and likely with a substantial dowry, Guadalupe Perea entered the home as a domestic worker and a Native woman. Although the last census enumeration before her marriage placed Guadalupe Perea among the servants of the Perea family, little evidence remains of her early life. According to the census, she was born, like her parents, in New Mexico in the auspicious year of 1848. Her first name quite likely alluded to the Treaty of Guadalupe Hidalgo, signed that same year between the United States and Mexico ending the Mexican War and resulting in the U.S. annexation of much of the greater Southwest. At the same time, the name Guadalupe may have referred to the Virgen de Guadalupe, the Spanish and Mexican religious icon and symbol of the commingling of Native and Christian religious beliefs.[20]

More important is the question of how and when Guadalupe Perea entered the Perea household. Her last name suggests that she may have been baptized by the family; baptisms, however, did not necessarily have to occur at a young age. Indeed, Guadalupe did not appear in either the 1850 or 1860 censuses, when she would have been two and twelve years old, respectively. During that same period, as mentioned, the Perea household included several servants, suggesting that Guadalupe may have become a member of the household and been subsequently baptized with the name Perea when she was in her teens. A further clue to Guadalupe's entrance into the Perea household is the fact that in 1870 she was listed as an "Indian" domestic servant. New Mexico had a long and inglorious tradition of Native servitude and slavery, stretching as far back as the entrance of the Spanish into the

Southwest. Countless Native women, men, and children of various tribes, including Pueblos, Navajos, Apaches, and Utes, entered Spanish homes, often as the result of direct slaving raids or as the booty of war.[21] While the practice of Native enslavement had ostensibly ended after the Civil War, wealthy Hispanos and Anglos alike continued to rely on Native domestic servants. Warfare between the American military and Native Americans continued in New Mexico throughout the nineteenth century, offering the wealthy ample opportunity to procure the services of Native servants. Thus Guadalupe Perea's entrance into the Perea household between 1860 and 1870 could quite easily have been the result of an enduring though still poorly documented New Mexican legacy.

Once within the Perea household, Guadalupe occupied a vastly different social and sexual position than her immediate predecessor, Dolores Chávez.[22] Indeed, Guadalupe's life was fraught with dangers virtually unknown to the Señora Chávez de Perea. As a Native servant in New Mexico, Guadalupe had little status in the Perea household. There is no evidence of personal wealth in the census schedules, and she is listed as being unable to read or write. Furthermore, as Ramón Gutiérrez and others have noted, sexual predation was far from unknown in such domestic situations.[23] Although there is little evidence that Guadalupe was raped or that she had been pregnant prior to her marriage to José Leandro, it is clear that Guadalupe Perea had few legal recourses in resisting the sexual advances of males in the Perea household. Unlike Dolores Chávez, she came into the Perea family not with a handsome dowry or the backing of a prestigious family, but as a servant and quasi-slave.

In a startling transformation, however, Guadalupe would exit the home as a señora. The transformation began when she married José Leandro Perea in 1878. Two years later, the 1880 census enumeration suddenly listed her not as "Indian" but as "white." Although the household included one "mestizo" and two "Indian" servants, Guadalupe appears "white," as do José Leandro and his children from the first marriage. Furthermore, nine-month-old José Leandro, Jr., presumably the son of Guadalupe and José, also becomes whitened, his racial category listed as "white," not as "mestizo" or of mixed heritage.[24] José Leandro was evidently not at all shy about recognizing publicly his marriage to Guadalupe. He not only bestowed his first name on their child, but quite openly named Guadalupe his legitimate wife in his will. She and their child figured prominently in the wealthy New Mexican's estate, receiving a considerable bequeathment.[25] After the death of José Leandro, upon her remarriage to George Harrison, a newspaper duly noted that Guadalupe Perea was a "wealthy and accomplished lady."[26] Clearly, much had changed in the decade between 1870 and 1880, as an illiterate Native American servant became a wealthy Hispana señora.

At the same time, for all her wealth and apparent status, Guadalupe Perea could not so easily enter New Mexico's ruling elite. New Mexican elites had for centuries defined themselves as not "Indian," and there is little to suggest that the Perea family was much different. The widowed Guadalupe, though the recipient after José Leandro's death in 1883 of a significant portion of the estate of one of New Mexico's wealthiest men, was also in several senses a marked woman. One threat may have come from the townspeople of Bernalillo and the Middle Rio Grande Valley, some of whom were perhaps resentful of the stranglehold José Leandro had laid upon the valley and who were thus eager to acquire a portion of his bountiful estate. Speculators, Hispano and Anglo alike, abounded in late nineteenth-century New Mexico, and Guadalupe could hardly have had the business experience of her late husband. The señora's most direct challenge, however, was likely from the rest of the Perea family, including Filomena, the influential daughter of José Leandro Perea, and Filomena's husband, Mariano Otero. Filomena Perea Otero, like the rest of her brothers and sisters, had already received a generous portion of her father's estate. Still, as direct heirs of José Leandro, the Oteros and other members of the Perea family must have seen Guadalupe as a usurper of the worst order, especially considering her "Indian" appearance and previous servant status. Their estimation of Guadalupe could only have worsened two years later in 1885, when she married an Anglo doctor from St. Louis, George Harrison.

Several reasons may have accounted for this second prominent cross-cultural marriage in the Perea family. First, Guadalupe may have wanted an Anglo husband to help her protect her wealth from legal challenges. Although census records suggest that between 1870 and 1880 Guadalupe had learned to read and write, she was nevertheless in 1885 barely a decade removed from being a lowly servant in a deeply stratified society. She may have chosen to marry Dr. George Harrison, an eastern-educated physician, at least in part as a strategic business decision. As an Anglo professional, George was presumably better acquainted with American legal codes and customs and could perhaps better safeguard the widow's newfound wealth.[27] More important, however, Guadalupe may have been pregnant at the time of her marriage to George Harrison. A newspaper account of Guadalupe and George's wedding in the fall of 1885 observed that the ceremony was small due to "the delicate condition of the wife's health."[28] "Delicate condition," of course, was likely a veiled reference to Guadalupe's evident pregnancy during the ceremony. Though the evidence is scanty, the probable father was her soon-to-be husband, George Harrison. Also unclear is the identity of Guadalupe's child. There is no mention in the historical record of a child born to Guadalupe Perea in 1885. She was already the mother of José Leandro Perea, Jr., born in 1879, and most records indicate the birth of only two children to the later Harrison household: Grover, born in 1887, and María, born in 1889 and dead two months later. If the "delicate condition of the wife's health" does indeed describe a pregnant Guadalupe, the widow may have had added incentive to marry the doctor from Missouri.

A marriage for Guadalupe would protect a reputation already tarnished by a rapid ascent from Native servant to señora and in serious danger from a child born out of wedlock. Furthermore, the pregnancy may have alienated Guadalupe from the remaining members of the Perea family and forced her to seek out allies from elsewhere in the community. It is perhaps no coincidence that George Harrison had moved to Bernalillo only recently and had no apparent business or familial ties to the region. Witness also the newspaper's observation that "few relatives and friends" attended the Harrisons' wedding. The doubled meaning of the newspaper account is most revealing. Guadalupe's delicate condition on the one hand made a small ceremony advisable for "the wife's health." On the other hand, the bride's "delicacy" may have so infuriated the rest of the Perea family that they refused to attend the wedding. Ultimately both reasons may have accounted for the absence of a large audience at the ceremony, as might the hint of sarcasm in the newspaper's description of Guadalupe as a "wealthy and accomplished lady."[29] In either case, Guadalupe Perea de Harrison ultimately succeeded in protecting her valuable estate from challengers near and far. Despite the frustration and anger undoubtedly felt by the rest of the Perea family at their continued inability to wrest from the Native usurper the remainder of José Leandro's beneficence, Guadalupe went to her grave with a sizable chunk of the old man's fortune.

At the age of forty-one, Guadalupe Harrison died in the fall of 1889 during the birth of her second child fathered by George Harrison. The infant girl, María Guadalupe, died soon afterward, and the Harrison family was left with the widower George and his motherless, two-year-old son, Grover. A newspaper reported that at Guadalupe's funeral, "a large concourse of sympathizing relatives and friends filled the building to its utmost capacity." Likewise, the paper observed that Guadalupe had been a "model wife and mother and [that] her memory in the home and in the community [would] long be an ointment poured forth."[30] Still, compared to the ceremony accompanying the death of Filomena Otero twenty years later, Guadalupe appears considerably less than a prominent society matron. Filomena's funeral included two sets of pallbearers, from the Ladies Sodality and the Ladies Altar societies of Albuquerque's Immaculate Conception Church, of which Filomena apparently had been a member for years.[31] Guadalupe, it seems, had not been a member of any social organizations, nor were any leading community figures mentioned as present at the ceremony despite the presence of six priests: aside from the grieving husband and children, no other family members were mentioned.

According to court documents, Guadalupe died without leaving a will, and Grover became her main beneficiary.[32] Like his mother, despite his promise of inherited wealth, Grover Harrison was never fully accepted among the New Mexican elite. After his father's remarriage, Grover was sent out of state to live with relatives. He lived with an aunt in Kansas City until he was twelve, when he moved to live with other relatives in St. Louis and began work at various odd jobs. He worked as an office boy in a law firm for a period and then entered the Nashotah Theological Seminary in Nashotah, Wisconsin. After a year in Wisconsin, Grover entered another seminary in Chicago in 1907. Two years later, at the age of twenty-two, he entered Harvard University as a freshman. According to court records, during his childhood and teenage years, Grover Harrison at times saw his father only once a year and made "very few short visits in New Mexico."[33] In his own words, Grover lived with "relatives a part of [the] time and with strangers the remainder."[34] A remark by a relative was propitious: "Grover," she told the young man, "be careful, you are alone."[35]

Grover's father, George Harrison, on the other hand, quickly rose to prominence within elite Hispano-Anglo circles in turn-of-the-century New Mexico. George's rapid rise, of course, was undoubtedly deeply indebted to his fortunate second marriage in 1890 to Margarita Otero. Like the Perea family, the Oteros provided a shining example of the rising coalition between Hispano elites and well-educated

Anglos. Margarita's mother, Filomena, of course, was the daughter of José Leandro Perea, and her father, Mariano S. Otero, served variously as territorial delegate to the U.S. Congress, member of territorial and local assemblies, and founding member of Albuquerque's Bank of Commerce, the bank not coincidentally where his son-in-law George Harrison would eventually become president.[36] Mariano Otero was also a nephew of Miguel Antonio Otero, Jr., the eventual territorial governor of New Mexico. Thus, with the influential backing of his father-in-law, George Harrison served as the president of Albuquerque's Bank of Commerce between 1892 and 1895 and was the president of both the New Mexico Medical Society and the territorial board of health. In 1901 Harrison represented Bernalillo County in the New Mexico legislative council.

When George Harrison, the widower of Guadalupe Perea, married Margarita Otero, the granddaughter of José Leandro Perea, in 1890, however, there was much more at stake than the aspirations of an Anglo social climber like George Harrison. Indeed, what is most striking about the intermarriage of Margarita Otero and George Harrison is not that theirs was a cross-cultural romance, but rather that their respective families were so intimately related. Margarita was, after all, a step-granddaughter to George's first wife, Guadalupe; in marrying Margarita, George was marrying the granddaughter of his first wife's dead husband. As executor of the estate of his wife Guadalupe, George was tantalizingly close to a sizable portion of José Leandro Perea's original estate, a portion seemingly denied the family by Don José's marriage to Guadalupe Perea. While George and Margarita were by ethnicity marrying out, in another sense, in terms of money—in terms of the estate of José Leandro Perea—they were just trying to keep it all in the family. Thus, after George Harrison married Margarita Otero in 1890, only one thing stood between the Perea-Harrison family and José Leandro's money: Grover Harrison.

The marriage of Margarita and George illustrates once again the critical role of gender and sexuality in the creation and maintenance of elite status in turn-of-the-century New Mexico. Unlike their forebears, this Hispano-Anglo elite did not rely directly on Spanish and Mexican land grants or the acquisition of U.S. military contracts and Santa Fe Trail trade. Instead, these elites began to rely on formalized legal codes, on territorial courts and skillful lawyers. At the same time, such emergent elites continued to turn to the well-worn strategies of marriage and intermarriage. They adapted the successful techniques of an older period (strategic marriages and intermarriages) to the changing demands of a new era (the need to understand more thoroughly the interworkings of the legal process). It is therefore no coincidence that John Baron Burg, the husband of Dolores Otero and brother-in-law to George Harrison and Margarita Otero, was an attorney and eventually a judge with a Georgetown University law degree. Nor is it a surprise that the intermarried George Harrison served as a territorial legislator in addition to his executive positions in banking and medicine. Further, it is little wonder that Frederico Otero, a son of Mariano and Filomena, was also educated at Georgetown before returning to New Mexico to take over his father's business, and that another son, Mariano Jr., attended the University of Notre Dame.[37] Whereas Mariano Otero a generation earlier had been schooled in St. Louis before entering the ranching business, later

Hispano and Anglo elites would be educated more specifically in the understanding and practice of the law.

It is all too appropriate, then, that a courtroom should be the next stop in this complex story. Between 1890 and 1908, while George and Margarita Harrison assumed their rightful positions atop New Mexican society, Grover Harrison was shipped from relative to relative and school to school throughout the Midwest. Then in 1908, shortly before Grover's twenty-first birthday, George Harrison paid his son a rare visit. Grover was at the time a student at the Western Theological Seminary in Chicago, living in a dormitory room. According to court records, George rented a room near the seminary and visited his son daily for more than a week. Grover later observed, "I saw more of him during that visit than I think I ever had seen of him before in my life."[38] During his stay in Chicago, George convinced his son to accept a settlement in the estate of his mother. As executor of Guadalupe Harrison's estate, of which Grover was the sole beneficiary, George was the administrator of several parcels of real estate in New Mexico and Missouri. When he attempted to convince Grover to take a piece of land in St. Louis in exchange for a release of the young man's claim on the estate of the late Guadalupe Harrison, George Harrison set the stage for a legal battle that would ultimately last over a decade, stretch over several states, and come to affect institutions as diverse as Harvard University, the Sailor's Haven of Charlestown, Massachusetts, and the Sisters of Loretto of Bernalillo, New Mexico.

The first major battle occurred in 1914, when the twenty-seven-year-old Grover Harrison took his father to court. The basis of the suit filed in Bernalillo County District Court in Albuquerque was George Harrison's alleged refusal to turn over to his son the young man's legitimate inheritance. In the preceding years, despite being denied entry into New Mexico's high society, Grover Harrison had managed to take advantage of the territory's newfound emphasis on formal legal codes. Like his cousins, he too was well educated, and he too had access to the legal system. Suspicious of his father's intentions, Grover hired lawyers on at least two occasions between 1908 and 1914, both times concerning the status of the estate left to him by his mother.[39]

As his numerous appearances as both plaintiff and defendant in county docket books between 1886 and 1914 suggest, George Harrison was also no stranger to the courtroom.[40] George, however, no longer had the support of the rest of the Perea-Otero family. By 1914 relations between George and the family had soured considerably. It is difficult to establish the cause of the friction, though it was serious enough by 1907 to prompt the Harrison family to leave New Mexico and what had been George's successful political career for a new home in Denver.[41] In fact, the relative who had told Grover that "he was alone," and implicitly that he was not to trust his father, was none other than Filomena Otero, George's mother-in-law. In the court case against his father, Grover testified that George had told him that "the Oteros had been against him [George] here in New Mexico and fought him."[42] Further proof of the enmity between George Harrison and the Otero family, and an added indication of the continuing significance of strategic marriage and intermarriage, was Grover Harrison's choice of lawyers. One of his three lawyers was none other than John Baron Burg, husband to Dolores Otero, son-in-law to Mariano and Filomena Otero, brother-in-law to George and Margarita Harrison, and, of course, related by marriage to José Leandro Perea. By having Burg, a prominent legal figure and soon to be a judge in Bernalillo County, defend Grover and not George, the Otero family signaled a final break with the good doctor and his family. They also, as we shall see, situated themselves quite nicely with respect to Grover's inheritance. For his part, George Harrison was hardly overmatched in his defense. He had hired a judge, E. A. Mann, and a U.S. district attorney, Summers Burkhart, to plead his case.

In the late spring of 1914, the verdict in the sensational trial was in. George Harrison was ordered to hand over more than one hundred thousand dollars to his son. In a sense, the ruling was a setback for the elites of the Perea-Otero family. Grover, the unwanted and half-Native son, had wrested Guadalupe's inheritance once again from the grasp of José Leandro's more proper heirs, represented here by George and Margarita Harrison. In a deeper sense, however, the verdict was a stunning victory for both the Perea-Otero family and the elites of the fledgling state.[43] The extent of that victory is evident in the brief will dictated by Grover Harrison in 1914 soon after the verdict. Now possessed of a significant fortune, Grover named but three beneficiaries: Harvard University received a quarter of his estate, one of his lawyers, George Howell, received another quarter, and the ubiquitous John Baron Burg received a full half of the estate. Grover, of course, must have been elated at his victory in court and perhaps understandably gave kindly to his attorneys and the university where he had received his education. At the same time, he had perhaps unwittingly placed within tantalizing reach of the Otero family a significant portion of José Leandro Perea's estate. Through John Burg and his wife, Dolores Otero Burg, the Otero family once again stood to inherit a sizable parcel of the Perea fortune. Once again, the ligatures of interracial marriage served to consolidate the power of upper-class New Mexicans.

Here, both the flexibility and the continuity of the emerging Anglo-Hispano elite are evident. George Harrison, once a stalwart member, had for whatever reason fallen out of grace with the Otero family. No longer trusting George, the Oteros—in 1914 with a second generation of sons and daughters in charge—placed their faith in John Burg to give them a chance at Guadalupe's portion of José Leandro's estate. Significantly, Burg's law firm was none other than Catron and Catron, one of the most fabled firms and names in territorial New Mexico. Thomas B. Catron had become a fabulously wealthy lawyer by exploiting the changing dynamics of land tenure in nineteenth-century New Mexico. A member of a powerful political machine, the notorious Santa Fe Ring, Catron had amassed a huge fortune in part through successfully defending settler land claims and taking as payment large tracts of real estate.[44] Catron frequently defended women, especially Hispanas, in their property claims, and it was perhaps in this venerable tradition that Catron and Catron, and John Burg, defended Grover Harrison.[45]

In other words, the lawyers standing beside Grover Harrison likely represented yet another in a long line of property snatches. Whereas Thomas Catron may have earlier been something of an anomaly in his exploitative use of the legal system, a quarter century later his literal and figurative heirs seem to have mastered the game, complete with its careful use of the marriage altar. Often bound by ties of interethnic marriage and shared purpose, this new generation, people like John Burg, Frederico Otero, and Charles Catron, embodied a new elite. In 1914, two years after the dawn of New Mexico statehood, these Anglos and Hispanos together seem to have consolidated even further their grip on the politics of the new state. Half of the one hundred thousand dollars that had passed from José Leandro Perea to Guadalupe Perea to Grover Harrison now depended on only one thing: the death of Grover Harrison.

In 1914, however, Grover Harrison had other plans both for his life and for his fortune. He was, for several reasons, anathema to the modernizing world of New Mexico's professional elites. In the first place, unlike, for example, the one-time territorial governor Miguel Otero, whose "dual-cultural background" allowed him to "toe the precarious line between the conflicting worlds of the New Mexican Hispano and the Yankee newcomers," Grover could not so easily reconcile his mixed ancestry.[46] Indeed, the son of the servant-señora, "Indian-Hispana-white" mother and Anglo father struggled mightily to sort out the divergent strands of his *coyote* identity.[47] Grover's relationship to religion offers one example of his ambivalence. Neither the Catholicism of his Hispano roots nor the Protestantism of his Anglo forebears took permanent hold on his life. Rather, his life seemed to synthesize the two faiths. As a young man, he studied in at least two seminaries. After his graduation from Harvard, he taught at the Episcopalian St. Stephen's School in Colorado and was ordained a Protestant minister there.[48] A second will, dictated in 1918, designated New Mexico's Sisters of Loretto as heirs, yet his suicide note was directed to an Episcopal minister.[49]

At the same time, Grover, better-educated than most elites in New Mexico, was far more artistic than his lawyerly and professional relatives. His suicide note reveals his inclination toward the literary, with the last line lifted directly from the final passage in Dickens's *Tale of Two Cities*: "the thing that I do is far, far better than I have ever done; the rest that I go to is far, far better than I have ever known." Dickens, of course, was the painfully logical choice of a boy whose youth, with few exceptions, was spent very much as a disinherited orphan. His love of literature also emerges in his 1918 will, where Grover designated Harvard University as the recipient of a generous sum to establish a Grover Harrison Prize in English. The prize, according to Grover, was to be presented to the "undergraduate who shall submit the best essay on a social subject."[50] Grover was also a writer. After his death, a newspaper reported that "several royalties are being paid Harrison for works of fiction," and that a publisher had made inquiries about a novel among the young man's belongings.[51] Thus, in both his ethnic ambiguity and religious eclecticism and his interest in literature and writing, Grover had little in common with the business and political inclinations of his relatives.

Most alienating, however, was probably Grover's sexuality. Religion and the arts may have distanced the young man from his family, and his Native American heritage was certainly not an exalted feature in turn-of-the-century New Mexico. Nevertheless what ultimately seemed to transform Grover from an eccentric outsider to

the black sheep of the family was the fact that Grover was likely gay. Evidence that
Grover Harrison pushed the boundaries of "normal," early twentieth-century (het-
ero)sexual behavior emerges from a variety of sources, including descriptions of the
events surrounding his death in 1919. Grover had been in the Colorado Springs
hospital room for observation after an arrest a week before and a previous suicide
attempt in his prison cell. According to newspaper accounts, he was arrested on
June 18, 1919, for "contributing to the degeneracy of young boys."[52] A police
officer claimed that Harrison was "an undesirable of the worst character who had
operated in [the] city during the previous tourist seasons."[53] The suicide and the
subsequent revelations of family fortune and intrigue made for relatively big news
in Colorado Springs and Albuquerque. One article noted suspiciously that Grover
had been "summarily dismissed" from his job at a war camp community service
site and that "the cause of this discharge was never made public."[54] Another implied
that he killed himself after "a serious charge had been preferred against him by the
mother of a young boy here."[55] Grover's suicide note alludes to those charges
brought against him. Addressed to the Reverend Chauncey Blodgett of Episcopal
Grace Church in Colorado Springs, Grover asked the man to inform several acquaintances of his "illness." He also argued, "I can only repeat that I am in no way
guilty."[56] Elsewhere he exclaimed, "I am innocent. Please, in deference to my
friends, keep all confidential."[57]

Taken alone, such evidence is hardly proof that Grover was gay. Indeed, George
Chauncey has demonstrated that the category "gay" was deeply contested throughout the early decades of the twentieth century. Unlike the contemporary binary of
hetero- and homosexuality, men's identities, according to Chauncey, were defined
more by notions of proper masculine and feminine behavior than by "the anatomical sex of their sexual partners."[58] Still, further evidence suggests Grover's familiarity with, if not actual membership in, the social world described in Chauncey's *Gay
New York*. In November 1918, six months before he committed suicide, Grover
drafted a second will, one that would presumably invalidate the earlier 1914 will.
Unlike the first, the second will offers a detailed glimpse inside Grover's short life.
It also provides compelling evidence that Grover Harrison was an intimate member
of an erotically charged, profoundly homosocial world stretching from coast to
coast and including sailors, college professors, and men of the church.

In the second will, male "dear friends" received the bulk of Grover's bequeathments. Morris Dallett of Philadelphia received half of the estate, and another quarter went to Felton Elkins of San Francisco. Grover asked either Elkins or William
Drayton of London to dispose of his ashes, noting that he was "confident that either
would have them placed near his residence."[59] Smaller gifts ranging from a gold
watch left to him by his mother, to a scarf pin of seven pearls and a pearl dress
shirt, to Moorish ash trays and Algerian coverings went to assorted friends such as
C. Gouveneur Hoffman of New York, Chaplain (Major) E. P. Newsom of the U.S.
army, and Professor George P. Baker of Harvard University.[60]

More suggestive are other bequeathments to certain individuals. For instance,
Professor Charles Townsend Copeland of Cambridge was the recipient of Grover's
complete collection of Shakespeare and "the Stratford Edition" of the poem *Venus*

and Adonis. According to one scholar, the poem is "a leading example of the erotic narrative tradition," contrasting as it does "the principle of erotic pleasure embodied in Venus . . . with the refinement of spirit expressed in Adonis."[61] One especially provocative stanza reads,

> "Fondling," she saith, "since I have hemmed thee here
> Within the circuit of this ivory pale
> I'll be the park, and thou shalt be my deer;
> Feed where thou wilt, on mountain or in dale;
> Graze on my lips, and if those hills be dry,
> Stray lower, where the pleasant fountains lie."[62]

That Grover would select Copeland as one of only two men in his will to receive a specific book, and the particularly sensual content of that book, suggest at the very least a certain measure of homoeroticism in the two men's relationship. The same may be said, though certainly with less precision, of Grover's relationship with Francis Severin Moulton of Rhode Island, to whom he gave his copy of the collected letters of John Keats. Keats may have been similarly evocative for Grover, considering both the author's passionate, turbulent life and his death at the age of twenty-five.[63]

Further evidence that Grover may have been gay emerges from the addresses of several of the beneficiaries of his will. Felton Elkins, the recipient of a quarter of the estate, was listed with an address at the Lambs Club in New York City. Although the Lambs Club is not one of the many clubs mentioned in Chauncey's study, the name is a curious one, especially considering that "lamb," along with "punk" and "kid," was one of the common terms for a "physically slighter [male] youth" involved in a sexual relationship with a "wolf," an "older and more powerful man."[64] Similarly intriguing is the ship's bell clock that Grover gave to Stanton King of the Sailors' Haven in Charlestown, Massachusetts, a group that had already received a sixty-fourth share of Grover's estate. Again, the proof is far from conclusive, yet sailors and seamen occupied prominent positions in the creation of a gay subculture in New York City in the early twentieth century, and there is little to suggest that a similar subculture did not exist along the Massachusetts coast as well.

In all, then, Grover's will charts a fascinating set of intimate and erotically charged male relationships stretching across both vast geographical distances and potentially, as in the case of sailors, deep class divides. Whether Grover Harrison was gay or not, however, is to a certain extent beside the point. In either case, as his arrest on "degeneracy" charges indicates, he led a life well outside the "normal" sexual confines of Colorado Springs, elite New Mexico, and perhaps even greater America. Positioned there on the outskirts of propriety, in his racial ambiguity, his religious indeterminacy, and his sexual transgressiveness, Grover had few people to defend his interests after his death.

For all its insight and bravado, Grover's 1918 will was ultimately overturned by a probate judge and the previous will, the one written in 1914 after his legal victory against his father, was authorized in its place. Grover had written his final will only six months before his suicide, and the circumstances surrounding his death must have played a role in the judge's decision. At the same time, as important as

Grover's sexual identity and supposed "illness" may have been in the dismissal of his 1918 will, there was likely a better explanation for the young man's posthumous reversal of fortune. Barely three days after his suicide, a familiar figure once again entered Grover's life (and death) and submitted the previous, 1914 will to the probate court.

That figure was none other than John Baron Burg, Grover Harrison's former attorney and a prominent member of the Otero family and New Mexico's ruling elite. On June 28, 1919, Burg, who was by now a federal judge, produced a copy of the 1914 will that had bequeathed half the estate to himself and the remainder to George Howell and Harvard University. According to newspaper accounts, Burg "expressed the opinion that the one filed by him would be upheld in court."[65] He was, fortunately for himself and his family, prophetic. Two months after Harrison's suicide, on August 10, 1919, Judge J. A. Garcia y Sanchez of Albuquerque "approved the Grover Harrison will filed by John Baron Burg."[66] As a result, the young man's substantial estate was not divided among the twenty-odd heirs mentioned in the 1918 will and scattered throughout the country. Instead, Grover's heirlooms, carved crucifixes, ship's bell clocks, and Stratford Editions were all likely auctioned away and the proceeds distributed along with the rest of the estate to Burg, George Howell, and Harvard University. The final, bitter tragedy in the life of Grover Harrison was that, for all his careful planning and thoughtful division of his belongings, his possessions were ultimately sold to the highest bidder and the proceeds divided up among a total of three beneficiaries.

John Burg and his wife, Dolores Otero Burg, received fifty thousand dollars, and Harvard undergraduates never got a shot at the Grover Harrison English prize. There are, however, three broader points that emerge from this tale of intermarriage and the transfer of property. First, this tale illustrates the importance of a multigenerational approach to questions of interracial sex and sexuality. Through such an approach one can see not only the triumphs of Guadalupe and Grover's transgressions, but the tragic and enduring cost of such rebellions. Guadalupe, recall, died when she was barely forty. Except for her last decade, she had experienced thirty years of servitude and domestic labor, not to mention the much greater threat of physical and sexual abuse. The apparent relative absence of close friends and relatives at both her wedding to George Harrison and her funeral suggests a life of isolation after her rise to señora status.

Like his mother, Grover endured a frequently tortuous relationship with his family. Court documents hint at Grover's alienation, such as the numerous childhood homes and his isolation from his father and stepfamily. Grover also grew up largely without Guadalupe, who died when he was two. In his suicide note, Grover invoked Guadalupe and his yearning to be with her once again. His embittered refusal in his 1918 will to allow his father or his father's family to "view [his] remains or to have any part in their interment" was done, according to Grover, "in justice to [his] dear mother." Ultimately, he blamed his father for the "ugly litigation suit" and for his feeling "very, very tired . . . as though every nerve in [his] body had been laid bare and sandpapered."[67] By viewing examples of intermarriage alongside the lives of mixed-heritage children, we have greater access both to broader patterns of change over time, such as New Mexico's post-railroad transformation, and to the personal relationships among kinship, gender, and ethnic identity. Grover Harrison may indeed have found himself in a hybrid landscape, a *coyote* poised on the borderlands of three ethnic cultures; yet it would be impossible to locate his position, let alone understand his life, without first looking at Guadalupe, his mother.

The second crucial aspect of this narrative is the intimate link between the power to rule in New Mexico and interethnic marriage. After the arrival of the transcontinental railroad in New Mexico, the tools needed to control the territory and its people changed at an accelerated pace. Law and legal expertise became increasingly critical skills for aspiring elites. Anglos and Hispanos had previously formed ruling coalitions in New Mexico, frequently through the use of strategic marriages. After 1880, however, a newly formalized and interconnected world began to demand new strategies and skills. Sex and love across racial and ethnic boundaries in New Mexico was a primary route that allowed elites to bridge successfully the old and the new worlds. Intermarriages between wealthy families and educated newcomers, such as Margarita Otero's wedding to George Harrison or the marriage of Dolores Otero and John Burg, were critical features of an emerging Hispano-Anglo elite in New Mexico. While the ruling elite was hardly static—witness the fall from grace of George Harrison—neither was it a mirage. The subtlety with which John Burg, Charles Catron, and the Otero family finally recovered Grover Harrison's portion of the estate of José Leandro Perea attests to the strength of this interethnic, profoundly gender-based coalition. In its reliance on legal expertise, political influence, and strategic marriages and intermarriages, the Anglo-Hispano elite that formed after 1880 endures to the present in New Mexico.

Finally, this story illuminates the challenge posed by individuals such as Guadalupe Perea and Grover Harrison to this emerging Anglo-Hispano elite. As a Native American servant, Guadalupe had little opportunity to enter New Mexico's high society, yet by marrying José Leandro Perea she came to control a considerable sum of money and property. While she did not seem to be welcomed into elite status, it is also possible that she actually refused membership in that world and did as she pleased with José Leandro's fortune. Her pregnancy and subsequent marriage to George Harrison were certainly not the behavior of a chastened and humble servant. Nor were the respectful words of her wedding and funeral notices, however tinged with sarcasm they may have been, the vitriolic abuse commonly turned upon lower-class Native Americans and Hispanos throughout the Southwest in the nineteenth century.[68] Her funeral was, after all, attended by six priests. To the likely dismay of the rest of the Perea family, Guadalupe Perea was hardly the model either of Native servitude or of Hispano-Anglo honor and status.

Guadalupe's son, Grover Harrison, even more than his mother, explicitly and implicitly challenged the dominance of New Mexico's emergent elite. He was *coyote*, mobile, and probably gay, and, as such, was hardly a proper representative of New Mexico's new elite order. He was of little use to an aspiring elite beholden to the law, professional expertise, and the use of marriage and intermarriage to solidify business and political alliances. Though he could obviously maneuver through the increasingly complicated world of New Mexico jurisprudence—as his lawsuit against his father indicates—religion, literature, and travel tempted him far more than courtrooms and politics. Uninterested in marriage, Grover also had little to offer elites in terms of newfound partners and co-conspirators. He would bring to high society no fiancée with handsome dowry, no bride with spectacular inheritance.

Instead, Grover Harrison threatened to spend his vast fortune on complete collections of Keats, pearl dress-shirts, or excursions to San Francisco, New York, and London. Though Grover's final will was eventually overturned, and his money returned in part to the Perea-Otero-Burg family, we should not underestimate the effect of this *coyote* in (black) sheep's clothing on his fellow New Mexicans. One hundred thousand dollars of the estate of José Leandro Perea nearly went to gay and straight individuals and institutions throughout the country. For a short time in New Mexico, accomplished ladies and *coyotes* like Guadalupe Perea and Grover Harrison refused to be ignored. For a brief period, their claims to elite status and wealth had to be taken seriously. It is such a legacy of insubordination and transgression that provides this tale of family intrigue and boundary crossing with its ultimate significance.

NOTES

The author would like to acknowledge the generous comments and support of Ramón A. Gutiérrez, Beth L. McLaughlin, María E. Montoya, and Virginia J. Scharff in the writing of this essay.

1. *Colorado Springs Evening Telegraph*, June 24, 1919, 1.

2. *Albuquerque Morning Journal*, June 25, 1919, 1.

3. Probate Record Index no. 1975, Grover William Harrison, Bernalillo County Courthouse, Albuquerque.

4. Unfortunately, terms such as "stepgrandfather" are the best ways to describe the complex relationships in the Perea-Harrison family.

5. Marc Simmons, *New Mexico: A Bicentennial History* (New York: W. W. Norton, 1977), 164.

6. See Ramón A. Gutiérrez, *When Jesus Came, the Corn Mothers Went Away: Marriage, Sexuality, and Power in New Mexico, 1600–1846* (Stanford: Stanford University Press, 1991).

7. Richard White, *"It's Your Misfortune and None of My Own": A New History of the American West* (Norman: University of Oklahoma Press, 1991), 267.

8. See especially the work of María E. Montoya on southeastern New Mexico, "Dispossessed People: Settler Resistance on the Maxwell Land Grant, 1860–1901" (Ph.D. diss., Yale University, 1993).

9. See Howard Lamar, *The Far Southwest, 1847–1912: A Territorial History* (New Haven: Yale University Press, 1966); Robert Larson, *New Mexico's Quest for Statehood, 1846–1912* (Albuquerque: University of New Mexico Press, 1968); and Victor Westphall, *Thomas Benton Catron and His Era* (Tucson: University of Arizona Press, 1973).

10. Gutiérrez, *When Jesus Came*, xxix.

11. Deena J. González, "The Spanish-Mexican Women of Santa Fé: Patterns of Their

Resistance and Accommodation, 1820–1880" (Ph.D. diss., University of California, Berkeley, 1986), 121.

12. U.S. Bureau of the Census, Manuscript Census Schedule, New Mexico, Bernalillo County, 1850.

13. "José L. Perea," in Donald S. Dreesen, *Nineteenth Century Pioneers of Albuquerque* (Albuquerque: Center for Southwest Research, University of New Mexico, 1991), unpaged.

14. Marc Simmons, *Albuquerque: A Narrative History* (Albuquerque: University of New Mexico Press, 1982), 215–16.

15. U.S. Bureau of the Census, Manuscript Census Schedule, New Mexico, Bernalillo County, 1850, 1860, 1870, 1880.

16. Raymond P. Salas and Margaret Leonard Windham, eds., *New Mexico Marriages, Church of San Antonio de Sandia, 1771–1864* (Albuquerque: New Mexico Genealogical Society, 1993), 42, 56.

17. Gutiérrez, *When Jesus Came*, 181–82.

18. Perea Family Genealogy, Perea Family Vertical File, Albuquerque Public Library Special Collections, Albuquerque.

19. Charles F. Coan, *History of New Mexico* (Chicago: American Historical Society, 1925), 72–73.

20. According to the legend of the Virgen de Guadalupe, *"un indio,"* Juan Diego, was the first to see the apparition of *la Virgen* and pass along her message to the rest of Mexico and Latin America. Her image subsequently has come to occupy a significant place in the Catholic iconography of the Southwest. Guadalupe's son, Grover, was probably named for Grover Cleveland, the president at the time of his birth.

21. Gutiérrez, *When Jesus Came*, 180–90.

22. In one respect, Guadalupe Perea had much in common with Dolores Chávez. Despite her wealth, much of Dolores's life was immersed not in the management of her family's vast estate, but in the more dangerous task of raising children. Sources vary on the number of her children, but it is clear that Dolores was barely fifty years old when she passed away in 1877. Likewise, Guadalupe died at forty-one shortly after giving birth to her third known child. The dangers of childbirth, if the lives of Guadalupe Perea and Dolores Chávez are any indication, threatened both wealthy and impoverished women in late nineteenth-century New Mexico; see Dreesen, *Nineteenth Century Pioneers.*

23. Gutiérrez, *When Jesus Came*, 184.

24. U.S. Bureau of the Census, Manuscript Census Schedule, New Mexico, Bernalillo County, 1880. According to one source, José Leandro Perea, Jr., died in 1888 at the age of nine, one year before the death of his mother, Guadalupe; see Dreesen, *Nineteenth Century Pioneers.*

25. Probate Record Book E, pp. 606–27, Bernalillo County Courthouse, Albuquerque.

26. *Albuquerque Morning Democrat*, Sept. 3, 1888, 4.

27. María Montoya has suggested that the nineteenth-century imposition of American laws of coverture in New Mexico may have ironically functioned to deprive married Hispanas of the ability to control their property and wealth; see María E. Montoya, "Identity, Power, and Property, or How the Beaubien Girls Lost Their Land" (paper presented at Pacific Coast Branch, American Historical Association, Maui, Hawaii, August 1995). Although Guadalupe Perea may have had more rights as a widow than she would have had as the wife of George Harrison, her Native American heritage and status as a former servant nevertheless deeply complicate the issue, especially considering the centuries of racial and class inequalities in New Mexico. Much more work needs to be done on women's property rights in the nineteenth-century American West.

28. *Albuquerque Morning Democrat*, Sept. 3, 1883, 4.

29. Ibid.

30. *Albuquerque Morning Democrat*, Oct. 22, 1889, 2.

31. *Albuquerque Morning Journal*, May 23, 1909, 3.

32. *Grover W. Harrison v. George W. Harrison*, 1914, Bernalillo County District Court, Civil Case no. 8624, State Records Center and Archives, Santa Fe.

33. Ibid., 191.

34. Ibid.

35. Ibid., 224–25.

36. "Mariano S. Otero," in Dreesen, *Nineteenth Century Pioneers*.

37. Coan, *History of New Mexico*, 545.

38. *Grover W. Harrison v. George W. Harrison*, 192.

39. Ibid., 205–06.

40. Bernalillo County Civil and Criminal Docket Books, Bernalillo County Courthouse, Albuquerque.

41. "George W. Harrison," in Dreesen, *Nineteenth Century Pioneers*.

42. *Grover W. Harrison v. George W. Harrison*, 224.

43. In 1912 New Mexico and Arizona were admitted as states to the Union. For New Mexico, it was the culmination of a struggle for statehood that had begun sixty years earlier with the end of the Mexican War; see Larson, *New Mexico's Quest for Statehood*.

44. See Westphall, *Thomas Benton Catron*.

45. Thanks to María Montoya for this valuable observation.

46. María E. Montoya, "The Dual World of Governor Miguel A. Otero: Myth and Reality in Turn-of-the-Century New Mexico," *New Mexico Historical Review* 67 (1992): 19.

47. Like "mestizo," *coyote* describes a person of mixed racial or ethnic heritage in New Mexico. It was originally one of the numerous specific racial categorizations under Spanish rule, but has come to represent any of a number of mixed ancestries.

48. *Colorado Springs Evening Telegraph*, June 19, 1919, 1.

49. Probate Record Index no. 1975, Grover William Harrison.

50. Ibid.

51. *Colorado Springs Gazette*, June 27, 1919, 5.

52. *Colorado Springs Gazette*, June 25, 1919, 3. The vagueness, however, of the charges brought against Grover, especially concerning his attraction to "young boys" of unspecified age, suggests that the thirty-two-year-old Harrison may have simply been associating with men near his own age.

53. *Colorado Springs Gazette*, June 19, 1919, 7.

54. *Colorado Springs Gazette*, June 26, 1919, 1.

55. *Colorado Springs Evening Telegraph*, June 19, 1919, 1.

56. *Colorado Springs Evening Telegraph*, June 24, 1919, 5.

57. *Colorado Springs Evening Telegraph*, June 19, 1919, 3.

58. George Chauncey, *Gay New York: Gender, Urban Culture, and the Making of the Gay Male World, 1890–1940* (New York: Basic Books, 1994), 97.

59. Probate Record Index no. 1975, Grover William Harrison.

60. Ibid.

61. John Roe, introduction to *The Poems: Venus and Adonis, The Rape of Lucerne, The Phoenix and the Turtle, The Passionate Pilgrim, A Lover's Complaint*, by William Shakespeare, ed. John Roe (Cambridge: Cambridge University Press, 1992), 3, 5.

62. Ibid., 6–7.

63. Probate Record Index no. 1975, Grover William Harrison.

64. Chauncey, *Gay New York*, 88.

65. *Albuquerque Morning Journal*, June 28, 1919, 3.

66. *Albuquerque Morning Journal*, Aug. 10, 1919, 6.

67. *Colorado Springs Gazette*, June 25, 1919, 3.

68. For New Mexico, see Sarah Deutsch, *No Separate Refuge: Culture, Class, and Gender on an Anglo-Hispanic Frontier in the American Southwest, 1880–1940* (New York: Oxford University Press, 1987); Pablo Mitchell, "Strangers in the Land: Marriage and Identity in a Nineteenth-Century Landscape" (unpublished paper, 1996); Montoya, "Dispossessed People"; and González, "Spanish-Mexican Women of Santa Fé." For elsewhere in the Southwest, see Albert Camarillo, *Chicanos in a Changing Society: From Mexican Pueblos to American Barrios in Santa Barbara and Southern California, 1848–1930* (Cambridge: Harvard University Press, 1979); Arnoldo De León, *They Called Them Greasers: Anglo Attitudes towards Mexicans in Texas, 1821–1900* (Austin: University of Texas Press, 1981); Lisbeth Haas, *Conquests and Historical Identities in California, 1769–1936* (Berkeley: University of California Press, 1995); and David Montejano, *Anglos and Mexicans in the Making of Texas, 1836–1986* (Austin: University of Texas Press, 1987).

Chapter Seventeen

The Reform of Rape Law and the Problem of White Men

Age-of-Consent Campaigns in the South, 1885–1910

Leslie K. Dunlap

> We have looked at the "Negro problem" long enough.
> Now the time has come for us to right-about-face and
> study the problem of the white man.
>
> —Lillian Smith (1945)[1]

In September 1886 the *Atlanta Constitution* publicized a matter its editors preferred to keep silent. In response to a national campaign to reform rape laws led by the Woman's Christian Temperance Union, the *Constitution* excoriated reformers for raising "forbidden subjects."

> It is nothing more nor less than a public indecency for a lot of women to be moving about, discussing such a matter, getting up petitions and signatures, and bringing the subject into such prominence as to make it common talk. There are some evils unfit for public discussion, and this is one of them . . . Some reforms are not to be spoken of in mixed company or mentioned in print.[2]

Women in the WCTU offered a trenchant retort. That very same issue of the newspaper, they pointed out, contained three explicit reports of alleged rape by black men, "dished up with startling headlines and needlessly disgusting particulars."[3] Why, editors of the national WCTU paper asked, were these crimes fit for public discussion, while the legal reform that they proposed was deemed off-limits for public consideration?

The forbidden subject was the sexual behavior of white men. White newspapers in the post-Reconstruction South featured lurid descriptions of alleged crimes committed by black men against women, especially white women.[4] In contrast, white dailies rarely mentioned white men's crimes against women, black or white. African Americans had long criticized white men's sexual behavior. But the WCTU's campaign to reform rape law, which peaked in the South in the early 1890s, marked the first time that organized southern white women drew public attention to white men's sexual conduct.[5]

Most historians have agreed with Ellen DuBois and Linda Gordon, who argue that late nineteenth-century sex reformers focused their anger on groups of men "other than their own husbands and fathers."[6] Yet this was certainly not the case for black women activists, who regularly and sometimes angrily called upon black men to reform their sexual conduct in the service of "respectability" and "racial uplift." Nor, for a period of time, did white sex reformers displace their criticism of male abuse of sexual power onto men outside their kin networks and social circles. In the WCTU's age-of-consent campaigns, white sex reformers in the South did not invoke charged stereotypes about black rapists or immigrant brothel keepers. In fact, especially in the early years of the campaign, for the most part they avoided descriptions of women facing danger at the hands of black and foreign-born men or roving strangers. This is surprising, considering that these campaigns coincided with an explosion of inflammatory racialized rape rhetoric by white supremacists, escalating violence against African Americans, and the WCTU's own well-known apologies for lynching.[7] Rather, this legal campaign revolved around the sexual behavior of those white men and boys who were assumed to be "respectable."[8] Native-born white men—that is, reformers' "own" husbands, fathers, and sons— became the focus of debate.

Following Elsa Barkley Brown's challenge to analyze relationships between white women and men "as shaped by race," this essay examines how white reformers' changing racial ideology shaped their sexual ideology and their practical plans for sex reform in the South.[9] Reform politics of the period brought labor and African American activists into tenuous coalition with WCTU reformers. These practical political alliances shaped sex reform in ways that distinguished them from later antiprostitution campaigns of the 1910s. Once disfranchisement quashed the reform movements that energized early age-of-consent campaigns, white women activists abandoned the African American and labor allies whose political activity had enabled them to challenge powerful white men. The solidification of segregation and white supremacy tempered white sex reformers' challenge; by 1910 reformers took pains to emphasize that white women were the primary focus of their reform efforts and that prostitution, not rape, constituted a threat to southern social order.

Southern white sex reformers, who had a distinctive stake in maintaining racial hierarchy, held white men accountable for both intraracial tension and interracial conflict. At the most immediate level, the sexual actions of many individual white men posed daily practical problems for black and white women, as well as black men. But for all these actors, elite white men's sexual power also indicated their systemic power over southern legal, political, and economic institutions. Challenging white men's sexual prerogatives, then, entailed confronting white men's political hegemony. Activists and scholars since Frederick Douglass and Ida B. Wells have argued that white southerners fashioned images of black male sexuality in response to African Americans' political agency.[10] So, too, were images of white male sexuality tied to the political power of white men.[11] Reformers' struggles to control the sexual conduct of white men were part and parcel of broader challenges to white men's political and economic control.

The efforts of African American activists and legislators set the precedent for white women's sex reform initiatives.[12] In the 1890s black women criticized white men's sexual behavior; unlike white women, they focused consistently on white men's aggression against all women. At the height of the age-of-consent debates, Ida B. Wells directed the public spotlight at white men's sexual crimes, publicizing the names of those who had raped black women and girls.[13] White men, she argued, were "not so desirous of punishing rapists as they pretend."[14] In 1905 the Baptist activist Nannie H. Burroughs offered an incisive assessment of public silence surrounding white men and rape:

> Why is it that we do not "hear" of the white men of the United States committing outrages upon white or black women? . . . White men in the United States were the first to begin the business of outraging women. They have outraged more women of both races than Negroes will ever outrage. . . . To publish such crimes perpetrated by them upon their own women would deprive their women of that protection of which the Anglo-Saxon delights to boast and which he wants his women to feel secure. . . . Let the thousands of white women whose mouths are shut by pride speak out.[15]

Burroughs and other black reformers further challenged white women's refusal to confront sexual abuse of African American women by white men. Frances Ellen Watkins Harper, a national superintendent of the WCTU who lectured to black audiences nationwide under its auspices, devoted a number of poems to the sexual and racial double standard that held black women accountable for white men's advances. Popular opinion held that white men's "crimes were only foibles, and these were gently told," she observed.[16] She warned white women to reform themselves, calling their "hate of vice a sham." But she also urged white women to reform "their" men. In "A Double Standard," a poem written from the perspective of a "fallen woman," she concluded with a barbed suggestion:

> Yes, blame me for my downward course,
> But oh! remember well,
> Within your homes you press the hand
> That led me down to hell.[17]

Harper not only indicated that white women associated intimately with immoral men, she also suggested that the sexual abuse of black women occurred under white women's noses—in their own homes. For example, she urged white reformers at an 1896 sex reform convention to include domestic servants in their social purity projects. Pronounced Harper, "no mistress of a home should be morally indifferent to the safety of any inmate beneath her roof."[18] For Harper and other reformers, white women, especially in their capacity as employers of domestic servants, were uniquely situated to protect black women but were not fulfilling these responsibilities. White women, they suggested, were complicit in white men's sexual offenses. As participants at a 1904 Atlanta University conference protested, domestic workers went "peculiarly unprotected" in white homes, since "the attitude of white women is not a protection, for many of them are indifferent to their husbands' or brothers' relations with Negroes."[19] These activists pushed white women, then, to assume responsibility for protecting black women against white men.

Black activists sought not only publicity but legal change as well.[20] Throughout the 1890s, African American politicians in the South sought sex legislation that would apply to African American women. Some, such as Texas representative Nathan Haller or Georgia legislator S. A. McIver, tried to ensure that bills for the "protection" or "reformation" of white girls explicitly included black girls as well.[21] Others took on white men directly, pursuing legislation that would penalize them for sex with African American women. At the same session where South Carolina lawmakers debated age of consent, for instance, Robert Smalls objected to a law that criminalized interracial marriage but left informal sexual activity unregulated, thereby enabling white men to define the terms of interracial sex and leaving black women unprotected. In a gesture rich with mockery, he proposed barring white men who cohabited with black women from holding office. White officeholders rejected his proposals by a large majority.[22] Like Smalls, other African Americans implied that the white men who framed the law might have a vested interest in stripping political rights from African Americans on the one hand, and leaving black women legally unprotected on the other. As a black newspaper wryly observed, "The very men who are abridging our rights are the ones who are ruining our daughters."[23]

The African American WCTU activist Frances Joseph-Gaudet bemoaned the effects of laws that criminalized interracial marriage but not interracial sex. Observing that "the law is not respected by some of the men of the race who have helped to make it," she challenged white women to take action. Abuse of black women would continue, she argued, "until the white woman rises in her might and demands a higher standard of morals from the men of her race."[24]

White women in the WCTU saw themselves as engaged in that very project, but they acted out of different motives. Age-of-consent campaigns in the South were part of a sweeping, nationwide sex reform program inaugurated in 1885 by the national WCTU.[25] Through the legal branch of the work, activists sought, in Frances Willard's words, "the passage of such laws as would punish the outrage of defenseless girls and women by making the repetition of such outrage an impossibility."[26] Specifically, the WCTU mobilized to amend rape statutes by raising the legal "age of consent." According to existing rape laws, most of which set the age at ten, a man who had sexual intercourse with a girl under that age would be punished as in the case of rape, whether or not she had consented and whether or not he had used force.[27] Through revised consent laws, reformers intended to render questions about a woman's sexual character moot in court, in order to nullify the popular defense strategy of claiming that a woman did not resist.[28] Most activists in this period took pains to distinguish between rape laws and laws regarding prostitution, although some confusion existed.[29]

For the most part white southern women used the same organizing tactics and language as their northern counterparts. Southern WCTU chapters immediately and eagerly pursued sex reform projects; by 1886, within one year after the national organization launched its sex reform program, every state WCTU in the South, with one exception, had organized a department of "social purity."[30] Yet the specific character of southern women's reform networks, race relations, and partisan politics in the South also influenced the timing and fate of age-of-consent legislation in the region.

White southern women were undoubtedly aware of black women's criticisms of the sexual conduct of white men, especially since their reform networks during this period brought them into interaction with African American educators, students, and activists. In the WCTU, which, although segregated, was the first biracial, interdenominational venture in women's politics in the South, there was considerable overlap between sex reform networks and interracial coalitions. Those white women prone to participate in race reform initiatives were also likely to be active in sex reform. In Georgia, for example, numerous white WCTU superintendents of social purity projects worked with black women in African American institutions, drawing upon "neo-abolitionist" networks forged in the crucible of Reconstruction.[31] White reformers promoted "White Shield" societies for African American women in Atlanta, where they aimed to "teach" students, mainly through moral exhortation, how to protect themselves from men's sexual advances.[32] Black organizers who led the state WCTU for African American women assuredly brought the problem of white men to white women's attention. White women sex reformers followed black women's lead by suggesting that the best solution to the "race problem" lay in reforming white men's sexual practices.

White and black southern women faced a new set of problems from white men in the post-Reconstruction period. While it is not clear that white men's sexual behavior changed, responses to white men's actions by women, police, judges, and juries did change. According to the historian Laura F. Edwards, during Reconstruction poor black and white women brought a steady flow of sexual violence cases before the courts, attesting to their increased political power.[33] "Redemption," the period in which elite white men beat back political challenges and reasserted control, reversed this trend.[34] As Edward Ayers's study of criminal justice in the South demonstrates, the conviction rate for white men, whatever the crime, declined after Reconstruction, even as it rose precipitously for African American men accused of crime.[35]

The impact of focusing on black men's alleged crimes, it seems, was to detract attention from those of white men. As the African American author Charles Chesnutt observed of the white popular fixation on the alleged rape of white women by black men, "from the hysterical utterances on the subject one would almost be inclined to believe that rape committed by a white man upon a white woman was scarcely any offense at all in comparison."[36] Indeed, white supremacist propaganda culminated in such bald declarations as "The lust of the white man makes no menace . . . toward the women of the South. The negro has a monopoly on rape."[37] Arrest statistics in at least one city—Savannah, Georgia—bear out the suggestion that white men's crimes against both black and white women went unnoticed by law enforcement officials: from 1899 to 1905 Savannah police arrested twenty black men for rape and three for seduction, but no white men whatsoever.[38] Since white men so consistently avoided punishment for rape, the WCTU's rape reform campaign can be viewed as a response to this neglect. White men increasingly unrestrained by law posed new threats to all southern women.

New political conditions also laid the groundwork for age-of-consent campaigns, and help to explain the timing and fate of this legislation in the South. During the 1890s women successfully introduced age-of-consent bills in every state; by 1910 fifteen of eighteen southern legislative bodies had modified their rape laws to some degree in response to organized popular pressure.[39] Georgia, the most notorious exception, did not pass a law raising the age from ten to fourteen years until 1918, despite the fact that women began petitioning the legislature to do so in 1887.

The sex reformers' success—be it simply introducing bills, pushing them through to a vote, or actually passing them—was tied to labor and African American political organization and independent party movement. Nationwide, Knights of Labor locals circulated thousands of petitions to raise the age of consent; in the South as well, WCTU members sought support from Knights in this campaign. Such legislation tapped into shared anxieties about exploitative bosses and sexual danger for women in the workplace. As WCTU literature explained, age-of-consent laws targeted the employer who "makes the price of [a working girl's] virtue the condition of her continued wages."[40] Alliance with working people pushed WCTU reformers to emphasize the economic aspects of women's sexual vulnerability. Memphis women, for example, tied their age-of-consent agitation to a broader economic program, combining labor and sex reform slogans in their call for "Equal Purity, Equal Pay for Equal Work, and Self-Possession of Womanhood."[41]

Sex legislation was among those political issues that could animate and unite organized white women, workers, and farmers. In Texas, age-of-consent reforms grew directly out of Populist politics. Mary Clardy, a Farmers' Alliance lecturer, Populist organizer, and laundress, began agitating for rape reform legislation in 1891.[42] Ellen Lawson-Dabbs promoted age-of-consent legislation in 1894 under the banner of the Texas Farmers' Alliance, People's Party, Knights of Labor, and WCTU.[43] In 1895 age-of-consent legislation was introduced by a Populist representative, and all the Populist legislators voted to raise the age. An opponent charged that the movement originated with "God forsaken Populistic Kansas . . . whose women are here now, the chief lobbyists for this amendment."[44]

Developments in North Carolina also suggest the connections between sex reform and other political challenges to conservative Democrats. WCTU activists in the state began appealing for new rape laws in 1887. Not until 1895, after black and white Populists and Republicans combined to seize a majority in the state legislature from Democrats, did they finally receive a hearing.[45] Notably, the most vigorous and vocal opponents of revising the rape law were also among the most staunch opponents of Populist and Republican reforms and were infamous for their obstructionist strategies.[46] The WCTU's opponents surely exaggerated the threat that WCTU reforms posed to the racial and economic status quo. Yet conservative allegations that the WCTU promoted labor radicalism and "social equality" testify to the challenge posed by such coalitions.[47]

Further evidence of rape reform's connections to the political challengers of the 1890s can be found in the political fate that befell those lawmakers who introduced age-of-consent bills in contrast to those who led the opposition. Age proponents mostly disappeared. In other words, those legislators who supported rape law reform were not among those who maintained power in the South well into the twentieth century. Conversely, contrary to the predictions of optimistic WCTU activists who maintained that opponents of rape reform "would be forever retired from public position," many of their antagonists went on to successful, and in some cases extremely long, political careers.[48] In Tennessee the notorious and belligerent opponent John A. Tipton was voted Speaker of the House the year after he declared that legal rape reform was unneccessary, since "the shotgun remedy was the best that had ever been invented for the protection of virtue."[49] In Alabama, Charles E. Waller, who led the opposition, enjoyed the exact same fate, as did Georgia representative Newton A. Morris.[50]

Georgia representative Joe Hill Hall of Macon best illustrates the staying power of statesmen who opposed sex reform. A strong opponent of raising the age of consent above ten years when a bill was first proposed in 1900, he remained an intransigent foe of sex reform (and woman suffrage) to the last. In 1917 he still held a seat in the state legislature, where he continued to ridicule proposals to revise the age-of-consent law, insisting that girls of ten must be held responsible for their sexual conduct.[51] Those men likely to introduce consent bills, then, generally did not demonstrate the political longevity of their opponents. Supporters' high turnover rate ensured that women reformers waged a constant battle to find new sponsors for their bills, while the opposition remained constant.

Opponents of age-of-consent reform benefited from keeping the issue quiet. The first step for white southern women who organized campaigns to raise the age of consent, then, was to claim a space for themselves in public discourse about sex, in order to change the law. Like the *Atlanta Constitution*, some newspapers did not deem this matter a fit subject for women to discuss publicly. As one editor patly put it, "THE LEAST TALKED ABOUT THE BETTER."[52] Reformers did not "break the silence" in frank terms. Faced with the resistance of such editors as well as their own standards of "respectable" womanhood, these women adopted verbal strategies of indirection in order to hold serious public debate about what they themselves referred to as "the unmentionable."[53] In fascinating comparison to what Darlene Clark Hine describes as middle-class black women's "culture of dissemblance," in which black women avoided public discussion of their private sexual practices even as they organized resistance to sexual exploitation, white women tiptoed around the subject of race and sex in the midst of a mass publicity campaign around the issue.[54]

Women first publicized the issue by canvasing communities and gathering signatures on petitions. Activists in every southern state exerted sustained pressure on state lawmakers by submitting such petitions virtually every year until the legislation passed. In Texas, one of the most well-organized states, almost fifty thousand citizens signed petitions requesting the 1891 state legislature to raise the age of consent from ten to eighteen years. Ten years later, the pressure was still on: reformers in Florida submitted over fifteen thousand signatures in support of this reform.

But the club meetings, sidewalks, and stores where reformers gathered signatures were not the only public spaces where this battle raged. Women brought their campaign into legislative halls.

Law was properly a matter for public discussion, women reformers maintained, not to be determined by men conversing alone behind closed doors. Out of the belief that "men will say in secret session things they would not say if they knew women to be present," women insisted that lawmakers publicly explain their reasons for not changing age-of-consent laws.[55] Reformers attended legislative hearings in blocs to make their claims in person, punctuating the proceedings with commentary, even hissing at times.[56] Legislators employed a variety of strategies to divert public attention from the matter, including inaction, evasion, and ridicule. Once age-of-consent bills were introduced, judiciary committees often simply rejected the proposed legislation, and the bills never came to a vote. When a bill made it to the floor, opponents used every stalling tactic available to them. One legislator even invented a new filibustering technique: making a show of bolting from the house when a vote was called.[57] As a last resort, legislators barred women from the galleries while they discussed age-of-consent bills.[58] This move echoed the trend in this period to bar women from courtrooms.[59] New laws enabling judges to clear the courtroom were in part a response to local WCTU chapters' practice of attending rape trials in a body.

Despite this resistance, reformers achieved some success, though not always on the terms that they had set. Southern lawmakers framed laws not necessarily in the ways women reformers intended. The opponents of rape reform shaped these laws just as much as reformers did. Legislators in most states made a distinction between rape and intercourse with an underage female. Referred to as the "age of protection," these laws set a higher age than the age of consent where sex with a woman would constitute a crime, but established milder penalties than for rape. Often no minimum penalty was established, and juries could recommend punishment by imprisonment or fines. No convictions would occur if the woman did not have a witness. Furthermore, when legislators named these bills, they shifted emphasis from men's behavior to the conduct of girls. They framed acts not to define the criminal action of men and prescribe penalties, but "to protect females of immature age and judgment from licentiousness," or "for the protection of girls and for the promotion of chastity," or "to establish the age of moral responsibility in girls."[60] This marked a departure from the WCTU's intent, which was to place responsibility for sexual encounters largely upon men.[61]

Reformers had a difficult time explaining the source and substance of this resistance. Although opposition in part stemmed from partisan allegiances, legislators did not represent a clear-cut body of interests. A legislator's occupation apparently had little bearing on his position: lawyers, farmers, and merchants were arrayed on both sides of the issue. Although lawmakers debated child labor throughout this period, no substantial correlation existed between support for raising the age of consent and support for child labor laws.[62] Nor can geography help explain patterns of support or opposition: legislators from upcountry regions and plantation belts could be found in both camps. What unified opponents was a commitment to a particular conception of manhood, one based on opposition to women participating in politics or using the law to protect themselves. Opponents claimed that age-of-consent legislation deprived white southern men of their time-honored "right" to protect white women through individual acts of vengeance.[63] But legislators also based their opposition on the perceived sexual interests of particular white men.

Ironically, opponents described white men not only as protectors of women, but also as potential victims of them.[64] They described certain women as unusually powerful, and boys—not girls—as in need of special protection. "Is there nothing to be done for our boys?" objected one editorialist. "Do we mean that an amarous [sic] Venus of 17 years shall entice, if she chooses, a stripling Adonis of 16?"[65] A Tennessee representative and self-proclaimed "father of boys as well as girls" protested that "he would not in the fear of God throw down the gate of blackmail against his sons." Another insisted that "he would not vote for a bill that would allow a designing prostitute to induce his boy into her house and make him a felon."[66] That a substantial number of opponents had teenage sons or were single themselves helps explain the prevalence of this particular line of argument. They understood that their sons were at risk of being constrained by age-of-consent laws.

They also apprehended that adult men, including themselves, would be subject to these laws as well. A group of North Carolina legislators protested in 1895 that changing the age of consent would "prove a snare to some unfortunate and unwary man . . . [and provide] an instrument of oppression in the hands of some scheming female."[67] Opponents expressed special alarm at the prospect of working women charging their employers with sexual abuse. As Texas senator William Bailey argued, raising the age above fourteen "gave rise to an opportunity for the typewriter girls and other females so disposed to blackmail their employers."[68] A Texas newspaper insinuated that opponents feared that domestic workers would use this legislation to their advantage, but consoled anxious lawmakers that "defamation" could not touch the truly virtuous employer.[69]

Opponents hinted that African American women, in particular, posed a threat to white men. One Tennesseean warned,

> All grades of society and all classes of population must be considered in such matters. To raise the age of consent . . . would enable loose young women, both white and black, to wreak a fearful vengeance on unsuspecting young men. . . . Who of us that has a boy 16 years old would be willing to see him sent to the penitentiary on the accusation of a servant girl?[70]

The Kentucky legislator A. C. Tompkins expressed an unrestrained, and probably representative, opinion: "We see at once what a terrible weapon for evil the elevating of the age of consent would be when placed in the hands of a lecherous, sensual negro woman!"[71] Yet overall, the white southern press was evasive when reporting on this feature of lawmakers' objections: newspapers reported on arguments of this type with innuendo.[72] According to a Texas daily, Senator Walter Tips refused to support raising the age of consent "because legislation of this kind affects all classes."[73] The South Carolina firebrand Ben Tillman, in uncharacteristic understatement, reportedly argued that opponents refused to raise the age of consent for white girls "because others were here."[74]

Legislators fully understood that black girls and women could potentially use the law to protect themselves from white men. Tennessee senator Ernest Bullock objected that the law would extend to "both white and colored."[75] In Mississippi an opponent explicitly argued "that this would enable negro girls to sue white men."[76] A. C. Tompkins based his opposition precisely on the lack of distinction the age of consent law made among women. According to Tompkins, "The laws of the United States place the negro female on the same plane with the white female, declaring them identical in every particular."[77]

With this lack of distinction in mind, lawmakers proceeded to make distinctions that would prevent black and working-class white women from effectively using these laws. Legislatures made provisions that the age-of-consent laws would include only women of "previously chaste character."[78] In the words of one lawmaker, "The law is only beneficial inasmuch as it protects the innocent girls of the state."[79] This shifted the burden of proof back onto a woman, who would not only have to prove in court that she was in fact "chaste," but further that she had a "reputation" for chastity.[80] Legislators and reformers understood that this "reputation" requirement would be particularly difficult for African American women to meet, considering long-standing white stereotypes about their sexuality.[81] Much like laws that prevented people whose grandfathers had not voted from voting themselves, this distinction was a way of writing racial distinctions into the law without using racial terminology.

Reformers objected strenuously to these clauses, arguing that the law had "teeth" only when women did not have to defend their character.[82] They condemned legislators for drawing legal distinctions between the "innocent" and the sexually experienced. As one reformer exclaimed after North Carolina legislators enacted a prior chastity clause, "Fancy stopping to discuss whether a child ten and one-half years old is a virgin or has outlawed herself by having once before met a male brute! Is this 'Southern chivalry'?"[83] An editorial in the African American journal the *Crisis* averred that through these clauses, southern lawmakers had "invented a [sure] method of damning the poor and helpless by making a distinction between 'chaste' and 'unchaste' children, the latter being given the least protection."[84]

Lawmakers' opposition to strict rape laws extended only to those that might affect white men. Apparently, opponents did not see a contradiction in their advocacy of castration for rapists in one instance, and their vigorous defense of "men's rights" in the age-of-consent debates. Across the South at this time, legislators considered bills that would enable juries to recommend castration for men convicted of rape or attempted rape.[85] These measures were clearly aimed at black men.[86] Many of the same newspapers that played down age-of-consent campaigns gave these other draconian proposals a considerable amount of publicity and warm support. Thus, a Georgia paper observed that a proposed castration law was "peculiarly adopted to Southern conditions."[87] In terrorist language, a Texas daily urged lawmakers to enact castration legislation for the protection of the "noble women of Texas" against black men.[88]

Notably, in a number of cases it was the opponents of WCTU efforts who introduced these castration bills in the heart of debate over age of consent.[89] Furthermore, a number of opponents proposed making penalties for attempted rape more broad—eliminating maximum limits to penalties and thereby giving juries greater power to determine punishments.[90] In the South, where "attempt to rape" might include even a passing comment by an African American man to a white woman, and where juries were composed exclusively of white men, indeterminate sentences increased white southerners' ability to mete out harsher sentences to black men than to white men convicted of the same crime.

In the words of one African American editor who opposed leaving punishment, especially death, to jurors' discretion, "It is needless to say that the discretion is never thrown against white men, however heinous their offenses." The problem white southerners faced in framing criminal law, he observed, was "a hard one—how to [make] the law and yet save the white man from its provisions."[91] In contrast to sex reformers, then, who wanted strict rape laws that would be universally and uniformly applied, their opponents wanted rape laws that could be selectively applied. In short, opponents wanted to limit both the number of women who could seek protection under the law and the number of men who would be affected by the law's provisions.

White women activists endeavored to close up the very loopholes that their opponents labored to maintain. They intended rape laws to extend comprehensive protection to women and to cover all men. Though they shared a commitment to white supremacy with their opponents, their means of solidifying white control differed: they meant to compel white men to uphold its principles. Quite simply, white women hoped to prevent white men from having sex with black women, and saw the age-of-consent laws as a means to stop them from doing so. Texas WCTU president Helen Stoddard made this clear in an address before a state senate committee:

> I have heard a whisper—it was hardly meant for my ears—that this bill would protect the colored girl. As I pass along the streets of our cities and see the mulatto children, I think the colored girl needs protection, and more than that, the Anglo-Saxon man needs the restraints of this law to help him realize the dignity and sacred heritage he possesses by being born into the dominant race of the world.[92]

Stoddard and her colleagues objected to any revisions in the proposed bill that "would withhold protection from the negro or colored girl against white men."[93] In a circular letter, Georgia WCTU organizers referred to "the fact that certain legislators had openly objected to the protection [that an age-of-consent] bill would afford colored girls." This, the WCTU commented, stood as "an added reason for the bill's passage."[94]

But reformers had rarely addressed the subject of sex between white men and black women in terms this direct. When they did, in marked contrast to their refusal to point fingers at African American men, many activists were ready to charge black women with immorality. In 1893 one activist editorialized, "I do not believe that negro men, *taking into consideration the low standard of morals among the women of the race*, are one whit more immoral than white men."[95] While the white women activists emphasized the victimization of young white women, they studiously avoided naming African American women as victims.[96]

Age-of-consent reformers presented themselves as protectors of "working girls" without ever alluding to what this meant in the South, where African American women constituted a large part of the labor force and the vast majority of domestic workers, and where many of these same white women unquestionably employed workers in their own households.[97] When one white proponent tentatively broached the question of domestic service and African American women's sexuality, she put the onus on black women, urging employers to "require" virtue on the part of the women who would work in their homes.[98] Not until the advent of southern interracial women's councils during World War I would organized white women frankly announce, "We acknowledge our responsibility for the protection of the Negro women and girls in our homes and on the streets."[99]

White women in the WCTU expressed a range of racial perspectives in their sex reform work, and these attitudes changed in relation to shifting political conditions. Three examples illustrate the complex sources of white women's criticisms of white men, and the impact of the rising tide of white supremacy on their sexual ideology. Martha Schofield, a transplanted Quaker who ran a school for African Americans in South Carolina, made an intriguing suggestion at an 1896 purity conference. Women in the WCTU, she declared, "are sharing a weariness of so much talk and preaching about keeping *race* purity. They know what enemy is in the household and through them it must be cast out." Schofield reproached white men for their sexual advances toward black women, directing her criticism at "sons of respectable parents," men who "moved in the best society," public officials, and ministers "who led colored school girls from the path of virtue." "There are no young lives in America that have as much to contend with as the young *colored women*," maintained Schofield. "One cannot conceive the feelings of . . . colored women who know they are never safe from the insults of white men." For Schofield, the problem and the solution lay with white men; she exhorted women to "lift men . . . to respect *all* women."[100]

A decade later, even as white supremacy campaigns and politically manufactured "black brute" rape rhetoric reached a violent climax in the 1906 Atlanta riot, some white reformers still trained their critical sights on white men. Two editorials by WCTU activists in response to a barrage of sensationalist newspaper accounts of a "Reign of Terror for Southern Women" indicate different approaches to the white man problem. Mary Latimer McLendon made public her doubt over white men's will or ability to "protect" white women, especially in view of their refusal to raise the age of consent in Georgia. Although she did not dispute white stereotypes about "negro brutes," McLendon argued that certain white public officials, such as corrupt policemen, posed "as great danger" to all women, "white, black, red and yellow," as black rapists purportedly did. McLendon, who advised men to "stop all this foolish talk about disfranchising the negro," suggested that women needed political power in order to protect themselves.[101] In effect, McLendon argued that white men's political conduct, not black men's sexual behavior, posed a threat to women.

Her fellow WCTU organizer Vara A. Majette—who later organized WCTU chapters among black women in Georgia in the 1920s and became a county juvenile court probation officer—also seized the opportunity to criticize white men. Majette's newspaper editorial appeared under the bold headline "The White Man to Blame." Unlike McLendon, who challenged white men's abuse of political and legal power, Majette focused her outrage on white men's betrayal of white supremacy. "Look at the hordes of mulatto children swarming in the cities, the towns and even the country," she protested, "and say how far is the white man responsible for conditions." Majette's white supremacist fury led her to lump black and white men together, even while she made a critical distinction about the nature of their crimes: "Accomplished by willing intercourse on the white man's part—brute force by the negro—the result is the same, outraged nature and degradation of our Southern blood!"[102]

Commitment to white supremacist ideals of "race purity" led Majette to deny that white men raped black women or that white women might have willing intercourse with black men. While McLendon's criticisms of white men grew out of dissatisfaction with man-made laws, Majette's proceeded out of the conviction that white men were violating God-given, immutable "biological" laws. Her belief that criminal law should uphold scientific "truths" indicated the eugenic turn that white women's sex ideology was taking in the aftermath of Reconstruction.

As McLendon's editorial suggests, many white women in age-of-consent campaigns combined their consideration of white men's sexual behavior with a challenge to white men's political dominance. In the strong words of the Missouri WCTU activist Clara Hoffman, some reformers concluded that "Sex gives bias to law. Men legislate favorable for men."[103] All of these white activists were less willing to conclude that race gives bias to law, much less to address how racial ideology shaped their own understanding of sexual relationships and their definition of sexual crime.

Women in the WCTU sustained their agitation through the early 1920s, persistently calling for a higher age of consent and more clearly defined penalties for rape. Campaigns after 1910 changed in character, however. Just as the post-disfranchisement southern political structure differed markedly from the immediate post-Reconstruction order, so too did sex reform of the later period differ from the earlier campaigns of the 1890s. Consent laws passed in this second stage of sex reform were not designated as rape laws, but rather constituted a different category of crime: criminal carnal knowledge.[104] Women, not men, became the targets of reform: now reformers described their mission in different terms, "to protect the girl both from the man and from herself."[105] Furthermore, white activists specified that their concerns extended exclusively to white women, concentrating their energies on the so-called white slave traffic. They shifted their focus from sexual harassment by white patriarchs and employers to the machinations of a clandestine and remote "traffic" in white women conducted by immigrants and strangers. WCTU organizers promoted sex reform in the name of "gospel eugenics," renaming the social purity department the Department of Moral Education and Race Betterment.

By 1945, when Lillian Smith sought to break what she saw as white southern liberals' perpetual silence about the "white man problem," the earlier challenge to white men's sexual behavior had largely vanished from public memory. Age-of-consent campaigns indicate, however, that the subject of white men's sexuality garnered a significant amount of critical commentary in the period from 1885 to 1910. White men's sexual behavior, and the laws regulating it, were the subject of widespread public comment within black communities as well as among white women, and occasionally became points of discussion between white and black reformers as well. But disfranchisement and the solidification of racial segregation had effectively ensured that white women were even less likely to listen to African American women's insights on the problem of white men. This made it easier for white men to pursue their most effective strategy of sexual power: silence.

NOTES

Thanks to Nancy Hewitt, Darlene Clark Hine, and Tera Hunter for comments on the first draft of this essay. Thanks also to Wallace Best, Marisa Chappell, Seth Cotlar, Josie Fowler, Jacalyn D. Harden, Martha Hodes, Anastasia Mann, Michele Mitchell, John Seawright, and especially Nancy MacLean.

1. Lillian Smith, "Addressed to White Liberals," in *Primer for White Folks*, ed. Bucklin Moon (Garden City, N.Y.: Doubleday, 1945), 484–87.

2. *Atlanta Constitution*, Sept. 17, 1886, 4.

3. *Union Signal*, Oct. 7, 1886, 2. The *Union Signal* remarked on an attempted rape of a black woman and two rapes of white women reported in the *Constitution* that day.

4. Jacquelyn Dowd Hall, " 'The Mind That Burns in Each Body': Women, Rape, and Racial Violence," in *Powers of Desire: The Politics of Sexuality*, ed. Ann Snitow, Christine Stansell, and Sharon Thompson (New York: Monthly Review Press, 1983), 328–49.

5. On private criticism of white men's sexual conduct in slavery, consult Deborah Gray White, *Ar'n't I a Woman? Female Slaves in the Plantation South* (New York: W. W. Norton, 1985), 40–43; Nell Irvin Painter, introduction to *The Secret Eye: The Journal of Ella Gertrude Clanton Thomas, 1848–1889*, ed. Virginia Ingraham Burr (Chapel Hill: University of North Carolina Press, 1990), 34–35, 55–66. On white women's later public campaigns against lynching, see Jacquelyn Dowd Hall, *Revolt against Chivalry: Jessie Daniel Ames and the Women's Campaign against Lynching* (rev. ed.; New York: Columbia University Press, 1993).

6. Ellen Carol DuBois and Linda Gordon, "Seeking Ecstasy on the Battlefield: Danger and Pleasure in Nineteenth-Century Feminist Sexual Thought," in *Pleasure and Danger*, ed. Carole S. Vance (London: Pandora, 1989), 38; David Pivar, *Purity Crusade: Sexual Morality and Social Control, 1868–1900* (Westport, Conn.: Greenwood, 1973).

7. For WCTU members' apologies for lynching, see, for example, *Voice* (New York), Oct. 28, 1890, p. 8, cols. 3–4; *Union Signal*, Oct. 28, 1897, 6; *Atlanta Constitution*, Dec.

22, 1898. For criticism, see "Miss Willard Pounds the Poor Negro," *Atlanta Times*, Nov. 15, 1890; Ida B. Wells-Barnett, *Crusade for Justice: The Autobiography of Ida B. Wells*, ed. Alfreda M. Duster (Chicago: University of Chicago Press, 1970), 136, 151–52, 201–11.

8. A wealth of important scholarship argues that nineteenth-century sex reform focused primarily on controlling the sexual behavior of girls and that legislation ostensibly designed to protect women ultimately resulted in coercive measures against them. See, for example, Hazel V. Carby, "Policing the Black Woman's Body in an Urban Context," *Critical Inquiry* 10 (1992): 738–55; Mary E. Odem, *Delinquent Daughters: Protecting and Policing Adolescent Female Sexuality in the United States, 1885–1920* (Chapel Hill: University of North Carolina Press, 1995).

9. Elsa Barkley Brown, " 'What Has Happened Here': The Politics of Difference in Women's History and Feminist Politics," *Feminist Studies* 18 (1992): 300. On sex reform and racial ideology in this period, see Evelyn Brooks Higginbotham, *Righteous Discontent: The Women's Movement in the Black Baptist Church, 1880–1920* (Cambridge: Harvard University Press, 1993), 185–229; Peggy Pascoe, *Relations of Rescue: The Search for Female Moral Authority in the American West, 1874–1939* (New York: Oxford University Press, 1990), 114–17; Mariana Valverde, " 'When the Mother of the Race Is Free': Race, Reproduction, and Sexuality in First-Wave Feminism," in *Gender Conflicts: New Essays in Women's History*, ed. Franca Iocavetta and Mariana Valverde (Toronto: University of Toronto Press, 1992), 3–26.

10. Martha Hodes, "The Sexualization of Reconstruction Politics: White Women and Black Men in the South after the Civil War," *Journal of the History of Sexuality* 3 (1993): 402–17.

11. See Gail Bederman, *Manliness and Civilization: A Cultural History of Gender and Race in the United States, 1880–1917* (Chicago: University of Chicago Press, 1995); Glenda Elizabeth Gilmore, *Gender and Jim Crow: Women and the Politics of White Supremacy in North Carolina, 1896–1920* (Chapel Hill: University of North Carolina Press, 1996), 61–89; Bryant Simon, "The Appeal of Cole Blease of South Carolina: Race, Class, and Sex in the New South," in this volume.

12. Hazel V. Carby, " 'On the Threshold of Woman's Era': Lynching, Empire, and Sexuality in Black Feminist Theory," in *"Race," Writing and Difference*, ed. Henry Louis Gates, Jr. (Chicago: University of Chicago Press, 1985), 301–16; Laura F. Edwards, "Sexual Violence, Gender, Reconstruction, and the Extension of Patriarchy in Granville County, North Carolina," *North Carolina Historical Review* 68 (1991): 237–60; Herbert G. Gutman, *The Black Family in Slavery and Freedom, 1750–1925* (New York: Pantheon, 1976), 393–95.

13. Ida B. Wells, "Color Line Justice," in *A Red Record* (Chicago: Donahue and Henneberry, 1895), 68–70.

14. Ida B. Wells, *Southern Horrors: Lynch Law in All Its Phases*, in *On Lynchings* (1892; reprint, New York: Arno Press, 1969), 11–12; Bederman, *Manliness*, 58–59. Reports on white men's sex crimes became a staple in African American newspapers. See, for example, "Chasing White Brute," *Savannah Tribune*, Nov. 10, 1900, p. 1, col. 6; *Savannah Tribune*, Nov. 17, 1900, p. 2, col. 1; *Voice of the Negro* 1, no. 6 (June 1904): 231.

15. *Voice of the Negro* 2, no. 2 (February 1905): 106–07.

16. Frances E. W. Harper, "The Contrast" (1854), in *The Complete Poems of Frances E. W. Harper*, ed. Maryemma Graham (New York: Oxford University Press, 1988), 20–21. See also idem, "An Appeal to My Countrywomen" (1894), in *Complete Poems*, 193–95.

17. Frances E. W. Harper, "A Double Standard" (1895), in *Complete Poems*, 176–78. On Harper's WCTU-sponsored social purity lectures, see *Spelman Messenger* 6, no. 2 (December 1889): 6; 6, no. 3 (January 1890): 6.

18. Frances E. W. Harper, "Social Purity—Its Relation to the Dependent Classes," in *National Purity Congress: Papers, Addresses, Portraits*, ed. Aaron M. Powell (New York: American Purity Alliance, 1896), 328–30.

19. "Some Notes on Negro Crime," *Proceedings of the Ninth Conference for the Study of Negro Problems*, ed. W. E. B. Du Bois (Atlanta: Atlanta University Press, 1904), 58, 65.

20. On earlier attempts by black politicians to pass laws legalizing interracial marriage but punishing white men for concubinage, see Gutman, *Black Family*, 399–402. On black women combating interracial marriage prohibitions in court, see Janice Sumler-Edmond, "The Quest for Justice: African American Litigants, 1867–1890," in *African American Women and the Vote, 1837–1965*, ed. Ann D. Gordon (Amherst: University of Massachusetts Press, 1997), 111–14.

21. *Atlanta Constitution*, Oct. 1, 1889, p. 8, col. 2; Tex. *House Journal* (1893), 621, 702.

22. *Charleston News and Courier*, Oct. 4, 1895; *News and Courier*, Nov. 23, 1895, p. 4, col. 3; *Colored American Magazine* 6, no. 4 (February 1903): 262.

23. *Savannah Tribune*, quoted in Clarence Bacote, "Negro Proscriptions, Protests and Proposed Solutions in Georgia, 1880–1908," *Journal of Southern History* 25 (1959): 479.

24. Frances Joseph-Gaudet, *He Leadeth Me* (New Orleans: Louisiana Printing Company, 1913), 121–24.

25. On these campaigns, see Odem, *Delinquent Daughters*, 8–37; Jane E. Larson, " 'Women Understand So Little, They Call My Good Nature "Deceit" ': A Feminist Rethinking of Seduction," *Columbia Law Review* 93 (1993): 374–472.

26. *Minutes of the National Woman's Christian Temperance Union, 12th Annual Meeting* (1885), 73–74.

27. For legal explanations of age-of-consent statutes, see, for example, Georgia Mark, "The Age of Consent," *Union Signal*, Dec. 3, 1885, 4–5; idem, "Morality vs. Law" (four-part series), *Union Signal*, Feb. 4–25, 1886.

28. Georgia Mark, "Some Legal Aspects of the Question," WCTU Social Purity Series, no. 12 (Chicago: Woman's Temperance Publication Association, n.d.), 9.

29. Georgia Mark, "A Few Hints on Legislative Work," *Union Signal*, Feb. 3, 1887, 4, clarified that "the term 'age of consent' can properly be used only with reference to crimes of violence." Mark carefully distinguished between laws relating to felonious assault and those relating to prostitution.

30. South Carolina was the lone exception; by 1887 all southern states reported social purity programs. *Minutes of the National WCTU, 13th Annual Meeting* (1886), xiv–xxxvii, appendix, xxxv–xlii. This essay includes the following in its discussion of the "South": the eleven former Confederate states, five former slaveholding states (Delaware, Kentucky, Maryland, Missouri, West Virginia), plus the District of Columbia and Indian Territory/Oklahoma.

31. On interracial cooperation between northern white and southern black Baptist women, see Higginbotham, *Righteous Discontent*, 88–119.

32. *Minutes of the Georgia WCTU, 6th Annual Convention* (1888), 8, 31; *Minutes of the Georgia WCTU, 12th Annual Convention* (1894), 37; *Spelman Messenger* 22, no. 7 (April 1906); 24, no. 8 (May 1908); 25, no. 1 (October 1908); 25, no. 8 (May 1909).

33. Edwards, "Sexual Violence"; idem, "The Disappearance of Susan Daniel and Henderson Cooper: Gender and Narratives of Political Conflict in the Reconstruction-Era U.S. South," in this volume.

34. Mary Frances Berry, "Judging Morality: Sexual Behavior and Legal Consequences in the Late Nineteenth-Century South," *Journal of American History* 78 (1991): 835–56; Peter W. Bardaglio, *Reconstructing the Household: Families, Sex, and the Law in the Nineteenth-Century South* (Chapel Hill: University of North Carolina Press, 1995).

35. Edward Ayers, *Vengeance and Justice: Crime and Punishment in the Nineteenth-Century South* (New York: Oxford University Press, 1984), 179.

36. Charles W. Chesnutt to Booker T. Washington, Aug. 11, 1903, in *"To Be an Author": Letters of Charles W. Chesnutt, 1889–1905*, ed. Joseph McElrath and Robert C. Leitz (Princeton: Princeton University Press, 1997), 185–91.

37. *Atlanta Georgian*, Aug. 21, 1906, p. 6, col. 1.

38. Savannah, Ga., *Municipal Reports*, 1899–1905 (excluding statistics for 1900). In this period Savannah police arrested a total of 15 black men for attempted rape compared to 3 white men, and 446 African Americans for "licentious conduct," compared to 9 whites.

39. Alabama (1897); Arkansas (1893); Delaware (1895); District of Columbia (1889); Florida (1887, 1901); Indian Territory (1898); Kentucky (1906); Louisiana (1896); Missouri (1889, 1895); Mississippi (1908); Maryland (1899); North Carolina (1895); Oklahoma (1890, 1895, 1910); South Carolina (1895); Tennessee (1893); Texas (1891, 1895); Virginia (1896); West Virginia (1891).

40. *Nashville Banner*, Jan. 21, 1893, p. 4, col. 3; "Outraged Womanhood," *Journal of United Labor*, April 9, 1887.

41. *Minutes of the Tennessee WCTU, 15th Annual Convention* (1896), 42. See also "Equal Pay for Equal Work," *Union Signal*, May 14, 1896, 8.

42. Mary Clardy, "The Mothers and the Senators," *Texas Christian Advocate*, April 23, 1891, p. 2, col. 5; Tex. House Journal (1891), 504; *Union Signal*, May 21, 1891, 10.

43. Ellen Lawson-Dabbs, "Reform Forces: Can They Unite?" *Union Signal*, March 28, 1893, 4,

44. *Austin Daily Statesman*, Feb. 9, 1895, p. 8, col. 3.

45. N.C. House Journal (1895), 63, 143–44; N.C. *Senate Journal* (1895), 631; *Public Laws of N.C.* (1895), chap. 295; Helen G. Edmonds, *The Negro and Fusion Politics in North Carolina, 1894–1901* (Chapel Hill: University of North Carolina Press, 1951).

46. Collins and Goodwin, *Biographical Sketches of the Members of the General Assembly of North Carolina, 1895* (Raleigh: Edwards and Broughton, 1895), 34, 35, 43. Opponent Frank Ray was the titular leader of the Democratic minority; suggestively, Ray later led opposition to a proposed "Jim-Crow bed law," which would fine white men for sexual intercourse with black women; Edmonds, *Negro and Fusion Politics*, 192.

47. For one such indictment, see *Charleston News and Courier*, undated clipping, Frances E. Willard Collection, box 7, folder 6, Frances E. Willard Memorial Library, Evanston, Ill.

48. *Nashville Banner*, March 3, 1893, p. 1, col. 2.

49. *Knoxville Daily Journal*, March 17, 1893, p. 1, col. 1; *Nashville Banner*, March 21, 1893, p. 4, cols. 1–2; Robert M. McBride, *Biographical Dictionary of the Tennessee General Assembly* (Nashville: Tennessee State Library and Archives, 1979), 2:910.

50. *Birmingham State Herald*, Jan. 22, 1897, p. 5, col. 1; Thomas M. Owen, *Dictionary of Alabama Biography* (Chicago: S. J. Clarke, 1921), 4:1722; Ga. House Journal (1902), 9–10.

51. *Atlanta Constitution*, Nov. 15, 1900, p. 9, col. 1; *Atlanta Journal*, Aug. 14, 1917,

p. 3, col. 2; Ga. *House Journal* (1901), 291; Ida Husted Harper, ed., *History of Woman Suffrage* (New York: Little and Ives, 1906), 6:126. Henry William Hopkins, a member of the "Original" Atlanta Ku Klux Klan in 1868 and a Reconstruction-era foe of "republican and negro misrule," who served in the state legislature from 1888 to 1918, presents another vivid case of long-standing opposition. See Henry William Hopkins, State of Georgia Biographical Questionnaires, microfilm drawer 154, box 6, Georgia Department of Archives and History, Atlanta.

52. *Charleston News and Courier*, Sept. 20, 1895, p. 2, col. 1.

53. In the words of Frances Willard, "I can not too earnestly urge that our Mothers Meetings and private conversations, to say nothing of our printed and spoken words, be carefully weeded clean from unsavory recitals, terrible examples, and all those technical expressions which, by base associations have become themselves impure." *Minutes of the NWCTU, 13th Annual Convention* (1886), 77.

54. Darlene Clark Hine, "Rape and the Inner Lives of Black Women: Preliminary Thoughts on the Culture of Dissemblance," *Signs* 14 (1989): 912–20; Deborah Gray White, "Private Lives, Public Personae: A Look at Early Twentieth-Century African American Club-women," in *Talking Gender*, ed. Nancy Hewitt, Jean O'Barr, and Nancy Rosebaugh (Chapel Hill: University of North Carolina Press, 1996), 105–23.

55. *Union Signal*, March 7, 1895, 12; *Nashville Banner*, Feb. 24, 1893, p. 4, col. 3.

56. Women's presence, or absence, at these sessions always elicited commentary from the press and legislators. See *Knoxville Daily Journal*, March 17, 1893, p. 1, col. 1; *Memphis Commercial*, March 17, 1893, p. 1, col. 5; *Charleston News and Courier*, Nov. 21, 1895, p. 1, col. 7.

57. *Austin Daily Statesman*, Feb. 9, 1895, p. 8, col. 2.

58. Miss. *House Journal* (1908), 277. One newspaper argued that "plainness of speech" necessitated "clearing the galleries of ladies and minors." *Memphis Commercial Appeal*, Feb. 1, 1908, p. 9, col. 2. See also Tenn. *Senate Journal* (1893), 560, 576; *Knoxville Daily Journal*, March 17, 1893, p. 1, col. 1; *Austin Daily Statesman*, Feb. 8, 1895, p. 8, col. 3.

59. In Georgia, for example, according to new laws, the court could be cleared "of all *or any portion* of the audience" in seduction or divorce cases, or cases where the evidence was "vulgar and obscene." *Georgia Public Laws* (1891), pt. 1, title 7, chap. 692; *Georgia Public Laws* (1895), pt. 1, title 5, chap. 182. The national WCTU encouraged women to attend rape trials to exert pressure for strict sentences.

60. Fla. *House Journal* (1887), 261; *Laws of Fla.* (1887), chap. 3760; N.C. *House Journal* (1895), 63; *Laws of North Carolina* (1895), chap. 295; N.C. *House Journal* (1917), 478.

61. *Union Signal*, Aug. 8, 1895, 4. For commentary on the distinction drawn by legislators between "age of consent" and "age of protection," see Susan B. Anthony and Ida Husted Harper, eds., *History of Woman Suffrage* (Indianapolis: Hollenbeck Press, 1902), 4:578–79.

62. I made a vote-by-vote comparison of support for child labor laws and age of consent in Alabama (1897), Georgia (1900), Mississippi (1908), and North Carolina (1895). Opposition usually extended to both child labor and protective sex reform, but a legislator's support did not necessarily extend to both. For instance, in Georgia forty-six of seventy-seven age-of-consent opponents had also voted against child labor legislation, but only twenty of seventy-one age-of-consent supporters had voted for child labor. See also Elizabeth Davidson, *Child Labor Legislation in the Southern Textile States* (Chapel Hill: University of North Carolina Press, 1939).

63. For invocations of the "unwritten law," see examples in *Nashville Banner*, March

31, 1893, p. 1, col. 4; *Arena* 14 (November 1895): 408; *Austin Daily Statesman*, Feb. 9, 1895, p. 8, cols. 2–3. See also Robert Ireland, " 'The Libertine Must Die': Sexual Dishonor and the Unwritten Law in the Nineteenth-Century United States," *Journal of Social History* 23 (1989): 27–44.

64. Age-of-consent debates brought out claims about mutual sexual agency and gender equality. One legislator argued that "All the honesty and purity does not belong to the female sex . . . all girls under 18 years of age are not pure, nor have they always mothers who are beyond reproach." *Austin Daily Statesman*, Feb. 9, 1895, p. 8, col. 3. See also Tenn. *House Journal* (1893), 446; *Knoxville Daily Journal*, March 17, 1893, p. 1, col. 1.

65. *Nashville Banner*, March 2, 1893, p. 4, col. 3.

66. *Knoxville Daily Journal*, March 17, 1893, p. 1, col. 1. See also *Nashville Banner*, March 31, 1893, p. 1, col. 4; *Austin Daily Statesman*, Feb. 8, 1895, p. 2, col. 1; *Birmingham State Herald*, Jan. 22, 1897, p. 5, col. 1; *Atlanta Constitution*, Nov. 15, 1900, p. 9, col. 1.

67. N.C. *House Journal* (1895), 63.

68. *Austin Daily Statesman*, Feb. 8, 1895, p. 8, col. 1.

69. Ibid., p. 2, col. 2.

70. *Nashville Banner*, March 11, 1893, p. 4, col. 3.

71. *Arena* 13 (July 1895): 220–23.

72. See Barbara Omolade, "Hearts of Darkness," in *Powers of Desire*, ed. Snitow, Stansell, and Thompson, 364, on white men's secrecy on these issues as a means of maintaining power.

73. Tips argued that Mexican and African American girls should not be included in this legislation. *Austin Daily Statesman*, Feb. 9, 1895, p. 8, cols. 2–3; *Arena* 14 (November 1895): 410.

74. Tillman supported raising the age to sixteen. *Charleston News and Courier*, Nov. 21, 1895, p. 1, col. 7.

75. *Nashville Banner*, March 31, 1893, p. 1, col. 4.

76. *Daily Clarion Ledger* (Jackson, Miss.), Jan. 12, 1908.

77. *Arena* 13 (July 1895): 223; *Arena* 11 (January 1895): 211.

78. N.C. *House Journal* (1895), 143–44, 152; Tenn. *House Journal* (1893), 443; *Austin Daily Statesman*, Feb. 8, 1895, p. 8, col. 1.

79. Bullock, quoted in *Nashville Banner*, March 31, 1893, p. 1, col. 4.

80. Tenn. *Senate Journal* (1893), 570–71, 575, 577–83; *Acts of Tennessee* (1893), chap. 129.

81. White, *Ar'n't I a Woman?* 27–61; Beverly Guy-Sheftall, *Daughters of Sorrow: Attitudes towards Black Women, 1880–1920* (Brooklyn: Carlson, 1990); Patricia Morton, *Disfigured Images: The Historical Assault on Afro-American Women* (Westport, Conn.: Greenwood, 1991).

82. *Union Signal*, Nov. 28, 1889, 8; *Arena* 14 (September 1895): 31–32; *Union Signal*, Feb. 3, 1887, 4.

83. *Arena* 14 (November 1895): 413.

84. *Crisis* 12 (August 1916): 165.

85. Ga. *Senate Journal* (1900), 75; Ga. *Senate Journal* (1901), 185, 236, 245, 272; Ga. *House Journal* (1901), 471, 595; *Atlanta Constitution*, Oct. 27, 1900, p. 1, col. 6; Tenn. *House Journal* (1895), 70, 76; Tex. *House Journal* (1893), 258.

86. For proposals to castrate sex criminals, "particularly negroes," see F. E. Daniel, "Should Insane Criminals or Sexual Perverts Be Allowed to Procreate?" *Medico-Legal Journal* 11 (1893–94): 275–92; T. D. Crothers, "Sexual Crimes and the Remedies," *Union Signal*, Aug. 26, 1897, 4.

87. *Enquirer-Sun* (Columbus, Ga.), Oct. 27, 1900, quoted in John Dittmer, *Black Georgia in the Progressive Era, 1900–1920* (Urbana: University of Illinois Press, 1977), 115.

88. *Austin Daily Statesman*, Jan. 19, 1895, p. 2, cols. 1–3; F. E. Daniel, "A Travesty on Religion and Law," *Austin Daily Statesman*, Jan. 25, 1895, p. 2, col. 3.

89. Tex. *Senate Journal* (1895), 131. But see Louisville *Courier-Journal*, Jan. 18, 1894, p. 1, cols. 1, 7.

90. For example, in Mississippi two-thirds of the senators and all of those representatives who voted against raising the age of consent supported a bill giving juries the discretionary power to make death the penalty for attempted rape. *Memphis Commercial Appeal*, Jan. 28, 1908, p. 10, cols. 1–2; *Daily Clarion-Ledger*, Feb. 7, 1908, p. 6, col. 2; Miss. *House Journal* (1908), 225, 277–78; Miss. *Senate Journal* (1908), 248, 327. See also Tex. *House Journal* (1893), 236; Tex. *Senate Journal* (1895), 47, 60, 93, 95, 108, 131, 506, 566; *General Laws of Texas* (1895), chap. 834.

91. "Southern Caste Laws," *Horizon: A Journal of the Color Line* 2 no. 3 (September 1907): 22.

92. Helen Stoddard, "The Age of Consent," *Houston Post*, Feb. 3, 1895, reprinted in Fanny L. Armstrong, *To the Noon Rest: The Life, Work and Addresses of Mrs. Helen M. Stoddard* (Butler, Ind.: L. H. Higley, 1909), 62. Notably, this portion of Stoddard's address was later omitted from an official history of the Texas WCTU, which included the rest of the speech. Mrs. W. M. Baines, *A Story of Texas White Ribboners* (n.p., 1935), 31–33.

93. Helen Stoddard, "Hillsboro Address, 1895," in Armstrong, *To the Noon Rest*, 83.

94. Methodist women passed a resolution calling for "the protection of the childhood and womanhood of Georgia without regard to race" in response to the WCTU letter. Lily Hardy Hammond, *Southern Women and Racial Adjustment* [1917], 2d ed. (Charlottesville: Surber-Arundale; John P. Slater Fund Occasional Paper no. 19, 1920), 12.

95. *Nashville Daily Banner*, March 15, 1893, p. 4, cols. 2–3.

96. If they referred to black women's sexual activity at all, they labeled it "prostitution," never countenancing the possibilities of sexual abuse. For example, *Minutes of the NWCTU, 14th Annual Convention* (1887), clxxvi. Ida B. Wells's agitation on the subject of white men's violence finally prompted Frances Willard to state that "the immoralities of white men in their relations with colored women are the source of intolerable race prejudice and hatred." *Minutes of the NWCTU, 21st Annual Convention* (1894), 130. For an objection to the view that "there is no such thing as rape on a colored girl," see John V. Smith, "The Age of Consent in Alabama," *Proceedings of the 19th Annual Meeting of the Alabama State Bar Association* (Montgomery: Brown Printing Company, 1896), xlix.

97. On age-of-consent legislation's benefits for girls "who work for a living," see *Arena* 14 (November 1895): 405; *Arena* 11 (January 1895): 214.

98. *Nashville Daily Banner*, March 15, 1893, p. 4, cols. 2–3.

99. Monroe N. Work, *Negro Yearbook: An Annual Encyclopedia of the Negro, 1921–1922* (Tuskegee, Ala.: Negro Yearbook Publishing Company, 1922), 7.

100. Martha Schofield, "Slavery's Legacy of Impurity," in *National Purity Congress*, ed. Powell, 174–78. Emphases in original.

101. *Atlanta Georgian*, Sept. 8, 1906, p. 9, cols. 1–2.

102. *Atlanta Georgian*, Sept. 1, 1906, p. 9, col. 5.

103. *Arena* 14 (September 1895): 32.

104. For example, see the contrast between *Acts of Tennessee* (1893), chap. 129; *Acts of Tennessee* (1901), chap. 19; *Acts of Tennessee* (1911), chap. 36. Note also the marked difference in language used in proposed bills in Ga. *House Journal* (1913), 201, 281; Ga. *House Journal* (1917), 386, 457; Ga. *Senate Journal* (1917), 637, 973.

105. *Union Signal*, Nov. 2, 1911, 10. Beginning as early as 1905, sex reformers began distinguishing themselves from earlier activists: "We do not advance the proposition that the girls who fall are all blameless and that the male is always to be held entirely responsible." *Union Signal*, April 27, 1905, 12. Odem analyzes this shift in *Delinquent Daughters*.

Chapter Eighteen

The Appeal of Cole Blease of South Carolina
Race, Class, and Sex in the New South

Bryant Simon

Joe Childers was a white southern millworker. He was described by a newspaper reporter as a "respectable laboring man" who enjoyed a "good reputation."[1] On the night of March 27, 1912, Childers met Joe Brinson and Frank Whisonant, both African Americans, near the train station in Blacksburg, South Carolina, a small town in the western Piedmont section of the state. For two of these men, the meeting proved tragic.

What happened that night among Brinson, Childers, and Whisonant will never be known. Depending on which account one believes, Childers either asked Brinson and Whisonant to get him a pint—or a quart—of whiskey or the two African Americans badgered the innocent white man until he finally agreed to buy liquor from them. The three men got drunk. According to Childers's version of the story, Brinson and Whisonant challenged him to chug all of the whiskey. Fearing for his safety, he drank as much as he could as fast as he could, but he could not drain the bottle. As Childers guzzled the rust-colored rotgut—or maybe it was clear white lightning— Brinson and Whisonant taunted him; when he did not finish, they grew quarrelsome. They dragged him to a cemetery and ordered him to take off his clothes. N. W. Hardin, a local attorney, recounted what he heard happened next: "They [Brinson and Whisonant] drew their pistols, cocked them and told Childers to open his mouth, and keep it open, that if he closed it, he would be shot on the spot." Then according to Hardin, Brinson made Childers perform oral sex on Whisonant.

Following this consensual or coerced sexual act, or what the press dubbed the "unmentionable act"—the phrase commonly used to hint at the rape or alleged rape of a white woman by an African American man—Childers "escaped." He ran straight to the police station to report the attack, and the chief of police quickly arrested Brinson and Whisonant. According to Hardin and as reported in the March 29 *Gaffney (South Carolina) Ledger*, they were charged with selling liquor, highway robbery, carrying a concealed weapon, assault with a deadly weapon, and sodomy. The next day the local magistrate fined the two men twenty dollars each. Some thought that the fine, which was roughly the equivalent of three weeks' wages for a textile worker, was too lenient. Regardless of the amount, Brinson and Whisonant had no money at all and were sent to jail.

The next morning E. D. Johnson of Blacksburg got up early and walked to the well in the center of the town square for water. Johnson discovered that the rope used to pull up the bucket was missing. Puzzled, he looked around; his eyes stopped at the stone and brick jail. The front door had been knocked down. Johnson peered inside and saw a broken padlock and an open cell. He must have known what had happened, and he ran to get the mayor. It did not take them long to find the missing rope and the missing prisoners.

"The job," wrote a reporter in the April 2 *Gaffney Ledger*, "had been done in a most workman-like manner." Brinson and Whisonant's cold and limp bodies dangled from the rafters of the blacksmith shop located just behind the jail. Bound hand and foot, both victims had been gagged, one with cotton, the other with rope. The killers had not wanted them to scream.[2]

Word of the lynching raced through the area, but the crime did not produce unanimity. It did not bring together, in the words of the sociologist and student of southern vigilantism Arthur Raper, "plantation owners and white tenants, mill owners and textile workers."[3] Rather, the killings stirred discord and division. "Law and order," worried the editor of the *Gaffney Ledger*, "has been flaunted" as "passions [became] inflamed and reason dethroned." "Every good citizen," he was certain, "deplored the crime." The newsman, however, had no sympathy for the dead. "Those were two bad negroes who were lynched in Blacksburg," he conceded. "But," he added, "those who outraged them became worse whites."[4]

No one, at least in public, named the "worse whites." Speculation, however, was rampant.[5] Many Blacksburg residents were convinced that the mob—totaling as many as a dozen or as few as six men—rode into town on horseback from the industrial towns and mill villages of Gaffney, Cherokee Falls, Hickory Grove, and King's Mountain. Others insisted that the killers were from Blacksburg. Though questions about where the murderers lived lingered, there was little doubt about what they did for a living. "My idea," wrote N. W. Hardin, "is that as Childers was a factory operative, the lynching was done by the operatives of the surrounding mills, trying to take care of their class." If millworkers committed the crime, townspeople were sure where the larger blame for the murders lay. "Some of the d——d fools are already saying," reported Hardin, "this is Bleasism." The *Gaffney Ledger* echoed this view. "If a majority of the people of South Carolina want Blease and Bleasism," the editor wrote of the lynching, "they will have it in spite of those who desire law and order."[6]

Bleasism was the term used by friends and foes alike to designate the political uprising of first-generation South Carolina millworkers. This electoral surge took its name from its standard-bearer, Coleman Livingston Blease. "Coley," as his loyal backers called him, had occupied the governor's office for a little more than a year and was preparing for his reelection drive when Brinson and Whisonant were killed. Although Blease did not play a direct role in the murders, commentators who linked him to the disorder in Blacksburg were, at least in part, right. Blease's racially charged, antireform campaigns and leadership style stirred up many of the same cultural, economic, and sexual anxieties that ultimately led some white working-class men to lynch African American men.

Let us for a moment speculate about what ran through the minds of the Blacksburg murderers. Despite the biracial, homoerotic overtones of the meeting at the railway station, the killers may have decided that Childers was "innocent" and that he had been "raped." The crime seems to have symbolized something more than one evening of horror in a cemetery. The alleged or imagined rape of the millworker Joe Childers may have represented in microcosm the assaults on white manhood posed by industrialization. Even more than the rape of a white woman, the rape of this white man by another man graphically represented male millworkers' deepest fears of emasculation. That the perpetrators were African Americans further magnified the offense. The alleged sexual attack not only erased the color line but also inverted the racial hierarchy, placing an African American man "on top," in a position of power over a white man. A few male textile workers appear to have made a connection between how the "rape" of Childers feminized him and how industrialization stripped them of control over their own labor and that of their families and, thus, over their manhood. Some southern white wage-earning men felt that industrialization placed them in the position of women, vulnerable and dependent, powerless at home and in the public sphere.

Recent scholarship on lynching and gender relations in the New South suggests that by murdering Joe Brinson and Frank Whisonant, the Blacksburg killers sought to reassert their manhood.[7] The same fierce determination to uphold white supremacy and patriarchy that led to the Blacksburg lynching was the driving force behind Cole Blease's electoral appeal. The same sexual and psychological anxieties that drew the lynch mob to the jail that spring night in 1912 brought many more men to the polls a few months later to vote for Blease. Middle-class South Carolinians—professionals and members of the emerging commercial elite—also connected the lynching in Cherokee County with Blease's political success. Both, they argued, stemmed from the collapse of "law and order" in the mill villages and demonstrated the need for reform.[8]

Southern historians have often identified white supremacy as the unifying thread of the New South. This was supposedly the one social principle that all white southerners agreed on.[9] Yet by the spring of 1912, most middle-class South Carolinians regarded lynching as a menacing signal of working-class disorder, not as a bright emblem of a unified community's resolve to defend white supremacy at any cost. Clearly, white southerners in the early part of the twentieth century were not of a single mind—not socially, not politically, and not even with regard to maintaining racial order.

However, for all their apparent "southernness," the anxieties that produced Bleasism and the Blacksburg lynching were not confined to South Carolina or, for that matter, to the American South. Across the United States and indeed the globe, the reconfiguration of production landscapes—the shift from fields to factories—jarred gender relations. Industrialization triggered an almost universal crisis of male identity. In South Carolina, the crisis of masculinity among first-generation mill hands aggravated race and gender relations and eventually spilled over into politics, dividing the state along class lines.[10]

South Carolina's turn-of-the-century mill-building crusade and white supremacy campaigns set the stage for Cole Blease's political emergence. In 1880 there were just over a dozen mills in South Carolina. Twenty years later, the number of textile factories had jumped to 115; in 1920 there were 184. As the mills of South Carolina multiplied, the labor force changed as well. At first, the mills employed mostly widowed women and their children, but as the industry grew and the rural economy stagnated, more and more men took jobs in the factories. As early as 1910, more than 60 percent of all millworkers were men.[11] Meanwhile, unlike other southern states, South Carolina did not disenfranchise poor white males, including property-less millworkers, when, in 1895, it prohibited African Americans from voting in the all-important Democratic Party primary.[12] By 1914, in fact, nearly one out of every seven Palmetto State Democrats lived in a mill village.[13]

Although Blease's mentor, the quasi-Populist leader of the state's disfranchising forces, Benjamin R. ("Pitchfork Ben") Tillman, had little use for industrial laborers—he once referred to them as that "damned factory class"—Cole Blease himself recognized the electoral harvest to be reaped in the textile communities.[14] As soon as Blease turned away from a career in law toward one in politics, he focused his attention on the mill hills around his hometown of Newberry. He spent time in village drugstores, in front of company stores, and at roadhouses, and he joined the clubs, fraternal organizations, and brotherhoods that textile workers belonged to. Sometime early in this century it was said, and no one disputed it, that Blease knew more mill hands by name than anyone else in the state.[15] He turned this familiarity into votes. In 1890 he was elected to represent Newberry County in the General Assembly. Twice, in 1910 and 1912, Blease triumphed in the governor's race. On several other occasions he won enough votes to earn a spot in the statewide second primary or runoff elections for governor. In all these contests, mill hands made up the bulk of Blease's support.[16]

Male textile workers did not just cast their ballots for Blease, they seemed devoted to him. When he stumped for votes on the mill hills, poking fun at elites and shouting the slogans of white supremacy, huge crowds greeted him with "tornado[es] of shrieks, yells, and whistles." Mill families named their children after Blease and hung his picture over their mantels. Laborers sang songs and wrote verses about their electoral favorite son. "If you want a good chicken," an upcountry poet was heard to say, "fry him in grease. If you want a good governor get Cole Blease." When a reporter asked a textile worker why he supported Blease, the man snapped, "I know I ain't goin' to vote for no aristocrat." Another mill hand once hollered, "Coley, I'd vote fer you even if you was to steal my mule tonight."[17]

The allegiance of millworkers to Cole Blease has baffled historians. Because he promoted white supremacy, derided national unions, rejected child labor restrictions, and lambasted compulsory school legislation, scholars have accused him of having "no program for the benefit of the factory workers" and of being nothing more than "a feather-legged demagogue." His detractors have contended that the reform policies Blease opposed could have freed the workers from the mill village's prison of poverty and that, even so, male textile laborers acted as pawns of their captors and squandered their votes on a racist, do-nothing politician. How, historians have wondered, could such perplexing behavior be explained? Ignorance and false consciousness were the answers most often given. V. O. Key argued in 1949 that poor whites were uneducated and rabidly racist and responded more to hollow appeals to white supremacy than to positive economic initiatives and well-intentioned social programs. A quarter of a century later, J. Morgan Kousser depicted Blease as a demagogue who "yelled so stridently" about African Americans that white laborers could not hear the anti–working-class message hidden underneath his racist tirades. For these two scholars and most other southern historians, the only legitimate form of class politics in the New South was biracial politics along the lines of Populism; if poor whites had better understood their world, they would not have allowed the artificial issue of race to disrupt the so-called natural alliance of southern have-nots—black and white—across the color line.[18]

In 1982 David L. Carlton reinterpreted Bleasism. Rather than measuring the electoral behavior of South Carolina workers against the ideal of biracial class collaboration and finding it wanting, Carlton contextualized this political surge. He maintained that Bleasism, unfolding against the rapid industrialization of the South Carolina upcountry, represented the politicization of cultural and social tensions between mill and town or, in other words, the rational, albeit sometimes unsavory, response of tradition-bound white southerners to the forces of modernization.[19]

According to Carlton, the "builders of a new state" preached to their fellow South Carolinians a gospel of regional renewal through mill building. Converting people to this creed required convincing them that industrialization would not lead the region down the road to ruin. Promoters promised "that a combination of the social controls of 'cotton mill paternalism' and the operatives' 'Anglo-Saxon' virtues would spare South Carolina the turmoil and class enmities of northern and British cities."[20] This faith in social harmony quickly faded. Well before the close of South Carolina's factory-building spree, many city and town dwellers concluded that, instead of being a civilizing influence on the rural-born workers, the mill villages were breeding grounds of disorder. Church and club meetings buzzed with warnings about the "cotton mill problem." They fretted about whiskey drinking, pool playing, prostitution, cock fighting, and gambling in the mill villages. Middle-class South Carolinians blamed poor white parents—not industrialization—for village lawlessness. Drunk and lazy, dirty and uneducated, mothers and fathers from the mills, it was charged, inculcated their innocent children with principles that could possibly distort the New South dream of prosperity into an ugly reality of disorder. Through public health programs, child labor restrictions, and compulsory school attendance legislation, reformers sought to uplift the children of the millworkers by intervening in their upbringing and teaching them the virtues of law and order, discipline and deference, sobriety and thrift. Furthermore, some reformers suggested that suffrage be limited to those white men who had already learned these lessons. Voting restrictions and interventionist reforms, David Carlton has argued, were the essence of South Carolina Progressivism.[21]

Carlton has shown that mill laborers resisted the progressive impulse. Consider the example of child labor legislation. Millworkers opposed these measures. Why would parents want their children to be permitted to work long hours in a steamy lint-filled factory? Money, Carlton explained, was part of the answer. Because of the southern textile industry's traditionally low wages, cotton mill families could not survive on one or even two paychecks. Quite often, children's wages prevented a family from falling into poverty. Workers also rejected middle-class reforms for ideological reasons. "Blease's supporters," Carlton wrote, "were spiritual, if not intellectual, heirs of an older America whose citizens viewed all concentrations of power as dangerous, and all government bureaucracies as corrupt and self-interested." Mill hands opposed progressive reforms and interpreted them as attacks on traditional notions of independence. Like English Luddites, South Carolina workers were, in Carlton's view, at war with the modern world, and they voted for Blease because he vowed "to wreck the social machinery being created by the middle classes."[22]

To be sure, Carlton has advanced the understanding of Bleasism. Nevertheless, the question of why workers opposed reform and voted in favor of Cole Blease deserves another look, one that takes into account Carlton's work along with the insights of feminism and gender studies of the last ten years. By reexamining the origins of the political insurgency of first-generation South Carolina millworkers, this time through the overlapping lenses of sexuality, gender, race, and class, a more complicated picture emerges. Race alone was not the stuff of the politics of South Carolina textile laborers; neither were notions of traditional independence nor the passions of antimodernism. Instead, as the grisly Blacksburg lynching suggested, the attitudes of workers combined race, class, and gender concerns. Workers' attitudes reflected private concerns about parental authority as well as public qualms about the actions of elected officials and self-appointed reformers. To male mill hands, politics was about power—in other words, about patriarchy and suffrage, economic autonomy and white supremacy. The public and private, therefore, were never as far apart for workers as they have been for historians. After gender and sexuality, personal anxieties and public fears, race and class are all incorporated into the analysis of wage laborers' motives for backing Blease, the result is a conceptual framework that reveals the political and social divide separating white working-class men from other white men in the New South.[23] South Carolina's new generation of industrial workers was certainly committed to independence, as Carlton has argued, but to most white men this meant more than living unencumbered from the modernizing state. Instead, their concepts of independence were interwoven with ideas about citizenship, race, economic autonomy, and masculinity. These ideas, moreover, were not static; rather, they shifted with changes in politics and the economy.

To South Carolina upcountry yeomen, who were the most likely ancestors of mill men and Blease backers, independence meant, above all else, political equality. Decades before the Nullification Crisis of 1832, planters and yeomen had reached an accord. They agreed to make slavery the law of the land and to scrap all but the most minimal property qualifications for voting, thereby enfranchising the vast majority of white men. Race and sex, not class, fixed the boundaries of citizenship. At the same time, ideas about suffrage and exclusion took on ideological dimensions that stretched far beyond the public arena of electoral politics. To be independent was to have the right to vote or, in other words, to be white and male. Those who could not vote were deemed to be dependent and unmanly. In antebellum South Carolina, African Americans and women made up the bulk of the state's adult "dependents," and self-serving white men argued that nature determined the rigid divide between voters and nonvoters, independents and dependents. White men were enfranchised because of their God-given superiority over childlike slaves and frail, emotional women. Domination in the political realm justified domination of women and children at home and African Americans in all aspects of life. White male notions of independence, therefore, were based not only on the right of all white men to vote but also on patriarchal control over the affairs of the household.[24]

However, claims about the natural superiority of white men failed to ease the fears of some yeomen about losing their basic political rights. Poor whites, in fact, did not completely trust wealthy planters, especially those who lived in grand style in the lowcountry, and indicated distrust of these men by calling them "aristocrats." *Aristocrats* was defined as *antidemocrats*—people who might, at any time, try to curtail the suffrage rights of ordinary people. Moreover, as Lacy K. Ford has explained, living day in and day out near enslaved people of African descent intensified yeomen's "fear[s] of submission and dependence." White male South Carolinians were unwilling to be reduced to the racialized and feminized status of dependents, so they clung to the right to vote, or to what one democrat called "the only true badge of the freeman."[25]

Antebellum notions about independence, masculinity, and suffrage were also enmeshed with ideas about control over the household and the economy. Before the Civil War, according to Lacy Ford, South Carolina yeomen adhered to the doctrines of "an inherited 'country-republican' ideology." Independence, in this view, was based on the pillars of political equality, economic autonomy, and patriarchal control over the public and private affairs of the household. Along with the vote, the surest guarantee of personal independence was a political economy based on "widespread ownership of productive property." If yeomen had assets—principally land, draft animals, farm implements, and a house—the aristocrats could not dictate to them. Divorced from the means of production, white men, whether they had the right to vote or not, could easily be reduced to dependency—that is, placed under the control of others and in the same position as women, children, and, worse yet, slaves. In such a position, they would no longer be independent and entitled to dominate. Under these conditions, the wealthiest and most aristocratic members of society might wrest from yeomen the social and political privileges of whiteness.[26]

Emancipation threw the intellectual universe of white yeomen into chaos. At that point, suffrage—that coveted distinction of independence and masculinity—was defined by sex alone. Not only did Reconstruction mark the end, however temporarily, of the white monopoly on public power, it also challenged prevailing ideas about white manhood. In this confusing new environment, some wealthy whites—so-called aristocrats—courted the votes of African Americans, implicitly acknowledging the manhood of ex-slaves.[27] Other whites, some rich, some poor, seemed unable to think about suffrage without also thinking about interracial sex.[28] Freedmen, they believed, saw political equality as a license to assault white women. White men responded with fury, especially after the Republican Party abandoned its Reconstruction policies in 1877. Intimidation at the polls, ballot box stuffing, late-night lynching, and the devious eight-box law were all designed by South Carolina Democrats to rob African Americans of the right to vote and to emasculate them in the process. Yet neither subterfuge nor violence worked, at least not entirely. African American men continued to vote well into the 1890s. Finally, in 1895, South Carolina adopted a new constitution that all but eliminated voting by black men in the state. Suffrage was once again defined by race and sex, and most white men over the age of twenty-one were entitled to vote.[29]

While the new constitution affirmed the political privileges of whiteness and maleness, the economic world of the yeomen was under attack. Beginning as early as the 1850s, the railroad crept into the South Carolina upcountry, bringing with it the possibilities and pitfalls of the market economy. Growing inequality, widely fluctuating cotton prices, and falling rates of property ownership among yeomen followed. Poor and middling farmers, nonetheless, held on to the "country-republican" vision of independence, but the changing relationships of production forced some shifts in this ideology.[30]

Whereas antebellum notions of independence rested on propertied independence, in the postbellum era ideas about independence depended increasingly on notions of control over others and on personal autonomy. No matter how much the market economy encroached on their lives, most plain white folks either held on to a small parcel of land or worked as free tenants. Either way, they owned and/or controlled the means of production and worked free from the supervision of others. White husbands and fathers continued to insist that they were the boss and that their wives and children should follow their commands. While women and children made vital contributions to the household economy, cooking and sewing, picking and hoeing, the cash crop—the source of family wealth—was the responsibility of the husband and father. Men were in charge of producing cotton for money, determining what to plant, how to allocate labor resources, and when to move. In the market-driven world of the New South, money, more than land or anything else, was the nexus of power. By defining their economic activities as those associated with money, men reasserted their control over the household in a changing world, even as they lost ownership of land.[31] As the propertied economic independence of poor whites slipped away, men also seem to have placed added stress on the privileges of whiteness and the virtues of patriarchy—of male control over dependent women and children. Plain folks insisted, perhaps more than ever before, that women, wealthy whites, and African Americans recognize their whiteness. It seemed that they interpreted any slight as a slap at their manhood, and they responded sometimes violently and sometimes politically. White supremacy, personal autonomy, and the control of dependents in public and private—these were the values of independence that poor white men brought with them from the countryside to the cotton mill world of South Carolina at the turn of the century.

Mill village life and labor challenged male conceptions of independence. Tending looms and operating carding machines stripped men of control of their own time and labor. The boss in the rural household now worked to the relentless rhythms of machines and to the angry bark of the foreman. Some even compared the factory regime to slavery. "They are trying to treat the help more like slaves than free people," protested T. V. Blair of Pelzer, South Carolina. S. F. Arthur of Langley added, "We do not have more showing than the negroes in slavery time." Mill hands deployed the metaphor of slavery to protest against the conditions in the mills and to articulate their fears about their growing dependence on the will of others. Without control over their own labor, male workers must have worried, as they had in the past, that maintaining their authority over others would be difficult.[32]

Wages, if they had been high enough to support the entire family, might have provided some men with a sense of compensation for their dwindling control.[33] Few mill men, however, earned enough to feed and clothe their families. Therefore, children and wives took up what southern mill hands revealingly labeled "public work"—that is, paid labor. Though fathers often disciplined their children on the shop floor, scolding those who misbehaved and urging slackers to work harder, they no doubt knew that the real authority rested with the foreman and the mill owner, men who were more powerful than they were.[34] Male mill hands familiar with the dynamics of the shop floor also knew that some supervisors used their power over hiring and firing to intimidate female workers sexually, which heightened the anxieties of fathers and husbands. Yet these men also understood that if they accused the supervisors of harassing their wives and daughters they risked losing their own jobs, and an unemployed worker was even less of a man than an underpaid one.[35]

The participation of dependents in the paid labor force realigned the balance of power within the family. Feeling enfranchised by their contributions to the household economy, working wives and children periodically challenged their husbands and fathers over the disposition of their wages. Sons and daughters, in particular, often demanded the right to spend part of their earnings on whatever they wanted.[36] How they spent their wages was also an issue in the family. Across the urban South in the first decades of the twentieth century, young workers, especially women, shaped a new heterosexual aesthetic. Cigarettes, bobbed hair, and shorter skirts were evidence of this trend. A refraction of the new city sensibilities quickly reached the mill hills. Some mill girls purchased the latest styles, went out with their friends, male and female, on Saturday nights, and skipped church on Sunday. Much more than their cousins back on the farms, young millworkers expressed themselves as independent and autonomous individuals culturally at odds with their fathers.[37]

While white mill men worried about their growing dependence and declining authority, all around them it seemed that African Americans were becoming more and more economically independent and assertive. To be sure, jobs inside the textile mills of South Carolina were reserved for whites, but African Americans made strides elsewhere. Between 1890 and 1910, for example, the number of black landowners in the Palmetto State steadily inched upward.[38] African Americans also registered other kinds of financial gains. Take the case of Archie Green of Walhalla, a town with a couple of textile mills in upcountry Oconee County. In 1915 Green, who was rumored to be the illegitimate grandson of John C. Calhoun, owned livestock, a small truck, and a neat house just across the tracks from Walhalla's main street. Local white officials praised Green's skills as a firefighter and rewarded him with a slew of municipal jobs. At one time, in fact, Green was in charge of a crew of white sanitation and street workers. When Green was accused some years later of sexually assaulting a Walhalla white woman who worked at a local mill, prominent whites rushed to his defense. Rather than punishing Green, they chastised the white woman, charging her with promiscuity.[39]

The doctrine of white supremacy, declared a Bleasite newspaper editor in 1917, "demanded that the LOWEST white man in the social scale is above the negro who stands HIGHEST by the same measurement."[40] But middle-class whites seemed to be turning away from this creed. At the same time that these uptown white men defended the character of African American men like Green, they disparaged working-class white men. Beginning as early as 1890, middle-class South Carolinians attacked the character of male laborers, questioning their worthiness as white men and patriarchs. The press portrayed "mill daddies" as "lazy, good-for-nothing wife beater[s] . . . and drunkard[s]." A Spartanburg journalist warned about "strong, hearty men . . . with several children, who move to a mill and strut around and form secret societies and talk big while their children support the family." "They say," the reporter added, "some of them spend one tenth of their children's earnings for whiskey." Shifting the burden of labor to their children, "cotton mill drone[s]," as some referred to mill fathers, sat around all day doing nothing. Occasionally, men of this sort left their seats in front of the company store and trudged off to the mill, not to tend looms, but to deliver lunch to their hardworking offspring. Before the machines started to whirl again, these "tin-bucket toter[s]" were back to swapping lies and taking their turn at the bottle. Though these ugly portraits of mill fathers twisted the truth, they nonetheless impressed reform-minded residents of South Carolina.[41]

"The character of part of the voting population has changed in recent years," remarked a South Carolina editor soon after the turn of the century, and not for the better, he probably meant. The group that most alarmed him and many other middle-class South Carolinians was the so-called unruly element among the mill hands. Reformers believed that they could take care of the children but wondered what could be done about the adults. Initially, a few spoke quietly of restricting the vote, of limiting the suffrage rights of the propertyless and illiterate, at least until they could be properly civilized. The emergence of Bleasism added urgency to this talk. For many, Cole Blease's electoral success—he finished a close second in the 1908 governor's race—confirmed what they had long suspected: that the poor unthinking multitude was ruled by the baser impulses rather than by reason and civility.[42] Bleasism, charged a Baptist minister, marked the "emergence of the Southern underworld." He added that it oozed from the sinister "whispers on the night corners in mill yards and at the crossroads."[43] The only way to stop Blease and to protect law and order, many argued, was to erase the names of his strongest supporters—illiterate and propertyless white men—from the voting rolls. Limiting suffrage would enable the "best" people of South Carolina to join together to reform the region without having to pander to the enfranchised "unruly element[s]." It was predicted that South Carolina would quickly become more modern and more efficient if society's most enlightened members were the only people permitted to vote. By pushing for voting restrictions, middle class reformers seemed to be calling for a wholesale renegotiation of white supremacy, hinting that bourgeois values, as well as race, should be the prerequisites for citizenship.[44]

The passions of the unthinking multitude alarmed middle-class women as well as men. The wives and daughters of the state's professional and commercial elite joined with schoolteachers and welfare workers to push for compulsory education, mandatory medical inspections, child labor restrictions, and prohibition. Many female reformers also advocated women's suffrage. Few, however, were radical democrats; instead they constructed a class-based appeal for the vote. They asked why uneducated white men with little financial stake in the system should be allowed to vote while well-informed white women did not have the franchise. In place of white male democracy, they proposed a sort of oligarchy of the best white people. Clearly, many white South Carolina suffragists had in mind a system of suffrage based on class and race, regardless of sex. Women's suffrage, if it fit this description, would destabilize sexual roles, making some working-class white men dependent on some middle-class white women in the public realm.[45]

For first-generation white workers, assaults on their independence and manhood seemed to be coming from every direction. Each mill hand dealt with the confusion of industrialization, low wages, waning parental authority, the growing assertiveness of women, middle-class hostility, and African American progress in his own way. Some gave up on the mill and returned to the countryside.[46] Others drank too much, and a few probably deserted their families.[47] A small number took out their frustrations on their wives and children. Domestic violence, as Christine Stansell has pointed out in another context, was not simply a reaction against dwindling status in the workplace but also a brutal "attempt to recapture and enforce . . . masculine authority."[48] Violence was not confined to the household; during the first two decades of the twentieth century, mill hands, along with white men and a few women from every side of town, assembled in lynch mobs. They killed African Americans who, they believed, wanted to wipe away the color line and undermine white masculinity.[49] Others spoke out for shorter working hours and higher pay, and a few joined trade unions and went out on strike.[50] Many, armed as they were with the vote, turned to politics—or, perhaps more accurately, politicians turned to them. The most famous of these politicians was Cole Blease.

In nearly a biennial ritual, between 1906 and 1916 textile workers went to the polls and voted for Cole Blease as a rock-solid bloc.[51] Blease brought male mill hands to the polls in record numbers because he honed a political message that gave public voice to their gathering resentments. He spoke to their concerns and frustrations in ways that made sense to them. He was, in the words of the Greenville journalist and longtime Blease-watcher James C. Derieux, their "mouthpiece," articulating their "unexpressed emotions, ambitions, and disgruntlements."[52] Like the Blacksburg lynching and yeomen's notions of independence, Blease's rhetoric fused issues of race, class, gender, sexuality, and state power.

Blease turned politics into theater, entertaining his audiences with guile and humor. However, there was always a point to Blease's antics. Usually it was to mock and belittle his opponents while building up himself and his followers. Lowcountry elites and middle-class South Carolinians, the reformers in particular, rather than the factory owners, caught the brunt of Blease's verbal blitzes. He was not impressed by their college degrees, big words, or their claims to selflessness; instead he dismissed them as "intellectuals," "fool theorists," "wise-looking old fossils," and members of the "holier than thou crowd." With a grin and wink he regularly stood on the stump and made light of the rule of law—that cardinal tenet of bourgeois ideology—by admitting to drinking bootleg whiskey every now and then. Each time he made this confession, his opponents tagged him as an ominous threat to law and order. Cole answered their forecasts of doom with charges of hypocrisy. "Why, I saw men up here last summer," he quipped in his 1913 inaugural address, "hollering, 'Law and Order,' yelling for 'Law and Order,' and 'We must redeem South Carolina.' " "I saw some of those same people down here at the State Fair drinking liquor and mixing it with coca-cola and betting on horses." "Who," Blease asked, "is going to redeem them?" The crowd chuckled.[53]

When he was not jabbing his opponents with pointed jokes, Blease smacked them with male bravado. He portrayed his opponents as unmanly "cowards," "belly crawlers," "pap-suckers," "nigger lovers," "molly-coddles," and "very small m[e]n."[54] Blease was especially scornful of women reformers and suffragists. He accused them of neglecting their homes and children so they could run around the state " 'doing society,' playing cards for prizes, etc." A supporter of Blease complained that female reformers wanted "to give us their dresses for our pants." Blease agreed. He opposed women's suffrage, hinting that the right to vote—to enter the public realm—might unsex women and lead to the unraveling of the social fabric. Women, Blease advised, should spend their time aiding "good men" rather then agitating for "drastic reforms."[55]

Aristocrats was one of Blease's favorite terms for his enemies.[56] By tagging his opponents as aristocrats, Blease tapped into a tradition of antielitism among the plain folk of South Carolina that stretched back to the antebellum era. Before and after the Civil War, *aristocrat* served as the pejorative term for wealthy lowcountry planters and their children who either wanted to restrict the suffrage rights of yeomen or entered into an unholy alliance with African Americans to blunt the political power of poor whites. "The fight I have tried to make and am making," Blease said of his battle against suffrage restrictions, "is to keep my friends in a position where they will not be oppressed, and to prevent a return to rule of the old aristocracy."[57]

At the same time, the image of the aristocrat conjured up gendered and class connotations. Blease's supporters had a clear image of how an aristocrat looked, sounded, and acted. Aristocrats were effete, wealthy men—dandies dressed in silk shirts and top hats with soft hands and coifed hair. Unlike real men, aristocrats did not work; instead they relied on others, typically their fathers, to provide for them. Also unlike real men, they lacked self-discipline: they drank, they smoked, they gambled, and they skipped church. Their thirst for excess extended to sex: they were insatiable, debauched, and without discipline. Not even the sanctity of marriage mattered. Some, in fact, never married at all, which made suspect the sexuality of aristocratic "confirmed bachelors."

"The best definition I know for aristocracy," Blease said in 1913, "is some fellow who does nothing, lives on his daddy's name and doesn't pay his debts." The aristocrats, Blease continued, fiddled away their nights watching decadent theater shows, yelling with delight at a foul-mouthed Yankee woman and a man dressed as "The Pink Lady." Just below the surface of Blease's attacks was the sly accusation that aristocrats subverted traditional gender roles. Because they placed themselves outside the boundaries of manly behavior, Blease warned, they posed a serious threat to patriarchy and white womanhood. As evidence of their deceit, Blease pointed to aristocrats' attempts to restrict the citizenship rights of poor whites. By depriving poor white men of their independence and manhood, they encouraged black men to consider themselves once again the political and social equals of white men. This was sure to produce a frightening rerun of Reconstruction. No "pure-blooded Caucasian," Blease asserted, would stand by and let this happen.[58]

Blease offered white laborers more than antiaristocratic rhetoric. Understanding some of the frustrations of male millworkers, he vowed to safeguard their suffrage rights and to uphold the privileges of race. Blease pledged his allegiance to the creed of white supremacy. He battled to make sure that all white males over the age of twenty-one could vote in the Democratic primary regardless of their background or income. He also endorsed legislation to bar African Americans from the textile mills, notwithstanding that by 1910 almost no mills would hire blacks for jobs inside the factories. Just to make sure that people knew exactly where he stood on employment, he fired every African American notary in the state.[59] Though Blease favored state action to bolster white supremacy, he opposed virtually all progressive reforms.[60]

Blease's fight against compulsory education laws was a case in point. These statutes would have required all children under the age of fourteen or sixteen to attend school. Blease scoffed at the reformers' humanitarian depiction of these education statutes. He portrayed these proposals instead as part of a broad campaign to reduce parental authority and to control mill people's private lives. Nature, he argued, determined that fathers and mothers, not the government, should oversee families. In opposition to a proposed compulsory education act, Blease said that cotton mill people "should be left alone . . . and allowed to manage their own affairs." "Compulsory education," he contended, "means disrupting the home, for it dethrones the authority of the parents and would place paid agents in control of the children which would destroy family government." "Of course I am opposed," he declared of a compulsory school bill on another occasion, "it comes . . . from some narrow-minded bigot who has made a failure in raising his own children . . . and now wants to attempt to raise somebody else's." Blease looked to the Bible to bolster his case. Not surprisingly he turned out to be a rather conservative theologian. He told a mill crowd, "The Bible says a great deal about obedience to parents and reverence for parents and believing in that Book and its teachings as I do, I say to the parents, for the sake of their children, our country, and for the future, keep within your own control the rearing and education of your own children." Blease's hostility toward compulsion did not mean that he opposed public education. In 1914 he called for higher pay for teachers, hiring more male instructors, improved libraries, longer school terms, and more "books, especially histories, by southern authors for southern children."[61]

Even more than compulsory education, progressive plans to mandate medical inspections of mill children provoked Blease. Proponents insisted that doctors' examinations of mill children would compensate for "the oversight of the child's environment" and would correct deformities that were "easily correctible" but were left unattended to by ignorant parents. Blease pointed to what he saw as the arrogance of the reformers, highlighting their tendency to treat mill men as less than men. "Do you not think," he asked lawmakers, "that every man in this State is able to care and has love enough for his children to care for and protect them?" "Have all the people and all classes of the people become imbeciles and children," he demanded, "that the Legislature at every turn must pass acts creating guardianships?" "Do you wish to . . . force every poor man," Blease continued, "to bow down to the whims of all the professions?"[62]

For Blease, sex—that is to say, deviant sexuality—linked the emerging middle class of the New South to the debauched and aging aristocracy. He asked what doctors would do with the information that they obtained during the medical inspections of mill children. Would they publicize their findings? If a mill girl suffered from an embarrassing ailment would they broadcast the news and turn the examination into yet another humiliating ritual for working people? "Do not say," Blease warned, "that every young girl in the State . . . without her consent, must be forced to be examined and her physical condition certified by her physician to some school teacher, to be heralded around as public property." The most dangerous aspect of the law, according to Blease, was that it would give morally lax elites the license to sexually abuse poor white women. Some "male physicians," a correspondent wrote to Blease in 1914, "boast openly that they can seduce their female patients." One even kept a diary, a supporter told the governor, of his sexual exploits with working-class girls. "If I had a daughter," Blease proclaimed, puffing out his chest, "I would kill any doctor in South Carolina whom I would be forced to let examine her against her will and mine." On the campaign trail, he promised South Carolina fathers that he would pardon any man convicted of murdering a doctor who "violat[ed] his daughter's modesty." In a final horrific charade of politically opportunistic logic, Blease wondered aloud about the role of doctor's assistants, "third parties," and "negro janitors." Would physicians, he asked, permit the "unmentionable crime"—the virtual rape of a white woman—by allowing voyeuristic black men to watch the medical inspections of mill girls?[63]

Once again, Blease turned the bourgeois conception of the world on its head. Reformers viewed medical examinations as a tool for creating a modern New South. In the minds of the middle classes, doctors were asexual individuals, pillars of the community, and architects of a more orderly universe. Blease laughed at these fawning characterizations. To him, doctors had the capacity for evil. Under the guise of morality, in fact, they and their reformer allies undermined morality and defiled innocent working-class women. Cole Blease would have none of this: he vigorously opposed the medical inspection bill and, in so doing, positioned himself as the millworkers' defender of decency, masculine honor, and white womanly virtue.

Blease tied together his assaults on elites and reformers and his appeals to white workers with the threads of race and gender. He accused the reformers of trying to place the "cotton mill men ... on the same basis as a free negro."[64] Laws that dictated who could vote and who could not and told mill parents when their children had to go to school and when they must stay at home violated the principles of independence, white equality, and patriarchal authority. Only blacks, minors, and women, not white men, Blease maintained, should have their behavior so rigidly regulated. To put white men in the same category as women, children, or African Americans was, according to Blease, to turn the natural order of the world upside down.

"I am no enemy of the negro but I believe in keeping him in his place at all times," Blease announced. That place, he told campaign crowds, expounding on his own crude version of the popular mythology of scientific racism, was established by the Almighty to be far below the position of any white man. According to Blease, morality—sexual morality to be precise—fixed the racial hierarchy. "The negro race has absolutely no standard of morality," he lectured in 1914. "They are, in that respect a class by themselves, as marital infidelity seems to be their more favorite pastime," he continued. Blease's world was immutable. He opposed spending white tax dollars on black schools. Educating a black person, he contended, would simply "ruin a good field hand, and make a bad convict."[65] He insisted that the immorality of blacks was ingrained and that black men in particular had to be watched at all times. "I tell you that it is not all quiet in South Carolina," Blease cautioned. In his imagination, "the black ape and baboon" lurked in the shadows waiting for the opportunity to rape a white woman. If this crime did take place, or even if there was a hint or a suggestion of an African American crossing the sexual color line, lynching was the only answer. Not to lynch, Blease contended, would only make other black men more brazen. To Cole Blease, then, those who joined the mobs were not disorderly or lawless, they were manly and moral. Those who questioned the principles of white equality and the need for the lynching were, like aristocrats and doctors, effete and dangerous. They had to be stopped.[66]

"Whenever the constitution of my state steps between me and the defense of the virtue of the white woman," Blease declared at the national governor's conference in 1912, "then I say to hell with the Constitution!" When it came to the defense of white women, there was a higher virtue than law and order. "The pure-blooded Caucasian will always defend the virtue of our women," Blease declared, "no matter what the cost." "If rape is committed," he continued, "death must follow!" Campaigning in 1910, he promised the crowds that he would never send out the militia to stop a lynching. "When mobs are no longer possible liberty will be dead," he averred on another occasion. Sometimes after a lynching, Blease celebrated the savage murder in public with a bizarre death dance. Through his grotesque gestures, he invited his audience to participate vicariously in the spectacle of vigilante justice.[67]

When white men joined lynch mobs and cheered Blease's ritual dances, they asserted not only their power over African Americans but also their control over their own homes and families. As Jacquelyn Dowd Hall and Gail Bederman have argued, "by constructing black men as 'natural' rapists and by resolutely and bravely avenging the (alleged) rape of pure white womanhood, Southern white men constructed themselves as ideal men: 'patriarchs, avengers, righteous protectors.' "[68] Blease spoke to the multiple meanings of lynching. In the summer of 1913 a supporter informed the governor of an alleged rape in Laurens. "The brute," he went on to explain, was captured and "tried before an honest jury." "It was not a mob," the supporter assured the state's chief executive, "but a crowd of determined men anxious to have justice meted out to one never more deserving of its fruits." "You did like men and defended your neighbors and put their black bodies under ground," Blease told the members of the Laurens County lynch mob, which according to reports included "many of the 'cotton mill boys' of Laurens Cotton Mill." He praised these criminals as well for "their defense of the white womanhood of our state—our mothers and our sisters."[69]

The Blacksburg lynching of Brinson and Whisonant described earlier took place fifteen months before the murders in Laurens. Both events demonstrated that sexual tensions, class issues, and vigilante justice were always tied together in the New South. Millworkers in each case took to the streets to defend their manhood and their whiteness. With regard to the Blacksburg lynching, some people believed that in Cherokee County blacks not only lay in wait to ravage white women but also assaulted white men like Joe Childers. These same men must have been worried about the fate of white womanhood, white manhood, and white supremacy if white men could not protect even themselves from black sexual predators. Male laborers in Blacksburg emphatically answered these doubts. They asserted their masculinity by murdering two black men for allegedly sexually humiliating a white millworker and thus all white millworkers. In the anxious world of the industrializing New South, interracial sexual contact of any kind—even if it was a homosexual act— that became public knowledge could easily threaten white independence and white manhood.[70] Though Blease did not dance for, or even condone, each and every lynching—and he did not comment on events in Blacksburg—he nonetheless understood why some poor white men executed black men, and these white men and thousands like them repaid him for his understanding with their votes.

But only some understood Blease this way. Clearly in the early part of the twentieth century, white South Carolinians were divided on questions of race, class, gender, and even lynching. These divisions eventually seeped into the political arena, fracturing the electorate into two rival camps: Bleasites and anti-Bleasites. Blease's message sounded different to each audience. Middle-class contemporaries detected nothing of substance in Blease's critique of society but the dissonant chords of demagoguery and disorder, lawlessness and anarchy. Male millworkers, on the other hand, interpreted Blease's rhetoric and actions to be a defense of their manhood against the forces of industrialization and the reform agenda of the Progressives. By voicing laborers' discontents and abusing those who demeaned them, Blease provided workers with a way to strike out at their perceived oppressors. Casting their ballots for Cole Blease, textile workers pressed their claims of patriarchal privilege and equality with all white men and asserted in the strongest language available to them that the economic and socially mighty did not control everything. "Even though Coley don't ever do a durn thing for us poor fellows," declared an Aiken laborer summing up the views of many of his millworker neighbors, "he does at least promise us somethin', and that's more than any of the others do."[71]

Blease rode to power on the backs of poor whites, especially mill hands like Joe Childers and the man quoted above. Once in office, he did almost nothing to enhance workers' material status, but his success at the polls, like the lynching in Blacksburg, exposes the discontents and aspirations of South Carolina's first generation of male textile laborers. These white men feared that their control over their families was dwindling and that their masculinity was under attack. Blease politicized them along class lines, but his mobilization produced a misogynist, racist, nonradical, and antireform version of class politics. He directed the ire of male workers against the middle classes, not against the mill bosses, and he aroused them to safeguard their manhood by blocking progressive changes, not by proposing reforms. Another politician might have urged workers to organize trade unions or called for child labor legislation linked to minimum wage statutes, but no one in South Carolina, at least not before the Great Depression, was heard articulating these positions. If there had been such a voice, Cole Blease's celebrations of white manhood and his harangues against African Americans, progressive reformers, and aristocrats drowned it out.

NOTES

1. *Gaffney (S.C.) Ledger*, March 29, 1912. The *Ledger* was Blacksburg's local paper.

2. This account of the Blacksburg lynching and reactions to it was reconstructed on the basis of N. W. Hardin to Governor Cole L. Blease, March 29, 1912, and W. W. Thomas to Blease, March 29, 1912 (telegram), both documents in folder—Cherokee County, 1911–1913, box 11, Cole L. Blease Papers (South Carolina Division of Archives and History, Columbia); *Gaffney Ledger*, March 29, April 2, 5, 9, 1912; and *Spartanburg Herald*, March 30, 1912. The above account relies on the Hardin letter and on newspapers; in other words, it relies on white sources. There are some minor disagreements and discrepancies in these accounts, but only minor ones. Of course, Whisonant and Brinson would probably have told a different story of the events that led up to their deaths, but they were never heard from.

3. Arthur Raper, *The Tragedy of Lynching* (Chapel Hill, 1939), 47.

4. *Gaffney Ledger*, April 4, 1912 (first two quoted sentences) and April 2, 1912 (last two quotations).

5. According to W. Fitzhugh Brundage's typology, the Blacksburg mob would probably be classified either as a "terrorist" mob—a group that lynched for economic or moral reasons—or as a "private mob." "Unlike terrorist mobs," Brundage writes, private mobs "organized to punish alleged criminal offenses, including crimes of a serious nature." See Brundage, *Lynching in the New South: Georgia and Virginia, 1880–1930* (Urbana, 1993), 17–48. In his detailed, quantitative study of lynching in South Carolina, Terence R. Finnegan fails to mention the Blacksburg lynching. According to Finnegan, lynchings with sexual-psychological overtones, like this one, were not the norm. Most lynching, he argues, took place for economic or political reasons—often because of a dispute between a white land-

owner and an African American tenant. See Finnegan, " 'At the Hands of Parties Unknown': Lynching in Mississippi and South Carolina, 1880–1940" (Ph.D. diss., University of Illinois, 1992). Some have attributed lynching to social and economic instability in the area in which the crime took place. Obviously, industrialization, the focus of this paper, was a forceful engine of change. Nonetheless, evidence from the U.S. census does not suggest other dramatic changes in Blacksburg and Cherokee County in the first decade or so of the twentieth century. For instance, population in the area climbed steadily, but not remarkably, in the years leading up to the murders. However, between 1900 and 1910 the population of the town of Blacksburg declined by almost 13 percent. In addition, there does not seem to have been a sudden shift in the overall structure of the rural economy of the county. In 1900, 61.1 percent of the county's residents, white and black, were tenants. The relative percent of white and African American tenants also remained about the same. By 1920 there was, it is worth noting, a slight increase in the number of African American landowners in Cherokee County. For information on population changes, see *Thirteenth Census of the United States*, vol. 3 *Population: Reports by States* (Washington, D.C., 1913), 643; and *Fourteenth Census of the United States*, vol. 1, *Population: Numbers and Distribution of Inhabitants* (Washington, D.C., 1921), 603. For information on the economic structure of the county, see *Twelfth Census of the United States*, vol. 5, *Agriculture*, part 1 (Washington, D.C., 1902), 118–19; *Thirteenth Census of the United States*, vol. 7, *Agriculture, 1909 and 1910. Reports by States, with Statistics for Counties* . . . (Washington, D.C. 1913), 508–15; and *Fourteenth Census of the United States*, vol. 6, part 2, *Agriculture: Report for States* (Washington, D.C., 1922), 276–77.

6. N. W. Hardin to Gov. Cole L. Blease, March 29, 1912; and *Gaffney Ledger*, April 2, 1912.

7. See, for example, Jacquelyn Dowd Hall, " 'The Mind That Burns in Each Body': Women, Rape, and Racial Violence," in Ann Snitow, Christine Stansell, and Sharon Thompson, eds., *Powers of Desire:The Politics of Sexuality* (New York, 1983), 328–49; idem, *Revolt against Chivalry: Jessie Daniel Ames and the Women's Campaign against Lynching* (New York, 1979); Gail Bederman, " 'Civilization,' the Decline of Middle-Class Manliness, and Ida B. Wells's Antilynching Campaign (1892–94)," *Radical History Review*, no. 52 (winter 1992): 5–30; Nancy MacLean, "The Leo Frank Case Reconsidered: Gender and Sexual Politics in the Making of Reactionary Populism," *Journal of American History* 78 (December 1991): 917–48; and Laura F. Edwards, "Sexual Violence, Gender, Reconstruction, and the Extension of Patriarchy in Granville County, North Carolina," *North Carolina Historical Review* 68 (July 1991): 237–60.

8. The growing divide between millworkers and the town classes has been explored by David L. Carlton, *Mill and Town in South Carolina, 1880–1920* (Baton Rouge, 1982). Many middle-class South Carolinians equated Bleasism with anarchy and lawlessness. See, for example, Joel F. Dowling to Blease, March 23, 1912, folder-Greenville County, 1911–1913, box 17; M. A. Moseley to Blease, March 15, 1912, folder-Spartanburg County, 1912–1913, box 34; and W. P. Caskey to Blease, March 23, 1912, folder-Lancaster County, 1912, box 21, all in Blease Papers.

9. For an excellent survey of the literature on postbellum southern politics and its emphasis on race, see Numan V. Bartley, "In Search of the New South: Southern Politics after Reconstruction," *Reviews in American History* 10 (December 1982):151–63.

10. For work on the crisis of masculinity in the South, see Joel Williamson, *The Crucible of Race: Black-White Relations in the American South since Emancipation* (New York, 1984); and Ted Ownby, *Subduing Satan: Religion, Recreation, and Manhood in the Rural South, 1865–1920* (Chapel Hill, 1990). See also Michael S. Kimmel, "The Contemporary

'Crisis' of Masculinity in Historical Perspective," in Harry Brod, ed., *The Making of Masculinities: The New Men's Studies* (Boston, 1987), 121–33; Peter N. Stearns, *Be a Man! Males in Modern Society* (New York, 1979); and Louise A. Tilly, "Connections," *American Historical Review* 99 (February 1994): 1–20.

11. For figures on mill building, see Ernest McPherson Lander, Jr., *A History of South Carolina, 1865–1960* (Chapel Hill, 1960), 83. See also Steve Shapiro, "The Growth of the Textile Industry in South Carolina, 1919–1930" (Ph.D. diss., University of South Carolina, 1972), 13–28. For figures on the number of male workers in the factories for the years 1850 to 1890, see *Report on Manufacturing Industries in the United States at the Eleventh Census: 1890*, part 3, *Selected Industries* (Washington, D.C., 1895), 188–89; for figures on male workers in 1900, see *Occupations at the Twelfth Census, Special Reports* (Washington, D.C., 1904), 385; and for the percentage of men in the textile mill workforce in 1910, see *Thirteenth Census of the United States, Taken in the Year 1910*, vol 4, *Population, 1910: Occupational Statistics* (Washington, D.C., 1914), 516–17.

12. For discussions of the white supremacy campaign in South Carolina, see George Brown Tindall, "The Campaign for the Disfranchisement of Negroes in South Carolina," *Journal of Southern History* 55 (May 1949): 212–34; V. O. Key, Jr., *Southern Politics in State and Nation* (New York, 1949), 548; J. Morgan Kousser, *The Shaping of Southern Politics: Suffrage Restriction and the Establishment of the One-Party South, 1880–1910* (New Haven, 1974), 50, 84–91; and Edward L. Ayers, *The Promise of the New South: Life after Reconstruction* (New York, 1992), 285–87. For debates about disfranchisement in the South as a whole, see C. Vann Woodward, *The Strange Career of Jim Crow*, 3d rev. ed. (New York, 1974); as well as Ayers, *Promise of the New South*; and Kousser, *Shaping of Southern Politics*. See also Howard N. Rabinowitz, "More Than the Woodward Thesis: Assessing *The Strange Career of Jim Crow*," and C. Vann Woodward, "*Strange Career* Critics: Long May They Persevere," *Journal of American History* 75 (December 1988): 842–68.

13. This figure for the number of mill hands who were eligible to vote was calculated by dividing the number of adult male workers in 1914 by the approximate number of white men over the age of twenty-one—in other words, the only eligible voters—in the state in 1914. This latter figure is an extrapolation. In order to derive this number, I calculated the difference between the number of men over twenty-one in 1910 and in 1920; then I divided this figure by ten and multiplied it by four. Finally, I added this number to the census figures from 1910 and arrived at an approximation of the number of white men over twenty-one in the state in 1914. For information on the number of textile workers, see *1914 Census of Manufactures*, vol. 1, *Reports by States* (Washington, D.C., 1914), 1414. For figures on voting-age males, see *Thirteenth Census of the United States* vol. 3, *Population: Reports by States* (Washington, D.C., 1913), 635–58; and the *Fourteenth Census of the United States*, vol. 3, *Population: Composition and Characteristics of the Population* (Washington, D.C., 1922), 923–27. On the numbers of voters in the mill villages of South Carolina in 1929, see also David L. Carlton, "The State and the Worker in the South: A Lesson from South Carolina," in David R. Chesnutt and Clyde N. Wilson, eds., *The Meaning of South Carolina History: Essays in Honor of George C. Rogers, Jr.* (Columbia, 1991), 188, 198 n. 8.

14. For the Tillman quotation, see Francis Butler Simkins, *Pitchfork Ben Tillman: South Carolinian* (Baton Rouge, 1944), 485.

15. A careful study of Blease's correspondence suggests that he belonged to or had close ties to the following organizations:the Independent Order of Odd Fellows, the Improved Order of Red Men, Loyal Order of Moose, Knights of Pythias, Protective Order of Elks, Woodmen of the World, and possibly even the Ku Klux Klan. On Blease and his extensive

contacts, consult Marjorie A. Potwin, *Cotton Mill People of the Piedmont: A Study in Social Change* (1928; reprint, New York, 1968), 32, 45, 98.

16. For election returns, see Frank E. Jordan, Jr., *The Primary State: A History of the Democratic Party in South Carolina, 1876–1962* (Columbia, n.d.), 25–30. See also *Columbia State*, Aug. 30, 1906, Aug. 29, 1908, Aug. 31, 1912, Aug. 27, 1914, and Sept. 13, 1916. David Carlton's sophisticated quantitative research suggests a strong correlation between the number of millworkers in a district and the vote in favor of Blease. Carlton, *Mill and Town*, 215–20, 273–75. Qualitative evidence also suggests a similar relationship. Blease supporters regularly reported that Blease was running well in the mill villages. S. M. Smith to Blease, n.d., folder—Edgefield County, 1911–1913, box 14; J. L. Harris to Blease, May 14, 1912, folder—Union County, 1911–1913, box 36; and Joshua W. Ansley, Feb. 28, 1911, folder—Anderson County, 1911–1913, box 4, Blease Papers.

17. I. A. Newby, *Plain Folk in the New South: Social Change and Cultural Persistence, 1880–1914* (Baton Rouge, 1989), 269; Carlton, *Mill and Town*, 2 (first quotation); story related to me by longtime South Carolina resident and noted genealogist Brent H. Holcomb (doggerel); David Duncan Wallace, *South Carolina: A Short History, 1520–1948* (Chapel Hill, 1951), 656 (quotation from textile worker); Osta L. Warr, "Mr. Blease of South Carolina," *American Mercury* 16 (January 1929): 29 (last quotation). For additional verses, see J. A. Wilson to Blease, March 3, 1911, folder—Greenwood County, 1911–1913, box 19; and Hilrey Sanford to Blease, n.d., folder—Anderson County, 1912, box 3, Blease Papers.

18. W. J. Cash, *The Mind of the South* (New York, 1941), 250 (first quotation); Warr, "Mr. Blease of South Carolina," 29 (second quotation); Key, *Southern Politics*, 130, 143–45; and Kousser, *Shaping of Southern Politics*, 236. For other views on Blease, see Cash, *Mind of the South*, 250–59; Simkins, *Pitchfork Ben Tillman*, 486–504, 536–49; Clarence N. Stone, "Bleaseism and the 1912 Election in South Carolina," *North Carolina Historical Review* 40 (winter 1963): 54–74; and Daniel W. Hollis, "Cole L. Blease and the Senatorial Campaign of 1924," *Proceedings of the South Carolina Historical Association* (1978): 53–68. To date, there is not a full-length biography of Blease. Perhaps this is because Blease's personal papers have not been found. There are nonetheless two unpublished accounts of different aspects of Blease's political career. Consult Ronald Burnside, "The Governorship of Coleman Livingston Blease of South Carolina, 1911–1915" (Ph.D. diss., Indiana University, 1963); and Anthony Barry Miller, "Coleman Livingston Blease" (M.A. thesis, University of North Carolina, Greensboro, 1971). The Blease historiography is summarized in Carlton, *Mill and Town*, 221–23.

19. Carlton, *Mill and Town*.

20. Ibid., 83–84. See also idem, " 'Builders of a New State': The Town Classes and Early Industrialization of South Carolina, 1880–1907," in Walter J. Fraser, Jr., and Winfred B. Moore, Jr., eds., *From the Old South to the New: Essays on the Transitional South* (Westport, Conn., 1981), 43–62. For the classic view of mill men as regional saviors, refer to Broadus Mitchell, *The Rise of Cotton Mills in the South* (Baltimore, 1921).

21. Carlton, *Mill and Town*, 132 (quoted phrase). For additional information and interpretations of Progressivism in South Carolina, see Mary Katherine Davis Cann, "The Morning After: South Carolina in the Jazz Age" (Ph.D. diss., University of South Carolina, 1984); Sandra Corley Mitchell, "Conservative Reform: South Carolina's Progressive Movement, 1915–1929" (M.A. thesis, University of South Carolina, 1979); Doyle W. Boggs, "John Patrick Grace and the Politics of Reform in South Carolina, 1900–1931" (Ph.D. diss., University of South Carolina, 1977); John Samuel Lupold, "The Nature of South Carolina Progressives, 1914–1916" (M.A. thesis, University of South Carolina, 1968); and Robert Milton Burts, *Richard Irvine Manning and the Progressive Movement in South Carolina*

(Columbia, 1974). For a review of southern Progressivism, refer to George Brown Tindall, *The Emergence of the New South, 1913–1945* (Baton Rouge, 1967), 219–84; Dewey W. Grantham, "The Contours of Southern Progressivism," *American Historical Review* 86 (December 1981): 1035–59; and William A. Link, *The Paradox of Southern Progressivism, 1880–1930* (Chapel Hill, 1992).

22. Carlton, *Mill and Town*, 224, 225.

23. Stephanie McCurry has looked at the intersection between the public and the private in antebellum South Carolina. See McCurry, "The Two Faces of Republicanism: Gender and Proslavery Politics in Antebellum South Carolina," *Journal of American History* 78 (March 1992): 1245–64. For other examples of mixing the public and private in the analysis of the South, see Martha Hodes, "The Sexualization of Reconstruction Politics: White Women and Black Men in the South after the Civil War," *Journal of the History of Sexuality* (1993): 402–17; and Nancy MacLean, *Behind the Mask of Chivalry: The Making of the Second Ku Klux Klan* (New York, 1994). Joan Scott has framed this whole question about links between the public and private quite broadly. See Scott, "On Language, Gender, and Working-Class History," *International Labor and Working Class History* 31 (spring 1987): 1–13.

24. For a discussion of the naturalization of difference, see Bederman, " 'Civilization,' the Decline of Middle-Class Manliness," 4–30. For observations on the links between household power and public authority, see Elizabeth Fox-Genovese, *Within the Plantation Household: Black and White Women of the Old South* (Chapel Hill, 1988).

25. For a discussion of the larger meaning of suffrage, see Eric Foner, "The Meaning of Freedom in the Age of Emancipation," *Journal of American History* 81 (September 1994): 442–43 (last quoted phrase on 443). On the ideology of race, see Barbara J. Fields, "Ideology and Race in American History," in J. Morgan Kousser and James M. McPherson, eds., *Region, Race, and Reconstruction: Essays in Honor of C. Vann Woodward* (New York, 1982), 143–77. See also recent literature on the construction of "whiteness." David R. Roediger, *The Wages of Whiteness: Race and the Making of the American Working Class* (London, 1991); Theodore W. Allen, *The Invention of the White Race*, vol. 1, *Racial Oppression and Social Control* (London, 1994); and Andrew Neather, " 'Whiteness' and the Politics of Working-Class History," *Radical History Review* 61 (winter 1995): 190–96. On the fears of white yeomen in South Carolina, see Lacy K. Ford, Jr., *Origins of Southern Radicalism: The South Carolina Upcountry, 1800–1860* (New York, 1988), 138–41 (quoted phrase on 138). For more on the yeomanry, see also Eugene D. Genovese, "Yeomen Farmers in a Slaveholders' Democracy," *Agricultural History* 49 (April 1975): 331–42; J. Mills Thornton III, *Politics and Power in a Slave Society: Alabama, 1800–1860* (Baton Rouge, 1978); and J. William Harris, *Plain Folk and Gentry in a Slave Society: White Liberty and Black Slavery in Augusta's Hinterlands* (Middletown, Conn., 1985).

26. Ford, *Origins of Southern Radicalism*, 49–51 (both quoted phrases on 50), 99–144. Nancy MacLean makes a similar argument about how the petite bourgeoisie of the South felt about the increased concentration of capital after World War I. See MacLean, *Behind the Mask*, 23–26.

27. See Ben Tillman's attacks on the aristocracy in Simkins, *Pitchfork Ben Tillman*, 70–71.

28. For more on sexual tensions and Reconstruction, see Hodes, "Sexualization of Reconstruction Politics," 402–17; and Edwards, "Sexual Violence," 237–60.

29. On the South Carolina constitution of 1895, see Kousser, *Shaping of Southern Politics*, 50, 84–91; Lander, *History of South Carolina*, 40–41; Tindall, "Campaign for the Disfranchisement," 228–29; and Simkins, *Pitchfork Ben Tillman*, chap. 20.

30. Lacy K. Ford, "Rednecks and Merchants: Economic Development and Social Ten-

sions in the South Carolina Upcountry, 1865–1900," *Journal of American History* 71 (September 1984): 294–318; and idem, "Yeoman Farmers in the South Carolina Upcountry: Changing Production Patterns in the Late Antebellum Era," *Agricultural History* 60 (fall 1986): 17–37. See also Steven Hahn, *The Roots of Southern Populism: Yeoman Farmers and the Transformation of the Georgia Upcountry, 1850–1890* (New York, 1983).

31. See Ayers, *Promise of the New South*, 202–07. Nancy MacLean also discusses control over the household and cash tenants. See *Behind the Mask*, 36. So too does Douglas Flamming in *Creating the Modern South: Millhands and Managers in Dalton, Georgia, 1884–1984* (Chapel Hill, 1992), 14–15.

32. T. V. Blair to Cole Blease, Nov. 30, 1914, folder—Anderson County, 1914, box 5; and S. E. Arthur to Blease, Jan. 19, 1914, folder—Aiken County, 1914, box 3, both in Blease Papers. See also Eric Foner's discussion of wage slavery in *Politics and Ideology in the Age of the Civil War* (New York, 1980), 59–63; and Roediger, *Wages of Whiteness*. Nancy MacLean makes a similar point about declining authority in *Behind the Mask*, 24.

33. On wage scales, see Gavin Wright, "Cheap Labor and Southern Textiles before 1880," *Journal of Economic History* 39 (September 1979): 655–80; and Kathy L. McHugh, *Mill Family: The Labor System in the Southern Cotton Textile Industry, 1880–1915* (New York, 1988). On southern mill men and their fears of declining patriarchy, see Jacquelyn Dowd Hall et al., *Like a Family: The Making of a Southern Cotton Mill World* (Chapel Hill, 1987), 152–53. See also a discussion of wages and masculinity in other settings and contexts in Margaret Hobbs, "Rethinking Antifeminism in the 1930s: Gender Crisis or Workplace Justice? A Response to Alice Kessler-Harris," *Gender and History*, (spring 1993): 4–15.

34. For discussion of masculinity and the workplace, see MacLean, "Leo Frank Case," 917–48; and Jacquelyn Dowd Hall, "Private Eyes, Public Women: Images of Class and Sex in the Urban South, Atlanta, Georgia, 1913–1915," in Ava Baron, ed., *Work Engendered: Toward a New History of American Labor* (Ithaca, 1991), 243–72.

35. On sexual harassment on the shop floor in the textile mills, see Newby, *Plain Folk in the New South*, 329–30; and Gary M. Fink, "Efficiency and Control: Labor Espionage in Southern Texiles," in Robert H. Zieger, ed., *Organized Labor in the Twentieth-Century South* (Knoxville, 1991), 25. For examples from a later period about a longtime supervisor who was well known for harassing young female employees, see J. H. Palmer to Kamanow, Sept. 11, 1935; J. L. Harding, "Preliminary Report of the Limestone Mill," June 20, 1935; and Roland Hill et al., to W. C. Hamrick, n.d., all three documents in file—Limestone Mill, box 75, series 402, Records of the National Recovery Administration (NRA), Record Group 9, National Archives, Washington, D.C.

36. On the disposition of wages and family tensions, see Hall et al., *Like a Family*, 62–63. Douglas Flamming has argued that southern women millworkers kept more of their wages than northern women millworkers. See Flamming, "Daughters, Dollars, and Domesticity: Family Wages and Female Autonomy in American Textiles, Evidence from the Federal Survey of 1908," Humanities Working Paper no. 153, California Institute of Technology (spring 1992).

37. MacLean, *Behind the Mask*, 31–33; Hall et al., *Like a Family*, 257; Jacquelyn Dowd Hall, "Disorderly Women: Gender and Labor Militancy in the Appalachian South," *Journal of American History* 73 (September 1986): 354–82; and idem, "O. Delight Smith's Progressive Era: Labor, Feminism, and Reform in the Urban South," in Nancy A. Hewitt and Suzanne Lebsock, eds., *Visible Women: New Essays on American Activism* (Urbana, 1993), 166–98. For northern examples, see Joanne J. Meyerowitz, *Women Adrift: Independent Wage Earners in Chicago, 1880–1930* (Chicago, 1988); and Kathy Peiss, *Cheap Amusements: Working Women and Leisure in Turn-of-the-Century New York* (Philadelphia, 1986).

38. In 1890 African Americans owned only 11.2 percent of the farms in South Carolina; twenty years later, the proportion reached 31.7 percent. See Ayers, *Promise of the New South*, 514. In his 1913 annual address to the legislature, Blease noted with alarm the growing number of African American landowners in the state. Burnside, "Governorship of Coleman Livingston Blease," 236–37.

39. For the story of Archie Green, see Finnegan, " 'At the Hands of Parties Unknown,' " 301–05.

40. Quotation from William Beard, the Bleasite editor of the *Abbeville Scimitar*, in Finnegan, " 'At the Hands of Parties Unknown,' " 173.

41. Characterizations of mill hands can be found in Newby, *Plain Folk in the New South*, 130–32 (first quoted phrase occurs on all three pages); and Carlton, *Mill and Town*, 208 (second quotation), 195 (quotations from Spartanburg journalist and all remaining quotations), and 205. Alabama town folks looked at industrial laborers through very similar lenses. See Wayne Flynt, *Poor but Proud: Alabama's Poor Whites* (Tuscaloosa, Ala., 1989), 107–09, 233. The same could be said of North Carolina elites. See Holland Thompson, *From the Cotton Field to the Cotton Mill: A Study of the Industrial Transition in North Carolina* (New York, 1906), 116; Jennings J. Rhyne, *Some Southern Cotton Mill Workers and Their Villages* (Chapel Hill, 1930), 85; and Douglas P. De Natale, "Bynum: The Coming of Mill Village Life to a North Carolina County" (Ph.D. diss., University of Pennsylvania, 1985), 325–27. For Georgia, see LeeAnn Whites, "The De Graffenried Controversy: Class, Race, and Gender in the New South,"*Journal of Southern History* 54 (August 1988): 449–78.

42. On suffrage restriction, see Carlton, *Mill and Town*, 225–27 (quotation on 226) and 229–31; and Miller, "Coleman Livingston Blease," 99–100.

43. Reverend John White from the *Golden Age*, Jan. 2, 1913, folder—Anderson County, 1913, box 3, Blease Papers. Blease supporters dutifully reported to the governor what they said about him: W. P. Caskey to Blease, March 23, 1912, folder—Lancaster County, 1912, box 21; and Joel F. Dowling to Blease, March 23, 1912, folder—Greenville, 1911–1913, box 17, both in Blease Papers.

44. For the two short quotations, see Link, *Paradox of Southern Progressivism*, 183; and Carlton, *Mill and Town*, 226, also 3–4, 226–27.

45. For information on reform and suffrage in South Carolina, see Antoinette Elizabeth Taylor, "South Carolina and the Enfranchisement of Women: The Early Years," *South Carolina Historical Magazine* 77 (April 1976): 115–26; idem, "South Carolina and the Enfranchisement of Women: The Later Years," *South Carolina Historical Magazine* 80 (October 1979): 298–310; Marjorie Spruill Wheeler, *New Women of the New South: The Leaders of the Woman Suffrage Movement in the Southern States* (New York, 1993), 110; and Link, *Paradox of Southern Progressivism*, 183–98. See also Joe L. Dubbert, "Progressivism and the Masculinity Crisis," in Elizabeth H. Pleck and Joseph H. Pleck, eds., *The American Man* (Englewood Cliffs, N.J., 1980), 303–20.

46. For examples of men who wanted to leave the mill villages because they worried about their dwindling control over their families, see Hall et al., *Like a Family*, 152.

47. On drinking in the mill village, see, for instance, B. E. Wilkins to Blease, July 11, 1911, folder—Spartanburg County, 1911, box 32; and J. R. Dean to Blease, Nov. 11, 1911, folder—Spartanburg County, 1911, box 33, both in Blease Papers. On desertion as well as drinking, see Hall et al., *Like a Family*, 165–68.

48. Stories of violence can be found in James Taylor Brice, "The Use of Executive Clemency under Coleman Livingston Blease, Governor of South Carolina, 1911–1915" (M.A. thesis, University of South Carolina, 1965), 12; Hall et al., *Like a Family*, 162, 166–67; and

Christine Stansell, *City of Women: Sex and Class in New York, 1789–1860* (New York, 1986), 76–83 (quotation on 78).

49. For accounts of lynching in South Carolina during these years, see Jack Simpson Mullins, "Lynching in South Carolina, 1900–1914" (M.A. thesis, University of South Carolina, 1961); Susan Page Garris, "The Decline of Lynching in South Carolina, 1915–1947" (M.A. thesis, University of South Carolina, 1973); and Finnegan, " 'At the Hands of Parties Unknown.' "

50. For workers' views on wages, hours, and unions, see J. T. Blassingame to Blease, June 19, 1914, folder—Greenville County, 1914, box 19; and C. P. Lackey to Blease, Dec. 29, 1913, folder—Spartanburg County, 1913, box 34, both in Blease Papers. See also Newby, *Plain Folk in the New South*, 542–46; and Melton A. McLaurin, "Early Labor Union Organizational Efforts in South Carolina Cotton Mills, 1880–1905," *South Carolina Historical Magazine* 72 (January 1971): 44–59.

51. For a brief overview of these primaries, consult Jordan, *Primary State*, 25–26. See also *Columbia State*, Aug. 30, 1906, and Aug. 29, 1908. For quantitative analysis of Blease's support on the mill hills, see Carlton, *Mill and Town*, 215–21, 273–75.

52. James C. Derieux, "Crawling toward the Promised Land," *Survey* 48 (April 29, 1922): 178.

53. Miller, "Coleman Livingston Blease," 136 (first quotation) and 65 (third quotation); W. H. Newbold to Blease, June 6, 1912, folder—Chester County, 1911–1912, box 11, Blease Papers (second quotation); Blease to William Woodward Dixon, May 24, 1912, folder—Fairfield County, 1911–1912, box 15, Blease Papers (fourth quotation); and South Carolina General Assembly, *House Journal*, 1913, p. 158 (quotations from the inaugural address). On Blease's drinking, see Blease to J. W. Ashely, April 21, 1913, folder—Anderson County, 1913, box 4, Blease Papers. For his response to law-and-order advocates, see Carlton, *Mill and Town*, 248–49.

54. For the phrases that Blease used to characterize his opponents, see Burnside, "Governorship of Coleman Livingston Blease," 294, 274; Miller, "Coleman Livingston Blease," 136, 65; and A. H. Walker to Blease, Feb. 10, 1912, folder—Anderson County, 1912, box 2, Blease Papers. For examples of Blease labeling his opponents, see Blease to J. C. Wilborn, June 6, 1912, folder—Chester County, 1911–1912, box 11; Blease to Charles H. Henry, Nov. 10, 1911, folder—Spartanburg County, 1911, box 33; and Blease to W. P. Beard, June 1; 1914, folder—Abbeville County, 1914, box 1, all three in Blease Papers; Wallace, *South Carolina*, 656; and Carlton, *Mill and Town*, 1–4.

55. Blease quoted in Carlton, *Mill and Town*, 239, 238; and his supporter quoted in Link, *Paradox of Southern Progressivism*, 189; see also Burnside, "Governorship of Coleman Livingston Blease," 99–100; Miller, "Coleman Livingston Blease," 136; Wheeler, *New Women of the New South*, 25–37; MacLean, *Behind the Mask*, 30–31; and Dubbert, "Progressivism and the Masculinity Crisis."

56. Miller, "Coleman Livingston Blease," 61, 113, 135–36; and clipping from the *Seneca Tri-County Harpoon*, circa 1913, folder—Anderson County, 1913, box 4, Blease Papers.

57. Blease to W. P. Beard, June 1, 1914, folder—Abbeville County, 1914, box 1, Blease Papers. For other examples of the language of aristocracy and the vocabulary of South Carolina politics, see Ford, *Origins of Southern Radicalism*, 109; and clipping from the *Seneca Tri-County Harpoon*, circa 1913, folder—Anderson County, 1913, box 4, Blease Papers. Anti-aristocratic attacks were part and parcel of Tillmanism. See Simkins, *Pitchfork Ben Tillman*, 70–71. For more on the laborite perception of aristocrats and their sexuality, see T. Fulton Gantt, *Breaking the Chains: A Story of the Present Industrial Struggle*, in Mary

C. Grimes, ed., *The Knights in Fiction: Two Labor Novels of the 1880s* (Urbana, 1986), 27–133.

58. Blease's gubernatorial inaugural address, Jan. 22, 1913, in *House Journal*, 158 (first quotation); and Miller, "Coleman Livingston Blease," 113, 43 (second quotation). For more on the mythology of Reconstruction in the twentieth-century South, see James Goodman, *Stories of Scottsboro* (New York, 1994), 52, 114.

59. For some of the measures supporting white supremacy that Blease endorsed, see Carlton, *Mill and Town*, 243–44; Blease to J. W. D. Bolin, May 9, 1912, folder—Cherokee County, 1911–13, box 11; J. A. McGill to Blease, Feb. 25, 1911, folder—Greenville County, 1911, box 17; J. L. Woodward to Blease, Feb. 11, 1914, and Blease to All County Board of Registers, attached to a letter to W. D. Grist, July 7, 1913, both in folder—Spartanburg County, 1913–14, box 39, all in Blease Papers. On the firing of all African American notary publics, see Milton B. McCuen to Blease, Jan. 20, 1912, folder—Laurens County, 1911–1913, box 22, Blease Papers.

60. On the surface and because of its seeming antistatism, Bleasism shared some common ground with the laborite ideology of voluntarism. While both perspectives rejected intrusive state action, voluntarism embraced trade unionism, and Bleasism eschewed it. "In its original conception," writes Michael Rogin, "the unifying theme of voluntarism was that workers could best achieve their goals by relying on their own voluntary associations. Voluntarism defended the autonomy of the international craft union against the coercive interference of the state. . . . it meant opposition to alliance with any political party as well as to positive state action." Rogin, "Voluntarism: The Political Functions of an Antipolitical Doctrine," *Industrial and Labor Relations Review* 15 (July 1962): 521–22. See also Gary M. Fink, "The Rejection of Voluntarism," *Industrial and Labor Relations Review* 26 (January 1973): 805–19; and Michael Kazin, *Barons of Labor: The San Francisco Building Trades and Union Power in the Progressive Era* (Urbana, 1989), 145–47.

61. Burnside, "Governorship of Coleman Livingston Blease," 255 (first quotation), 17–19 (fourth quotation on 18), 38 (fifth quotation), 216–17; Mitchell, "Conservative Reform," 213 (second quotation); Warr, "Mr. Blease of South Carolina," 31 (third quotation); and Miller, "Coleman Livingston Blease," 37, 88–89. See also Blease's gubernatorial inaugural address, Jan. 22, 1913, *House Journal*, 1913, p. 158.

62. Carlton, *Mill and Town*, 236 (first two quotations); and Newby, *Plain Folk in the New South*, 383 (all other quotations).

63. On the medical inspection bill, see Newby, *Plain Folk in the New South*, 381–84 (first quotation on 383); Miller, "Coleman Livingston Blease," 37, 88–89; Carlton, *Mill and Town* 236–39 (third quotation, "third parties," and last quotation all on 237); J. J. Contey to Blease, March 5, 1914, folder—Clarendon County, 1914, box 12, Blease Papers (second quotation); Wallace, *South Carolina*, 660 (quotation from Blease on the campaign trail); Burnside, "Governorship of Coleman Livingston Blease," 216–17 ("negro janitors"); and South Carolina General Assembly, *House Journal*, 1912, pp. 1089–92. See also J. L. Darlington to Blease, n.d., folder—Greenville County, 1911–1913, box 18, Blease Papers. For a regional perspective on working-class resistance to medical inspections, see Link, *Paradox of Southern Progressivism*, 208–11.

64. Carlton, *Mill and Town*, 245. See also Blease to C. W. Templeton, Jan. 12, 1914, folder—Greenville County, 1914, box 19, Blease Papers.

65. Brice, "Use of Executive Clemency," 37 (first quotation); Burnside, "Governorship of Coleman Livingston Blease," 39, 74–91 (second quotation on 75); *Charleston News and Courier*, Aug. 16, 1910 (third quotation); Blease to J. W. D. Bolin, May 9, 1912, folder—

Cherokee County; 1911–1913, box 11; and W. L. Abernathy to Blease, Feb. 12, 1914, folder—Chester County, 1914, box 12, both in Blease Papers. For more on Blease's racial ideology from a later period, refer to *Anderson (S. C.) Blease's Weekly*, May 27, 1926. For a wider context, see I. A. Newby, *Jim Crow's Defense: Anti-Negro Thought in America, 1900–1930* (Baton Rouge, 1965).

66. Warr, "Mr. Blease of South Carolina," 25–26; Burnside, "Governorship of Coleman Livingston Blease," 39, 74–91 (first quotation on 76); and Carlton, *Mill and Town*, 246–49 (second quotation on 246). Blease further elaborated on his view of lynching in *Los Angeles Sunday Times*, a clipping of which is attached to a letter from W. O. Grist to Blease, Jan. 1, 1913, folder—York County, 1913–1914, box 38, Blease Papers. Blease was not alone in his view of lynching. See Fitz McMaster, a newspaperman, to H. Brown of New York, June 18, 1930, Fitz Hugh McMaster Papers, South Caroliniana Library, University of South Carolina, Columbia.

67. After Blease made this statement at the governors' conference, the national press picked up the story and editorial pages buzzed with Blease's words. Miller, "Coleman Livingston Blease," 38, 43 (second quotation), 57, 59–60 (first quotation); and *New York Times*, Aug. 27, 1915 (third quotation).

68. Bederman " 'Civilization,' the Decline of Middle-Class Manliness," 13 (Bederman's paraphrase of Hall). On the broader meaning of lynching in the twentieth-century South, see Williamson, *Crucible of Race*, 183–89; Hall, " 'The Mind That Burns in Each Body,' " 328–49; idem, *Revolt against Chivalry*; MacLean, "Leo Frank Case," 917–48; and Edwards, "Sexual Violence," 237–60.

69. John M. Cannon to Blease, Aug. 12, 1913, Blease to John M. Cannon, Aug. 13, 1913, and Blease to W. T. Crews, Aug. 18, 1913, all three in folder—Laurens County, 1913, box 22, Blease Papers; and Carlton, *Mill and Town*, 247–48 (last quotation on 247). In an interesting side note, it appears that several of the workers who participated in the murder were fired, and they protested to Blease. See Albert E. Sloan et al. to Blease, Aug. 21, 1913, folder—Laurens County, 1913, box 22, Blease Papers.

70. On the idea that in the New South lynching must follow all sexual contacts between whites and blacks, see the arguments in the Scottsboro case presented in Dan T. Carter, *Scottsboro: A Tragedy of the American South* (Baton Rouge, 1969); Hodes, "Sexualization of Reconstruction Politics," 416–17; and Harper Lee, *To Kill a Mockingbird* (Philadelphia, 1960).

71. Derieux, "Crawling toward the Promised Land," 178; and Warr, "Mr. Blease of South Carolina," 25–32 (quotation on 29).

Chapter Nineteen

Remapping the Black/White Body
Sexuality, Nationalism, and Biracial Antimiscegenation Activism in 1920s Virginia

Barbara Bair

In 1924 a white Richmond activist named Louise Burleigh sat down to write a detailed letter to her fiancé, John Powell, about her lobbying efforts on behalf of the Racial Integrity Act, which was debated and passed by the Virginia General Assembly in that year. Powell was among those who had most ardently addressed the assembly in favor of the legislation, and Burleigh had worked extensively with politicians and grassroots white supremacist activists behind the scenes in order to secure its passage.

Virginia's antimiscegenation legislation found its place in American law among similar state legislative acts across the country. In effect, it codified white supremacists' definition of whiteness. Louise Burleigh's close colleague, Earnest Sevier Cox, called it the "most perfected legal expression of the white ideal," and a response to the "need for a re-defining of 'white person.' "[1] Interracial marriage was already criminalized and punishable by imprisonment under Virginia laws of the 1870s. The 1924 act went further, building on 1910 legislation stipulating who was "white" and who was "black." The 1924 act stated that the "term 'white person' shall apply only to the person who has no trace whatsoever of any blood other than Caucasian, but persons who have one-sixteenth or less of the blood of the American Indian, and no other non-Caucasic blood shall be deemed white persons."[2] Virginians born after 1912 were required to file certificates testifying to their racial heritage, and no individuals of differing certification were to be allowed licenses to marry. The successful passage of the act made white supremacists' beliefs in racial difference a formal political construct, sanctioned by law and subject to enforcement through police authority. In enacting this definition of whiteness, white supremacists sought to prevent not only consensual interracial unions and sexual liaisons but the continued passing of people of mixed African American, Native American, and white heritage into educational institutions and neighborhoods, employment, professional opportunities, and civic positions. The act was about sex and mating. It was also about the composition of color and power within the body politic.

The Racial Integrity Act and related legislation were introduced with crucial grassroots lobbying from the all-white members of the Anglo-Saxon Clubs of America (ASCOA), an offshoot of the Ku Klux Klan headquartered in Richmond, Virginia. The ASCOA had circulated grassroots petitions in favor of the 1924 act and had been instrumental in its introduction in the legislature. John Powell was a founder of the organization and leader of the main Richmond branch. Louise Burleigh, a playwright and theater director, was his unofficial lieutenant. But Burleigh, Powell, and their cohorts in the ASCOA were not alone. They worked in the mid-1920s with coalition support from local and national representatives of the Universal Negro Improvement Association (UNIA), the Harlem-based black nationalist and Pan-Africanist organization originally founded by Marcus Garvey and Amy Ashwood in Jamaica. In the 1920s the UNIA had dozens of local chapters in the cities and small towns of Virginia.

The events and issues surrounding this conjoining of strange political bedfellows in support of the legislation of whiteness offer a historical context in which to examine the specificity of 1920s ideas about race and the body. It is a particularly useful context in which to deconstruct the ways in which sexuality was used both as a locus for social control and as a symbolic image for white and black nationalist desires. At issue in the propaganda surrounding the legislation and the activism that supported it—for both the black and the white parties involved—was a racialized female body and its larger meaning within the body politic.

Louise Burleigh and the ASCOA

The ASCOA was founded in September 1922 after factionalization and corruption in the national administration of the Ku Klux Klan made the Richmond elites who were Klan activists wish for an independent organization. The group had organized twenty-five chapters or local posts by the time of its first state convention in 1923, including groups at the University of Virginia and Virginia's other major colleges. Two years later, in 1925, there were thirty-six active posts. The Anglo-Saxon Clubs were self-styled (like the second, revitalized Klan) as patriotic associations. Like its parent organization, the ASCOA was officially an all-male movement.[3] The members eschewed heavy-handed or ungentlemanly tactics of overt racial political oppression (such as the violent intimidation of African Americans who might attempt to vote) or the secretive racial terrorism and lynchings associated with the old Klan. They did so while favoring the official institutionalization of strict notions of racial difference, all in the name of improved civilization. They worked at maintaining or introducing Jim Crow segregation of people of differing races in public places, immigration restriction, English-only laws, and antimiscegenation laws. They were concerned about black competition with, or undercutting of, poor white labor and thus favored the repatriation of African Americans to Africa.

In a stated departure from old Klan politics, the ASCOA operated under a cloak of modernism and intellectualism. Its members—among whom were professional teachers, physicians, artists, writers, public health officials, and patrons of the arts—

embraced scientific racism and used its biological theories to support their own rubric of supposedly unimpassioned objectivity. A report in the July 22, 1923, *Richmond Times-Dispatch* identified the scientific community as one of the main audiences for Earnest Sevier Cox's publications. Cox, trained in sociology at the University of Chicago, drew on observations made while working as a laborer in Africa to support his social Darwinist theories of hierarchies of civilizations.[4] In 1926 Burleigh used the language of eugenics—and of final solutions—to support her lobbying efforts for racial legislation in Virginia. In a letter to the editor of the *Boston Evening Transcript*, which had criticized what was happening in Virginia, Burleigh wrote, "The realization, which has been crystallizing both in the North and in the South, that the race problem is a biological one, has presented additional difficulties in practical details of present action ('the racial legislation now before the Virginia General Assembly'), and, to offset these difficulties, a brighter hope for an ultimate solution." She amplified this supposedly depoliticized biological stand-point in the rest of her letter:

> Just as the theory, once widely accepted in the North, that no fundamental difference kept the races apart, has been losing ground in actual experience, so, also in the course of experience, the South's confidence that widely divergent heredities would keep the races distinct has lost ground. The North no longer considers the problem exclusively an ethical one; the South is beginning to see that it is not political. With scientific advance and the study of Eugenics, it was inevitable that it should assume its proper biological aspect. The present program before the General Assembly of Virginia is based upon this fact. White Supremacy has given place to Racial Integrity as an ideal. The measures aim to cut off any infusion of non-white blood through intermarriage; to check illicit mixing by making carnal communication between the races a felony; [and] to emphasize the distinction between the races by avoiding even an appearance of social intermingling.

Burleigh further stated that the best solution to this situation was the one "advocated by Jefferson, Madison, Monroe, Webster, and Abraham Lincoln"—namely, to give the "Negro the hope of a future" by "encouraging the further colonization of Liberia by American Negroes."[5] After recommending repatriation, she went on to talk about the preoccupation the ASCOA had with minute legal definitions of race as a method of excluding people of color from free choice in sexual activity as well as in civil opportunities.

For the ASCOA, the provisions of the 1924 Racial Integrity Act were not tight enough, and their activism in the 1920s after the act had passed was focused on securing even more stringently defined legislation. Burleigh worked on such efforts in 1926, 1928, and 1930. The ASCOA successfully lobbied for the 1926 Massenburg Bill, which mandated segregated audiences for public performances and was targeted at Hampton Institute, where mixed-race audiences and groups of performers (for example, a black conductor of an all-white glee club) drew ASCOA pickets and demonstrations. The greatest effort was expended in favor of new racial integrity bills that would further restrict the definition of "white" beyond the one-sixteenth rule used in the successful 1924 act. The 1926 effort for such a bill failed when, as the *New York Times* pointed out, whites noticed that it would "classify as 'colored' some of the most distinguished families of Virginia," not to mention some of the members of the Virginia legislature.[6]

In finishing her 1926 letter to the *Transcript*, written in the middle of this AS-COA campaign, Burleigh spoke of the obsession that her ASCOA colleague, the Bureau of Vital Statistics official W. A. Plecker, had about Indian people who qualified under the 1924 law as "white" but who were really—according to the "one drop" rule—"black." "These 'Indian' groups were a stepping stone in the path from Black to White," Burleigh wrote, from "Indianoid negro to Negroid Indian, Negroid Indian to plain Indian, plain Indian to Indianoid white, whose marriage to a white person established his position in the white class."[7] Plecker was vocal on the issue. He carried on a crusade in Virginia, with the help of ASCOA members, to ferret out individuals of African American or African-Indian-American heritage who were passing, especially those with children attending "white" public schools. Burleigh worked hand in hand with Plecker in these endeavors and helped to draft and revise bills in favor of a 100-percent definition of whiteness to be presented by the assembly. Plecker, meanwhile, had already reported his opinions about the danger of "triple intermixing" of white, black, and Indian, in "Shall America Remain White?" a speech he delivered to the Southern Medical Association's annual meeting in New Orleans in November 1924. The connection between eugenic constructions of personal identities and racial engineering of populations that Burleigh alluded to in her letter to the editor was not lost on the doctors who heard Plecker speak. One of them responded from the audience to Plecker's address by suggesting a sterilization law, similar to those that some leading mental health experts sought to apply to mentally retarded people, in order to "eventually eliminate the negro."[8]

Louise Burleigh knew what she was talking about when she addressed the issue of northern racial prejudice in her letter to the *Transcript*. She had been born in 1889 into an upper-middle-class New England family and was educated at Thayer Academy in Braintree, Massachusetts, and Radcliffe College. Her father, Robert F. Burleigh, was a Hopkinton, New Hampshire, physician. Burleigh became deeply involved in the little-theater movement at Radcliffe. She was one of the founders of the well-known Workshop 47 and helped produce plays as a member of Radcliffe's Idler's Club. Like many other politically active white women in the Progressive period and the 1920s, Burleigh was a strong defender of white women's rights at the same time that she assumed the exclusion of people of color, male and female, from gaining the very sorts of advantages she felt were merited by her own kind. Burleigh described her time at Radcliffe as a revolutionary period in the education of (white) women, during which female drama students deliberately broke gender and status divisions between Radcliffe and Harvard—particularly by breaking into producing and directing positions previously monopolized by men.[9] Upon graduation in 1912, Burleigh became involved in New England repertory theater. Although her early work as a playwright dealt with psychological, modernist, and social reform subjects, her specialty became the adaptation of Elizabethan material for community plays and pageants. During the World War I era Burleigh became an important promoter of regional and local theater and of children's productions. In her book *Community Theatre* (1917), she championed public parks and services as important aspects of urban reform and argued for recognition of the parallels between the collaborative aspects of mounting community arts productions, with native-born and ethnic-immigrant urban dwellers learning to work together, and the exercise of grassroots democracy.[10]

Burleigh came to Richmond in 1919 to work as a director and manager of the Richmond Little Theatre League. She also created the Queene's Children, a Richmond children's theater group that toured small rural towns in Virginia and West Virginia. She helped Powell collect Anglo-American folk songs for rural areas of Virginia, taught university extension courses, and lectured widely on Elizabethan drama and the use of Anglo-Saxon folk themes in community theater. Her letters to Powell make it clear that she viewed her grassroots theatrical work and her interest in the preservation of Anglo-American folk song as extensions of her white supremacist politics. Performances she organized to tour small Virginia towns, she noted, helped to spread the message that Anglo-Saxonism was the taproot of American civilization and subtly encouraged common white folk to champion her own notions of supremacist cultural hegemony.

Her support for racial integrity legislation came out of no Victorian prudery of the body. One of her major professional preoccupations during the time she was working with the ASCOA was the adaptation of fellow Richmonder James Branch Cabell's 1919 novel, *Jurgen*, for the stage. *Jurgen* had been subjected to censorship by the New York Society for the Suppression of Vice in 1920 because of its supposedly pornographic content. The censorship may well have been fueled by the highly public rumors of the bisexuality of the novel's author. The attempted suppression of the book made Cabell for a time the darling of the New York literati. Cultural critics including H. L. Mencken and Carl Van Doren welcomed the controversy over the book's content as a means of publicly advocating Jazz Age notions of freer sexuality in general, and the potency of liberated female sexuality in particular—a decidedly non-Victorian concept. Burleigh apparently had no difficulty with the bawdiness of Cabell's work, and she could easily embrace its dominant themes of male chivalry and the simultaneous idealization and objectification of women. These themes translated easily from the medieval setting of Cabell's novel to the cultural milieu in which the ASCOA existed—and to the habit Powell and his cohorts had of endorsing a knight-like vision of themselves in relation to white southern ladyhood.

Allegorical idealization was clearly one thing and interracial sex another. While chagrined at the suppression of *Jurgen*, which so promoted their own Anglo-Saxon values, Burleigh and Earnest Sevier Cox were in the forefront of advocating censorship of the 1926 film adaptation of Charles Wadell Chesnutt's 1900 book, *The House behind the Cedars*, a novel in which a light-skinned black female protagonist must choose between white and black lovers. They argued for the film's suppression by the Virginia Board of Censors on the grounds that its depiction of interracial sexuality was at odds with what Burleigh described in her statement as the "accepted standard in Virginia" and specifically of the mores codified by the 1924 Racial Integrity Act.[11]

After a long courtship and close political partnership, Burleigh married John Powell in 1928. Like Burleigh, Powell combined political activism with the application of white supremacy to the arts. Powell was born in Richmond in 1882, the son of the head of the prestigious Richmond Female Seminary. He proved himself a child prodigy at the piano, and after earning a degree at the University of Virginia, studied in Vienna and made his concert debut in Berlin in 1907, followed by an acclaimed European tour. He debuted in the United States at Carnegie Hall in 1913, and throughout the period of his ASCOA activism was an internationally renowned pianist and poster boy for Steinway pianos. In radio broadcasts, articles, and concert talks and in the White Top Folk Festival classes, which he and Burleigh helped to found in 1931, he promoted the idea that Anglo-Saxon folk songs were the true basis of American nationalist music, and that black music was a bastardization of white musical constructs. His compositions—including *Sonata Teutonica and Rhapsodie Negre* (which he dedicated to Joseph Conrad and *The Heart of Darkness*)—were conscious and direct expressions of his white supremacist theories about American civilization and culture. He emphasized black primitivism and pseudo-Freudian ideas of the association of blackness with the natural, the wild, the dangerously unhindered, and the subconscious.[12]

The gender-and-power politics of Louise Burleigh's role in the ASCOA were very similar to those of Elizabeth Tyler in the Ku Klux Klan of the early 1920s. Marion Monteval, a former member of the KKK who wrote an internal exposé of Klan operations, called Tyler the "friend, companion, associate, and partner of E. Y. Clarke in all his enterprises of exploitation."[13] A similar pattern of male-female partnership in leadership was also evident in the UNIA portion of the antimiscegenation and repatriation lobby that developed in Virginia in the 1920s: the man was recognized as the public spokesperson and figurehead of a grassroots movement, but much of the actual day-to-day operations of that movement was orchestrated outside the public eye by a woman, with whom the male leader was romantically involved. And just as the ASCOA had arisen out of white supremacist Virginians' disgust with the shenanigans of top KKK leadership, so the real roots of the coalition between the UNIA and the ASCOA lay in the reconstituted Klan.

Enter Amy Jacques Garvey and the UNIA

Under pressure from Justice and State Department officials who were investigating his alleged radicalism and seeking means for his deportation, Marcus Garvey took a decided turn to the right in 1922. In June he and his fiancée and personal secretary, Amy Jacques, traveled to Atlanta, where he met with acting Imperial Wizard Edward Young Clarke and his aide Elizabeth Tyler at KKK headquarters. Among the issues discussed were the mutual race-purity goals of the two organizations and their common opposition to the agenda of the NAACP, which included social equality, racial assimilation, and racial rights. Garvey traveled directly from his meeting with the Klan leaders to Virginia, where he made a public appearance in Norfolk. The black nationalist–white supremacist alliance that formed in Virginia in the mid-

1920s was a direct outgrowth of the line of political logic Garvey had expressed in arranging the Atlanta meeting. His editorial on race purity and the KKK, published in the June 27, 1922, *Negro World*, was a virtual manifesto of the platform the UNIA utilized in the 1925 coalition.[14] Garvey believed that the Klan represented in bold relief the true feelings of the majority of white Americans on race. He told audiences at the UNIA's Liberty Hall in New York that "every second white man in this country is a member of the KKK" and that the invisible empire was well manifested in the workings of the government of the United States.[15] In addition to his conviction that African Americans could never receive justice under such conditions, he linked white majority endorsement of Klan repression to labor relations, and specifically to the practice of industrial employers to favor white labor over black.[16] The remedy, for Garveyites, was to abandon false hopes of social and political equality in America and to create a separate black homeland in Africa. Eschewing coalition with liberal black assimilationists or the black Left, Garvey turned to the white supremacist Right to find allies to help further his separatist vision.[17]

Garvey was incarcerated in the Atlanta Federal Penitentiary during the most intense period of coalition building between the UNIA and the ASCOA over legislation in Virginia. Indeed, the fact of his imprisonment (and his desire to gain white support for his release) was a key factor in the formation of that coalition. Garvey was arrested on mail fraud charges stemming from the sale of Black Star Line stock in 1922 and was tried and convicted in 1923. He was imprisoned, after appeals failed, in early 1925. The coalition formed through Cox, Burleigh, and Powell began in the spring of 1925. The importance of Garvey's jeopardy in regard to his imprisonment and impending deportation is key to understanding the motivations of the UNIA's turn to the right and its willingness to try alliances with white supremacists during this period. Much of the early radical or militant content of UNIA rhetoric disappeared after the State Department and the Bureau of Investigation successfully infiltrated the Garvey movement and used legal avenues to place limitations on Garvey's actions and movements. Part of the UNIA's linkage to white supremacist groups was an (as it turned out, mistaken) effort to convince government authorities that the movement was not radical and to win support from white lobbyists for Garvey's release from prison without deportation.[18] White supremacist leaders in Virginia—including John Powell, Earnest Sevier Cox, and W. A. Plecker—all urged the federal government to change its mind about Garvey and allow him to remain to work in the United States.[19] Despite this tactic in allying with the white supremacist Right, Garvey was deported directly upon his release from the federal penitentiary in late 1927 and was never allowed to reenter the United States. Meanwhile, most of the actual grassroots organizing done in Virginia with the ASCOA was accomplished not by Garvey himself, but by his second wife, Amy Jacques Garvey, whom he had married a month after the 1922 meeting with Clarke and Tyler.

Amy Jacques Garvey was born to a middle-class family in Jamaica in 1896. She moved to the United States in 1917 and became involved in the Garvey movement in New York the following year. She soon became Garvey's personal assistant, traveling with him on UNIA organizational tours, and was office manager of the UNIA's headquarters in Harlem. During the period of Garvey's arrest, trial, and imprisonment in the early 1920s, Jacques Garvey emerged as the premier propagandist of the Garvey movement. Just as Burleigh handled ASCOA affairs while Powell was out of the state on tours, so did Jacques Garvey step in for her absent husband.

Both Jacques Garvey and Burleigh were leading propagandists for their respective movements. In addition to traveling widely to local UNIA divisions as a speaker, lobbying government officials for her husband's release, and editing the women's page of the UNIA's *Negro World* newspaper, Jacques Garvey edited and compiled the influential *Philosophy and Opinions of Marcus Garvey* (published in two volumes in 1923 and 1925). The second volume of *Philosophy and Opinions* was the most significant propaganda piece produced by the movement. In it, arguments regarding miscegenation and the injustice of Garvey's plight existed side by side with advertisements for publications that were favorites in ASCOA circles.[20] Intended in part to sway public opinion in favor of Garvey's release from prison, it represented the most comprehensive statement of the UNIA's position on race purity.

During the time she was preparing *Philosophy and Opinions*, Jacques Garvey became actively involved in supporting white supremacist efforts in Virginia regarding racial purity and repatriation. Earnest Sevier Cox was the connective link that initially brought the UNIA and the ASCOA together. Already a close ally of Louise Burleigh, he became a political colleague and friend of Amy Jacques Garvey as well. After UNIA members in St. Louis and Detroit became interested in Cox's publications, Amy Jacques Garvey contacted him directly in May 1925 and sent him some UNIA pamphlets.[21] The letter marked the beginning of a long correspondence that extended, sporadically, until Cox's death in the mid-1960s.[22] In June 1925, Marcus Garvey wrote to Cox that "your letter and pamphlet have been brought to my attention by my wife . . . I endorse and support your views and hope for closer cooperation between [the] two societies." A week later he reported to Cox that he was dispatching Amy Jacques Garvey to Virginia and that although she was "of slight mixed blood . . . she understands thoroughly the question and the opposition."[23] Cox invited Jacques Garvey to come to Richmond and went himself to talk to the local UNIA division members. John Powell—who went to Georgia to lobby the state legislature to enact legislation similar to Virginia's 1924 bill—visited Marcus Garvey at Atlanta Federal Penitentiary in June 1925.[24] In July Cox attended a Richmond UNIA meeting and read aloud from the pages of *Philosophy and Opinions*. Amy Jacques Garvey came to Richmond in August to interview Cox. She facilitated the attendance of Powell, Burleigh, Cox, and other ASCOA members at a meeting of the local Richmond UNIA. She also helped arrange for John Powell to give a major address on race purity at Liberty Hall, the UNIA's main meeting place in Harlem, on October 28, 1925; Jacques Garvey gave the speech introducing him on that occasion.[25] At Garvey's direction, she revised the compilation of *Philosophy and Opinions* in November 1925 to insert a copy of Powell's New York speech and also included an advertisement for Earnest Sevier Cox's two major works, the book *White America* and the pamphlet *Let My People Go*—which Garvey had already lavished with praise.[26] The book and the pamphlet were privately published under the auspices of Cox's Richmond-based White America Society, and both became best-sellers in UNIA divisions in the North. In an epigraph, Cox described *Let My People Go* (which sold over seventeen thousand copies in its first two months) as "A message from white men who wish to keep the white race white, to black men who wish to keep the black race black, including the terms of an alliance between these groups against the whites who wish to mix with the Negroes and the Negroes who wish to mix with the whites." He dedicated the pamphlet to "Marcus Garvey, a martyr for the independence and integrity of the Negro race."[27] When the newly compiled second volume of *Philosophy and Opinions* came out early in 1926, Amy Jacques Garvey sent copies of it to the members of the Virginia General Assembly.[28]

Amy Jacques Garvey was also instrumental in the UNIA-ASCOA coalition on repatriation. She worked hard in Virginia on behalf of a resolution drafted by Cox in favor of repatriation introduced to the Virginia General Assembly in 1926. She presented the text of the resolution as a major plank at the UNIA convention in Detroit in March 1926 and urged UNIA members to take copies of the resolution, and upon "their return to their communities they would form committees whose duty it would be to draft resolutions along similar lines and get influential white persons in their districts to send such resolutions to their State Assemblies, which in turn would memorialize the Congress, so that in three months resolutions would be going to Congress from all parts of the country, thereby forcing action by the Congress."[29]

Meanwhile, on the white supremacist side of the coalition, Earnest Sevier Cox was an almost daily visitor in Louise Burleigh's home on North Plum Street in Richmond. Burleigh helped to ghostwrite and edit Cox's numerous publications advocating racial separatism and warning of the eugenic evils of "amalgamation." Among other things, she distributed copies of *White America*, so that while Amy Jacques Garvey was ordering and distributing *Let My People Go* through UNIA circles and placing an advertisement for *White America* in the back of her edited book, Burleigh was busy sending out the same book to white supremacists. The March 1925 revised edition of the book contained, among other things, an appendix reprinting the 1924 Racial Integrity Act.[30] Just as Amy Jacques Garvey brought Cox's work to Marcus Garvey's attention, Burleigh apparently was responsible for making Cox and Powell aware of Marcus Garvey and his political platform. She wrote to Powell about a European article concerning the Garvey movement in 1922, observing that "It seems to me that ESC [Earnest Sevier Cox] ought to have it, as it bears directly upon the questions which are his particular field."[31] Just as Amy Jacques Garvey reported on her activities in telegrams and visits to Garvey in prison, so Burleigh gave detailed descriptions of her lobbying in letters to John Powell and sent him clippings of the events. While Jacques Garvey was host to Powell at the UNIA gathering in New York, Burleigh attended programs sponsored by the Richmond UNIA division. She was one of the fifteen or so ASCOA representatives who attended UNIA officer William Sherrill's talk at the Sharon Baptist Church, sponsored by the Richmond UNIA division in September 1925, and she wrote to Marcus Garvey that she "found Sherrill's talk . . . one of the most stirring experiences I have ever had. . . . We wished all Richmond could have heard him."[32] She aided Powell in the preparation of his supremacist speeches and newspaper articles and facilitated his trip to the UNIA meeting in Harlem. It was often she, not Powell, who handled correspondence with UNIA members in Virginia when those members turned to Powell's Anglo-Saxon Clubs for support in their local endeavors.[33]

In thus promoting movement rhetoric in separate but parallel ways, Amy Jacques Garvey and Louise Burleigh were actively instigating a process of political remapping.[34] In the antimiscegenation campaign, many of the racial purity arguments were focused on the female body. The female body—the body of the black woman for Garveyites, and the body of the white woman for the white supremacists—was in turn a powerful symbolic emblem for nationalist goals and desires.

The Body and the Nation

When Burleigh and the white supremacists spoke of the white female body, they spoke of an idealized South and, by extension, the glorification of an Anglophilic concept of the roots of white civilization in a legendary Anglo-Saxon past. When Garveyites spoke of the black female body, they spoke of black independence from white oppression and, by extension, an Afrocentric concept of the roots of black civilization in ancient Egypt and Ethiopia. Both used metaphors of rape and discussion of literal sexual racial intermixing as referents to a larger nationalist political debate. Both made the ideological connection between the immediate/biological and the future/political, between woman's body and the future state of the black or white nation. For them, remapping sexual access to women according to racial boundaries was a direct and conscious equivalent to remapping the racial composition and power relations of the continents of North America and Africa.

The white female body was a referent to what Cox and Burleigh so succinctly termed a "White America"; the black female body to Garveyites' vision of a redeemed Africa liberated from white colonial rule. By taking an old argument—familiar from Ku Klux Klan rhetoric of the nineteenth century and from African American women's antilynching campaigns—the members of UNIA divisions and the Anglo-Saxon Clubs made the leap from discussion of women's bodies as a kind of property over which black men and white men battled for access and control (often using the vocabulary of protection) to far-reaching political goals of controlling actual territory or empires.

UNIA speeches, pageants, parades, poetry, and songs idealized Africa as a black woman who had been defiled by white colonial invasion, and signified black liberation from colonial domination as black male rescue of this raped and captive woman. At the August 1922 international UNIA convention held in Harlem in the same summer as the Garveys' meeting with Clarke and Tyler, Garveyite women literally embodied the UNIA vision of a precolonial, predefiled Africa. They put on a fashion promenade and pageant representing "women of African nobility," with UNIA leader Henrietta Vinton Davis as the Queen of Sheba and other women representing the empresses, queens, and princesses of Dahomey, Abyssinia, Basutoland, South Africa, Nigeria, Sierra Leone, Angola, and several other African countries. At the same time, the political connection between lost nationhood and lost power, miscegenational sexual defilement, and the black woman in need of black male succor found expression in poems about black womanhood that Garvey wrote from his prison cell. The imagery Garvey used of white colonialism as rape and the redemption of Africa as the black man coming to the rescue of the molested black woman was common throughout UNIA speeches and editorials.[35]

For the ASCOA, rhetoric surrounding the sexual purity of the white woman was similarly a racial mapping of sexuality for political purposes. Just as Garveyites sought a reversal of the sins of slavery and the African diaspora through racial separatism and repatriation, and glorified a mythic black African civilization that predated white incursion, so the ASCOA was fixated on a pre-emancipation South in which the hierarchies of white supremacy were entrenched by the authority of law, and white southern manhood was unsullied by the invading forces of the pro-emancipation North. The Anglophilic ASCOA specifically looked to the origins of white southern culture in the Anglo-Saxon past, and mythologized that era of English history. Thus the two groups used metaphors of the female body to convey two visions of nationalism: for Garveyites, a black empire in postcolonial Africa, and for the ASCOA, an all-white South free to revel culturally in its Anglo-Saxon antecedents. For the UNIA, antimiscegenation was a watchword for black autonomy, race pride, and revolution. For the ASCOA, it was a hierarchical code of control in the service of the preservation of white supremacy. The symbols that gave the two groups common ground for political action were ultimately emblematic of opposite intent: for the UNIA, they represented a politics of change and rebellion; for the ASCOA, they represented a politics of the prevention of change or the revocation of privilege.

In Garveyite thinking on the antimiscegenation issue, the ethos of protection was specifically transferred from black male guarding of the black female body to black power through nationhood—a regained and protected African empire. The property metaphor was transferred from the black woman to literal black territory in Africa, and the debate became about African American masculinity. Survival and liberation, Garvey assured UNIA members, were a matter of "demanding our portion as MEN." The *Negro World* staff member H. G. Mugdal similarly called for territorial boundary lines to be drawn regarding the "PURITY of the NEGRO WOMANHOOD . . . if the whites have us to do nothing with their womanhood let them not have anything to do with ours."[36]

Perhaps the most succinct statement of the UNIA's position on the race purity and miscegenation nexus was the credo "What We Believe," written by Garvey a few months before the passage of the Racial Integrity Act, and printed in the January 19, 1924, edition of the *Negro World*. The credo stated that the UNIA "advocates the uniting and blending of all Negroes into one strong healthy race. It is against miscegenation and race suicide." It called for race pride and unity among blacks, and stated that the "purity of the Negro race and the purity of the white race" should be preserved. It was "against rich blacks marrying poor whites" and "rich or poor whites taking advantage of Negro women." It embraced the "spiritual

Fatherhood of God and the Brotherhood of Man" and the "rights of all men." In closing, it advocated the "social and political physical separation of all people to the extent that they promote their own ideals and civilization, with the privilege of trading and doing business with each other" in service of the "promotion of a strong and powerful Negro nation."

The creation of viable separate black economic and educational institutions—which was another part of the UNIA program in Virginia—was directly related to the UNIA's stand on racial purity as a means of protection and respect for black women. It related specifically to removing black women from work in domestic households where they were subject to the whims of white employers. Amy Jacques Garvey and the women of the UNIA went further than this masculine-related property-and-protection model to argue a position of rights for women and of women's abilities independent of men.

On the white supremacist side, Burleigh, Cox, and Powell mourned the lost sovereignty of the pre–Civil War South. Replacing the overt violence of the supremacist language of the nineteenth century, they shifted from (but did not entirely abandon) an emphasis on imperiled white womanhood and the image of the black male rapist, and used in its place a eugenics framework of degeneration, notions of cycles of civilization, and what they saw as a threatened devolution of the species. At the center, for them, remained the white female body, because their obsession in thinking about miscegenation was focused mainly on the coupling of white women and black men.

ASCOA members greeted with denial reminders from African Americans of the problems inherent in the image of the pure white lady of civilization that was at the center of ASCOA thought. An anonymous letter to John Powell, which Louise Burleigh handled while he was out of town, addressed just this issue. Handwritten and enclosed in a typed envelope with no return address, the 1925 letter was sent to Powell in care of the white *Richmond Times-Dispatch*, a paper that Louise Burleigh later heard opponents of the 1926 repatriation and racial integrity legislation refer to as "under Powell's thumb." Across the envelope, Burleigh wrote to Powell, "This needs no answer, but I wish I could have one." The letter outlined the very tenets regarding women, men, and interracial sex that were emphasized by the UNIA. "In all your propaganda regarding racial relations, it appears that you are aiming to vindicate the white man," the writer observed, laying the blame for miscegenation on white men: "In the days of slavery in America, white men forced Negro women to bed with them. If they resisted or resented they were flogged, or sold. The same rule is in force today, only in a different way." The writer noted that "Colored women have to work in private families and cafeterias, hotels, and other such places," where they were subjected to white male sexual advances, and forced to choose between complying in order to keep their jobs and income, and refusing and being fired. The legal system was no recourse, nor was reporting the harassment: "They have no protection if they report the case to the courts. . . . If she reports to the head of the house or to the police, they don't take her word." "The white man is more eager for colored women than the Negro man is for white women," the writer concluded. "White men started this mixed color," and they are trying to "keep at it" by "using racial integrity as a veil to protect them, and at the same time defile our race. If a white man insults a Negro woman on the street and a Negro man aim to protect her, the Negro man is arrested, some charge placed against him, fined or put in jail." The letter closed with a question that was more of a statement: "Is it fair."[37]

The prevailing metaphoric concept at play in the ASCOA and the UNIA was of the body as contested terrain, subject to invasion by "others" and thus to the compromise of masculinity. It was also thought of as a literal form of physical property over which males fought for rights of exclusive access. In this sense, the KKK and the ASCOA used the specter of the black male rapist and the imperiled white woman. The UNIA addressed the more real threat of the defiled black woman subjected to the white harasser or colonizer. Largely lost in the respective politicizations of the black and white female body was the idea of consensual sex and love relationships between individuals of different races.

As the "What We Believe" credo implied, Garvey was as interested in black men who would seek white "trophy" wives as he was in white men who sexually assaulted black women, especially black working women, who, like the anonymous writer of the letter to Powell, were especially vulnerable because the lack of alternative employment (in black-owned businesses or homes) placed them in positions of dependence on white domestic employers. In this, concerns of property, possession, and economic ascendancy were firmly entwined with the sexual. On the issue of black men looking for white wives, Garvey penned an editorial entitled "A Racial Weakness" that focused on well-to-do black male professionals and planters in the West Indies who married white women and transferred their fortunes to the other race, thereby weakening their own race financially and emotionally.[38]

While the UNIA castigated black men who would desire white women at the same time that it decried white male violence against black women, both the Garveyites and the white supremacists focused their main arguments regarding interracial sex on male choice and either black or white female victimization. They left the notion of female choice—the black woman who would choose a white man, or the white woman who would choose a black man—on the periphery of the debate. When women's consensual desire was acknowledged as an element in the miscegenation issue, it was usually referred to obliquely. Powell touched on it at the end of a speech he gave at the ASCOA post in Newport News, Virginia. He described an unofficial survey he conducted by spending forty-five minutes standing on a street corner (the intersection of Second Street and Broad Street in Richmond), during which he counted some "200 Negro passerbys" of whom "only 5 were black," and observed (what was to him) a disturbing trend toward greater social equality in the form of black and white social address and attire. He concluded with what he identified as the most disturbing observation of all—the "increase in the number of hybrids born of white women," adding, "This matter is too abhorrent to be discussed in the public press."[39]

Burleigh and Powell were obsessed with preventing racial intermixing out of concern for the maintenance of white privilege and Anglo-Saxon cultural hegemony, stating a fear that if interracial sex were to go on unchecked, it would mean the "mongrelization" of the nation and the loss of (using the language of breeding and science) the superior, purebred species. For them the issue was degeneration. For the Garveyites, the issue was extinction. For many ASCOA members, the future hung on a balance between the two. The head of the Newport News ASCOA chapter wrote President Calvin Coolidge in 1927 to say that "we will later have either complete amalgamation or a bloody war of extermination of the blacks and negroids by the whites."[40]

Of Genocide and Degeneration: Burleigh's "Dark Cloud"

The UNIA pointed to miscegenation, along with white violence, the declining birth rate and rising mortality rates of blacks, and white exploitation of black labor leading to chronic impoverishment and starvation as part of a system of genocide against people of the African diaspora. They believed that separatism, including independent black economic development and the avoidance of interracial relationships, combined with selective repatriation to Africa and work on behalf of the political sovereignty of African nations and their independence from colonial rule, was the only means by which to ensure black survival. At root, then, in the UNIA support of antimiscegenation legislation was the commitment to prevent the dying out of the black race in the United States and a political prelude to the future establishment of an all-black Africa.

Louise Burleigh combined the themes of degeneration and genocide in an unpublished short story that gives voice to the very kind of white supremacist fears regarding miscegenation that underlay the ASCOA support for racial integrity legislation. "Dark Cloud" is a gothic horror tale about the white female body, interracial sex, and mistaken racial identity.[41] It is undated, but the idea almost certainly occurred to Burleigh while she was in Connecticut in the summer of 1925. As Burleigh wrote to Powell, "I've been prowling among the Confederate books since I came, getting data on the colour subject, and with great success." One such book was Nehemiah Adams's *Sable Cloud* (1861). She wrote gleefully that the book was "a defense—not of slavery, but of the South's position. . . . It contains all sorts of wonderful things, whix the most delightful is the repeated statement 'What can we do with them if freed?' I am just arriving at a delightful justification of slave-holding on the basis of biblical authority."[42]

"Dark Cloud" relates both to the African American literary genre of stories of passing—the classics of James Weldon Johnson and Nella Larsen, Dorothy West's "Mammy," or Frances Harper's *Iola Leroy*—and to stories by white authors using the birth of a baby to reveal secrets of racial identity (most notably, Kate Chopin's "Desiree's Baby"). "Dark Cloud" was Burleigh's artistic answer, in fiction, to the themes Powell embedded in his musical compositions, and reveals a great deal about the paradigms of white racism that lay behind Burleigh's political activism.

In Burleigh's story, a happily married white New England woman—aptly named Alicia Fairchild—goes south with her brown-eyed, blonde, curly-headed little girl only to find out that her supposedly white husband's mother was a very black woman. Before this revelation is made, Fairchild is immersed in an unfamiliar and surreal world that is described by Burleigh as embodying the dark side of the psyche: to go from North to South, from white to black is to cross over into the irrational, the beastly, the fearsome and ominous—into what Burleigh terms the "substance of nightmares." Burleigh switches between metaphors of contamination and illness and those of devolution and bestiality to frame her white heroine's perceptions of darkness. Black characters are compared to worms and maggots, to howling and writhing demons. They are associated with the evil and hellish, the primitive, the occult, the childlike and instinctive, the secret and conniving. As in Chopin's story, where mother and baby die when faced with the stigma of their apparent blackness, knowledge of her own part in miscegenation for Burleigh's protagonist means death. Emblematic of white civilization itself, her taintedness from her trip across the color line leads to her downfall. Her dawning self-awareness of the true racial dynamics of her sexuality (that she, a white woman, has been having sexual relations with a black man) means the reversal of physical agency and the loss of her former state of personal integrity, in which she was described as having the "purity of a nun." As the story progresses, her body degenerates from that of an adult, capable human being to one more akin to a child, then an animal, and finally, a prostrate zombie. As with her white female body, so, implies Burleigh, lies the fate of the nation.

The white woman goes to the church where her mother-in-law's funeral is taking place. While a white pastor gives a sermon on the racial harmonies of slavery in contrast to the sad effects of black dependence without white patronage since emancipation, she looks around. The horror builds inside her as she realizes in slow steps that her husband's mother is black and a former slave; that her husband is therefore black as well; that their marriage is a situation of miscegenation; and that their daughter is the product of interracial sex, and kin to the "dark creatures" she has been encountering since she came South. Her experience becomes one of redefining the "other" all around her. The husband she loved and admired deeply until her recent discovery is suddenly transformed into a "rabid" rapist in her mind's eye. The fact of his blackness and his deception regarding his racial identity reverse the consensual aspects of their sexual relations in her mind. Miscegenation in Burleigh's scenario is thus by definition rape. In the end, the white wife confronts and kills her husband. Even more grisly, Burleigh brings the character of the previously beatific little daughter to an end that can only be described as deeply sadistic. Once "white," now "black," the little girl not only changes color, but in effect is made to change species. Once a toddling child, she is at story's end described as "whining like some little animal" scurrying "off on all fours." Ultimately she is left behind to be consumed by fire inside the locked-up church, which a toppled candle ignites into flames.

In choosing the inferno method of elimination for the mixed-race child, Burleigh alluded to a classic Ku Klux Klan image in defense of whiteness—the fiery cross. While Burleigh's concern in the story was primarily with white degeneration through contact with blackness, she proved the UNIA's point regarding the ultimate motivations of white supremacists. Her story's denouement spoke directly to the conviction within the UNIA that the full expression of genuine white supremacy would mean genocide. Garveyites recognized in the ASCOA's legal campaign of racial "purification" the implications that were so well voiced on an individual level in Burleigh's short story. One of the passages Amy Jacques Garvey chose to include in *Philosophy and Opinions* was Garvey's admonition that black people hold themselves

> in readiness for that great catastrophe that is bound to come—that of racial extermination at the hands of the stronger race. . . . The attitude of the white race is to subjugate, to exploit, and if necessary exterminate the weaker peoples with whom they come in contact. They subjugate first . . . then exploit, and if they will not stand for SUBJUGATION nor EXPLOITATION, the other recourse is EXTERMINATION.[43]

The kind of racial remapping of the female child who looks white and turns out to be one-quarter black that Burleigh used as the premise of "Dark Cloud" was exactly what the Virginia antimiscegenation legislation was all about. Not only did the ASCOA seek to prevent current and future interracial unions, they desired to expose African Americans who were the descendants of those who had crossed the lines of race in the past. The white supremacists loved to talk about how contact with blackness would mean the death of white civilization. For Garveyites in the racial integrity coalition, the opposite was true. Their participation was based on a recognition that remaining in the United States meant for African Americans a future of injustice and genocide, based on the model already so painfully manifested by Native Americans in their contact with whites. As Garvey noted in a 1924 address to a session of an international UNIA convention in Harlem, "As I can see it, the white man is determined to kill this race of ours. I know it, it is only a question of time, of another hundred years when this race of ours will be dead as the Indian."[44] The Native American past was a foretaste of the African American future. For them, ultimately, antimiscegenation politics was a step toward helping all black people avoid the fate of the black man in Burleigh's story.

For Garveyites, antimiscegenation legislation and its implications for the protection of black women's honor were a strategy aimed toward a more important goal—winning white governmental support for repatriation, the realization of the Garveyite call for "Africa for the Africans." The same coalitions that worked for antimiscegenation legislation in the 1920s would reunite to work for repatriation legislation in the 1930s.

For the ASCOA and its propagandists, the position represented in the Racial Integrity Act, with its definition of whiteness under force of law, was a link between the nativism, racism, and xenophobia of the 1920s and the final solution paradigm of Hitler's Europe. As World War II opened and progressed, John Powell's nieces corresponded with each other about the genocidal aspects of Hitler's campaign of racial purity, and recognized in it the basic premises that had motivated their uncle in his earlier activism. Powell had written in an ASCOA treatise in 1923 that one of the goals of the ASCOA was the "fundamental and final solutions to our racial problems in general, most especially of the Negro problem."[45]

It was not until the 1950s and 1960s that the full ramifications of the 1920s racial debate were played out in formal politics. The *Brown v. Board of Education* ruling of 1954 sparked a new wave of white supremacist resistance to black opportunity, and the Powells joined in with those who virulently opposed the desegregation of Virginia's public schools. While Amy Jacques Garvey continued to correspond warmly with Earnest Sevier Cox about UNIA affairs in Jamaica and his own life in Richmond, Marcus Garvey had died in London in 1940. His influence, however, was far-reaching, and he was recognized as an inspiration by leaders of anticolonial independence movements in Africa and the Caribbean who recognized the call for black political sovereignty that lay behind the UNIA's position regarding miscegenation.

The antimiscegenation legislation of 1924 (supplemented by further specifications of race in acts passed in 1930 and 1932) was brought crashing down, fittingly, by the court action of the case of two Virginians, Mildred Delores Jeter Loving, a black woman, and her husband, Richard Perry Loving, a white man. Issued warrants of arrest in 1958 and convicted in 1959 of violating Virginia's antimiscegenation statutes, they contested the ruling. The result was the overthrow of the Racial Integrity Act by the United States Supreme Court in 1967, on the grounds that it violated Fourteenth Amendment rights to equal protection and due process under the law. The ruling nullified all remaining laws in the United States forbidding interracial marriage.

NOTES

Research was supported by grants from the Virginia Center for the Humanities and the Virginia Historical Society.

1. Earnest Sevier Cox, *White America* (Richmond: White America Society, 1923; rev, ed., 1925), 393, 394.

2. For the text of the act, see "The New Virginia Race Integrity Law," in Cox, *White America*, appendix 3, 393–95. The one-sixteenth exception was made because of the large number of elite white families in Virginia who wanted to make a genealogical claim to ancestral ties with Pocahontas.

3. Aside from Burleigh's dedication to the movement, I have found no evidence of an organized female auxiliary to the ASCOA such as existed in the Ku Klux Klan.

4. After working in Africa and traveling in different parts of the world, Earnest Sevier Cox moved to Richmond in 1920 and became friends with Louise Burleigh and John Powell. Although he claimed not to be a formal member of the ASCOA, he represented the group at public meetings and was a frequent participant in ASCOA affairs. He formed the White America Society, a paper organization, about the same time that Powell created the ASCOA as a membership group. Cox worked for decades to secure state and federal backing for African repatriation. Although he was successful in winning support from the Virginia General Assembly, the federal legislation he helped promote never came to fruition. Cox published copiously through his White America Society vanity press. His works include *Lincoln's Negro Policy* (1938), *Teutonic Unity* (1951), *Black Belt around the World at the High Tide of Colonialism* (1963), and numerous articles, interviews, and pamphlets. His papers are at the William R. Perkins Library, Duke University. The major biographical source is Ethel

Hedlin, "Earnest Cox and Colonization: A White Racist's Response to Black Repatriation, 1923–1966" (Ph.D. diss., Duke University, 1974). See also William Edwards, "Racial Purity in Black and White: The Case of Marcus Garvey and Earnest Cox," *Journal of Ethnic Studies* 15 (1987): 117–42. On the Virginia legislation and changing theories of race in the 1920s, see Peggy Pascoe, "Miscegenation Law, Court Cases, and Ideologies of 'Race' in Twentieth-Century America," in this volume.

5. Louise Burleigh to editor, *Boston Evening Transcript*, March 8, 1926, typescript, box 3, John Powell Papers, Alderman Library, Special Collections, University of Virginia, Charlottesville (hereafter JPP, UVA).

6. The *New York Times* article was reprinted in the *Negro World*, Feb. 20, 1926.

7. Burleigh to editor, *Boston Evening Transcript*. On Plecker's career and the activities surrounding the racial integrity actions of the ASCOA, see Richard B. Sherman, "The Last Stand: The Fight for Racial Integrity in Virginia in the 1920s," *Journal of Southern History* 56 (1988): 69–92; and J. David Smith, *The Eugenic Assault on America: Scenes in Red, White and Black* (Fairfax, Va.: George Mason University Press, 1993).

8. *Anglo-Saxon Clubs of America* (Richmond: ASCOA, [1926?]), Rare Book Collection, Alderman Library, UVA.

9. For a sympathetic overview of Burleigh and her artistic career that does not deal with her involvement in white supremacist politics, see Elizabeth Copeland Norfleet, "Louise Burleigh Powell: An A
rtist in the World of the Theatre, on Stage and behind the Scene," *Richmond Quarterly* 6 (1983): 22–27. See also Burleigh's *Community Theatre in Theory and Practice* (Boston: Little, Brown, 1917) and her papers and writings in JPP, UVA.

10. Burleigh's gender and class politics are evident in her numerous creative works, including her prison reform drama, *Punishment: A Play in Four Acts* (New York: Henry Holt, 1916), written with Edward Hale Bierstadt.

11. Statement of Louise Burleigh regarding "The House of [behind] the Cedars," n.d., ca. 1926, box 3, JPP, UVA.

12. On John Powell, see clippings and correspondence in his papers, JPP, UVA. Laudatory published profiles include Vera Palmer, "John Powell, the Composer: An Intimate Story of that Richmonder's Compositions," *Richmond* 15 (1929): 17–18, 34; Ernest Mead, "The John Powell Collection at the University of Virginia," *UVA Newsletter* 49 (Nov. 15, 1972): 9–12; and Pocahontas Wight Edmunds, *Virginians Out Front* (Richmond: Whittet and Shepperson, 1972), 336–79. For Powell's politics and the impact of his racial views on his musical career, see R. D. Ward and Edgar E. MacDonald, "John Powell: A Retrospect," pts. 1 and 2, *Richmond Literature and History Quarterly* 2 (spring 1980): 27–34; (summer 1980): 21–29. For contemporary African American perspectives on Powell, see Joel Rogers, "Virginia 'Nordic Blood Purists' Reveal Their Scheme to J. A. Rogers," *Norfolk Journal and Guide*, March 6, 1926, 1; and James Weldon Johnson, "Powell Is Asked to Define What Is 'Anglo-Saxon,' " *World* 3 (February 1924): 8. See also F. P., "John Powell, Noted Pianist-Composer, Gives Views on Negro Music, Its Use and Abuse," *Musical Courier*, May 3, 1930, 8; and Powell's program notes to "Rhapsodic Negre" (1921), box 2, JPP, UVA. Powell's racist writings are copious; see, for example, "Is White America to Become a Negroid Nation?" *Richmond Times-Dispatch*, July 22, 1923; and *The Breach in the Dike: An Analysis of the Sorrells Case Showing the Danger to Racial Integrity from Intermarriage of Whites with So-Called Indians* (Richmond: Anglo-Saxon Clubs of America, [1926?]).

13. Marion Monteval, *The Klan Inside Out* (Claremore, Okla.: Monarch, 1924), 23, Peabody Collection, Special Collections, Hampton University. See also Kathleen Blee,

Women of the Klan: Racism and Gender in the 1920s (Berkeley: University of California Press, 1991), 19–23.

14. See also *Negro World*, March 24, Nov. 17, 1923, April 19, July 12, Aug. 9, 1924.

15. *Negro World*, Dec. 22, 1923.

16. "Negroes Driven from Industrial Centres—Plan of the Future," *Negro World*, Sept. 22, 1923.

17. Garvey voiced the flip side of the ASCOA stance on black and white labor and black civil ascendancy in American society. "Negroes," Garvey said,

> get busy building a nation of your own, for neither Europe nor America will tolerate us as competitors in another half century. Let's get busy now, and, like the KKK and Knights of Columbus, fight for those ideals that are possible—not to ever see a black President, Governor, Cabinet Officer or Mayor . . . but . . . to build up Africa, where our race will have the opportunity to rise to the highest positions in society, industry and government ("The Wonders of the White Man in Building America," *Negro World*, Oct. 27, 1923).

18. On Garvey's political strategy and documentation of his period in prison, see Barbara Bair, "Garveyism," in *Encyclopedia of the American Left*, ed. Mari Jo Buhle, Paul Buhle, and Dan Georgakas (New York: Garland, 1990), 253–55; and Robert A. Hill and Barbara Bair, eds., *The Marcus Garvey and Universal Negro Improvement Association Papers*, vol. 6 (Berkeley: University of California Press, 1989).

19. See, for example, Charles Berkeley to Calvin Coolidge, March 23, 1927; Earnest Sevier Cox to Coolidge, March 23, 1927; S. R. Church to Coolidge, March 18, 1927; W. A. Plecker to Coolidge, March 19, 1927; and George N. Wise to Coolidge, March 24, 1927, all reprinted in *Marcus Garvey Papers*, ed. Hill and Bair, 6:515, 516, 525, 527–28, 529–30.

20. Amy Jacques Garvey, *Philosophy and Opinions of Marcus Garvey*, 2 vols. (reprint, New York: Atheneum, 1986). Amy Jacques Garvey was the associate editor of the *Negro World* newspaper. She introduced the "Our Women and What They Think" page and edited it from 1924 to 1927; spearheaded the UNIA's lobbying effort for the release of Garvey from prison; traveled to UNIA divisions around the United States and gave regular orations at Liberty Hall; countered the male-dominant rhetoric of the UNIA as articulated by Garvey with a woman's rights agenda, and printed feminist news of women's activities on the *Negro World* women's page; carried on UNIA affairs at Garvey's direction during the period of his imprisonment, and after his deportation in 1927 accompanied him on an organizational tour of Europe. The marriage deteriorated in the mid-1930s and the couple separated; however, as a widow Jacques Garvey continued to champion Garveyism from her home in Kingston, and she published her memoirs, *Garvey and Garveyism*, in 1963. Earnest Sevier Cox was among those to whom she sent a personal copy.

21. Amy Jacques Garvey to Earnest Sevier Cox, May 18, 1925, Earnest Sevier Cox Papers, Special Collections, William R. Perkins Library, Duke University (hereafter ESC, DU).

22. See ESC, DU, and Amy Jacques Garvey's papers in the Marcus Garvey Memorial Collection, Special Collections, Fisk University.

23. Marcus Garvey to Earnest Sevier Cox, June 2, 10, 1925, ESC, DU. In a July 25, 1925, letter to Cox, Garvey referred to the NAACP and its like as "hybrid agitators" and told him, "The White America Society, Anglo-Saxon Clubs, and Ku Klux Klan have my full sympathy in fighting for a pure white race even as we are fighting for a pure Negro race." See also Garvey to Cox, Aug. 8, 1925, praising *White America*, speaking of Amy Jacques Garvey's impending visit to Cox, and sending best wishes to Powell and Plecker for their

work on "the cause." It should be noted that this alliance did not go on without internal dissent on the part of Garveyites—groups of UNIA members in both Richmond and New York were appalled by the coalition.

24. Georgia passed its own law defining who met the criteria of being a white person and who was considered a person of color in 1927. (See *Acts and Resolutions of the General Assembly of the State of Georgia* (Atlanta: State of Georgia, 1927), 272.

25. Amy Jacques Garvey spoke in lieu of the formal introductory text prepared by Garvey, which did not arrive in New York in time for the meeting, but was published as the introduction to Powell's speech when it was reprinted in the *Negro World*, Nov. 7, 1925. Powell's speech and Marcus Garvey's introductory letter were reprinted in Garvey, *Philosophy and Opinions*, 2:338–49.

26. Cox's *White America* presented the argument that civilization exists on the basis of race and that race migrations and racial intermixing were the cause of the decline of great civilizations, and advocated racial separatism and repatriation as the only hopes for avoiding the decline of white society in America. His *Let My People Go* (Richmond: White America Society) was published in 1925.

27. Cox, *Let My People Go*, 3, 4.

28. This was to aid Cox in his efforts to have the Virginia General Assembly memorialize Congress in support of African American repatriation to Liberia. The UNIA had also been pushing for federal support of repatriation—including the gathering of grassroots petitions presented to President Calvin Coolidge in 1924. Despite Cox's many efforts, the colonization resolution was not passed in Virginia until 1936. See Garvey to Cox, Jan. 11, 1926, Feb. 4, 1926, ESC, DU.

29. *Negro World*, March 27, 1926. Both Cox and Amy Jacques Garvey remained strong supporters of repatriation, and in the 1930s Cox spearheaded Virginia backing for the Greater Liberia Bill introduced in the U.S. Senate by Theodore Bilbo of Mississippi. The bill was the occasion of another black-white coalition between a contingent of the UNIA, headed by a woman, and the white supremacist Right. See Hedlin, "Earnest Cox and Colonization"; and Michael W. Fitzgerald, " 'We Have Found a Moses': Theodore Bilbo, Black Nationalism, and the Greater Liberia Bill of 1939," *Journal of Southern History* 63 (1997): 293–320. On the Greater Liberia Bill, see also the Theodore Bilbo Collection, University of Southern Mississippi, Hattiesburg.

30. On Burleigh editing Cox's writings, see Burleigh to Powell, ca. Oct. 2, ca. Oct. 14, ca. Nov. 3, ca. Nov. 6, and Dec. 11, 1925; March 25, Dec. 14, 1926, box 3, JPP, UVA.

31. Burleigh to Powell, Aug. 16, 1922, box 3, JPP, UVA.

32. Louise Burleigh to Marcus Garvey, Sept. 17, 1925, box 3, JPP, UVA. On Sherrill's appearance, see *Richmond Planet*, Sept. 19, 1925. Sherrill and Garvey had a severe falling out in the next months, and by March 1926 there was a major split in the Garvey movement between those loyal to Garvey and Amy Jacques Garvey and those loyal to Sherrill's leadership in New York.

33. See, for example, Louise Burleigh to Marcus Garvey, Sept. 17, 1925; Marcus Garvey to John Powell, Sept. 26, 1925; and Louise Burleigh's reply to Caleb Robinson to John Powell, March 26, 1926, box 3, JPP, UVA.

34. I refer here especially to those feminist and cultural theories relating colonial geographies to the body; see, for example, Alison Blunt and Gillian Rose, eds., *Writing Women and Space: Colonial and Postcolonial Geographies* (New York: Guilford, 1994); Terry Threadgold and Anne Cranny-Francis, eds., *Feminine Masculine and Representation* (Sydney, Australia: Allen and Unwin, 1990); Andrew Parker, Mary Russo, Doris Somner, and Patricia Yeager, eds., *Nationalisms and Sexuality* (London: Routledge, 1992); and Rosalyn Duprone

and Robyn Ferrell, eds., *Cartographies: Poststructuralism and the Mapping of Bodies and Spaces* (Sydney, Australia: Allen and Unwin, 1991).

35. Garvey's 1927 poem "The Black Woman" is an ode to Africa as the Queen of Sheba. See Tony Martin, *Poetical Works of Marcus Garvey* (Dover, Mass.: Majority Press, 1983), 44–45. In "The Song of the Negro Maid" Garvey wrote of the black woman defying the white man's claim on her chastity (69). See also, for example, Amy Jacques Garvey's editorial on "the rape of their motherland" in "The White Man and Africa," *Negro World*, Oct. 25, 1924. When Liberia rejected the UNIA colonization plan, deported UNIA experts, and turned to the Firestone Rubber Company as a major investor, Garvey lambasted the betrayal as the "Rape of the Republic of Liberia," *Negro World*, Sept. 6, 1924.

36. Garvey, *Philosophy and Opinions*, 1:9. H. G. Mugdal, "Negro Race Purity," *Negro World*, July 12, 1930.

37. Anonymous letter to John Powell, March 1, 1925, box 3, JPP, UVA.

38. *Black Man* 2 (August 1937): 8. Garvey's writing on this issue in London was ironic, since he himself was accused by his wife of consorting with a white woman after he relocated the UNIA headquarters to England. On the issues of whiteness as a form of property and the systems of racialized privilege, see Cheryl L. Harris, "Whiteness as Property," *Harvard Law Review* 106 (1993): 1709–91.

39. *Newport News Daily Press*, Nov. 9, 1924.

40. Charles C. Berkeley to Calvin Coolidge, March 23, 1927, reprinted in *Marcus Garvey Papers*, ed. Hill and Bair, 6:528.

41. "Dark Cloud," typescript, box 32, JPP, UVA.

42. Burleigh to Powell, postmarked July 23, 1925, box 3, JPP, UVA.

43. Garvey, *Philosophy and Opinions*, 1:12, 13.

44. *Negro World*, Aug. 23, 1924.

45. Smith, *Eugenic Assault on America*, 54–55; see also *What Are We Striving For?* (Richmond: ASCOA, 1923), 4, and Powell's Dec. 2, 1923, *New York World* article.

Part V

Twentieth Century

Chapter Twenty

The Prison Lesbian

Race, Class, and the Construction of the Aggressive Female Homosexual, 1915–1965

Estelle B. Freedman

In the mid-twentieth century, the subject of lesbians in prison began to attract both scholarly and popular attention in the United States.[1] After World War II, criminologists depicted lesbian inmates as menacing social types. In popular culture, as well, women's prisons became synonymous with lesbianism. The emergence of the prison lesbian as a dangerous sexual category, and its changing contours over time, provide a unique historical window on the social construction of homosexual identity.

The prison lesbian also reveals a complex reconfiguration of the class and racial meanings attached to sexuality in modern America. In the early twentieth century, most prison literature equated female sex crime almost entirely with prostitution and rarely inquired into the homosexual activities of delinquent women. As criminologist Charles A. Ford puzzled in 1929, despite widespread evidence of lesbian relationships within women's reformatories, very few studies had been written about the subject. When authors did mention homosexuality, they usually identified black women as lesbian aggressors and white women as temporary partners. By the 1960s, psychologists and criminologists had become intrigued with lesbianism in prison, publishing books and articles on the subject and suggesting that homosexuals "present the greatest sexual problem" in women's prisons. Unlike the earlier literature, the later studies extended the lesbian label to white women, emphasizing the threat of their aggressive homosexuality.[2]

The following exploration, first of the criminological literature and then of the records of the Massachusetts Reformatory for Women, analyzes these simultaneous shifts in the conception of the prison lesbian. From an initial association with African American women, the image of the aggressive female homosexual extended after World War II to include white working-class prisoners as well. At the same time, greater public scrutiny of prison lesbianism, and concern about its "contaminating" effect on the society at large, intensified the process of labeling female homosexuality in women's prisons and beyond their walls.

*

A small body of historical literature provides a context for investigating the prison lesbian. Alongside earlier studies of middle-class women's romantic friendships and their medical reclassification as perversion in the twentieth century, a rudimentary narrative of working-class lesbian identity and community is now emerging. In brief, it suggests that in industrializing America, economic necessity led some working-class women to "pass" as men and sometimes marry other women; in the early twentieth century, some single working-class women pooled resources and lived together as couples in urban, furnished-room districts. For African American women, the Harlem Renaissance fostered a sexually experimental subculture that offered a measure of tolerance for homosexual relationships. During World War II, women's workforce and military participation intensified a process of homosexual community formation. Even in the postwar decade, when the hostile cold war climate condemned homosexuals as subversive, a public, working-class lesbian bar culture became increasingly visible.[3]

The prison system provides another location for understanding not only working-class lesbian history but also the importance of race and class relations within this history. By the 1920s, almost every state and the federal government had established a separate adult women's reformatory.[4] The majority of inmates came from working-class backgrounds and were often daughters of immigrants; only a small minority were African American.[5] Most of the reformatory inmates had been sentenced for "crimes against public order," including drunkenness, vagrancy, and a variety of prostitution-related offenses once labeled "crimes against chastity." Many of the educated and professional women who worked in the reformatories sought to "uplift" the sexual morality of female inmates. Until the 1940s, however, women's prison authorities concentrated on diverting inmates from *heterosexual* acts prohibited by law—especially prostitution. They rarely mentioned lesbianism as a problem, and most women's prison officials ignored evidence of homosexuality among inmates. This lack of interest contrasted with the approach of administrators of men's prisons, who frequently labeled and punished homosexuality.[6]

The one exception to the disavowal of lesbianism in women's prisons highlights the racial construction of the aggressive female homosexual in the early twentieth century. Beginning in 1913, criminologists, psychologists, and state officials denounced one form of lesbian relationship—cross-race romances between black and white inmates—for disrupting prison discipline. These accounts usually represented African American women prisoners as masculine or aggressive and their white lovers as "normal" feminine women who would return to heterosexual relations upon release from prison. The earliest criminological study of lesbianism in prison described the practice of "nigger loving" by young white women committed to reformatories. Author Margaret Otis explained that "the love of 'niggers' " had become a tradition in which black inmates sent courtship notes to incoming white inmates. The ensuing relationships ranged from the casual to those of an "intensely sexual nature." Despite this intensity, Otis claimed, once released the white girls rarely had contact with "the colored race," nor, presumably, with women lovers.[7]

Observations of interracial lesbianism recurred within women's prisons over the following decades. An officer at the New York State Reformatory for Women at

Bedford Hills testified in 1915 that "the colored girls are extremely attractive to certain white girls." Another official explained that these relationships had existed since the founding of the reformatory in the nineteenth century, but recent over-crowding had made them more frequent. Blaming unrest at the reformatory on these liaisons, an investigative committee recommended the segregation of black inmates at Bedford Hills. Its rationale echoed the sexual fears that underlay Jim Crow institutions in the South. The committee held that segregation was necessary not simply "because of the color line" but because "the most undesirable sex rela-tions grow out of this mingling of the two races." Even though these homosexual relationships did not lead to the kind of amalgamation most feared by white su-premacists, namely, mixed-race offspring, the thought that white women would reject heterosexuality entirely—and thus reject their racial duty to reproduce—was intolerable. Even segregation, however, did not discourage interracial homosexual unions or lessen the mythology surrounding black women's sexual aggression. Black-white relationships persisted noticeably in New York prisons, for example, fifteen years after the Bedford Hills investigation.[8]

In writing about interracial lesbian relationships, criminologists emphasized the ways that race substituted for gender in women's prisons. Black women took the role of "husbands," white women of "wives" in the New York reformatory Ford studied in the 1920s. Samuel Kahn later quoted a New York City inmate who claimed, "There are more colored daddies and more white mamas" in the city jails. In 1943 one scholar reasoned that Negroes were sexually attractive to whites "be-cause the White girls interpret the Negro aggression and dominance as 'maleness' " and because the blacks' "uninhibited emotional expressions and some of their phys-ical characteristics (dark skin) seem to enhance the sex attraction of the Negro girls."[9] In a 1941 fictional portrayal of a segregated women's reformatory in the South, novelist Felice Swados incorporated the stereotype of black lesbian aggres-sion. Inmate lore described "a cute blonde with dimples" who "got to going around with niggers." The woman wound up in the hospital after "a great big black" woman "got too hot. Went crazy. Just tore her insides out."[10]

Explanations of interracial attractions in terms of "male" aggression by black women mirrored, in part, the then-dominant theories of homosexuality as a form of gender inversion.[11] At the same time, assigning the male aggressor role to black women and preserving a semblance of femininity for their white partners racialized the sexual pathology of inversion. In this interpretation, white women were not really lesbians, for they were attracted to men, for whom black women temporarily substituted. Thus, the prison literature racialized both lesbianism and butch/femme roles, implicitly blaming black women for sexual aggression and, indeed, homosex-uality by associating them with a male role.

Whether or not these explanations accurately reflected women inmates' own erotic systems, the official interpretations reinforced long-standing associations among race, sexuality, and gender roles. In the nineteenth century, for example, medical authorities had regarded African women's genitals as pathological and, according to Sander Gilman, they even associated "the concupiscence of the black" with "the sexuality of the lesbian." Because lesbian then connoted both maleness and a lack of feminine virtue, the label effectively denied gender privileges to black women. Like the cultural assignment of strong, even insatiable, sexual desire to African American women, the identification of black women as aggressive butch lesbians rested on a denial of their womanhood.[12]

Similarly, twentieth-century criminologists often correlated race, sexual deviance, and aggression. Theories of black women's greater criminality rested in part on a model of sexual inversion, in which black women more easily engaged in "male" aggressive behaviors. As one criminal psychiatrist explained in 1942, "colored females" predominated among aggressive women criminals, because the "accepted ideological codes of Harlem" condoned violence on their parts, especially if related to a love triangle. The writer identified one other pattern of aggressive female felonies, which he labeled "lesbian homicides." Presumably referring to black or white women, in these cases "murder obviously afforded an unconscious destruction of the murderess' own homosexual cravings." Another study of working-class black women suggested that homosexuality was prevalent among black prostitutes because both prostitution and homosexuality stemmed from a "fundamental inability" to accept the "feminine role."[13]

White women clearly participated in lesbian relations in prisons and no doubt with white as well as black partners. Yet the early twentieth-century criminological literature on white women's sexuality invariably discussed prostitution, not homosexuality. Even as psychoanalytic concepts filtered into American criminology, it was white women's heterosexual deviance that attracted attention. As historian Elizabeth Lunbeck has shown, in the early twentieth century, the new diagnosis of sexual psychopathy—a term implying uncontrollable libidinal instinct that would later become a code for male homosexuality—at first applied to *heterosexually* active white women. Because psychologists presumed that black women were naturally promiscuous, they did not label them as diseased psychopaths.[14] Throughout the 1920s and 1930s, the growing literature on psychopathic crime rarely addressed lesbianism. A 1934 study of psychopathic women, for example, found that only a few cases could be classified as homosexual. As late as 1941 one criminologist argued that juvenile homosexuality was more common among male than female offenders, while "[h]eterosexual delinquency is by far the girl's premier offence." Even as a "lesbian taboo" within marital advice literature warned middle-class women to remain heterosexual or risk becoming abnormal deviants, few writers portrayed white lesbians as dangerous criminals.[15]

The paucity of either scholarly or popular attention to lesbianism among women in prison did not necessarily reflect the extent of the practice between 1915 and 1940. The few criminologists who did observe women's relationships in prison documented a sexually active and often racially constructed lesbian subculture. In the New York City House of Detention, for example, women prisoners engaged in "bull diking," and their love affairs included regular tribadism. At other institutions, "wives" and "husbands" found ways to send sexually explicit love letters to each other. "You can take my tie/You can take my collor/But I'll jazze you/'Till you holler," one black husband wrote to "My dearest Wife Gloria," who responded, "Sugar dady if I could sleep with you for one little night, I would show you how much I hon[es]tly and truly I love you." Other inmates scratched their "friend's" initials on their skin and smuggled contraband presents in their bras. The administrator of one reform school recalled that white girls aggressively pursued black girls, a pattern rarely reported in the criminological literature.[16]

For the most part, women's prison administrators either tolerated these lesbian relationships or denied their existence. When physician Samuel Kahn published the first book-length study of prison homosexuality in 1937 (based on research conducted a decade earlier), he seemed dismayed to report that at the New York City Women's Workhouse, in contrast to the men's division, "the homosexuals have been unclassified and are not segregated . . . so that they all mingle freely with the other inmates." Even though Kahn sought out lesbians to interview, neither the woman warden nor the male priests at the workhouse were willing to identify inmates as homosexuals. In *Five Hundred Delinquent Women*, the classic 1934 study of women prisoners conducted at the Massachusetts women's reformatory, criminologists Sheldon Glueck and Eleanor Glueck never referred to lesbianism.[17]

Women's prison administrators may have been reluctant to call attention to the subject of homosexuality because many of them were single professional women who maintained close personal bonds with other women and could be vulnerable to charges of lesbianism. According to the superintendent of several reform schools for girls, in the 1920s women prison workers recognized the problem of homosexuality but never openly talked about it. One superintendent who lectured inmates of a girls' reformatory about the dangers of homosexuality was pressured into resigning in 1931, in part because she addressed such an "embarrassing subject" and in part because she accused both staff members and local businesswomen of "immoral relationships." In 1931 officials preferred to be silent about these possibilities for lesbianism rather than to call attention to them.[18]

The disinclination to acknowledge lesbianism in prison lasted until the 1940s, when both prison administrators and criminologists began to express more concern about female homosexuality. The reasons for a gradual shift in awareness included increased arrests for prostitution during World War II and consequent prison overcrowding. Some prostitutes were also lesbians, while the doubling up of women in cells may have intensified lesbian activity. A growing lesbian subculture centered around predominantly white working-class bars may have heightened identity for some women who wound up in jails and prisons. Aside from any actual increase in lesbian activity in prison, fears about the dangers of female sexual expression escalated during wartime, especially targeting white women as the purveyors of venereal disease to soldiers or as seductive saboteurs. It was in this context that female homosexuality in general, and among white women in prisons, came under closer scrutiny.

A new consciousness about prison lesbianism appeared, for example, among the superintendents of women's institutions, who met annually to discuss common problems. Several of them had acknowledged black-white sexual liaisons in institutions previously, but for the most part the superintendents had been concerned about heterosexual irregularities among inmates. Only during the 1940s did they introduce the topic of how to manage homosexual relationships in institutions. At one annual conference, for example, they questioned their guest speaker, Margaret Mead, about "how much we should worry about homosexuality." Although Mead advised them to "keep it down as much as possible," the anthropologist—who had herself been sexually involved with women—also argued that female homosexuality was much less socially dangerous than male homosexuality because women tended toward "more or less permanent relationship[s] in which one person looks after the welfare of the other, makes them silk underwear, etc. The male homo-sexuality, on the other hand, is exploitive and promiscuous—it is not a paired sexuality." Mead believed that women's relatively benign institutional homosexuality was a temporary substitute for heterosexual relations. Unlike earlier writers, however, she did not identify any racial patterns in lesbian role playing. Her tolerant attitude, echoed by other speakers, counseled adequate recreation and social stimulation as diversions from homosexuality in prison.[19]

In the post-war decade, however, the relative tolerance that had characterized the treatment of prison lesbianism gradually gave way to greater surveillance and ultimately to condemnation. The shift from lack of interest to fascination with the prison lesbian can be seen within U.S. popular and political culture shortly after World War II. In the 1950s, *True Confessions* magazine sensationalized accounts of "love-starved girls in reform school," while pulp novels incorporated women's prison seduction scenes. Hollywood produced a series of women's prison films, replete with lesbian innuendo. In contrast to the earliest women's prison films, in which the lesbian was portrayed as comic and benign, a dangerously aggressive lesbian criminal now threatened the innocence of young women, as in the 1950 film *Caged*. At the same time, politicians began to target "aggressive female homosexuals" in prison as a serious threat to moral order. During the 1950s they invoked images of lesbians in prison as part of a larger cold war campaign to discredit liberal reformers for being soft on perversion, as on communism.[20] By the late 1950s women who formed homosexual relationships in prison had become stock cultural characters associated with threats to sexual and social order. At the same time, black women ceased to be the primary suspects as prison lesbians. Class marking seemed to be replacing earlier race marking, making both black and white working-class women more vulnerable to charges of deviance, while still exempting middle-class women. By the 1960s the criminological literature no longer relied on an exclusively racial definition of lesbians and emphasized the social threat of white lesbian activity.

These changes coincided with a larger cultural emphasis on both the power of female sexuality and the need to contain it within domestic relationships among white and middle-class Americans. Reflecting the rhetoric of cold war America, which sought to identify internal enemies who threatened social order, the post-war clinical literature on lesbianism elaborated on the image of the aggressive female homosexual, but it rarely targeted black women. The new stereotype drew upon earlier concepts of the male sexual psychopath, whose uncontrolled, often violent sexuality threatened to disrupt social order. In contrast to earlier studies that had posited little relationship between psychopathy and lesbianism, writers now suggested "the possibly greater tendency of the [female] psychopaths to engage in sex acts with other girls." New psychoanalytic theories also contributed to the image of a dangerous, promiscuous lesbian. One writer, for example, differentiated between those female homosexuals who simply preferred the company of women and a rarer group containing "the more dangerous type—the promiscuous Lesbian who passing quickly and lightly from affair to affair, usually with physical relations, may cause great harm and unhappiness." Just as the male psychopath was invariably portrayed as white, and often middle-class, the dangerous lesbian was no longer marked as a racial minority but appeared to be white, although usually working-class.[21]

Along with serious psychological studies, pseudoscientific works of the 1950s conflated the lesbian and the woman criminal. In her study of post-war lesbian imagery, historian Donna Penn has summarized the portrayals of the lesbian found in popular works, such as Frank Caprio's *Female Homosexuality*, as the "promiscuous, oversexed, conquering, aggressive dyke who exercised masculine prerogative in the sexual arena." Like the prostitute, the lesbian now spread moral contagion. In Penn's view, the demonization of the sinister, working-class lesbian helped shift the meaning of female homosexuality away from the "Boston marriages" and innocent romantic friendships of middle-class women.[22]

The prison literature confirms Penn's analysis but suggests a racial, as well as class, realignment in the demonology of lesbianism. The dangerous lesbian had moved away from a racially specified aggressive invert. Even though interracial unions continued to characterize women's prison life, by the 1950s it was the homosexuality of white women prisoners that became the object of intense scrutiny. Larger social trends contributed to this racial shift, including the gradual sexualization of white women in popular culture and the emergence of visible white, working-class lesbian institutions in the post-war period—such as the bar culture studied by Madeline Davis and Elizabeth Lapovsky Kennedy.[23] The prison lesbian now appeared not primarily as an African American but more typically as a white woman, albeit one who may have sexually crossed a racial boundary in the process of becoming homosexual. Of either race, she became the "unnatural woman" personified, a threat to other inmates and to women outside the prison. If earlier tolerance had rested on an assumption of the natural depravity, or inherent sexual inversion, of black women, it is not surprising that the revelation of white women's lesbianism in prison would sound an alert, a warning about the potential degeneration of theoretically "true" womanhood. Indeed, by the mid-1950s institutional tolerance gave way to a call to "sort out the real homosexual" in prison through psychological testing and to "segregate those who show strong homosexual inclinations," with no reference to race.[24]

A good example of the new attitude toward prison lesbianism appeared in a 1956 popular book written by Katharine Sullivan, a conservative member of the Massachusetts parole board. According to Sullivan, "No age or race is immune to the temptations of homosexuality in prisons." Moreover, the prison lesbians she described had violent, almost animalistic, characters. Jealousies led to "hand-to-hand fights or even free-for-alls." If separated from a lover, Sullivan warned, the surviving partner "may suffer an acute attack of homosexual panic, with violent screaming and frothing at the mouth, followed by a period of wan anxiety."[25]

In contrast to earlier writers, Sullivan firmly believed that once a woman engaged in homosexual acts in prison she quickly became "addicted" and built her life around the practice after release. In one example, a young white parolee named Mary learned about the "doll racket" in prison and now wanted nothing to do with men. Visited on parole, she sported a new boyish haircut, no makeup, wore boys' clothes, and, significantly, had set up a household with two black women. Unlike the "nigger lovers" described by Otis in 1913, who rejected interracial relations after release, Mary continued to associate with black women on the outside. She even adopted a butch identity that had been racially specific to black women in the past. Earlier racial stereotypes continued to operate as well. Sullivan depicted Mary's black roommates as the antithesis of natural women: they were "large," "rangy," and sloppily dressed in jeans and T-shirts. Mary, she implied, had descended into an interracial netherworld from which she would emerge an addicted lesbian. Indeed, Mary declared that when she turned twenty-one she intended to "leave home and go to live permanently in one of the big cities in America, where Lesbians flourish." Sullivan clearly wished to prevent white women like Mary from being exposed to homosexuality in prison; she seemed much less concerned about the black women who adopted male styles.[26]

By the time the prison lesbian became the subject of extensive academic inquiry in the 1960s, race had practically disappeared from the scholarly research agenda. Sociological accounts of the "problem" of the prison lesbian described widespread homosexuality in women's institutions and focused on the butch-femme role system that organized prison life, but like other supposedly "race-blind" works of the period, they evaded race, even when it influenced their findings.[27] The two classic case studies that appeared in the 1960s—David A. Ward and Gene G. Kassebaum's *Women's Prison: Sex and Social Structure* and Rose Giallombardo's *Society of Women: A Study of a Women's Prison*—avoid mentioning race in their descriptions of prison social life and sexual roles. Giallombardo's discussion of fictive marriage patterns among women prisoners never referred to race, even though her kinship diagrams, read closely, reveal that the majority of "marriages" were interracial.[28] In short, race may have continued to play a role in the erotic life of prisoners, but observers presented a lesbian world that, lacking racial markers, appeared to be entirely white.[29]

The racial shift in the construction of the prison lesbian, taken together with other evidence of postwar moral panics, suggests deep-seated cultural anxieties about the instability of white heterosexuality. Although focused on working-class women who wound up in prison, and who were forming a lesbian subculture in various cities, the discourse reached a broader public. Literary critic Lynda Hart has argued that the historical construction of the lesbian has often projected a "secret" sexual identity on to working-class women, as well as women of color, while it simultaneously speaks loudly to fears about the sexuality of middle- and upper-class women. In post-war America, as popular and commercial culture elaborated upon white women's sexual availability, and when effective medical treatment of venereal disease made prostitutes seem less threatening than in the past, several new bound aries appeared to help shore up white, marital heterosexuality. The outlaws included the frigid career woman, the black welfare mother, and the prison lesbian.[30]

A case study of the Massachusetts Reformatory for Women further illustrates both the changing racial construction of the aggressive female homosexual and the shift from a period of institutional denial or tolerance to one of labeling and strict surveillance. The reformatory, founded in 1877, typically housed between three hundred and four hundred adult female prisoners, the vast majority of whom served two-to-five-year terms for minor offenses against public order, such as drunkenness or prostitution (often coded as vagrancy or "lewdness"). As in most northern reformatories, until the 1960s the population was overwhelmingly white. The institution had a scattered history of liberal administrations aimed at uplifting so-called fallen women. Miriam Van Waters, who became the reformatory superintendent in 1932, expanded on this mission by providing education, social welfare services, psychiatric counseling, and work opportunities outside prison.

As in other institutions, the earliest references to lesbian relations at the Massachusetts reformatory noted attractions between white and black inmates. In the 1930s, when Van Waters detected "black-white manifestation of homosexuality," she followed the advice of writers such as Charles Ford and attempted to divert the black inmates by "stressing their prestige in Dramatics, Spirituals, [and] Orchestra." Other staff members also learned of romantic liaisons between inmates during the 1930s. One officer informed Van Waters of inmate gossip about the "doll" situation—the prison code for lesbian—and noted "the fuss the white girls make over the colored girls." A few years later, when Van Waters noted no "overt white-white" relationships, she identified several interracial couples.[31]

Van Waters and her staff distinguished between true homosexuality and temporary attractions. They believed the former could be detected by the Rorshach test; in the absence of such "positive evidence" they assumed that only the boredom of prison routine stimulated unnatural interest in same-sex relationships. An active program of classes and clubs attempted to channel the energies of both black and white prisoners into what the staff considered healthier recreations. Nonetheless, underground homosexual unions survived. Newcomers quickly learned about "dolls," and love letters circulated among inmates. In 1938, for example, when an inmate tried to use her fear of sexual advances to convince the parole board to release her from the reformatory, she submitted love letters from other women to support her case. In addition, officers occasionally discovered two women in bed together, a problem that escalated during World War II, when increased prison commitments led to overcrowding.[32]

Prison records also reveal contradictory attitudes toward lesbian relationships on the part of reformatory and court officials. The former were reluctant to label women as homosexuals, while the latter were willing to impose harsh penalties for openly lesbian relationships. The case of Marie LeBlanc, a white woman of French Canadian background, illustrates psychiatric tolerance within the institution and the punitive response of parole boards and courts.[33] LeBlanc had become sexually involved with Eleanor Harris, another white inmate. The prison psychiatrist who "treated" her saw no reason not to recommend her for parole. When parole agents learned that, after release, LeBlanc had been sleeping with Eleanor Harris and her husband, they revoked LeBlanc's parole "for the best interests of herself and the community." She returned to prison for a year, then left on parole again. This time she reportedly became involved with another former inmate, Jane MacGregor. The court convicted LeBlanc of "Open and Gross Lewdness" and sentenced her to another two years in the reformatory because of her lesbian relationship.[34]

Jane MacGregor's records further highlight the conflicting policies toward lesbianism. According to a reformatory psychiatrist, MacGregor had "no preference" between "hetero- and homosexual experience." Because she was "not the aggressive one" in the latter, he did not consider her a true lesbian. Even after officers discovered MacGregor in bed with another inmate, the psychiatrist emphasized her need for mother love and recommended, "It is far better to have some of these intense feelings directed toward an officer where the activity can be controlled than toward another student [inmate]." Only after MacGregor repeatedly appeared in bed with other women did prison officials fear that she was "in danger of becoming a true homosexual." Despite efforts to divert her interests in women into athletics and the care of animals (to "help take care of her need to demonstrate affection"), the psychiatrist eventually concluded that MacGregor was in fact "strongly homosexual." Nonetheless, he supported her request for parole. The more conservative parole board revoked her release, explaining that she "engaged in homosexual activities to such an extent that she is unable to adjust in employment."[35]

The inmates clearly knew that reformatory officials were reluctant to label same-sex relations, as the case of Barbara Jones illustrates. A white woman, Jones had been committed to prison for idle and disorderly conduct, which may have meant prostitution. At the reformatory she tended to pair off with a "colored inmate," laboring to maintain the relationship by "coveting [sic] favor with small gifts." The staff tried to discourage the pairing by transferring Jones to a living division apart from her friend. Annoyed by the move, Jones wrote to a staff member with the expectation of tolerance and understanding: "You told me one time if I didn't want people to complain to you about my actions I shouldn't make them so obvious," she explained. "I didn't this time. It was purely what people thought. True, I was carrying on an affair, but I certainly wasn't loud about it."[36]

The relative tolerance toward homosexuality among staff at the Massachusetts Reformatory for Women could not survive long after World War II. Just as the psychological and popular literature began to emphasize a sinister, even predatory, lesbian, conservative Massachusetts politicians seized on the prison lesbian to discredit the unusually liberal reformatory administration. The investigation of an inmate suicide in 1947 led to reports of a "doll racket" at the reformatory, giving the Massachusetts Department of Corrections an opportunity to launch a series of probes of Superintendent Van Waters's administration. Among their complaints they charged that "many of the inmates receiving special favors are 'known' homosexuals or dangerous psychopaths." Although Van Waters denied the charges, the politicians exploited them in the press, using prison lesbianism as a sensational-istic wedge with which to expose Van Waters's liberal attitudes toward rehabilita-tion.

Like the federal officials who soon outlawed the employment of homosexuals on the grounds that they spread corruption in the government, Massachusetts officials claimed that homosexuals corrupted the young women of the state. Instead of pros-titution, which had so disturbed an earlier generation of Americans, homosexuality now represented the great destroyer of young women's virtue. As Senator Michael LoPresti told the press, "Supt. Van Waters' administration of the Women's Refor-matory has been more damaging to the morals and mental health of young girls than has the operation of White Slavery in all New England over the same period of time."[37] In 1949, when the commissioner of corrections dismissed Van Waters from office, he charged

> That you have known of and failed to prevent the continuance of, or failed to know and recognize that an unwholesome relationship has existed between inmates of the Reformatory for Women which is called the "doll racket" by inmates and some officer personnel; the terms "stud" and "queen" are used with implied meanings, and such association has resulted in "crushes," "courtships," and homosexual practises [sic] among the inmates in the Reformatory.[38]

Although the grounds for dismissal included Van Waters's allowing inmates to work for pay outside of the institution and hiring former inmates on the reforma-tory staff, the homosexual motif ran throughout the charges, fueling sensational newspaper coverage of the issue.

During several months of public hearings, Van Waters successfully defended her policies, in part by minimizing the existence of homosexuality at the reformatory, in part by deferring to psychiatric authorities when asked about homosexual ten-dencies among inmates. Typical of her strategic evasion was this response to hostile interrogation about whether certain acts or personal styles revealed homosexual tendencies:

> That, sir, is so distinctly a medical and technical question that I would not presume to answer it. One of the first things we are taught is that a homosexual tendency must be distinguished from a homosexual act. A homosexual tendency may be completely re-pressed and turned into a variety of other expressions, including a great aversion to emotion.

By invoking the power of psychiatry, Van Waters acknowledged the shifting mean-ing of homosexuality, from an act to an identity and from a crime to a mental disorder. At the same time, she tried to avoid a labeling process that would mark close friends, mannish women, and those who had crushes on other inmates as confirmed homosexuals. Responding to further questions, she explained that a woman's mannish dress and preference for men's jobs resulted from early childhood neglect, not homosexual desire.[39]

Whether consciously or not, Van Waters's testimony represented a form of resis-tance to the use of accusations of homosexuality to discredit nonconforming women. Rather than sacrifice some "mannish" women or close female friends by calling them either homosexuals, latent homosexuals, or women with homosexual tendencies, she firmly opposed labeling. At the same time, like psychologists of the period, she did so by accepting a definition of true homosexuality as a pathology.

When the superintendent evaded the labeling of homosexuality, she also side-stepped implicit questions about her own sexual identity. In her personal life, Van Waters had refused to label her love for a woman as a form of homosexuality, despite her long-term romantic partnership with Geraldine Thompson, who was known publicly only as a wealthy benefactor and a supporter of Van Waters's reforms. So too she hesitated to assume that other women who appeared to fit the definition really were homosexuals, a term she reserved for women's pathological, although curable, sexual aggression toward other women.[40]

In March 1949 a special panel appointed by the governor exonerated Van Waters of all charges and reinstated her as superintendent. During the two years of publicity concerning the "doll racket" at Framingham, however, the image of the homosexual woman criminal had been widely disseminated by both local and national media coverage of the Van Waters hearings. In the aftermath of the Van Waters case, prison lesbianism came under greater scrutiny, with white as well as black women subject to the charge. A few months after the hearings, for instance, the Massachusetts Parole Board taunted a white woman they suspected of homosexuality, interrogating her about whether she ought to have a sex-change operation because of her "boyish swagger."[41] In addition, popular media further stereotyped inmates as lesbians. The Van Waters case directly inspired *Caged*, the prototypical women's prison film, in which older, aggressive lesbians compete for access to an innocent young inmate. The lurid *True Confessions* tales of reform school lesbians also followed in the wake of the Van Waters case.

The image of the "aggressive homosexual," along with greater surveillance by the Massachusetts Department of Corrections and the public, helped erode the earlier tolerance toward prison lesbianism among Framingham staff. In the 1950s, despite Superintendent Van Waters's continuing belief that healthy recreation could divert women from situational homosexuality, the reformatory capitulated to the antihomosexual climate by attempting to transfer lesbians out of the institution. Previously, even evidence of homosexual relations did not disqualify an inmate as a candidate for parole. Now, however, when a white woman on parole "made a connection with a married woman with the result that the woman left her husband," Van Waters's staff refused to keep her at the reformatory. Labeled "hard core," these women were now transferred to county jails to serve their additional terms without benefit of reformatory programs.[42]

These efforts to weed out hard-core lesbians did not protect the Massachusetts Reformatory for Women from further political scrutiny. In July 1957 an escapee fighting extradition claimed that alcohol, drugs, and homosexuality made her afraid to return to the reformatory. Newspapers had a field day with the ensuing investigation. "Charge Sex Fiends, Boozers Run Wild in Women's Prison" and "Girl Inmates 'Wed' in Mock Prison Rites," the headlines read. A committee chaired by a conservative woman legislator accused "aggressive homosexuals" of "escaping, assaulting officers and practicing unnatural acts!" The committee recommended greater security as well as the segregation of "aggressive homosexuals and belligerent non-conformists." Even though such activity was "not rampant" at the reformatory, the legislators argued that the "real factor to be considered here" was "not the extent but the fact that it appears to have been overlooked." They stated that "there have been mock marriages; there have been unnatural acts witnessed and reported by members of the staff, and there have been numerous indications of parolees carrying this type of activity outside the institution in association with others who had never participated in such actions before."[43] Because these lesbians—significantly unidentified by race—were believed to corrupt other inmates and spread homosexual contagion into the broader society, officials now called for sexual, rather than racial, segregation. By 1959, after Van Waters had retired, the Massachusetts Reformatory for Women instituted a lecture on sexuality for young inmates in which a psychiatrist warned them away from experimenting with lesbianism, because "[i]t is a sick way of life" and one that could never lead to happiness.[44]

As in the larger society, in which McCarthy-era campaigns identified homosexuals as the source of communist subversion and moral ruin, so too in the microcosm of the women's prison the lesbian became a scapegoat for the demise of institutional order and gender propriety. The very term "women's prison" would long evoke an image of lesbian aggression. The association of lesbianism and criminality may have served as a warning to women who might be tempted to acknowledge their homosexual desires. To do so meant, in part, to become part of a criminal underworld, to lose both class and, for white women, race privilege, to descend into an underworld vulnerable to the control of police and parole agents. The prison lesbian thus represented an inverse of the ideal white woman of the 1950s, the "reprivatized" suburban housewife who served rather than challenged men.[45]

The shifting racial construction of the prison lesbian, in which the role of sexual aggressor extended from black to all working-class inmates, raises larger historical questions about race and sexuality. Although the sources reveal little about how either black or white lesbians constructed their own identities, or about racial distinctions in the treatment of lesbians in prison, they do point toward a fluidity in the racial construction of sexual boundaries. After the 1940s, prostitution and promiscuity seemed less problematic for white working-class women than they had before; white unwed mothers, for example, could now be forgiven and "cured." In contrast, homosexuality among white working-class women loomed larger as a threat to social order, as evidenced by the negative portrayals of bar dykes, lesbian athletes, and prison lesbians. At the same time, for working-class black women, homosexual aggression now attracted less attention than did the newly emergent image of the black unwed mother on welfare. Seen together, the literature on deviance reacted against both white women's rejection of reproductive heterosexuality (lesbianism) and black women's "excessive" reproductive activity (illegitimacy).[46]

Specific historical contexts in the post-war period can help explain this shift, including the development of penicillin, which lessened fears about prostitutes, and the increased social costs of out-of-wedlock births, in light of the establishment of government aid to dependent children. The pattern of reaction, however, can be found much earlier in American history, especially during the race suicide scare at the turn of the twentieth century, when mass immigration triggered admonitions to middle-class white women to bear children lest the foreign-born dominate American society. Similarly, the shifting sexual and racial demonizations during the 1940s responded in part to the continued northern migration of blacks. In addition, wartime economic opportunities may have contributed to fears about women usurping male prerogatives, so that the aggressive white lesbian became a symbol of excessive female independence.

The representation of the prison lesbian also suggests how class became a clearer marker of sexual identity. Middle-class women who resisted the labeling of lesbianism—as did Miriam Van Waters—may have avoided social stigma for themselves and protected some of the women under their supervision. Nonetheless, the image of the aggressive female homosexual made these reformers vulnerable to political attacks that eventually weakened their moral authority and lessened their ability to protect working-class lesbians in prison. At the same time, the emergence of the malignant image of the criminal lesbian widened the class gulfs among women. Many white women who loved other women gladly claimed their race and class privilege by disassociating themselves from a category that included bar lesbians and criminals. In the process, these middle-class women often denied their own desires or insured their own social isolation. For those who did acknowledge their lesbianism, maintaining middle-class status meant rejecting any affiliation with working-class lesbians and with the butch-femme roles that had been pathologized by the 1950s.[47]

It was the prison lesbian, however, who paid the highest price for the greater cultural recognition of women's sexual desires and the weakening of middle-class women's public authority. Once ignored or tolerated, the prison lesbian became a symbol of social disorder, not unlike the prostitute of an earlier period. Even as subsequent generations of middle-class women first rejected the models of criminality and sickness in favor of lesbian feminism, and more recently have elaborated a subversive "outlaw" identity, women in prison have continued to suffer from the older cultural construction. Prison lesbians, a 1987 study proclaimed, are "more criminalistic, more feministic and more aggressive" than other prisoners. These stereotypes help explain why lesbians serve longer terms than nonlesbians and why prison officials continue to treat lesbians more harshly than other women. The greater vulnerability of prison lesbians is suggested, as well, by the fact that implications of lesbianism have been part of the prosecution strategy in 40 percent of the cases of women currently awaiting execution in the United States.[48] The serious consequences of the persistent conflation of lesbianism and aggressive criminality are rarely addressed by either contemporary feminists or penologists, for working-class women in prison remain largely invisible in critiques of sexual injustice. Ignoring the historical construction of the aggressive female homosexual, however, allows the specter of the prison lesbian to continue to police class and sexual boundaries, both inside and outside of prison walls.

NOTES

I am grateful to Martha Mabie for research assistance and to Allan Berube, Susan K. Cahn, John D'Emilio, Sharon Holland, Susan Krieger, Elaine Tyler May, Joanne Meyerowitz, Peggy Pascoe, Leila Rupp, and Nancy Stoller for their extremely useful comments on earlier versions of this essay.

1. Although courts have rarely sentenced women to prison for homosexual acts, lesbianism has long been associated with both crime and insanity. In the nineteenth century, women who passed as men were sometimes arrested and jailed, but it was their defiance of gender roles rather than sexual acts that labeled them criminals. See San Francisco Lesbian and Gay History Project, " 'She Even Chewed Tobacco': A Pictorial Narrative of Passing Women in America," in *Hidden from History: Reclaiming the Gay and Lesbian Past,* ed. Martin Bauml Duberman, Martha Vicinus, and George Chauncey, Jr. (New York: New American Library, 1989), 183–94. Lesbians have often been institutionalized in mental hospitals and sometimes in reform schools. For an example of a young woman sent to reform school because she was a lesbian, see Madeline Davis and Elizabeth Lapovsky Kennedy, *Boots of Leather, Slippers of Gold: The History of a Lesbian Community* (New York: Routledge, 1993), 59. On the historical association between female criminality, insanity, and lesbianism, see Lynda Hart, *Fatal Women: Lesbian Sexuality and the Mark of Aggression* (Princeton: Princeton University Press, 1994), esp. 4–28. Hart argues that the incidence of imprisonment for lesbianism has been masked because crimes labeled "lewdness" or prostitution in fact referred to lesbianism. On this point, see Ruthann Robson, *Lesbian (Out)law: Survival under the Rule of Law* (Ithaca, N.Y.: Firebrand Books, 1992). On associations between women criminals, insanity, gender inversion, and lesbianism in specific historical cases, see Lisa Duggan, "The Trials of Alice Mitchell: Sensationalism, Sexology, and the Lesbian Subject in Turn-of-the-Century America," *Signs* 18 (summer 1993): 791–814; and Claire Bond Potter, " 'I'll Go the Limit and Then Some': Gun Molls, Desire, and Danger in the 1930s," *Feminist Studies* 21 (spring 1995): 46.

2. Charles A. Ford, "Homosexual Practices of Institutionalized Females," *Journal of Abnormal Psychology* 23 (January-March 1929): 442; Elizabeth M. Kates, "Sexual Problems in Women's Institutions," *Journal of Social Therapy* 1 (October 1955): 187. Other later studies include Mary A. Kopp, "A Study of Anomia and Homosexuality in Delinquent Adolescent Girls" (Ph.D. diss., St. Louis University, 1960); James Stephen Howard, "Determinants of Sex-Role Identifications of Homosexual Female Delinquents" (Ph.D. diss., University of Southern California, 1962); Seymour L. Halleck and Marvin Hersko, "Homosexual Behavior in a Correctional Institution for Adolescent Girls," *American Journal of Orthopsychiatry* 32 (October 1962): 911–17; William G. Miller and Thomas E. Hannum, "Characteristics of Homosexuality in Involved Incarcerated Females," *Journal of Consulting Psychology* 27 (June 1963): 277; Max Hammer, "Homosexuality in a Women's Reformatory," *Corrective Psychiatry and Journal of Social Therapy* 4 (May 1965): 168–69; David A. Ward and Gene G. Kassebaum, *Women's Prison: Sex and Social Structure* (Chicago: Aldine, 1965); and Rose Giallombardo, *Society of Women: A Study of a Women's Prison* (New York: John Wiley, 1966). For a discussion of the criminological literature on race and gender in reform schools for girls, see Kathryn Hinojosa Baker, "Delinquent Desire: Race, Sex, and Ritual in Reform Schools for Girls," *Discourse* 15 (fall 1992): 41–61.

3. On middle-class lesbian history, see, for example, Lillian Faderman, *Surpassing the Love of Men: Romantic Friendship between Women from the Renaissance to the Present* (New York: William Morrow, 1981); and idem, *Odd Girls and Twilight Lovers: A History*

of Lesbian Life in Twentieth-Century America (New York: Columbia University Press, 1991); Carroll Smith-Rosenberg, "The Female World of Love and Ritual: Relations between Women in Nineteenth-Century America," *Signs* 1 (autumn 1975): 1–29; Nancy Sahli, "Smashing: Women's Relationships before the Fall," *Chrysalis* 8 (summer 1979): 17–27; and Leila J. Rupp, " 'Imagine My Surprise': Women's Relationships in Historical Perspective," *Frontiers* 5 (fall 1980): 61–70. On working-class lesbian history, see, for example, Jonathan Katz, ed., *Gay American History: Lesbians and Gay Men in the U.S.A.* (New York: Thomas Cromwell, 1976), esp. "Passing Women," 209–81; San Francisco Lesbian and Gay History Project; Eric Garber, " 'T'Ain't Nobody's Bizness': Homosexuality in 1920s' Harlem," in *Black Men/White Men*, ed. Michael J. Smith (San Francisco: Gay Sunshine Press, 1983); Allan Berube, *Coming Out under Fire: The History of Gay Men and Women in World War Two* (New York: Free Press, 1990); Madeline Davis and Elizabeth Lapovsky Kennedy, "Oral History and the Study of Sexuality in the Lesbian Community: Buffalo, New York, 1940–1960," *Feminist Studies* 12 (spring 1986): 7–26, and idem, *Boots of Leather, Slippers of Gold*; John D'Emilio, *Sexual Politics, Sexual Communities: The Making of a Homosexual Minority in the United States, 1940–1970* (Chicago: University of Chicago Press, 1983). On medicalization, see George Chauncey, Jr., "From Sexual Inversion to Homosexuality: Medicine and the Changing Conceptualization of Female Deviance," *Salmagundi*, nos. 58–59 (fall–winter 1983): 114–46; and Jenny Terry, "Lesbians under the Medical Gaze: Scientists Search for Remarkable Differences," *Journal of Sex Research* 27 (August 1990): 317–39.

4. On the founding, populations, and administrations of the reformatory prisons, see Estelle B. Freedman, *Their Sisters' Keepers: Women's Prison Reform in America, 1830–1930* (Ann Arbor: University of Michigan Press, 1981).

5. More African American women served sentences in state prisons than in reformatory prisons. In 1923, for example, black women constituted 64.5 percent of the women in custodial prisons but only 11.9 percent of the inmates of women's reformatories. See Nicole Hahn Rafter, *Partial Justice: Women in State Prisons, 1800–1935* (Boston: Northeastern University Press, 1985), 146, table 6.5. The overrepresentation of women of color in the prison population is evident from 1950 U.S. census data on institutional populations. Out of a total of approximately 13,000 adult women prisoners, 56 percent were white and 44 percent were labeled "non-white." White women were incarcerated at a rate of 10.8 per 100,000 in the population; "nonwhite" women's rate was 68.8 per 100,000. See National Institute of Mental Health, *Psychiatric Services and the Changing Institutional Scene, 1950–1985*, DHEW Publication (ADM) 77–433 (Washington, D.C.: Government Printing Office, 1977), 24–25, 60–62, 63–67. For a rare historical analysis of African American women's prison experience, see Anne M. Butler, "Still in Chains: Black Women in Western Prisons, 1865–1910," in *"We Specialize in the Wholly Impossible": A Reader in Black Women's History*, ed. Darlene Clark Hine, Wilma King, and Linda Reed (Brooklyn: Carlson, 1995), 321–34.

6. On the concerns of male prison administrators, see, for example, Samuel Kahn, *Mentality and Homosexuality* (Boston: Meador, 1937), a study of New York City penal institutions conducted in the 1920s; and, for Massachusetts, Maurice Winslow, Superintendent, Norfolk Prison Colony, to Arthur T. Lyman, Commissioner of Corrections, 17 Aug. 1939, "Administrative Correspondence" file, Human Services, Corrections, Reference Files, series 1137x, Massachusetts State Archives, Boston.

7. Margaret Otis, "A Perversion Not Commonly Noted," *Journal of Abnormal Psychology* 7 (June–July 1913): 112–16.

8. Freedman, *Their Sisters' Keepers*, 139–40; see also Ruth Alexander's discussion of the Bedford Hills inquiry in *The "Girl Problem": Female Sexual Delinquency in New York*,

1920–1930 (Ithaca: Cornell University Press, 1995), 91–92. On the impact of "race suicide" fears on white women, who were urged to bear children, and black women, who were subject to sterilization, see Elaine Tyler May, *Barren in the Promised Land: Childless Americans and the Pursuit of Happiness* (New York: Basic Books, 1995), chaps. 2–3.

9. Ford, 442–47; Kahn, 123–24; Theodora M. Abel, "Dominant Behavior of Institutionalized Subnormal Negro Girls: An Experimental Study," *American Journal of Mental Deficiency* 67 (April 1943):429.

10. Felice Swados, *House of Fury* (Garden City, N.Y.: Doubleday, Doran and Co., 1941), 40–41. Swados implicitly criticized her white characters' racist objectification of black women. At the same time, however, the platonic interracial love she favored in the novel served to underscore the pathology of lesbianism.

11. See Chauncey; and Faderman, *Odd Girls*, chap. 2.

12. Sander Gilman, "Black Bodies, White Bodies: Toward an Iconography of Female Sexuality in Late Nineteenth-Century Art, Medicine, and Literature," in *"Race," Writing, and Difference*, ed. Henry Louis Gates, Jr. (Chicago: University of Chicago Press, 1986), 237. On the exclusion of black women from the category "woman," see Evelyn Brooks Higginbotham, "African-American Women's History and the Metalanguage of Race," *Signs* 17 (winter 1992): 256–58. On the historical association of blacks and hypersexuality, see also Winthrop Jordan, *White over Black: American Attitudes toward the Negro, 1550–1812* (Baltimore: Penguin Books, 1969). A parallel association among nonprison lesbians appears in gynecological literature from the 1930s that described the black lesbian as having a long, erectile clitoris; according to Jennifer Terry, the description "occupied an analogous position to the common representation of black men as having unusually long penises, signifying an ideological link between blackness and hypersexuality." See Terry, 334.

13. John Holland Cassity, "Socio-Psychiatric Aspects of Female Felons," *Journal of Criminal Psychopathology* 3 (April 1942): 600. The author also discussed infanticide and prostitutes who attacked their pimps (597–604); see also idem,"Personality Study of 200 Murders," *Journal of Criminal Psychopathology* 2 (January 1941): see esp. 303. On prostitutes, see Margaret Brenman, "Urban Lower-Class Negro Girls," *Psychiatry: Journal of the Biology and Pathology of Interpersonal Relations* 6 (August 1943): 321.

14. Elizabeth Lunbeck, " 'A New Generation of Women': Progressive Psychiatrists and the Hypersexual Female," *Feminist Studies* 13 (fall 1987): 538; and, idem, *The Psychiatric Persuasion: Knowledge, Gender, and Power in Modern America* (Princeton: Princeton University Press, 1994), 194, 204–07, 297–98.

15. Frances Strakosch, *Factors in the Sex Life of Seven Hundred Psychopathic Women* (Utica, N.Y.: State Hospitals Press, 1934), 61–62; Maurice A. R. Hennessy, "Homosexual Charges against Children," *Journal of Criminal Psychopathology* 2 (April 1941): 529. On the middle-class "lesbian taboo," see Christina Simmons, "Marriage in the Modern Manner: Sexual Radicalism and Reform in America, 1914–1941" (Ph.D. diss., Brown University, 1982).

16. Ford; Otis; Florence Monahan, *Women in Crime* (New York: I. Washburn, 1941), 224–25. On working-class women who first learned about lesbianism while in a girls' reformatory or a women's prison, as well as lesbians who worked as prostitutes and served time in women's prisons, see, for example, the report on "bulldiking" written by Perry M. Lichtenstein, the physician at the New York City Tombs. His article, "The 'Fairy' and the Lady Lover," from the *Medical Review of Reviews* 27 (August 1921): 369–74, is extracted in Jonathan Ned Katz, *Gay/Lesbian Almanac: A New Documentary* (New York: Harper Colophon, 1983), 402–03; Rusty Brown, "Always Me," in *Long Time Passing: Lives of Older Lesbians*, ed. Marcy Adelman (Boston: Alyson, 1986), 144–51; Davis and Kennedy, *Boots*

of Leather, Slippers of Gold, 60, 96ff, 329; and Joan Nestle, "Lesbians and Prostitutes: An Historical Sisterhood," in *Sex Work: Writings by Women in the Sex Industry*, ed. Frederique Delacoste and Priscilla Alexander (San Francisco: Cleis, 1987), 231–47.

17. Kahn, 24; Sheldon Glueck and Eleanor Glueck, *Five Hundred Delinquent Women* (New York: Alfred A. Knopf, 1934). In a 1932 study of a reformatory for girls, sociologist Lowell Selling labeled the pervasive wife/husband interracial relationships as nonpathological "pseudohomosexuality," in contrast to a mere two percent of the inmates characterized by "overt homosexual existence." He recognized, however, that the latter group was "usually shrewd enough to conceal this relationship from the authorities." See Lowell S. Selling, "The Pseudo Family," *American Journal of Sociology* 37 (May 1932): 247–53.

18. Women who studied or worked within women's reformatories who had long-term female partners include former Bedford Hills reformatory staff member Jessie Taft, who lived with Virginia Robinson, and Miriam Van Waters, who had a long-term relationship with philanthropist Geraldine Thompson. Democratic Party politician Molly Dewson and social worker Polly Porter met when they both worked at a Massachusetts girls' reformatory. See Estelle B. Freedman, *Maternal Justice: Miriam Van Waters and the Female Reform Tradition* (Chicago: University of Chicago Press, 1996), chap. 9; Susan Ware, *Partner and I: Molly Dewson, Feminism, and New Deal Politics* (New Haven: Yale University Press, 1987), 55. On reform schools in the 1920s, see Monahan, 223–24. The 1931 case involved the superintendent of the Alabama State Training School for Girls and is detailed in clippings files labeled "Reformatories-Ala.-Girls" in the Southern History Department at the Birmingham, Alabama, Library. I am extremely grateful to Susan K. Cahn for sharing this material with me.

19. Minutes of the Conference of Superintendents of Correctional Institutions for Women and Girls, 1944, p. 21, file 587, Miriam Van Waters Papers, Schlesinger Library, Cambridge, Mass. (hereafter MVW Papers). Note that Mead concluded that in the postwar period, "For the first time in our lives, we are going to face society that has more women than men in this generation, and female homosexuality will be a problem, not alone in the institutions but in society at large." In 1942 the women superintendents also heard a paper by Caroline Zachery on "Problems of Homosexuality in the Institutions"; in 1943 they invited an Austrian psychoanalyst to discuss "Female Homosexuality in Correctional Institutions" (file 420, MVW Papers).

20. "I Lived in a Hell behind Bars," *True Confessions*, March 1954, 32. Pulp novels include James Harvey, *Degraded Women* (New York: Midwood Tower, 1962); and Ann Aldrich, ed., *Carol in a Thousand Cities* (Greenwich, Conn.: Gold Medal Books, 1960). The 1932 women's prison film, *Ladies They Talk About*, had a brief scene portraying a comic butch lesbian; in *Caged* a sinister butch attempted to seduce a young woman played by Eleanor Parker, who was nominated for an Academy Award as best actress for her part. Other 1950s women's prison films include *Girls in Prison* and *Reform School Girl*. (I am grateful to Joanne Meyerowitz for calling to my attention the series of articles in *True Confessions*, to Allan Berube for reminding me of the pulp novels, and to Andrea Davies for a tape of *Ladies They Talk About*.) On changing depictions of homosexuality in film, see Vito Russo, *The Celluloid Closet: Homosexuality in the Movies* (New York: Harper and Row, 1981); for an analysis of contemporary films about lesbians in prison, see Karlene Faith, *Unruly Women: The Politics of Confinement and Resistance* (Vancouver: Press Gang Publishers, 1993), 259–62.

21. A. M. Shotwell, "A Study of Psychopathic Delinquency," *American Journal of Mental Deficiency* 51 (July 1946): 57–62; Albertine Winner, "Homosexuality in Women," *Medical Problems* 218 (July–December 1947): 219–20.

22. Donna Penn, "The Sexualized Woman: The Lesbian, the Prostitute, and the Containment of Female Sexuality in Post-War America," in *Not June Cleaver: Women and Gender in Postwar America, 1945–1960*, ed. Joanne Meyerowitz (Philadelphia: Temple University Press, 1994). On a corresponding association of female athletes with aggressive masculinity, see Susan K. Cahn, *Coming on Strong: Gender and Sexuality in Twentieth-Century Women's Sport* (New York: Free Press, 1994), esp. chap. 7.

23. For an inmate's observation of interracial relations in a women's prison, see Elizabeth Gurley Flynn, *The Alderson Story: My Life as a Political Prisoner* (New York: International Publishers, 1963), 178–79. Flynn, like novelist Felice Swados, considered the sexualization of black women by white inmates as a form of racism, which she called " 'white chauvinism' masquerading as 'love,' in interracial lesbian relations' " (178). Interracial lesbian relationships outside of prison may have become more common during the 1950s. See Davis and Kennedy, *Boots of Leather, Slippers of Gold*; and Audre Lorde, *Zami: A New Spelling of My Name* (Trumansburg, N.Y.: Crossing Press, 1983). Lorde observed a predominance of black butches and white femmes in 1950s bar culture. On the nexus of race and sexual roles in Lorde's work, see Katie King, "Audre Lorde's Lacquered Layerings: The Lesbian Bar as a Site of Literary Production," in *New Lesbian Criticism: Literary and Cultural Readings*, ed. Sally Munt (New York: Columbia University Press, 1993), 51–74.

24. Kates, 188, 190.

25. Katharine Sullivan, *Girls on Parole* (Boston: Houghton Mifflin/Riverside Press, 1956), 111–19.

26. Ibid., 111–21.

27. Ruth Frankenberg describes a shift from an essentialist race consciousness in early twentieth-century American society to a "color-blindness" that she labels "color evasiveness" and "power evasiveness." Her categories well describe the social science literature on women's prisons in the 1960s. See Ruth Frankenberg, *White Women, Race Matters: The Social Construction of Whiteness* (Minneapolis: University of Minnesota Press, 1993), 13–15. On shifting racial paradigms in modern America, see also Michael Omi and Howard Winant, *Racial Formation in the United States: From the 1960s to the 1990s*, 2d ed. (New York: Routledge, 1994).

28. Ward and Kassebaum, 136, 197–200; Giallombardo, 177, fig. 2; 183, fig. 3. (Six of the ten "marriages" between women diagrammed consisted of interracial couples, three others were between white women [two of them "divorced"] and one other between black women.) The only passing reference to race suggested that whites were slightly overrepresented as butches, blacks as femmes, an observation rarely found in this literature. For examples of reform school literature that similarly ignores, or evades, race, see Halleck and Hersko; and Sidney Kosofsky and Albert Ellis, "Illegal Communication among Institutionalized Female Delinquents," *Journal of Social Psychology* 48 (August 1958): 155–60.

The absence of any discussion of race in these studies does not reflect the prison population. Giallombardo's figures on prior commitments, broken down by race, reveal that over 40 percent of the Alderson prison population was "Negro." The assumption of a liberal "race-blind" approach during the 1960s may have represented a reaction to earlier social scientific arguments linking biological race and criminality. Ward and Kassebaum, for example, explicitly reject biological explanations of homosexuality, although they tend to substitute psychoanalytic interpretations (104 n. 4 and passim). Both studies are sympathetic to their subjects, resisting the demonization of lesbians in popular literature in favor of a functionalist explanation of the sexual and familial roles assumed by women prisoners.

For evidence of the continued eroticization of race in female correctional institutions, see Barbara Lillian Carter, "On the Grounds: Informal Culture in a Girls Reform School" (Ph.D.

diss., Brandeis University, 1972), chap. 6. In this study, a black female observer found that "the *single* most important factor" determining butch/femme roles was race. Disproportionate numbers of blacks became "Butches and high status girls; and whites, equally disproportionately, became Femmes and lower status girls" (128).

29. Thus far I have found only one passing reference to Mexican American lesbians in prison. See Michela Robbins, "The Inside Story of a Girls Reformatory," *Collier's*, 30 Oct. 1953, 74–79, cited in Baker, 59. The juvenile delinquency and post–1945 women's prison literature may provide richer sources for a multiracial account.

30. Hart, 107–09, 117. On postwar sexual regulation, see Estelle B. Freedman, " 'Uncontrolled Desires': The Response to the Sexual Psychopath, 1920–1960," *Journal of American History* 74 (June 1987): 83–106; Elaine Tyler May, *Homeward Bound: American Families in the Cold War Era* (New York: Basic Books, 1988), esp. chap. 4; D'Emilio; and Ricki Solinger, *Wake Up Little Susie: Single Pregnancy and Race before Roe v. Wade* (New York: Routledge, 1992).

31. Miriam Van Waters (hereafter MVW), handwritten notes, 11 Apr. 1938, file 241, and Helen Schnefel to MVW, 4 Oct. 1932, file 177, MVW Papers.

32. Dr. Pavenstedt, Report on student 16590, 1943–47, and 18572, 30 Mar. 1948, in McDowell Exhibits, 20 Feb. 1949 and 21 Feb. 1949, file 251; interview by Mr. Swanson, 19 Jan. 1949, file 251, MVW Papers.

33. All inmate names have been changed.

34. McDowell Exhibits 125, 125A, 18 Feb. 1948, file 251, MVW Papers.

35. MacGregor eventually married a man she had met in a local jail, but she continued to pursue lesbian relationships. McDowell Exhibits 126, 16A, 20 Feb. 1949, file 251, MVW Papers.

36. McDowell Exhibits 125, 125 and 126, 126A, 129, 129A, 18 Feb. 1949, file 251, MVW Papers.

37. Elliot E. McDowell to MVW, 28 July 1948, file 250 and Van Waters, "Superintendent's Answers," 1 June 1948, file 248, MVW Papers; LoPresti quoted in "Sherborn Probe," *Boston Herald Traveller*, 9 June 1948; "Immorality Charged at Reformatory," *Boston Herald Traveller*, 13 Sept. and 15 Sept. 1948; *Boston Evening American*, 10 Nov. 1948. On the cultural context for associating homosexuality with communism, see D'Emilio; and May, *Homeward Bound*.

38. McDowell to MVW, 7 Jan. 1949, file 201, MVW Papers.

39. John O'Connor, "Van Waters Rejects Inmate Sex Charge," *Boston Herald*, 1 Jan. 1949, 1.

40. Rumors about Van Waters's sexuality are discussed in MVW to Ethel Sturges Dummer, 26 Sept. 1948, file 825, Ethel Sturges Dummer Papers, Schlesinger Library, and in letters from a former inmate to MVW, 1 June 1948, file 195, and from Harry R. Archbald to MVW, 7 Feb. 1949, file 203, both in MVW Papers. For a full discussion of Van Waters's interpretation of lesbian identity and the political response to rumors of her own homosexuality, see Freedman, *Maternal Justice*, esp. chaps. 9, 12, 14, and 15.

41. Peg O'Keefe to MVW, 15 June 1949, file 215, MVW Papers.

42. A. Perry Holt, Jr., Deputy Commissioner, to Commissioner Reuben L. Lurie, 21 May 1954, in "Escapes" Framingham, Human Services, Corrections, Reference Files, series 1137x, Commonwealth of Massachusetts Archives.

43. "Report of the Special Committee Authorized to Study the Reorganization of the Correctional System," Commonwealth of Massachusetts House Document 3015 (Boston, 1958), 12–13, 56–59, 60, located in Framingham File, Human Services, Corrections, Reference Files, series 1137x, Commonwealth of Massachusetts Archives.

44 "Remarks Made by Anne L. Clark, M.D., at Hodder Hall, Massachusetts Correctional Institution for Women, Framingham, Massachusetts, on Wednesday, May 13, 1959," file 69, pp. 2–7, Massachusetts Society for Social Hygiene Papers, Schlesinger Library. I am grateful to Donna Penn for calling my attention to this document. On the segregation of lesbians in contemporary women's prisons, see Faith, 216; and Robson, 108.

45. On men's efforts to "reprivatize" women in the 1950s, see Wini Breines, *Young, White, and Miserable: Growing Up Female in the Fifties* (Boston: Beacon Press, 1992), 36. For alternative historical interpretations of women's lives in the 1950s, see Meyerowitz.

46. On differential treatment of white and black unwed mothers, see Solinger; and Regina Kunzel, *Fallen Women, Problem Girls: Unmarried Mothers and the Professionalization of Social Work, 1890–1945* (New Haven: Yale University Press, 1993). On bar dykes, see Davis and Kennedy, *Boots of Leather, Slippers of Gold.* For a discussion of lesbianism and women's sports, see Cahn, esp. chap. 7. At the same time, sterilization efforts in the South shifted their targets from white to black women. See Rebecca R. Lallier, " 'A Place of Beginning Again': The North Carolina Industrial Farm Colony for Women, 1929–1947" (M.A. thesis, University of North Carolina, 1990). I am grateful to Susan K. Cahn for this reference.

47. On the persistence of class divisions among lesbians through the 1970s, see Faderman, *Surpassing the Love of Men*, chap. 7; Davis and Kennedy, *Boots of Leather, Slippers of Gold*, esp. 4, 138–45; Katie Gilmartin, " 'The Very House of Difference': Intersections of Identities in the Life Histories of Colorado Lesbians, 1940–1965" (Ph.D. diss., Yale University, 1995); and Susan Krieger, *The Mirror Dance: Identity in a Women's Community* (Philadelphia: Temple University Press, 1983), chap. 11.

48. Robson, 109–10, and idem, "Convictions: Theorizing Lesbians and Criminal Justice," in *Legal Inversions: Lesbians, Gay Men, and the Politics of Law*, ed. Didi Herman and Carol Stychin (Philadelphia: Temple University Press, 1995); Faith, 216.

Chapter Twenty-One

Mixing Bodies and Cultures
The Meaning of America's Fascination with Sex between "Orientals" and "Whites"

Henry Yu

On June 19, 1897, the Reverend Walter Ngon Fong, pastor of the Methodist Mission of San Jose and a recent graduate of Stanford University, was married. He and his bride, the new Mrs. Emma Fong, exchanged their vows in a small, quiet ceremony in Denver, Colorado.

Walter Fong had been an exceptional student at Stanford: he had served as the president of the Nestorian Debating Society and had consistently received high grades.[1] It was not, however, his academic achievements that had distinguished him. While studying in Palo Alto, Walter Fong had been the only Chinese student in the whole of Stanford University. After he graduated, his life continued to be marked by distinction. Fong became a lawyer in San Francisco and the head of the Chinese Revolutionary Party in the United States. Fong's professional status marked him as a rare, educated elite at a time when the majority of Chinese in America were merchants, laborers, or servants.[2] Fong's shining public status, however, was overshadowed by an even greater personal achievement. For a Chinese male in the United States in 1897, just being able to marry was a rare accomplishment. An overwhelming percentage of the Chinese in America at the turn of the century were men—about 85,000 compared to a little more than 4,500 women. Labor migration had been the initial impetus for Chinese immigration to America in the 1860s and 1870s. The demographic pattern had been frozen by exclusionary federal legislation in the 1870s and 1880s, which had been explicitly designed to keep Chinese women out of the United States. American legislators believed that without Chinese women, Chinese men would be unable to establish families and therefore would never be allowed to settle in America.[3]

Yet there was even more that was exceptional about Walter Fong. Though he lived and worked in the Bay area, Fong had not been able to marry in his home state—California law prohibited him and his new bride from receiving a marriage license. The reason? Emma Fong was "white." In 1880 California's Civil Code had been amended to prohibit the issuance of any marriage license to a white person and a "Negro, Mulatto, or Mongolian." Most other states on the Pacific coast had also enacted "antimiscegenation" laws during this period. The Fongs were forced to travel to Colorado, one of the few western states without such laws, in order to sanction their union.[4]

Mrs. Emma Fong was herself an exceptional woman. Almost exactly twenty-five years after her wedding day, she related her autobiography in a series of articles in the *San Francisco Bulletin*. Entitled (in a manner recognizable to modern readers of tabloid magazines) "My Oriental Husbands—The story of a San Francisco girl, who married a Chinese graduate of Stanford University, and a year after his death became the wife of his lifelong friend, a Japanese instructor of the University of California, by Emma Fong Kuno," the story she told was amazing to the *Bulletin's* readers, and more than a little controversial. She described the angry denunciations she had suffered, and the widespread condemnation of her spousal choices. Most of all, however, she detailed what it had been like to live with her two "Oriental" husbands: what the differences were between Chinese men and Japanese men, how they treated her, and how different they were, both from each other and from "white" Americans.[5]

The story of Walter Fong, his best friend, Professor Kuno, and their wife, Emma, is an interesting entrance into the social phenomena of interracial sex, love, and marriage between Asian Americans and "white" Americans in the twentieth century. The purpose of this essay, however, is not to explore the social dimensions of interracial sex and love. Such relations did occur, and with some frequency throughout the nineteenth and twentieth centuries. What is of much greater interest is just how interesting "white" Americans, and in particular "white" intellectuals, found such relationships.[6]

There was a peculiar fascination with sex between "Orientals" and "whites," particularly between "Oriental" men and "white" women, which was disproportionate to the small number of publicly reported cases.[7] The marital history of Emma Fong Kuno is a perfect example. Her autobiographical story, which was published in installments to take maximum advantage of the anticipated readership, caused a great stir. The day after her series ended on June 14, 1922, the *Bulletin* published an editorial attack on intermarriage between races, and Emma Fong Kuno's text began its long life as a central piece in discussions about interracial love between "Orientals" and "whites." In 1924 the story became a key document in the massive Survey of Race Relations conducted by American social scientists on the West Coast. In 1946 her autobiography was reprinted by the Social Science Institute of Fisk University as part of a series of exemplary social documents concerning race relations and the social adjustment of "Orientals." This story, and a handful of other documented cases of intermarriage between Asian Americans and "white" Americans, became the focus for a fascination that American social science would have with sexual relations across racial boundaries.

The purpose of this essay is to explore the ways in which these social scientists defined and structured their interest in interracial sex—what it meant to them, how it fit into their conceptions of culture, race, and racial relations, how it reflected their ideological hopes and dreams for America. Beyond the individual examples of intermarriage between "Orientals" and "whites," which show little pattern except for a stubborn peculiarity unique to each case, I am much more interested in examining the scholarly fascination with sexual relations across racial boundaries. Social scientists thought that by examining an individual case of an "Oriental" man and a "white" American woman, they could learn something about race relations between "Orientals" and "whites" in general. This assumption led to an intense examination of individual cases of racial intermarriage, and attempts to find and gather as many of these cases for analysis as possible. This essay will focus on social scientists' interest in intermarriage in order to explore their theories about the importance of race and culture. A larger goal is to provide a historical context for scholarly interest in "intermarriage" and interracial sex. Recent studies of intermarriage have looked to the phenomenon as one fraught with great social meanings, just as have studies in the past. Perhaps outlining some of the reasons that intermarriage as a topic has historically been so hotly pursued will lead to more critical examinations of contemporary fascinations with interracial sex.[8]

Throughout the twentieth century, intermarriage has been conceptualized in two ways: as the meeting point of different things, and as the ultimate erasure of the difference between things. Like a pendulum, the interest in intermarriage between "Orientals" and "whites" has swung from an emphasis in the 1920s upon exotic couples who were different from each other, to an obsession in the 1950s with homogenization and hybridization as a means of solving the problems of racial difference, and back and forth again in the last three decades between intermarriage as a sign of difference and interracial children as a sign of hybridization.

From the first large-scale appearance of Chinese in America in the 1850s, through the rise of Japanese immigration at the turn of the century, and up until the 1920s, the dominant public reaction of the American social body, and of the educated elite, was a fear and abhorrence of Asian immigrants. A few capitalists (such as Leland Stanford—whose money, much of it made through the labor of Chinese railroad workers, founded Stanford University) and missionaries welcomed Asian immigrants as malleable laborers or potential converts. However, anti-Asian activists succeeded in arousing a fear of an "Asiatic invasion" or a "yellow peril" overwhelming "white" workers and, potentially, American civilization itself. When Emma Fong Kuno's marital history was first published in 1922, the text and the subsequent attacks on it plugged into a larger context of debates over racial competition and fears about the long-term survival of the "white race." Racial death and the end of "white" supremacy and civilization were often prophesied. In the competition among the races, "whites" were warned to fear the alleged reproductive advantage of "Mongolians," who were believed to be more fertile, but intellectually and physically inferior.

Racial thinking, in the form of biological theories of "Mongolian" inferiority or arguments for the supremacy of "white" civilization over the barbarity of "Oriental" civilization, was criticized in the late 1910s and in the 1920s from a number of points of view. Cultural pluralists such as Randolph Bourne and Horace Kallen argued for an inclusive vision of America that maintained the stark differences of various immigrant communities; social scientists and anthropologists such as William I. Thomas and Franz Boas began to propagate theories of culture that stressed understanding different communities from the inside or "native" perspective.

The consequent rise in fascination with those people or communities that were most different from native-born Americans placed a value on the exotic, and was accompanied by an interest in intermarriage between those who were similar and dissimilar. The very conception of "intermarriage," or contact between "races" and "cultures," depended upon the acceptance of a boundary that marked the stark difference between one group and another. If one does not accept the validity of this boundary as actually marking meaningful difference (in contrast to the idea, for instance, that such a boundary is arbitrary and the people on each side are much more similar than different), any interest in interracial or intercultural contact would be pointless and devoid of meaning. In other words, only in positing that there is a difference between two sets of people, and that this difference has great meaning, does someone come to be interested in examining the relations between people whom they define as different.

Intermarriage stood at the most intimate point along these boundaries of difference, and American social scientists in the 1920s even went so far as to make it the ground zero in their attempts to quantify and measure the amount of difference between cultures. In theories about what they labeled "social distance," sociologists asserted that the quantity of difference between cultures was equal to the degree of intimacy and abhorrence that members of one group felt toward the other.[9] In this way, sexual relations and reproduction came to represent the most intimate of social relations, equated with the most profound lack of measurable distance (both physical and social) between two races or cultures.

What began in the 1910s and 1920s as a fascination with the exotic became by the 1940s and 1950s a desire to erase the exotic, and in the 1970s and to the present day, has come to echo again the eroticization of difference that marked early social scientists' definitions of race and culture. The initial commodification of exotic difference in the 1910s and 1920s, which began with the "culture" concept, remained confined to a small group of scholars. Within more common social understandings of America, the value of difference remained secondary to a dominant "melting pot" ideal that emphasized the assimilation and disappearance of such differences. These opposing conceptions of the desirability of difference, however, shared an emphasis on the importance of boundaries. The belief in the validity of cultural difference and cultural boundaries played a central role in conceptions of social interaction in America. It was just that in some cases a value was placed upon the desirability of the exotic, while in others the desire was for the erasure of such differences.

The 1950s were marked by a belief in America as potentially homogeneous, and social scientists at that time debated the desirability of the "melting pot" as the goal of American progress. Its *possibility*, though, was unquestioned. The utopian dream of consensus and an opposing dystopian nightmare of bland homogeneity both relied on a belief in the possibility of erasing difference. Intermarriage, as a symbol for the ultimate extinction of all cultural and physical difference, assumed a centrality and importance for very different reasons than it did during the 1920s. Now, instead of encapsulating the meeting of two unlike things (and therefore valuable for being a symbol of difference), intermarriage contained the possibility of erasing difference in its union of unlike things.

By the 1970s the fascination with intermarriage had come to focus again upon the meeting of dissimilar things. In the 1960s and 1970s attacks on the "melting pot" as a desirable goal brought with them a return to a celebration of difference and "ethnicity." With the triumph of "multiculturalism" as a banner word to eclipse the homogeneity of the "melting pot," the initial commodification of difference that cultural theorists and pluralists had created in the 1920s blossomed into a full-scale commercialization of difference. The mass marketing of ethnicity and cultural difference has brought to America a curious blend of homogeneous market goods sold through an appeal for exotic attributes. Advertisements show interracial couples (who represent difference in their dissimilar bodies) wearing identical clothing, or "hybrid" children (perhaps the Japanese American term "hapa" children is more pleasant) tingeing mass-produced products with the touch of exoticism. Multiculturalism as a commercial strategy has evinced a fascination with interracial sex and love that parallels the initial commodification of ethnicity created by the early social scientists.

The American intellectual fascination with interracial sex, love, and marriage points to larger transformations in the social understandings of race, culture, and exotic ethnicity in America. The social meaning of intermarriage has reflected the dominance of theories of biological race at the turn of the century, the liberal enthusiasm for cultural pluralism in the early part of the century, a liberal debate over homogeneity in the middle of the century, and the triumph of ethnic identity and multiculturalism in recent years. Intermarriage has always served as the most focused example of what interracial and intercultural relations mean. The possibility of both difference and similarity, and therefore a tension between exoticism and a desire for homogeneity, has always existed within the idea of intermarriage. Because of this tension, discussions of intermarriage have served as a means for encapsulating larger definitions of social relations in America.

At the same time, the fascination with sexual relations between "Orientals" and "whites" cannot be understood without taking into account the obsession and abhorrence that could be invoked by fantasies of interracial sex. Social scientific knowledge was created within the context of widespread curiosity about "miscegenation," and the social scientists' interest in the love lives of "Orientals" and "whites" takes on new meaning when understood in relation to more popular conceptions of interracial sex.

American social scientists, particularly those from the University of Chicago's department of sociology, extensively documented and explored cases of sexual contact between "Orientals" and "whites" during the twentieth century.[10] In the 1920s sociologists from the University of Chicago, the University of Southern California, and the University of Washington made intermarriage between "Orientals" and "whites" one of the major aspects of their Survey of Race Relations on the West

Coast. From the 1920s to the 1960s, a number of doctoral students in sociology at the University of Chicago, some of whom were Chinese American or Japanese American, continued to focus on intermarriage as one of the key aspects of race relations between "Orientals" and "whites" in America. The original theories produced during the 1920s continue to structure the ways in which race and culture are understood by social theorists to the present day.[11]

During the Survey of Race Relations between 1924 and 1926, American social scientists and the missionary social reformers who gave them financial backing decided to study what they labeled the "Oriental problem" on the West Coast. Anti-Japanese agitation at the time, and anti-Chinese movements of the 1860s and 1870s, had rallied "white" Americans of the laboring classes against "Oriental" and "Asiatic" immigration, blaming Asian American workers for the difficult social and economic position of "white" workers. Anti-Asian legislation such as the federal Chinese Exclusion Act of 1882, California's Anti-Alien Land Acts of 1917 and 1923, and the federal National Origins Acts of 1924 discriminated racially against Chinese and Japanese immigrants and enjoyed widespread public support.[12] Anti-Asian publications such as Valentine McClatchy's *Sacramento Bee* used the term "yellow peril" to describe the threat of Asian immigrant labor competing with "white" laborers migrating at the same time to the West Coast. A long history of lynching, violence, and rioting against Asians had provided a legacy of racial strife that social reformers and sociologists defined as the "Oriental problem" in America. One of the major interests of both the missionaries and the sociologists centered upon intermarriage between the "races."

In 1923 Robert Park, one of the leaders of the Chicago school of sociology, was enlisted by Protestant missionaries to direct an "objective" survey to study the "facts" of the "Oriental problem" on the West Coast. Park and his fellow sociologists believed that they could study an inflammatory issue such as the "yellow peril" with the detached air of a biologist studying a plant, maintaining critical distance from the conflicts surrounding the "Oriental problem" in America. It is no surprise that their attempts to maintain an "unbiased" and "uncontroversial" approach proved impossible, despite their rhetoric of "scientific objectivity." Even during the 1920s the claims of social science for "value-neutral" and "nonpartisan" research were a matter of bitter debate. The facade of "objectivity" proved the most difficult to maintain when the sociologists began to study the heated topic of interracial sex.

The intellectual interest of the sociologists and missionaries in the subject of intermarriage must be placed in the context of a wider curiosity about "miscegenation." Academic interest in the sexual relations of Chinese and Japanese American men with "white" women was inextricably tied to a widespread fear of the sexual behavior of "Oriental" men. No matter how enraged or emotional West Coast anti-Asian activists became over the issue of "Oriental" immigration in general, they became even more enraged with the subject of interracial sex—the idea of "mongrelization" and "dirty Orientals" lewdly fondling "white" women. The "yellow peril" rhetoric that infused pulp magazines and dime novels did not try to rationalize unfair labor competition or overly efficient farming practices; it dwelled instead upon "Oriental" men preying on helpless "white" women. Perhaps best realized in

Sax Rohmer's fictional character Fu Manchu, pulp magazines and novels depicted
"Orientals" as scheming men with long fingernails, waiting in ambush to kidnap
"white" women into sexual slavery.[13] Just as lurid were the denunciation of, and
obsession with, "Oriental" women, as expressed through descriptions of them as
"prostitutes" and "sex slaves."

The sexual threat of individual "Oriental" men and women stood for the larger
threat of the "Oriental race." Would America be purely "white" in the future, or
would the sexual threat of the "yellow peril" turn Americans into a "mongrel
race"?[14] Interracial sex was a taboo subject that seemingly everyone—"white" and
"Oriental"—wanted to think about and read about, yet only pornographic novels
or pulp fiction dared to explore. It is hard to recover just how hot a topic it was,
how incensed people became about it, how fascinated and obsessed. Even in the
sociologists' self-conscious attempts to write rhetorically neutral texts during the
Survey of Race Relations, the wider context of prurient interest in interracial sex
could not be ignored. Early on in the survey, the missionary J. Merle Davis, secretary of the Survey of Race Relations, asked Park to produce a sample questionnaire
to pass around in an effort to drum up interest and financing for the survey. Park
chose to give him an extensive document on "interracial marriage." Davis raved
about the public response to the questionnaire:

> I have had fifty copies of this document mimeographed here in Seattle and am using
> them with people who are vitally interested. It is significant to note that *practically*
> *everyone is crazy to get a copy*, and it is plain that there is much more interest in this
> topic than appears on the surface.
>
> This document has already *revived the drooping interest* of some of our leaders here
> in Seattle, and will be useful with every group, as a concrete evidence of the spirit and
> method of approach to some of these difficult problems.
>
> You certainly made a happy choice in the subject of the first questionnaire. *From*
> *the way folks act or react to it, one would be led to believe that most of these good*
> *people at one time or another had had serious thoughts about marrying a Chinese or*
> *Japanese.*[15]

Davis made hundreds of copies and sent them out in an effort to elicit donations
for the survey. The missionaries did not pass on the opportunity to capitalize on
interracial marriage as the technique to retool their flaccid fund-raising efforts.
What was this amazing document that could revive "drooping interest" in the survey? What questions did it ask that would warrant such a response from inquiring
minds up and down the Pacific coast? What did people want to know about interracial marriage and sex?

In fact, the questionnaire seems quite sedate, and never probed very deeply into
the roots of sexual attraction between "races." But it is important to consider the
different perspectives that anti-Asian activists brought to their readings of the
questionnaire—they focused in on the provocative aspects of interracial sex:

> Of what height and coloring is the American woman married to an Oriental? Is it a
> type closely approximating that of the Oriental women? What kind of Oriental man

does the American woman marry? Is he American in appearance? What seems to be the basis of the physical attraction? Are the American women who have married Orientals wholesome and conventional people? Do any of them belong to marked psychological types, the romantic, the neurotic, etc.?[16]

Anyone and everyone who ever wanted to know why "white" women would ever be attracted to "Oriental" men could identify with these questions. The "romantic" type and the "neurotic" type, who were being suggested as possible marriage partners, were obviously not the same as "wholesome and conventional people."

Park and the sociologists were also very interested in the class aspects of interracial marriage, asking whether the woman was of the same economic or social level as the man, and whether her status was raised or lowered by the union. Again, such an interest from the point of view of the sociologists was a neutral and seemingly dispassionate inquiry into the social and economic background of the lovers. Yet coupled with the question of whether the American woman was of a "conventional" and "wholesome" type, the inquiring mind of the reader could quickly tour the slums and ghettoes of urban America. Was she "white trash," or a prostitute perhaps? Was she somehow gaining status by marrying an "Oriental" of a better class when no "white" man would marry her?

These possibilities were hinted at by the line of questioning. The assumption that it would be an "Oriental" man marrying a "white" woman was telling, refracting the "yellow peril" fears that most "Orientals" in the United States were men who posed a sexual threat to "white" women, and that the few "Oriental" women were prostitutes believed unfit for marriage. While there were more Chinese American males in the United States in 1924 than there were females, the sex ratio of the Japanese was much more even; the basis for the questionnaire's assumption of a "white" woman marrying an "Oriental" man thus had as much to do with popular preconceptions of protecting "white womanhood" as it did with demographics.

The interracial marriage questionnaire allowed for a wide range of interpretations that differed from the author's intended meanings. Robert Park was purportedly interested in intermarriage for reasons having to do with social acceptance of the couple and their children. For instance, there were numerous questions about how other people regarded the marriage and its offspring, and family and community reactions were polled. Yet although the questionnaire was designed to elicit a history of people's attitudes about interracial marriage, the numerous fascinated readers could find their own interests within it. Those people obsessed with the question of interracial sexual relations could, for example, find hints of their own erotic fantasies in the text of the questionnaire.

Indeed, the interracial marriage document was deliberately provocative, and Park was aware of the potential ways in which it could be read. Having been a newspaper reporter and having been in charge of public relations at Booker T. Washington's Tuskegee Institute in Alabama, Park considered himself an expert on the range of receptions a text could invoke. Prior to writing the questionnaire, Park had responded coolly to Davis's request for a public relations release concerning the survey. Park believed that it was better to keep the survey's exact nature under wraps, so people could supply their own understandings of its purpose.[17] He believed in the technique of generating public interest through the hype of secrecy. Davis, however, convinced Park that there was a danger of anti-Asian agitators assuming that the survey would be pro-"Oriental," and thus refusing to cooperate. Instead of a press release, Park wrote the questionnaire.[18]

The questionnaire was a masterful text designed to arouse everyone's desire for more information about interracial marriage—it appealed to the sociologists' and missionaries' needs for enlightened knowledge at the same time that it stimulated the worst fears and obsessions of anti-Asians. The interest of Chinese and Japanese Americans was also piqued, and like nativists who could go on and on about the threat of "Oriental" men to "white" women, Chinese and Japanese Americans responded to the surveyors' questions about intermarriage with a clarity that revealed long reflection on the matter.

The Survey of Race Relations had actually begun with little intention of addressing intermarriage. In the formative stages of the survey in 1923, long before Park became involved, Sidney Gulick, a prominent missionary and supporter of Asian immigrants, had questioned Davis about the survey's apparent lack of interest in intermarriage:

> I am a little surprised that . . . so slight a reference is made to the question of intermarriage. As yet this has not become a burning question because American-born Japanese have not yet grown up to the marrying age to any considerable numbers. In ten years the situation will change. And unless some pretty thorough work has been done upon it in a thoroughly scientific way, I fear it will become one of the burning questions which politicians will capitalize and make the basis of much trouble.
>
> I am not sure however that it will be wise for your survey group to touch it. If in some way you could provide for a distinct study of the question by experts and then deliberately exclude the subject from your field of investigation, it might be wise.[19]

Gulick was being slightly disingenuous when he remarked that intermarriage was not a "burning question" at that time; his warning to Davis to keep the investigation of intermarriage quiet or even separate indicated that he recognized the subject's volatility. What he really meant was that for the missionaries, intermarriage had not yet become the solution to the "Oriental problem" that they hoped to find. Racial intermarriage represented to both missionaries and sociologists the point of most intimate social contact, and thus the true successful end of American assimilation. The inevitable logic of intermarriage was rarely discussed outside of personal letters, however, precisely because it was such an incendiary topic. The subject of intermarriage became one of the largest and most intensely scrutinized aspects of the Survey of Race Relations, but no one made the mistake of publicly declaring just why everyone was so obsessed with it.

The missionaries were the most open in declaring the reasons for their interest in intermarriage. For them, intermarriage symbolized the successful end of assimilating Asians into "white" America. The missionaries believed it was the last hurdle in proving that "Orientals" were being "Americanized," and Sydney Gulick had even used a picture of a Japanese American man married to a "white" woman as "proof" that the assimilation of Japanese in America was possible. If "white" women were accepting "Oriental" men as spouses, then America was truly a "melting pot."[20]

The missionaries were not alone in understanding intermarriage as the ultimate proof of the success of American assimilation. Robert Park recognized the reason that both sociologists and missionaries were fascinated with the topic: "[we] should study carefully the circumstances under which the legislation forbidding inter-racial marriage came to be passed. If the Japanese are not permitted to intermarry in the United States, we will always have a race problem as long as they are here."[21] Park was interested in intermarriage for two reasons. First, he understood intermarriage as the focal point of all race relations, the distillation and symbol of two different cultures coming into intimate contact. Whatever tensions there were between two groups' cultures and social attitudes, he believed the marriage between two individuals carrying those attitudes would certainly be the place to explore the dynamic of those tensions. The relationship between a man and a woman of two different "races" was the perfect experiment for discovering how different "cultures" and "races" could coexist. What changes in attitude were required? How was "race consciousness" overcome?

Park was not interested in whether the children of such "hybrid" relationships would be biologically inferior or superior—he was certain that such a question needed no answer except to discredit those who were claiming the genetic inferiority of such children. He was, however, interested in the children of intermarriages as "cultural" products, as the embodiment of two social groups in contact. Did either community ignore the children or ostracize them? Did either community cut off ties with the married couple? What about the families of the couple? These were the interesting questions for Park, and they tied into his second reason for research into intermarriage as the ultimate solution to the problem of "race prejudice." If physical differences such as skin color were the symbolic markers that allowed people to abstract their awareness of different "races," then physical "amalgamation" would eventually remove these racial markers.

This interest in intermarriage as a biological homogenizer was purely theoretical, and Park never advocated it as the ultimate solution. Indeed, his belief that "cultural assimilation" was the sufficient end of the "melting pot" did not result from personal fears of interracial marriage, but rather derived from his emphasis on the validity of "cultural assimilation" as a purely "social" phenomenon. The fact that the Japanese and Chinese in America were not permitted to intermarry with "whites" was disturbing to him not because "hybrid" children would never be produced, but because it indicated that the social interaction between the "races" was still not intimate enough. Assimilation in the cultural sense was obviously not taking place.

The emphasis that sociologists placed on intermarriage as a cultural phenomenon, and the consequent de-emphasis placed on its physical component, paralleled the missionaries' emphasis on conversion as a matter of faith. Protestant missionaries, in their desire to convert and Americanize "Orientals" and other people who were "racially" different from "Americans" (a term they used to mean "white"), came up with the idea of assimilation in a spiritual sense. As a matter of conscious faith and acts of piety, the missionaries' version of American assimilation had little to do with the physical body. Social scientists paralleled this separation of the physical body from the definition of assimilation by promoting the concept of "culture," which they defined as divorced from the biology of the body. Intermarriage, for Park and the sociologists, was more interesting as a social phenomenon than as a biological act. Indeed, if the concept of assimilation was to be a purely cultural interaction, then it was improper to discuss the body as anything except the site of cultural mixture.

The interest of American social science in sexual contact between "Orientals" and "whites" occupied a significant portion of the Survey of Race Relations research. In files coded "IM" for "intermarriage," documents touching on sex between "Oriental" and "white" Americans made up about ten percent of the four hundred or so life histories and interviews that the surveyors collected. The sociologists believed that their examination of sexual relations between individual "Orientals" and "whites" was of great consequence for the future of American society. Sex between individuals of different "races" would produce children who were both "American" and "Oriental" in culture, just as social contact in general between different "races" could lead to a society that was culturally "half-white" and "half-Oriental." Sexuality and sexual reproduction between individuals became the focal point for concerns about the metaphorical "reproduction" of the social body as a whole. Just as individual "Orientals" could stand as symbols for the larger threat of a "yellow peril" overtaking "white" civilization, sexual relations at the level of individual man and woman symbolized general social relations in American society.

Even after the survey ended in 1926, interracial marriage and sex remained a major subject of interest for American social scientists. Both missionaries and social scientists during the 1920s had explored the possibilities of intermarriage as the ultimate solution to the racial conflicts of the United States, but the incendiary reactions to the issue had limited their public discussions of interracial sex. They had, however, carefully used the "burning" interest in intermarriage to provoke interest and generate funding for the survey.

Robert Park had believed that actual "hybrid" children were unnecessary for the "melting pot" of America to work. For Park, the intimate contact of intermarriage was synonymous with close social communication, and this communication was enough for the elimination of "social" and "physical distance" between the "races." Society could overcome racial prejudice and discrimination without eliminating the physical characteristics that marked racial difference. The actual biological products of sexual union remained for Park interesting but unnecessary.[22]

By the 1950s some Chicago sociologists studying the "Oriental problem" in America had become convinced that "social" or "cultural assimilation" between racial groups in the United States was not enough to eradicate racial prejudice. The writings of one social theorist, the Chinese American sociologist Rose Hum Lee, serve as an example of how an emphasis on the actual products of interracial sex, rather than the mere act, could shift the discourse on intermarriage from ideas about difference to hopes about the creation of sameness. Rose Hum Lee finished her doctorate at the University of Chicago in 1947, and by 1956 had achieved the height of a prolific career at Roosevelt University in Chicago by becoming the first woman, and the first Chinese American, to head a sociology department at an American university.[23]

Rose Hum Lee had begun her career emphasizing that cultural assimilation was enough to end racial prejudice, but by the end of the 1950s she had begun to despair of Park's emphasis upon culture. Lee's analysis contained one major difference from those of earlier sociologists. Robert Park's answers to the "Oriental problem" had emphasized that on a theoretical level, social assimilation was inevitable. Interracial relationships were merely singular instances of more general cultural interactions. Rose Hum Lee offered a more concrete prescription for the ultimate solution to America's "race" problems: the universal physical mixing of individuals.

Lee wrote in 1956 about the difficulties of being a Chinese American in the United States. Racial prejudice had led to a socially marginal existence, caught outside of American society. Social acculturation and assimilation into the larger American society, she believed, provided the answer to such feelings of marginality on the part of the "cultural hybrid":

> Culture conflict is responsible for his marginal feelings, composed of guilt, depression, instability, anxiety and frustration. These feelings are more pronounced in the second, or marginal, generation of settlement in a new society than in the one preceding it and in the ones to follow. When the "cultural gaps" are closed, so to speak, the cultural hybrid no longer poses a problem to himself and others. This is brought about by the processes of acculturation and assimilation.[24]

Lee added to the standard definition of "cultural assimilation" the eradication of all physical evidence of foreignness. "Ideally," she went on to say, "the completion of the processes includes the mixing of cultures and genes so that there are truly no 'dissimilar people.' "[25]

Rose Hum Lee's extolling of the need for biological race-mixing in order to remove all physical traces of difference was extreme even in the 1950s. This vision of the assimilation process went far beyond what might be termed the "culturalist" theories of the Survey of Race Relations sociologists. Physical differences, Park had said, had nothing to do with differences between the "races" except for the cultural consequences of seeing physical difference. It was self-consciousness caused by awareness of physical difference, not any physical difference in itself, that was at the root of racial awareness. Culture was a purely mental and social phenomenon. For Park, the ultimate "melting pot," which lay at the end of the assimilation cycle, was built purely out of shared memories and experiences—actual physical amalgamation was extraneous and unnecessary. Studying intermarriage and its importance to social relations, therefore, did not necessitate interest in the sexual act nor in its products.

In her early writings during the late 1940s and early 1950s, Rose Hum Lee had stayed well within the theoretical bounds of the "Oriental problem" as it had been defined and discussed by Robert Park and the sociologists of the Survey of Race Relations. By 1960, after fifteen years as a sociologist, and after struggling for her entire career with the inability of the Chinese in the United States to be accepted as completely "American," Rose Hum Lee argued for an absolute commitment to "integration." This term had never been important in the lexicon of the sociologists who had studied the "Oriental problem" in the 1920s, and Lee also used the term in a completely different manner than its current usages in the 1950s. "Integration" had become a political banner word, invoking a debate and battle over racial segregation and civil rights, and so it comes as a surprise that the way in which Lee used the term was completely outside of that context. Lee meant "integration" as a shorthand for the entire Chicago description of social assimilation and the race prejudice that blocked it: "The final objective of integration is a culturally homogeneous population," she wrote. "The barrier to complete integration is racial distinctiveness."[26]

Lee's vision of a physically as well as culturally homogeneous America, without a trace of "foreignness" or "distinctiveness," may not have been a nightmare in the context of 1950s America; after all, political and social conformity was still a general ideal rather than the object of scorn that William Whyte outlined in his 1956 work, *The Organization Man*.[27] Lee's idea of a homogeneous America was a utopian dream reflecting her own struggles against everything she saw as blocking the assimilation of Chinese Americans. By the time she published *The Chinese in the United States of America* in 1960, Lee saw the eradication of physical and cultural distinctiveness as the only way ultimately to eliminate both "white" racial prejudice and the "clannish" tendencies of many Chinese in America. Interracial sex was to be the process of fusion that would de-race America.

In many ways, Lee's move away from Park's emphasis on cultural assimilation toward a call for physical amalgamation signaled a fundamental weakness in the social scientists' model of culture in America. The existence of racial awareness and the consciousness of physical difference were of such permanence in American social life that racial boundaries were considered by Lee to be insurmountable through cultural means. Intermarriage, because it had been conceived as the meeting point between biological and cultural conceptions of racial contact, could embody a switch in emphasis from cultural to physical components.

Social scientists in the 1920s had defined intermarriage in such a way that it relied upon an awareness of differences in physical bodies, while seemingly emphasizing only the cultural aspects of the contact between those bodies. They seemed to erase the importance of the biological by focusing upon culture, but by choosing sexuality and sexual reproduction as the site of closest cultural contact, the sociologists placed an awareness of biology at the center of any definition of cultural difference. Sexual contact between two physical bodies did not necessarily result in the social institution of marriage, but the social scientists collapsed interracial sex and interracial marriage into the same category in order to emphasize the greater social meanings of sexual contact between individuals.[28]

Rose Hum Lee, living in a body that would never be accepted as anything except different, could see no way out of America's racial dilemma short of racial homogenization. Rose Hum Lee saw herself as straddling the marginal space between an exotic "Orient" and a "white" America. Though born and raised in Butte, Montana, she never felt fully accepted, and played the role of a translator and interpreter of the Chinese experience to interested Americans. Rose Hum Lee was forced to exoticize herself, and though she managed a successful academic career, her call for a time when "the cultural hybrid no longer poses a problem to himself and others" can be seen as referring as much to herself as it did to Chinese Americans in general.[29] To Lee, the "cultural hybrid" was not enough; only an actual "physical hybrid" would be free from racial discrimination. Rose Hum Lee saw "intermarriage" as the ultimate answer to the problem of racial prejudice and strife; interracial sex was the penultimate act that would produce the physically indistinguishable children of a "melting pot" America.

The meanings that "interracial sex" carried for American social thinkers seemed to go far beyond a prurient interest in sex across the color line. In the end, though, despite the multitude of meanings that interracial sex could convey, American social scientists and reformers could never escape the prurience of their own interest in the subject. They were fascinated by its connotations, and their obsession with exploring its hidden dimensions reflected a larger concern with its erotic and exotic potential. "Orientals" were the exotic "other" against which "white" Americans on the West Coast could measure themselves. "Orientals" were also an erotic fantasy, a mystery to be explored, the object of "white" men's loathing and "white" men's lust (and less apparent in images of popular culture, the object of "white" women's loathing and lust).

American sociologists' fascination with intermarriage between the "races" has always been more than social theory. The interest of social scientists in "interracial sex" inhabited the dark and liminal space connecting the sexuality of researchers and the social research they produced. The denial of such a connection has always been a precondition for the claims for validity of such social research, but it is a denial that speaks to the same tension between fascination and loathing that has marked the meanings of "miscegenation" in modern America. "White" social scientists consistently denied their personal fascination with exotic "Orientals."

For most of the past 150 years in America, Asian Americans have been represented as exotic "Orientals," the opposite of everything "American." As the embodiment of the exotic, "Orientals" have also been eroticized, objectified, and desired for being mysterious and different. This eroticization must be understood as the flip side of the loathing and fear that "white" Americans have also borne toward "Orientals"; the source of the desire is the same as that of the fear. It is because "Orientals" have been defined as different that they have attracted such attention.

The exoticization of "Orientals" was an act that always contained the possibility of smooth interchange between fear and lust. Loathed for being different, "Orientals" have always been desired at the same time for being different. If "Orientals" embodied the exotic, eroticization opened up the possibility of subsuming that difference within the sexual act. The tension still exists between a fascination with the exotic and a desire to unify America through similarity. Intermarriage remains the symbol for the meeting of difference and the ultimate disappearance of difference.

It is interesting to speculate about the possible reaction that Walter and Emma Fong's story might have generated if they had married in the 1990s rather than the 1890s. What would sociologists find fascinating about their history? Perhaps social scientific interest in Walter Fong would begin with his exceptional accomplishments; he was a perfect example of a "model minority." A highly educated, "overachieving" Asian American with a professional career, Walter Fong could serve as the poster boy for social scientific and political arguments that Asian Americans perform better than other minority groups in terms of education and income.[30] The clincher would be his achievement of the ultimate symbol of acceptance into American society—his "white" wife. The perfect flourish to cap his achievements, the educated Emma Fong would represent acceptance and assimilation into "white" America.

The intimate connection between social acceptance and intermarriage might be best contained in a saying common in the 1970s that "sansei marry blondes." The notion that third-generation Japanese Americans were "marrying out" in significant numbers (backed by demographic reports of rates of exogamy among Japanese Americans that exceeded 50 percent) led to fears of "racial death," as well as hopes for the ultimate amalgamation of America. This time, the fears were articulated most vocally among Japanese Americans, who prophesied the eventual disappearance of their community.[31] For some community activists, intermarriage was the most extreme form of "selling out" to the American dream of assimilation and trying to "become white." For other Japanese Americans, intermarriage with "whites" was simply another indication that they had achieved acceptance and success in the larger American society.

There is a history to the idea that intermarriage between Asian Americans and "whites" is a meaningful symbol. It has represented the fulfillment of a certain "American dream," the "melting pot" process of turning difference into similarity. Among both "whites" and Asian Americans, intermarriage has appeared as both a sign of success in assimilation and a dangerous process of "race-mixing" and "cultural loss." Intermarriage was seen to represent both difference and the erasure of difference. Although Robert Park and his fellow social scientists insisted that culture was a mental phenomenon—a matter of consciousness divorced from physical attributes—the prime marker of cultural difference has almost always been the body. American sociologists, in fighting racial thinking based on theories of biological inferiority or superiority, argued for the concept of "culture," one of the most influential and important constellations of ideas in twentieth-century America.[32] Theories about cultural assimilation triumphed both among social scientists and within popular thinking by the 1950s, succeeding in defining culture as absolutely nonbiological. Culture as a purely mental phenomenon, a result of consciousness and of acts caused by consciousness, was seen as the perfect road toward a homogenized melting pot.

The sociologists, however, could never break the connection between biological difference and their own awareness of cultural difference. They mapped different cultures onto different sets of bodies. This initial mapping worked because discrete sets of people who looked, for instance, "Oriental" did on the whole come from specific areas in Asia. In comparing Asian Americans to people who came from other places, "white" American social observers could homogenize the widely variant "cultural" practices of all "Orientals."[33] They could then imagine that intermarriage would eventually erase the cultural differences between "Orientals" and "whites." Rose Hum Lee, however, recognized that it was not the existence of cultural difference that was the obstacle to social assimilation; racial thinking remained despite intimate social relations between the "races." Indeed, the erotic allure of sexual relations could be driven by the very awareness of racial difference that sociologists thought the sex act would erase.

An awareness of the physical markers of biology is still a part of American consciousness, and so there remains a masked connection between bodies and culture. It is only because of our fine-tuned awareness of bodily difference that our fascination with intercultural sex and marriage makes sense. As long as Americans connect cultural difference with physical difference, we shall equate the racial with the cultural, and we shall remain fascinated with the idea of sex across racial boundaries.

NOTES

Funding for the research project that formed the basis for this essay was provided by fellowships from the Social Sciences and Humanities Research Council of Canada, the Mellon Foundation, the Woodrow Wilson Society of Princeton University, the Institute of American Cultures at UCLA, the Academic Senate of UCLA, and the University of California's Humanities Research Institute at Irvine.

1. The story of Walter Fong and Emma Fong Kuno was originally published in the *San Francisco Bulletin*, May 24–June 14, 1922. Copies were collected by the Survey of Race Relations on the West Coast in 1923; Papers of the Survey of Race Relations, box 24, major document 53, Hoover Institution Archives, Stanford University. The story was reprinted in a Fisk University collection, *Social Science Source Documents No. 4: Orientals and Their Cultural Adjustment. Interviews, Life Histories and Social Adjustment Experiences of Chinese and Japanese of Varying Backgrounds and Length of Residence in the United States* (Nashville: Social Science Institute, Fisk University, 1946).

2. According to Judy Yung's work on U.S. census manuscripts, about 7.5 percent of San Francisco Chinese men in 1900 were professionals; see Yung, *Unbound Feet: A Social History of Chinese Women in San Francisco* (Berkeley: University of California Press, 1995), 301.

3. Numbers from 1940 U.S. census. See Yung, *Unbound Feet*, 303; and Sucheng Chan, "Exclusion of Chinese Women, 1870–1943," in *Entry Denied*, ed. Sucheng Chan (Philadelphia: Temple University Press, 1991), 95.

4. Yung, *Unbound Feet*, 29; Dick Megumi Ogumi, "Asians and California's Anti-Miscegenation Laws," in *Asian and Pacific American Experiences: Women's Perspectives*, ed. Nobuya Tsuchida (Minneapolis: Asian/Pacific American Learning Resource Center and General College, University of Minnesota, 1982), 6. By the 1920s, antimiscegenation laws forbidding marriage between "Orientals" and "whites" had been enacted in California, Washington, Oregon, Nevada, Montana, and Idaho. California's law remained in effect until after World War II. On the effects of the Congressional Cable Act of 1922, see Chan, "Exclusion of Chinese Women," 128–29.

5. I use the term "Oriental" not because I condone its use as a name or marker, but because it reflects a specific historical usage and category. The current usage for people who

can trace their heritage back to Asia or the Pacific Ocean is "Asian/Pacific Islanders," a label that encompasses Chinese, Japanese, Filipino, Korean, Samoan, Hawaiian, Vietnamese, Cambodian, Thai, Indonesian, and other such ancestry. The term "Asian American," which replaced "Oriental" in the 1970s, still works for many of the same people who were formerly known as "Orientals." There has been a voluminous literature on the history of the term "Oriental," spurred especially by Edward Said's *Orientalism* (New York: Vintage, 1978). For a larger discussion of American "Orientalism," particularly in the form of social scientific definitions, see Henry Yu, *Thinking about "Orientals": Race, Migration and the Production of Exotic Knowledge in Modern America* (Oxford University Press, manuscript in progress). I use the term "white" for that constellation of people who benefit by being defined as different from those Americans of "color." I have also initially highlighted the terms "race," "interracial," and "hybrid" as a way of demarcating them as terms dependent on definitions of racial difference in America. For the central role of race in American history, see Michael Omi and Howard Winant, *Racial Formation in the United States* (New York: Routledge, 1986). See also David Roediger, *The Wages of Whiteness: Race and the Making of the American Working Class* (London: Verso, 1991); Tomás Almaguer, *Racial Fault Lines: The Historical Origins of White Supremacy in California* (Berkeley: University of California Press, 1994); Alexander Saxton, *The Rise and Fall of the White Republic* (London: Verso, 1990); Virginia Domínquez, *White by Definition* (New Brunswick: Rutgers University Press, 1986).

6. Social scientists in the 1920s equated "white" with "American," and thus understood Emma Fong, born in Canada, as the "American" in an interracial relationship between an "American" and an "Oriental." She is an example of how easy it was for "white" immigrants to America, particularly from Canada or Great Britain, to assume and be given the identity of "American." For the wedding, see *San Francisco Chronicle*, June 20, 1897; *Denver Rocky Mountain News*, June 20, 1897.

7. For other examples of stories of interracial love and marriage collected by the survey, see Papers of the Survey of Race Relations, box 28, major document 222, "Progeny of Jap-White Union Amaze," from *San Francisco Examiner*, Nov. 11, 1922; box 28, major document 223, from *San Francisco Call*, Dec. 1, 1921; box 28, major document 224, from *San Francisco Examiner*, March 20, 1923.

8. I am not arguing that studies of intermarriage have no validity, just that there has been a long history of assuming that studying intermarriage will say a great deal about America as a whole. See essays in Maria P. P. Root, ed., *Racially Mixed People in America* (Newbury Park, Calif.: Sage, 1992); Larry Hijame Shinagawa and Gin Yong Pang, "Asian American Panethnicity and Intermarriage," *Amerasia Journal* 22 (1996): 127–52; and a historian's valiant attempt to use intermarriage as a way of devaluing the salience of ethnic identity, Paul R. Spickard, *Mixed Blood: Intermarriage and Ethnic Identity in Twentieth-Century America* (Madison: University of Wisconsin Press, 1989). See also Colleen Fong and Judy Yung, "In Search of the Right Spouse: Interracial Marriage among Chinese and Japanese Americans," *Amerasia Journal* 21 (1995–96): 77–98. Of course an interracial couple or their friends may not consider the relationship to have much to do with "race" at all, but rather as related to mutual attraction based upon, for example, common hobbies or similar personal outlooks.

9. "Social distance" was more than a metaphor to Chicago sociologists. In an effort to arrive at "accurate" measurements of social distance, Emory Bogardus asked "Northern European whites" to rate "Japanese, Chinese, Hindus, Mexicans, Armenians, and thirty-five other races" according to the "primary reactions that they experienced toward each race." For example, if the "whites" would willingly "intermarry" with the Japanese, this reaction

would be assigned a numerical value of 1.0; if they would have Japanese as "chums," this would garner a 2.0; allowing the Japanese to be neighbors on their street would be a 3.0, fellow workers a 4.0, fellow citizens a 5.0, and at the farthest point of antipathy, 6.0 if the respondent wanted to exclude the Japanese from the country. Bogardus then asserted, for instance, "that the Chinese are put 4.28 groups away from complete intimacy and understanding, and that the English are put only 0.27 of a group away." Here, sexual relations marked ground zero for measurement of the "social distance" between two groups. See Emory Bogardus, "Social Distance: A Measuring Stick Gaging Racial Antipathies on the Coast—and Elsewhere," *Survey Graphic* 56 (May 1926): 169; and Robert Park, "The Concept of Social Distance," *Journal of Applied Sociology* 8 (1924): 340.

10. On the Chicago school of sociology, see Barbara Ballis Lal, *The Romance of Culture in an Urban Civilization: Robert E. Park on Race and Ethnic Relations in Cities* (London: Routledge, 1990); Lester R. Kurtz, *Evaluating Chicago Sociology: A Guide to the Literature, with an Annotated Bibliography* (Chicago: University of Chicago Press, 1984); Fred H. Matthews, *Quest for an American Sociology: Robert E. Park and the Chicago School* (Montreal: McGill University Press, 1977); and Robert E. L. Faris, *Chicago Sociology, 1920–1932* (San Francisco: Chandler, 1967).

11. On the role of Chinese and Japanese American sociologists in producing knowledge about "Orientals" in America, see Henry Yu, "Thinking about 'Orientals': A History of Race, Migration, and Modernity in Twentieth-Century America" (Ph.D., diss., Princeton University, 1995).

12. On anti-Asian agitation on the West Coast, see Sucheng Chan, *Asian Americans: An Interpretive History* (Boston: Twayne, 1991); and Ronald Takaki, *Strangers from a Different Shore* (New York: Penguin Books, 1989); see also Alexander Saxton, *The Indispensable Enemy: Labor and the Anti-Chinese Movement in California* (Berkeley: University of California Press, 1971).

13. Sax Rohmer was the pseudonym of Arthur Sarsfield Ward, who wrote a series of novels, beginning with *The Insidious Dr. Fu-Manchu* (New York: McKinlay, Stone, and McKenzie, 1913), involving the nefarious Fu Manchu, an evil "Oriental" genius out to conquer the world.

14. On the exoticization of "Orientals" in America, see John Kuo Wei Tchen, "Modernizing White Patriarchy: Re-viewing D. W. Griffith's Broken Blossoms," in *Moving the Image: Independent Asian Pacific American Media Arts*, ed. Russell Leong (Los Angeles: UCLA Asian American Studies Center and Visual Communications, 1991), 133–43; and James Moy, *Marginal Sights: Staging the Chinese in America* (Iowa City: University of Iowa Press, 1993). On the portrayal of Asian women in the media, see Renee Tajima, "Lotus Blossoms Don't Bleed: Images of Asian Women," in *Making Waves: An Anthology of Writings by and about Asian American Women*, ed. Asian Women United of California (Boston: Beacon, 1989), 308–17. On the exoticization of Asians in literature, see William Wu, *The Yellow Peril: Chinese Americans in American Fiction, 1850–1940* (Hamden, Conn.: Archon Books, 1982); and Stuart Creighton Miller, *The Unwelcome Immigrant: The American Image of the Chinese, 1785–1882* (Berkeley: University of California Press, 1969).

15. Davis to Park, Nov. 21, 1923, box 13, Park Correspondence, Papers of the Survey. Emphasis added.

16. Original of the full Intermarriage Document, box 6, Papers of the Survey. The questionnaire, which was only a portion of the larger document discussing "racial intermarriage," was reprinted in Emory Bogardus, *Introduction to Social Research* (Los Angeles: Suttonhouse, 1936).

17. Letters between Park and Davis, Dec. 1923, box 13, Park Correspondence.

18. There had been a debate among the survey organizers over the desirability of using the "red flag" of interracial sex to provoke interest; see letters between Davis and George Gleason, March 17, 20, 25, 1924, General Correspondence Folder, box 13, Papers of the Survey.

19. Sidney Gulick to Davis, July 12, 1923, box 11, Davis Correspondence, Papers of the Survey.

20. In a book supporting Japanese immigration to the United States, Gulick had included a picture of Mr. Otto Fukushima, an "American Japanese," and his wife, who was labeled in parentheses "American"—meaning "white." See Sydney L. Gulick, *The American Japanese Problem: A Study of the Racial Relations of the East and the West* (New York: Scribner's Sons, 1914), 131.

21. Park to Davis, April 29, 1924, box 13, Park Correspondence.

22. Franz Boas evinced a more pessimistic view than Park on the effectiveness of cultural assimilation, wondering if it would ever be possible to get rid of racial prejudice as long as there were visual physical differences, and thus suggesting that intermarriage was the long-term solution to racial awareness. See Boas, "The Problem of the American Negro," *Yale Review* 10 (January 1921): 392. Some Chicago sociologists were more interested than Park in actual sexual relations. In the 1930s, while conducting research for his Ph.D. dissertation on Chinese male laundry workers, the Chinese American sociologist Paul Chan Pang Siu examined sexual relations between Chinese American men and "white" women. See Siu, *The Chinese Laundryman: A Study of Social Isolation*, ed. John K. W. Tchen (New York: New York University Press, 1987).

23. On Rose Hum Lee, see Biographical File, Roosevelt University Archives, Chicago; private letters and papers in the possession of her daughter, Elaine Lee; interviews by Henry Yu with her brother, Ralph Hum, Oct. 1992; and with a roommate at the University of Chicago, Beulah Ong Kwoh, Jan. 1992.

24. Rose Hum Lee, "The Marginal Man: Re-evaluation and Indices of Measurement," *Journal of Human Relations* (1956): 27–28.

25. Lee, "The Marginal Man," 28.

26. Rose Hum Lee, *The Chinese in the United States of America* (Hong Kong: Hong Kong University Press, 1960), 406.

27. William F. Whyte, *The Organization Man* (New York: Simon and Schuster, 1956).

28. For instance, they might have focused instead on more idiosyncratic founts of desire, using Freudian notions that emphasized the individual's psychic history. The attraction between individuals of different "races" might have lost any greater social meaning if it were reduced, for example, to such personal factors as a man looking for the traits of his mother, or desire for someone similar to an earlier partner as a way of working out the failure of previous relationships. It is telling that the Chicago sociologists on the whole avoided psychoanalytic modes of analysis precisely because of their emphasis on the cultural meanings of interracial sex and marriage.

29. Lee, "The Marginal Man," 28.

30. The rise of the idea of Asian Americans as a "model minority" can be traced back to social scientific studies just after World War II that traced the success Japanese Americans had achieved in rebounding from internment. See William Abel Caudill, "Japanese American Acculturation and Personality" (Ph.D. diss., University of Chicago, 1950); Setsuko Matsunaga Nishi, "Japanese American Achievement in Chicago: A Cultural Response to Degradation" (Ph.D. diss., University of Chicago, 1963); William Petersen, "Success Story, Japanese-American Style," *New York Times Magazine*, Jan. 9, 1966; and idem, *Japanese-Americans: Oppression and Success* (New York: Random House, 1971); Martin Kasindorf et al., "Asian

Americans: A Model Minority," *Newsweek*, Dec. 6, 1982, 39–43; David Bell, "The Triumph of Asian Americans," *New Republic*, July 1985, 24–31. What began as a social scientific focus on post-internment Japanese Americans spread to Chinese Americans and then to the Asian immigrants who came after 1965.

31. For statistics, see Akemi Kikamura and Harry H. L. Kitano, "Interracial Marriage: A Picture of the Japanese Americans," *Journal of Social Issues* 29 (1973): 67–81.

32. For one of the earliest and most interesting discussions of culture in modern American history, and the difficulty of using an analytical concept that itself arose during the period being studied, see Warren Susman, *Culture as History: The Transformation of American Society in the Twentieth Century* (New York: Pantheon, 1984).

33. Physical markers no longer serve as very good indicators of cultural and geographic origin, and perhaps never did. Even seventy years ago, the birth of second-generation Asian Americans made generalizations based on "cultural" origin difficult, but increases in the numbers of both native-born and immigrant Asian Americans have made any argument about the cultural similarity of Asians untenable. For early social scientific fascination with the American-born generation of "Orientals," see William C. Smith, "Born American, But—" *Survey Graphic* 56 (May 1, 1926): 167; idem, "The Second Generation Oriental-American," *Journal of Applied Sociology* 10 (1925–26): 160; idem, "The Second Generation Oriental in America" (preliminary paper prepared for the second General Session, Institute of Pacific Relations, July 15–29, 1927).

Chapter Twenty-Two

Miscegenation Law, Court Cases, and Ideologies of "Race" in Twentieth-Century America

Peggy Pascoe

On March 21, 1921, Joe Kirby took his wife, Mayellen, to court. The Kirbys had been married for seven years, and Joe wanted out. Ignoring the usual option of divorce, he asked for an annulment, charging that his marriage had been invalid from its very beginning because Arizona law prohibited marriages between "persons of Caucasian blood, or their descendants" and "negroes, Mongolians or Indians, and their descendants." Joe Kirby claimed that while he was "a person of the Caucasian blood," his wife, Mayellen, was "a person of negro blood."[1]

Although Joe Kirby's charges were rooted in a well-established—and tragic—tradition of American miscegenation law, his court case quickly disintegrated into a definitional dispute that bordered on the ridiculous. The first witness in the case was Joe's mother, Tula Kirby, who gave her testimony in Spanish through an interpreter. Joe's lawyer laid out the case by asking Tula Kirby a few seemingly simple questions:

> *Joe's lawyer:* To what race do you belong?
> *Tula Kirby:* Mexican.
> *Joe's lawyer:* Are you white or have you Indian blood?
> *Kirby:* I have no Indian blood.
>
> . . .
>
> *Joe's lawyer:* Do you know the defendant [Mayellen] Kirby?
> *Kirby:* Yes.
> *Joe's lawyer:* To what race does she belong?
> *Kirby:* Negro.

Then the cross-examination began.

> *Mayellen's lawyer:* Who was your father?
> *Kirby:* Jose Romero.
> *Mayellen's lawyer:* Was he a Spaniard?
> *Kirby:* Yes, a Mexican.
> *Mayellen's lawyer:* Was he born in Spain?
> *Kirby:* No, he was born in Sonora.
> *Mayellen's lawyer:* And who was your mother?
> *Kirby:* Also in Sonora.

Mayellen's lawyer: Was she a Spaniard?

Kirby: She was on her father's side.

Mayellen's lawyer: And what on her mother's side?

Kirby: Mexican.

Mayellen's lawyer: What do you mean by Mexican, Indian, a native [?]

Kirby: I don't know what is meant by Mexican.

Mayellen's lawyer: A native of Mexico?

Kirby: Yes, Sonora, all of us.

Mayellen's lawyer: Who was your grandfather on your father's side?

Kirby: He was a Spaniard.

Mayellen's lawyer: Who was he?

Kirby: His name was Ignacio Quevas.

Mayellen's lawyer: Where was he born?

Kirby: That I don't know. He was my grandfather.

Mayellen's lawyer: How do you know he was a [S]paniard then?

Kirby: Because he told me ever since I had knowledge that he was a Spaniard.

Next the questioning turned to Tula's opinion about Mayellen Kirby's racial identity.

Mayellen's lawyer: You said Mrs. [Mayellen] Kirby was a negress. What do you know about Mrs. Kirby's family?

Kirby: I distinguish her by her color and the hair; that is all I do know.[2]

The second witness in the trial was Joe Kirby, and by the time he took the stand, the people in the courtroom knew they were in murky waters. When Joe's lawyer opened with the question, "What race do *you* belong to?" Joe answered, "Well . . . ," and paused, while Mayellen's lawyer objected to the question on the ground that it called for a conclusion by the witness. "Oh, no," said the judge, "it is a matter of pedigree." Eventually allowed to answer the question, Joe said, "I belong to the white race I suppose." Under cross-examination, he described his father as having been of the "Irish race," although he admitted, "I never knew any one of his people."[3]

Stopping at the brink of this morass, Joe's lawyer rested his case. He told the judge he had established that Joe was "Caucasian." Mayellen's lawyer scoffed, claiming that Joe had "failed utterly to prove his case" and arguing that "[Joe's] mother has admitted that. She has [testified] that she only claims a quarter Spanish blood; the rest of it is native blood." At this point the court intervened. "I know," said the judge, "but that does not signify anything."[4]

From the Decline and Fall of Scientific Racism to an Understanding of Modernist Racial Ideology

The Kirbys' case offers a fine illustration of Evelyn Brooks Higginbotham's observation that, although most Americans are sure they know "race" when they see it, very few can offer a definition of the term. Partly for this reason, the questions of what "race" signifies and what signifies "race" are as important for scholars today as they were for the participants in *Kirby v. Kirby* seventy-five years ago.[5] Historians have a long—and recently a distinguished—record of exploring this question.[6] Beginning in the 1960s, one notable group charted the rise and fall of scientific racism among American intellectuals. Today their successors, more likely to be schooled in social than intellectual history, trace the social construction of racial ideologies, including the idea of "whiteness," in a steadily expanding range of contexts.[7]

Their work has taught us a great deal about racial thinking in American history. We can trace the growth of racism among antebellum immigrant workers and free-soil northern Republicans; we can measure its breadth in late nineteenth-century segregation and the immigration policies of the 1920s. We can follow the rise of Anglo-Saxonism from Manifest Destiny through the Spanish-American War and expose the appeals to white supremacy in woman suffrage speeches. We can relate all these developments (and more) to the growth and elaboration of scientific racist attempts to use biological characteristics to scout for racial hierarchies in social life, levels of civilization, even language.

Yet the range and richness of these studies all but end with the 1920s. In contrast to historians of the nineteenth- and early twentieth-century United States, historians of the nation in the mid- to late twentieth century seem to focus on racial ideologies only when they are advanced by the far Right (as in the Ku Klux Klan) or by racialized groups themselves (as in the Harlem Renaissance or black nationalist movements). To the extent that there is a framework for surveying mainstream twentieth-century American racial ideologies, it is inherited from the classic histories that tell of the post-1920s decline and fall of scientific racism. Their final pages link the demise of scientific racism to the rise of a vanguard of social scientists led by the cultural anthropologist Franz Boas: when modern social science emerges, racism runs out of intellectual steam. In the absence of any other narrative, this forms the basis for a commonly held but rarely examined intellectual trickle-down theory in which the attack on scientific racism emerges in universities in the 1920s and eventually, if belatedly, spreads to courts in the 1940s and 1950s and to government policy in the 1960s and 1970s.

A close look at such incidents as the *Kirby* case, however, suggests a rather different historical trajectory, one that recognizes that the legal system does more than just reflect social or scientific ideas about race; it also produces and reproduces them.[8] By following a trail marked by four miscegenation cases—the seemingly ordinary *Kirby v. Kirby* (1922) and *Estate of Monks* (1941) and the pathbreaking *Perez v. Lippold* (1948) and *Loving v. Virginia* (1967)—this article will examine the relation between modern social science, miscegenation law, and twentieth-century American racial ideologies, focusing less on the decline of scientific racism and more on the emergence of new racial ideologies.

In exploring these issues, it helps to understand that the range of nineteenth-century racial ideologies was much broader than scientific racism. Accordingly, I have chosen to use the term *racialism* to designate an ideological complex that other historians often describe with the terms "race" or "racist." I intend the term *racialism* to be broad enough to cover a wide range of nineteenth-century ideas, from the biologically marked categories scientific racists employed to the more amorphous ideas George M. Fredrickson has so aptly called "romantic racialism."[9] Used in this way, "racialism" helps counter the tendency of twentieth-century observers to perceive nineteenth-century ideas as biologically "determinist" in some simple sense. To racialists (including scientific racists), the important point was not that biology determined culture (indeed, the split between the two was only dimly perceived), but that race, understood as an indivisible essence that included not only biology but also culture, morality, and intelligence, was a compellingly significant factor in history and society.

My argument is this: During the 1920s, American racialism was challenged by several emerging ideologies, all of which depended on a modern split between biology and culture. Between the 1920s and the 1960s, those competing ideologies were winnowed down to the single, powerfully persuasive belief that the eradication of racism depends on the deliberate nonrecognition of race. I will call that belief *modernist racial ideology* to echo the self-conscious "modernism" of social scientists, writers, artists, and cultural rebels of the early twentieth century. When historians mention this phenomenon, they usually label it "antiracist" or "egalitarian" and describe it as in stark contrast to the "racism" of its predecessors. But in the new legal scholarship called critical race theory, this same ideology, usually referred to as "color blindness," is criticized by those who recognize that it, like other racial ideologies, can be turned to the service of oppression.[10]

Modernist racial ideology has been widely accepted; indeed, it compels nearly as much adherence in the late twentieth-century United States as racialism did in the late nineteenth century. It is therefore important to see it not as what it claims to be—the nonideological end of racism—but as a racial ideology of its own, whose history shapes many of today's arguments about the meaning of race in American society.

The Legacy of Racialism and the Kirby Case

Although it is probably less familiar to historians than, say, school segregation law, miscegenation law is an ideal place to study both the legacy of nineteenth-century racialism and the emergence of modern racial ideologies.[11] Miscegenation laws, in force from the 1660s through the 1960s, were among the longest lasting of American racial restrictions. They both reflected and produced significant shifts in American racial thinking. Although the first miscegenation laws had been passed in the colonial period, it was not until after the demise of slavery that they began to function as the ultimate sanction of the American system of white supremacy. They burgeoned along with the rise of segregation and the early twentieth-century devotion to "white purity." At one time or another, forty-one American colonies and states enacted them; they blanketed western as well as southern states.[12]

By the early twentieth century, miscegenation laws were so widespread that they formed a virtual road map to American legal conceptions of race. Laws that had originally prohibited marriages between whites and African Americans (and, very occasionally, American Indians) were extended to cover a much wider range of groups. Eventually, twelve states targeted American Indians, fourteen Asian Americans (Chinese, Japanese, and Koreans), and nine "Malays" (or Filipinos). In Arizona the *Kirby* case was decided under categories first adopted in a 1901 law that prohibited whites from marrying "negroes, Mongolians or Indians"; in 1931 "Malays" and "Hindus" were added to this list.[13]

Although many historians assume that miscegenation laws enforced American taboos against interracial sex, marriage, more than sex, was the legal focus.[14] Some states did forbid both interracial sex and interracial marriage, but nearly twice as many targeted only marriage. Because marriage carried with it social respectability and economic benefits that were routinely denied to couples engaged in illicit sex, appeals courts adjudicated the legal issue of miscegenation at least as frequently in civil cases about marriage and divorce, inheritance, or child legitimacy as in criminal cases about sexual misconduct.[15]

By the time the *Kirby* case was heard, lawyers and judges approached miscegenation cases with working assumptions built on decades of experience. There had been a flurry of challenges to the laws during Reconstruction, but courts quickly fended off arguments that miscegenation laws violated the Fourteenth Amendment guarantee of "equal protection." Beginning in the late 1870s, judges declared that the laws were constitutional because they covered all racial groups "equally."[16] Judicial justifications reflected the momentum toward racial categorization built into the nineteenth-century legal system and buttressed by the racialist conviction that everything from culture, morality, and intelligence to heredity could be understood in terms of race.

From the 1880s until the 1920s, lawyers whose clients had been caught in the snare of miscegenation laws knew better than to challenge the constitutionality of the laws or to dispute the perceived necessity for racial categorization; these were all but guaranteed to be losing arguments. A defender's best bet was to do what Mayellen Kirby's lawyer tried to do: to persuade a judge (or jury) that one particular individual's racial classification was in error. Lawyers who defined their task in these limited terms occasionally succeeded, but even then the deck was stacked against them. Wielded by judges and juries who believed that setting racial boundaries was crucial to the maintenance of ordered society, the criteria used to determine who fit in which category were more notable for their malleability than for their logical consistency. Genealogy, appearance, claims to identity, or that mystical quality, "blood"—any of these would do.[17]

In Arizona, Judge Samuel L. Pattee demonstrated that malleability in deciding the *Kirby* case. Although Mayellen Kirby's lawyer maintained that Joe Kirby "appeared" to be an Indian, the judge insisted that parentage, not appearance, was the key to Joe's racial classification: "Mexicans are classed as of the Caucasian Race. They are descendants, supposed to be, at least of the Spanish conquerors of that country, and unless it can be shown that they are mixed up with some other races, why the presumption is that they are descendants of the Caucasian race."[18] While the judge decided that ancestry determined that Joe Kirby was "Caucasian," he simply assumed that Mayellen Kirby was "Negro." Mayellen Kirby sat silent through the entire trial; she was spoken about and spoken for but never allowed to speak herself. There was no testimony about her ancestry; her race was assumed to rest in her visible physical characteristics. Neither of the lawyers bothered to argue over Mayellen's racial designation. As Joe's lawyer later explained, "The learned and discriminating judge . . . had the opportunity to gaze upon the dusky countenance of the appellant [Mayellen Kirby] and could not and did not fail to observe the distinguishing characteristics of the African race and blood."[19] In the end, the judge accepted the claim that Joe Kirby was "Caucasian" and Mayellen Kirby "Negro" and held that the marriage violated Arizona miscegenation law; he granted Joe Kirby his annulment. In so doing, the judge resolved the miscegenation drama by adding a patriarchal moral to the white supremacist plot. As long as miscegenation laws regulated marriage more than sex, it proved easy for white men involved with women of color to avoid the social and economic responsibilities they would have carried in legally sanctioned marriages with white women. By granting Joe Kirby an annulment rather than a divorce, the judge not only denied the validity of the marriage while it had lasted but also in effect excused Joe Kirby from his obligation to provide economic support to a divorced wife.[20]

For her part, Mayellen Kirby had nothing left to lose. She and her lawyer appealed to the Arizona Supreme Court. This time they threw caution to the winds. Taking a first step toward the development of modern racial ideologies, they moved beyond their carefully limited argument about Joe's individual racial classification to challenge the entire racial logic of miscegenation law. The Arizona statute provided a tempting target for their attack, for under its "descendants" provision, a person of "mixed blood" could not legally marry anyone. Pointing this out, Mayellen Kirby's lawyer argued that the law must therefore be unconstitutional. He failed to convince the court. The appeals court judge brushed aside such objections. The argument that the law was unconstitutional, the judge held, "is an attack . . . [Mayellen Kirby] is not entitled to make for the reason that there is no evidence that she is other than of the black race. . . . It will be time enough to pass on the question she raises . . . when it is presented by some one whose rights are involved or affected."[21]

The Culturalist Challenge to Racialism

By the 1920s, refusals to recognize the rights of African American women had become conventional in American law. So had refusals to recognize obvious inconsistencies in legal racial classification schemes. Minions of racialism, judges, juries, and experts sometimes quarreled over specifics, but they agreed on the overriding importance of making and enforcing racial classifications.

Lawyers in miscegenation cases therefore neither needed nor received much courtroom assistance from experts. In another legal arena, citizenship and naturalization law, the use of experts, nearly all of whom advocated some version of scientific racism, was much more common. Ever since the 1870s, naturalization lawyers had relied on scientific racists to help them decide which racial and ethnic groups met the United States naturalization requirement of being "white" persons. But in a series of cases heard in the first two decades of the twentieth century, this strategy backfired. When judges found themselves drawn into a heated scientific debate on the question of whether "Caucasian" was the same as "white," the United States Supreme Court settled the question by discarding the experts and reverting to what the justices called the opinion of the "common man."[22]

In both naturalization and miscegenation cases, judges relied on the basic agreement between popular and expert (scientific racist) versions of the racialism that permeated turn-of-the-century American society. But even as judges promulgated the common sense of racialism, the ground was shifting beneath their feet. By the 1920s, lawyers in miscegenation cases were beginning to glimpse the courtroom potential of arguments put forth by a pioneering group of self-consciously "modern" social scientists willing to challenge racialism head on.

Led by cultural anthropologist Franz Boas, these emerging experts have long stood as the heroes of histories of the decline of scientific racism (which is often taken to stand for racism as a whole). But for modern social scientists, the attack on racialism was not so much an end in itself as a function of the larger goal of establishing "culture" as a central social science paradigm. Intellectually and institutionally, Boas and his followers staked their claim to academic authority on their conviction that human difference and human history were best explained by culture. Because they interpreted character, morality, and social organization as cultural, rather than racial, phenomena and because they were determined to explore, name, and claim the field of cultural analysis for social scientists, particularly cultural anthropologists, sociologists, and social psychologists, they are perhaps best described as culturalists.[23]

To consolidate their power, culturalists had to challenge the scientific racist paradigms they hoped to displace. Two of the arguments they made were of particular significance for the emergence of modern racial ideologies. The first was the argument that the key notion of racialism—race—made no biological sense. This argument allowed culturalists to take aim at a very vulnerable target. For most of the nineteenth century, scientific racists had solved disputes about who fit into which racial categories by subdividing the categories. As a result, the number of scientifically recognized races had increased so steadily that by 1911, when the anthropologist Daniel Folkmar compiled the intentionally definitive *Dictionary of Races and Peoples*, he recognized "45 races or peoples among immigrants coming to the United States." Folkmar's was only one of several competing schemes, and culturalists delighted in pointing out the discrepancies between them, showing that scientific racists could not agree on such seemingly simple matters as how many races there were or what criteria—blood, skin color, hair type—best indicated race.[24]

In their most dramatic mode, culturalists went so far as to insist that physical characteristics were completely unreliable indicators of race; in biological terms, they insisted, race must be considered indeterminable. Thus, in an influential encyclopedia article on "race" published in the early thirties, Boas insisted that "it is not possible to assign with certainty any one individual to a definite group." Perhaps the strongest statement of this kind came from Julian Huxley and A. C. Haddon, British scientists who maintained that "the term *race* as applied to human groups should be dropped from the vocabulary of science." Since Huxley was one of the first culturalists trained as a biologist, his credentials added luster to his opinion. In this and other forms, the culturalist argument that race was biologically indeterminable captured the attention of both contemporaries and later historians.[25]

Historians have paid much less attention to a second and apparently incompatible argument put forth by culturalists. It started from the other end of the spectrum, maintaining not that there was no such thing as biological race, but that race was nothing more than biology. Since culturalists considered biology of remarkably little importance, consigning race to the realm of biology pushed it out of the picture. Thus Boas ended his article on race by concluding that although it remained "likely" enough that scientific study of the "anatomical differences between the races" might reveal biological influences on the formation of personality, "the study of cultural forms shows that such differences are altogether irrelevant as compared with the powerful influence of the cultural environment in which the group lives."[26]

Following this logic, the contrast between important and wide-reaching culture and unimportant (but biological) race stood as the cornerstone of many culturalist arguments. Thus the cultural anthropologist Ruth Benedict began her influential 1940 book, *Race: Science and Politics*, with an analysis of "what race is *not*," including language, customs, intelligence, character, and civilization. In a 1943 pamphlet coauthored with Gene Weltfish and addressed to the general public, she explained that real "racial differences" occurred only in "nonessentials such as texture of head hair, amount of body hair, shape of the nose or head, or color of the eyes and the skin." Drawing on these distinctions, Benedict argued that race was a scientific "fact," but that racism, which she defined as "the dogma that the hope of civilization depends upon eliminating some races and keeping others pure," was no more than a "modern superstition."[27]

Culturalists set these two seemingly contradictory depictions of race—the argument that biological race was nonsense and the argument that race was merely biology—right beside each other. The contradiction mattered little to them. Both arguments effectively contracted the range of racialist thinking, and both helped break conceptual links between race and character, morality, psychology, and language. By showing that one after another of these phenomena depended more on environment and training than on biology, culturalists moved each one out of the realm of race and into the province of culture, widening the modern split between culture and biology. Boas opened his article on race by staking out this position. "The term race is often used loosely to indicate groups of men differing in appearance, language, or culture," he wrote, but in his analysis, it would apply "solely to the biological grouping of human types."[28]

In adopting this position, culturalist intellectuals took a giant step away from popular common sense on the issue of race. Recognizing—even at times celebrating—this gap between themselves and the public, they devoted much of their work to dislodging popular racial assumptions. They saw the public as lamentably behind the times and sadly prone to race "prejudice," and they used their academic credentials to insist that racial categories not only did not rest on common sense, but made little sense at all.[29]

The Monks Case and the Making of Modern Racial Ideologies

This, of course, was just what lawyers challenging miscegenation laws wanted to hear. Because culturalist social scientists could offer their arguments with an air of scientific and academic authority that might persuade judges, attorneys began to invite them to appear as expert witnesses. But when culturalists appeared in court, they entered an arena where their argument for the biological indeterminacy of race was shaped in ways neither they nor the lawyers who recruited them could control.

Take, for example, the seemingly curious trial of Marie Antoinette Monks of San Diego, California, decided in the Superior Court of San Diego County in 1939. By all accounts, Marie Antoinette Monks was a woman with a clear eye for her main chance. In the early 1930s, she had entranced and married a man named Allan Monks, potential heir to a Boston fortune. Shortly after the marriage, which took place in Arizona, Allan Monks declined into insanity. Whether his mental condition resulted from injuries he had suffered in a motorcycle crash or from drugs administered under the undue influence of Marie Antoinette, the court would debate at great length. Allan Monks died. He left two wills: an old one in favor of a friend named Ida Lee and a newer one in favor of his wife, Marie Antoinette. Ida Lee submitted her version of the will for probate, Marie Antoinette challenged her claim, and Lee fought back. Lee's lawyers contended that the Monks marriage was illegal. They charged that Marie Antoinette Monks, who had told her husband she was a "French" countess, was actually "a Negro" and therefore prohibited by Arizona law from marrying Allan Monks, whom the court presumed to be Caucasian.[30]

Much of the ensuing six-week-long trial was devoted to determining the "race" of Marie Antoinette Monks. To prove that she was "a Negro," her opponents called five people to the witness stand: a disgruntled friend of her husband, a local labor commissioner, and three expert witnesses, all of whom offered arguments that emphasized biological indicators of race. The first so-called expert, Monks's hairdresser, claimed that she could tell that Monks was of mixed blood from looking at the size of the moons of her fingernails, the color of the "ring" around the palms of her hands, and the "kink" in her hair. The second, a physical anthropologist from the nearby San Diego Museum, claimed to be able to tell that Monks was "at least one-eighth negroid" from the shape of her face, the color of her hands, and her "protruding heels," all of which he had observed casually while a spectator in the courtroom. The third expert witness, a surgeon, had grown up and practiced medicine in the South and later served at a Southern Baptist mission in Africa. Having once walked alongside Monks when entering the courthouse (at which time he tried, he said, to make a close observation of her), he testified that he could tell that she was of "one-eighth negro blood" from the contour of her calves and heels, from the "peculiar pallor" on the back of her neck, from the shape of her face, and from the wave of her hair.[31]

To defend Monks, her lawyers called a friend, a relative, and two expert witnesses of their own, an anthropologist and a biologist. The experts both started out by testifying to the culturalist position that it was impossible to tell a person's race from physical characteristics, especially if that person was, as they put it, "of mixed blood." This was the argument culturalists used whenever they were cornered into talking about biology, a phenomenon they tended to regard as so insignificant a factor in social life that they preferred to avoid talking about it at all.

But because this argument replaced certainty with uncertainty, it did not play very well in the *Monks* courtroom. Seeking to find the definitiveness they needed to offset the experts who had already testified, the lawyers for Monks paraded their own client in front of the witness stand, asking her to show the anthropologist her fingernails and to remove her shoes so that he could see her heels. They lingered over the biologist's testimony that Monks's physical features resembled those of the people of southern France. In the end, Monks's lawyers backed both experts into a corner; when pressed repeatedly for a definite answer, both reluctantly admitted that it was their opinion that Monks was a "white" woman.[32]

The experts' dilemma reveals the limitations of the argument for racial indeterminacy in the courtroom. Faced with a conflict between culturalist experts, who offered uncertainty and indeterminacy, and their opponents, who offered concrete biological answers to racial questions, judges were predisposed to favor the latter. To judges, culturalists appeared frustratingly vague and uncooperative (in other words, lousy witnesses), while their opponents seemed to be good witnesses willing to answer direct questions.

In the *Monks* case, the judge admitted that his own "inexpert" opinion—that Marie Antoinette "did have many characteristics that I would say . . . [showed] mixed negro and some other blood"—was not enough to justify a ruling. Turning to the experts before him, he dismissed the hairdresser (whose experience he was willing to grant, but whose scientific credentials he considered dubious); he passed over the biologist (whose testimony, he thought, could go either way); and he dismissed the two anthropologists, whose testimonies, he said, more or less canceled each other out. The only expert the judge was willing to rely on was the surgeon, because the surgeon "seemed . . . to hold a very unique and peculiar position as an expert on the question involved from his work in life."[33]

Relying on the surgeon's testimony, the judge declared that Marie Antoinette Monks was "the descendant of a negro" who had "one-eighth negro blood . . . and ⅞ Caucasian blood"; he said that her "race" prohibited her from marrying Allan Monks and from inheriting his estate. The racial categorization served to invalidate the marriage in two overlapping ways. First, as a "negro," Marie Antoinette could not marry a white under Arizona miscegenation law; and second, by telling her husband-to-be that she was "French," Marie Antoinette had committed a "fraud" serious enough to render the marriage legally void. The court's decision that she had also exerted "undue influence" over Monks was hardly necessary to the outcome.[34]

As the *Monks* case suggests, we should be careful not to overestimate the influence culturalists had on the legal system. And, while in courtrooms culturalist experts were trying—and failing—to convince judges that biological racial questions were unanswerable, outside the courts their contention that biological racial answers were insignificant was faring little better. During the first three decades of the twentieth century, scientists on the "racial" side of the split between race and culture reconstituted themselves into a rough alliance of their own. Mirroring the modern dividing line between biology and culture, its ranks swelled with those who claimed special expertise on biological questions. There were biologists and physicians; leftover racialists such as physical anthropologists, increasingly shorn of their claims to expertise in every arena *except* that of physical characteristics; and, finally, the newly emerging eugenicists.[35]

Eugenicists provided the glue that held this coalition together. Narrowing the sweep of nineteenth-century racialist thought to focus on biology, these modern biological experts then expanded their range by offering physical characteristics, heredity, and reproductive imperatives as variations on the biological theme. They were particularly drawn to arenas in which all these biological motifs came into play; accordingly, they placed special emphasis on reforming marriage laws. Perhaps the best-known American eugenicist, Charles B. Davenport of the Eugenics Record Office, financed by the Carnegie Institution, outlined their position in a 1913 pamphlet, *State Laws Limiting Marriage Selection Examined in the Light of Eugenics*, which proposed strengthening state control over the marriages of the physically and racially unfit. Davenport's plan was no mere pipe dream. According to the historian Michael Grossberg, by the 1930s, forty-one states used eugenic categories to restrict the marriage of "lunatics," "imbeciles," "idiots," and the "feebleminded"; twenty-six states restricted the marriages of those infected with syphilis and gonorrhea; and twenty-seven states passed sterilization laws. By midcentury, blood tests had become a standard legal prerequisite for marriage.[36]

Historians have rather quickly passed over the racial aspects of American eugenics, seeing its proponents as advocates of outmoded ideas soon to be beached by the culturalist sea change. Yet until at least World War II, eugenicists reproduced a modern racism that was biological in a particularly virulent sense. For them, unlike their racialist predecessors (who tended to regard biology as an indicator of a much more expansive racial phenomenon), biology really was the essence of race. And unlike nineteenth-century scientific racists (whose belief in discrete racial dividing lines was rarely shaken by evidence of racial intermixture), twentieth-century eugenicists and culturalists alike seemed obsessed with the subject of mixed-race individuals.[37]

In their determination to protect "white purity," eugenicists believed that even the tightest definitions of race by blood proportion were too loose. Setting their sights on Virginia, in 1924 they secured passage of the most draconian miscegenation law in American history. The act, entitled "an Act to preserve racial integrity," replaced the legal provision that a person must have one-sixteenth of "negro blood" to fall within the state's definition of "colored" with a provision that

> It shall hereafter be unlawful for any white person in this State to marry any save a white person, or a person with no other admixture of blood than white and American Indian. For the purpose of this act, the term "white person" shall apply only to the person who has no trace whatsoever of any blood other than Caucasian; but persons who have one-sixteenth or less of the blood of the American Indian and have no other non-Caucasic blood shall be deemed to be white persons.

Another section of the Virginia law (which provided for the issuance of supposedly voluntary racial registration certificates for Virginia citizens) spelled out the "races" the legislature had in mind. The list, which specified "Caucasian, Negro, Mongolian, American Indian, Asiatic Indian, Malay, or any mixture thereof, or any other non-Caucasic strains," showed the lengths to which lawmakers would go to pin down racial categories. Within the decade, the Virginia law was copied by Georgia and echoed in Alabama. Thereafter, while supporters worked without much success to extend such laws to other states, defenders of miscegenation statutes added eugenic arguments to their rhetorical arsenal.[38]

Having been pinned to the modern biological wall and labeled as "mixed race," Marie Antoinette Monks would seem to have been in the perfect position to challenge the constitutionality of the widely drawn Arizona miscegenation law. She took her case to the California Court of Appeals, Fourth District, where she made an argument that echoed that of Mayellen Kirby two decades earlier. Reminding the court of the wording of the Arizona statute, her lawyers pointed out that "on the set of facts found by the trial judge, [Marie Antoinette Monk] is concededly of Caucasian blood as well as negro blood, and therefore a descendant of a Caucasian." Spelling it out, they explained,

> As such, she is prohibited from marrying a negro or any descendant of a negro, a Mongolian or an Indian, a Malay or a Hindu, or any of the descendants of any of them. Likewise . . . as a descendant of a negro she is prohibited from marrying a Caucasian or descendant of a Caucasian, which of course would include any person who had any degree of Caucasian blood in them.

Because this meant that she was "absolutely prohibited from contracting valid marriages in Arizona," her lawyers argued that the Arizona law was an unconstitutional constraint on her liberty.[39]

The court, however, dismissed this argument as "interesting but in our opinion not tenable." In a choice that speaks volumes about the depth of attachment to racial categories, the court narrowed the force of the argument by asserting that "the constitutional problem would be squarely presented" only if one mixed-race person were seeking to marry another mixed-race person, then used this constructed hypothetical to dodge the issue:

> While it is true that there was evidence that appellant [Marie Antoinette Monks] is a descendant of the Caucasian race, as well as of the Negro race, the other contracting party [Allen Monks] was of unmixed blood and therefore the hypothetical situation involving an attempted alliance between two persons of mixed blood is no more present in the instant case than in the Kirby case. . . . The situations conjured up by respon-

dent are not here involved . . . Under the facts presented the appellant does not have
the benefit of assailing the validity of the statute.

This decision was taken as authoritative. Both the United States Supreme Court and
the Supreme Judicial Court of Massachusetts (in which Monks had also filed suit)
refused to reopen the issue.[40]

Perhaps the most interesting thing about the *Monks* case is that there is no reason
to believe that the public found it either remarkable or objectionable. Local reporters who covered the trial in 1939 played up the themes of forgery, drugs, and
insanity; their summaries of the racial categories of the Arizona law and the opinions of the expert witnesses were largely matter-of-fact.[41]

In this seeming acceptability to the public lies a clue to the development of modern racial ideologies. Even as judges narrowed their conception of race, transforming an all-encompassing phenomenon into a simple fact to be determined, they
remained bound by the provisions of miscegenation law to determine who fit in
which racial categories. For this purpose, the second culturalist argument, that race
was merely biology, had far more to offer than the first, that race was biologically
indeterminable. The conception of race as merely biological seemed consonant with
the racial categories built into the laws, seemed supportable by clear and unequivocal expert testimony, and fit comfortably within popular notions of race.

The Distillation of Modernist Racial Ideology: From Perez to Loving

In the *Monks* case we can see several modern racial ideologies—ranging from the
argument that race was biological nonsense to the reply that race was essentially
biological to the possibility that race was merely biology—all grounded in the split
between culture and biology. To distill these variants into a unified modernist racial
ideology, another element had to be added to the mix, the remarkable (in American
law, nearly unprecedented) proposal that the legal system abandon its traditional
responsibility for determining and defining racial categories. In miscegenation law,
this possibility emerged in a case that also, and not coincidentally, featured the
culturalist argument for biological racial indeterminacy.

The case was *Perez v. Lippold*. It involved a young Los Angeles couple, Andrea
Perez and Sylvester Davis, who sought a marriage license. Turned down by the Los
Angeles County clerk, they challenged the constitutionality of the California misceg-
enation law directly to the California Supreme Court, which heard their case in
October 1947.[42]

It was not immediately apparent that the *Perez* case would play a role in the
development of modernist racial ideology. Perhaps because both sides agreed that
Perez was "a white female" and Davis "a Negro male," the lawyer who defended
the couple, Daniel Marshall, did not initially see the case as turning on race categorization. In 1947 Marshall had few civil rights decisions to build on, so he tried
an end-run strategy: he based his challenge to miscegenation laws on the argument
that because both Perez and Davis were Catholics and the Catholic Church did not

prohibit interracial marriage, California miscegenation law was an arbitrary and unreasonable restraint on their freedom of religion.

The freedom-of-religion argument made some strategic sense, since several courts had held that states had to meet a high standard to justify restrictions on religious expression. Accordingly, Marshall laid out the religion argument in a lengthy petition to the California Supreme Court. In response, the state offered an even lengthier defense of miscegenation laws. The state's lawyers had at their fingertips a long list of precedents upholding such laws, including the *Kirby* and *Monks* cases. They added eugenic arguments about racial biology, including evidence of declining birth rates among "hybrids" and statistics that showed high mortality, short life expectancies, and particular diseases among African Americans. They polished off their case with the comments of a seemingly sympathetic Roman Catholic priest.[43]

Here the matter stood until the California Supreme Court heard oral arguments in the case. At that session, the court listened in silence to Marshall's opening sally that miscegenation laws were based on prejudice and to his argument that they violated constitutional guarantees of freedom of religion. But as soon as the state's lawyer began to challenge the religious freedom argument, one of the court's associate justices, Roger Traynor, impatiently interrupted the proceedings. "What," he asked, "about equal protection of the law?"

> *Mr. Justice Traynor:* . . . it might help to explain the statute, what it means. What is a negro?
>
> *Mr. Stanley:* We have not the benefit of any judicial interpretation. The statute states that a negro [Stanley evidently meant to say, as the law did, "a white"] cannot marry a negro, which can be construed to mean a full-blooded negro, since the statute also says mulatto, Mongolian, or Malay.
>
> *Mr. Justice Traynor:* What is a mulatto? One-sixteenth blood?
>
> *Mr. Stanley:* Certainly certain states have seen fit to state what a mulatto is.
>
> *Mr. Justice Traynor:* If there is 1/8 blood, can they marry? If you can marry with 1/8, why not with 1/16, 1/32, 1/64? And then don't you get in the ridiculous position where a negro cannot marry anybody? If he is white, he cannot marry black, or if he is black, he cannot marry white.
>
> *Mr. Stanley:* I agree that it would be better for the Legislature to lay down an exact amount of blood, but I do not think that the statute should be declared unconstitutional as indefinite on this ground.
>
> *Mr. Justice Traynor:* That is something anthropologists have not been able to furnish, although they say generally that there is no such thing as race.
>
> *Mr. Stanley:* I would not say that anthropologists have said that generally, except such statements for sensational purposes.
>
> *Mr. Justice Traynor:* Would you say that Professor Wooten of Harvard was a sensationalist? The crucial question is how can a county clerk determine who are negroes and who are whites.[44]

Although he addressed his questions to the lawyers for the state, Justice Traynor had given Marshall a gift no lawyer had ever before received in a miscegenation case: judicial willingness to believe in the biological indeterminacy of race. It was no accident that this argument came from Roger Traynor. A former professor at

Boalt Hall, the law school of the University of California, Berkeley, Traynor had been appointed to the court for his academic expertise rather than his legal experience; unlike his more pragmatic colleagues, he kept up with developments in modern social science.[45]

Marshall responded to the opening Traynor had provided by making sure that his next brief included the culturalist argument that race was biological nonsense. In it, he asserted that experts had determined that "race, as popularly understood, is a myth"; he played on the gap between expert opinion and laws based on irrational "prejudice" rooted in "myth, folk belief, and superstition"; and he dismissed his opponents' reliance on the "grotesque reasoning of eugenicists" by comparing their statements to excerpts from Adolf Hitler's *Mien Kampf*.[46]

Marshall won his case. The 1948 decision in the *Perez* case was remarkable for many reasons. It marked the first time since Reconstruction that a state court had declared a state miscegenation law unconstitutional. It went far beyond existing appeals cases in that the California Supreme Court had taken the very step the judges in the *Kirby* and *Monks* cases had avoided—going beyond the issue of the race of an individual to consider the issue of racial classification in general. Even more remarkable, the court did so in a case in which neither side had challenged the racial classification of the parties. But despite these accomplishments, the *Perez* case was no victory for the culturalist argument about the biological indeterminacy of race. Only the outcome of the case—that California's miscegenation law was unconstitutional—was clear. The rationale for this outcome was a matter of considerable dispute.

Four justices condemned the law and three supported it; altogether, they issued four separate opinions. A four-justice majority agreed that the law should be declared unconstitutional but disagreed about why. Two justices, led by Traynor, issued a lengthy opinion that pointed out the irrationality of racial categories, citing as authorities a virtual who's who of culturalist social scientists, from Boas, Huxley, and Haddon to Gunnar Myrdal. A third justice issued a concurring opinion that pointedly ignored the rationality or irrationality of race classifications to criticize miscegenation laws on equality grounds, contending that laws based on "race, color, or creed" were—and always had been—contrary to the Declaration of Independence, the Constitution, and the Fourteenth Amendment; as this justice saw it, the Constitution was color-blind. A fourth justice, who reported that he wanted his decision to "rest upon a broader ground than that the challenged statutes are discriminatory and irrational," based his decision solely on the religious freedom issue that had been the basis of Marshall's original argument.[47]

In contrast, a three-justice minority argued that the law should be upheld. They cited legal precedent, offered biological arguments about racial categories, and mentioned a handful of social policy considerations. Although the decision went against them, their agreement with each other ironically formed the closest thing to a majority in the case. In sum, although the *Perez* decision foreshadowed the day when American courts would abandon their defense of racial categories, its variety of judicial rationales tells us more about the range of modern racial ideologies than it does about the power of any one of them.[48]

Between the *Perez* case in 1948 and the next milestone miscegenation case, *Loving v. Virginia*, decided in 1967, judges would search for a common denominator among this contentious variety, trying to find a position of principled decisiveness persuasive enough to mold both public and expert opinion. One way to do this was to back away from the culturalist argument that race made no biological sense, adopting the other culturalist argument that race was biological fact and thus shifting the debate to the question of how much biological race should matter in determining social and legal policy.

In such a debate, white supremacists tried to extend the reach of biological race as far as possible. Thus one scientist bolstered his devotion to white supremacy by calling Boas "that appalling disaster to American social anthropology whose influence in the end has divorced the social studies of man from their scientific base in physical biology."[49] Following the lead of eugenicists, he and his sympathizers tried to place every social and legal superstructure on a biological racial base.

In contrast, their egalitarian opponents set limits. In their minds, biological race (or "skin color," as they often called it) was significant only because its visibility made it easy for racists to identify those they subjected to racial oppression. As Myrdal, the best-known of the mid-twentieth-century culturalist social scientists, noted in 1944 in his monumental work, *An American Dilemma*,

> In spite of all heterogeneity, the average white man's unmistakable observation is that *most Negroes in America have dark skin and woolly hair*, and he is, of course, right. . . . [the African American's] African ancestry and physical characteristics are fixed to his person much more ineffaceably than the yellow star is fixed to the Jew during the Nazi regime in Germany.[50]

To Myrdal's generation of egalitarians, the translation of visible physical characteristics into social hierarchies formed the tragic foundation of American racism.

The egalitarians won this debate, and their victory paved the way for the emergence of a modernist racial ideology persuasive enough to command the kind of widespread adherence once commanded by late nineteenth-century racialism. Such a position was formulated by the United States Supreme Court in 1967 in *Loving v. Virginia*, the most important miscegenation case ever heard and the only one now widely remembered.

The *Loving* case involved what was, even for miscegenation law, an extreme example. Richard Perry Loving and Mildred Delores Jeter were residents of the small town of Central Point, Virginia, and family friends who had dated each other since he was seventeen and she was eleven. When they learned that their plans to marry were illegal in Virginia, they traveled to Washington, D.C., which did not have a miscegenation law, for the ceremony, returning in June 1958 with a marriage license, which they framed and placed proudly on their wall. In July 1958 they were awakened in the middle of the night by the county sheriff and two deputies, who had walked through their unlocked front door and right into their bedroom to arrest them for violating Virginia's miscegenation law. Under that law, an amalgam of criminal provisions enacted in 1878 and Virginia's 1924 "Act to preserve racial integrity," the Lovings, who were identified in court records as a "white" man and a "colored" woman, pleaded guilty and were promptly convicted and sentenced to a year in jail. The judge suspended their sentence on the condition that "both accused leave . . . the state of Virginia at once and do not return together or at the same time to said county and state for a period of twenty-five years."[51]

In 1963 the Lovings, then the parents of three children, grew tired of living with relatives in Washington, D.C., and decided to appeal this judgment. Their first attempts ended in defeat. In 1965 the judge who heard their original case not only refused to reconsider his decision but raised the rhetorical stakes by opining: "Almighty God created the races white, black, yellow, malay and red, and he placed them on separate continents. And but for the interference with his arrangement there would be no cause for such marriages. The fact that he separated the races shows that he did not intend for the races to mix." But by the time their argument had been processed by the Supreme Court of Appeals of Virginia (which invalidated the original sentence but upheld the miscegenation law), the case had attracted enough attention that the United States Supreme Court, which had previously avoided taking miscegenation cases, agreed to hear an appeal.[52]

On the side of the Lovings stood not only their own attorneys, but also the National Association for the Advancement of Colored People (NAACP), the NAACP Legal Defense and Education Fund, the Japanese American Citizens League (JACL), and a coalition of Catholic bishops. The briefs they submitted offered the whole arsenal of arguments developed in previous miscegenation cases. The bishops offered the religious freedom argument that had been the original basis of the *Perez* case. The NAACP and the JACL stood on the opinions of culturalist experts, whose numbers now reached beyond social scientists well into the ranks of biologists. Offering both versions of the culturalist line on race, NAACP lawyers argued on one page, "The idea of 'pure' racial groups, either past or present, has long been abandoned by modern biological and social sciences," and on another, "Race, in its scientific dimension, refers only to the biogenetic and physical attributes manifest by a specified population. It does not, under any circumstances, refer to culture (learned behavior), language, nationality, or religion." The Lovings' lawyers emphasized two central points: miscegenation laws violated both the constitutional guarantee of equal protection under the laws and the constitutional protection of the fundamental right to marry.[53]

In response, the lawyers for the state of Virginia tried hard to find some ground on which to stand. Their string of court precedents upholding miscegenation laws had been broken by the *Perez* decision. Their argument that Congress never intended the Fourteenth Amendment to apply to interracial marriage was offset by the Supreme Court's stated position that congressional intentions were inconclusive. In an attempt to distance the state from the "white purity" aspects of Virginia's 1924 law, Virginia's lawyers argued that since the Lovings admitted that they were a "white" person and a "colored" person and had been tried under a section of the law that mentioned only those categories, the elaborate definition of "white" offered in other sections of Virginia law was irrelevant.[54]

On only one point did the lawyers for both parties and the Court seem to agree: None of them wanted to let expert opinion determine the outcome. The lawyers for

Virginia knew only too well that during the twentieth century the scientific foundations of the eugenic biological argument in favor of miscegenation laws had crumbled, so they tried to warn the Court away by predicting that experts would mire the Court in "a veritable Serbonian bog of conflicting scientific opinion." Yet the Lovings' lawyers, who seemed to have the experts on their side, agreed that "the Court should not go into the morass of sociological evidence that is available on both sides of the question." "We strongly urge," they told the justices, "that it is not necessary." And the Court, still reeling from widespread criticism that its decision in the famous 1954 case *Brown v. Board of Education* was illegitimate "sociological jurisprudence," was not about to offer its opponents any more of such ammunition.[55]

The decision the Court issued was, in fact, carefully shorn of all reference to expert opinion; it spoke in language that both reflected and contributed to a new popular common sense on the issue of race. Recycling earlier pronouncements that "distinctions between citizens solely because of their ancestry" were "odious to a free people whose institutions are founded upon the doctrine of equality" and that the Court "cannot conceive of a valid legislative purpose . . . which makes the color of a person's skin the test of whether his conduct is a criminal offense," the justices reached a new and broader conclusion. Claiming (quite inaccurately) that "We have consistently denied the constitutionality of measures which restrict the rights of citizens on account of race," the Court concluded that the racial classifications embedded in Virginia miscegenation laws were "so directly subversive of the principle of equality at the heart of the Fourteenth Amendment" that they were "unsupportable." Proclaiming that it violated both the equal protection and the due process clauses of the Fourteenth Amendment, the Court declared the Virginia miscegenation law unconstitutional.[56]

Legacies of Modernist Racial Ideology

The decision in the *Loving* case shows the distance twentieth-century American courts had traveled. The accumulated effect of several decades of culturalist attacks on racialism certainly shaped their thinking. The justices were no longer willing to accept the notion that race was the all-encompassing phenomenon nineteenth-century racialist thinkers had assumed it to be; they accepted the divisions between culture and biology and culture and race established by modern social scientists. But neither were they willing to declare popular identification of race with physical characteristics (like "the color of a person's skin") a figment of the imagination. In their minds, the scope of the term "race" had shrunk to a point where biology was all that was left; "race" referred to visible physical characteristics significant only because racists used them to erect spurious racial hierarchies. The Virginia miscegenation law was a case in point; the Court recognized and condemned it as a statute clearly "designed to maintain White Supremacy."[57]

Given the dependence of miscegenation laws on legal categories of race, the Court concluded that ending white supremacy required abandoning the categories.

In de-emphasizing racial categories, they joined mainstream mid-twentieth-century social scientists, who argued that because culture, rather than race, shaped meaningful human difference, race was nothing more than a subdivision of the broader phenomenon of ethnicity. In a society newly determined to be "color-blind," granting public recognition to racial categories seemed to be synonymous with racism itself.[58]

And so the Supreme Court promulgated a modernist racial ideology that maintained that the best way to eradicate racism was the deliberate nonrecognition of race. Its effects reached well beyond miscegenation law. Elements of modernist racial ideology marked many of the major mid-twentieth-century Supreme Court decisions, including *Brown v. Board of Education*. Its effects on state law codes were equally substantial; during the 1960s and 1970s, most American states repealed statutes that had defined "race" (usually by blood proportion) and set out to erase racial terminology from their laws.[59]

Perhaps the best indication of the pervasiveness of modernist racial ideology is how quickly late twentieth-century conservatives learned to shape their arguments to fit its contours. Attaching themselves to the modernist narrowing of the definition of race to biology and biology alone, conservative thinkers began to contend that, unless their ideas rested solely and explicitly on a belief in biological inferiority, they should not be considered racist. They began to advance "cultural" arguments of their very own, insisting that their proposals were based on factors such as social analysis, business practicality, or merit—on anything, in other words, except biological race. In their hands, modernist racial ideology supports an Alice-in-Wonderland interpretation of racism in which even those who argue for racially oppressive policies can adamantly deny being racists.

This conservative turnabout is perhaps the most striking, but not the only, indication of the contradictions inherent in modernist racial ideology. Others run the gamut from administrative law to popular culture. So while the U.S. Supreme Court tries to hold to its twentieth-century legacy of limiting, when it cannot eradicate, racial categories, U.S. government policies remain deeply dependent on them. In the absence of statutory definitions of race, racial categories are now set by the U.S. Office of Management and Budget, which in 1977 issued a "Statistical Directive" that divided Americans into five major groups—American Indian or Alaskan Native, Asian or Pacific Islander, Black, White, and Hispanic. The statistics derived from these categories help determine everything from census counts to eligibility for inclusion in affirmative action programs to the drawing of voting districts.[60] Meanwhile, in one popular culture flash-point after another—from the Anita Hill/Clarence Thomas hearings to the *O. J. Simpson* case, mainstream commentators insist that "race" should not be a consideration even as they explore detail after detail that reveals its social pervasiveness.[61]

These gaps between the (very narrow) modernist conception of race and the (very wide) range of racial identities and racial oppressions bedevil today's egalitarians. In the political arena, some radicals have begun to argue that the legal system's deliberate nonrecognition of race erodes the ability to recognize and name racism and to argue for such policies as affirmative action, which rely on racial categories to overturn rather than to enforce oppression. Meanwhile, in the universities, a growing chorus of scholars is revitalizing the argument for the biological indeterminacy of race and using that argument to explore the myriad of ways socially constructed notions of race remain powerfully salient. Both groups hope to do better than their culturalist predecessors at eradicating racism.[62]

Attaining that goal may depend on how well we understand the tortured history of mid-twentieth-century American ideologies of race.

NOTES

This article was originally presented at the Organization of American Historians annual meeting in 1992, and it has benefited considerably from the responses of audiences there and at half a dozen universities. For especially helpful readings, suggestions, and assistance, I would like to thank Nancy Cott, Karen Engle, Estelle Freedman, Jeff Garcilazo, Dave Gutiérrez, Ramón Gutiérrez, Eric Hinderaker, Marcia Klotz, Dorothee Kocks, Waverly Lowell, Valerie Matsumoto, Robyn Muncy, David Roediger, Richard White, the Brown University women's history reading group, and the editors and anonymous reviewers of the *Journal of American History*.

1. Ariz. Rev. Stat. Ann. sec. 3837 (1913); "Appellant's Abstract of Record," Aug. 8, 1921, pp. 1–2, *Kirby v. Kirby*, docket 1970 (microfilm: file 36.1.134), Arizona Supreme Court Civil Cases (Arizona State Law Library, Phoenix).

2. "Appellant's Abstract of Record," 12–13, 13–15, 15, *Kirby v. Kirby*.

3. Ibid., 16–18.

4. Ibid., 19.

5. Evelyn Brooks Higginbotham, "African-American Women's History and the Metalanguage of Race," *Signs* 17 (winter 1992): 253. See Michael Omi and Howard Winant, *Racial Formation in the United States: From the 1960s to the 1990s* (New York, 1994); David Theo Goldberg, ed., *Anatomy of Racism* (Minneapolis, 1990); Henry Louis Gates, Jr., ed., *"Race," Writing, and Difference* (Chicago, 1986); Dominick LaCapra, ed., *The Bounds of Race: Perspectives on Hegemony and Resistance* (Ithaca, 1991); F. James Davis, *Who Is Black? One Nation's Definition* (University Park, 1991); Sandra Harding, ed., *The "Racial" Economy of Science: Toward a Democratic Future* (Bloomington, 1993); Maria P. P. Root, ed., *Racially Mixed People in America* (Newbury Park, 1992); and Ruth Frankenberg, *White Women, Race Matters: The Social Construction of Whiteness* (Minneapolis, 1993).

6. Among the most provocative recent works are Higginbotham, "African-American Women's History"; Barbara J. Fields, "Ideology and Race in American History," in *Region, Race, and Reconstruction: Essays in Honor of C. Vann Woodward*, ed. J. Morgan Kousser and James M. McPherson (New York, 1982), 143–78; Thomas C. Holt, "Marking: Race, Race-Making, and the Writing of History," *American Historical Review* 100 (February 1995): 1–20; and David R. Roediger, *Towards the Abolition of Whiteness: Essays on Race, Politics, and Working Class History* (London, 1994).

7. On scientific racism, see Thomas F. Gossett, *Race: The History of an Idea in America* (Dallas, 1963); George W. Stocking, Jr., *Race, Culture, and Evolution: Essays in the History of Anthropology* (1968; Chicago, 1982); John S. Haller, Jr., *Outcasts from Evolution: Scientific Attitudes to Racial Inferiority, 1859–1900,* (Urbana, 1971); George M. Fredrickson, *The Black Image in the White Mind: The Debate on Afro-American Character and Destiny, 1817–1914* (New York, 1971); Thomas G. Dyer, *Theodore Roosevelt and the Idea*

of Race (Baton Rouge, 1980); Carl N. Degler, *In Search of Human Nature: The Decline and Revival of Darwinism in American Social Thought* (New York, 1991); and Elazar Barkan, *Retreat of Scientific Racism: Changing Concepts of Race in Britain and the United States between the World Wars* (Cambridge, Eng., 1992). On the social construction of racial ideologies, see the works cited in note 6, above, and Ronald T. Takaki, *Iron Cages: Race and Culture in Nineteenth-Century America* (New York, 1979); Reginald Horsman, *Race and Manifest Destiny: The Origins of American Racial Anglo-Saxonism* (Cambridge, Mass., 1981); Alexander Saxton, *The Rise and Fall of the White Republic: Class Politics and Mass Culture in Nineteenth-Century America* (London, 1990); David R. Roediger, *The Wages of Whiteness: Race and the Making of the American Working Class* (London, 1991); Audrey Smedley, *Race in North America: Origin and Evolution of a Worldview* (Boulder, 1993); and Tomás Almaguer, *Racial Fault Lines: The Historical Origins of White Supremacy in California* (Berkeley, 1994).

8. On law as a producer of racial ideologies, see Barbara J. Fields, "Slavery, Race, and Ideology in the United States of America," *New Left Review* 181 (May–June 1990): 7; Eva Saks, "Representing Miscegenation Law," *Raritan* 8 (fall 1988): 56–60; and Collette Guillaumin, "Race and Nature: The System of Marks," *Feminist Issues* 8 (fall 1988): 25–44.

9. See especially Fredrickson, *Black Image in the White Mind.*

10. For intriguing attempts to define American modernism, see Daniel J. Singal, ed., *Modernist Culture in America* (Belmont, 1991); and Dorothy Ross, ed., *Modernist Impulses in the Human Sciences, 1870–1930* (Baltimore, 1994). For the view from critical race theory, see Brian K. Fair, "Foreword: Rethinking the Colorblindness Model," *National Black Law Journal* 13 (spring 1993): 1–82; Neil Gotanda, "A Critique of 'Our Constitution Is Color-Blind,'" *Stanford Law Review* 44 (November 1991): 1–68; Gary Peller, "Race Consciousness," *Duke Law Journal* (September 1990): 758–847; and Peter Fitzpatrick, "Racism and the Innocence of Law," in *Anatomy of Racism*, ed. Goldberg, 247–62.

11. Many scholars avoid using the word *miscegenation*, which dates to the 1860s, means race mixing, and has, to twentieth-century minds, embarrassingly biological connotations; they speak of laws against "interracial" or "cross-cultural" relationships. Contemporaries usually referred to "antimiscegenation" laws. Neither alternative seems satisfactory, since the first avoids naming the ugliness that was so much a part of the laws and the second implies that "miscegenation" was a distinct racial phenomenon rather than a categorization imposed on certain relationships. I retain the term *miscegenation* when speaking of the laws and court cases that relied on the concept, but not when speaking of people or particular relationships. On the emergence of the term, see Sidney Kaplan, "The Miscegenation Issue in the Election of 1864," *Journal of Negro History* 24 (July 1949): 274–343.

12. Most histories of interracial sex and marriage in America focus on demographic patterns, rather than legal constraints. See, for example, Joel Williamson, *New People: Miscegenation and Mulattoes in the United States* (New York, 1980); Paul R. Spickard, *Mixed Blood: Intermarriage and Ethnic Identity in Twentieth-Century America* (Madison, 1989); and Deborah Lynn Kitchen, "Interracial Marriage in the United States, 1900–1980" (Ph.D. diss., University of Minnesota, 1993). The only historical overview is Byron Curti Martyn, "Racism in the United States: A History of the Anti-Miscegenation Legislation and Litigation" (Ph.D. diss., University of Southern California, 1979). On the colonial period, see A. Leon Higginbotham, Jr., and Barbara K. Kopytoff, "Racial Purity and Interracial Sex in the Law of Colonial and Antebellum Virginia," *Georgetown Law Journal* 77 (August 1989): 1967–2029; George M. Fredrickson, *White Supremacy: A Comparative Study in American and South African History* (New York, 1981), 99–108; and James Hugo Johnston, *Race Relations in Virginia and Miscegenation in the South, 1776–1860* (Amherst, 1970), 165–90.

For later periods, see Peter Bardaglio, "Families, Sex, and the Law: The Legal Transformation of the Nineteenth-Century Southern Household" (Ph.D. diss., Stanford University, 1987), 37–106, 345–49; Peter Wallenstein, "Race, Marriage, and the Law of Freedom: Alabama and Virginia, 1860s–1960s," *Chicago-Kent Law Review* 70, no. 2 (1994): 371–437; David H. Fowler, *Northern Attitudes towards Interracial Marriage: Legislation and Public Opinion in the Middle Atlantic and the States of the Old Northwest, 1780–1930* (New York, 1987); Dick Megumi Ogumi, "Asians and California's Anti-Miscegenation Laws," in *Asian and Pacific American Experiences: Women's Perspectives*, ed. Nobuya Tsuchida (Minneapolis, 1982), 2–8; and Peggy Pascoe, "Race, Gender, and Intercultural Relations: The Case of Interracial Marriage," *Frontiers* 12, no. 1 (1991): 5–18. The count of states is from the most complete list in Fowler, *Northern Attitudes*, 336–439.

13. Ariz. Rev. Stat. Ann. sec. 3092 (1901); 1931 Ariz. Sess. Laws ch. 17. Arizona, Idaho, Maine, Massachusetts, Nevada, North Carolina, Oregon, Rhode Island, South Carolina, Tennessee, Virginia, and Washington passed laws that mentioned American Indians. Arizona, California, Georgia, Idaho, Mississippi, Missouri, Montana, Nebraska, Nevada, Oregon, South Dakota, Utah, Virginia, and Wyoming passed laws that mentioned Asian Americans. Arizona, California, Georgia, Maryland, Nevada, South Dakota, Utah, Virginia, and Wyoming passed laws that mentioned "Malays." In addition, Oregon law targeted "Kanakas" (native Hawaiians), Virginia "Asiatic Indians," and Georgia both "Asiatic Indians" and "West Indians." See Fowler, *Northern Attitudes*, 336–439; 1924 Va. Acts ch. 371; 1927 Ga. Laws no. 317; 1931 Ariz. Sess. Laws ch. 17; 1933 Cal. Stat. ch. 104; 1935 Md. Laws ch. 60; and 1939 Utah Laws ch. 50.

14. The most insightful social and legal histories have focused on sexual relations rather than marriage. See, for example, Higginbotham and Kopytoff, "Racial Purity and Interracial Sex"; Karen Getman, "Sexual Control in the Slaveholding South: The Implementation and Maintenance of a Racial Caste System," *Harvard Women's Law Journal* 7 (spring 1984): 125–34; Martha Hodes, *White Women, Black Men: Illicit Sex in the Nineteenth-Century South* (New Haven, 1997); and idem, "The Sexualization of Reconstruction Politics: White Women and Black Men in the South after the Civil War," in *American Sexual Politics: Sex, Gender, and Race since the Civil War*, ed. John C. Fout and Maura Shaw Tantillo (Chicago, 1993), 59–74; Robyn Weigman, "The Anatomy of Lynching," in *American Sexual Politics*, ed. Fout and Tantillo, 223–45; Jacquelyn Dowd Hall, " 'The Mind That Burns in Each Body': Women, Rape, and Racial Violence," in *Powers of Desire: The Politics of Sexuality*, ed. Ann Snitow, Christine Stansell, and Sharon Thompson (New York, 1983), 328–49; Kenneth James Lay, "Sexual Racism: A Legacy of Slavery," *National Black Law Journal* 13 (spring 1993): 165–83; and Kevin J. Mumford, "From Vice to Vogue: Black/White Sexuality and the 1920s" (Ph.D. diss., Stanford University, 1993). One of the first works to note the predominance of marriage in miscegenation laws was Mary Frances Berry, "Judging Morality: Sexual Behavior and Legal Consequences in the Late Nineteenth-Century South," *Journal of American History* 78 (December 1991): 838–39. On the historical connections among race, marriage, property, and the state, see Saks, "Representing Miscegenation Law," 39–69; Nancy F. Cott, "Giving Character to Our Whole Civil Polity: Marriage and the Public Order in the Late Nineteenth Century," in *U.S. History as Women's History: New Feminist Essays*, ed. Linda K. Kerber, Alice Kessler-Harris, and Kathryn Kish Sklar (Chapel Hill, 1995), 107–21; Ramón A. Gutiérrez, *When Jesus Came, the Corn Mothers Went Away: Marriage, Sexuality, and Power in New Mexico, 1500–1846* (Stanford, 1991); Verena Martinez-Alier, *Marriage, Class, and Colour in Nineteenth-Century Cuba: A Study of Racial Attitudes and Sexual Values in a Slave Society* (Ann Arbor, 1989); Patricia J. Williams, "Fetal Fictions: An Exploration of Property Archetypes in Racial and Gendered Contexts," in *Race in America:*

The Struggle for Equality, ed. Herbert Hill and James E. Jones, Jr. (Madison, 1993), 425–37; and Virginia R. Domínguez, *White by Definition: Social Classification in Creole Louisiana* (New Brunswick, 1986).

15. Of the forty-one colonies and states that prohibited interracial marriage, twenty-two also prohibited some form of interracial sex. One additional jurisdiction (New York) prohibited interracial sex but not interracial marriage; it is not clear how long this 1638 statute was in effect. See Fowler, *Northern Attitudes*, 336–439. My database consists of every appeals court case I could identify in which miscegenation law played a role: 227 cases heard between 1850 and 1970, 132 civil and 95 criminal. Although cases that reach appeals courts are by definition atypical, they are significant because the decisions reached in them set policies later followed in more routine cases and because the texts of the decisions hint at how judges conceptualized particular legal problems. I have relied on them because of these interpretive advantages and for two more practical reasons. First, because appeals court decisions are published and indexed, it is possible to compile a comprehensive list of them. Second, because making an appeal requires the preservation of documents that might otherwise be discarded (such as legal briefs and court reporters' trial notes), they permit the historian to go beyond the judge's decision.

16. Decisions striking down the laws include *Burns v. State*, 48 Ala. 195 (1872); *Bonds v. Foster*, 36 Tex. 68 (1871–1872); *Honey v. Clark*, 37 Tex. 686 (1873); *Hart v. Hoss*, 26 La. Ann. 90 (1874); *State v. Webb*, 4 Cent. L. J. 588 (1877); and *Ex parte Brown*, 5 Cent. L. J. 149 (1877). Decisions upholding the laws include *Scott v. State*, 39 Ga. 321 (1869); *State v. Hairston*, 63 N.C. 451 (1869); *State v. Reinhardt*, 63 N.C. 547 (1869); *In re Hobbs*, 12 F. Cas. 262 (1871) (No. 6550); *Lonas v. State*, 50 Tenn. 287 (1871); *State v. Gibson*, 36 Ind. 389 (1871); *Ford v. State*, 53 Ala. 150 (1875); *Green v. State*, 58 Ala. 190 (1877); *Frasher v. State*, 3 Tex. Ct. App. R. 263 (1877); *Ex Parte Kinney*, 14 F. Cas. 602 (1879) (No. 7825); *Ex parte Francois*, 9 F. Cas. 699 (1879) (No. 5047); *Francois v. State*, 9 Tex. Ct. App. R. 144 (1880); *Pace v. State*, 69 Ala. 231 (1881); *Pace v. Alabama*, 106 U.S. 583 (1882); *State v. Jackson*, 80 Mo. 175 (1883); *State v. Tutty*, 41 F. 753 (1890); *Dodson v. State*, 31 S.W. 977 (1895); *Strauss v. State*, 173 S.W. 663 (1915); *State v. Daniel*, 75 So. 836 (1917); *Succession of Mingo*, 78 So. 565 (1917–18); and *In re Paquet's Estate*, 200 P. 911 (1921).

17. Individual racial classifications were successfully challenged in *Moore v. State*, 7 Tex. Ct. App. R. 608 (1880); *Jones v. Commonwealth*, 80 Va. 213 (1884); *Jones v. Commonwealth*, 80 Va. 538 (1885); *State v. Treadaway*, 52 So. 500 (1910); *Flores v. State*, 129 S.W. 1111 (1910); *Ferrall v. Ferrall*, 69 S.E. 60 (1910); *Marre v. Marre*, 168 S.W. 636 (1914); *Neuberger v. Gueldner*, 72 So. 220 (1916); and *Reed v. State*, 92 So. 511 (1922).

18. "Appellant's Abstract of Record," 19, *Kirby v. Kirby*.

19. "Appellee's Brief," Oct. 3, 1921, 6, *Kirby v. Kirby*.

20. On the theoretical problems involved in exploring how miscegenation laws were gendered, see Pascoe, "Race, Gender, and Intercultural Relations"; and idem, "Race, Gender, and the Privileges of Property: On the Significance of Miscegenation Law in United States History," in *New Viewpoints in Women's History: Working Papers from the Schlesinger Library 50th Anniversary Conference, March 4–5, 1994*, ed. Susan Ware (Cambridge, Mass., 1994), 99–122. For an excellent account of the gendering of early miscegenation laws, see Kathleen M. Brown, *Good Wives and Nasty Wenches: Gender, Race, and Power in Colonial Virginia* (Chapel Hill, 1996).

21. "Appellant's Brief," Sept. 8, 1921, *Kirby v. Kirby*; *Kirby v. Kirby*, 206 P. 405, 406 (1922). On *Kirby*, see Roger Hardaway, "Unlawful Love: A History of Arizona's Miscegenation Law," *Journal of Arizona History* 27 (winter 1986): 377–90.

22. For examples of reliance on experts, see *In re Ah Yup*, 1 F. Cas. 223 (1878) (No. 104); *In re Kanaka Nian*, 21 P. 993 (1889); *In re Saito*, 62 F. 126 (1894). On these cases, see Ian F. Haney Lopez, *White by Law: The Legal Construction of Race* (New York, 1996). For reliance on the "common man," see *U.S. v. Bhagat Singh Thind*, 261 U.S. 204 (1923). On *Thind*, see Sucheta Mazumdar, "Racist Responses to Racism: The Aryan Myth and South Asians in the United States," *South Asia Bulletin* 9, no. 1 (1989): 47–55; Joan M. Jensen, *Passage from India: Asian Indian Immigrants in North America* (New Haven, 1988), 247–69; and Roediger, *Towards the Abolition of Whiteness*, 181–84.

23. The rise of Boasian anthropology has attracted much attention among intellectual historians, most of whom seem to agree with the 1963 comment that "it is possible that Boas did more to combat race prejudice than any other person in history"; see Gossett, *Race*, 418. In addition to the works cited in note 7, see I. A. Newby, *Jim Crow's Defense: Anti-Negro Thought in America, 1900–1930* (Baton Rouge, 1965), 21; and John S. Gilkeson, Jr., "The Domestication of 'Culture' in Interwar America, 1919–1941," in *The Estate of Social Knowledge*, ed. JoAnne Brown and David K. van Keuren (Baltimore, 1991), 153–74. For more critical appraisals, see Robert Proctor, "Eugenics among the Social Sciences: Hereditarian Thought in Germany and the United States," in *Estate of Social Knowledge*, ed. Brown and van Keuren, 175–208; Hamilton Cravens, *The Triumph of Evolution: The Heredity-Environment Controversy, 1900–1941* (Baltimore, 1988); and Donna Haraway, *Primate Visions: Gender, Race, and Nature in the World of Modern Science* (New York, 1989); 127–203. The classic—and still the best—account of the rise of cultural anthropology is Stocking, *Race, Culture, and Evolution*. See also idem, *Victorian Anthropology* (New York, 1987), 284–329.

24. U.S. Immigration Commission, *Dictionary of Races or Peoples* (Washington, 1911), 2. For other scientific racist classification schemes, see *Encyclopedia Britannica*, 11th ed., s.v. "anthropology"; and *Encyclopedia Americana: A Library of Universal Knowledge* (New York, 1923), s.v. "ethnography" and "ethnology."

25. Franz Boas, "Race," in *Encyclopedia of the Social Sciences*, ed. Edwin R. A. Seligman, 15 vols. (New York, 1930–35), 27; Julian S. Huxley and A. C. Haddon, *We Europeans: A Survey of "Racial" Problems* (London, 1935), 107.

26. Boas, "Race," 34. For one of the few instances when a historian has noted this argument, see Smedley, *Race in North America*, 275–82.

27. Ruth Benedict, *Race: Science and Politics* (New York, 1940), 12; Ruth Benedict and Gene Weltfish, *The Races of Mankind* (Washington, D.C., 1943), 5; Benedict, *Race*, 12.

28. Boas, "Race," 25–26.

29. See, for example, Huxley and Haddon, *We Europeans*, 107, 269–73; Benedict and Weltfish, *Races of Mankind*; Benedict, *Race*; and Gunnar Myrdal, *An American Dilemma: The Negro Problem and Modern Democracy* (New York, 1944), 91–115.

30. The *Monks* trial can be followed in *Estate of Monks*, 4 Civ. 2835, Records of California Court of Appeals, Fourth District (California State Archives, Roseville); and *Gunn v. Giraudo*, 4 Civ. 2832. (Gunn represented another claimant to the estate.) The two cases were tried together. For the seven-volume "Reporter's Transcript," see *Estate of Monks*, 4 Civ. 2835.

31. "Reporter's Transcript," vol. 2, pp. 660–67, vol. 3, pp. 965–76, 976–98, *Estate of Monks*.

32. Ibid., vol. 5, pp. 1501–49, vol. 6, pp. 1889–1923.

33. Ibid., vol. 7, pp. 2543, 2548.

34. "Findings of Fact and Conclusions of Law," in "Clerk's Transcript," Dec. 2, 1940, *Gunn v. Giraudo*, 4 Civ. 2832, p. 81. One intriguing aspect of the *Monks* case is that the

seeming exactness was unnecessary. The status of the marriage hinged on the Arizona mis-cegenation law, which would have denied validity to the marriage whether the proportion of "blood" in question was "one-eighth" or "one drop."

35. For descriptions of those interested in biological aspects of race, see Stocking, *Race, Culture, and Evolution,* 271–307; I. A. Newby, *Challenge to the Court: Social Scientists and the Defense of Segregation, 1954–1966* (Baton Rouge, 1969); and Cravens, *Triumph of Evolution,* 15–55. On eugenics, see Proctor, "Eugenics among the Social Sciences," 175–208; Daniel J. Kevles, *In the Name of Eugenics: Genetics and the Uses of Human Heredity* (New York, 1985); Mark H. Haller, *Eugenics: Hereditarian Attitudes in American Thought* (New Brunswick, 1963); and William H. Tucker, *The Science and Politics of Racial Research* (Urbana, 1994), 54–137.

36. Charles B. Davenport, *Eugenics Record Office Bulletin No. 9: State Laws Limiting Marriage Selection Examined in the Light of Eugenics* (Cold Spring Harbor, 1913); Michael Grossberg, "Guarding the Altar: Physiological Restrictions and the Rise of State Intervention in Matrimony," *American Journal of Legal History* 26 (July 1982): 221–24.

37. See, for example, C[harles] B[enedict] Davenport and Morris Steggerda, *Race Crossing in Jamaica* (1929; Westport, 1970); Edward Byron Reuter, *Race Mixture: Studies in Intermarriage and Miscegenation* (New York, 1931); and Emory S. Bogardus, "What Race Are Filipinos?" *Sociology and Social Research* 16 (1931–32): 274–79.

38. 1924 Va. Acts ch. 371; 1927 Ga. Laws no. 317; 1927 Ala. Acts no. 626. The 1924 Virginia act replaced 1910 Va. Acts ch. 357, which classified as "colored" persons with one-sixteenth or more "negro blood." The retention of an allowance for American Indian "blood" in persons classed as white was forced on the bill's sponsors by Virginia aristocrats who traced their ancestry to Pocahontas and John Rolfe. See Paul A. Lombardo, "Miscege-nation, Eugenics, and Racism: Historical Footnotes to *Loving v. Virginia,*" *U. C. Davis Law Review* 21 (winter 1988): 431–52; Richard B. Sherman, " 'The Last Stand': The Fight for Racial Integrity in Virginia in the 1920s," *Journal of Southern History* 54 (February. 1988): 69–92; and Bair, in this volume.

39. "Appellant's Opening Brief," *Gunn v. Giraudo,* 12–13. This brief appears to have been prepared for the California Supreme Court but used in the California Court of Appeals, Fourth District. On February 14, 1941, the California Supreme Court refused to review the Court of Appeals decision. See *Estate of Monks,* 48 C.A. 2d 603, 621.

40. *Estate of Monks,* 48 C.A. 2d 603 at 612–15; *Monks v. Lee,* 317 U.S. 590 (*appeal dismissed,* 1942, 711 (*reh'g denied,* 1942); *Lee v. Monks,* 62 N.E. 2d 657 (1945); *Lee v. Monks,* 326 U.S. 696 (*cert. denied,* 1946).

41. On the case, see *San Diego Union,* July 21, 1939–Jan. 6, 1940. On the testimony of expert witnesses on race, see *San Diego Union,* Sept. 21, 1939, 4A; Sept. 29, 1939, 10A; and Oct. 5, 1939, 8A.

42. *Perez v. Lippold,* L.A. 20305, Supreme Court Case Files (California State Archives). The case was also known as *Perez v. Moroney* and *Perez v. Sharp* (the names reflect changes of personnel in the Los Angeles County clerk's office). I have used the title given in the *Pacific Law Reporter,* the most easily available version of the final decision: *Perez v. Lippold,* 198 P. 2d 17 (1948).

43. "Petition for Writ of Mandamus, Memorandum of Points and Authorities and Proof of Service," Aug. 8, 1947, *Perez v. Lippold*; "Points and Authorities in Opposition to Issu-ance of Alternative Writ of Mandate," Aug. 13, 1947; "Return by Way of Demurrer," Oct. 6, 1947; "Return by Way of Answer," Oct. 6, 1947; "Respondent's Brief in Opposition to Writ of Mandate," Oct. 6, 1947, all in *Perez v. Lippold.*

44. "[Oral Argument] On Behalf of Respondent," Oct. 6, 1947, pp. 3–4, *Perez v. Lippold.*

45. Stanley Mosk, "A Retrospective," *California Law Review* 71 (July 1983): 1045; Peter Anderson, "A Remembrance," *California Law Review* 71 (July 1983): 1066–71.

46. "Petitioners' Reply Brief," Nov. 8, 1947, pp. 4, 44, 23–24, *Perez v. Lippold.*

47. *Perez v. Lippold*, 198 P. 2d at 17–35, esp. 29, 34.

48. Ibid., 35–47.

49. For the characterization of Franz Boas, by Robert Gayres, editor of the Scottish journal *Mankind Quarterly*, see Newby, *Challenge to the Court*, 323. On *Mankind Quarterly* and on mid-twentieth-century white supremacist scientists, see Tucker, *Science and Politics of Racial Research.*

50. Myrdal, *American Dilemma*, 116–17.

51. *Loving v. Commonwealth*, 147 S.E. 2d 78, 79 (1966). For the *Loving* briefs and oral arguments, see Philip B. Kurland and Gerhard Casper, eds., *Landmark Briefs and Arguments of the Supreme Court of the United States: Constitutional Law*, vol. 64 (Arlington, 1975), 687–1007. Edited cassette tapes of the oral argument are included with Peter Irons and Stephanie Guitton, eds., *May It Please the Court: The Most Significant Oral Arguments Made before the Supreme Court since 1955* (New York, 1993). For scholarly assessments, see Wallenstein, "Race, Marriage, and the Law of Freedom"; Walter Wadlington. "The Loving Case: Virginia's Antimiscegenation Statute in Historical Perspective," in *Race Relations and the Law in American History: Major Historical Interpretations*, ed. Kermit L. Hall (New York, 1987), 600–634; and Robert J. Sickels, *Race, Marriage, and the Law* (Albuquerque, 1972).

52. *Loving v. Virginia*, 388 U.S. 1, 3 (1967); Wallenstein, "Race, Marriage, and the Law of Freedom," 423–25, esp. 424; *New York Times*, June 12, 1992, B7. By the mid-1960s some legal scholars had questioned the constitutionality of miscegenation laws, including C. D. Shokes, "The Serbonian Bog of Miscegenation," *Rocky Mountain Law Review* 21 (1948–49): 425–33; Wayne A. Melton, "Constitutionality of State Anti-Miscegenation Statutes," *Southwestern Law Journal* 5 (1951): 451–61; Andrew D. Weinberger, "A Reappraisal of the Constitutionality of Miscegenation Statutes," *Cornell Law Quarterly* 42 (winter 1957): 208–22; Jerold D. Cummins and John L. Kane, Jr., "Miscegenation, the Constitution, and Science," *Dicta* 38 (January–February 1961): 24–54; William D. Zabel, "Interracial Marriage and the Law," *Atlantic Monthly* 216 (October 1965): 75–79; and Cyrus E. Phillips IV, "Miscegenation: The Courts and the Constitution," *William and Mary Law Review* 8 (fall 1966): 133–42.

53. Kurland and Casper, eds., *Landmark Briefs*, 741–88, 847–950, 960–72, esp. 898–99, 901.

54. Ibid., 789–845, 976–1003.

55. Ibid., 834, 1007.

56. *Loving v. Virginia*, 388 U.S. at 12.

57. Ibid., 11.

58. The notion that American courts should be "color-blind" is usually traced to Supreme Court Justice John Harlan. Dissenting from the Court's endorsement of the principle of "separate but equal" in *Plessy v. Ferguson*, Harlan insisted that "Our Constitution is color-blind, and neither knows nor tolerates classes among citizens." *Plessy v. Ferguson*, 163 U.S. 537, 559 (1896). But only after *Brown v. Board of Education*, widely interpreted as a belated endorsement of Harlan's position, did courts begin to adopt color blindness as a goal. *Brown v. Board of Education*, 347 U.S. 483 (1954). On the history of the color blindness ideal, see

Andrew Kull, *The Color-Blind Constitution* (Cambridge, Mass., 1992). On developments in social science, see Omi and Winant, *Racial Formation in the United States*, 14–23.

59. *Brown v. Board of Education*, 347 U.S. at 483. The Court declared distinctions based "solely on ancestry" "odious" even while upholding curfews imposed on Japanese Americans during World War II; see *Hirabayashi v. United States*, 320 U.S. 81 (1943). It declared race a "suspect" legal category while upholding the internment of Japanese Americans; see *Korematsu v. United States*, 323 U.S. 214 (1944). By 1983 no American state had a formal race-definition statute still on its books. See Chris Ballentine, " 'Who Is a Negro?' Revisited: Determining Individual Racial Status for Purposes of Affirmative Action," *University of Florida Law Review* 35 (fall 1983): 692. The repeal of state race-definition statutes often accompanied repeal of miscegenation laws. See, for example, 1953 Mont. Laws ch. 4: 1959 Or. Laws ch. 531; 1965 Ind. Acts ch. 15; 1969 Fla. Laws 69–195; and 1979 Ga. Laws no. 543.

60. The fifth of these categories, "Hispanic," is sometimes described as "ethnic," rather than "racial." For very different views of the current debates, see Lawrence Wright, "One Drop of Blood," *New Yorker*, July 25, 1994, 46–55; and Michael Lind, *The Next American Nation: The New Nationalism and the Fourth American Revolution* (New York, 1995), 97–137.

61. *People v. O. J. Simpson*, Case no. BA 097211, California Superior Court, Los Angeles County (1994).

62. See, for example, Kimberlé Williams Crenshaw, "Race, Reform, and Retrenchment: Transformation and Legitimation in Antidiscrimination Law," *Harvard Law Review* 101 (May 1988): 1331–87; Dana Y. Takagi, *The Retreat from Race: Asian-American Admissions and Racial Politics* (New Brunswick, 1992), 181–94; and Girardeau A. Spann, *Race against the Court: The Supreme Court and Minorities in Contemporary America* (New York, 1993), 119–49. See note 5, above. On recent work in the humanities, see Tessie Liu, "Race," in *A Companion to American Thought*, ed. Richard Wightman Fox and James T. Kloppenberg (Cambridge, Mass., 1995), 564–67. On legal studies, see Richard Delgado and Jean Stefancic. "Critical Race Theory: An Annotated Bibliography," *Virginia Law Review* 79 (March 1993): 461–516.

Chapter Twenty-Three

Speaking of Race

Sarah Patton Boyle and the "T. J. Sellers Course for
Backward Southern Whites"

Jennifer Ritterhouse

After more than fifteen years as a freelance writer, Sarah Patton Boyle usually sat down at her typewriter with a sense of ease, ready to let her thoughts work themselves out as she went along. In the summer of 1950, she approached her typewriter with a new idea. A daughter of one of the "first families" of Virginia and the wife of a University of Virginia professor, Boyle had been a more or less unquestioning participant in the South's Jim Crow system for all of her forty-four years. She had accepted the indoctrination of her youth, an aristocratic training that encouraged amiability and benevolence toward African Americans but also demanded a strict adherence to caste rules. By the time her education was complete, Boyle later reflected, "I was as close to a typical Southern lady as anyone ever is to a typical anything. My mind had many partitions and my heart many levels. I was a mixture of high idealism and contradictory practice, of rigid snobbery and genuine human warmth."

In July 1950, when Boyle's husband, Roger, brought home the news that a young black attorney named Gregory Swanson was expected to win his test case for admission to the University of Virginia law school, the levels and partitions of Boyle's segregated conscience collapsed. "The South had somehow committed enormous injustice," she suddenly thought. The fact that a qualified Virginian, a man who had already graduated from an out-of-state law school and passed the state bar exam, had to sue to be admitted to the university was proof. As she pursued this new line of thinking, Boyle felt an urge to reach out to Swanson in welcome. She also felt troubled, the "clamoring" of her "Southern code" reminding her that her impulses were improper, that her sudden recognition of the injustice of segregation was precisely the sort of heresy that might lead to "social equality," or what she herself disdained as "familiarity with Negroes." If her conversations within the university community had not convinced her that many white southerners privately agreed that segregation was unjust, Boyle might never have reached out to Swanson at all. Despite her reservations, she translated Charlottesville's quiet acceptance of Swanson's admission into a belief that the "majority of *educated* Southerners were ready to throw off the yoke of injustice to Negroes whenever it was called to their attention." To her mind, it was only whites' fear of standing alone against convention that kept them silent against the inner pressure of their democratic principles. "Being a writer," Boyle later explained, "I inevitably burst into words. . . . 'Dear Mr. Swanson,' I began, feeling queer and proud. This was the first time I had ever addressed a Negro as Mister."[1]

Self-consciously typing these first few words, Sarah Patton Boyle could not have predicted how much her life would change as a result of her decision to write to Gregory Swanson. Over the next two decades, this self-described "typical Southern lady" became the most outspoken white integrationist in Virginia. She wrote hundreds of magazine articles and letters to the editors of Virginia newspapers in hopes of persuading white readers not only to accept, but to welcome the removal of all racial barriers. She also spoke to any group that would listen, including the Commission on Public Education that Virginia's conservative governor, Thomas B. Stanley, appointed shortly after the Supreme Court's decision in *Brown v. Board of Education* was announced. In February 1955, as Virginia lurched toward a state policy of "massive resistance" and school closings, Boyle gained national attention when an article that she had originally called "We're Readier Than We Think" appeared in the *Saturday Evening Post* under the inflammatory title "Southerners Will *Like* Integration." Despite the hostility the article engendered and her own growing disillusionment with white southerners' unwillingness to change, Boyle continued her efforts in the late 1950s and early 1960s. She helped to found the Virginia Council on Human Relations in 1955 and traveled throughout the state almost continuously for the next three years, lecturing, establishing discussion groups, and raising funds for both this new interracial organization and the NAACP. She also embraced the direct-action techniques pioneered by a younger generation of activists and eventually went to jail for her part in a 1964 sit-in at a St. Augustine, Florida, motel. In 1962 Boyle's autobiography, *The Desegregated Heart*, became a nationwide best-seller, carrying her message of human brotherhood to thousands of readers.

Although many historians are familiar with Boyle's book, Boyle has not received as much scholarly attention as many other white southern women who took part in the black freedom struggle. One reason for this neglect has to do with timing. Born in 1906, Boyle was less than a decade younger than Katherine Du Pre Lumpkin and Lillian Smith and only three years younger than Virginia Durr. Nevertheless, by the time Boyle began to question segregation in the early 1950s, Lumpkin, Smith, Durr, and a number of other white southern women had been active in the interracial movement for decades and had openly challenged segregation for years.[2]

Boyle's change of heart coincided more closely with the transformative experiences of considerably younger women, such as Casey Hayden, Sue Thrasher, and Constance Curry, yet their backgrounds and motivations were very different. Unlike the generation of white southern women who came of age in the late 1950s and early 1960s and who joined the Student Nonviolent Coordinating Committee (SNCC) and other civil rights groups, Boyle began her crusade against segregation on her own as a well-established matron with two young sons, ailing dependent parents, and a lifelong commitment to her upper-crust Virginia heritage. Her initial overture to Gregory Swanson was motivated largely by class pretensions and a self-styled "maternalism" that she later repudiated. On reflection, Boyle felt that she had supported Swanson's cause "automatically as a mother champions her child" because the "best Southerners always had taken care of their Negroes."[3] Thus, while most other white southern women who participated in the civil rights movement "came to it first through the Church," Boyle acted first in a secular sphere, and her initial impulses, though informed by her Christian beliefs, were rooted in a class-based sense of *"noblesse oblige."*[4]

Gradually, Boyle's activism guided her to a deeper Christian faith, and her primary purpose in writing her autobiography was to recount this spiritual journey. Because her greater faith in God resulted from her total loss of faith in human beings, however, Boyle found her new orthodoxy to be incompatible with the realpolitik of the late 1960s. Rather than turning from the black freedom struggle to the women's movement, as many of her younger female colleagues did, Boyle retired from public life in 1967.

Although Sarah Patton Boyle never identified herself as a feminist, her story is most significant for the light it can shed on certain feminist political concerns, particularly the relationship between public and private life and the question of how individuals can build coalitions across race and gender lines. Perhaps more than any other white southern liberal, Patty Boyle began her crusade against segregation thinking that she would find an untapped reservoir of love for African Americans in white southerners' hearts. Instead, she found a friendship with the African American newspaper editor T. J. Sellers that can serve as a model for making political alliances in a world where even potential allies seldom "love" one another. Boyle's decision to call Gregory Swanson "Mister"—to take a political stand that required her to address someone of another race equally or not at all—was a first attempt at frank communication across race lines. As her stormy relationship with Swanson reveals, it was also a miserable failure, in part because Boyle remained convinced of her own social superiority in reaching out to a black man, but also because she failed to consider the gender implications of her efforts. Slowly, Boyle learned that black southerners did not appreciate whites' limited and paternalistic "love" for them and that white southerners had so tainted the concept of "love" between white women and black men that it seriously hindered her efforts to "sow love" between blacks and whites.[5] It was not through "love" of any of these varieties, but in her friendship with T. J. Sellers that Boyle finally succeeded in sustaining a dialogue across race and gender differences. Because it allowed each of them to grow personally and politically while maintaining individual autonomy and difference, Boyle and Sellers's friendship offers an instructive precedent at a time when even those who share basic political commitments find communication and coalition building at best problematic.

Patty Boyle might have been less disappointed by her inability to change white southerners had she remembered all that had gone into her own conversion experience. In her 1962 autobiography, Boyle described a number of minor but unsettling incidents prior to 1950 that had primed her for the epiphany that the news of

Gregory Swanson's lawsuit sparked. What she did not describe was the "terrible shock" she had experienced in the late 1940s when she and her husband, Roger, discovered that they had grown very far apart. "[T]he world just fell out from under me," Boyle explained in a 1994 interview, still reluctant to discuss a private emotional crisis almost thirty years after she and Roger finally divorced in 1965. "I had become Christian before that," she added, "but only verbally so really. . . . it was just a sort of repetition thing." Brought up in the Episcopal Church, Boyle had become interested in Eastern religions and spiritualism as a young adult, turning away from the church temporarily "just because it was such a bore." Her conflicts with Roger pushed her toward a deeper Christian faith because, as she described it in retrospect, God was "the only permanent thing left in my life"; "I had no place to turn but God."[6]

By turning to God, Boyle was also returning to the religious beliefs of her childhood and the moral teachings of her father, an Episcopal minister who had worked to improve educational opportunities for blacks. In fact, Robert Williams Patton's career in black education made it somewhat difficult for Boyle to explain why she had failed to question the southern racial order for so long. From 1920 until his retirement in 1940, Patton had served as the executive secretary of the American Church Institute for Negroes, an Episcopal Church affiliate that operated seven normal and industrial schools in the South, as well as the Bishop Payne Divinity School in Petersburg, Virginia, and St. Augustine's College in Raleigh, North Carolina.[7] Although he shared the paternalistic assumptions that many whites brought to their educational work, Patton was progressive for his time and place, and his views presumably ought to have had some effect on his daughter's developing racial consciousness. According to Boyle's own, perhaps self-serving account, this was not the case. Her father "was very enlightened for his day," she acknowledged in *The Desegregated Heart*. "But what chance had such stray thoughts against impressions gathered from our whole social pattern? Besides," she insisted, "my father's work kept him away from home nine tenths of the time." "He would stop by, of course," Boyle added in an interview. "And he was crazy about my mother. He was wild about her and he didn't want anything but to see her when he came and that communicated itself. He was not very popular with me, to tell you the truth."

In addition to resenting her father's neglect, Boyle claimed to have found a more compelling role model in her mother, who did not share her husband's progressive racial views. Instead, Janie Stringfellow Patton "loved Negroes . . . with the same deep tenderness she lavished on her riding horse, her dogs, and other pets," and she taught her daughter that being a "lady" meant keeping a proper social distance between herself and African Americans. She also taught Patty that Robert Patton's liberal attitudes were "for ministers"—and, by implication, men—"only."[8]

Whether or not her father's racial views actually had as little potential to shape her early life as she suggested, Boyle did draw a great deal of strength from Robert Patton's example in later years. Despite his frequent absences, Patton had instilled in his daughter a sense of social responsibility that mingled with her sense of personal dissatisfaction in the late 1940s. "My father had often said, 'If you see a public need which isn't being met . . . that probably means it's *your* job,' " Boyle noted in *The Desegregated Heart*. Long before she ever heard of Gregory Swanson, Boyle's private emotional conflicts and resurgent Christian faith seem to have put her on the lookout for some kind of public job. "I've never been confronted with one full-sized job that I thought was worth doing with my full strength," she wrote to a friend and spiritual advisor in 1948. "I'm a potential fanatic who has not yet found my cause."[9] Little more than a year later, Boyle would begin to feel an exhilarating sense of calling.

By the time she wrote to Gregory Swanson, that vocation had less to do with her own compassionate impulses than with an eagerness to express the views of a new-found community of sympathetic whites. When news of Swanson's lawsuit hit the headlines, Boyle began to ask her close female friends and other educated, middle-class white women in Charlottesville how they felt about having a black student at the University of Virginia. Combined with evidence from recent polls of southern educators and university students, Boyle's informal canvass was enough to convince her that a significant number of white southerners were desegregationists at heart. Her first letter to Swanson reflected that conviction. "Dear Mr. Swanson," she began,

> I feel impelled to speak for the many Southerners who are silently on your side. . . . Many more than you probably believe sincerely want you to come and will be consistently glad that you are here. Even some of those who are not glad will be filled with respect for your willingness to bear and to suffer so that those who follow you will be less burdened and freer from pain. Salaam. More power to you. And good luck!

Confident in her newly discovered community of white moderates, Boyle was not daunted when several of her friends discouraged her from sending a copy of the letter to the *Richmond Times-Dispatch*.

She was, however, shaken by Swanson's response. "He said he was looking forward to our being great friends and to many other enjoyable relationships at the University," she wrote in her autobiography. "This implied social equality! Something gripped me with digging, cold fingers. Clearly I had already made Swanson FORGET HIS PLACE!" She would have to make it clear to him that, despite her sympathy, the two of them remained on opposite sides of a societal wall. Like generations of white southern liberals before her, Boyle hoped for a racial equality that would preserve racial separation in most of its forms.[10]

To make matters worse, in her effort to maintain social distance, Boyle inadvertently misled Swanson about her intentions. "I wish there were some way we could know each other personally," she wrote in a subsequent letter. "I want us to very much. But I don't quite see how it can be done. It would be humiliating to us both to be clandestine about it, and would be unwise to be open about it. For us there can be no middle road between those two, for there's no privacy where I live." As Boyle acknowledged in her autobiography a dozen years later, "Almost any woman, even though half-witted, could be expected to see in my remarks the implication they might carry for a man." At the time, she could not see the sexual implications of her words at all. "There are two distinct schools in handling the Southern interracial sex problem," she explained. "One consists in warnings against 'the bestial

nature of Negroes.' This school makes white girls super-sex-conscious and continually on their guard." The other school simply ignored the fact that black men were
members of the opposite sex, encouraging white girls "to regard them rather as one
does male dumb animals." According to Boyle, the "latter method was used with
me."[11]

If Boyle was in fact so unconscious of white southerners' perpetual furor over
interracial sex, Gregory Swanson was not. A twenty-six-year-old graduate of Howard University Law School, Swanson had agreed to serve as the plaintiff in an
NAACP test case designed to build on the Supreme Court's recent decision in *Sweatt
v. Painter*, the ruling that had desegregated the law school at the University of
Texas. Remembered in Charlottesville as a somewhat reluctant leader, Swanson also
had serious doubts about this effusive white faculty wife who seemed both to invite
and to repel. By the time he started classes in late September, he had begun to
answer Boyle's warm letters and phone calls in deliberately cold and sullen tones.[12]

Boyle found Swanson's increasing reticence all the more troubling because she
could not perceive its cause. He "confronted [her] with a blankness" that she knew
must be intentional when they met for the first time in the lobby of Swanson's hotel.
She described their clipped conversation in *The Desegregated Heart*: Had he understood her last letter? "Yes, perfectly." Would he help her with a magazine article
that she wanted to write about him? "Yes, a biographical sketch would be mailed
to [her] within two days." Then, a week or so later, as Swanson read over the draft
of Boyle's article, "We Want a Negro at the UVA," his impassivity broke down.
"You intend to publish *that?*" he demanded angrily. A moment later he was gone.

Boyle could not understand Swanson's reaction. To her, the piece seemed to be
"a clear-cut, straightforward statement from a faculty wife expressing one hundred
per cent approval of Swanson, and good will in regard to the whole movement
toward equal rights for Negroes." A decade later her assessment would be different.
Rereading the article in preparation for writing *The Desegregated Heart*, she
marked more than a dozen places where her article was offensive either in word
choice or by implication. She had begun by asserting her credentials as a white
southerner in a tone that implied that she felt no remorse for the South's crimes
against its black citizens. She had also tried to whitewash the University of Virginia,
implying that only state law and a benevolent concern for Swanson's welfare had
prevented his admission. Worst of all, throughout the article she had depicted Swanson and his family as good-natured colored folk who harbored "not a trace of
defiance" against segregation. A freelance writer who knew her audience well, Boyle
had hoped to minimize opposition by describing Swanson as the sort of genial and
nonthreatening black person whom no reasonable white person could mind having
around.

In fact, Boyle's concern for white opinion meant that she was bound to offend
Swanson sooner or later. She not only talked down to him, but also presumed to
speak *for* him in a manner that implied a community of feeling that did not exist.
"I'll bet you agree with me that the surest step toward getting what we want is to
be grateful—*visibly* grateful—for what we get," she wrote in one typical letter, not
recognizing that the only "we" for whom these words made sense were paternalistic

whites like herself. She came closer to the truth when she titled her proposed article "We Want a Negro at the UVA."

As Boyle later learned, her title had offended Swanson almost as much as the article itself. He had no doubt as to which "we" she was speaking for, though he may have doubted the existence of a significant white liberal community, silent or not. What annoyed him was her suggestion that she and other whites wanted only one Negro, an exception, to enjoy the right to educational opportunities that ought to be available to all. "If you didn't intend this singling out, why didn't you use the plural?" Swanson asked her when they met again at an NAACP meeting in 1953—apparently one of the few clarifying conversations they ever had, especially after Swanson returned to his law practice in Martinsville, Virginia, in early 1951.[13] Although she attributed her title primarily to chance, by 1953 Boyle had begun to understand why a seemingly trivial matter of word choice could be so important.

"White and colored Southerners both use English terms, but often the meanings we give them are as separated as our lives," she explained in a chapter of her autobiography entitled "The Semantic Barrier." "Often as a Negro friend and I talked together it was as though we spoke different languages. Worse! For when persons address each other in different tongues, they are at least aware that they do not understand what is being said." Painfully, Boyle discovered that race inflected even her most ordinary statements in ways that she could not anticipate. Her "semantic barrier" resulted from race's function as a "metalanguage" that gave her words meanings that she did not consciously intend. As the historian Evelyn Brooks Higginbotham has argued, race "serves as a 'global sign.' . . . By continually expressing overt and covert analogic relationships, race impregnates the simplest meanings we take for granted. It makes hair 'good' or 'bad,' speech patterns 'correct' or 'incorrect.' " In Boyle's case, race made her description of Swanson as "quiet and easy-going" into a portrait of an Uncle Tom, and her advice to Swanson to "keep your neck in" came across as either a sexual innuendo or a warning not to get too "uppity," or both. Because of her "semantic barrier," however, Boyle could not imagine why her words were proving offensive. Only an obvious break in communications could alert her to the misunderstanding, as when Swanson rejected her article.[14]

Bewildered by Swanson's reaction, Boyle showed the article to several white friends in Charlottesville, only to discover that "Southern white liberals do not necessarily know any more about the Negro whose side they are on than do the segregationists who oppose him." None of the men and women she consulted had close friends who were black; some were strictly "library liberals" who "had not even attempted a conversation with an educated Negro." Only Boyle's family doctor was perceptive enough to be critical, pointing out the sexually suggestive paragraph in her letter. "Why obviously he thought you were making passes at him," he told her, an idea that seemed "so preposterous" to Boyle at the time that she "didn't even consider it." No closer to understanding Swanson's anger, Boyle finally turned to T. J. Sellers.

Boyle had telephoned Sellers, the editor of a local black weekly then called the *Roanoke Tribune*, once before to offer to help him find Swanson a place to live in

Charlottesville. Although they had never met, she asked Sellers if, as a professional editor, he would give her a "brutally frank" critique of "We Want a Negro at the UVA." His reply was a litany of white liberalism's shortcomings. "Point by point," Boyle recalled in her autobiography, "he laid my Southernisms bare": gradualism, paternalism, "the one hundred per cent Southern conviction that 'privileges' were not for Negroes." Sellers's final statement was his most damning. He closed the letter by warning Boyle that "There is a New Negro in our midst who is insisting that America wake up and recognize the fact that he is a man like other men. He is entirely out of sympathy with the gross paternalism of the 'Master class' turned liberal"—liberal as, Sellers knew, Patty Boyle had only recently become.

Boyle read Sellers's letter with astonishment and indignation. Never had she been addressed in such a manner, not by a man and especially not by a man who was black. All together, it was enough to send her staggering, breathless, against her living room wall. Still, she had asked for a frank appraisal. She reread the letter, forcing herself to consider Sellers's points. As she put it in her autobiography, "Only two facts emerged: First, that I was thoroughly misunderstood by Negroes; second, that they were thoroughly misunderstood by me." She wrote Sellers to thank him for his honesty and to inform him that, given the depths of her miscomprehension, she would refrain from speaking out on race relations in the future.[15]

As Boyle explained in *The Desegregated Heart*, she "wasn't to get off so easily." T. J. Sellers wrote her another letter to apologize for hurting her feelings and to ask her not to withdraw from the battle for equal rights. Her reply sparked another round of letters and another disagreement. Although she left Sellers's third, conciliatory letter unanswered, Boyle continued to think about his appeal to "Keep up the good fight." As autumn passed into winter and winter into spring, her heart slowly "drew together" and then, in April 1951, "burst suddenly outward, spilling over the pages in an article addressed to Negroes." "Forgive us a little more," she pleaded, hoping against hope that integration could be accomplished in the South, not simply by changes in law, but through mutual compassion and the patient and painstaking removal of all the barriers of fear and resentment that kept black and white southerners apart. Sure that she would earn but another rebuke, she mailed the manuscript to T. J. Sellers.

She need not have worried. Even in the midst of their disagreements, Boyle and Sellers were learning how to speak to one another. Their successful communication depended, in large part, on Sellers's ability to address Boyle in a way that created a community of feeling, rather than simply presuming it, as she had done in her letters to Swanson. Accustomed to working with whites in the Charlottesville Interracial Commission, Sellers knew where to find common ground with white southerners and how to communicate the moral imperative embedded in that commonality. "Bits of Mr. Sellers' letters haunted me," Boyle later wrote.

> He had said that citizens like myself were needed. And he had closed one letter with the admonition, "Keep up the good fight." My father's dying words had been St. Paul's contented avowal, "I have fought the good fight; I have finished the course; I have kept the faith."

The good fight. Yes, it was! Even though the Negroes doing the fighting bore no resemblance to those I had loved all my life, they were right, and my beloved South was wrong. They were right, and that made it my fight, too.

By drawing on a biblical language that was also the language of Boyle's father, Sellers became for Boyle a moral exemplar much as her father had been. His friendship, and especially his ability to speak truth to her in language that was familiar and compelling, allowed her to complete the political transformation that she had begun.

Sellers's ability to speak to Boyle in her own language also prevented them from having the same kind of sexual misunderstandings that she had experienced with Gregory Swanson. Perhaps because he was older and more used to dealing with whites, Sellers never made the mistake Swanson made of underestimating Patty Boyle's naiveté. As a result, their friendship did not suffer, despite the fact that it developed within the context of a white hysteria about sexual relations between white women and black men that would seem to have made a nonsexualized discourse between them all but impossible. Sellers knew enough to take Boyle's potentially suggestive statements at face value, especially after she showed him her correspondence with Swanson, and he maintained a reserve that sometimes troubled her but also allowed their friendship to grow. In addition, Sellers tried to keep Boyle out of local interracial groups in the early 1950s, ostensibly because he thought that she could be more effective as an unaffiliated moral spokeswoman, but perhaps also because he recognized that her sexual obtuseness could easily lead to misunderstandings, as it would a few years later.

Sellers did not disparage the heartfelt article Boyle sent him in April 1951. Instead, he published it in his newspaper and the two became friends. Soon after, he also agreed to undertake Boyle's reeducation: as she put it in her autobiography, "to teach me the facts which had been omitted from my education, to help me bridge my chasm of segregation and knock down my segregation walls."[16] For more than a year, Boyle visited Sellers's office weekly for discussions that they only half-jokingly called the "T. J. Sellers Course for Backward Southern Whites." Taking southern interracialists' oft-stated commitment to black-white dialogue much farther than most white liberals had ever been willing to go, Boyle and Sellers talked about everything, from his cynicism about white society to her unconscious offenses of speech and behavior. When Sellers moved to New York City to edit the *Amsterdam News* in 1953, they continued their conversation in dozens of letters that now provide a rich source for understanding what lay behind Boyle's civil rights activism in the 1950s and 1960s. More than anything else, Boyle hoped to speak to other white southerners in the same transformative way that Sellers had spoken to her. First, though, she had to learn not to speak as the southern lady that she had been trained to be.

Born in Charlottesville in 1911 and educated in Virginia's segregated public schools, Thomas Jerome Sellers knew just as much about white southerners' race training as Boyle did. Slowly but surely, despite her hurt feelings, he cleared away the wreckage of Boyle's collapsed southern code, overturning stereotypes and relieving her of the paternalistic assumptions that she had brought to the Swanson case. Although he was a founding member of the Charlottesville Interracial Commission, Sellers had never agreed with its cautious approach. He believed deeply in the principles of equality and justice that underlay American democracy, and he had little patience for whites' failure to recognize blacks' constitutional rights. In a 1950 editorial, for example, Sellers boldly asserted that blacks had "always been opposed to every form of segregation—not because we saw any special blessing in mingling with our white fellow Americans and not because we favored intermarriage either. But because segregation has meant discrimination, oppression, and double standards of justice." His uncompromising position made him a valuable leader in Charlottesville; as one observer put it, "If Charlottesville's black community was discouraged by the local NAACP and the Interracial Commission's failure to attack segregation head on, it found solace in Sellers's frank editorials. . . . Sellers left no doubts about his views."[17]

If Sellers's outspokenness makes his decision to befriend a naive white idealist like Boyle somewhat surprising, it is clear that her plaintive request for an education appealed to his moral sense. Sellers valued whites' contributions to the struggle for racial equality, and he cited the example of Mary White Ovington, one of the founders of the NAACP, in an early letter to Boyle. Boyle's naive but earnest efforts at self-betterment also brought out the dedicated teacher in him. After graduating from Virginia Union University with a degree in history in 1939, Sellers had taught for one year in a rural elementary school before joining the staff of the *Norfolk Journal and Guide*. He later returned to teaching after many years as a journalist and worked for the New York City public school system for more than two decades before his retirement in 1980. Asked in 1994 about his first impressions of Patty Boyle, Sellers suggested that his willingness to teach was the natural result of Boyle's willingness to learn. "I thought she was a well-meaning and highly intelligent white lady who wanted to help," he reflected. "I also thought she had something to contribute to this struggle for human rights," a belief he maintained throughout the 1950s and 1960s, as his letters to Boyle reveal.[18]

However much potential Sellers saw in her, in 1951 Patty Boyle still had a long way to go. She was utterly naive about race relations, not to mention the role of race in the political and economic structures of the post-war South. Even on the personal level, Boyle scarcely knew what she was getting herself into when she enrolled in the "T. J. Sellers Course for Backward Southern Whites." Sellers seemed to fit the part of the "mean Nigra" she had been warned against as a child. "His face habitually wore an angry, bitter look," she wrote in her autobiography, "and a small scar on his lip added to the effect of a dangerous man, not to be trifled with."[19] As Boyle soon learned, Sellers was not a mean man, but a man who had been compelled to fight for every ounce of respect he had ever gotten, a man for whom masculinity was synonymous with race pride. "The struggle for better human relations is not primarily a struggle to get better treatment for poor downtrodden Negroes," Sellers explained to Boyle in one particularly revealing letter; "it is a struggle to recognize the basic concept upon which our civilization is based—that men, all men, and all mankind must regard themselves as brothers. I spent so many weary years trying to get across the thought to well meaning members of the other race [that] I never needed or wanted or fought for pity." "I fought against the kind of stupidity," he continued, "in pitiful blacks and whites, that saw no merit in anything nonwhite."[20] The nature of Boyle's activism suggests just how far she took Sellers's ideas.

"Having learned that Negro leaders resent [white southerners'] possessive protectiveness nearly as much as our snow-blind injustices," Boyle explained in her autobiography, "I strongly suspected that some preferred to fight for their freedom without the white man's help. Wouldn't it be more wrong than right to help them do a job which they wanted to do alone?" Drawing on what Sellers had taught her, she decided very early in her crusade what she thought the answer to this question was. "If I wasn't now fighting to help 'our Negroes' (having learned that they weren't ours) but to defend a Christian ideal and a democratic principle," she determined, "then it was irrelevant whether Negroes wanted me in the battle or not."

Boyle's belief in "corporateness"—a true integration that was the opposite of the personal and societal disintegration that resulted from human beings' inability to love one another—motivated her throughout her civil rights career. As she explained in *The Desegregated Heart*, she saw her role in the 1950s as that of a "mediator, peacemaker ... restorer of the Southern Utopia of heart- and soul-satisfying interracial relationships, but on a higher plane than before—a plane where equality would rule over all, and each group would accept the other with the self-giving hearts of children."[21] She described her vision of this "plane" often in her letters to T. J. Sellers. "To fight for integration for the Negro's sake [is] pure idiocy," she wrote in March 1953. "It doesn't make a bit of sense unless done on principle, for the good of the nation, and with the full knowledge that . . . you are doing Negroes no favor in opening white doors. . . . This is a fight for right in the ABSTRACT, and if you don't stay on the 'plane' all the time your reward will be ten burned fingers. But," she continued, reiterating how much her crusade meant to her emotionally, "on the 'plane' it is the most exciting thing in the world."[22]

Even in 1953 Sellers could sense the danger of abstraction inherent in Boyle's approach. He saw the civil rights struggle as a fight for democracy more than redemption; if Boyle was defending a "Christian ideal and a democratic principle," for him the order of significance of these two values was reversed. Nevertheless, he understood how important it was for Boyle to connect her fight to a moral vision, just as he himself had a vision of equality and justice for all. "Stay on the 'plane,' " he wrote back. "You need the moral courage that cannot be obtained from any other source. But continue to fight like 'hell' because this problem must be attacked with the fury that only Hades can provide."[23]

As much as they agreed on the need, Boyle and Sellers disagreed on what "fighting like hell" ought to mean. Because it was Swanson's reaction and not a negative response from white southerners that had led Boyle to abandon "We Want a Negro at the UVA," she found it relatively easy to maintain her belief in the good will of white southerners, despite Sellers's protests. "I concede that you know more about Negroes than I do," she insisted in their discussions. "Isn't it obvious, then, that I must know more about whites than you?" "No," Sellers would reply, "because I'm a sophisticated newspaper man and you're a naive idealist. . . . I'd be a sucker if I listened to you." Confident that it was "worse to be a cynic than a sucker," Boyle set out to prove that white southerners really loved African Americans and would stop oppressing them as soon as someone pointed out that their laws and their behavior were, in fact, oppressive.[24] Some small percentage of whites might actually hate African Americans, she admitted, but on the whole white southerners seemed to feel a strong affection for blacks that was not unlike the emotional bond between parent and child. Her goal, as she explained it to a colleague in July 1951, was "not only to bring an end to segregation and to other forms of discrimination through pressure from *white* as well as colored Southerners, but also to bring about a better understanding between two races whom segregation has alienated, but who normally love each other."[25]

Given her belief in a natural, albeit unequal, "love" between blacks and whites, Boyle was particularly interested in combating media reports that tended to focus on racial conflict whenever the issue of desegregation came up. Most of her early writings on race relations highlighted examples of good will and what she called "bootleg nonsegregation," evidence that black and white southerners could live together peacefully if the legal barriers of segregation were removed. She followed this strategy of accentuating the positive throughout the early 1950s, publishing dozens of articles in religious periodicals such as the *Christian Century* and deluging local and regional newspapers with letters to the editor under both her own name and those of other sympathetic whites. She also wrote two biweekly columns for Sellers's *Roanoke Tribune*, one a review of encouraging surveys and opinion polls called "Facts and Figures of Good Will," the other a question-and-answer series called "From behind the Curtain" by "A White Southerner." "By autumn, 1954, my published writings on integration were close to a gross," Boyle wrote in 1962. "I wanted now to try again to deliver my message in a top-circulation national periodical"—"again" because, to add to Gregory Swanson's horror, "We Want a Negro at the UVA" had been slated for publication in *Reader's Digest*. Beginning with Charlottesville's calm response to Swanson's admission and selecting several examples of "bootleg nonsegregation" from her files, Boyle pieced together a new article under the title "We're Readier Than We Think" and mailed it off.

At the same time, she was anxiously waiting to see what effects the *Brown* decision, announced a few months earlier in May 1954, would have. Unlike many white liberals who had rejoiced at the Supreme Court's ruling, Boyle had been shocked by its failure to set a deadline for desegregating the public schools. She was certain that this "fatal error" would deliver the South, "like a gift-wrapped package, to the rabid race baiters."[26] Still, she tried to be optimistic. When Virginia's newly appointed Commission on Public Education called a hearing on the problem of school desegregation in November 1954, she thought she had found the prominent local forum she needed. As the historian James Hershman notes, Boyle was "more outspoken and controversial" than any of the other whites who spoke at the commission's two-day public hearing in Richmond. She asserted that, "under proper leadership," the silent majority of white southerners would accept and even welcome integration, an argument that enraged many in her audience, including one woman who accosted her as she left the podium, angrily accusing her of trying to "mongrelize" the white race.[27]

Boyle continued to meet opposition—the first white opposition she had yet encountered—in the months that followed, and much of the criticism she faced took a similarly sexualized form. In February 1955 her new article appeared in the *Saturday Evening Post*, catapulting her to national prominence but also sensationalizing her views in a way that was destined to stir up white hostility. "Southerners Will *Like* Integration," the rewritten title screamed, while just below it a blown-up photograph of Boyle standing next to two black male medical students who had followed in Gregory Swanson's footsteps suggested, at least to segregationists' minds, what *she* liked about having African Americans at the University of Virginia. Although the article had been meant to reassure white southerners that "if we believe in justice and equality for all, we are not only on the side of right but also on the side of the majority," many readers never got beyond this picture and the title. Over the next few months, Boyle received dozens of letters from white opponents who accused her of everything from being a communist to looking like Eleanor Roosevelt. White newspapers across the South joined the attack, disputing her arguments and alleging that she had betrayed her native region for financial gain—a charge that Boyle found particularly annoying because her family had sustained a substantial loss of income when she gave up freelance writing for women's magazines in favor of unpaid work as a civil rights advocate. No matter what else they said about her, however, virtually all Boyle's critics accused her of the same heinous crime, the white southern woman's ultimate transgression: desiring black men.[28]

Not only an idealist but also reticent about sex, Boyle was hardly prepared for the opposition her article aroused. The hostility of her critics shocked her, despite the fact that she also received many letters of support. Even more upsetting was her realization that many white liberals were unwilling to take a stand against Virginia state leaders' policy of "massive resistance" to the *Brown* decision, a policy that eventually closed public schools in Charlottesville, Norfolk, Front Royal, and Prince Edward County. Instead, as Boyle recalled with a certain bitterness almost forty years later, "the longer the thing went on, the more of them ran for cover."[29] This seemed particularly true in Charlottesville, where Boyle's efforts to attract former members of the Southern Regional Council and other interracial groups into the new Virginia Council on Human Relations (VCHR) sparked less enthusiasm than she expected. Meanwhile, a special session of the Virginia legislature voted in August 1956 to grant Governor Thomas B. Stanley the authority to close any school that desegregated and to fund private schools. To Boyle's dismay, this legislation met little opposition in Charlottesville, while segregationist forces were becoming increasingly vocal and organized. In addition to various forms of intimidation directed at the black community, white leaders in the VCHR received threatening letters and phone calls and saw their meetings broken up by the white demagogue John Kaspar and the local Seaboard White Citizen's Council. At the end of August 1956 Boyle and two other whites also found burning crosses in their yards, a memento of her crusade that Boyle later hung on her living room wall.

As disturbing as these attacks were, Boyle continued to be most troubled by liberal and moderate whites' failure to stand up for the democratic principles that she was certain they held. The mood of resignation among whites in Charlottesville confounded her at least as much as the newly elected Governor J. Lindsay Almond's decision to close Charlottesville schools in the fall of 1958. Suddenly the shock of seeing schools actually close awakened whites who would have never supported desegregation in its own right. As a new coalition of white moderates moved to reopen the schools on a basis of limited integration in the fall of 1958, the NAACP strategically asked Boyle and other outspoken white liberals to step aside. Having given her "heart and strength, mind and soul for an integration accomplished with love and grace . . . in a land where justice was done when injustice was seen," Boyle acknowledged that the legal battle for school desegregation had been won, but felt that "all that I had fought for was lost."

By the time Charlottesville's schools reopened in 1959, Patty Boyle had learned a painful lesson: white southerners were nowhere near as "ready" for integration as she had originally thought. She became less and less comfortable around whites, even as she became less and less welcome in white social circles in Charlottesville. By the late 1950s she began to accept the widespread white opinion that one white moderate voiced: "You don't belong with us; you belong with the Negroes."[30]

At the same time, however, Boyle was also becoming increasingly disillusioned with blacks. Working in local interracial groups, she had discovered that individual black men and women were not always as "superior" as she expected them to be, despite the moral superiority of their cause. "A lot of the men made passes at me for one thing," she insisted in later years, adding that she had never mentioned this in her writings because she "felt that one thing I wasn't going to do was to add to the bad stereotype" of the sexually dangerous black male.[31] Whether or not black men were actually making passes at Boyle is a complicated question, given the fact that many white southern women at midcentury might construe even a glance from a black man as a sexual threat. Certainly, Boyle thought the discomfort she was experiencing had a basis in reality, and although she never wrote publicly about black men's "passes," she did make an effort to defend her interpretation of them as such.

Her explanation, meant to establish her innocence in misleading Gregory Swanson, focused on a lesser-known current in the socialization of white southern girls that taught them to ignore the possibility of interracial sex altogether. In her autobiography, Boyle labeled this countercurrent the "sex-suppression school" and suggested that, while "no data is available which offers a clue to whether the majority of southern white women learned" in it or in the better-known "super-sex-conscious school," "many of my friends belonged to my school, and joined me in thinking that persons taught the other way were unpleasantly evil-minded." "I have yet to find a Negro who knows even of the existence of the sex-suppression school," she continued, T. J. Sellers's apparent insight into Boyle's naiveté notwithstanding. "Resultant misunderstandings are virulent."[32]

Self-serving as Boyle's account of the "sex-suppression school" might be, it does help to explain sexual misunderstandings—whatever their exact nature—for which she ultimately took the blame. "I was very unself-conscious sexually," she admitted in a 1994 interview. "I had this Southern contradiction thing. I flirted a lot, but I didn't mean it as an invitation." Unable to recognize the suggestiveness of her own behavior at the time, Boyle found anything that seemed suggestive on the part of black men to be particularly disheartening. "I expected the leaders to have high purposes," she reflected, "and when they related to me on the lowest level while talking the highest level, it was just one shock after another." Faced with hostility from whites and frequent misunderstandings with black men, Boyle lost virtually all inspiration for the black freedom struggle by the late 1950s.

Her relationships with black women seem to have added to her despair. "[O]ne of the chief black women leaders in Charlottesville . . . pulled a complete deception on me . . . and pretended to work on getting out the vote [for a local fair-housing referendum] and didn't do it," Boyle remembered bitterly. "So, I found they were telling me lies. The men were making passes at me and all this. And I almost threw in the sponge there because of my disillusion in black people. But then," she added, skipping ahead to the story of spiritual renewal that she would tell in the third section of *The Desegregated Heart*, "as I began to lean more and more on orthodox Christianity, I began to feel again that you just couldn't count on people anyway and I mustn't think in terms of people. My assignment was from God, what he wanted me to do, and that was what enabled me to go on."[33]

Although Boyle's account of blacks' "deceptions" is obviously one-sided, the fact of her disillusionment remains. And certainly black activists had reason to be less than transparent to her. As the Charlottesville NAACP president George Ferguson explained, one always had to "be very careful of people who became so enthused overnight." Ferguson doubted Boyle longer and harder than most, long after, as one of Boyle's white friends described it, "Patty had burned all of her bridges, and the white community had utterly abandoned her" so that "the black community had to realize she was sincere, however strange she always remained to them." To Ferguson and likely to others, Boyle "forever remained a 'grandstander' using race relations as a 'stepping stone to make some money,' " despite the fact that many other African Americans in Charlottesville felt that "she 'wrote just lovely' and 'had a Christian heart.' "[34] Whatever the range of African American opinion, Boyle felt utterly betrayed because, as she later admitted, "I think I needed and wanted to believe in [blacks'] superior virtue at that point." At the time, she knew only that

> the people that I had trusted were deceiving me all over the place, in one way or another, black people, and this I had not expected at all. So in a way it was the same kind of a crushing blow that I had got[ten] from my husband because I had assumed certain virtues in them which turned out to be only pretense.

"This was why I valued T. J. so," Boyle concluded. "T. J. told you what he was thinking. There was no question about that. So that gave me something I could hold onto."[35]

T. J. Sellers's friendship did indeed give Boyle something to hold on to during the roughest period of her crusade. Disillusioned as she was, she could always rely on

Sellers for empathy, if not always for approval. They achieved what the philosopher Stanley Cavell has called a "perfectionist" friendship, one characterized by

> a mode of conversation, between . . . friends, one of whom is intellectually authorita-
> tive because his life is somehow exemplary or representative of a life the other(s) are
> attracted to, and in the attraction of which the self recognizes itself as enchained . . .
> and a process of education is undertaken . . . in which each self is drawn on a journey
> of ascent to a further state of that self, where the higher is determined not by natural
> talent but by seeking to know what you are made of and cultivating the thing you are
> meant to do.[36]

Even before Boyle began to encounter opposition in the mid-1950s, she and Sellers had made quite a journey. He had transformed her perspective on race relations (although not as completely as he might have hoped), and as a result, she had found the cause she had been searching for in the late 1940s. Sellers, too, had benefited from their conversation, even though he remained skeptical of Boyle's optimistic views. "I think it is a good time for me to tell you how much you have aided my own education," he wrote to Boyle in March 1955. "I think you should know that you helped me to destroy the ugly and mean and distorted picture that once came to my mind whenever I heard the word 'South.' "[37]

Even as he thanked her for giving him a little more faith in humanity, however, Sellers reserved the right to disagree with Boyle and especially to reject her tendency to idolize him as a "superior" human being. "Will you ever forgive me," Boyle had written to him just a month earlier, days before her controversial *Saturday Evening Post* article hit the stands,

> if I now confide that more than anything else it was the constant object lesson that in
> the South a man like you could be kept in a relatively subordinate position when he
> was obviously bursting at the seams with contributions which he could make to our
> world—more than anything it was this which made me feel that no sacrifice was too
> great which might contribute to the alteration of such a system.

Although her intentions are ambiguous, Boyle was apparently trying to push their friendship to a more personal level—to compel Sellers to admit that he cared for her as a person and not merely as a student—by confessing that it was her admiration for him as a "superior" individual that had made her want to change her society's unfair rules. Sellers's reply—that he had "always lived in a highly competitive society [and] always liked and welcomed competition"—hardly lived up to Boyle's expectations. Suddenly deluged by angry responses to her article, Boyle was hoping not for gratitude perhaps, but for affirmation from her mentor for "a letter the total implication of which was probably the most complimentary I have ever written." "Please don't be so hard to get along with," she wrote in her next letter, assuring Sellers that she was already having enough trouble dealing with the hate mail and the hostile reviews her article had generated.

A few days later, Boyle would need Sellers's affirmation even more, as she became increasingly distraught over blacks' failure to respond to the article that had earned her so much enmity from whites. "[W]hat would your reaction be if you were in my position and had received . . . not one word from the NAACP [?]" she wrote, thoroughly disheartened. "My reaction is that you don't undertake this kind of thing for the purpose of winning appreciat[ion] and support. . . . Also, that I am defending the right, not the people. But this last is only a half truth. You can't be human and altogether separate the right from the people, for there is no right and wrong without the people who suffer and strive. Oh, Boss," she concluded, addressing Sellers with the affectionate inversion of southern racial idiom that she had begun using while working for him at the *Tribune*, "if you were here I would cry so hard on your shoulder. I'm so tired of being a white lady."[38]

Boyle became increasingly "tired of being a white lady" as her crusade wore on. Her sense of social displacement drove her all the more resolutely to the "plane," just as her marital troubles had driven her to a more committed Christianity in the late 1940s. She gradually lost faith in all people, black and white alike, because she considered human beings in general to be unable to live up to her own supposedly high moral standards. Recognizing her loss of empathy for human weakness, she admitted that she simply "found it impossible to believe in anyone merely because he or she had not *thus far*" disappointed her.[39] "Spiritually bankrupt," Boyle decided to put her faith in God, eventually "separating the right from the people" much more than she had once thought possible. "When I began to have all this trouble," she remembered almost forty years later, "my Christianity was still [focused on] human virtue. I still believed in good people. I didn't accept the doctrine [that] there is no such thing as a good person, that all goodness is an expression of God." As she encountered opposition and dissent, however, Boyle began to "get really orthodox." "I believed that the only good was God's direct action . . . and that was when I made my real flip-over and began to be interested only in knowing God more and better."[40]

Although Boyle tended to think of her new orthodoxy as a "flip-over," it was also a heightening of her commitment to the "plane." Confronted with the hate mail sparked by "Southerners Will *Like* Integration," she had written to Sellers as early as May 1955 of her need "to step up to a plane of thinking and feeling which is entirely removed from the plane on which this type of attack is formulated." Even then, she wanted "to live in the land of principles and universal values, where individuals merge into humanity and humanity is an expression of God."[41] Clearly, Boyle's attempt to "rise above" the disillusionments she was encountering in the mid-1950s was a strategy to allow her to continue to participate in the struggle for African Americans' rights—and she did continue for almost a decade longer, speaking, writing, and taking part in the marches and demonstrations of her younger black and white colleagues. Soon, though, she also began to realize that her thinking was far removed from the political and economic level at which the South's race problems would have to be solved. "I spend more time higher on 'the Plane' each year," she wrote to Sellers in November 1957. "I don't know whether you would like me any more or not. You might think me not enough in this world."[42]

Boyle was right; Sellers was concerned about her spiritual distance from the civil rights cause. Though he continued to believe that the black freedom struggle was "everybody's struggle for the ultimate good of everybody," he also recognized that

Boyle's increasingly moralistic approach left little room for agency on the part of blacks. "[T]rying to touch the consci[ence] of Southern white folks by play-acting like Jesus Christ is downright ludicrous when Negroes are in the supporting roles," he wrote to Boyle in July 1960, insisting that "a hymn chanting, bible toting Negro does not produce a dramatic effect on the thinking of Southern white folks because hymn chanting and bible toting are important parts of the stereotype picture that they already have of Uncle Tom's grandchildren."[43]

As this letter suggests, Sellers's complaint was not only with Boyle, but also with the methods of the early civil rights movement. He simply found it hard to believe that demonstrators would be able to change whites' thinking as much as many activists hoped. "We can help educate our [white] friends not by sitting in at hot dog counters demanding the chance to spend a quarter, but by WALKING AWAY, and staying away, from all counters, everywhere that are not willing to give us the respect and consideration and courtesy that the 20 million dollars spent by American Negroes each year should deserve," he told the audience at a Charlottesville Freedom Fund dinner in November 1962. Sellers also advocated self-reliance and, when necessary, self-defense, insisting that "America, as a nation, and individual American citizens, must have the power and the fortitude and the willingness to strike back, and strike back hard, if the other fellow becomes violent. This is a good old American credo," he concluded, "which our friends may understand and respect more than they have, so far, understood and respected the late Prophet Gandhi's 'Soul Force' concept."[44] In fact, while it would be a mistake to identify T. J. Sellers as an early proponent of Black Power thinking, it is clear that a moral suasion approach to the civil rights movement contrasted rather sharply with both his strong sense of racial identity and his pragmatism.

Education had always been Sellers's preferred weapon in the black freedom struggle, one he wielded both in his newspaper editorials and in the various jobs he held in the New York City public schools after he left the *Amsterdam News* in 1956. His vision was not of a redeemed white society—although that certainly would have been nice—but of a strengthened black citizenry able to compete and succeed in America as a result of improved educational opportunities and the eradication of racial barriers. Given his more earthly and racially based vision, Sellers could have little sympathy when Boyle told him that she wanted to live in the place "where individuals merge into humanity," that she was "tired of being a white lady," that she was "thinking seriously of dying my skin brown."[45] To him, such statements suggested her failure to understand both the social and economic foundations of white supremacy and the irony of her own exercise of white prerogative in choosing to be black. Sellers made this connection poignantly in a 1968 letter about Boyle's friend John Howard Griffin, a white man who had shaved his head and dyed his skin to experience "what it is like to be a Negro in a land where we keep the Negro down."[46] "I have always thought that it would have been poetic irony," Sellers wrote,

> if the dye had remained on and if the hair had grown back nappy and if it had been impossible for him to relate that this was all a gag—and he had then been forced to

remain black all of his natural life, without the benefit of literary noblesse oblige! I don't know for sure, but there is a possibility that he might have spent his senility making gasoline bombs and tossing them into liquor stores instead of making lectures to church groups on the restlessness in dark America.[47]

Although Boyle's commitment to the black freedom struggle was certainly no "gag," her increasing spiritual distance from the political and economic realities of race relations in America sometimes left Sellers feeling more than a little annoyed. Nevertheless, Patty Boyle and T. J. Sellers remained friends. It is in that fact, as well as in the spiritual awakening her autobiography touched off in many readers, that Sarah Patton Boyle's legacy rests. Boyle and Sellers were extraordinary, not only because they found common ground, but also because they never let a lack of common ground put an end to their conversation. They shared, in Boyle's words, "the habit of stating facts, feelings and convictions exactly as we saw them, which explains both our conflicts and our ability to cooperate with each other."[48] What they did not share was "love," especially not in the narrow and heterosexist sense in which the term is usually applied to relationships between men and women, and in fact not even to the extent that "love" requires individuals to agree with one another more often than not.

Patty Boyle was not looking for love when she asked T. J. Sellers to reeducate her—or if she was, Sellers made it clear from the beginning that she was not going to find it. As Boyle recorded in her autobiography, Sellers's response to her plea for enlightenment was characteristically blunt: "All right—provided you approach the assignment as an objective student of sociology and not as a white lady slumming!"[49] And therein, perhaps, lies the secret to their successful communication, in both personal and political terms. As Carolyn Heilbrun acknowledges in *Writing a Woman's Life*, Stanley Cavell's concept of perfectionist friendship offers a better standard for evaluating relationships between men and women than the "indications of happy marriage that romance and the patriarchy have taught us." Though not a marriage in any traditional sense, Boyle's friendship with T. J. Sellers turned out to be a far more "meet and happy conversation" than her actual marriage to Roger Boyle had been.[50] Unlike segregationists, unlike Boyle herself in her miscommunications with Swanson and other black men, Boyle and Sellers could, by thinking in terms of friendship, think far enough beyond the teachings of their racist and patriarchal society not only to imagine but to sustain an intimate, nonsexual relationship across race and gender lines.

More important, Boyle and Sellers maintained their friendship, which was also a political alliance in that it motivated Boyle as an activist and author, without sacrificing their differences. As Sara Evans has argued, we need to recognize that conflict and difference are "constitutive of public life," no matter how appealing the brotherhood or sisterhood ideal. "Within private/familial life one gives and receives unconditional love," Evans reminds us (although her view of family life is a bit idealistic). "Within public life one operates out of self-interest and has a right to demand respect but not love." Nevertheless, reformers of recent decades, including the younger generation of activists with whom Boyle aligned herself in the 1960s, have tended to make just such an impossible demand. "Within the new left," Evans explains, "public life was never conceptualized as distinct from, even if dynamically related to, private life. . . . Identity politics, in effect, proposed that political communities were conceptualized as familylike. In practice, where differences existed, they were denied or subordinated." Liberating as the movements of the 1960s and 1970s proved for some, the conflation of public and private and the denial of difference limited the possibilities for further change. Those, like Boyle, who expected to find love and acceptance in the public sphere have become disillusioned. Others whose experience of oppression led them to make absolute moral claims have "found it difficult to negotiate, build lasting alliances, or deal with the uncertainties and moral ambiguities of actual politics," difficulties that have enervated reform initiatives across the board.[51]

Patty Boyle's emotional demands on the public sphere were great and her disillusionment came early. That she was seeking love in her activism is made all the more clear by the fact that, in the "foxhole Christianity" to which her activism drove her, she felt she had found it. "My primary purpose in this book," she explained in *The Desegregated Heart*, "is to share my discovery that to have joy and peace we must love, and that in the last extremity we can love only by means unfamiliar to most of us"—means that included a total subordination of self and of political purpose to the perceived will of God.[52]

If Boyle seems to fit Evans's model of activist burnout in one respect, however, her friendship with Sellers is a different and more positive story. Boyle could not accept Sellers's near-total lack of faith in white southerners in the early 1950s, even as she gratefully accepted his instruction in the "T. J. Sellers Course for Backward Southern Whites." Her optimism, her insistence on speaking to white southerners' better selves, resulted in much disillusionment, but it also helped to prepare the way for future progress as the nonviolent protests of the late 1950s and early 1960s took shape. Meanwhile, Sellers could not fault Boyle for her deeply held religious convictions, even if he seriously doubted the political effectiveness of her moral appeal. Even years later, long after the ideological shifts of the Black Power movement led Boyle to retire from activism, months after her quiet death at the age of eighty-seven gave him the last word in their conversation, Sellers rejected the idea that Patty Boyle's moral crusade ever became "too abstract" to be relevant to the people she was trying to help. "Mrs. Boyle was crusading for a change of heart," he asserted. "Her appeal for human brotherhood was an honest attempt to help ALL Americans become better human beings. I will always remember her for her honest efforts in this regard."[53]

NOTES

I would like to thank Jacquelyn Dowd Hall and Suzanne Lebsock for their steadfast engagement and invaluable assistance with this essay. Thanks also to Anne Firor Scott, Glenda Gilmore, Kirsten Wood, and Leigh Edwards, who commented on later drafts. I am grateful to Martha Hodes for her thoughtful editing and to the University of North Carolina at Chapel Hill for financial support.

1. Sarah Patton Boyle, *The Desegregated Heart: A Virginian's Stand in Time of Transition* (New York: William Morrow, 1962), 29, 50–51, 56. For a compelling discussion of "social equality," see Nell Irvin Painter, " 'Social Equality,' Miscegenation, Labor and Power," in *The Evolution of Southern Culture*, ed. Numan V. Bartley (Athens: University of Georgia Press, 1988), 53–54.

2. Kathleen Murphy Dierenfield discusses Boyle's contributions as a white liberal in "One 'Desegregated Heart': Sarah Patton Boyle and the Crusade for Civil Rights in Virginia," *Virginia Magazine of History and Biography* 104 (1996): 251–84. On white women's involvement in the interracial movement, see Jacquelyn Dowd Hall, *Revolt against Chivalry: Jessie Daniel Ames and the Women's Campaign against Lynching*, rev. ed. (New York: Columbia University Press, 1993), 59–106 and passim; and Mary E. Frederickson, " 'Each One Is Dependent on the Other': Southern Churchwomen, Racial Reform, and the Process of Transformation, 1880–1940," in *Visible Women: New Essays on American Activism*, ed. Nancy Hewitt and Suzanne Lebsock (Urbana: University of Illinois Press, 1993), 296–324. A direct comparison between Boyle's autobiography and the autobiographical works of Lumpkin, Smith, and Durr would prove interesting for a future study: see Katharine Du Pre Lumpkin, *The Making of a Southerner* (1946; reprint, Athens: University of Georgia Press, 1981); Lillian Smith, *Killers of the Dream* (1949; reprint, New York: W. W. Norton, 1994); Hollinger F. Barnard, ed., *Outside the Magic Circle: The Autobiography of Virginia Foster Durr* (Tuscaloosa: University of Alabama Press, 1985).

3. Boyle, *Desegregated Heart*, 117, 52. For Boyle's use of "maternalism," see *Desegregated Heart*, 58.

4. Sara Evans, *Personal Politics: The Roots of Women's Liberation in the Civil Rights Movement and the New Left* (New York: Vintage, 1980), 35. For Boyle's sense of "noblesse oblige," see *Desegregated Heart*, 6, 117.

5. The phrase "sow love" comes from a prayer of St. Francis of Assisi that Boyle took as her motto in the first years of her crusade. See *Desegregated Heart*, 121.

6. Sarah Patton Boyle, interview by Jennifer Ritterhouse, Jan. 7, 1994, Arlington, VA. Tapes in author's possession.

7. On Robert Patton's career, see Robert W. Patton, "An Inspiring Record in Negro Education" (New York: National Council of the Protestant Episcopal Church, 1940). James D. Anderson discusses some of the American Church Institute schools and offers a compelling critique of white educators' paternalism in *The Education of Blacks in the South, 1860–1935* (Chapel Hill: University of North Carolina Press, 1988).

8. Boyle, *Desegregated Heart*, 14; Boyle, interview; Sarah Patton Boyle to W. Lester Banks, Sept. 4, 1951, Sarah Patton Boyle Papers (no. 8003), Special Collections Department, University of Virginia Library, Charlottesville. All letters cited in this essay are from the Boyle Papers unless otherwise noted.

9. Boyle, *Desegregated Heart*, 94. Boyle to Rev. Chad Walsh, quoted in Joanna Bowen Gillespie, "Sarah Patton Boyle's *Desegregated Heart*," in *Beyond Conventions: Southern Women Series*, vol. 3, ed. Janet Coryll, Sandra Treadway, Martha Swain, and Elizabeth Turner (Columbia: University of Missouri Press, 1998).

10. Boyle, *Desegregated Heart*, 54–58. For a recent overview of the South's white liberal tradition, including white liberals' reluctance to challenge segregation, see John Egerton, *Speak Now against the Day: The Generation before the Civil Rights Movement in the South* (New York: Alfred A. Knopf, 1994). See also Morton Sosna, *In Search of the Silent South: Southern Liberals and the Race Issue* (New York: Columbia University Press, 1977).

11. Boyle, *Desegregated Heart*, 78–79.

12. Dierenfield, "One 'Desegregated Heart,' " 257; Boyle, *Desegregated Heart*, 64.

13. Boyle, *Desegregated Heart*, 64–65, 72, 73, 84, 126–27. Swanson later moved to Washington, D.C., where he worked in the Chief Counsel's Office of the Internal Revenue Service. He and Boyle corresponded on a few occasions, but were never close. For example, Boyle did not know that he was married and the father of two girls until 1961, when she wrote to ask for permission to quote from one of his letters in *The Desegregated Heart*. Their correspondence survives in the Boyle Papers (no. 8003).

14. Boyle, *Desegregated Heart*, 126–30; Evelyn Brooks Higginbotham, "African-American Women's History and the Metalanguage of Race," *Signs* 17 (1992): 25. Boyle discussed the semantic barrier between blacks and whites in more detail in her second book, an interracial etiquette manual entitled *For Human Beings Only* (New York: Seabury Press, 1964). For a feminist perspective on communication across difference, particularly the perils of attempting to speak for someone else as Boyle attempted to speak for Swanson, see Linda Alcoff, "The Problem of Speaking for Others," *Cultural Critique* 20 (winter 1991): 5–32.

15. Boyle, *Desegregated Heart*, 82–85.

16. Ibid., 86–87, 93, 97, 102.

17. Both quotations are from Bradley Charles Mittendorf, "From Discussion to Confrontation: Defining Race Relations in Charlottesville before the *Brown* Decision" (M.A. thesis, University of Virginia, 1993), 35–36, 38. Sellers's statement appeared in the *Roanoke Tribune*, Dec. 8, 1950.

18. Boyle, *Desegregated Heart*, 86; T. J. Sellers to Jennifer Ritterhouse, Nov. 8, 1994, letter in author's possession.

19. Boyle, *Desegregated Heart*, 102–03.

20. T. J. Sellers to Sarah Patton Boyle, Nov. 28, 1955.

21. Boyle, *Desegregated Heart*, 118, 121.

22. Boyle to Sellers, March 24, 1953.

23. Sellers to Boyle, March 29, 1953.

24. Boyle, *Desegregated Heart*, 137.

25. Boyle to Dennis N. Haughton, July 1, 1951. Haughton was the pastor of Mt. Zion Baptist Church in Cheriton, Virginia.

26. Boyle, *Desegregated Heart*, 189, 179.

27. James Howard Hershman, Jr., "A Rumbling in the Museum: The Opponents of Virginia's Massive Resistance" (Ph.D. diss., University of Virginia, 1978), 57; Boyle, *Desegregated Heart*, 196.

28. Sarah Patton Boyle, "Southerners Will *Like* Integration," *Saturday Evening Post*, Feb. 19, 1955, 134. For a description of white reactions to the article and Boyle's struggle with the *Post* over its title, see Boyle, *Desegregated Heart*, 200–254; and Dierenfield, "One 'Desegregated Heart,' " 265–71. Although Boyle received one thousand dollars for "Southerners Will *Like* Integration," she usually worked without pay and started accepting honorariums for her speeches only in the late 1950s. Her correspondence is full of references to her lack of time and money as well as occasional complaints about the strain of her household duties, which included raising two sons and nursing her mother-in-law through terminal cancer in the early 1950s.

29. Boyle, interview.

30. Quotations are from Boyle, *Desegregated Heart*, 288, 284. A number of secondary works recount the history of "massive resistance" in Virginia from various perspectives, including Benjamin Muse, *Virginia's Massive Resistance* (Bloomington: Indiana University Press, 1961); Robbins L. Gates, *The Making of Massive Resistance: Virginia's Politics of Public School Desegregation, 1954–1956* (Chapel Hill: University of North Carolina Press, 1962); James W. Ely, Jr., *The Crisis of Conservative Virginia: The Byrd Organization and*

the Politics of Massive Resistance (Knoxville: University of Tennessee Press, 1976); and Hershman, "Rumbling in the Museum." On school desegregation in Charlottesville, see Dierenfield, "One 'Desegregated Heart,' " 276–81; and Anna Holden, *The Bus Stops Here: A Study of School Desegregation in Three Cities* (New York: Schocken, 1974).

31. Boyle, interview.

32. Boyle, *Desegregated Heart*, 79–80.

33. Boyle, interview.

34. Kathleen Anne Murphy, "Sarah Patton Boyle and the Crusade against Virginia's Massive Resistance" (M.A. thesis, University of Virginia, 1983), 19, 54–55, 41. The first and third quotations are from Murphy's interview with George Ferguson, Nov. 7, 1980. The second quotation is from her interview with Jane Foster, Dec. 5, 1980. See also Dierenfield, "One 'Desegregated Heart,' " 274.

35. Boyle, interview.

36. Stanley Cavell, *Conditions Handsome and Unhandsome: The Constitution of Emersonian Perfectionism* (Chicago: University of Chicago Press, 1990), 6–7. I have omitted the parenthetical numbering in Cavell's original for the reader's convenience. For an excellent overview of Cavell's philosophical writings, see Stephen Mulhall, *Stanley Cavell: Philosophy's Recounting of the Ordinary* (New York: Oxford University Press, 1994).

37. Sellers to Boyle, March 11, 1955.

38. In order, quotations are from Boyle to Sellers, Feb. 10, 1955; Sellers to Boyle, Feb. 11, 1955; Boyle to Sellers, Feb 19, Feb. 14, Feb. 19, 1955.

39. Boyle, *Desegregated Heart*, xii.

40. Boyle, interview.

41. Boyle to Sellers, May 10, 1955.

42. Boyle to Sellers, Nov. 13, 1957.

43. Sellers to Boyle, April 10, 1967, July 30, 1960.

44. T. J. Sellers, "The Task before Us Now" (speech given at Freedom Fund dinner, Charlottesville, Nov. 21, 1962), Sarah Patton Boyle Papers (no. 8003).

45. Boyle to Sellers, May 10, Feb. 19, 1955, Feb. 20, 1956.

46. John Howard Griffin, *Black Like Me* (New York: Houghton Mifflin, 1960), 5.

47. Sellers to Boyle, Feb. 19, 1968.

48. Boyle to Jennifer Ritterhouse, Nov. 2, 1993, in author's possession.

49. Boyle, *Desegregated Heart*, 102.

50. Carolyn Heilbrun, *Writing a Woman's Life* (New York: W. W. Norton, 1988), 95. Although Cavell's ideas apply to relationships of many kinds, Heilbrun limits her discussion to marriage, drawing on Cavell's *Pursuits of Happiness: The Hollywood Comedy of Remarriage* (Cambridge: Harvard University Press, 1981). For Cavell's analysis of John Milton's argument that "a meet and happy conversation is the chiefest and noblest end of marriage," see *Pursuits of Happiness*, 87.

51. Sara Evans, "Women's History and Political Theory: Toward a Feminist Approach to Public Life," in *Visible Women*, ed. Hewitt and Lebsock, 124, 131.

52. Boyle, *Desegregated Heart*, xi.

53. Sellers to Ritterhouse, Nov. 8, 1994.

Chapter Twenty-Four

Crossing Oceans, Crossing Colors
Black Peace Corps Volunteers and Interracial Love in Africa, 1961–1971

Jonathan Zimmerman

One morning in 1966, the black Peace Corps volunteer Gloria Myklebust walked into her classroom of Cameroonian students and delivered a stunning announcement: she was marrying a white American. Immediately, hands shot up. "Please, Madam, I don't understand," one youngster pleaded. "How can you marry the enemy?" Flooded with news reports of racial strife in the United States, Cameroonians presumed that Myklebust would never befriend—let alone betroth—an American of a different color. As the ensuing months confirmed, however, her African hosts fully accepted black-white marriages. Such unions were a fairly common sight on the continent, where many elites returned from foreign study with white spouses. For the remainder of Myklebust's Peace Corps service, then, her choice of partner drew little comment. "[F]olks accept you for who you are, not what you are," she recalled. "I felt that most keenly in Africa."

But the feeling quickly dissipated when Myklebust returned to America with her husband, a fellow Peace Corps volunteer. Relatives in each family questioned the decision to marry across the color line. As the civil rights movement shaded into Black Power, meanwhile, several African American acquaintances charged Myklebust with diluting the pride and "purity" of her race. But the most difficult experience was the routine harassment the couple received from strangers, especially whites. Told that their Virginia hotel lacked king-sized beds, the Myklebusts requested two single beds next to each other. Then they went out for lunch, returning to find that the beds had been separated. The pattern repeated itself for the next few days: whenever the couple left their room, the white hotel clerks rearranged it.[1]

Pushed together and then apart, the beds provide an apt metaphor for interracial Peace Corps romances in Africa during the 1960s. The handful of black volunteers on the continent rarely had the opportunity to date each other, since they were dispersed across two dozen countries.[2] Nor did they sustain many long-term relationships with Africans, whose gender roles and expectations often proved too different from their own. So they paired off with white volunteers, who seemed far less "foreign" in an overseas environment than they had at home. "The white volunteers had more in common with us, as African Americans, than they did with

Nigerians," noted another black Peace Corps veteran, "and we had more in common with the white Americans than with the Nigerians." Both American races "had the freedom to . . . treat people as people," a third black volunteer added, "and if relationships happen, they happen."[3]

The frequency of these unions is difficult to determine three decades after the fact. Of the thirty-nine black Peace Corps veterans I interviewed, almost half reported that they had dated whites in Africa.[4] All but three said that interracial relationships were both more common and less conflicted than they were in the United States. For couples like the Myklebusts, then, "coming home" meant a new and excruciating encounter with America's oldest dilemma. Preaching unity across the races, civil rights advocates often balked when lovers applied this principle in its most intimate form. So did Black Power adherents, whose calls for "race pride" and "self-determination" spawned a searing ambivalence on issues of sex. Race pride seemed to dictate against black-white unions, which could only retard African American unity and integrity. But self-determination suggested that blacks should be free to pursue any destiny they chose, including romance or marriage with members of another race.[5]

Meanwhile, white Americans stood virtually united against interracial sex and marriage. A host of opinion polls confirmed this antipathy, which softened only slightly by the end of the decade. Interracial couples suffered harsh abuse on the streets and chronic discrimination in housing, employment, and the law. Sixteen states still banned interracial marriages in 1967, when the Supreme Court's *Loving v. Virginia* decision struck down such measures. "Almighty God created the races . . . and he placed them on separate continents," the original trial judge in *Loving* had written. "And but for the interference with his arrangement there would be no cause for such marriages." Returning to the continent of their ancestors, black Peace Corps volunteers conclusively refuted this separatist dogma. But for America's own "history of oppression," as one volunteer called it, no cause prevented blacks and whites from living—and loving—together.[6]

In his "Weekly Report to the President" for January 23, 1962, the Peace Corps's first international director anxiously announced the Corp's first interracial marriage. A few days earlier, the Nigeria volunteers Yvette Burgess ("black—from New York," the director noted) and Charles Polcyn ("white—from Michigan") had exchanged vows. Now came the difficult part: public relations. "They have . . . informed their parents and we have been warned to expect some 'noisy objections,' " Sargent Shriver told his brother-in-law John F. Kennedy. "If the parents call, I shall speak to them personally." Perhaps Shriver feared that the couple's parents would contact the press, where reports of miscegenation in the Peace Corps would make hot copy indeed. They would also sully his young agency's fastidious image, which Shriver polished and guarded as if it were a jewel.[7]

In Nigeria, likewise, the Peace Corps tried to keep the new couple out of the news. When an African reporter took pictures at their wedding, for example, a fellow volunteer paid him to relinquish them. "We really believed in the Peace Corps," explained Burgess, the African American bride. "We understood that back home, this would make a big problem." Before they could wed, in fact, Burgess and Polcyn were required to consult with a U.S. embassy lawyer about marriage laws in America. Since neither of their native states banned black-white unions, the Peace Corps allowed the wedding to proceed. But it also made a conscious decision to soft-pedal the event, even as the agency advertised its commitment to "human justice" and "equal opportunity." Heralding a new age of interracial harmony, the Peace Corps could not afford to espouse interracial matrimony as well.[8]

Here it echoed America's early civil rights movement, which also struggled to evade the thorny issue of sex across the color line. In 1957 Martin Luther King, Jr., sounded the movement's essential dream: a "beloved community," bringing every race and creed into a single, unified whole. "Our ultimate goal," King declared, "is genuine intergroup and interpersonal living—*integration*." The following year, however, he took pains to distinguish this vision from the frightful specter of miscegenation. "[T]he continual outcry concerning intermarriage is a distortion of the real issue," he cautioned. "[T]he Negro's primary aim is to be the white man's brother, not his brother-in-law." Repeated frequently for white audiences, this quip was born less of conviction than calculation. King himself had once contemplated marriage to a white lover, railing in private against "the cruel and silly forces in life that were keeping two people from doing what they most wanted to do." Given whites' historic hostility to intermarriage, however, any public plea on its behalf seemed certain to doom other quests for justice. "Defend interracial marriage on principle!" scoffed one civil rights advocate. "Principle costs too much." If blacks asserted this right, she argued, "[t]here would be no integrated swimming pools, no mixed schools, no public accommodations. . . . Only the burning cross. Only the rope." When whites inquired whether he secretly desired to marry their daughters, a second African American added, the best answer was also the simplest: no.[9]

As the 1960s wore on, this "conspiracy of silence" proved increasingly untenable. American rates of intermarriage nearly doubled during the decade, while interracial dating probably increased at an even faster clip.[10] Entering college and the professions in record numbers, blacks had far greater opportunities to meet—and marry—whites. Another common venue for interracial dating was the civil rights movement itself, where southern blacks worked side by side with young whites from the North. Throwing King's caution to the wind, some activists openly celebrated black-white romance as the "ultimate expression" of his integrationist ideology. Symbolically, at least, "interracial sex became . . . conclusive proof of their right to membership in the 'beloved community,' " as Doug McAdam has argued. Yet these relationships were often marked less by liberation than by exploitation, placing a wedge—not a bridge—between the races. White women found it "much harder to say no to the advances of a black guy because of the strong possibility of that being taken as racist," recalled one participant. They also clashed heatedly with black women, who suffered "grave feelings of inferiority" at being passed over by African American men, as the essayist Calvin Hernton wrote in 1965. Despite their rhetoric of freedom, then, few couples managed to escape the maelstrom of anger, guilt, and jealousy that swirled around interracial sex.[11]

Similar problems afflicted Peace Corps training sites, which also brought black and white recruits into close, extended proximity. Many of these volunteers were veterans of the civil rights movement: for example, roughly five percent of participants in the "Freedom Summer" campaign of 1964 went on to join the Peace Corps. "Have you been arrested five times in the last five months for sitting in?" asked a 1965 brochure, tongue barely in cheek. "Do you think we should ban the bomb, integrate Mississippi into the United States, abolish the State Department and turn the Met over to folksingers? The Peace Corps is just your cup of espresso." Whereas civil rights projects drew heavily from both races, however, the vast majority of Peace Corps recruits were white. Many training groups included just one or two African Americans, while several others had none. For black volunteers, then, their first "culture shock" frequently occurred not in Africa but in America—at their Peace Corps trainings, usually held on northern college campuses. This choice of site only increased blacks' sense of isolation, since most of them came from the South. "That really scared me, to get out there in the middle of nowhere with all these whites," recalled the volunteer Patricia Eaton. "I was very uncomfortable."[12]

For black female trainees, especially, sexual tensions compounded their discomfort. As if to underscore the taboo on interracial love, a Peace Corps psychologist asked Eaton what she would do if a white volunteer made a pass at her. Wise to his game, she happily played along. "They all respect me," Eaton responded with a laugh, omitting mention of the white trainee who had, in fact, propositioned her. "We've never had that problem, and I don't foresee that problem." Elsewhere, however, black-white romances spawned a palpable climate of envy and recrimination. After dating the same Jewish man at their training, the African American Esther White and her white rival exchanged angry racial epithets. At still a third site, meanwhile, the black volunteer Gerald Durley and a white counterpart actually came to blows over the issue. "I just thought he tried to be a little too friendly with some of the black girls," Durley recalls. "It was the same old white man's attitude, and it's troubling. It's quite troubling."[13]

As in the civil rights movement, the sharpest fears surrounded relations between black men and white women. At the conclusion of a dance with the black volunteer William Seraile, a white trainee was shocked to find that his arm was still around her. "Bill," she said, insistently, *the music stopped.* " Whites were "very ambivalent" on the entire subject, Seraile recalled: they "were trying to be super-liberal, but they might have their own reservations, too." Another white recruit confided that she had "this thing . . . about Negroes," but feared that acting on her attraction would cause the Peace Corps to dismiss her. At least one white woman at the training had already been "deselected," allegedly for having an affair with a black man. Still other whites worried about sexual advances from blacks, especially in Africa. One woman asked the black trainee David Closson how she should respond if an African placed his hand on her thigh. That would depend on her feelings, Closson replied; if she did not favor the suitor, "tell him, 'Get your black hands off my butt.' " The white volunteer blushed, claiming she could never say such a thing. In the same circumstance, Closson pointed out, she would surely reprimand a black American like himself. "But you're different," the woman protested. "He's African, and I don't want him to think of me as a racist."[14]

Well before they went overseas, then, white trainees were already distinguishing black Peace Corps volunteers from their African hosts. Indeed, whites transferred many of their fears and anxieties about black Americans onto Africans: Africans were sexually promiscuous; Africans lusted after white women; and Africans would use racial blackmail to corner their prey. "There was the stereotypical notion that [Africans] were just waiting for these young girls to come over to devour them, and seduce them," Closson recalled. "That sexual thing always came up." Against this backdrop, black-white Peace Corps romances must have seemed fairly innocuous: whatever worries whites felt about dating black Americans, they paled next to the far more stringent taboos against sex with an African. In subtle ways, Peace Corps officials helped reinforce this contrast. They were hardly eager to promote interracial dating or marriage among volunteers, as the Burgess-Polcyn incident shows. But they made it clear that romance with foreigners was even worse, flatly warning one group of female trainees to "stay away from African men." Women—especially white women—well understood that "black Peace Corps volunteers were safer than the black males over there," as one African American recalled. Only in Africa, however, would either race of Americans feel truly safe to love the other.[15]

Before he joined the Peace Corps, LaCharles James had dated only one white woman. When James walked hand in hand with her across the Kansas University campus, heads would turn. One afternoon, a group of students actually stood up and applauded as the couple strolled by. Playing to the crowd, James threw his arm around his partner—a tall, striking redhead—and kissed her. "It was fun appreciation," James remembered. "There weren't a lot of interracial couples on campus." Not everyone appreciated the fun, of course. When James and his girlfriend paid a call on his relatives, his grandmother burst into a rage. "Don't bring this white girl in my home," she exploded. The next day, the shaken pair returned to college. Praised by their peers, they were shunned by their families; mascots at school, they were pariahs at home.[16]

Yet in Africa, James found, interracial romance was an altogether "different experience." Neither celebrated nor censured, "it felt like . . . a normal kind of thing." Africans rarely remarked upon it, another volunteer confirmed, except to ask whether it was permitted in America. "The African gives less than a damn whether an African marries a white woman," added George Carter, the Peace Corps's first director in Ghana. "The white man, the white person in the U.S. . . . resents the marriage." A black New Yorker, Carter had wed a white woman before he came to Africa. Now, for the first time, they could appear in public without provoking stares and slurs. "Nobody paid any attention to us in Ghana," Carter recalled. "Lots of people pay attention to you in Queens."[17]

Given their own history of white rule, of course, Africans were hardly color-blind. To speed his way through traffic, for example, Carter sometimes asked his wife to ride in the back of their car. "With this white lady in back, I could drive by everyone," Carter recalled. "That's a carry-over from colonial days. The white person had status and the black didn't." Interracial marriage was a legacy of colonialism, as well. British and French educators sent thousands of Africans to school in

Europe, where they frequently married across the color line. So black-white unions were "an accepted procedure," another Peace Corps official wrote, especially among members of the elite. Back in America, blacks who took white spouses were often vilified for trying to "move up" the social ladder. But in Africa they had already reached the top: indeed, several national rulers returned from overseas study with white wives. A foreign spouse signified the successful achievement of high status, not the craven desire for it.[18]

Saturated with reports of white southern bigots beating defenseless demonstrators, Africans tended to regard black Americans as uniformly oppressed, impoverished, and degraded. Insofar as they remarked on black volunteers dating whites, then, they expressed surprise that the Peace Corps—or the white volunteers—would allow it. "People ask me why I'm discriminated against, why the white man in America doesn't like the black man, and how they would be treated if they went to America," the Senegal volunteer Ellis Franklin told a 1965 interviewer. "[A] lot of them want to know if I could marry a white girl." When Franklin responded affirmatively, they refused to believe him. "[N]o matter what you say, they've got an answer of their own," he remarked. "Every time they find a new picture of the hoses or the dogs in Mississippi or something, they bring it over to the house to show me."[19]

Actually, very few black volunteers had ever dated whites in America. Most of them were from the South, where the mere suggestion of interracial sex still provoked paroxysms of rage and violence. Just a few years earlier, Mississippians had murdered fourteen-year-old Emmett Till for flirting with a white woman; across the country, blacks described a dangerous situation with the aphorism, "that would be like slapping a white woman on the buttocks in Mississippi." In parts of Alabama, meanwhile, it was illegal for black men to "socialize"—let alone sleep—with females of another race. Up North, blacks enjoyed somewhat more freedom to date and marry across the color line. Even there, however, threats of violence often hounded interracial lovers. In 1963 a mixed-race couple in Long Island had a cross burned on their lawn and a bomb taped to their window; in suburban Chicago another pair had swastikas painted on their garage. Hardly the downtrodden souls that Africans imagined, American blacks had indeed made massive gains in education, employment, and civil rights. Yet these advances were simply not matched in the areas of dating and marriage, where—for the most part—Jim Crow still ruled.[20]

Despite their confident claims of progress in America, meanwhile, many black volunteers recalled harboring secret and shameful feelings of racial inferiority. When Africans described them as weak and helpless, volunteers adopted what Charles Gray called a "defensive posture." Beneath the surface, however, they sometimes wondered whether the charges were true. "In the classroom, in the schoolbooks, in going shopping, in how the neighborhood was configurated—there were so many subconscious messages [that] if you're black, you're not as good," one volunteer recalled, describing her childhood. "I thought less of myself because of the country that I was in." Peace Corps training often heightened this perception, since white volunteers were generally better educated than blacks. "I really had an inferiority complex," another African American acknowledged. "The whole fact that I was going to be in competition with whites . . . really blew my mind." Like the ever-present threat of physical violence, this feeling often poisoned American interracial relationships. To stifle it, some black volunteers simply stayed away from whites. Others struggled desperately for their approval and affection, hoping—against all odds—to win back in sex what they had lost in society.[21]

In Africa, however, the senses of danger and inferiority both melted away. Black volunteers mingled easily with whites, never eliciting the threats and epithets that were de rigueur back home. "It was not unusual," explained Homer Butler, who married a white volunteer he met in Togo. "You weren't looked at or discriminated against." Accosting Yvette Burgess and Charles Polcyn in a post office, a Nigerian asked them if they were "from different tribes"; on another occasion, a group of Africans asked Burgess why she was "traveling with this white man." When she identified Polcyn as her husband, however, they said, simply, "Oh"—and walked away. Otherwise, for two years, their different races never drew a comment. "If things worked out and we had an attraction, things worked out and we had an attraction," recalled Carl Meacham, who dated white volunteers in Liberia. "The Liberians couldn't care less."[22]

Eventually, volunteers like Meacham came to agree: race did not matter, at least not in matters of love. Dating whites was a "novelty" at first, he acknowledged, especially for an Alabama native like himself. "But after a while," he noted, "you find out that women are women." Indeed, another black volunteer added, "*people are people*": whatever their color or culture, human beings were all endowed with the same basic capacities, flaws, and desires. In Africa, then, blacks cast off any lingering feelings of subservience that they had suffered back home. "I could no longer be put in . . . that traditional place of black folks in America," recalled J. Fletcher Robinson, after serving as the Peace Corps's doctor in Tanzania. "I just had no sense of inferiority, or being defined by somebody else." In neighboring Kenya, likewise, the volunteer Leon Dash came to appreciate "the commonness of humankind"—and the speciousness of racial hierarchies. "I began to see, very close up, that we're all really very similar," Dash remarked. "You realize there's nothing inferior about you."[23]

Similarly, blacks found, white volunteers tended to discard their own sense of racial privilege when they left home. "[T]hey were just more open, more loose, less *white*," remembered Robinson. "A lot of the American experience in terms of race was erased . . . in Africa."[24] To be sure, racial tensions still flared on occasion.[25] In a new and often strange environment, however, black and white volunteers were less likely to replay their old conflicts than to discover their "many commonalities"—including an attraction to each other. "My sense was that the whites had the freedom to do what they probably had wanted to do before," another African American explained. "They were so constrained . . . in America." As long-held taboos came crashing down, both races exulted in their new sexual liberty. "They had never lain next to a naked black man before," recalled LaCharles James, describing his affairs with white women. "And I'd just hear these comments over and over again—your skin. I love your skin, black skin." After the initial thrill wore off, however, white and black volunteers came to share the African view of interracial sex: it was "no big deal." Indeed, another African American remarked, volunteers seemed to be "losing [their] perspective on skin color"—and loving each other without regard to it.[26]

By contrast, volunteer romances with Africans were often rife with acrimony. Female volunteers of both races bridled at African promiscuity and plural marriage. Others resented the persistent advances of many African men, who "used the whole black American kind of thing with the white volunteers—if you don't go to bed with me, it means that you're a racist," one African American recalled. A local magazine even ran an article explaining "how to make out with American Peace Corps volunteers," explicitly prescribing such guilt-driven blackmail. Black volunteers, meanwhile, risked charges of betrayal rather than bigotry from snubbed African suitors. If she said yes, Anne Wortham noted, she was a "biological soulmate"; but if she said no, she was "another one of those American bitches"—and a race traitor to boot. "It infuriates me that there are those who would dare to hide behind such phantom identifications to satisfy their own lust," Wortham wrote to a friend in America.[27]

For male volunteers, meanwhile, "African promiscuity" represented a mythic allure rather than a persistent annoyance. Both black and white men arrived with deeply ingrained stereotypes about "loose" African women. As in America, however, a sharp double standard often governed sexual relations on the continent: whereas African males were free to cavort as they pleased, African females were not. "It was a lot of parlor-type dating," recalled Walter Agers, a black volunteer in Nigeria. "That was the rudest awakening for everyone, no matter what your race was." Another Nigeria volunteer, Charles Gray, lived near some young women whose father literally locked them up each night. Gray would chat with them through barred bedroom windows, a stark symbol of their unassailable chastity. Elsewhere, some volunteers found truth to the claim that African women were "free" sexual beings. "It was expected for a woman to have a man, it was expected to flirt, and make eyes, and go to bed," LaCharles James recalled with a laugh. "I mean, the courtships were *very short*!" But so were relationships, which frequently foundered upon the partners' unequal economic resources. Some African women wore Western clothes and developed "jive" affectations, all in the hope of luring an African American husband—and a free ticket to the United States. "You had to be really conscious . . . that you're not exploiting something, just because it's familiar to you," Agers remembered. "A lot of times [women] would act like, hey, I'm hip, I've been there. And you'd be doing the same thing. . . . But it's not real, in the sense that you want to build a relationship."[28]

Ironically, then, volunteer romances with Africans were often plagued by the same problems as interracial unions at home: unequal status, unfulfilled expectations, and unspoken resentments. Meanwhile, unofficial Peace Corps policy continued to discourage them. "There is . . . ample indication of affairs involving female volunteers and Togolese men," wrote a worried agency evaluator in 1963. "There are affairs involving female volunteers and volunteer men. There are affairs involving volunteer men and Togolese women. And there is a bit of VD." Yet the Peace Corps tended to interdict the first type of relationship much more strongly than the other two, dismissing several women volunteers for "multiple sexual relationships" with Africans. By contrast, a male volunteer who contracted venereal disease from an African was simply given a lecture on "sexual responsibility" and sent back to work. For women, these reprimands reinforced an unspoken but unmistakable message: regardless of their race, fellow volunteers were safer sex partners than Africans.[29]

Most of all, though, common values and experiences drew them together. "We were dependent upon each other, because we were all in a situation that was different," noted one black volunteer. "So necessity is the mother of invention." For Americans of different races, especially, this meant a new appreciation for the attributes they shared. "You would tend to bond [when] everything else is so foreign to you," another African American explained. "At least we speak the same language." Upon their return home, however, interracial Peace Corps couples would find themselves labeled "foreign." Even worse, they discovered, America lacked any other language to speak about them.[30]

For the volunteer Homer Butler and his white girlfriend, Andrea, the first sign of trouble appeared during their first African vacation. Starting in Togo, where the pair met, they planned to travel all the way down to the tip of the continent. When they reached the Congo, however, Andrea received a visa to continue on to South Africa—and Homer did not. "It was a rude awakening," he remembered. "I had this great belief in America. I thought they'd let me in *because* I was American." To the South Africans, however, he was simply a "Negro"—and a miscegenator at that. After the Nationalist victory of 1948, South Africa had banned all black-white sex and marriage for the first time in its history. It was hardly interested in hosting an interracial couple, even for a few days.[31]

During these same years, of course, America was removing its own legal barriers against race mixing. Between 1948 and 1967, fourteen states repealed their bans on intermarriage. Sixteen other states had their laws struck down by the Supreme Court's *Loving* decision, which declared forthrightly that antimiscegenation codes violated "the principle of equality" at the core of the Constitution. As the Butlers discovered upon their return that same year, however, black-white couples remained stark aberrations in American society. Despite the dire predictions of white racists, no mass run to the altar occurred in the wake of *Loving*: indeed, Mississippi did not celebrate its first black-white wedding until over three years later. In the North, likewise, the new legal climate did not signal a corresponding change in attitudes or practices. As the Butlers drove across the Delaware River, a policeman pulled them over—ostensibly for speeding, but actually to see what a black man was doing with a white woman. To assist them in exactly this type of situation, the minister who wed the Butlers had insisted that they carry full documentation of their marriage. But while the couple avoided potential hassles with the law, they could not evade the perpetual stares of strangers—everywhere. "[P]eople looked at us constantly," Homer Butler recalled. "That was quite a difference from Africa."[32]

Inevitably, for interracial couples, the first strange looks came from family members. In 1964 newspapers carried reports of a white female volunteer who had married a Nigerian. Her parents were "perturbed," one journalist noted matter-of-factly, while "some of their Kentucky neighbors have raised eyebrows." Upon meeting their future son-in-law, however, they quickly warmed to him. "Once you see a man," the bride's father remarked, "he becomes a man." A similar pattern marked many family reactions to marriages between black and white volunteers: initial shock and repugnance, followed by gradual respect and acceptance. Yvette Burgess's parents had always warned her against dating across the color line, especially because one of her great-aunts had been raped by a white man and later committed suicide. When she announced her wedding to Charles Polcyn, then, they were stunned. "They have owned you," complained her mother, a New York native. "I don't see how you can have them touch you." Eventually, Burgess's mother grew to accept her choice of partner. "She just got over it," Burgess recalled. "[I]f I was happy, she was waving the American flag." Hailing from an all-white town in Wisconsin, Polcyn's family was even more outraged by the news of his marriage. When they finally encountered his wife, they found that they liked her—and their frosty demeanor began to melt.[33]

But outside their families, as Calvin Hernton has emphasized, mixed-race couples remained "*fugitives* in American society." Rooted in "fear of other people," parental opposition to interracial marriages tended to fizzle after parents met the spouses. But most other Americans never actually spoke with black-white couples; instead, they simply looked. Wherever the couples went—the grocery store, the laundromat, the park, the movies—eyes trailed them. The pattern was so pervasive, and so irritating, that interracial couples gave it their own name: "the stare." Whites watched more closely, it seemed, but blacks were hardly exempt from the fixation. "[W]henever the subject, let alone the fact, is encountered," Hernton observed in 1971, "everybody, white and black, gets uptight."[34]

To be sure, mixed volunteer couples caused less of a stir in larger cities. Settling in Washington, D.C., Homer and Andrea Butler found that the nation's capital "was a little different than the everyday U.S." in the easy way it accepted interracial unions. In New York, meanwhile, black-white couples formed a recognizable feature of the social landscape: they wore a "certain uniform," Yvette Burgess recalled, marked especially by thong sandals and other "hippie" fashions. Even here, however, Burgess and her white husband had a hard time adapting. For whereas New Yorkers viewed interracial love as a political statement, a self-conscious snub at mainstream society, returning Peace Corps volunteers approached it the way Africans did: as normal. "We didn't see ourselves as a unit set up for rebellion," Burgess explained. "We saw ourselves as simply a couple." So they were "perceived oddly" by the interracial community, where every act of love was also regarded as a call to arms. "We didn't meet in a movement, we didn't meet in a political organization, and gravitate toward one another as part of our expression of that political attitude," Burgess added. "We were trying to fit, and find a place to live, and be. Just like anyone else."[35]

In America, however, no such place could be found. As interracial dating and marriage increased, slowly but steadily, so did the sense of "rebellion" that surrounded it—especially among African Americans. After personally desegregating the University of Georgia, for example, Charlayne Hunter-Gault found that many of her own friends were "wildly disapproving" of her white lover. So the couple decided to get married, "an act of love and defiance" against critics of every color. "We would show them, and all the hypocrites of the world, how we lived by our beliefs," Hunter-Gault wrote, "and didn't just pay them lip service." To some militants, meanwhile, sex with whites was a way to strike back at America rather than to sustain its historic promise. In one of the most notorious diatribes of the era, the Black Panther leader Eldridge Cleaver even described interracial rape as an "insurrectionary" act. "It delighted me that I was defying and trampling upon the white man's law, upon his system of values, and that I was defiling his women," wrote Cleaver, in prison for sex crimes. "I felt I was getting revenge." (Often ignored was Cleaver's admission, on the very next page, that he was wrong.) For African Americans of every persuasion, then, sex across the color line became a highly political statement. Although returning Peace Corps volunteers declared it "normal" and "natural," America's distinctive racial history made it special—and controversial.[36]

Worst of all, black volunteers found, still other voices condemned mixed-race romance as a capitulation—not a challenge—to white rule. In the Black Power movement, especially, blacks who took white lovers were blasted for practicing "daytime nationalism" and "nighttime integration." African American women often spearheaded the charge, complaining that black men "go along with the white man's value system" when they date outside the race. Yet interracial sex and marriage had its male critics, too, led by the redoubtable Malcolm X. Denouncing blacks who married across the color line as "stool pigeons" and "Uncle Toms," he claimed that the very impulse reflected a pathological wish to please their oppressors. Such charges placed returning black Peace Corps volunteers in a classic double bind: whereas some observers praised them as proud rebels for dating whites, others reviled the same practice as insufficiently rebellious. Like the old joke about a patient hurrying to his psychiatrist, they were anxious if early, hostile if late, and compulsive if punctual. Everybody had a diagnosis—and cure—for the "problem" of interracial love, which cast such a long and painful shadow over America's past.[37]

Still, history was not destiny: however dim, signs of change were on the horizon. In the last book he wrote before his death, Martin Luther King, Jr., denounced a white liberal who supported racial equality but did not want her daughter to marry a black man. Earlier in his career, of course, King tried to avoid the issue altogether. Now, rather than denying interracial sexual attraction, he addressed it straight on. "This lady could not see that her failure to accept intermarriage negated her claim to genuine liberalism," King wrote in 1967. "The question of intermarriage is never raised in a society cured of the disease of racism." Here, as in many other realms, King moved into near-accord with his alleged opposite, Malcolm X. As late as March 1964, Malcolm restated his steadfast opposition to mixed-race marriages. But then, like black Peace Corps volunteers, he visited Africa—and changed his views. "I found out during my travels that it wasn't such a big deal to most folk," he told an interviewer later that year, in an almost perfect echo of African American volunteers. "I mean, peeping into bedrooms to find out the color of couples in bed is a sick American pastime." Asked by another reporter whether he still condemned love between the races, Malcolm laughed. "How can anyone be against love?" he responded.[38]

How, indeed?

NOTES

1. Gloria Myklebust, interview by Jonathan Zimmerman, Feb. 16, 1994, audiotape, side 1, tape 1, Returned Peace Corps Volunteer Collection, John F. Kennedy Library, Boston (all interviews with former Peace Corps volunteers are recorded on audiotape and unless otherwise specified are deposited in the Returned Peace Corps Volunteer Collection); Jonathan Zimmerman, "Beyond Double Consciousness: Black Peace Corps Volunteers in Africa, 1961–1971," *Journal of American History* 82 (1995): 1027.

2. Although the Peace Corps did not keep racial records during its first decade, recruiters and other officials estimated that about a thousand African Americans served in the agency between 1961 and 1971. Roughly two-thirds went to Africa, where they never constituted more than a tiny fraction of any given country's volunteer force. For example, Sierra Leone's first thirty-seven volunteers included just one black person, while Cameroon's first fifty had two. The first two Peace Corps groups in Nigeria had only one African American each; the initial contingent in Niger had none. Zimmerman, "Beyond Double Consciousness," 1000, 1004–05.

3. Collie Coleman, interview by Jonathan Zimmerman, Jan. 19, 1994, side 1, tape 1; Charles Gray, interview by Jonathan Zimmerman, Feb. 2, 1994, side 2, tape 1. See also Carolyn Payton, interview by Jonathan Zimmerman, Feb. 3, 1994, side 1, tape 1.

4. Since there is no official list of African Americans in the Peace Corps during the 1960s, I had to locate them using agency photographs and publications. Identifying roughly two hundred blacks who served as volunteers or administrators, I obtained addresses for about half of this total and sent each individual a letter that described my project and requested assistance. More than fifty people responded; eventually I taped oral histories with thirty-nine of them. All but four of these interviews are on deposit at the John F. Kennedy Library in Boston. Zimmerman, "Beyond Double Consciousness," 1002.

5. There is no comprehensive history of American interracial sex and marriage in the 1960s and 1970s. The best place to start is Paul Spickard, *Mixed Blood: Intermarriage and Ethnic Identity in Twentieth-Century America* (Madison: University of Wisconsin Press, 1989), 235–342. For contemporary accounts, see Beth Day, *Sexual Life between Blacks and Whites: The Roots of Racism* (New York: Crowell, 1972); Grace Halsell, *Black/White Sex* (New York: Morrow, 1972); Eldridge Cleaver, *Soul on Ice* (New York: Dell, 1968); Calvin Hernton, *Sex and Racism in America* (1965; reprint, New York: Anchor, 1988); idem, *Coming Together: Black Power, White Hatred, and Sexual Hang-Ups* (New York: Random House, 1971); Clotye M. Larsson, *Marriage across the Color Line* (Chicago: Johnson, 1965); Charles Stember, *Sexual Racism: The Emotional Barrier to an Integrated Society* (New York: Elsevier, 1976); Joseph R. Washington, *Marriage in Black and White* (Boston: Beacon Press, 1970); and Doris Y. Wilkinson, *Black Male/White Female: Perspectives on Interracial Marriage and Courtship* (Cambridge, Mass.: Schenkman, 1975). A brief but eloquent summary of this literature appears in David W. Southern, *Gunnar Myrdal and Black-White Relations: The Use and Abuse of An American Dilemma, 1944–1969* (Baton Rouge: Louisiana State University Press, 1987), 283–87. On the transition from "civil rights" to "Black Power," see Clayborne Carson, *In Struggle: SNCC and the Black Awakening of the 1960s* (Cambridge:

Harvard University Press, 1981); Benjamin Muse, *The American Negro Revolution: From Nonviolence to Black Power, 1963–1967* (Bloomington: Indiana University Press, 1968); and especially Allen J. Matusow, "From Civil Rights to Black Power: The Case of SNCC, 1960–1966," in *Twentieth-Century America: Recent Interpretations.* ed. Barton J. Bernstein and Allen J. Matusow (New York: Harcourt, Brace, and World, 1969). For critiques of this paradigm, see Steven F. Lawson, "Freedom Then, Freedom Now: The Historiography of the Civil Rights Movement," *American Historical Review* 96 (1991): esp. 462–63; and William L. Van Deburg, *New Day in Babylon: The Black Power Movement and American Culture* (Chicago: University of Chicago Press, 1992), esp. 24. See also Zimmerman, "Beyond Double Consciousness," 1000–1001.

6. Spickard, *Mixed Blood*, 292–93; Robert J. Sickels, *Race, Marriage, and the Law* (Albuquerque: University of New Mexico Press, 1972), 64; Washington, *Marriage in Black and White*, 93; Leon Dash, interview by Jonathan Zimmerman, Jan. 13, 1994, side 1, tape 2. For a lucid discussion of the *Loving* case in a broader historical context, see Peggy Pascoe, "Miscegenation Law, Court Cases, and Ideologies of 'Race' in Twentieth-Century America," in this volume.

7. Sargent Shriver, memo, Jan. 23, 1962, Weekly Report to the President folder, box 2, Peace Corps Microfilm Hard Copy Collection, Kennedy Library. Charles Polcyn was from Wisconsin, not Michigan. Yvette Burgess, interview by Jonathan Zimmerman, June 8, 1996, side 1, tape 1. For general overviews of the Peace Corps in the Shriver years, see Irving Bernstein, *Promises Kept: John F. Kennedy's New Frontier* (New York: Oxford University Press, 1991), 259–79; Gerard T. Rice, *The Bold Experiment: JFK's Peace Corps* (South Bend, Ind.: University of Notre Dame Press, 1985); Coates Redmon, *Come as You Are: The Peace Corps Story* (San Diego: Harcourt Brace Jovanovich, 1986); and Karen Schwartz, *What You Can Do for Your Country: An Oral History of the Peace Corps* (New York: Morrow, 1991), 27–46.

8. Burgess, interview, side 2, tape 2; Robert Sargent Shriver, Jr., "Commencement Address, North Carolina A. & T. College," typescript, June 1, 1963, p. 6, Speeches of Sargent Shriver, Peace Corps General Collection, Peace Corps Library, Washington, D.C.; Paul Geren and Franklin H. Williams, memo, Nov. 10, 1961, Subcabinet Group on Civil Rights—Peace Corps folder, box 13, Harris Wofford Papers, Kennedy Library. See also Zimmerman, "Beyond Double Consciousness," 1008–09.

9. Ira G. Zepp, Jr., *The Social Vision of Martin Luther King, Jr.* (Brooklyn: Carlson, 1989), 211; *A Testament of Hope: The Essential Writings of Martin Luther King, Jr.*, ed. James Melvin Washington (San Francisco: Harper and Row, 1986), 478; Albert I. Gordon, *Intermarriage: Interfaith, Interracial, Interethnic* (Boston: Beacon Press, 1964), 269; Taylor Branch, *Parting the Waters: America in the King Years, 1954–1963* (New York: Simon and Schuster, 1988), 89; Larsson, *Marriage across the Color Line*, vii, 39.

10. Stember, *Sexual Racism*, 106; Hernton, *Sex and Racism*, 20–21; Spickard, *Mixed Blood*, 280–82. For an analysis of more recent patterns, see Matthijs Kalmijn, "Trends in Black/White Intermarriage," *Social Forces* 72 (1993): 119–46.

11. Doug McAdam, *Freedom Summer* (New York: Oxford University Press, 1988), 93, 105–06; Sara Evans, *Personal Politics: The Roots of Women's Liberation in the Civil Rights Movement and the New Left* (New York: Alfred A. Knopf, 1979), 80–81; Hernton, *Sex and Racism*, 165. See also Mary Frances Berry and John W. Blassingame, *Long Memory: The Black Experience in America* (New York: Oxford University Press, 1982), 139; Rhoda Lois Blumberg, *Civil Rights: The 1960s Freedom Struggle* (Boston: G. K. Hall, 1991), 153; Mary King, *Freedom Song: A Personal Story of the 1960s Civil Rights Movement* (New York: Morrow, 1987), 464; Allen J. Matusow, *The Unraveling of America: A History of Liberalism*

in the 1960s (New York: Harper and Row, 1986), 351; and Spickard, *Mixed Blood*, 281–82.

12. Joan Downs, "Black/White Dating," in *The Black Male in America: Perspectives on His Status in Contemporary Society*, ed. Doris Y. Wilkinson and Roland L. Taylor (Chicago: Nelson-Hall, 1977), 207; McAdam, *Freedom Summer*, 187; Robert Johnson, "Sit Ins Boring? Try the Peace Corps," *Peace Corps News* 4 (autumn 1965), Special College Supplement; David Riesman, "Two Views," *Peace Corps Volunteer* 6 (October 1968): 4; "More Black Volunteers Sought by Peace Corps," unidentified clipping, 1969, Minorities-Recruiting folder, Peace Corps General Collection; Patricia Eaton, interview by Jonathan Zimmerman, March 15, 1994, side 1, tape 1. See also Zimmerman, "Beyond Double Consciousness," 1010. According to Doug McAdam, almost 25 percent of Freedom Summer veterans worked as "full-time activists" afterward; counting the Peace Corps, nearly 30 percent did so. Hence we can infer that roughly five percent of the campaign's participants joined the Peace Corps.

13. Eaton, interview, side 1, tape 1; Esther White Kaufman, interview by Jonathan Zimmerman, Jan. 30, 1994, side 1, tape 1; Gerald Durley, interview by Jonathan Zimmerman, March 2, 1994, side 1, tape 1.

14. William Seraile, interview by Jonathan Zimmerman, Jan. 27, 1994, side 1, tape 1; Alan Weiss, *High Risk/High Gain: A Freewheeling Account of Peace Corps Training* (New York: St. Martin's, 1968), 90, 185; David Closson, interview by Jonathan Zimmerman, Feb. 1, 1994, side 1, tape 1.

15. Closson, interview, side 1, tape 1; Julius A. Amin, *The Peace Corps in Cameroon* (Kent, Ohio: Kent State University Press, 1992), 214 n; LaCharles James, interview by Jonathan Zimmerman, March 1, 1994, side 1, tape 2.

16. James, interview, side 1, tape 2.

17. Ibid.; "Confessions of a Portuguese Dodger Rooter," *Spectrum* (Senegal) 1 (winter 1965): 5; George Carter, interview by Jonathan Zimmerman, March 21, 1994, side 2, tape 1.

18. Carter, interview, side 2, tape 1; Minutes, Nov. 7, 1962, Director's Staff Meeting folder, box 1, Peace Corps Microfilm Hard Copy Collection; Spickard, *Mixed Blood*, 302–03. See also Homer Butler, interview by Jonathan Zimmerman, Feb. 15, 1994, side 2, tape 1. My ideas about African perceptions of race have been heavily influenced by Kwame Anthony Appiah, *In My Father's House: Africa in the Philosophy of Culture* (New York: Oxford University Press, 1992).

19. Zimmerman, "Beyond Double Consciousness," 1018–19; "Confessions of a Portuguese Dodger Rooter," 5. See also Myklebust, interview, side 1, tape 1; Gray, interview, side 2, tape 1.

20. Hernton, *Sex and Racism*, 20, 69–70; Frank A. Petroni, "Interracial Dating—The Price Is High," in *Interracial Marriage: Expectations and Realities*, ed. Irving R. Stuart and Lawrence E. Abt (New York: Grossman, 1973), 129–30; Spickard, *Mixed Blood*, 296; Studs Terkel, *Race: How Blacks and Whites Think and Feel about the American Obsession* (New York: New Press, 1992), 395. On the Till incident and its legacy, see Stephen J. Whitfield, *A Death in the Delta: The Story of Emmett Till* (New York: Free Press, 1988).

21. Gray, interview, side 2, tape 1; Patricia Darrah, interview by Jonathan Zimmerman, Feb. 1, 1994, side 1, tape 1; Eaton, interview, side 1, tape 1. On feelings of inferiority among black volunteers, see also Dash, interview, side 1, tape 2; Ed Smith, interview by Jonathan Zimmerman, Feb. 5, 1994, side 1, tape 1 (in Jonathan Zimmerman's possession); C. Payne Lucas, interview by Jonathan Zimmerman, March 14, 1994, side 2, tape 1.

22. Butler, interview, side 2, tape 1; Burgess, interview, sides 1 and 2, tape 2; Carl Meacham, interview by Jonathan Zimmerman, March 23, 1994, side 1, tape 1.

23. Meacham, interview, side 1, tape 1; Myklebust, interview, side 2, tape 1; J. Fletcher Robinson, interview by Jonathan Zimmerman, Feb. 23, 1994, side 2, tape 1; Dash, interview, side 1, tape 2. See also Lucas, interview, side 2, tape 1; "Needed: Abroad or at Home?" *Peace Corps Volunteer* 6 (July–August 1968): 9; Zimmerman, "Beyond Double Consciousness," 1026–27.

24. Robinson, interview, side 2, tape 1. See also Gray, interview, side 2, tape 1; Coleman, interview, side 2, tape 1; Minutes, July 23, 1964, National Advisory Council folder, box 3, Gerald Bush Papers, Kennedy Library.

25. See, for example, Seraile, interview, side 1, tape 1; Durley, interview, side 1, tape 1; Ed Smith, *Where To, Black Man?* (Chicago: Quadrangle Books, 1967), 44; William Mercer, Jr., "On 'Minority Volunteer,'" *Peace Corps Volunteer* 7 (February 1969): 23.

26. Payton, interview, side 1, tape 1; Gray, interview, side 2, tape 1; James, interview, side 1, tape 2; Butler, interview, side 2, tape 1; Kaufman, interview, side 2, tape 1.

27. Evelyn Davis, interview by Jonathan Zimmerman, Jan. 27, 1994, side 2, tape 1; Marilyn Turner, interview by Jonathan Zimmerman, Feb. 25, 1994, side 1, tape 1; Butler, interview, side 2, tape 1; Anne Wortham, interview by Jonathan Zimmerman, March 4, 1994, side 2, tape 1. See also Amin, *Peace Corps in Cameroon.* 147–49; Zimmerman, "Beyond Double Consciousness," 1024.

28. Walter Agers, interview by Jonathan Zimmerman, Jan. 31, 1994, side 2, tape 1; Gray, interview, side 2, tape 1; James, interview, side 2, tape 1; Meacham, interview, side 2, tape 1. But see also Matthew Plummer, interview by Jonathan Zimmerman, Feb. 24, 1994, side 2, tape 1.

29. Milton Viorst, ed., *Making a Difference: The Peace Corps at Twenty-Five* (New York: Weidenfeld and Nicolson, 1986), 69; James, interview, side 2, tape 1 and side 1, tape 2. On the Peace Corps's policies regarding volunteers and sex, see Redmon, *Come as You Are*, 96–97; Rice, *Bold Experiment*, 231–34; and Lawrence H. Fuchs, *"Those Peculiar Americans": The Peace Corps and American National Character* (New York: Meredith Press, 1967), 120–21. Although it does not address Africa, Fuchs's book provides an especially vivid illustration of the Peace Corps's double standard on questions of sex in the 1960s. Fuchs reports that ten female volunteers in the Philippines were dismissed "for misbehavior connected with romance and sex" during the Peace Corps's first two years, whereas not a single male volunteer was fired for this type of offense.

30. Coleman, interview, side 2, tape 1; Payton, interview, side 1, tape 1.

31. Butler, interview, side 2, tape 1; George M. Fredrickson, *White Supremacy: A Comparative Study in American and South African History* (New York: Oxford University Press, 1981), 98.

32. Spickard, *Mixed Blood.* 295; Peter Irons and Stephanie Guitton, *May It Please the Court: The Most Significant Oral Arguments Made before the Supreme Court since 1955* (New York: New Press, 1993), 288; Beth Day, "The Hidden Fear," in *The Black Male in America*, ed. Wilkinson and Taylor, 204; Butler, interview, side 2, tape 1.

33. Ralph Blumenfeld, "Kentucky Girl Weds a Nigerian with Parents' Blessing," *New York Post*, Dec. 28, 1964, Peace Corps—Africa Microfiche, Schomburg Clipping Collection, Schomburg Center for Research in Black Culture, New York Public Library, New York, N.Y.; Burgess, interview, sides 1 and 2, tape 1. See also Myklebust, interview, side 2, tape 1; Ophelia Gona, interview by Jonathan Zimmerman, Jan. 14, 1994, side 2, tape 1.

34. Hernton, *Sex and Racism*, xviii; Gona, interview, side 2, tape 1; William Barry Furlong, "Interracial Marriage Is a Sometime Thing," in *The Blending American: Patterns of Intermarriage*, ed. Milton L. Barron (Chicago: Quadrangle Books, 1972), 121; Berry and Blassingame, *Long Memory*, 135–36; Hernton, *Coming Together*, 150.

35. Butler, interview, side 2, tape 1; Burgess, interview, sides 1 and 2, tape 2. On interracial communities in New York and elsewhere, see the essays in Larsson, *Marriage across the Color Line*.

36. Charlayne Hunter-Gault, *In My Place* (New York: Farrar Straus, 1992), 239, 241–42; Cleaver, *Soul on Ice*, 14–15. See also Furlong, "Interracial Marriage," 122; Stember, *Sexual Racism*, 110–11. In *Colored People: A Memoir* (New York: Alfred A. Knopf, 1994), 195, Henry Louis Gates, Jr., describes his own interracial love affair during this era as a "vague political statement."

37. Stember, *Sexual Racism*, 110, 112; *Black Nationalism in America*, ed. John H. Bracey, Jr., et al. (Indianapolis: Bobbs-Merrill, 1970), 418; Myklebust, interview, side 2, tape 1; Meacham, interview, side 2, tape 1; James Bartley, interview by Jonathan Zimmerman, Feb. 16, 1994, side 2, tape 1; Werner Sollors, *Beyond Ethnicity: Consent and Descent in American Culture* (New York: Oxford University Press, 1986), 192.

38. Martin Luther King, Jr., *Where Do We Go from Here: Chaos or Community?* (Boston: Beacon Press, 1967), 89; Malcolm X, *By Any Means Necessary*, ed. George Breitman (New York: Pathfinder Press, 1970), 9, 118; Jan Carew, *Ghosts in Our Blood: With Malcolm X in Africa, England, and the Caribbean* (Chicago: Lawrence Hill Books, 1994), 35. See also Alex Haley, *The Autobiography of Malcolm X* (New York: Grove Press, 1965), 424. On the evolving agreement between King and Malcolm, see especially James H. Cone, *Martin and Malcolm in America: A Dream or a Nightmare* (Maryknoll, N.Y.: Orbis Books, 1991).

Index

Aaron (slave), 72–73, 74–77, 78–79, 82, 86

abolitionism and antislavery, 22, 116, 151, 153, 191–212, 241, 254–66, 309n.17. *See also individual names; names of organizations*

abortion, 108n.23

Adair, James, 104–05

adultery, 103, 105, 109n.47, 113, 120, 152, 164, 171, 174, 175, 182

advertising, 448

affirmative action, 482–83

Africa and Africans, 254; and American Indians, 13, 15, 17, 18, 72, 73, 74, 75–76, 77, 79, 84, 402; and Christianity, 63, 64–65; and English, 95, 106; and immigration, 25; and Spanish, 17, 18, 20; and whites, 73, 77, 80, 244, 401, 514–29;. *See also* colonization; Pan-Africanism; racial identity; repatriation; slavery; *names of countries*

African Americans: and American Indians, 13, 15, 16, 72–90, 107n.6, 402; free, under slavery, 64, 73, 74, 77, 84, 114, 116, 118, 119–120, 141, 156, 157, 158, 164–90, 193, 194, 199, 201, 297, 303, 304, 317; and gender, 282, 285, 294–95, 297, 298, 306; and racial identity, 17, 22, 23, 25, 239, 242, 464, 468, 469, 472, 474, 475, 477, 479, 480, 482; as slaveowners, 167, 168, 169, 177, 178, 182; and whites, 25, 26, 50–51, 60–71, 112–38, 141–63, 164–90, 191–212, 213–34, 237–53, 254–66, 267–93, 294–312, 313–27, 352–72, 373–98, 399–419, 423–43, 464–90, 491–513, 514–529. *See also* blackness; citizenship; civil rights; emancipation; freedpeople; slavery.

African diaspora, 409, 412

age-of-consent laws, 352–72

Alabama, 118, 119, 122, 124–25, 126, 358, 395n.41, 440n.18, 475, 519, 520. *See also* Mobile; Tuskegee Institute

Alaska, 482

Albuquerque, N.M., 331, 333, 335, 339, 340, 341, 344, 346

Alcott, Louisa May, 257, 263

Alden, John, 107n.7

Algonkian Indians, 10

"amalgamation," 191–92, 193, 194, 200, 207–08, 407, 412, 453

American and Foreign Anti-Slavery Society, 199

American Anti-Slavery Society, 194, 195, 196, 198

American Church Institute for Negroes, 494

American Colonization Society, 193. *See also* colonization

American Freedman's Inquiry Commission, 257–58

American Indians, 25; and African Americans, 13, 15, 16, 72–90, 107n.6, 402; and Africans, 13, 15, 17, 18, 72, 73, 74, 75–76, 79, 84, 402; and Anglo-Americans, 11, 72–73, 74–75, 76–78, 79, 80, 81, 82, 83–85, 331–51; and Canadians, 37, 39, 40–41, 43–44, 45, 46–48, 51; in colonial Louisiana, 10, 35–59; and English, 10, 13, 20, 91–111; and French, 10, 13, 17, 35–59, 95, 100–01, 110n.61; and gender, 39, 79, 82, 83, 84; in New Mexico, 331–51; and racial identity, 237, 242, 260, 399, 402, 464–65, 468, 475, 482; as slaves, 39–40, 41, 336–37; as slaveowners, 15; and Spanish, 13, 17, 18; and whites, 10, 11–15, 16, 17, 20–21, 35–59, 80, 91–111, 134nn.48 and 50, 331–51, 399, 402, 414. *See also names of tribes*

Americanization, 452, 453

American Revolution, 21, 116, 133n.38. *See also* revolutionary era

Ames, Jessie Daniel, 239

Anglicans and Church of England, 61, 63–64, 65, 67, 100, 104

Anglo-Americans: and American Indians, 11, 72–73, 74–75, 76–78, 79, 80, 81, 82, 83–85, 331–51; and Hispanos, 331–51; and racial categories, 18, 25. *See also* British; England; whites

Anglo-Saxon Clubs of America (ASCOA), 400–04, 405, 406–08, 409–12, 414

Anglo-Saxonism, 22–24, 259, 260, 261, 354, 362, 377, 403, 404, 408, 409, 411, 466

antebellum era, 11–17, 21–22, 116–21, 141–63, 164–90, 191–212, 213–22, 242–46, 258, 267, 268, 269, 278, 279, 285, 296–97, 298, 299, 300, 304, 308n.7, 314–17, 323–24, 378–79, 380, 384, 466

anthropology, 24, 446, 470, 472, 473, 474, 477, 479. *See also individual names*

Anti-Alien Land Acts, 449